CHARACTER AND COPS

CHARACTER AND COPS
ETHICS IN POLICING

Sixth Edition

Edwin J. Delattre

The AEI Press

Publisher for the American Enterprise Institute

WASHINGTON, D.C.

Distributed by arrangement with the Rowman & Littlefield Publishing Group, 4501 Forbes Boulevard, Suite 200, Lanham, Maryland 20706. To order call toll free 1-800-462-6420 or 1-717-794-3800. For all other inquiries please contact AEI Press, 1150 Seventeenth Street, N.W. Washington, D.C. 20036 or call 1-800-862-5801.

Library of Congress Cataloging-in-Publication Data

Delattre, Edwin J.
    Character and cops : ethics in policing / Edwin J. Delattre. —6th ed.
        p. cm.
    Includes bibliographical references and index.
    ISBN 978-0-8447-7224-0 (cloth)
    ISBN 978-0-8447-7225-7 (pbk: alk. paper)

    1. Police ethics—United States. 2. Police Psychology—United States.
3. Police—United States—Social conditions. I. Title.

    HV7924.D45 2006
    174'.93632—dc23
                                                                    2011017712
13 14 15   3 4 5

The Library of Congress has already catalogued earlier editions as follows:

Fifth edition   ISBN 978-0-8447-4217-5 (pbk.)
Fourth edition   ISBN 0-8447-4153-1 (pbk.)
Third edition   ISBN 0-8447-3973-1 (pbk.)
Second edition ISBN 0-8447-3868-9 (cloth)
                        ISBN 0-8447-3686-4 (pbk.)
First edition   ISBN 0-8447-3685-6 (cloth)

Printed in the United States of America

To my mother, Donna Marie Delattre, and to the memory of
my father, Jules Irvey Delattre

The fourth edition is dedicated to the memory of
John P. O'Neill
February 6, 1952–September 11, 2001

The fifth edition is dedicated to my wife—Alice Boggs Delattre

The sixth edition is dedicated to the memory of Larry Brown—
man of integrity, faithful friend of fifty-five years—
and his intrepid wife, Judy.

Contents

Foreword to the Sixth Edition

David R. Bores

In 1989, Patrick Murphy eloquently inscribed the foreword to the first edition of *Character and Cops*. His words accurately predicted the book's significance and are just as applicable now as when he first wrote them. Mr. Murphy's opening statement remains a tribute to Dr. Edwin J. Delattre; the book, he wrote, "makes a major contribution to the body of knowledge essential for police to play their rightful part in the struggle of society against injustice."

Indeed, we are now in a position to assess how prophetic this statement was in light of the impact Dr. Delattre has had on those charged with maintaining the public trust of policing in a free society. I shall address the subject of his future legacy later. But first, it might be instructive to recall some of the more significant challenges we have faced over the past two decades as members of what Mr. Murphy referred to as the "unprofessional profession." For it is because of these and many other challenges that we have become ever more mindful of the profound gratitude we owe Dr. Delattre for the wisdom found in the pages of this book, wisdom that has helped us better navigate the ethical dilemmas arising from these events.

Since 1989, we have been blessed (or cursed) by the increased capability of an unlimited variety of technological advancements. From a full range of less lethal weapons to the marvels of computer technology that change almost daily, we are the beneficiaries of an unending parade of new products that allow us to be more efficient at service delivery, more protective of our officers' safety, and less injurious to those who may require our coercive authority. We have also made much progress in attracting more female and minority officers to our ranks, as well as in promoting more of them to positions at the highest levels of our profession.

But while we have made great advances—spending millions of dollars purchasing the wares of the police-industrial complex, selecting highly dedicated officers from a much better pool of qualified job applicants, and subscribing to the tenets of equal employment opportunity for all by basing advancement on individual abilities rather than prejudice and political interference—we have been comparatively slow to acknowledge that police are not solely responsible for maintaining public order and preventing crime. We have only reluctantly transitioned to community policing and only recently come to accept what Dr. Delattre told us years ago: "Our civilization does not . . . survive by accident."

Accordingly, we have stopped passively waiting before responding to the lawbreakers of our communities. Now we take a proactive outlook toward crime, an approach suggested by James Q. Wilson and George L. Kelling in their 1982 article, "Broken Windows." Today, we more widely   accept that police must purposefully engage law-abiding citizens and community groups to proactively challenge those who do evil, find the root causes behind social issues, and become more creative at neighborhood problem solving. We also see more clearly why our Founding Fathers insisted upon local control over government agents. To be sure, there are some who are quick to criticize the consequences of political decentralization and the fragmentation and inefficiencies that result from some seventeen thousand disparate police departments. However, few dispute that the multiplicity of departments has afforded our citizens the opportunity to better influence their local police officers. Police can now more effectively respond to threats by tailoring service delivery to satisfy specific needs of local jurisdictions.

Another example of our reluctance to change is even more deeply rooted than our unwillingness to embrace community policing. Since 1979, the Commission on Accreditation for Law Enforcement Agencies has spearheaded the requirement that all police departments elevate their administrative practices, operational procedures, methods of management, and service-delivery measures by adopting national accreditation standards. This effort initially met with tepid results. Fortunately, in recent years, more and more departments have willingly engaged in the accreditation process, while many states have vigorously advanced the adoption of agency-wide standards by developing certification programs with the structures necessary to evaluate departmental compliance.

In the twenty-two years since the first edition of *Character and Cops* was published, we have also been forced to confront terrorist acts that have had a profound effect on our country. From the actions of locally born terrorists such as Timothy McVeigh in Oklahoma City to the horrific attacks instigated by noncitizens in the name of Islam on 9/11, policing is now charged with the immense mission of homeland security. Fortunately, the virtues of community policing and the formation of police-citizen partnerships can help us prevent future domestic and international attacks.

Just as the Oklahoma City and World Trade Center bombings significantly expanded our law enforcement obligations to protect the homeland, the massacre at Columbine High School drastically changed how we respond to those who are actively attempting to kill or injure members of the general public. This one event, more than any other, resulted in a collective recognition that in active-shooter situations, first-responding officers can no longer wait for those specially trained and equipped to handle immediate life-threatening situations. Rather, the duty to react decisively and effectively falls to on-duty line officers.

While we have witnessed countless examples of heroic officers willing to rush into harm's way for strangers, the many other criminal challenges we have faced over the past two decades remain daunting. Illegal drugs, gangs, cyber crime, meth labs, pill mills, human trafficking, and identity theft represent just a few of the newer threats that our profession has learned to confront. Added to these are the formidable social dilemmas posed by illegal immigration and the increasing belief among many state governments that it is now up to local police to address this problem. Finally, there is the looming possibility that many departments may soon face increased labor unrest over the curtailment of public-sector unions and their member benefits. And even though these current challenges are great, they must be confronted with fewer resources because far too many jurisdictions are contending with officer furloughs, layoffs, and cutbacks due to declining tax revenues.

In the past twenty-two years, we have also been forced to confront our dark side. The beating of Rodney King by rogue police officers is seared in our memories and is a constant reminder of how the video camera has forever changed public and media access to the actions of officers on the street. The horrific torture of Abner Louima in New York City is likewise an indelible black mark on our record representing the painful truth that there are some within our ranks who have the potential for indescribable evil.

Fortunately, these incidents of individual officer brutality and use of illegal force have been few. What has been more common is the application of unjust tactics and physical coercion to achieve "noble" outcomes. The Rampart scandal in Los Angeles and the Katherine Johnson shooting in Atlanta are just two examples of how willing some officers are to greatly exceed their authority in an effort to suppress criminal activity. In both cases, we are again reminded how otherwise honorable officers can be persuaded to violate their oaths of office, not for personal gain, but in the mistaken belief that it is permissible to ignore the constitutional guarantees to which all citizens are entitled as long as the ends that are achieved overshadow the means that are used.

One of the lasting consequences of this so-called noble cause corruption in our profession has been to force all police administrators to reconsider the use of statistics as the principle way to measure organizational effectiveness. As long as well-meaning officers believe that their professional survival depends on impressive statistics, especially in front of their peers during COMPSTAT presentations, they will be tempted to bend the rules to produce information that will keep them off the radar screens of their supervisors. These and other recent abuses of police authority have brought the threat of federal oversight to the operations of local police departments. If it can be shown that a pattern and practice of excessive force exists within an agency, then the Department of Justice has the legal authority either to ensure that appropriate administrative and operational changes are made to bring the department into compliance with federal guidelines or to impose appropriate legal sanctions on that agency.

To be sure, policing in a free society is not easy. It is made even tougher for police supervisors by virtue of their leadership role. Pastor Andy Stanley, in his book *The Next Generation Leader: Five Essentials for Those Who Will Shape the Future*, warned: "As a leader, our talents and giftedness have the potential to take us farther than our character can sustain us." There is little doubt that failings of character have made policing tougher for our fellow officers and civilian workers. The International Association of Chiefs of Police has reported that the biggest stress producer among our rank-and-file employees is poor supervision. I submit that the key contributing reason for our leadership problems is the absence of trust of men and women in many departments for their supervisors.

Quite simply, the painful fact remains that even the most honorable among us have weaknesses and are vulnerable to the temptations of anger, lust, greed, and peer pressure. The antidote we need to take more seriously is what Dr. Delattre has so rightly prescribed—a "stiffening spine" or an "invisible senate" consisting of men and women "throughout the ranks who perceptibly stand for the highest ideals of the profession and will not bear in silence their being betrayed or forsaken" so that there will rise "leadership from within that refuses to be ground down by external politics or internal cynicism."

So, let us ponder what is to be the future legacy of *Character and Cops*. Thousands of police executives and peace officers have been influenced by its wisdom; countless officers have studied it for promotional exams; and untold numbers of students have been exposed to its tenets in the classroom. Dr. Delattre writes in these pages that it is his "hope that the book will be of use to police and others in the broad domains of law and politics who seek to bear faithfully the public trust." This is a most humble understatement from a wise teacher who has given so much more. *Character and Cops* is a classic, an unparalleled repository of knowledge that will continue to influence the lives and careers of peace officers, elected officials, and members of the legal profession for generations. Without question, we and those who replace us will continue to be inspired by this book to raise our professional and private standards of conduct so that we are, in fact, worthy stewards of the public trust.

Dr. Delattre has spent countless hours riding in the front seats of patrol cars with line officers and gone fearlessly into harm's way to observe firsthand what policing is all about. He is a courageous individual who has adamantly confronted the hypocrisy and abuse of authority so prevalent in high places of public decision making. On behalf of academics and police practitioners alike, I thank him, fondly and respectfully, for epitomizing the very virtues that he so unabashedly admonishes us to emulate.

DAVID R. BORES
Chief of Police, Woodstock, Georgia
April 2011

Foreword to the First Edition

Patrick V. Murphy

Edwin J. Delattre's *Character and Cops* illuminates hundreds of moral problems faced regularly by police officers and managers. It makes a major contribution to the body of knowledge essential for police to play their rightful part in the struggle of society against injustice.

Policing as an emerging profession dedicated to justice under law will be strengthened by these well-reasoned analyses of actual problems of the street and headquarters. This book will stimulate citizens, elected officials, journalists, and, most important, police practitioners to take a harder look at their functions as fundamental elements of a free society.

Understandably, *Character and Cops* is about good and evil. It faces squarely the fact that without individuals of good character and institutions that apply high ideals to daily practice, the goals of liberty, order, and justice cannot be achieved. It offers neither compromise nor comfort to betrayals of the public trust by anyone in government. Professor Delattre is intolerant of double standards and of time-worn excuses for incompetence, avoidable character faults, and corruption.

It is a privilege to be a police officer in a democratic society. Government of the people, by the people, and for the people is possible only with the assistance of the police. In a modern urban industrial environment, the people could not maintain social control with an all-volunteer system. An insufficient number of able-bodied citizens would contribute time to stand guard, to settle disputes, to investigate accidents and crimes, to arrest offenders, to testify in court, to organize communities in the prevention of crime, and to aid the sick, injured, lost, abused, disturbed, homeless, abandoned, and evicted. The tasks are too complex. Highly developed organizations functioning twenty-four hours every day are necessary. Under a government by the people, however, all citizens have an obligation to participate in the maintenance of order, while delegating to police officers, whose salaries they pay, their collective authority to enforce the law.

The patrol officer who orchestrates the contributions of all the people to the maintenance of order is an essential member of the community. Without order, there is neither freedom nor civilization. The neighborhood beat officer can accomplish little alone. She or he gets the job done through others—parents, relatives, neighbors, teenagers, teachers, clergy, social workers, employers, community leaders, prosecutors, judges, and probation and parole officers. The job description of a police officer resembles that of a manager more than a worker. Although the community, not the officer, is the boss, the officer as the one authorized to use force must sometimes resort to intimidation to accomplish the mission.

Since they can have a profound effect on individual lives, such awesome responsibilities should be entrusted only to people of good character, who will exercise discretion in making decisions. Insufficient guidance has been available to those who must grapple with the moral implications involved in resolving disputes, confronting violence, making arrests, issuing citations, detaining disturbed persons, separating families, protecting children, aiding the poor, and other confrontations with unpredictable behavior. This valuable volume sheds light on the nature of the judgment and character required to meet those duties. Wisdom and integrity—and the virtues of justice, temperance, courage, compassion, honesty, fortitude, and restraint—are described succinctly and shown to be irreplaceable in policing.

Yet the decency of police will not of itself accomplish the essential purposes of our country. As the author understands, two hundred years into the "great experiment," American democracy is thriving—except in the inner cities. The dimensions of problems elsewhere are within the normal range for an advanced society. Where the underclass is concentrated in densely populated urban enclaves, however, individuals are deprived of their right to life, liberty, and the pursuit of happiness to an extent that must be considered abnormal. Criminal victimization, disorder, and fear abound, and violent crime rates are many times the national average. People are unable to exercise social control over their neighborhoods. Government of, by, and for the people is not a reality. The 90 percent of the people who are law abiding are powerless when drug dealers control the streets and use their enormous profits to corrupt and to exert influence.

After the most remarkable achievement in integration in the history of free people, after so many who had been excluded became empowered within the brief period of thirty years, the six largest cities have four black mayors and five black police chiefs. Regrettably, their departments—like those of the other major cities—cannot bring justice and freedom to all of their citizens. Since self-government can be realized only when community exists, large concentrations of poor people—weak in the leadership potential of the middle class—look to the police to assist them in becoming a community of free people. They need to be well informed about crime patterns and resident criminals to protect themselves and one another. The police, in partnership with the people, must ensure that criminals do not intimidate them and that the rule of law supersedes the threat of fear.

In practice, individual officers, chiefs, and entire departments are prevented from taking actions that would serve those goals. Improper political interference in police matters by elected officials, political party leaders, or campaign contributors is a common problem. Nepotism and favoritism, as well as discrimination against well-qualified persons in hiring, assigning, promoting, and disciplining, are far from rare. Professional standards that might be invoked to correct such abuses or to support highly principled practitioners are not universally available or accepted. Many chiefs are stymied in their effort to provide better service by indefensible provisions of collective bargaining contracts.

The police are the "unprofessional profession." They possess the powers and discretion associated with a profession, but they are not a profession. Although they are making progress, professionalism will remain unachievable until the states and federal government provide a support structure. The most fundamental weakness in crime control is the failure of federal and state governments to create a framework for local policing. Much of what is wrong with the police is the result of the absurd, fragmented, unworkable nonsystem of more than 17,000 local departments.

Police officers are victims of the nonsystem. Conscientious officers become demoralized and generate the cynicism that permits callousness and indifference. They are frustrated by irrational management and illogical variations in policies and practices. A four-year college degree should be required for every officer to do work that calls for all of the strengths and resources of a profession.

More harm results from the crazy quilt of thousands of uncoordinated, ineffective agencies than from the misbehavior of poorly motivated officers. Many who succumb to the temptations of graft, laziness, and minimal productivity were once highly motivated but were overcome by poor management, weak leadership, and a lack of fulfillment. For the ideal of justice to be faithfully served, police, prosecutors, legal defenders, judges, court systems, jails, prisons, and probation and parole officers must become participants in a system of crime control.

An honest and fully professional police community would acknowledge in its police education the root causes of crime—poverty, unemployment, underemployment, racism, poor health care, bad housing, weak schools, mental illness, alcoholism, addiction, single-parent families, teenage pregnancy, and a society of selfishness and greed. The profession would acknowledge as well that police have in the past routinely served as the instruments of discrimination in American life. They broke their oath of office by depriving people of the protection of the law because of their race. The complicity of the beat officer, the detective, and the chief was necessary to sustain virulent discrimination in housing, education, employment, and public accommodation.

The police are now better educated, more restrained, and more representative of the communities they serve. In the forty-three years since I entered the New York City Police Department, ethical standards have soared. The ability of the police to fulfill their sacred trust will improve as a lucid sense of ethical standards is developed. Professor Delattre's work with and about police is a powerful ally for all in public service and academic life who care about such standards.

PATRICK V. MURPHY
Former commissioner of the New York City Police
Department and president of the Police Foundation
April 1989

Acknowledgments

I am indebted to the following people for their help with the sixth edition of *Character and Cops*. I have relied on them and benefited from their knowledge, wisdom, and counsel.

John Agresto
Joe Anderson
Merrill Anderson
Sue Autry
David Barnes
Dan Brennan
Judy Brown
Stephen Carlabino
Paul Ciesinski
Larry Crosby
Arnie Daxe Jr.
Lou Dekmar
Syd and Doris Eisen
Andrea Elkon
Darcy Evans
Jerry Fain
Ron Gibson
David Glick
Richard Goldberg
Bob Gretschel
Charles Griswold
Jim Harris
P .J. Ivanhoe
Ruth Johnson
Ed Keller
Tony Kirk

Joe Koletar
Joe Loszinski
Jim McMahon
Ron Miller
Rick Myers
Richard and Wini Myrick
Ron Naples
Tony Narr
Rufus Oliver
Kevin Paletta
Kelly Rosnow
Bill Russell
John Silber
Al Simmons
Jon Sisk
Mike Smathers
Rick and Patty Smith
Darrel Stephens
Ed and Deborah Styles
Ed Sulzbach
Ed Tully
Tam Vieth
Rod and Carol Ward
Chuck Wexler
Bill Wians
Walt Wywadis

I appreciate assistance from the Georgia Association of Chiefs of Police, the Canadian Association of Chiefs of Police, and participants in the Police Executive Research Forum's Senior Management Institute for Police and in Law Enforcement Executive Development programs.

Many police and law enforcement personnel and veterans spoke with me in confidence. While I cannot name them here, I am grateful for their insights and their trust.

I am especially grateful to Ken Watson, who advised me on legislation and court rulings essential to "From War Veterans to Peace Officers." Laura Harbold, the manager of the AEI Press at the American Enterprise Institute, brought encouragement, patience, and intelligence to the project that I thoroughly appreciate. David R. Bores was the first chief to broach the subject of a sixth edition covering this material and was echoed by other chiefs. His thoughts along the way have been right on the mark. As always, my wife, Alice, worked closely with me throughout the research, writing, and typing.

CHARACTER AND COPS

1

Introduction

The romance of police activity keeps in some sense before the mind the fact that civilization itself is the most sensational of departures and the most romantic of rebellions. By dealing with the unsleeping sentinels who guard the outposts of society, it tends to remind us that we live in an armed camp, making war with a chaotic world, and that the criminals, the children of chaos, are nothing but the traitors within our gates. . . . The romance of the police force is thus the whole romance of man. It is based on the fact that morality is the most dark and daring of conspiracies. It reminds us that the whole noiseless and unnoticeable police management by which we are ruled and protected is only a successful knight-errantry.

—G. K. Chesterton[1]

Chesterton's description of police activity as romance will strike some people responsible for enforcing the law and keeping the peace as naïve, or at least incomplete. Police work involves boredom, suffering, anxiety, danger, and disappointment as much as romance, challenge, satisfaction, and success.

Still, despite much literature that describes police as cynical, alienated, disaffected, and unhappy, my own experience with police of all ranks indicates that many love their work and find great fulfillment in it. They understand, with Chesterton, that civilization does not come into existence or survive by accident, and they take seriously their place in sustaining it.

Civilization depends on people who are committed to civility and decency. Not everyone is. People have a mixture of motives; some are high-minded, and some are not. Even the best among us have weaknesses. Some of us are downright dangerous—to ourselves, to other people, or to both.

Human beings are neither angels nor beasts, and they differ in attitudes, beliefs, motives, purposes, and ambitions. This makes civilization difficult

1

to create and preserve. For the same reason, there must be "unsleeping sentinels who guard the outposts of society." Simply put, civilization cannot defend itself: people must stand up for it. The specific people who are on the front lines—the police—are thus essential to civilized life, even though there are limits to what they can do.

In the end, of course, the citizens must do much for themselves in their own daily behavior and in educating the young. No police force can safeguard the ideals of civility and decency from a public determined to destroy them or lacking the courage to stand up for them. But even when many citizens are basically respectful of each other and of the law, there is never enough decency, never enough restraint, to enable people to live well together without someone who can step in when civility breaks down. So some of us must be entrusted to guard the public safety, to enforce the laws, to keep the peace, and to help the helpless.

The age-old dream of living together free from tyranny is the most daring romance of mankind. We want to be free and at the same time to enjoy security. This is the context in which morality in law enforcement takes shape. We want police and law enforcement institutions that merit our trust, respect, and confidence.

Within this context, I have tried to address the kinds of moral questions most often raised by police and others in the criminal justice system with whom I have worked over the past twenty-five years. The chapters are self-contained, but common threads of argument run throughout. I have also tried where appropriate to explain how to think conscientiously about moral questions and public policy issues.

I have addressed the following broad questions: What is excellence of character? Particularly, what are wisdom and integrity, and how are they related to specific aspects of character, such as justice, courage, temperance, and compassion? How does personal virtue figure in the fulfillment of the mission of police? How should problems of infidelity to the public trust—whether in corruption or in abuse of authority, power, and discretion—be addressed? What basic principles of morality apply to police acceptance of gratuities, to uses of deception and force, to treatment of informants, to selective enforcement of the law, to drug testing, and to preparation of reports and testimony? What are just and wise policies for recruitment, selection, reward, and promotion of personnel? How are police to analyze the moral dimensions of public policy debates, such as those concerning the legalization of narcotics? How can police education and training most effectively promote respect for moral ideals? What should decent people do about hard cases where moral ideals seem to be, or actually are, in unresolvable conflict? How can people draw out the best in themselves when suffering heartache and discouragement?

Chapter 2 describes personal character and shows how morality concerns good character and right action. It emphasizes connections between wisdom and integrity in public and private life. Chapter 3 describes the ideals of a constitutional republic and the mission of police in such a republic. Chapter 4 expands on the nature of the police mission by explaining the idea of public trust and describing the kinds of people who are qualified to serve the public. Chapter 5 focuses on the nature, place, and limits of discretion in policing. Chapter 6 discusses corruption, hypotheses about its causes, and the power of individuals to resist it. The chapter distinguishes legitimate higher standards from illegitimate "double" standards. Chapter 7 treats effective uses of authority for reform. Chapter 8 addresses departmental leadership, personnel policies, burnout, and affirmative action. It concludes with recommendations for sound recruiting, selection, and advancement. Chapter 9 describes and analyzes the moral dimensions of public policy debates, focusing on the specific debate about legalization of narcotics. It denies that legalization can solve our problems, and it concludes that morally overriding reasons do not exist for legalization.

Chapters 10 through 12 are devoted explicitly to police training in relation to good character and good judgment. The chapters proceed from fundamentals of ethics through progressively more subtle deliberation about moral questions to the problems of tragedy and "noble cause" corruption. They emphasize the formation of habits of virtue, including the habit of reasoning well about issues that call for deliberation, and thus highlight the need for command personnel, academy instructors, and field training officers who can bridge the gap between moral ideals and the realities of the streets. Chapter 13 is a reflection on the place of wisdom and character in facing the death of a friend, partner, or loved one; the bereavement of others; and the aftermath of deadly force. Chapter 14 describes the morality of aspiration by which we take our lives seriously.

Chapter 15 addresses the dangerous, and false, assertion that police departments are mere microcosms of society. That mistake has undermined proper recruitment and education of police and impaired high standards in policing. Chapter 16 treats juvenile crime, gang recruitment, and gang predation as serious threats to public safety requiring the combined efforts of police and criminal justice officials; civic and youth organizations; the media, corporations, and foundations; parents and personnel from religious, medical, and educational institutions. Using the O. J. Simpson trial as an example, chapter 17 explains why police departments are obligated to refuse to assent to the reduction of individuals to mere members of groups—including racial or ethnic groups. Chapter 18 explains how public service and individual conscience are intertwined and describes the responsibilities of police leaders to their subordinates when questions of conscience or religious belief arise. Chapter 19 shows how a steady decline in individual willingness to exercise peer pressure on the side of morals, manners, and reputable conduct has led to a coarsening of modern life. To meet the complex duties of policing in the twenty-first century, police departments must teach their personnel the differences, for example, between legitimate and illegitimate profiling and establish unambiguous policies for action. Chapter 20 addresses obligations of police and law enforcement personnel that arise from the threat—and the execution—of terrorist atrocities and acts of war against civilian populations. Chapter 21 describes ethics in action—professional excellence in the investigation of mass murder at Columbine High School, the reform of policing in the Rampart Division of the Los Angeles Police Department, gang intelligence and enforcement in the Fairfax County, Virginia, Police Department, and the work on public safety and individual privacy in the New York State Office of Homeland Security.

Honorable and conscientious police work is performed every day by countless command and patrol personnel throughout America. I have witnessed their work time and again: I have seen police apply patience and good judgment to prevent violent conflict; and I have seen them endure racial and ethnic abuse with equanimity rather than add to tension.

I have worked with departments where officers routinely inform citizens who try to bribe them, "We don't do that here." I have seen officers expose themselves to danger to protect the innocent and seen them suffer harm from sudden violence by the very people they were protecting; I have seen police sprayed with the vomit of homeless drunks rather than let them fall to the pavement. I have observed their efforts to help youths recover their lives from addiction and futility; I have seen police work the streets seeking information to identify and apprehend suspects in violent crimes; I have observed their respect for civil rights even in extended undercover investigations of organized crime; and I have seen them make arrests without force when conflict seemed virtually inevitable.

I have seen police use force to subdue the perpetrators of crimes when no lesser means would suffice and witnessed their anguish afterward, even when there was absolutely no reason for remorse or self-criticism. I have enjoyed their humor when things seemed terribly unfair: For example, an officer who was unjustly attacked by reporters, after a harrowing chase to apprehend a suspect, remarked to me, "Man, what a job we could have done if we had known as much as those reporters." I have been touched by police efforts to bring comfort and assurance to old, mentally frail people who were terrorized by their own imaginations.

I have likewise met sly, greedy, cowardly, mean, unreliable, and brutish police. I have witnessed the effects of individual, rogue corruption and violence and of institutionalized corruption and brutality. I have seen people recruited who were never fit to be police in the first place and learned of their subsequent betrayal of the badge. And I have listened to their excuses and rationalizations for failings, sometimes accompanied by excuses from their peers, departments, and political officials.

I have also learned of the work of honorable judges, legislators, prosecuting attorneys, and defense lawyers and seen the good effects of their probity on the criminal justice system. And I have been taught the scams of corrupt attorneys and judges and their impact on police—as well as the effects of legislative corruption, incompetence, cowardice, and greed.

Accordingly, I have written this book in awareness that policing, like all other walks of life, includes people who are worthy of their authority and responsibilities and people who are not. It is my hope that the book will be of use to police and others in the broad domains of law and politics who seek to bear faithfully the public trust.

2

Excellence of Character

It is a matter of real importance whether our early education confirms in us one set of habits or another. It would be nearer the truth to say that it makes a very great difference indeed, in fact all the difference in the world.

—Aristotle[1]

No one who does not already care about being a good person and doing what is right can have a serious ethical question. A person must have achieved a disposition to do the right thing in the right way at the right time for the right reasons before any moral perplexities can arise.

First and Second Nature

No one is born with formed character. Whatever the injustices of the human condition, everyone, regardless of background, race, or sex, enters the world with a full portion of ignorance; and all of us die with much of that ignorance intact.

As infants, we are curious and responsive. Our behavior as babies—such as crying when another baby cries—suggests that the roots of sympathy and social awareness run very deep in us.

At the same time, as infants we are often bent on the immediate gratification of every desire, indifferent to the extent of our demands on others. We have yet to develop a sense of self; our character remains to be formed. We are impulsive. This is what some thinkers call our *first nature* as human beings.

Babies are born with neither good *nor* bad character. Normal people, as they grow, learn, and are trained, develop better or worse dispositions and habits of conduct. They come to have a *second nature*.

Obviously, we are born with a potential for good character—and for the dispositions and habits that make up bad or weak character. Because we are born in ignorance of moral ideals, however, we must be instructed and trained if we are to achieve a good second nature. As philosopher J. O. Urmson expressed it, "If we are normal human beings and not incapacitated by some abnormal defect, then whether we acquire a good or bad character depends on the kind of upbringing we get."[2]

Aristotle observed that "habit is a second nature" and quoted the Greek poet Evenus: "I say that habit's but long practice, friend, And this becomes men's nature in the end."[3] Everyone develops a second nature—whatever becomes natural to do and feel in recurrent situations. The fulfillment of our potential for character excellence depends on the habits "our early education confirms in us."

Environment, however, is not sufficient to give a person good character. The habits of feeling, action, and judgment that constitute good character depend on personal self-discipline and powerful aspiration to become a good person, all of which must finally be drawn from within.

Still, children exposed primarily to bad examples seldom acquire good character. They tend to develop habits of self-indulgence and disregard for others, and they often become dangerous.

It is difficult to nurture respect for moral ideals in adults who have not learned self-discipline as children. Adult programs that focus on ethical problems are fruitless unless the students take questions of decency seriously. Without a prior disposition to decency, discussion of moral dilemmas cannot forge a second nature better than our impulsive first nature, and it is not likely to change the bad habits of our second nature.

Anyone who has played sports knows it is easier to develop good habits—hitting a baseball or cue ball—if we have not already developed bad ones. Bad habits are hard to break. Likewise, moral education, training, and habituation have the best chance when they begin early in life, preferably in a setting that emphasizes love and inspires trust. Although the family may be the best setting, an effective sense of kinship, mutual responsibility, nurture, and support can be built into whole communities, as in ancient Greece, in some Israeli kibbutzim, and in some neighborhoods, schools, and churches.

The idea that acquiring good character is comparable to acquiring a skill is not new. Aristotle observed that "people's characters take their bias from the steady directions of their activities. . . . It is these persistent activities in certain directions that make them what they are."[4] J. O. Urmson explained:

> Paradoxical though it may sound, one learns to play the piano by playing the piano, and to ride a bicycle by riding one. Before one has acquired the art or skill one acts in accordance with the instructions of a teacher, who tells us what to do, and one does it with effort. Gradually by practice and repetition it becomes effortless and second nature. In the same way, one is trained as a child (if lucky in one's parents and teachers) to become truthful, generous, fair, and the like. . . . If properly trained one comes to enjoy doing things the right way, to want to do things the right way, and to be distressed by doing things wrongly.[5]

A wholesome upbringing does not, however, lead inevitably to character excellence. But without training and habituation in youth, change for the better is difficult. As the philosopher Immanuel Kant observed, "If a man be allowed to follow his own will in his youth, without opposition, a certain lawlessness will cling to him throughout his life."[6]

Learning—and living up to—high standards is not easy, any more than learning to play the piano is easy. Philosopher John Stuart Mill criticized teaching the young *only* what can be made pleasurable. When the young are not required "to learn anything but what has been made easy and interesting, one of the chief objects of education is sacrificed." That system of teaching, he added, was "training up a race of men who will be incapable of doing anything which is disagreeable to them."[7] Learning in youth to control our impulses often is disagreeable, but character education does not otherwise succeed.

Character *can* be reformed later in life. Even mature adults do change habits of alcohol and food consumption, for example. Still, one suspects that they must have achieved some self-control beforehand.

The indispensability of moral habituation to moral excellence as second nature is disclosed in the very idea of character. Philosopher Alasdair MacIntyre wrote that a person's character is "his set of dispositions to behave systematically in one way rather than another, to lead one particular kind of life."[8] Character excellence, Urmson added, is the set disposition "to do what reason determines is the best course of action"[9] rather than to allow unconsidered desires and feelings to hold sway. It is made up of habits of feeling and acting in the right way, at the right time, toward the right people—and for the right reasons. Thus, the person of good character will not be inordinately angry about someone's cutting him off in a traffic jam but will be infuriated by the sale of illicit drugs to children.

Such habits are acquired by initiation and instruction from others—in the telling of stories; the explanation of decent behavior; the introduction to heroes, heroines, and villains; the exposure to the meaning of fundamental ideals; and the discussion of questions.

This is true not only for children but also for adults and thus for police. Listening and talking—and frequently reading and writing—can be basic instruments of moral and intellectual maturation. Political scientist William Ker Muir Jr. observed in *Police: Streetcorner Politicians* that grasping "the nature of human suffering" and achieving moral strength "depends in part on developing an enjoyment of talk."[10] This enjoyment draws us into closer association and gives us a chance to learn from each other—and to discern how to meet the moral demands of our work better than we can in isolation. Great teachers throughout history have emphasized the place of dialogue in education. Socrates told his fellow citizens that discussing excellence every day is the most beneficial of all activities.

Habits of virtue are acquired by observation and imitation of others, by rejection of behavior that falls short, and above all by practice over time at behaving well.

Character and Police

Obviously, all police and law enforcement agencies want to recruit candidates of good character and to encourage the best in them, but how should good character be understood?

The Bad Character. Imagine an officer who comes upon an undetected burglary and can steal goods and blame the burglar, even if the burglar later denies stealing those goods. A person of bad character will seek opportunities to profit by victimizing others. Other people exist for him only to be used for his own advantage. Whatever he may have been taught about right and wrong has nothing to do with the conduct of his life. He feels no shame in abusing his authority. The so-called meat-eaters are dangerous to life and property, they are often shrewd, and they are invariably rapacious and without conscience. Such persons must simply be weeded out by background investigations, by observant academy instructors, by careful field training officers, and so on.

In 1980, Miami, Florida, adopted a policy requiring that two hundred new police be recruited immediately, with 80 percent to be minority residents of Miami. Many of the recruits were utterly unsuited to be police, as background investigations and the warnings of academy instructors confirmed at the time. Sloppy field training, inadequate supervision, and an ineffective Internal Affairs Division permitted them to behave with contempt for the law. By 1988, more than a third of them had been fired. Twelve members of a group known as the River Cops had been convicted of crimes ranging from drug trafficking to murder. Many of these recruits became police to profit from illegal activity with drugs.[11]

The Uncontrolled. A person who is uncontrolled in some aspects of his character may behave like a person of bad character, if his passion for gain overrides his regard for the law. A person who is weak willed and vulnerable to childish temptations may be teachable but does not belong in a position of public trust. Such "grass eaters" cannot trust themselves under pressure from peers or in circumstances of illicit opportunity and may fall into progressively worse behavior. They can be "reached"; they "have a price."

Some of the "Buddy Boys" of the Seventy-seventh Precinct of the New York Police Department in Brooklyn served with honor for years. When they saw drug dealers making huge profits and flouting the law, however, they began to bust drug dealers to steal their money, and they finally stole and dealt drugs themselves. Any habits of decency they had formed succumbed to the temptations of revenge against street dealers and of easy money, as they rationalized their conduct by the timeworn excuse that "others do it."[12]

The Self-Controlled. Persons with greater self-discipline may report a crime, protect the remaining property, and so on, but resent the higher standard of conduct to which they are held. They may be gnawed by feelings that they could have profited and that others are getting away with illegality and enjoying more material goods. Such officers may feel a persistent tension between duty and desire and become desperately unhappy because acquisitiveness draws them even as they do what they *should*. A department should provide support and leadership to foster admirable behavior in the face of temptation and discouragement.

The Excellent. Finally, there are persons of excellent character, who have acquired habits of trustworthiness that have become integral to their lives. They respect and even love honesty, which has become second nature. Such persons behave in the same way as the self-controlled or self-disciplined person in that they do their duty, but they enjoy peace of mind in knowing who they are and what they stand for. Such persons can be said to be truly incorruptible, with no temptation to steal because money is "only green paper." Persons of such character are fit to bear the trust of public office in law enforcement.

In different aspects of their character, individuals reveal themselves to be of more than one of the four types described above. A person may be self-controlled in matters of money, for example, but uncontrolled in drinking. And character in general may range along a continuum from those who are remorseless; to those who cannot resist temptation but are ashamed of it; to the self-controlled, who find little fulfillment and who may be influenced more by fear of detection or sanctions than by duty, regard for others, or honor; and finally to those with an excellence of character that is deeply fulfilling.[13]

Acquiring Character. The unregulated desires of youngsters for, say, cake can easily overshadow their appreciation for justice and fair play in its distribution. When two children are to share a single portion of cake, we may let one divide it and the other choose the first piece. The first child may cut the cake evenly only to avoid losing the lion's share—motivated by advantage rather than fairness—but by such exercises the child learns respect for fair shares.

We try to give children practice in behaving fairly and in acquiring a sense for the feelings of other people. In games and sports, we witness their frustration when they cannot have their way or cannot do what they try to do, and we try to help them find more fun in winning with a fair field and no favors than in ruining the game or triumphing by cheating. We help children mature until they enjoy the fulfillment that comes of treating others fairly and find the peace of mind that accompanies a just life.

A police officer's fitness to wear the badge depends on the acquisition of habits of just behavior. A just officer will see that providing special—even if legal—services in return for gratuities takes time and unjustly deprives other members of the public of the attention they deserve. Officers who respect justice will have nothing to do with racial prejudices, will not exceed their authority in the exercise of discretion, abuse the powers of their office, falsify reports, or give perjured testimony.

None of these considerations is more important than the use of force. William Ker Muir argues that good police officers not only understand human suffering but also resolve the tension between respect for justice and the use of coercion to achieve it.[14] Respect for justice holds them back from using threats when reasoned persuasion will suffice, from force when threats will suffice, and from greater force when lesser force will suffice. Habits of restraint differ, however, from excessive caution, timidity, and irresoluteness.

There is fulfillment in acting with fairness toward others and peace of mind in knowing one has neither exceeded one's authority nor been more coercive than a situation demanded. The use of force is never as satisfying to a person of excellent character as a resolution by persuasion and reason, and a person in whom justice has become second nature reflects this in his behavior.

We admire individuals who resist a strong temptation to strike in vengeance or to deceive for personal gain. But as in the case of honesty, our highest esteem goes to the person who is above such temptation, for whom justice has become second nature.

Another crucial aspect of character formation is associated with temperance. Intemperate people pursue pleasure inordinately—whether through sex, alcohol, food, or drugs. Because pleasure is by definition enjoyable, temperance is self-control despite the allure. Temperate persons are not indifferent to pleasure, nor do they reject recreation, relaxation, and amusements, but they choose pleasures that contribute to well-being.

Self-control is also an essential part of courage and fortitude, at least *in extremis*. Courageous officers facing life-threatening situations hardly take pleasure in them, but will not run away and leave a partner or an innocent bystander exposed. They find fulfillment in not allowing fear to dictate their behavior. Shakespeare's insight—the coward dies a thousand deaths, but the brave man only one—holds.

Courage is not only physical, of course. Police officers may know that a partner is corrupt, that some of their superiors are "on the pad," or that fellow officers brutalize suspects. Decent officers may fear the contempt of their colleagues if they refuse to participate or blow the whistle.

Courageous persons will not tolerate such abuses even if they have to blow the whistle covertly rather than openly. To inform on a partner one likes and may admire in other respects and as a result to be rejected and isolated by peers is not enjoyable. No one wants to be thought a "rat" rather than a "stand-up guy," even by colleagues so corrupt that by the latter expression they mean a crooked cop.

A colleague who *deserves* to be a friend, however, would not compromise a partner. The betrayal of office is an affront to honesty and justice as well as to friendship. Courage here means fearing the right thing—dishonorable conduct—more than contemptible forms of peer pressure.

Balanced Perception. Two kinds of wholeness are related to excellent character. The first consists of a balanced perception of how to make the best of circumstances. On a domestic violence call, police officers must be courageous in ending the violence, just in their treatment of the combatants, temperate in their use of force, compassionate to the victims, respectful of the limits to discretion, honest, timely, and properly equipped and with sufficient backup. But they also need a sense of how all these factors are related. When they conflict, sound judgment of their relative importance is needed.

In a given case, compassion may give a victim comfort that falsely minimizes the danger of future beatings. The unvarnished truth may cause panic. Complete honesty may suggest that the more abusive party has no need to fear the law. And so on. Judgment and a sense of proportion about what the situation calls for may be called wisdom in the practical affairs of life.

Integrity. The second kind of wholeness related to good character is integrity. Excellent qualities of character must become integral, not just to certain parts of our lives, but to our entire lives, both public and private. Integrity means wholeness, being one thing through and through, much as homogenization is to milk. Persons of integrity by definition have made certain kinds of excellence integral to all of their lives.

A person of integrity is the same person in public and in private. Accordingly, integrity as an ideal flies squarely against the now popular idea that we live public lives on one plane and personal lives on another, and that these are essentially separate and subject to different principles of conduct.

Every human life is the life of a person; for this reason, all life is personal life. Personal life has both public and private dimensions, but these dimensions are parts of a single person. Don L. Kooken, who served as captain of the Indiana State Police and chairman of the Department of Police Administration at Indiana University, stressed this point: "Habits that are formed in the home and among working associates are reflected in a policeman's relations with the public. . . . One cannot be a gentleman in public and a cad in private."[15]

But integrity is not achieved just by being any one thing through and through. A person can, after all, be a cad both in public and private. In urban ghettos and elsewhere there are sociopaths, drug dealers, crack addicts, and terrorists who are one thing through and through, the same in public and private, but who are not people of integrity.

Danish theologian Soren Kierkegaard observed that "purity of heart is to will one thing." Though this is true in important ways, we would not say that a crack addict who wills one thing—his or her next hit of crack— is a person with purity of heart. What then is the wholeness that gives a person integrity?

No one achieves the full measure of integrity whose life falls under the dominion of gluttony, lust, sloth, pride, greed, anger, or envy, to cite a justly famous catalog of self-destroying sins. Moral wholeness cannot be achieved by anyone who commits murder, adultery, rape, theft, or perjury, or who is foul-mouthed, or whose thoughts and feelings are covetous, rancorous, or hateful. Along the same lines, we would not call morally whole a person who is foolish or unjust, reckless or cowardly, or who is without any sense of charity or has no faith in anything or anybody.

All such flaws are affronts to character excellence as a whole, and therefore to integrity. No one is without fault in every respect, but all the same, the aspiration to achieve integrity as fully as we can is the highest calling of a life well lived.

A simple test tells us how much integrity matters to us. In *The Republic*, Plato tells the story of the magical ring of Gyges, which can make whoever wears it invisible. The question is, How would you behave differently if you could make yourself invisible? When people do wrong, they try to make themselves as invisible as they can; they are motivated more by fear of detection than by integrity. Only a person who is good enough to care about behaving rightly, and not just about being caught, can become better.

The Morally Important and the Morally Problematic

What is morally important must be learned to understand what is morally problematic, whether in the moral instruction of children or the professional education and training of police or people in other walks of life. A person who lacks concern for others cannot appreciate moral questions about when deception is morally obligatory, right, or excusable. A person who has no sense of justice cannot understand disagreements about merit and affirmative action in personnel policies. A person who has no ideals cannot understand why they must not be betrayed through cowardice or laxity, or how ideals can conflict with one another.

Police executives, academy instructors, senior officers, and others in law enforcement can, of course, teach how to think through moral questions. We can show how to take stock, make a considered judgment, and respond effectively. We can teach that people deserve to be treated as valuable in themselves, just because they are people, and not merely as instruments. We can teach that we do what is right because it is right and not out of fear of detection or punishment. We can describe the way a fair-minded person deliberates about his behavior, that he is likely to ask, "What if everyone behaved as I propose to behave—would that be possible or would it be self-defeating?"

If a person considers lying for profit and asks whether everyone could do so, he sees that if everyone lied for personal advantage, then no one would trust anyone else where personal interests were involved, and no one could lie successfully. He can see that his own lie can be effective only if others do not lie, so if he lies he becomes a moral parasite who treats himself as having privileges others do not exercise. No fair-minded person is willing to treat himself with such favoritism. We can explain, as well, that such moral reasons are the most important reasons in deciding what to do.

Yet in teaching how to plan and implement responses to situations, we are, above all, refining intelligence. Powerful intelligence without good character is notoriously dangerous; because it spurns regard for others and for morality, it may be acquired by the successful contract killer, the shrewd drug dealer, or the corrupt public official.

Since the ideal is a combination of wisdom with good character, our instruction must be established by practice. Practice at behaving rightly establishes skillfulness, and with skill comes greater enjoyment; thus does our potential for good character—that element of the dove that is woven into our frame—come into the combination. Such experience at behaving well cannot be replaced by less intimate methods of instruction, and certainly not by holier-than-thou moralizing that implies a person of excellent character must shun every enjoyment of life. Practice and encouragement are necessary to moral wisdom because the proof of the quality of moral life is in living it.

The mission of policing can safely be entrusted only to those who grasp what is morally important and who respect integrity. Without this kind of personal character in police, no set of codes, rules, or laws can safeguard that mission from the ravages of police misconduct. No one need choose to be a police officer or to bear the public trust; but those who do so—no matter how naively and no matter how misguided their original expectations—must acquire the excellence of character necessary to live up to it.

3

The Mission of Police

Pride grows in the human heart like lard on a pig.
                                                    —Aleksandr Solzhenitsyn[1]

The accumulation of all powers legislative, executive and judiciary, in the same hands, whether of one, a few, or many, and whether hereditary, self-appointed, or elective, may justly be pronounced the very definition of tyranny.
                                                    —James Madison[2]

The mission of police in the United States, as in the other democracies, is to play a rightful part in the nation's "experiment in ordered liberty."

The Experiment in Ordered Liberty

The United States was established as a constitutional republic in which no person or group could rise to absolute power. Our experiment in government answerable to the public tests whether a country can maintain order *and* protect liberty. Powers are separated among executive, legislative, and judicial branches, each intended to serve as a check and a balance on the others and to be impervious to economic dominion by the private sector, just as the private sector is safeguarded from tyranny of government. Powers are balanced so that no person or agency can function without restraint.

When a country cannot provide order, its people are victimized by factions—whether in the rebellion in Massachusetts in 1786 (which led George Washington to conclude that America was on the verge of anarchy) or in the drug wars in the streets of our cities two centuries later. Yet when order is brought by the destruction of liberty, the people are victimized by tyrants.

17

Order with liberty cannot succeed if the government or the governed indulge themselves as they wish. Our ordered liberty is an experiment in the rule of laws that are impartial and that apply to governors and governed alike. James Madison, the father of our Constitution, stressed the burden this places on us:

> In framing a government which is to be administered by men over men, the great difficulty lies in this: you must first enable the government to control the governed; and in the next place oblige it to control itself.[3]

Since the rule of law requires the keeping of peace, America's government is also an experiment in law enforcement and peacekeeping. It is an experiment in whether policing can promote security and serve liberty for the sake of what Madison identified as the ultimate purpose of government:

> Justice is the end of government. It is the end of civil society. It has ever been and ever will be pursued until it be obtained, or until liberty be lost in the pursuit.[4]

The drafters of the Constitution were actively concerned about immoderation by both government and individuals. Alexander Hamilton cautioned in 1781 that government must have "a proper degree of authority to make and execute the laws with vigour," for "too little leads to anarchy."[5] Too much, he believed, leads to tyranny. In 1787 Benjamin Rush was even more direct about the dangers of making government too weak to protect citizens from each other:

> In our opposition to monarchy, we forgot that the temple of tyranny has two doors. We bolted one of them by proper restraints; but we left the other open by neglecting to guard against the effects of our own ignorance and licentiousness.[6]

The tension between order and liberty persists wherever men and women care about justice. Though a country dedicated to justice may tilt one way or the other, the experiment depends on the animating conviction, as constitutional scholar Robert Goldwin has explained, that while people are not angels, they are still "good enough to govern themselves."[7]

The founders knew that the system they framed was imperfect, that even good people are motivated by self-interest, and that all of us make grievous mistakes. No nation can hope to become perfect, without any abuses of freedom. Efforts to prevent every social evil have often led to worse excesses—including religious and political persecution.[8]

Justice in a society rests on restraint, by government and by the citizenry. Laws provide both a guide and a motive for such restraint for the good of everyone.

Disorder and Injustice

When I describe these American traditions to police, they point to the injustices suffered by many citizens:

> It is not just when perpetrators go free to repeat their crimes, or when victims know that their assailants walk the streets with impunity. Our country cannot be complacent when the bare minimum of civilized order is destroyed in ghettos by drug dealers and street criminals, and when ghetto children are deprived of all opportunity for healthy growth and worthwhile aspiration. It is not just when a known perpetrator in custody possesses information essential to saving the life or sanity of an innocent victim and will not divulge it in interrogation that gives undue priority to the perpetrator's civil rights.

They are right, of course. Immoderation, license, and violence in America are pressing, perhaps now more than ever before. If citizens' rights are largely secure from governmental excesses, they are not safe from individual and group excesses. Although interests and ambitions inevitably conflict among human beings, diversity in America has gone far beyond the legitimate boundaries of pluralism.

Pluralism means the range of views held by reasonable people of goodwill who restrain self-interest. Today, our diversity includes individuals and groups with no regard for civility, decency, and legality. The enforcement of law is a crushing problem in the face of deep divisions over what the laws should be and over the claim of law to our respect. When a country's most privileged citizens break the law—as in public corruption and white collar crime—and crime rates in urban areas put the entire public at risk, the situation is very serious.

Street crime has become mindlessly vicious in our time. Charles Silberman noted:

> The most disturbing aspect of the growth in "street crime" is the turn toward viciousness, as well as violence, on the part of many young criminals. A lawyer who was a public defender noted for her devotion to her clients' interests, as well as her legal ability, speaks of "a terrifying generation of kids" that emerged during the late 1960s and early 1970s. When she began practicing, she told me, adolescents and young men charged with robbery had, at worst, pushed or shoved a pedestrian or shopkeeper to steal money or merchandise; members of the new generation kill, maim, and injure without reason or remorse.[9]

Police, along with many ghetto residents, are exposed to this violence every day. Describing the Henry Horner Homes on Dameon Street in Chicago, Adam Walinsky wrote:

> Dominant authority is exercised by the gangs: organized groups, led by men of thirty or forty, organizing and recruiting down to the age of eight. . . . The gangs engage in regular and constant warfare for control of the drug and vice trades . . . armed with pistols, rifles, automatic weapons, and occasional grenades. . . . Children dodge machine gun crossfire as they leave school. . . . Women and children are mugged by youths of all ages. . . . Eight-year-olds, serving as drug salesmen, have been shot in the foot to encourage greater effort. . . . Children grow as in the midst of a war. . . . The children almost routinely witness friends and acquaintances shot and bleeding to death in the street. . . . The neighborhood has no place to buy food. . . . Move out? This is not the worst housing

project in Chicago. Even if there is room in another, the Housing
Authority assigns better apartments only when bribed. . . . In
Detroit, the police do not keep count of shot children; the news-
papers counted 270 last year.[10]

These citizens live and die deprived of the liberty and justice the
Constitution is intended to secure for them. They live, in Chesterton's words,
"in an armed camp . . . a chaotic world" in which "criminals, the children of
chaos," visit tyrannical terror upon them every day. The *Wall Street Journal*
noted the rise of vigilantism in America in the burning down of crack houses
in Detroit, Miami, and the South Bronx, and in the lethal beatings of muggers:

Vigilantes return . . . whenever citizens come to believe that the
law enforcement agencies don't work. Right now, the vigilantes are
back, especially in this country's most beleaguered, drug-infested
central city neighborhoods. . . . The police fail because the lawyers
won't let them succeed. The lawyers prevail because liberal jurists,
cheered on by columnists and editorial writers intent on expanding their notions of civil rights, have erected a vast legal jungle
gym of evidentiary procedures, subjected police conduct to extensive second-guessing, and eliminated nearly all discretion from
the cop on the beat—for example, by outlawing vagrancy
laws. . . . The system of criminal justice . . . is failing the people
who need it most.[11]

Although police can still exercise discretion on the beat, the problems
of the criminal justice system are real. Many officers—and prosecutors—
consider specific laws self-defeating. When police officers arrest a person
who throws his narcotics to the ground, the officers may momentarily lose
sight of the package. But if they testify in court that they did so, the case is
likely to be dismissed. Some officers perjure themselves rather than lose the
case. If an officer admits that he lost sight of the drugs, some police, attorneys, and judges infer that his testimony has been bought by the dealers.

Lawmakers sometimes present police with unenforceable laws or fail to
provide the funds necessary for enforcement. Courts issue rulings that
impose unreasonable standards of proof, undermining public respect for

law. Greater wisdom in legislators and judges will be required to square the balance between order and liberty, together with more communication to the public by police organizations, as in the growing opposition to easy purchase of cheap handguns. Convincing testimony by the public about the erosion of its safety must be joined with widespread participation in the electoral process.

Since inefficiency cannot be entirely avoided, however, the system will remain imperfect. Safeguarding rights of due process interferes with efforts to detect criminal activity, apprehend perpetrators, and secure convictions. The separation of powers does not place a premium on expediency. Tyranny does—and the results are terrifying.

Against Tyranny

The Marxist Sandinista government of Nicaragua failed to provide any economic security—or hope—to its people. Students carried their desks to and from school to prevent their being stolen; school toilets were stolen. Robbers armed with AK457 rifles prowled neighborhoods stealing everything from manhole covers to clothes hung out to dry. Neighbors kidnapped each other's dogs for ransom.[12] Yet so tyrannical was the government that at a ceremony "opening the sugar harvest Agrarian Reform Minister Jaime Wheelock threatened a gathering of sugar workers . . . , 'If anyone raises a strike banner here, we will cut off his hands.'"[13]

In Iran, under the Ayatollah Khomeini, mass executions and torture were routine. Iranian government documents confirmed approximately 12,000 executions in the second half of 1988. Women were executed, or beaten until the skin fell off their feet, raped by police, and disfigured with acid—and their children were slaughtered—for appearing in public with their faces uncovered. Public officials extorted bribes for release from prison: $125 for the crime of an exposed lock of hair; $900 for wearing fingernail polish.[14]

Such remorseless arrogance of power was not new, though tyrants of our time may exercise greater dominion by their use of modern bureaucracies and technologies. Such perpetrators of evil seem capable of immense self-deception; they persuade themselves that whatever they do is justified by circumstances.

On the strength of his experience under tyranny, Aleksandr Solzhenitsyn maintained that "to do evil a human being must first of all believe that what he's doing is good."[15] William Parker said something similar when he became chief of police of Los Angeles in 1950:

> As practicing policemen we are familiar with the fact that the average criminal does not believe that he is doing wrong. As he views the situation, he is doing right. However faulty his premises, however weak his logic, and however transitory his beliefs, he acts in accord with his own concepts.[16]

Although those statements omit that right and wrong are simply of no consequence for some people, they do highlight human capacities for self-deception and self-aggrandizement, and for judging oneself favorably. Awareness of these tendencies lies at the base of America's doctrine of separation of powers. When self-righteousness or remorselessness joins with unrestrained power, injustice and terror become inevitable. By restraining the power that resides in any individual or group, the worst horrors may be avoided.

Many tyrants, as in the postczarist Soviet Union, celebrated the unrestrained exercise of power. Solzhenitsyn explained:

> The supreme accuser—in other words, the Prosecutor General— informs us that the All-Russian Central Executive Committee . . . "pardons and *punishes*, at its own discretion *without any limitation whatever.*" For example, a six-month sentence was changed to ten years. . . . All of this, Krylenko explains, "shows the superiority of our system over the false theory of the separation of powers. . . . It is very good that the legislative and executive power are not divided by a thick wall as they are in the West. All problems can be *decided quickly.*"[17]

Those who want to unite the powers of government believe that its purpose is to perpetuate itself or extend its power. This is the reason the Soviet secret police—the Cheka—was empowered to do anything to preserve the dictatorship (ostensibly, in the interest of the public) and the reason the

Communist party, led by Lenin, claimed that its mistreatment of the people was necessary for the revolution. The viciousness of that dogma continued to be seen in the Soviet Union as dissidents were imprisoned, freedoms of religion and press denied, and due process mocked in show trials. The United States was established in opposition to such arbitrary deprivation of life and liberty.

Still, we may be tempted by expediency to "decide things quickly," without a lot of technicalities and restraints. Confronted with merciless criminals who savage innocent victims, we may feel justified in taking illegal shortcuts.

But expediency pushes us onto dangerous ground. Expediency of the worst kind insists that "the end justifies the means" and that "might makes right." In a setting such as the former Soviet Union, the courts were not concerned for justice, law, extenuating circumstances, or guilt or innocence. They proceeded "on the basis of considerations of expediency," as Solzhenitsyn explained. He continued:

> That was the way it was in those years: people lived and breathed and then suddenly found out that their existence was inexpedient. And it must also be kept in mind that it was not what he had done that constituted the defendant's burden, but what he *might* do if he were not shot now. "We protect ourselves not only against the past but also against the future."[18]

This is the way unrestrained power works. Expediency favors punishing the innocent to ensure that the guilty do not go free; it presumes the guilt of the accused, and it accuses anyone whose ideas or behavior are inconvenient to the tyrant. It imposes punishments that do not fit the crime. But punishing the innocent does not ensure that the guilty will also fall into the net. The presumption of guilt is therefore not only unjust but also impractical.

In fact, the presumption of guilt and the power to punish without due process may not even be significant deterrents to some kinds of crimes. Sir Leon Radzinowicz, then director of Cambridge University's Department of Criminal Science, reported that "no national characteristic, no political regime, no system of law, police, justice, punishment, treatment, or even terror has rendered a country exempt from crime."[19] His point was confirmed by figures released in August 1988 by Igor Karpets, then director of the All-Union Scientific Research Institute of Soviet Legislation. Karpets described a high incidence of embezzlement in the Soviet Union in the 1960s and 1970s "when many people confused their own pockets with those of the state." In 1987, 95,000 were convicted of hooliganism, and nearly 5,000 were convicted of premeditated murder for the first half of that year.[20]

In America we have chosen the presumption of innocence out of regard for justice and for the importance of the individual. For all its deficiencies, our system exhibits greater respect for the dignity of humanity than any other ever devised. Within it, police are charged to respect the lawful liberty of the people while applying authority, good judgment, and power to see that order and peace do not collapse under individual or group excesses. The role of police in the experiment in ordered liberty must be respected to grasp the specifics of their mission.

Mission

Some authorities, politicians, and citizens' groups say that the primary work of police is crime prevention. Others emphasize peacekeeping and maintenance of order. Some stress the enforcement of the law and the apprehension of perpetrators; others stress social services. Some scholars are especially interested in police work with juveniles, while other scholars and practitioners claim that this work should be done by separate agencies. Social movements, as during Prohibition, cast the police as enforcers of morals, and legislation can have the same effect. And some people expect the police to combat every social ill.

The police cannot do everything expected of them by everyone. In ghettos where social ills are worst and street crime is relentless, the problems require extreme remedies, which go far beyond anything the police can deliver. Citizens who appeal to the police suffer reprisals from the gangs, which are so powerful that enforcement of the law and protection of the public are largely impossible.

Attitudes have changed since the late James Baldwin characterized police in the ghetto as an occupying army. Because of drugs, gangs, and guns, many ghetto citizens want more and better police protection, not less.

More crime is intraracial than interracial—simply because of the proximity of potential victims—and the innocent victims of ghetto crimes know it.

The desperation of ghetto residents makes their expectations of the police unrealistic. In the South Bronx, I once accompanied police to a tenement where a woman had been bitten by a Great Dane. Other residents were frightened, and the owner of the dog—which never had any shots for distemper or rabies—wanted it removed. Children skated noisily through the halls on discarded metal food containers. As the police arrived, residents assured each other, "It's all right now, everything will be OK now, the police are here."

Of course, it was not all right. Emergency calls were coming from other areas of the precinct; the victim expected police to transport her to a hospital that was within easy walking distance; and the residents expected the police to substitute for the ASPCA and take the dog away. The two officers explained what they could and could not do, saw that the dog was confined, told the victim how to get to the hospital, and notified the ASPCA to collect the dog as soon as possible. Then they rushed to another call.

Unrealistic expectations of the police are not confined to ghettos. In 1988 citizens of Tampa, Florida, learned that a convicted rapist, who had cut off the arms of a victim, was living there after being released from prison in another state. In televised proceedings, many citizens became abusive when police explained that they could not violate the man's civil rights and drive him away. "I pay your salary, and you're supposed to protect me," they said. "It's your job."

Most knowledgeable accounts of police mission stress law enforcement, peacekeeping, and delivery of social services. The Police Foundation, for instance, observed in 1972, "The Foundation fully realizes that improved police services must strike a *balance between effective crime fighting and humane efforts to keep the peace*."[21] David A. Hansen, who served as supervising captain of the Daly City, California, Police Department, affirmed that view: "The keeping of the peace and the protection of life and property by those who are police officers—this is the police function."[22] Professor Lee W. Potts rehearsed data confirming this view in actual practice:

> One of the common findings of the volume of data developed on the police in the late 1960s and early 1970s was the falseness of the belief that law enforcement dominates police work. . . .

> Rather than being primarily a law enforcement officer, the aver-
> age policeman is primarily a peace officer. His time is spent per-
> forming public services such as directing traffic and escorting
> vehicles or performing social welfare services such as dealing
> with the mentally deranged, attempted suicides, domestic crisis
> intervention, and neighborhood disputes.[23]

Potts added that this multiplicity of responsibilities can cause tensions
for officers, since law enforcement duties may require "their coercive role to
be paramount" while "as peace officers, they most often find their public
servant role to be paramount."[24]

As Potts suggested, the mission "to protect and to serve" is not so simple as it may appear when emblazoned on a patrol car. The two functions
require common skills, but they require distinct and separate skills as well.
Furthermore, law enforcement frequently involves legal and institutional
guidelines more rigorous than do police duties in peacekeeping and other
social services.

In 1936 August Vollmer, a pioneer of modern American policing, wrote
that "the original purpose of police organizations was protection against the
occurrence of major crimes and the apprehension of perpetrators of such
offenses." Although he believed that this remained the primary duty of the
police, he insisted that

> police departments are also called upon to perform every con-
> ceivable kind of service. No federal or state law or city ordinance
> is passed which does not call for the attention of some police
> organization. Responsibility for sick, injured, and missing per-
> sons, for the insane and the feeble-minded, as well as the inves-
> tigation of suicide cases, is assigned these public agents. At any
> time of the day or night, citizens may report suspicious persons
> or circumstances and request action by the police. In times of
> disaster, strikes, or riots, it is the duty of the police to preserve,
> if possible, or to restore, peace and order.[25]

In 1978 Charles Silberman described how the diverse functions of the
police are interrelated, in terms of work by sociologist Egon Bittner:

There are common denominators to almost all the situations I have described that make them uniquely a police responsibility. To begin with, the police are called because they are available— twenty-four hours a day, seven days a week. . . . More important, the police are called because of a sense of urgency; what unites the various situations with which police deal is the fact that someone thought emergency help was needed to prevent injury, loss, harm, disorder, or inconvenience. [Egon] Bittner writes that whether a police officer is preventing someone from jumping off a bridge, rescuing people from a burning building, dispersing a crowd that might hamper the firemen, settling a domestic dispute or barroom brawl, breaking up a robbery in progress, or arresting a suspected burglar, the incident involves *"something-that-ought-not-to-be-happening-now-and-about-which-someone-had-better-do-something-now."* . . . Most important of all, the police are called into urgent situations because they, and only they, are empowered to use force to set matters right. . . . Much of the artistry of police work lies in the ability to handle explosive situations without resorting to force. But the fact that the police can use force is uppermost in the minds of those who call on them for help; it also directly affects the way other people behave.[26]

Within that rough consensus about manifold functions are many disagreements about priorities. But police are expected to fulfill their obligations "professionally"—that is, competently and honestly, and with accountability to supervisors for their performance. Disagreements abound about the appropriate levels of autonomy and authority of police administrators, elected officials, and citizen review boards and of the public itself.

Still, the law enforcement community and scholars of policing agree that the police cannot fulfill their mission without effective communication with the citizenry and without public support. Maintaining the best relations with the public, however, and having a near monopoly on the legitimate use of force make police walk a fine line. Both police and scholars recognize with Egon Bittner that "no amount of public relations work can entirely abolish the sense that there is something of the dragon in the dragon slayer."[27]

Police often sense that people draw into themselves when the police are around. That is, perhaps, the reason the social life of many police officers centers on the companionship of other officers. They share in the tradition of St. George, because they have the authority to use force, even deadly force, though for most officers the need is rare.

But police must remember that their mission is more complicated than St. George's, and if they work well, they will convey much more to the public than the image of a mere slayer of dragons. Police, after all, work in a chain of command; they abide by laws, departmental policies, and court rulings; they cooperate with internal affairs units; and they make reports. Moreover, they have to enforce laws, prevent crimes, maintain order, deal with the media, use informants responsibly, provide a range of services to those in need, testify in court, and be alert to the safety of their colleagues as well as of the public. Any police officer who conveys an image of being solely a dragon slayer causes needless risk to himself and to everyone around him.

Public Confidence

Some problems *cannot* be solved by sensitive communication. No one can be persuaded by reason to be reasonable—a person must be predisposed to reason even to listen. Even in intellectual debates, passions run so high as to make civility impossible. Discussions about abortion, arms control, federal policy, or constitutional reform are as likely to exacerbate as to relieve differences. We must be realistic to grasp the demands of police work.

The history of war and violence is not simply a history of failed communication. Some wars occur because nations do understand each other and know that they cannot be brought into harmony by diplomatic means. That was the case in World War II. In private life and in police work, self-defense and the protection of the innocent sometimes require immediate and sufficient force, both in the enforcement of the law and in dealing with the domestic and neighborhood disputes. The distinction between law enforcement and peacekeeping can never be absolute.

Public trust depends not only on communication but on many kinds of performance by the police, including the use of such powers as are minimally required. Ineffectiveness in protecting, for example, abused wives and children is as likely to erode trust as failure to communicate with sensitivity.

In early 1988 while riding with patrol officers in Atlanta, I asked what had been the best thing to happen to police in the past two years. The reply, interestingly, had nothing to do with salaries, benefits, or other personnel matters. Without hesitation—and with the concern for protection of the public that typifies fine police officers—one responded, "The Domestic Violence Act." He explained that many women abused by husbands or boyfriends would not press charges out of fear of reprisals. Domestic violence statutes enable police to become complainants and make arrests when they believe that assault has been committed, without action by the woman.

In such cases, arrest (and possibly prosecution) may be no more effective as a deterrent than separation and counseling, despite research studies that indicate otherwise.[28] But the legislation increases the alternatives to sensitive communication immediately available to the officer and surely safeguards some victims in a way that communication cannot.

Obviously, police civility, freedom from prejudice, realistic patience, and so on are essential to communication and to fulfillment of mission, but critics who fear police use of force above all else have missed an essential point. We allow police to use force because we prefer a disinterested party to have this authority, rather than allow those impassioned by involvement to use force against each other. The use of reasonable force by an authorized official for a legitimate purpose—even if extreme force is required—is not the same as the brutal use of force or as police brutality. Undue reliance on communication when force is needed jeopardizes innocent citizens and police officers.

Police necessarily exercise some discretion in their duties. Not only do they decide which available methods are most useful in a given situation; they must also decide which laws to enforce and when. As the President's Commission on Law Enforcement and Administration of Justice observed in 1967, "[T]he police do not have the resources to enforce all criminal provisions equally." Every police officer quickly learns that he cannot enforce every law to the letter and still enjoy public support. People who generally obey the laws resent excessive strictness. Since laws, as well as policies and procedures, are often ambiguous, police officers must often "make [their] own resolution instantly, under stress, and often without advice" in matters that only years of litigation may ultimately resolve.[29]

In 1947 Elijah Adlow, an associate justice of the Boston Municipal Court, wrote: "Police problems are immediate. The policeman . . . must make his decision right now. His judgment is called into play now. His discretion is taxed. He cannot reserve the matter for some future time."[30] Similar discretion is exercised by—and similar ambiguities are set before— police executives.

How important are these duties and their conscientious fulfillment to the "experiment in ordered liberty"? August Vollmer went too far in saying that "democracy's strongest reliance is the police."[31] Democracy's strongest bulwark is the citizens themselves and their self-governance in a constitutional republic. Vollmer himself observed that "laws never have been an effective substitute for human virtues."[32] He echoed the observation of the ancient Roman statesman Cicero, "Laws without habits are in vain."

The importance of citizens' virtue to a constitutional republic has never been more beautifully captured than by Joseph Story, a founder of the Harvard Law School, who served on the Supreme Court from 1811 to 1845. His *Familiar Exposition of the Constitution of the United States*, written in 1840 and perhaps the greatest book ever written for teaching high school civics, concluded:

> Let the American youth never forget that they possess a noble inheritance, bought by the toils, and sufferings, and blood of their ancestors. . . . It may, nevertheless, perish in an hour, by the folly, or corruption, or negligence of its only keepers, THE PEOPLE. Republics are created by the virtue, public spirit, and intelligence of the citizens. They fall, when the wise are banished from the public councils, because they dare to be honest, and the profligate are rewarded, because they flatter the people, in order to betray them.[33]

Although the people are the ultimate basis for the experiment, the behavior of government officials—especially those as visible as the police— has a profound effect on public attitudes. The citizens are unlikely to escape cynicism if government officials routinely show bad judgment, prejudice, or greed. As Charles Silberman put the matter:

If street crime threatens the social fabric of American life, governmental crime destroys the political fabric by undermining the trust and belief in the legitimacy of government on which our entire political system is based. "Our government is the potent, the omnipresent teacher," Justice Louis D. Brandeis wrote. "For good or ill, it teaches the whole people by its example. Crime is contagious. If the government becomes a lawbreaker, it breeds contempt for the laws; it invites every man to become a law unto himself; it invites anarchy."[34]

Honorable, competent, fair performance by police, however, is no guarantee of public confidence. Since current images of police are drawn largely from television programs bearing little resemblance to reality, public expectations are bound to be unrealistic. Furthermore, some people are convinced that all public officials everywhere are corrupt, cowardly, ambitious, or interested only in political survival.

A person or an institution should not be preoccupied with public image. Inordinate concern for it can lead to indifference about how well we are actually doing. Public opinion may be uninformed and irrational and may be manipulated by demagogues.

Sportswriter Grantland Rice named Knute Rockne's Notre Dame running backs after the Four Horsemen of the Apocalypse, and other sportswriters picked this up. Fearing that his running backs might grow overconfident, Rockne put in a scrub offensive line. When his backs were stopped cold by the defense, Rockne shouted, "Show 'em your press clippings, boys, show 'em your press clippings!"

Wise leaders will not assess their performance simply by media coverage. They should ask themselves, "If my critics knew everything I know— all the facts and relevant evidence, some of which are confidential—would they believe that a conscientious public servant could do the things I am doing?" If the answer is yes, then they have good reason to continue their course of action. If not, then they should conduct a serious review.

Policing has become more professional since the 1930s, when Vollmer said, "In America, law enforcement is generally held in contempt, and policing is [taken as] one of our national jokes."[35] But a constitutional republic must be able to survive adverse public opinion toward government in general and police in particular. If our nation were too frail to survive governmental malfeasance or unjustified public mistrust of government, it would have collapsed already. Although many citizens have realistic expectations of police, police and other government officials are obliged to conduct themselves so as to give no reason for public mistrust. By example, they teach respect for law, liberty, peace, and justice. Every day, they must face the plight of victims, the anguish of the helpless, the inevitability of unsolved crimes, the ambiguity of the laws, the limits of what reason and persuasion can accomplish, the necessity of using coercion and force, and danger, including possible death—and they must do so in a manner that inspires public confidence. They must stand in harm's way for people who by national tradition distrust authority and power.

This is a challenge that, like most ideals, can only be approximated in practice. Consider the kind of person it takes to live up to it. As Leonard V. Harrison observed in his 1934 study, *Police Administration in Boston*:

> There are few vocations which, if adequately performed, require so much of a man—physical courage, tact, disciplined temper, good judgment, alertness of observation, and specialized knowledge of law and procedure. . . . Not only physical courage but strong moral fiber is required of the policeman. He is at war with thieves, fences, and sharpers of every sort who will stop at nothing to avoid interference by the police. These underworld characters are skilled in every form of trickery and deception needed to compromise a weak policeman. . . . But physical courage and moral stamina are not enough. A policeman may be courageous in the face of danger, or have strong defenses against corrupting influence, and yet be too indolent or too ignorant to perform many kinds of work which make no demands on his admirable qualities.[36]

Codes of Ethics and Personal Character

Harrison described the good police officer as a professional, a person of fine character and specially trained abilities. The spirit of such professionalism is captured in the "Law Enforcement Code of Ethics," published by the International Association of Chiefs of Police:

LAW ENFORCEMENT CODE OF ETHICS

As a Law Enforcement Officer, my fundamental duty is to serve mankind; to safeguard lives and property; to protect the innocent against deception, the weak against oppression or intimidation, and the peaceful against violence or disorder; and to respect the Constitutional rights of all men to liberty, equality, and justice.

I will keep my private life unsullied as an example to all; maintain courageous calm in the face of danger, scorn, ridicule; develop self-restraint; and be constantly mindful of the welfare of others. Honest in thought and deed in both my personal and official life, I will be exemplary in obeying the laws of the land and the regulations of my department. Whatever I see or hear of a confidential nature or that is confided to me in my official capacity will be kept ever secret unless revelation is necessary in the performance of my duty.

I will never act officiously or permit personal feelings, pre-judices, animosities, or friendships to influence my decisions. With no compromise for crime and with relentless prosecution of criminals, I will enforce the law courteously and appropri-ately without fear or favor, malice or ill-will, never employing unnecessary force or violence and never accepting gratuities.

I recognize the badge of my office as a symbol of public faith, and I accept it as a public trust to be held so long as I am true to the ethics of the police service. I will constantly strive to achieve these objectives and ideals, dedicating myself before God to my chosen profession . . . law enforcement.[37]

Some police object to portions of this code as too demanding or too vague. They point to the great difficulty—or impossibility—of safeguard-ing lives and protecting the innocent from deception and the weak from intimidation *and* of simultaneously acting within the laws in respecting everyone's right to privacy and liberty. They add that in extreme danger, they are not calm, even though they may act with courage. Some police ask whether an "unsullied" private life means that they should not live with a lover. Some insist that they cannot prevent feelings from influencing their decisions, that they have to compromise on crime to maintain informants, and that acceptance of small gratuities is customary.

The code expresses ideals whose demands must be weighed with the wisdom of experience and tested judgment. Police should do all that they can to safeguard the public within the limits of their authority. They should try to form habits of self-control in dangerous situations that reduce the likelihood of panic even if they do not produce calmness. Police can ask whether their private lives impair their performance in office, compromise their authority, or force them to live a lie. If others knew, would they be ashamed, and would their colleagues question their decency? Not all feelings need be excised. Decisions ought to be influenced by the feelings of a person of good character, by habits of justice, courage, compassion, and so on. And the proper uses of informants and the acceptability of gratuities should be thoroughly treated by departmental policies.

So understood, the code is trustworthy as a general guideline, conveying the spirit of fidelity to the public trust, although no code can take the place of good character and wisdom. At the request of police commissioners, I tried in 1987 to capture this spirit, in a letter, in a concise way that would provide guidance both to newcomers and to experienced patrol and command personnel:

> When a citizen pins on a police badge, he *voluntarily* agrees to bear the public trust. He is entrusted to protect the safety and the rights of his fellow members of society.
>
> To provide these protections, the officer is given special authority and powers. He has the authority to investigate other people, to abridge their normal liberties, and to use force when necessary.
>
> There are two basic limits to the rightful use of his authority and powers by the police officer. First, it is wrong for the officer to use his office for personal profit or gain, wrong for him to accept any favor that places his own advantage above the welfare

of the public. Second, it is wrong for the officer to violate the Constitution or the laws in the performance of his work.

Some officers are offered favors by citizens who hope for preferential treatment at a later time. Those who accept such favors dishonor themselves and the badge. Likewise, officers are confronted with monstrous crimes and rightly want to get perpetrators off the streets. But they have no right to behave illegally to accomplish this purpose. The police officer must abide by the laws guaranteeing citizen rights to the fullest extent of his training and understanding of them.

Beyond these requirements, the officer must bring personal qualities to his work that the badge cannot provide for him. The most important qualities are common sense and common decency. He should never expose himself needlessly to danger, he should maintain his physical fitness and his skillfulness in the use of the tools of his work, and he should pay attention to the needs of the people he serves.

Living up to the public trust is demanding work. It can involve disappointment, weariness, and stress. These are the facts of life in police work. But this is the work each police officer has chosen for himself.

The (City) Police Department is obligated to provide the best possible training and support for its officers throughout their careers. When the officer pins on the badge, he becomes a public servant, but he also becomes a member of the Department.

Although persons in official life find guidelines useful, codes of ethics do not motivate all people to behave well. They assist only people who already want to do so. Public office holders, such as police, need genuinely to want to serve the public and to become good at their work. They cannot eliminate self-interest from their lives, nor can they be infallible. But they must be of reasonably good character, and they must know their mission and be dedicated to it.

Both individual character and codes of ethics must be sustained by departmental policies and by the conduct of command personnel. Even when men and women are virtuous, even when they behave with high standards of conscience, they benefit from responsible supervision and instruction designed to help them become better. They deserve superiors and peers who assess their performance with care and make departmental expectations clear. If the leadership and the experienced personnel do not show that they take ethics violations seriously, their codes will be treated as worthless platitudes.

4

The Public Trust and Probity

Friends and Fellow Citizens,

The period for a new election of a citizen to administer the executive government of the United States being not far distant . . . your thoughts must be employed in designating the person who is to be clothed with that important trust. . . . In the discharge of this trust, I will only say that I have, with good intentions, contributed towards the organization of the government the very best exertions of which a very fallible judgment was capable.

—George Washington[1]

In his Farewell Address to the People of the United States in September 1796, George Washington emphasized that a public office is a public trust. He recognized that no person is expected to be infallible; indeed, to suppose that anyone *can* be infallible in the conduct of public or private life is arrogant and dangerous. The public trust, rather, calls for "good intentions" and the "very best exertions."

Public servants must *intend* and *resolve* to put the public good above private advantage for anyone—self, family, friends, political allies, factions, or interest groups. They are obliged to identify the public good and to serve it; this is the sort of "exertion" that public office demands. John Adams wrote that such devotion to the well-being of the public interest "must be Superior to all private Passions. Men must . . . be happy to sacrifice their private Friendships and dearest Connections, when they stand in Competition with the Rights of Society."[2]

On this account, public office is a high, demanding calling, which calls for the very best from us. To appreciate trust in public life, we begin with its place in private life, where nothing is more basic.

Private Trust

Trusting persons is a serious matter, since it gives other people the power to affect by their words and actions our feelings, interests, and well-being. Accordingly, we choose friends, husbands, and wives whom we believe we can trust; our most intimate bonds to others are forged of many things—chemistry, affection, shared interests, common ideals—but trust is always present. Indeed, genuine intimacy cannot be imagined without trust. We can be sexually involved with people we do not trust and enjoy the company of rogues, but lust and mere companionship are far from the genuine intimacy that joins our lives to the lives of others.

Betrayal thus causes deep resentment, anger, and heartache. To trust others is to believe they will not forsake us—not that they will be perfect or infallible, but that they will use good judgment with us—and that they will neither sacrifice us for some private advantage, nor use us as mere instruments of some hidden desire, nor neglect to consider us. We believe that those we trust will treat our interests and feelings as though they were their own. Few disappointments run deeper than that of misplaced trust, and few lives are as barren as those from which mutual trust is absent.

We also entrust important interests to our doctors, lawyers, priests, ministers, rabbis, and teachers. We expect them to serve as trustworthy agents of our well-being and to behave on our behalf as we would behave for ourselves if we knew enough—that is, as professionals.

We are rightly resentful when they let us down. A doctor who brings a hangover to work, a lawyer who gouges, or a minister or teacher who takes sexual advantage of others offends us. We trust professionals to give us their best, in the spirit of the Hippocratic Oath: "Whatever houses I visit, I will come for the benefit of the sick, remaining free of all intentional injustice, of all mischief, and in particular of sexual relations with both female and male persons, be they free or slaves. Whatever I see or hear in the course of the treatment . . . I will keep to myself."

Much of daily life depends on trust in strangers. We can decide where we will live, but we can seldom decide who will share a sidewalk with us, or a bus or subway ride, or the lanes of a highway. When strangers—such as drunk drivers—disregard our well-being, they betray the trust required for people to live together securely. Few experienced people trust strangers any further than they have to, but persons cannot live together when they cannot trust each other at all. People who survive without trust do so in a condition resembling war.

The Public Trust

Just as we cannot all be our own architects, electrical contractors, doctors, and lawyers, we cannot serve entirely as our own government. Even in a constitutional republic where the people are the ultimate repository of authority, we must delegate that authority to public officials. People cannot live together without government, or promote the common good—or even the common defense—without government. If private life without trust is barren, our common life in liberty without trustworthiness in government is impossible.

Because the people must rely on government, the persistent questions throughout history are: How should government be constituted? and How should public officials be authorized to hold office? The people have often had little choice in the matter; government has consisted of hereditary monarchs or of tyrants whose only claim to authority was power. Even today, many governments rest mainly on military or economic dominion.

America, by contrast, derives authority from the consent of the people. "No man is good enough to govern another man without that other's consent," as Abraham Lincoln expressed it. "I say this is the leading principle—the sheet anchor of American republicanism."[3] If we must trust those who govern us, we should be able to decide who they will be.

Since most of our government officials are strangers to us, we cannot choose them as we do doctors or lawyers, let alone friends. Elected officials are rarely chosen by a majority of the people or even of the eligible voters. The majority of those who do vote generally compose a small portion of the population. Appointed officials, such as judges and police, are even more distant from any direct public choice.

The spirit of service essential to avoiding majority or minority tyranny requires that every official seek to deserve the public trust he may not actually possess. However effective the checks and balances of government, however extensive the prevention of abuses of power by government, the government itself will be less than trustworthy unless individual officials try to be worthy of the trust they bear.

As James Madison wrote to Thomas Jefferson in 1788, while the Constitution was being considered for ratification by the states, "Wherever there is an interest and power to do wrong, wrong will generally be done, and not less readily by a powerful and interested party than by a powerful and interested prince."[4] Laws and sanctions cannot always prevent individuals from using the powers of office for private gain, so we must trust to the quality and decency of our officials.

Appalling incompetence and dishonor undermine private as well as public institutions. Fraud in savings and loan companies has been said to have reached epidemic proportions, for example, and allegations of bribery and of the illicit use of inside information has been charged against defense contractors and the Pentagon itself.

At a Roofers Union racketeering trial in Philadelphia, tape recordings revealed an elected municipal court judge, a top official of the federal Occupational Safety and Health Administration, and two police officers accepting bribes while in office.[5] An Atlanta-based Drug Enforcement Administration agent was arrested in Washington, D.C., after police observed him buying drugs on the street.[6]

After the conviction of three elected Philadelphia judges and the naming of sixteen others in various investigations, Senator Arlen Specter called for judges to be appointed because so many judicial candidates are on the ballot that the public cannot be informed about them.[7] At the same time, twenty-eight New York City restaurant inspectors were accused of extortion.[8] The New York Times reported, "There are now more than 100 cases each year in state and federal courts in which law enforcement officials are charged or implicated in drug corruption."[9]

Few have ever maintained that human beings can be trusted to behave well unless they are held accountable. In the eighteenth century, republican agrarian John Taylor of Caroline said: "The more a nation depends for its liberty on the qualities of individuals, the less likely it is to retain it. By expecting publick good from private virtue, we expose ourselves to public evils from private vices."[10]

This skepticism seems less realistic than the position of the British historian Lord Acton, who observed that "power tends to corrupt, and absolute power corrupts absolutely." A century earlier, the American Founding Fathers established absolute limits on absolute power in our Bill of Rights. Notably, both they and Acton said not that power corrupts, but that power offers temptations to corrupt that some resist. They believed that the well-being of a constitutional republic *does* depend on the virtue of citizens and their officials. John Adams believed strongly in the necessity of good morals and manners for republican government: In 1776 he wrote to a friend that there was "so much rascality, so much venality and corruption, so much avarice and ambition" among men "*even* in America" that there might not be "virtue enough to support a republic."[11]

The propensity to misuse authority led the eighteenth-century Scottish philosopher Francis Hutcheson to write that "the constituting of civil power is *the most important transaction* in human affairs," and for that reason, we have a right to insist that the obligations of public servants are "very high and sacred."[12] "The rights of rulers," he said, are "less divine than those of the people, as the former are destined for the preservation of the latter."[13]

While realizing that corrupt governments that treat the public with disdain or that permit anarchy do immense harm, Hutcheson also recognized that even well-structured governments rely on officials to respect the public interest. Crimes by public officials are so pernicious, he said, that they warrant more severe punishment than private crimes. Although he approved of pardons and legal immunity for ordinary criminals, to break up gangs and to secure useful information, he urged that "for crimes against the publick rights of a people, or for gross abuses of power . . . there should be no impunity."[14] In a word, violation of the public trust is unpardonable.

Many officials, however, have never succumbed to temptation at the expense of the public. Federal agents, for example, regularly walk away from bribes greater than their lifetime earnings. This better side of human nature often emerges in police conduct, as indicated by the wife of Jim Giza, a street cop in Baltimore:

> When he puts on his uniform he creates a barrier between himself and the rest of mankind. And he does that out of choice and a willingness to risk difference because he believes he can make a difference. . . . So when I hear critical, accusatory, and snide comments about police, I react. Police are not freaks, they are

people like the rest of us—with families and mortgages, taxes and car payments. The only difference is that they have chosen a profession that puts them in daily contact with those elements of society we would like to forget, a profession that few of us would choose but which all of us depend on.[15]

Joanne Giza told as well of "the shootings, the cuttings, the rapes, the drugs, the life he witnessed with its poverty and hopelessness and fear."[16] She confirmed the willingness of some to bear the public trust faithfully while their families share in their sacrifices, unsung and uncompensated. Their lives bear out novelist Tom Wolfe's observation that cynicism is "a cowardly form of superiority," because it implies that I do not have to try my best, on the false grounds that nobody else tries.

The demands of fidelity to the public trust for police today may be greater than in earlier periods. Much of what is worst in America today grows in a poverty that many free people—not slaves—in Colonial America were spared. Forrest McDonald wrote, "The vast majority of American families held a comfortable amount of land, and poverty of the depth that was common in Europe was all but unknown."[17] Historian Marvin Meyers added that the founders knew that the experiment in ordered liberty itself could be threatened in the future by poverty:

> The republican remedy for factional violence, injustice, and confusion was far from perfect, Madison recognized; and it would meet its real test in the future when America, like other nations, accumulated a propertyless mass of citizens.[18]

Poverty has come to a portion of the American people with a vengeance, frequently accompanied by disenfranchisement, ignorance, brutality, and alienation from government. The poor are likely to feel powerless to call government to their aid. Such feelings and circumstances make them mistrustful of the police. James Madison observed that "the most rational government will not find it a superfluous advantage to have the prejudices of the community on its side."[19] Where circumstances are dreadful, prejudices run the other way, so police must make the greatest effort to serve this public and to be worthy of their trust, out of not charity but justice. Although police cannot by themselves deliver the benefits of a just society to those who are helpless through no fault of their own, they can offer service and respect. And they must resist not only bribes and the like but the temptation to give up as well.

The daily experience of police confirms the positions of Hutcheson, Madison, and the others on offices of public trust. Their philosophic points apply in practice.

Competence

As many cases show, a police officer without an understanding of people will not deal competently with conflict, while one who has it can calm adversaries and ease tension.

A particularly well coordinated and mutually trusting team, consisting of an older officer with more formal education and a very observant learner, was called late one afternoon to a domestic disturbance in a trailer park. A woman with her small daughter, inquiring about a trailer rental, had parked in a tenant's space. Upon returning from work, the man flew into such a rage that she fled into a trailer and was afraid to come out. When we arrived, the police escorted her and the child to their car and directed them to another parking space. Then the officers approached the tenant, a big man who was obviously tired. He assured the police that he had politely asked the woman to move her car and could not imagine why she called the police.

Arguing with him about the facts or suggesting that he was a liar might make future problems for the prospective tenant. Instead, the senior officer said, "I really don't know how you did it. When I come home from work, I'm bushed, and if somebody parked in my space, I'd be so damned mad, I'd probably raise hell." The man grew red in the face and spewed out his real feelings, using the grossest profanity, until he realized that he had given himself away and stopped abruptly.

The police might have rubbed it in but did not. The senior partner paused and then said, "Look, we know everybody has to put up with a lot of crap. We do, you do, and so does that woman over there. She's desperate for a home for herself and her daughter, and none of the spaces is marked, so she didn't know it was yours. She seems like a person who wouldn't do it on purpose. Maybe you could give her a break."

By not putting the man in a defeated position, the police gave him the opportunity to walk over to the woman and apologize. She apologized in turn and thereby led the way to a decent resolution of the conflict. But the man's wife arrived and interrupted with a diatribe against police in general, while insisting that her husband never was abusive, never used foul language, and never threatened anyone. After the police cocked an eyebrow, however, the husband shook his head, and the reconciliation continued.

That kind of competence is indispensable to serving the public well. In this instance, it also prevented any tension that might have arisen from the fact that of all the people involved, only the senior officer was black. I have seen other officers become involved in pointless arguments that only made people stick to their stories no matter how absurd.

Trustworthiness

Much police literature stresses common sense as the basis of competence. More to the point is the good sense in allowing others to keep their self-respect rather than humiliating them needlessly. This is a simple application of the golden rule.

Undercover police have been reported to let prostitutes undress before arresting them for solicitation. Mature people do not use their positions for foolish self-indulgence, however, or allow prurience to interfere with their judgment.

Albert A. Seedman, who served for thirty years in the New York City Police Department, from patrolman to chief of detectives, told of his colleagues' habitual decency:

> Ray McGuire, the captain who had run the squad for years, was famous for his integrity. . . . One Friday, just before Christmas in 1947, Seedman helped lug into the Safe and Loft office dozens of cartons of toys that had been recovered from a hijacking case. There were dolls, teddy bears, stuffed animals of all kinds.
>
> Ray McGuire, busy overseeing the operation, suddenly looked up and saw that it was close to three o'clock. "I'm never going to get to lunch," he said. "I was going to stop at Macy's

to pick up some toys for my girls." One of the detectives mentioned he had to do the same at Macy's. McGuire handed him a twenty-dollar bill. "Pick up a pair of dolls for me, will ya?"

If there were two dolls in that office, there were two thousand. . . . Yet I doubt it ever occurred to McGuire that a pair would never be missed. Or that the owner would be delighted to make them a gift.[20]

The habit of not even considering greedy behavior, of not speculating about ways to profit from office, prevents such conduct from "ever occurring" to us.

The same habits apply to bribery. An offer of a bribe is deeply insulting. That someone believes you can be bought is enough to stir anger (which must be concealed to prosecute the suspect). For any decent person, rejection of the offer requires no deliberation. For anyone tempted by such offers, the central questions are: Is this behavior worthy of me? Is it consistent with the reasons for which I respect myself? Do I have a price? If such questions are not sufficient, more compelling questions are, Am I willing to be viewed with contempt, however tactfully, by the person who has bribed me, and to deserve it? Am I willing to be bought—for I am being bought, not merely rented—by such a person? What would the people who love me think? What about the people whose respect I cherish and want to deserve?

Elijah Adlow explained:

> The policeman who accepts a gratuity or solicits a bribe from a racketeer must remember that he is dealing with a man who is not renting his soul for a day but is taking title to it for life. Once his hands are tainted he can no longer assert his authority with dignity and without restraint. . . . For a policeman who weighs the offer of a bribe it is wise to remember that only a consciousness of freedom from the taint of suspicion insures true peace of mind.[21]

For people of mature habits of trustworthiness, these reflections are unnecessary, but for people who aspire to such maturity they can be useful. And for people who are greedy—or intemperate in other ways—they are not likely to serve as much of a constraint. People who conceal their own greed from themselves usually are good at other kinds of self-deception and live comfortably with other betrayals of the public trust. For those without conscience, the only remedy is to cast them out.

Similar points can be made about self-pity, cowardice, and injustice. Like intemperance, these faults arise from inordinate self-love. Those who pity themselves—who believe, for example, that their jobs are too hard, or that the world is not sufficiently sensitive to their needs and desires—probably do not think straight about how to do their jobs well and how to live up to the trust others place in them.

Self-pity tends to obscure the importance of earning one's own respect. As one police officer remarked after he had been imprisoned for burglary: "The real truth is, after ten years on the force, I'm afraid I had reached the point of feeling, 'Nobody else cares, and why the hell should I?'"22 The answer to his question is simple: You should care because it is your life, not theirs; your self-respect that is at stake, not theirs; your oath of office that is in the balance, not theirs. By allowing self-pity to influence us, we give away control of our lives. Self-pity is that tempting voice that says, "It's all right . . . go ahead . . . nobody cares."

Cowards betray their obligations and forsake other people because they are inordinately concerned about their own survival, be it physical or occupational. They do not rise to their duties, because they fear the consequences. Failure to control fear, rather than fear itself, makes them cowards. They fear dying more than dishonor, fear losing their jobs more than failing in their duties, and fear suffering harm more than causing harm to others by their neglect or flight.

People can be unjust in many ways, but all of them involve failure to consider others. Whether it takes the form of prejudice, racism, sexism, pursuit of more than a fair share, or indifference to facts and evidence, injustice is an affront to decency.

In summary, immaturity and self-indulgence are incompatible with the trust of public office. We all have weaknesses, of course, but we also have obligations to root them out when they impair our capacity to serve faithfully. Individuals must do this for themselves; no laws or policies can do it for them, although specific institutional policies may either encourage our best or indulge our worst selves.

We can help each other to become worthy of the public trust. Seedman saw that Captain McGuire's honesty about the children's dolls was so natural that it was unforgettable to his colleagues: "One example like that is better than a year's supply of lectures, memos, and threats from the Commissioner's office on the need for honesty in the ranks."[23]

Policies and procedures for accountability are, however, important. Patrick V. Murphy, the commissioner of police in New York City who established the policy of cooperation with the Knapp Commission investigations of police corruption, stressed that institutional improvement cannot be based simply on conscience: "In reality, the [detective] bureau was an independent breakaway entity, with its own laws, customs, and marching orders. From the reform's point of view, accountability meant nothing to the detectives if they only had to answer to their consciences."[24]

How people behave, however, usually matters more than what they say. Even children sense hypocrisy. Officials whose behavior belies their words get the contempt they deserve from their colleagues. Moreover, moralizing can be offensive and tiresome and may sound self-righteous. Paying attention to the behavior of others is less likely to breed resentment.

In this regard, English novelist Thomas Hardy was right to say, "Persons with any weight of character carry, like planets, their atmospheres with them in their orbits."[25] They do so naturally, as Captain McGuire did, not by pretension.

Able leaders understand that nobody can really serve as an example by *trying* to do so. When we see an attempt to set an example, we suspect it is phony and not deeply rooted. People become real exemplars, trusted and looked up to, by being what they appear to be.

Roman thinker Cicero pointed out, "Socrates was perfectly right when he declared that there is a direct shortcut to winning a reputation: 'Make yourself the sort of man you want people to think you are.'"[26] Greek historian Xenophon reported that Socrates gave this advice: "If you want to be thought good at anything, the shortest and safest and most reputable way is to try to make yourself really good at it."[27] And James Madison wrote of his brother, "If he wishes to establish himself in the good will of the Country, the only durable as well as honorable plan will be to establish a character that merits it."[28]

5

Discretion

"You see," he [King Arthur] said, "Might is not Right. But there is a lot of Might knocking about in this world, and something has to be done about it. It is as if People were half horrible and half nice. Perhaps they are even more than half horrible, and when they are left to themselves they run wild . . . without reference to justice. Then the horrible side gets the uppermost, and there is thieving and rape and plunder and torture. The people become beasts."

—Terence Hanbury White[1]

Discretion is the authority to make decisions of policy and practice. In policing, discretion often includes command or patrol authority to decide which laws shall be enforced, and when, where, and how. It also includes authority to decide which means of helping the helpless, maintaining order, and keeping the peace are best suited to particular circumstances. Discretion is a special kind of liberty—the freedom to make decisions that affect the lives of others, which other citizens are not empowered to make. Special liberties entail special duties.

Judgment and Rules

Just as liberty should not indulge what is worst in human beings, neither should discretion indulge the unrestrained exercise of might. Might does not make right; if it did, the powerful could tyrannize over the weak, or the evil over the good, without objection.

Police are granted discretion because no set of laws and regulations can prescribe what to do in every possible circumstance. The possibilities are too numerous for us to have rules for everything that may happen.

49

Trying to make a rule for everything demeans our ability to apply our intelligence. When a bureaucracy becomes rule bound, it is like a person who is muscle bound; it can do less because it lacks flexibility.

Those who believe that people should be bound by institutional rules and mandatory responses neglect the complexity of our lives. They sometimes ignore the facts that must be taken into consideration to achieve justice, and they seem to believe that people cannot exercise good judgment.

When Mahatma Gandhi committed acts of civil disobedience in hope of reform in India, he was convicted of sedition. Eager to show British rule at its worst, he asked for the severest penalty from the court. But the judge understood that Gandhi was a man of exceptional civility and decency. A harsh sentence would *appear* as unjust as it actually was and would therefore be both morally wrong and politically foolish. He therefore chose a lesser penalty, one within the limits of his discretion.

The fear of discretion in government in general is strongest in regard to police discretion. According to Professor Emeritus Herman Goldstein of the University of Wisconsin–Madison Law School, this fear arises from concern over "the awesome power of the police," their reputation "for exceeding their legal authority," and their abuse of "existing discretion."[2] Many high-ranking police in America say in private that police themselves have brought on such criticisms. The history of policing in America includes disregard for the limits of discretion, violation of civil rights, brutality, and arrogance. Some police know of problems of sadism among their fellows as well.

Those issues are crucial. Their importance is reflected in their emphasis at the very beginning of the 1984 *Standards Manual of the Law Enforcement Agency Accreditation Program*:

> Written policy should set forth the enforcement policy of the agency, define the limits of individual discretion and provide guidelines for the exercise of such discretion. Because the concept of discretion defies rigid codification, officers should be trained in how to exercise the broad discretionary authority they have been granted. . . . The written directive should identify the authority of sworn officers to use alternatives to arrest (e.g., citations, summonses, referral, informal resolution, and warning) to address the

variety of problems they confront. . . . The directive should encompass the use of all types and kinds of force. . . . [A]n officer may use deadly force only when the officer reasonably believes that the action is in defense of human life, including the officer's own life, or in defense of any person in immediate danger of serious physical injury. . . . Definitions of "reasonable belief" and "serious physical injury" should be included.[3]

Some command personnel cite the *Miranda* ruling as an example of judicial reaction to police excesses and believe that policing is better for it. Goldstein described positions taken by other institutions, some of which rejected "the concept that police can and must exercise discretion." For example,

- A local chapter of the American Civil Liberties Union challenged the policy of a police administration intended to regulate the use made of street interrogations by arguing that police have no basis for questioning citizens unless there are grounds for making an arrest.

- A state supreme court found a law enforcement officer guilty of nonfeasance for his failure to initiate a criminal prosecution where evidence of the violation came to his attention.

- A state attorney general held that a police chief cannot limit the authority of his personnel to use deadly force within the bounds of existing statutes.

- A newspaper editorial condemned the local police chief for rising above the law in setting down guidelines that would result in his officers' arresting curfew violators only under certain conditions.

- Another newspaper editorial condemned a chief for pointing out that the enforcement of a newly enacted ordinance regulating massage parlors would have to compete with other demands for police manpower.

- A group of citizens in Berkeley, Calif., in 1973, obtained enough signatures to have an ordinance placed on the ballot that in effect instructed the Berkeley Police Department to give a low priority to the enforcement of marijuana laws. After its adoption, however, the state attorney general filed suit.[4]

Such actions usually stem from the belief that the accountability of police to the public is best preserved by minimizing discretion from the outset. Accountability was stressed, for example, in the 1987 report by the Philadelphia Police Study Task Force, *Philadelphia and Its Police: Toward a New Partnership*:

> The police are agents of the community and are therefore accountable to it. . . . Implicit in this relationship is the expectation that the police will feel morally responsible to the community, not just to themselves.[5]

The report did not suggest that the principle of accountability in itself reduces discretion. Virtually everyone agrees with the principle as such. The issue is not whether the principle is right, but how it should be applied, and whether the positions taken by the ACLU and the others above are wise applications of it.

Because its explicit mission is to protect liberty, the ACLU tends to obliterate the distinction between grounds for questioning and grounds for arrest. If we focus solely on protection of liberty, we neglect the public safety, so we must pay heed to both liberty and public safety, which sometimes conflict. For this reason, discretion cannot be eliminated in distinguishing between grounds for questioning and grounds for arrest. The ACLU protects liberties but takes too narrow a position on police discretion.

The instance of the state supreme court seems to deny that some cases of lawbreaking should not be prosecuted—or at least that police can make that judgment. Its concern is probably to avoid favoritism and discrimination—a worthwhile purpose, but again, too narrow. For if police could make no such judgments, enforcement would be unconditional and therefore unjust. It would offend public sentiment and thus render police ineffective. The newspaper editorial about curfew violations is too narrow in its perspective in the same way. The second editorial, about regulating massage parlors, is too narrow as well, because resources and manpower are always limited. The writer presumes that all legislation is accompanied by funding adequate to enforce it.

The state attorney general's objection to a police chief's making departmental limits on the use of force more confining than existing statutes takes law seriously. But it risks impairing police performance by assuming that laws are always clear. And the Berkeley ordinance about marijuana tells the police that the will of the majority is above the law.

In each case, the perspective is too narrow to accommodate the range of ideals that morality must take into account. Such steps do not promise a citizenry that laws will be enforced justly or wisely, peace kept securely, or safety maintained effectively. They lead not to a government of laws that is just but to one that treats everyone the same, no matter what. Sameness is not justice, for justice is sensitive to differences in context and detail. Justice is blind in the sense that it knows no favorites, not that it spurns evidence. An officer who does not arrest when a crime has been committed in a barroom brawl where no one is competent enough to offer reliable testimony, or when a summons is as effective for the public safety, has exercised judgment. Laws and regulations cannot possibly cover every instance with sensitivity to the circumstances.

Properly conceived, laws and regulations are not cynical, but realistic. They set boundaries to discretion; they frequently say what divides rightful and wrongful uses of authority. But they leave broad domains within which to decide which alternative is the best.

As Kenneth Culp Davis, professor emeritus at the University of San Diego School of Law, observed, "A patrolman should not have discretion about overall enforcement policy but should have discretion to do the needed individualizing in applying the policy made by his superiors to the facts and circumstances of each particular case."[6] Most law enforcement studies have reached the same conclusion. As mentioned, the Commission on Accreditation of Law Enforcement Agencies did so in 1984, the President's Crime Commission did in 1967, and the American Bar Association's Project on Standards for Criminal Justice and the Law Enforcement Assistance Administration's National Advisory Commission on Criminal Justice Standards and Goals did in 1973. Since the late 1960s most such groups have also advocated the establishment of rulemaking procedures within each department, so that rules are not idiosyncratic, unilaterally alterable, or so secret that the public cannot learn what they are.

The International Association of Chiefs of Police, the Arizona State University Project on Law Enforcement Policy and Rule-Making, and others have provided guidance for both substance and procedure.

Command personnel must establish departmental policies in writing to avoid discriminatory performance by subordinates. They must make policies that take into account the facts of daily enforcement, and they must have the courage to say what they mean. The policies cannot be false, tongue-in-cheek, or so unrealistic that they cause disbelief, such as one that requires total enforcement of all criminal laws. Limited manpower and budgets, proper use of informants, public sentiment, and policies of prosecutors and judges must all be taken into account in deciding what a department should enforce. Full enforcement is unrealistic and impracticable. As Davis wrote in *Police Discretion*:

> The plain reality is that from the beginning of American government, a gap has existed between statutory law and enforced law. When legislative bodies learn that enforcement officers are enforcing something less than the enacted law . . . they generally express their appreciation to the enforcement agencies for contributing to a sensible system. Almost all legislators are fully aware that the system would not be sensible if every criminal statute were enforced according to its letter.[7]

He added that "the police accomplishment in escaping the full enforcement legislation is a very considerable one, for which the police deserve much credit" and without which "the system of criminal justice would be insufferable."[8]

Some argue that the police usurp the authority of the legislature by determining which laws to enforce. If police enforce laws that are unpopular or foolish, it is also argued, then adverse public reaction will motivate the legislature to change the laws. Normally such arguments imply that selective enforcement leads to corruption, in that unpopular laws against prostitution, gambling, double-parking, after-hours sale of alcohol, and the like may be manipulated by the police for bribes and payoffs.

Such arguments seem unpersuasive, partly because in most places resources are insufficient for total enforcement. Furthermore, adverse public reaction to enforcement is much more likely to be directed at police than at lawmakers, who are often slow to admit, let alone correct, their mistakes. Although selective enforcement can deteriorate into uneven, unjust, and corrupt enforcement, the elimination of discretion is a poor preventive.

As with enforcement, truthful policies within which officers can responsibly exercise discretion are a basic obligation of command. Fulfillment of that obligation enables openness and obstructs corruption by increasing the possibility of acting on the words the department says it lives by.

In policing, as in all public service, the place where discretion ends must be known and respected. Two factors are involved. A person can know that he is not allowed to go beyond a certain point, respect that limit, and still show bad judgment when he has the authority to decide. And a person can know how to handle difficult situations and still be contemptuous of limits. The challenge is to achieve respect for the limits and wisdom in acting within them.

Respect for Limits

Respect for limits is a matter of fundamental attitudes, which have been succinctly drawn by theologian Reinhold Niebuhr in *The Children of Light and the Children of Darkness*.[9] He distinguished people who will do anything, at anyone's expense, to accomplish their purposes—good or bad—from people who restrain themselves in the pursuit of their goals. The former he called the children of darkness—for example, the Nazis—and the latter, the children of light.

Obviously, no children of darkness belong in policing or anywhere else in public service. But in the tradition of America's founders, Niebuhr stressed that a child of darkness in each of us—our passions and desires, our ambitions and commitments—tempts us all toward excesses. No children of light can be trusted in public service either, if they believe that they have no capacity for misconduct, no propensity to excess.

In a way, naïve children of light are as dangerous as the children of darkness. Their naïveté about the tendency of power to corrupt limits their own humility, obscures to them their own fallibility, and may lead to the kind of prideful self-righteousness that typifies tyrants.

Persons who can be trusted to exercise discretion are the children of light who are wise about human nature as it exists in themselves. They respect limits and recognize that they may be tempted to exceed them.

Respect for limits cannot excuse laxity, indifference, laziness, or timidity in the exercise of rightful authority. Public officials who are too lazy to do their duty, or too fearful of confrontation or controversy to use their authority, may not be as dangerous as those who violate the laws and the rights of the citizens, but they endanger all the same. Intemperance in the exercise of discretion is like other forms of intemperance—it consists of doing too much or too little.

Citizen complaints and departmental investigations of police performance involve accusations of both excess and deficiency. In New York, after the racial violence in Howard Beach, one Harlem priest in 1988 referred to the police as "a bunch of thugs gone wild."[10] Police everywhere are familiar with complaints that they fail to respond to calls quickly enough.

No amount of conscientious performance will satisfy everyone. Not even heroic diligence will transform the world and eliminate its evils. Even after police officers give up their early expectations to "help change things" and "get drugs off the street," and after they reach a point where they realize "that's not gonna happen,"[11] they are still obliged to deliver their best every day.

Few actions erode the confidence of the public or of the police in their own department as much as the indifference of command officers to misconduct by their personnel. Stories are commonplace of police who are protected while drunk on duty. A former New York officer and later a major city chief told of a New York cop who "had a notorious drinking problem; he would pass out on the sidewalk, like the grimiest wino, in full uniform and in broad daylight. His colleagues would haul him in to the station house time and again, protecting him and coddling him."[12] Other police have told of their own excesses being indulged by fellow officers. One estimated that "fellow officers stopped him for drunken driving fifteen times. Not once . . . was he arrested. Fifteen times he was taken home, followed home, or allowed to drive home. 'The job afforded me lots of ways to stay active in alcoholism,' he says."[13]

Confidence also erodes when officials play favorites among their personnel. A 1987–88 investigation in Washington, D.C., compelled the police chief to reprimand two high-ranking officials for actions beyond their authority, including possible falsification of data, that "contributed to the perception that there are improprieties and favoritism in the department's drug-screening process."[14]

Policies and Laws

Some policies and laws—such as a law against robbery or a policy prohibiting conflict of interest—are established to reinforce behavior that would be automatic for a decent human being. They clarify the limits to rightful action, which if not obvious to common sense or decency, need to be learned. A police officer needs a sense of relevant laws, regulations, and departmental policies in order to abide by them. Their proliferation, therefore, can reduce respect for limits, if the lists become so long that officers cannot learn them. They are then as likely to sneer at the whole business as to try to identify the fundamentals.

As every parent knows, if rules make a show of being complete, someone will respond to novel circumstances with, "You didn't forbid it, and so I will do it." Excessive attention to the letter can kill the spirit. At the opposite extreme, vague and ambiguous laws and policies, conflicting laws at different levels of government, and laws, regulations, and policies that impede the performance of duty tend to have the same effect. Most destructive are laws that require unreasonable standards of proof to dispel reasonable doubt. Yet since vagueness, ambiguity, conflict, and difficulty are unavoidable, they do not excuse intemperance in the exercise of discretion. No one can blame his own failures on the imperfections of the system.

Public officials are nonetheless obliged to reduce or avoid imperfections to the extent possible. Legislators should draft laws as lucidly as they can and should consult members of the executive branch about problems in enforcing those laws. Law enforcement officials must identify ambiguities and conflicts and advise their personnel about departmental expectations. Leaving everyone to his own devices is trusting to luck.

Clearly, some conflicts of law cannot be resolved by police alone, as shown by "kidnappings" by parents of their own children in custody disputes. A woman who won temporary custody of her son in California, for example, moved to Louisiana where she was granted permanent custody at the same time that her husband was awarded custody by the California courts, so he kidnapped the boy. That dispute could be resolved at the federal level only if Congress enacts new legislation.[15] Until then, police in different states will be called upon to enforce conflicting rulings.

Other problems arise over court rulings on the Fourth Amendment. In 1985, for example, Judge Patricia M. Wald of the U.S. Court of Appeals for the District of Columbia argued that the Supreme Court had "rewritten fourth amendment law"[16] in two cases:

> In *Illinois v. Gates*, the Court discarded all the old rules for deciding what constituted probable cause sufficient to obtain a search warrant and adopted a new "common sense," nontechnical, omnibus rule based on the "totality of circumstances" in each case. In *United States v. Leon*, the Court held that evidence obtained in an unconstitutional search could still be admitted . . . if the police officers, however mistaken, did not act dishonestly or recklessly in drawing up the affidavits submitted to the magistrate and if they could reasonably have believed that probable cause existed for the warrants, even if in fact it did not.[17]

Judge Wald observed that the "totality of circumstances/reasonable belief" standards will lead to lengthy deliberations in the lower courts over "whether the police behaved reasonably in conducting unreasonable searches."[18] Obviously, police are required to exercise discretion in seeking warrants for arrest, in assessing probable cause for warrantless arrests, and in the "balancing of the competing interests"[19] in stopping and frisking a suspect. As Judge Wald noted: "[I]n some of these contexts, courts have worked out rules interpreting the concept of reasonableness. . . . In others, such as determining whether an officer's observations will support probable cause for an arrest, the great variety of situations in which the problem arises has made this task more difficult."[20]

Their trend may increase the discretion of judges in lower courts more than discretionary authority elsewhere. It will not make judgment easier for police in the streets, because it will not make explicit any general guides to conduct.

Many codes of conduct and commentators on police work echo O. W. Wilson's "Square Deal Code" of Wichita, Kansas, in advocating a policy "never to arrest if a summons will suffice; never to summons if a warning would be better." The lesser means is conceived to be the most temperate and justifiable, the least likely to exceed the limits even where they are vague.

Determining whether a lesser means "will suffice" or "would be better" depends on what is to be accomplished. Means are sufficient or not to the achievement of specific ends, and judgment is required to establish which ends are to be pursued in specific circumstances.

Howard Cohen, former associate dean of the College of Arts and Sciences at the University of Massachusetts, Boston, emphasized that police authority "can be, at once, highly specific and exceedingly vague. It is specific insofar as it is conferred by statute with respect to law enforcement . . . and vague in the areas of peacekeeping and public safety where the variety of activities expected of the police is, typically, not legislated."[21] The tasks of police, said Cohen, do not come with convenient labels that identify them as cases of law enforcement or peacekeeping or public safety. Police "regularly step into situations in which neither their objectives nor their functions are particularly obvious."[22]

He referred to the case of George Kirkham, a university instructor who decided to become a police officer. While patrolling a ghetto, Kirkham's field training officer, D'Angelo, called two men, whom Kirkham could not see, out of an alley and ordered one of them to get "on the car" in position to be searched. When he told Kirkham to do the same with the other man, Kirkham hesitated, even though the second man's hands were in his pockets and he acted confused. D'Angelo then ordered the man, at gunpoint, to "get on the car." After his search of the first man uncovered a revolver, D'Angelo handcuffed him while Kirkham searched the second suspect and felt a soft, spongy object in his sock. He asked D'Angelo whether to run a record check before releasing him, but D'Angelo ordered him to find out what was in the sock. "We can't do that," Kirkham objected, thinking of the restrictions against further search implied by the Supreme Court decision in Terry v. Ohio. D'Angelo then removed the spongy object, which he identified as a plastic bag filled with small packets of heroin, and arrested the second man.[23]

Cohen's analysis was that Kirkham

> understood this encounter primarily, if not exclusively, in terms
> of law enforcement. . . . D'Angelo, on the other hand . . . seemed
> to be treating this encounter as a matter of public safety. . . . He
> was not . . . acting from ignorance of the law. . . . D'Angelo saw
> two dangerous people, one of whom turned out to be armed. All
> of his street sense told him they were probably drug users and
> dealers. . . . A gun and a small quantity of heroin were removed
> from the street. D'Angelo . . . was exercising his authority as a
> peacekeeper in the name of public safety.[24]

Cohen found Kirkham's behavior unquestionable, but he did question whether D'Angelo's actions were justified and whether his means could appeal to the end of public safety. This is a specific instance of the general question whether ends justify means.

He offered four standards that must be met for an end to justify means: (1) The end itself must be good. (2) The means must be a plausible way to achieve the end. (3) There must be no alternative, better means to achieve the same end. (4) The means must not undermine some other equal or greater end.[25]

Those standards are implicit in O. W. Wilson's injunction to use lesser means that "will suffice" to achieve their ends. They make explicit a general theory of means and ends within which practitioners do their work.

Cohen concluded, at least for some circumstances, that D'Angelo's behavior satisfied the first three conditions: Public safety is good, as is removing heroin from the streets; illegal searches by experienced officers are likely to turn up enough heroin to make them worthwhile; and confiscation of drugs is sometimes a more effective control than legal arrests and convictions that end in suspended sentences, probation, and the like. Thus, Cohen concluded that the real issue was whether D'Angelo's behavior was consistent with criterion four: The means must not undermine some other equal or greater end.

What ends were at risk in D'Angelo's conduct? "First, the enforcement of law, including the law of search and seizure and narcotics laws; and, second, police adherence to, and respect for, due process of law." Those ends were betrayed, but were they of equal or greater status than the end of public safety—heroin control? Cohen argued as follows:

> By undermining the legal process of administration of the law of search and seizure and narcotics laws, D'Angelo contribute[d] to the conditions of secrecy and police isolation that foster corruption in narcotics enforcement and, presumably, further entrench the use of heroin. Even if D'Angelo [was] an honest and well-intentioned officer, his methods, if permitted to flourish, [would] undermine his own goals. I conclude that D'Angelo . . . overstepped his peace-keeping authority and [was] not justified in doing so.[26]

That is hardly a surprising conclusion. Although extraordinary steps are sometimes demanded, police work can scarcely be rendered exempt from the constraints intended to protect citizens from routine suspension of their rights.

Police, including beginners, should learn that serving multiple purposes will not justify riding roughshod over any of them, especially when limits are so fundamental to police authority. Cohen's four tests can be useful for the routine treatment of the public, including dope dealers and other suspected criminals. But in unpredictable circumstances, the simpler principles of lesser means and respect for law may have more application.

Most law enforcement executives I have worked with take Cohen's analysis for granted. They instruct personnel that ends do not justify means and that violation of citizen rights is rarely professional or effective. Furthermore, one excess often leads to another. If officers violate citizens' rights, they must conceal their behavior alone or bring others, including superiors, into complicity with them. If convictions are sought, false reports, perjury, and cynicism and self-contempt may follow. Deception undermines trust among colleagues and disrupts efforts at conscientious performance. Moral wisdom includes recognition that excess begets excess; once officers are on it, they can find the slope very slippery.

Kirkham's regard for legal rights was admirable, but what of his hesitancy and second-guessing of his partner? When D'Angelo called the two men from the alley, one was armed, so the other could have been as well.

Yet when Kirkham hesitated with the second suspect, whose hands he could not see, D'Angelo drew his revolver and took control—even though he was already dealing with the first suspect. Kirkham's embarrassment and dallying placed his partner and himself in jeopardy. His concern about *Terry v. Ohio* should not have left him or his partner exposed. Once in a situation, two officers should not be at cross-purposes, at least not until the immediate danger is addressed. If disagreement is unavoidable, so be it, but not during risk of violence.

In an analogous situation in private life, I once ate with a friend at an oyster house and gave a $10 bill to the counter man, who returned change for $20. When I persisted in trying to correct the error, I learned that he understood little English. His boss heard me, rushed up to us, began shouting recriminations at the man, and threatened to fire him. As my friend and I left, he turned to me and said, "Ed, I never saw one man risk so much harm to another out of concern for his own character."

His analysis was instructive; I had been so determined to be honest that I neglected the harm I might do to the counterman. I could have left the extra change on the bar and gone quietly. Then, when the error was detected at day's end, the counterman would have had the money to make it up. My end was worthwhile, but my means, though well intentioned, were inappropriate.

If the stranger at an oyster bar deserves such consideration, our colleagues at work deserve even more. Police who work as partners have an absolute necessity for mutual trust, and one must not needlessly jeopardize the other out of concern for his own character. Kirkham should have gotten the situation under control first, and then thought about what to do next, especially since D'Angelo's decision to stop and frisk was legitimate. Otherwise, character can be damaged by failure to meet the trust of a colleague and to see to a partner's interests as though they were one's own. Perhaps D'Angelo should never have thrust the inexperienced Kirkham into the situation, but once there, each person must give priority to the danger to the other, as well as to the suspects. Allowing a situation to get out of hand jeopardizes them, too, though Kirkham ignored this.

Most police would not view the question whether D'Angelo's behavior was excessive and unproductive as a difficult one. They are, however, concerned about discretion in the use of force, especially deadly force, and how police should be instructed in it.

In one of my classes on ethics in law enforcement, an experienced uniformed officer said: "You know, Mr. Delattre, most of us don't want to shoot people. We don't even like to hurt people." Most of my work with police confirms this. For example, two patrol officers with whom I was riding were called about 8:00 p.m. to a bar between white and black sections of a midwestern city. Violence had occurred there before, and the owner had killed a patron.

In that case, the owner had thrown out a man who threatened to "go home and get my rifle and come back and kill you." The owner called the dispatcher and said that he would have to shoot the man if he returned. The officers entered the bar from opposite ends, then joined the bar owner in scanning the street. The man was walking toward the bar with a long object in hand, concealed in brown wrapping paper. When he saw the police and ran, one officer ran after him while the other took the car and started up the alley behind the bar. The foot patrolman informed him by radio that the suspect had entered a Camaro driven by another man and that they were coming down the alley. As the police car blocked the Camaro, it slid to a stop sideways in a small parking area; the foot patrolman ran to within a few feet of the car, drew his revolver, and ordered the suspect from the car, while the other officer covered him. The driver came out with his hands up, shouted that he knew nothing, and threw himself face against a wall. The suspect hesitated, then came slowly from the car and raised the object until it pointed at the shins, the knees, and then the midsection of the officer. Both officers shouted, "Drop it, drop it, drop it!" Finally, the suspect dropped the bag, which as it rattled to the pavement disclosed not a rifle but a long iron bar. Back-up patrol arrived and took the suspect downtown.

The officers continued their tour. They were shaken by the episode but did not discuss it until after the shift. I had believed that the suspect had a rifle or shotgun in the bag, and so had they. The officer who had allowed the suspect to point the object and apparently threaten his life said, "Well, I wasn't sure he had a gun, but I thought he did, and I thought he was going to shoot." Then he added, "At the end, I was pulling the trigger. I honestly thought I was pulling it hard enough to fire, but I released it as he dropped the bag. I was lucky—that he didn't have a gun and that I didn't shoot him."

He meant that he was lucky, not because he had escaped media fallout or a departmental investigation, but because he did not have to live with his having shot an unarmed man. Although he exposed himself to grave danger and had every reason to believe the man to be armed, he "didn't want to shoot people."

This officer was in no sense soft on crime or an apologist for criminals, and he held no social theories that rendered people blameless for their conduct. Although young, he had several years of experience and a fine record. He simply tried to avoid ever using more force than necessary in the performance of his duty. And so he held out against firing, hoping against hope that the suspect would not shoot.

In that confrontation, I believe that he exposed himself to the threat of being killed beyond anything required by duty or prudence. I remember vividly my cold fear of what seemed about to happen to him. The event unfolded very fast, but it seemed endless.

I have met other police like him. Some have never needed to draw a weapon. A few have been hurt trying to quiet domestic fights without hurting anyone. Some have successfully ended gunpoint confrontations without firing. Some have given enormous benefit of doubt to suspects, erring, if they err at all, on the side of danger to themselves.

Other police show few signs of such excellence. Much police literature, both popular and scholarly, focuses on excess use of force, including deadly force. For many who have reached middle age, visions of police brutality against nonviolent civil rights demonstrators are indelible, as are memories of the 1968 Chicago Democratic convention. And no one who follows the news can be unconcerned about errors of judgment, or apparent ill will, in policing.

Force and Deadly Force

Since police departments have very different records, we should look at laws and policies that may reduce the use of inordinate force and at attitudes about force that do not belong in policing.

Roger Wertheimer, a PhD who served as deputy sheriff of Multnomah County, Ore., drafted a general code of conduct that "tries to clarify the most general do's and don'ts of police use of force. For example, one paragraph categorically prohibits threatening or causing harm for the purpose of retaliation, or as a means of coercing a suspect, or in response to verbal abuse or exhibitions of disrespect, or as a means of procuring information or evidence."[27]

In offering these prohibitions, Wertheimer echoed the injunctions of the Wickersham *Report on Lawlessness in Law Enforcement*, completed in 1931. There, August Vollmer wrote with respect to third-degree techniques in interrogation:

> While third-degree methods are most frequently practiced by policemen and detectives, there are cases in which prosecuting officers and their assistants participate in them. To the contention that the third degree is necessary to get the facts, the reporters aptly reply in the language of the present Lord Chancellor of England (Lord Sankey): "It is not admissible to do a great right by doing a little wrong. . . . It is not sufficient to do justice by obtaining a proper result by irregular or improper means." Not only does the use of the third degree involve a flagrant violation of law by the officers of the law, but it involves also the dangers of false confessions, and it tends to make police and prosecutors less zealous in the search for objective evidence. As the New York prosecutor quoted in the report said, "It is a short cut and makes the police lazy and unenterprising." Or, as another official quoted remarked: "If you use your fists, you are not so likely to use your wits." We agree with the conclusion expressed in the report, that "The third degree brutalizes the police, hardens the prisoner against society, and lowers the esteem in which the administration of justice is held by the public."[28]

Recognition by police of the need for binding limits is essential to their education and training. But many statutory provisions on police use of force are either so permissive or so vague, Wertheimer said, that they leave police in need of clear and useful departmental policies. "Few citizens have any realistic conception of how much and what kinds of force are necessary to accomplish certain tasks safely," he said, and "still fewer citizens appreciate that a policeman is not likely to respect a rule he views as a threat to his own self-respect because it bars him from effective action."[29] Wertheimer cited *Oregon Revised Statutes* 163.100 as a typical case of inadequate legislation:

> The killing of a human being is justifiable when committed: (1) By public officers or those acting in their aid and assistance and by their command: (a) When necessarily committed in overcoming resistance to the execution of a legal duty. (b) When necessarily committed in retaking persons charged with or convicted of crimes who have escaped or been rescued. (c) When necessarily committed in arresting a person fleeing from justice who has committed a felony.[30]

And *Oregon Revised Statutes* 133.280 states:

> Means of Effecting Arrest: If after notice of intention to arrest the defendant, he either flees or forcibly resists, the officer may use all necessary and proper means to effect the arrest.[31]

The second statute offers no guidance about the meaning of *necessary* and *proper*. The first does not oblige an officer to shoot at a felon or escaped prisoner who flees, but it functions within "a statutory requirement that the department and its officers faithfully execute their duties and fulfill their functions."[32] Thus, the first is largely useless with respect to the discretion of officers, who need to know what their departments expect. The second, to the extent that it suggests that fleeing felons are to be stopped, militates against restraint.

In this context, Wertheimer's revision of his department's rules and procedures manual included the following paragraph:

> Members will use deadly force with maximum restraint. . . . The use of deadly force against a human being is unwarranted unless there is a preponderant evidence that the person will attack another human life.[33]

It also specified the particulars of the two circumstances permitting the use of deadly force:

The first circumstance is that the officer "has no reasonable alternative means of protecting himself or another person against a clear and present danger of death or serious injury from an unjustifiable attack." The second and more debatable circumstance specified is that the officer has no reasonable alternative means of preventing an escape or effecting an arrest and capture and (a) he has good reason to believe that the subject is a violent and dangerous public menace, (b) the arrest, capture, or prevention of an escape is lawful, (c) the subject is known to be an adult, (d) the subject is known to have committed a felony, (e) the officer exerts every reasonable effort to make known his authority and purpose to the subject.[34]

Wertheimer cautioned that those policies are imperfect. They are compromises, efforts to take into account, for example, concerns about imminent peril and about the age of offenders, the protection of innocent life and regard for the life of the felon. They were drafted in part on the rationale that Oregon had abolished capital punishment and that past misdeeds alone could not therefore justify the use of deadly force. He denied that such departmental policies could be implemented everywhere, and he insisted that each department should review with care its own legislation, past policies, and history of the use of force to determine where problems persist. Wertheimer's policies are in accord with standards of the Commission on Accreditation of Law Enforcement Agencies. They say, for example, that "a 'fleeing felon' should not be presumed to pose an immediate threat to life in the absence of actions that would lead one to believe otherwise, such as a previously demonstrated threat to or wanton disregard for human life."[35]

Finally, the manual gave officers the discretionary authority to decide whether to use deadly force when the circumstances permitted it:

> Even when a member is permitted . . . to use deadly force, he may refrain from doing so if he deems it advisable in a particular case. A member will not be censured if a subject is not apprehended after all reasonable methods except deadly force have been used, and the member deems the use of deadly force inadvisable.[36]

The idea, clearly, was that error on the side of restraint is better than error on the side of excess.

Critics may think that this allows too much discretion, or that it does not rightly identify all the cases where deadly force might be used, or that it allows too little discretion, or is imprecise about imminent peril, and so on. What matters most, though, is that the department met its obligations to address fundamental issues of policy in a way that both respects limits and advances the exercise of discretion within those limits. For the wise implementation of law and policy in the daily work of police, that kind of conscientiousness is irreplaceable.

Anticipation and Planning

Crises in judgment and discretion can be avoided by anticipating situations in which questions of duty and rightful conduct arise. Facing them when there is time to think can result in better reactions when there is no time and can forestall dilemmas about what to do, not only in uses of force but also in other police work.

For example, in 1988 northwest Washington, D.C., had been the scene of fourteen sexual attacks in four years for which one man may have been responsible. The crimes showed similarities, as did descriptions of the attacker. The *Washington Post* reported, "In the aftermath of each attack, there has been another similarity: District Police issued no immediate statement warning residents, even though the assailant remains at large."[37]

The police were uncertain that there was a single attacker. The *Post* said that those cases "underscore a debate over whether and when it serves residents to warn them that a serial criminal is preying on a community. 'It's always been one of the most difficult issues to deal with: When do you go out and make a public release?'" one police official asked. "While police warnings can raise community awareness . . . they can spawn 'copycat' crimes or merely cause the assailant to change the method or location of his attacks."[38]

The police were criticized by residents, who noted that other departments, as in Fairfax, Virginia, and Prince George's County, Maryland, operate on a different policy: "If we think there's a pattern, we put it out to the public." The public may respond with heightened awareness and take precautions to avoid the circumstances of the attacks—by locking doors and windows, for example, or staying away from certain neighborhoods or streets. These gains seem to the departments to outweigh the risk that apprehension of the criminals may be made more difficult.[39]

The issue was taken out of the hands of the D.C. police when the media gave it attention. Whether the police were right or wrong not to publicize the cases, they then faced the same result as if they had gone public except that they also became the subject of public criticism.

To avoid such results, police officials can review the effects of policies on the apprehension of perpetrators, the protection of the public, and so on. They can make continuing efforts to secure good, candid relations with the media, community leaders, and neighborhood associations. By making these routine, they can explain their policies when no specific case is in progress, as well as find out the opinions of those they serve. They can ask the media to cooperate in stressing police warnings to the citizenry.

Such steps are better than having no clear policies or policies the public does not know. When the steps are taken apart from a climate of fear, they may be less newsworthy in the eyes of the media, but they are a conscientious means of parrying the charge that the public had no way of knowing how police operate.

Finally, law enforcement personnel sometimes object that the standards they are expected to meet in their use of authority and discretion seem unfair. A few have complained to me that although others are innocent until proven guilty, police seem to be presumed guilty by the citizens and the media whenever accused.

Some people are simply prejudiced against police and any other form of authority. Others are prejudiced in favor of them. When authority, power, and discretion are granted to public officials, however, rational people presume that they will not use more than they need for their legitimate purposes, because rational people would never grant more authority or discretion to abridge liberty or use force than they believed necessary. The presumption is not of guilt but of official respect for restraint. Citizens expect public officials to justify their uses of authority or power when questions arise.

As Wertheimer insisted, citizens may be naïve in assessing how much authority and force are in fact needed. For this reason, the education of the public—not only by police, but by other public officials, schools, and others—is essential. But citizens are right to expect restraint, because each one risks being victimized by official excess.

Since prejudice is always unfair and presumption of guilt is prejudicial, it is therefore unfair. But there is nothing unfair in a presumption of respect for limits and an expectation that the burden of proof will be met by officials who have authority and use it. That presumption amounts to insistence that might does not make right, that officials will bear the public trust faithfully, and that they will accept the onus of showing that they are doing so. Those who have no stomach for such ordeals of the public trust should choose another line of work.

6

Public Corruption for Profit

Richard Rich. But every man has his price!
Thomas More. No-no-no.
R. Rich. But yes! In money, too.
T. More. (with gentle impatience) No, no, no.
R. Rich. Or pleasure. Titles, women, bricks-and-mortar, there's always something.
T. More. Childish.

—Robert Bolt[1]

The only thing that is incorruptible is personal character that refuses to be corrupted. An incorruptible person, as Aristotle observed, "is truthful in word and deed just because truthfulness has become second nature with him." Such a person, "who is truthful even in matters where nothing depends on his veracity, will be still more careful of the truth when something does depend on it."[2] The person of incorruptible character has no price.

Incorruptibility

Good character includes a conception of what is worthy of oneself. Persons who truly have no price consider it beneath them to give in to temptations for illicit gratification or profit. Peer pressure, weakness in others, impulse, opportunity, and personal rationalization or consolation do not excuse lapses of character.

A person who is incorruptible and who respects ideals of due process and limits to the rightful use of power is different from a fanatic. Fanatics, such as terrorists on suicide missions, cannot be diverted from their purpose, but they disdain the restraint essential to justice, liberty, and decency in law enforcement.

Incorruptibility is a form of personal freedom that consists of control of one's life in accordance with standards of excellence and self-respect that are more important than anything else, including life itself. No other disposition makes our lives our own, and no other disposition can make anyone trustworthy to the very end. Although few of us may ever reach full incorruptibility, we all should keep its nature clearly before us.

Cynicism and Consolation

Complaining that no one is incorruptible, that everyone has a price, is a time-worn excuse. If the cynicism were true, then our experiment in ordered liberty simply could not long endure. Neither could we identify any trustworthy public officials except by assuming that their price had never been offered.

A popular little book of counsel to young men and women explained in 1797:

> Men who transgress the rules of justice are not destitute of pallia-tives for their conduct. "In these times," they say, "the practice of every kind of dishonest trick is so universally prevalent, that were we scrupulously to abstain, inevitable ruin would be the conse-quence." Be it remembered, this libel . . . is not ours; it is quoted from men who . . . urge it as an excuse for conduct their own hearts do not approve and their tongues will not otherwise justify.[3]

History is full of stories of persons who have had the character to resist all sorts of powerful temptations. When the ancient Athenians put Socrates on trial, he could have persuaded them to spare him if he repented asking philosophical questions in public and promised never to do so again. Socrates told them, however, that his accusers might have the power to banish him or to kill him but not to do him real harm. Since betrayal of his convictions about his duties as a citizen would have made him a worse man, he declined to make a deal. They executed him, but they could not "reach" him, even by offering him life.

Thomas More, in Robert Bolt's play, was beheaded by Henry VIII on the strength of perjured testimony by Richard Rich. Rich had a price, but More did not. To save himself, More had only to put his hand on a Bible and tell a simple lie, but he remained silent.

In the 1960s and 1970s, hundreds of American POWs in Hanoi were offered freedom to return to America if they would provide information and false "confessions" of war crimes. They refused except after torture, and then said only as much as they had to. Many suffered in solitary confinement, manacled, for years rather than betray themselves, each other, or their country.

Thousands of police officers similarly cannot be reached by temptations to forsake duty for profit or for personal safety. The natural desires to live, rather than to die, and to live in some comfort have not eroded their sense of duty. They own their own lives, and they will not sell them to anything or anybody. Each of them is incorruptible, certainly in the sense described by Frederick Elliston and Michael Feldberg: None will accept "money or money's worth for doing something he is under a duty to do anyway, that he is under a duty not to do, or to exercise a legitimate discretion for improper reasons."[4]

Many who do have a price cushion their weaknesses in false consolation. As novelist-philosopher Iris Murdoch wrote:

> The chief enemy of excellence in morality is personal fantasy:
> the tissue of self-aggrandizing and consoling wishes and dreams
> that prevents one from seeing what is there outside one. . . .
> Almost everything that consoles is a fake.[5]

We human beings, of course, show remarkable capacity to excuse our worst excesses and negligence and to console ourselves that we are blameless for our own misdeeds. We blame our parents for how we were raised or embrace social and political ideologies that tell us that "the system" is always to blame.

Corrupt public officials—including corrupt police—in particular seek consolation by blaming "the system" for their own misconduct. Some police say that planting evidence, obtaining confessions illegally, submitting false reports, and committing perjury are necessary to take criminals off the streets, but even if they were, they would be inexcusable lawbreaking. Respected command personnel throughout America flatly deny that such means are necessary. They, like experienced patrol personnel, know that criminals continue to commit criminal acts and, if not apprehended for one crime, will often be apprehended and convicted—legally—for another.

Self-consolation attends laxity and negligence as well. Some police may be lax in enforcing traffic laws on the excuse that many traffic violations go undetected and unpunished and that competent patrol officers would never engage in a pursuit that constituted a greater hazard than the violation did. That is no excuse for laxity, however, when it is safe and prudent to stop and warn, ticket, or arrest violators.

Higher Standards and Double Standards

Some police seek consolation by claiming that they are victims of a double standard, unfairly discriminated against. For instance, police complain that random testing unfairly identified them as drug users because airline pilots, railroad personnel, and heavy-equipment operators are not similarly tested. The point, however, is that certain drugs are illegal, and that those in a position to endanger others impair their capacities by using them. If airlines, railroads, and other industries are lax about such matters, so much the worse for all of us; their laxity must not determine the trustworthiness of private or public officials. If police departments insist on higher standards than others, they are better institutions.

Those who serve the public must hold to a higher standard of honesty and care for the public good than the general citizenry does. Anyone likely to pursue self-interest and public or private excess—even in ways tolerated among the citizenry—does not belong in government.

A higher standard is not a double standard. Persons accepting positions of public trust take on new obligations and are free not to accept them if they do not want to live up to the higher standard. A higher standard as such is not unfair; granting authority to an official without it would be unfair to the public.

Since double standards are unfair standards, the distinction between them and higher standards should be maintained by command officers and teachers. Otherwise, they lose their justification for legitimate standards of performance in public office.

When police complain about double standards (and are not just confused about legitimate higher standards), they may refer to standards for police that differ from those for other officials. Police who enforce the laws, they say, should have the same standards as legislators who make the laws.

Some public officials fuel that resentment, as Senator Patrick J. Leahy did on March 31, 1988, on the *MacNeil/Lehrer NewsHour*, when he insisted that the U.S. attorney general, under investigation for possible illegal and unethical conduct, should either resign or take a leave of absence. "This is not a case where he is running the Department of HUD or something like that," the senator said. "He embodies the justice system in this country. He's the chief law enforcement officer of this country." The senator was then asked, "If you were the subject of an investigation, which you thought was in some way tarnishing your office that you hold, or the public respect for your office, would you step down, or resign, or step aside temporarily, if you knew in your heart that you were innocent?" He replied, "If I was running the Department of Justice, with the responsibility of that, of course I would have to step aside."

By implication, Leahy proposed a double standard that calls for greater trustworthiness from law enforcement officials than from other executive branch officials and from legislators. But if law enforcement executives cannot fulfill their duties because of high levels of public mistrust, neither can others in government. Lawmakers are impaired in representing their constituents.

One difference, however, is relevant. A senator can be voted out of office, but a police officer or attorney general cannot. For that and other reasons, many thoughtful people believe that all who bear the public trust cannot be judged—and punished—by the same standards and methods. They argue that a police officer should be judged by a higher standard than a legislator because police carry weapons and are more dangerous. Police "make law in the streets and can more readily violate rights." Also, police are more visible to the public, and "the example they set is more important."

Police do apply distinctive powers to the lives of citizens and are much more visible than many other government officials. The powers of judges or legislators are, however, no less important and have no less impact on the public. Legislative and judicial regulation of institutions and individuals reaches further now than ever before into American life, and the example they set matters no less; much of the cynicism of school children and college students stems from classroom study of media reports of corruption and bad judgment in high elective office. The behavior of lawmakers sets an example for them—and for police. If lawmakers and judges care about how police behave, they should not behave in ways they consider wrong for police.

Although police should not be judged and punished differently, the work of law enforcers does differ from that of lawmakers. Some of those differences suggest the appropriateness of different responses to misconduct.

When a police officer falsifies a report to preserve a chain of evidence, he is subject to departmental discipline. A legislator who manipulates data to the point of lying in floor debate is not subject to discipline. He is made accountable by the rebuttal of other lawmakers—if they take their jobs seriously—and by voter rejection. The methods of accountability differ because the work of police and lawmakers is not the same. Although it is wrong for both to lie, the institutional remedies are necessarily different. Neither set is entirely effective, since many police and many lawmakers are not actually held accountable for lies.

Stressing such differences is an argument not for double standards but for appropriately different policies and procedures in different institutions. That some public servants will inevitably betray the public makes it more essential that others not do so. Immoral behavior in government is not an excuse for others to imitate it but rather a compelling reason not to. Under such circumstances, high moral aspiration is needed more than ever.

Still, rationalization and self-consolation accompany even the worst kinds of behavior by police. Gerald Clemente, a former police captain in Massachusetts who stole and sold police promotion examinations and also became a bank robber, said: "I became corrupt by going on the police force. . . . [T]o be a part of that police force . . . you had to be a thief. You had to steal. Otherwise, they want nothing to do with you."[6] Officer Bob Rathbun, one of the Buddy Boys of Brooklyn who stole money and dealt in drugs, was frustrated by his job and his superiors:

> They destroyed me mentally. They did. 'Cause every time I did
> something good, they did something to turn around and say no
> good. . . . I looked around . . . and I saw who was doing what, and

they're getting away with anything, and they seem to be getting
along with every boss. So I must be doing something wrong.

A fellow officer, Henry Winter, who rationalized that stealing money from
drug dealers was "a means of getting back" at them, said he learned from his
own corruption "never to become a cop, not in the City of New York, no
never. Never get involved, never. Don't get involved. That's the lesson."[7]

Although such police may succeed in deceiving themselves, they were
a disgrace to the badge, and their explanations are a fake. Public officials
occupy a station of trust, which entails incorruptibility. Nothing like greed
is compatible with the trust of other people.

All trustworthy command and patrol personnel grasp the difference
between policing and the criminal justice system. They have duties of law
enforcement and peacekeeping irrespective of the outcome of their work.
Whether or not the suspects they arrest are prosecuted or receive only a nom-
inal penalty is absolutely irrelevant. Emotional involvement in cases is
dangerous because it encourages bitterness when they do not turn out as
desired. Resentment can turn into the self-deception and self-consolation of
the Buddy Boys.

The best police tolerate abuse from the citizenry without personal animosity that tempts them toward retaliation and self-indulgence. Their character protects them from self-destructive frustration. An experienced black police
officer described a not unusual situation in which a terribly frustrated individual, in tears of rage at his mistreatment by another person, screamed "pig" and
racial epithets at the officer: "Look, I know how he felt, and I figured he would
be swearing at anybody who came on the scene. It wasn't anything about me,
or my color, or even my uniform. I was just handy." In this instance as in "more
dangerous situations in the [housing] projects," he explained, a police officer
has to recognize that people are often pretty close to their own limits of tolerance and self-control. "You have to try to give people enough room to do what
you want them to do and not press the issue in a way that just makes things
worse. Even very dangerous people who prey on others have feelings of pride
and anger like the rest of us, and you have to allow them some room."

I am often told that we cannot expect everyone in public life to be like
that, nor can we recruit police for that level of self-mastery. After all, history
also reveals that decent people at the highest levels of government fall into

corruption and suffer a decline of personal character and the loss of moral purpose. The real issue, it is said, is to try to eliminate those things that corrupt or at least to combat their effects. But efforts to prevent corruption that rest on changes in environment, external inducements to honesty, and sanctions against dishonesty are poor substitutes for personal character. They cannot take the place of the deep and unshakable conviction that corruption is dishonorable and that dishonor is truly worse than death.

Hypotheses about Corruption

If greed is simple, the variety of temptations to which police and other public officials succumb is not. Hypotheses about the causes of corruption abound, together with the array of proposed remedies. The main positions are that police corruption is caused by society at large, by influences within police departments, or by a disposition toward corruption in individuals who become police. I call the first position the society-at-large hypothesis, and scholars call the second the structural, or affiliation, theory and the third the rotten-apple, or affinity, theory.

The Society-at-Large Hypothesis. O. W. Wilson gave voice to the society-at-large view in accounting for the history of police corruption in Chicago:

> This force was corrupted by the citizens of Chicago. . . . It has been customary to give doormen, chauffeurs, maids, cooks, and delivery men little gifts and gratuities. . . . It is felt that the level of service . . . depends on these gratuities.
>
> Now, there was little difficulty in transferring the concept from servants to *public* servants. It was natural to include policemen. . . .
>
> Unfortunately, it was easy to extend this to the offering of gratuities to policemen who would perform little favors that were not legal. . . . A certain progression of events follows. Some of the more grasping policemen would, shall we say, make themselves available for gratuities. Businessmen and others came to understand that the policemen now *expected* the gratuities.[8]

Such practices led to small bribes, Wilson explained; truckdrivers, for example, would clip money to their drivers' licenses to avoid traffic citations. As petty bribery became commonplace, police would make frivolous traffic stops to get the bills:

> The practice of accepting payoffs from businessmen and drivers was extended to more serious crimes. If a policeman caught a burglar with a big haul, he would take part of the haul and let the burglar go. "If I arrest this man," the policeman would rationalize, "he will be released on bond. The money will go to a bondsman and a lawyer to fix up the case." The officer reasoned that he might just as well have that money himself. Now we come to the final act of the grim business. . . . Suppose you caught a thief with no money. You could bargain with him. You could get him to perform future burglaries with you or for you, and offer him protection in exchange for a share of the haul.[9]

Wilson was warning, too, of the slippery slope (or moral career) hypothesis: that corruption begins with apparently harmless and well-intentioned practices and leads over time—either in individuals or in departments as a whole—to all manner of crimes-for-profit. When Wilson became superintendent of police in Chicago in 1960, he told the people of the city that "the same kind of special consideration that they were buying for small amounts, could, by the same logic, be purchased by criminals and crime syndicates for larger amounts. . . . When people realized that they were part of the pattern of corrupting Chicago police, they cut it out."[10]

Although Wilson's belief that citizens stopped seeking "special consideration" is not confirmed by the facts, his analysis shows how a police department can be hurt by the desire by ordinary citizens for special services and then for illegal ones. His description of police rationalization shows how corruption becomes routine when police believe that other parts of the criminal justice system are corrupt. When police believe that a violator will buy relief from a corrupt judge, they may sell relief themselves. Oliver Revell, former executive assistant director of investigations at the FBI, described such judicial corruption as "a significant problem in causing police corruption" because "where the judges are corrupt, police corruption has virtually always followed. It is nearly inevitable."

Wilson saw that cleaning up the Chicago police would require a strong and systematic method of addressing citizen complaints and a powerful internal affairs division to investigate charges. Such a division must be as assiduous in its defense of falsely accused police as in its disclosure of corrupt ones; Wilson understood that presumption of the guilt of his own men was self-destructive and self-defeating.

Believing that remedies for corruption could not be found outside police forces, he opposed political intrusion and civilian review boards:

> Discipline . . . is a function of command. It should not be divorced from operational responsibility. The answer to the problem of police misconduct and corruption is not the creation of an outside disciplinary agency. The answer is the creation of the right kind of a system within the force, consisting of men who know and understand police work, to protect the innocent and punish the guilty.[11]

Even those who concur acknowledge that external investigations in Chicago in the late 1960s show that Wilson's methods were not altogether successful. Still, with few exceptions, police officials find truth in the slippery slope hypothesis. The prevailing view in my experience is that corruption must be nipped in the bud by policies prohibiting *all* gratuities.

This policy denies that there is "honest graft," a notion advanced, in typically self-serving fashion, by George Washington Plunkitt of Tammany Hall. Rejecting blackmail, extortion, and bribery in public life, he attempted to justify the use of political office—and especially insider information—for profit. He believed that politicians could rightfully give contracts to friends, indulge cost overruns, and buy up land where parks or roads would be built. "Ain't it perfectly honest to charge a good price and make a profit on my investment and foresight?" he asked. "Of course it is. Well, that's honest graft."[12] As one former police official put the point, however, "There is no honest dollar except your salary. Everything else compromises you somehow."

Police everywhere know that the symbol of the gratuity is the free cup of coffee. A rather jaded police captain, upon learning that I was writing a book about police ethics, said, "Oh, God, not another book about the free cup of coffee." We shall return to the issue of gratuities below.

The Structural or Affiliation Hypothesis. The society-at-large hypothesis bears a strong resemblance to the structural (or affiliation) hypothesis. Arthur Niederhoffer, author of *Behind the Shield: The Police in Urban Society*, wrote:

> Actual policemen seem to accept graft for other reasons than avarice. Often the first transgression is inadvertent. Or, they may be gradually indoctrinated by older policemen. Step by step they progress from a small peccadillo to outright shakedown and felony.[13]

Niederhoffer appealed to the account of "a Denver policeman involved in the police burglary scandal of 1961," who claimed to have learned from senior officers when he was a rookie to take payoffs:

> So the rookie . . . is turned over to a more experienced man for breaking in. . . . He knows he is being watched. . . . He is eager to be accepted. . . . The older man stops at a bar, comes out with some packages of cigarettes. . . . He explains that this is part of the job. . . . So he, the rookie, goes into a Skid Row bar and stands uncomfortably at the end, waiting for the bartender to acknowledge his presence and disdainfully toss him two packages of cigarettes.
>
> The feeling of pride slips away, and a hint of shame takes hold. One thing leads to another for the rookies.[14]

Niederhoffer shared the widely held view that police loss of faith in mankind generally spawns individual and departmental corruption. He concurred with William A. Westley that

> the policeman's world is spawned of degradation, corruption, and insecurity. He sees men as ill-willed, exploitative, mean and dirty; himself a victim of injustice, misunderstood and defiled. He tends to meet those portions of the public which are acting

contrary to the law or using the law to further their own ends. He is exposed to public immorality. He becomes cynical. His is a society emphasizing the crooked, the weak and the unscrupulous. Accordingly, his morality is one of expediency and his self-conception one of a martyr.[15]

According to Niederhoffer, those conditions lead to anomie in police departments, to which the "typical adaptation" is cynicism: "It consists of diffuse feelings of hate and envy, impotent hostility, and the sour-grapes pattern." Cynicism is "a state of mind in which the anomie of the police organization as a whole is reflected in the individual policeman."[16] Niederhoffer's position is traceable to sociologist Emile Durkheim's account of anomie, a pathological condition of alienation from society and its constraining influences of law and morality. It means loss of any sense of solidarity with the collective sentiments and positive norms of society.

The structural account of police corruption is described by its advocates, sociologists Julian B. Roebuck and Thomas Barker:

Police corruption is best understood not as the exclusive deviance of individual officers, but as group behavior guided by contradictory sets of norms linked to the organization to which the erring individuals belong, i.e., organizational deviance.[17]

The view is that corruption emerges among police because deviant behavior is regarded as appropriate within the police department. Many studies confirm that young police are socialized by their senior colleagues in traditions of corruption within the department. According to that view, corruption depends on secrecy; thus, police reform can be achieved best by external review, by civilian boards, or by elected and appointed public officials. Police commissioners often lack sufficient authority and resources, however, to combat corruption from within. According to Mark Pogrebin of the University of Colorado's Graduate School of Public Affairs and Burton Atkins of Florida State University: "Very few police expect repercussions from their involvement in corrupt exchanges. They are not deterred by the law enforcement apparatus of which they are a part, nor do they fear departmental sanctions for their illegal behavior."[18]

Pogrebin and Atkins added that external remedies also encounter obstacles:

> The assuredness of punishment either on the part of the district attorney or another outside investigative body is usually lacking, therefore permitting corrupt activities on the part of police to endure. Internal control appears to prove insignificant and external control has proven to be successfully challenged by local Police Benevolent Associations.[19]

The hypothesis of structural deviance and the attendant perplexity about remedies are not complex: (1) If a young person of high ideals but little exposure to realities that challenge naive expectations of human decency (2) enters a world that exposes the worst in people and (3) is trained and influenced by senior colleagues who have lost faith in police work, and (4) if the young person must establish some mutual trust and reliance with colleagues who use their work to line their own pockets and to get their share of what all others are grabbing as fast as they can, and (5) if their superiors are unlikely to support efforts to behave honorably, and (6) the likelihood of sanction for corruption is negligible, (7) *then* the young person will probably accept the status quo and join in corrupt practices, perhaps with initial feelings of shame, but ultimately without remorse. The difficulty of remedy is equally transparent: When cynical persons on both sides of the law profit from an alliance, and when the ability of police command to force the issue is constrained, those persons will use any means to preserve the status quo and to prevent reform from outside.

No one has to conduct massive studies to know these things. They are amply demonstrated in history, political theory, and daily experience. Still, they do not confirm that police are universally cynical; clearly, a great many are not. Nor do they show that disappointed expectation is sufficient to make anyone corrupt. Many patrol and command personnel whose expectations of people have been lowered by years of experience would never take a dime that did not belong to them. Not even great disappointment in the citizenry in itself can make police corrupt; to become corrupt, police officers must give up on themselves, not just on others.

The Rotten-Apple Hypothesis. Some argue that the affiliation (or structural) hypothesis neglects important roots of corruption. The Chicago
Crime Commission, for example, "placed an emphasis on the type of police
officer on the force . . . in examining the major causes of police criminal
behavior. . . . The commission concluded that poor recruitment methods
permitted many men to enter the department who were not suited for
law enforcement work. The commission recommended that all police
candidates be subjected to a complete character investigation."[20] This
"rotten-apple" hypothesis, critics reply, ignores socializing influence within
departments and is too individualistic, like "the analogous free-will explanation of criminal behavior."[21]

The rotten-apple argument has, however, been confirmed repeatedly
by cases of corruption within departments—for example, the discovery of
the River Cops and others in Miami, Fla., which was expected to lead
to removal of a tenth of the department. By the early 1980s, Miami had
become a volatile city: "A savage turf war among cocaine traffickers
provided a daily litter of corpses. And that was just one of the developments
that left a shell-shocked citizenry screaming for more police. Another was
that Cuban neighborhoods were becoming explosively overcrowded." In
May 1980 "a race riot ripped through the black Liberty City ghetto."

In that year, officials decided to double the size of Miami's police department; within two years, two hundred new officers were hired. Those newcomers were not adequately trained or supervised; officers with less than a
year's experience became field training officers and made recommendations
whether newcomers should pass probation. Seventy-five percent of the
officers "since accused of wrongdoing or complicity have come from this
poorly trained group. . . . Ten . . . have pleaded guilty to murder-conspiracy
or drug trafficking charges."[22] After two more officers were convicted of
racketeering, cocaine possession, and conspiracy, a police official said that he
was "proud of the jury" and that more arrests would follow.[23]

The crimes included robberies, burglaries, millions of dollars in profits,
and conspiracy to murder a drug dealer who became a state's witness.
According to a former chief, "The rush to expand . . . seems to have led to
a willingness to overlook past behavior in background checks that at other
times would have been judged unacceptable." The president of Miami's
Fraternal Order of Police added, "When you're on the line offering your

life for $25,000 a year and you see these cocaine cowboys getting off on light sentences and getting off on probation, it becomes opportunity for the employee who's a little weak-willed."[24]

Few, if any, of those police were corrupted by more experienced police, who had little contact with them. Instead, the newcomers continued to frequent bars they had patronized before becoming police, the haunts of drug dealers. Supervision was lax, even nonexistent.

The frenzy of indiscriminate hiring, inadequate training, and poor supervision eroded personnel standards of the Miami Police Department until even illiteracy was no disqualification. Such betrayals of standards would have the same effects on any police department, regardless of the ethnic background of the newcomers, because so many thoroughly unfit individuals became police.

Neither the structural theory nor the rotten-apple theory is adequate by itself, nor are the theories mutually exclusive. The variety of corruption in public life gives plausibility to each in specific circumstances. But neither must we therefore accept Niederhoffer's account of anomie or the structuralist idea that men and women are not free to avoid corruption. The incompleteness of each position is clear; the structural argument cannot account for those who remain uncorrupted in corrupting environments; and the rotten-apple argument fails to explain how decent persons fall victim to circumstances. It also fails to account for those who lose their moral standards because they lack the imagination or intellect to control corrupting environments.

Some corrupt police are remorseful and tell the truth when they say that they "just didn't know how to say no" to partners who led them to corruption. Others had no idea what to do when they discovered corruption in their command structure. Part of their moral decline may be a matter of practical ignorance. In a few cases, I believe that the decline occurred partly because they knew too little about how to acquire power within institutions to combat abuses by supervisors, not because they were predisposed to corruption. For the clean members to join together to reverse peer pressure and to constrain others from corruption is a sophisticated political art, never learned by many police, especially at the patrol level. Standing for high principle need not mean standing alone, as students of politics know.

Departmental Supervision

Departmental structures and administrative policies can teach officers of integrity that they are not alone. Appropriate policies can thwart temptations toward corruption.

Bob Leuci, the subject of the book *Prince of the City: The True Story of a Cop Who Knew Too Much*[25] in New York, started on the road to corruption when he and his colleagues secretly used illegal wiretaps on drug dealers. When this surreptitious information enabled them to find drugs and make arrests, their successes led to accolades, to lack of supervision, to extensions of their tours of duty in narcotics, and to an insulated, cocoonlike environment. The officers then began keeping the money they found when arresting dealers, and later they kept and sold the drugs.

Closer supervision of the officers by command personnel might have prevented the wiretaps at the outset. Routine examination of informants by supervisory personnel could have served as a check on police activities. Mandating rotation of personnel assignments could have prevented insulation and the misconduct it made possible. Reassigning personnel whenever they are promoted and assigning them on the military model to fixed terms known at the beginning to be three years or so would have been useful. The expense of such practices in giving greater training to more people is small compared with that of corruption in law enforcement. If followed all the time as a way of safeguarding the police, such practices will not be seen as merely distrust or a reaction to corruption.

Although departmental structure does make a significant difference, especially in assignment and supervision, the structural hypothesis goes far beyond that. Its greatest weakness is to suggest that we are mere creatures of circumstance, that we can be courageous, honest, just, and temperate only so long as our circumstances do not become too difficult, and that we can have integrity only so long as it does not cost too much.

In my experience, many have greater fortitude than that. There is truth in the venerable beliefs that "fortitude even conquers fortune" and that "the art of living well consists principally of bringing good out of evils we may have to encounter."[26]

Still, such mature character is a great deal to expect of a teenager or someone in his early twenties. Habits of excellence can be developed by that age, for many young people do behave justly, courageously, honestly, and temperately, but their inexperience can make them too credulous toward senior colleagues whose good faith they take for granted. Misled about what qualifies as decent behavior, they may enter on a slippery slope. Their moral and emotional fortitude may be untested, as well, even if they are disposed toward right conduct, but their main weakness is likely to arise from inexperience. Those facts have implications for recruitment, education, training, and supervision. To forestall the young from stepping onto a slippery slope, two admonitions by former New York City Police Commissioner and Police Foundation President Patrick V. Murphy should be stressed. First, except for your paycheck, there's no such thing as a free buck.[27] Second, eliminating or reducing police corruption was always more important than convicting organized crime figures, even the overlords—the dons.[28] If that position is made clear, recruits may learn from the first day that behavior accepted by police personnel is not always acceptable.

Gratuities and the Slippery Slope

As we have seen, O. W. Wilson, Patrick V. Murphy, and many other experienced officials have contended that the slippery slope of corruption begins with any gratuity, including the well-known free cup of coffee. Many officers disagree, as do some scholars. Historian Michael Feldberg, for example, said that "small vices have small effects, and we need not begrudge police officers their free cup of coffee, half-priced meals, and the sense of welcome that they convey. . . . They are a relatively innocent transaction in a work universe in which the standard form of reciprocity . . . is extortionate rather than hospitable."[29]

Some restaurant owners do intend the free coffee or the reduced meal price as a kindness to police they judge to be underpaid, but others, more or less subtly, expect something in return. Some clearly want the police presence, but others want illegally parked customers to be left alone, and so on.

Police have told me that insurance companies reduce theft and robbery premiums on restaurants with a visible police presence and raise them where gratuities are prohibited. Although those officers believed that, a

survey of major companies suggests that they were wrong. Insurance companies sometimes prefer to insure restaurants with a central alarm system
or with a security guard, but rates are not affected (even when off-duty
police are hired as guards). Restaurant owners may tell police otherwise,
but they are never so motivated.

Some police view the free coffee as a hospitality, and others view it as
their right. Some always leave a tip as large as the price of the coffee plus
the normal tip and expect nothing in return; others leave no tip. Most
shopowners and waitresses can tell the difference in police attitudes, and so
can the police themselves. Some restaurant personnel clearly believe that
the police would be rude to refuse their hospitality, and so do some police.
But the police who think that they have a right to the coffee do not much
care about rudeness.

My experience leads me to conclude that, for some police, the small
kindness—like making fresh coffee when the police arrive in the middle of
the night—is just that. It is not like a tip for a bellhop, and it is not the beginning of a slippery slope. Since the intentions of the restaurant personnel are
often equally innocent, police acceptance and appreciation are not illicit.
Other police believe themselves deserving of special consideration because
they feel underpaid or burdened with too much hardship in their work. If
that attitude resembles self-pity, it can be a sign of vulnerability to a slippery
slope. The free coffee may not cause the vulnerability, but it may, by indulging
it, lead to worse things.

What, then, should be a department's policy? It should tell the truth: Not
everyone who accepts free coffee steps onto a slippery slope that leads to more
serious corruption, but some do, and some is too many. Although Wilson and
others may not be entirely right about bellhops and maids (if they do a poor
job unless tipped, they probably will not keep their jobs long), they are right
that members of professions do not take gratuities. If police want the status
of professionals, they should view being tipped as a threat.

Accordingly, departmental policy should treat all gratuities as unacceptable. They undermine public respect and cause resentment—costs that police
in general must pay. In this sense, the free coffee is much too expensive.
Young officers should take nothing except their compensation rather than
be faced later with questions about how far to go. Once that becomes the
issue, the matter has gone too far.

Some police departments compromise by permitting officers to accept free coffee and meals within their assigned districts but not elsewhere. That practice risks injustice in the distribution of benefits to police and jealousy among them over areas of assignment. If police departments require officers to sign checks for free coffee, many restaurant employees do not bother to submit them. Some police mock the policy by routinely signing illegibly or by writing the name of the chief or someone else.

Under a chit system, if a restaurant provides free coffee to an officer, it can seek reimbursement from the city. Thus, the officers retain the free coffee, but the city, not the restaurant, is the benefactor. The system is supposed to remove incentives to corruption. I would rather have the city and the police department make known that gratuities are prohibited. Any money available for a chit plan can be placed in the salary pool for police, who can decide how to spend it.

The question where the slope begins is no more emphasized in police literature than where it ends. Lawrence W. Sherman of the Crime Control Institute offered a hypothetical moral decline, beginning with the acceptance of minor perks, such as the free cup of coffee, which leads to complacency about accepting a free drink after hours from a bartender, to bribes for traffic violations, then to money from gamblers and prostitutes, and finally to graft from narcotics. Sherman insisted that such a decline presupposes circumstances that enable it, and he concurred with Ellwyn R. Stoddard's suggestion that "most policemen stop at a certain stage of deviance on the basis of group definitions of 'limits.'"[30]

But what makes up the "group" that defines the "limits"? Surely not the police force as a whole, or the Buddy Boys could never have accepted their final limits. Once a group begins to push to the limits, it may continue to press until few, if any, boundaries are left.

Furthermore, Sherman's identification of the coffee as a perk begs the question. By definition, a perquisite is a legitimate benefit, "expected or promised, held or claimed as an exclusive right" by virtue of a job, such as a residence for a college president. If a police officer thinks of the coffee in that way, he may think the same way about other benefits to which he has no right. A kindness is not a perquisite and therefore cannot suggest other perquisites except to a person who is confused about rights. Still, for those who can never have too much of a good thing, bad thinking can turn little vices into bigger ones.

According to the Knapp Commission in New York City, many police stop at a certain point on the slippery slope and go no further:

> Corruption, although widespread, is by no means uniform in degree. Corrupt policemen have been described as falling into two basic categories: "meat-eaters" and "grass-eaters." . . . The meat-eaters are those policemen who . . . aggressively misuse their police powers for personal gain. The grass-eaters simply accept the payoffs that the happenstances of police work throw their way.[31]

But why do police become grass-eaters at all, if they lack the greed and contempt for decency necessary to become meat-eaters?

Character and Free Will

Professor Herman Goldstein reported the commission's view, endorsed by Mark Pogrebin and Burton Atkins among others, that "the grasseaters may not, in a corruption-dominated department, be acting out of free choice. . . . One strong impetus encouraging grasseaters to accept relatively petty graft is, ironically, their feeling of loyalty to their fellow officers. Accepting payoff money is one way for an officer to prove that he is one of the boys and that he can be trusted." Officers who refuse such payoffs may not be "fully accepted into police fellowship."[32] As one former police executive put the point to me, "You know a department is in trouble when 'He's OK, you can trust him' means 'He's on the take, too.'"

Some officers say that they became corrupt because they feared for their lives if they did not. They feared that others would not assist them in an emergency or that active reprisals would be taken against them. Officer Crystal Spivey, who was videotaped accepting a $500 payoff to protect a drug dealer in the Buddy Boys scandal, said: "I'm a victim here . . . because of [Officer] Henry Winter coercing me, over several months, to get involved in some kind of a dirty deal. . . . I began to feel afraid that being on his bad side would put me in a very life-threatening situation." She could not complain to IAD about corrupt senior personnel because she said: "There were pretty big connections . . . that guys had in the precinct, who were corrupt, with the Internal Affairs Division. And if you made a complaint against them, they would know about it."[33]

William Phillips, a corrupt cop who became a witness for the Knapp Commission, said that it is "true everywhere" that "a stand-up cop won't be an informer" because deviation from the corrupt norms of the department will be "punished, promptly."[34]

Even if one accepts those rationalizations (and many experienced command personnel do not) and even if police do slide into corruption for peer approval, to say they are "not acting out of free choice" is bad sociology.

When police find that they cannot enjoy the approval of their fellows—and cannot rely on others for protection in dangerous situations—unless they are willing to forgo honesty, they are faced with a choice. No matter how great the pressure, it is their choice, and they are responsible for making it.

It is not their fault that the department suffers from corruption, and it is disgraceful that any police officer should be faced with such a choice, but it is a choice, and they must make it. Freedom of choice does not mean freedom from pressure or from conflict of loyalty, conflict of desire and duty, or conflict of one felt duty with another. If freedom meant that, our only free choices would be those made in a vacuum, and we are never in a vacuum.

A person subjected to torture who can bear no more and must yield has no choice. But a person who has much to lose from choosing honor over peer approval—in the circumstances the Knapp Commission described, for example—does have a choice and, one way or the other, makes it.

This is not to say that being incorruptible is easy or safe. Most of us face difficult choices of this sort in public and private life: Who has not wanted to protect a friend from the consequences of some error of judgment or misconduct? And who can fail to understand the temptation of a chief of detectives who allegedly falsified reports to make his son appear to be working as a police informant when he was arrested for drug dealing? Making such choices is evidence that we are free, not that we are not responsible for our conduct under pressure.

We teach children when faced with peer pressure in favor of promiscuous sex or dangerous drugs to "just say no." Children yearn for peer acceptance at least as strongly as adults do, and yet we expect them to have what it takes to say no to behavior that would shame or harm them. We insist that they are free to choose, even though the choice may be hard.

Children are exposed to tremendous peer pressure not to be tattletales that is sometimes reinforced by adults who suspect they are becoming whiners who "run to Mama" whenever they cannot get their way. But we try to combat peer pressure that conceals bad behavior within the group. We may not sufficiently explain to children that, if playmates are doing dangerous things, we want to be told, and that this differs from "telling mommy" about every dispute over a toy. As a result, some reach adulthood unable to distinguish tattling from rightful disclosures of misconduct that require courage. They think of all disclosure as a sign of weakness, even when it reveals the serious misbehavior of others, and they overlook that their duty in accepting a position of public trust implies a refusal to tolerate corruption in silence.

That confusion also arises among college students at institutions with honor systems, which require students to behave honestly and to inform officials whenever they witness a violation. Honor is understood to include intolerance of dishonor in others. Some might feel like a tattletale to tell on someone else and might fear that others would blame them for what happened to their friends.

The honest reply is that *tattletale* is a dirty word if it refers to whiners or cowards or to those who lack the strength to make their way with their peers. But if it means a person who has the courage to disclose serious wrongdoing, then it is not. Others may blame that person if their friends are punished for misconduct, but refusing to tolerate dishonor is neither whining nor cowardice. It is near the heart of our conception of honorable life, which includes the courage to accept contempt from those who should know better. Those who behaved dishonorably are responsible for whatever happens to them, not the person who would not yield to dishonor by silence.

Those who bear the public trust must see the difference between a refusal to tolerate dishonor and "tattling" in the bad sense. And those who bow to peer pressure at the expense of fidelity to the police mission are bad risks for the laws and the people, even though disclosure of police misconduct may require immense courage—and may destroy the whistleblower's career.

But will there not always be some who take the path of least resistance? Of course. And will there not always be those who truly believe that their obligations to fellow officers override their obligations to abstractions, like the laws, the public, and the public trust? Probably. And, given the things police suffer together, given the need for high morale and mutual trust, how can we have both mutual loyalty and whistle-blowing?

Loyalty among specific men and women is something to be prized, but it is not the purpose of law enforcement; and it must be subordinate to the purposes for which police are given authority and power. If colleagues had a duty to conceal each other's violations of office, it would make the duties of office subordinate to personal kinship. Upsetting the order of duties in this way is as misguided—and contemptible—as would be a command officer's thrusting an inexperienced patrolman into peril to spare a more qualified friend. If the command officer said later, "I did it out of loyalty to my friend," we would conclude that he was unworthy of command, that he played favorites, and that he was more interested in protecting his friends than in protecting the citizens, as he and his friend were obliged to do.

Someone might reply that the command officer jeopardized people, but routine corruption jeopardizes no one. As Albert Seedman, a veteran of the New York City Police Department, explained, however, some investigations of dangerous felonies are impaired because police cannot seek information from other police for fear word will reach the suspects. Of one murder case, he observed:

> Normally, I'd have called the local police routinely to find out what they knew about a suspect, but bookmaking was the one line of work where I didn't dare. . . . A bookmaker could not operate without at least tacit approval of local police. Like the folks who bet, most cops just do not regard gambling as a genuine crime. That's why so many of them can justify not enforcing the law in this one area. In any event, I was afraid that asking the Suffolk County Police about [the suspect] would be like shouting in his ear.[35]

Corruption has long tentacles, which may cause harm at unpredictable times and places. Blithe tolerance of "harmless" corruption should therefore always be avoided.

"But my life depends on my fellow officers. I don't want to be betrayed as Serpico was, or left to die for lack of assistance." The judgment of Patrick V. Murphy and others is that "there was never the slightest speck of evidence" suggesting that New York police officers were trying to rub out whistle-blower Frank Serpico. "His shooting was . . . thoroughly investigated by all of the people who obviously would want to make hay out of it, like the District Attorney, the FBI, reporters, and the police department's own internal affairs division."[36]

Even so, any officer cast into the wilderness by endemic corruption deserves great compassion. The most hardened command personnel ought to be unwilling to allow that to happen. To prevent it, they must root out corruption ruthlessly, out of feeling for their fellow officers as much as justice. No person's life ought ever to be on the line for the sake of graft.

7

Authority and Reform in Controlling Corruption

Everything secret degenerates, even the administration of Justice; nothing is safe that does not show it can bear discussion and publicity.

—Lord Acton[1]

Corruption has few easy remedies. According to an old truth, if the bad cannot corrupt the good, it will seek to drive the good out or destroy it. The bad seeks ways to cloak itself in secrecy, among police as much as anyone else.

Historian James F. Richardson has written about departments where corruption has run deep:

> The habit of secrecy came from the policeman's sense of public pressure and hostility, which required solidarity among the police to protect themselves. Men were not to talk about department business to outsiders, and, above all, they were not to inform on a fellow officer. In the department Westley surveyed, many policemen were willing to commit perjury to avoid informing on colleagues guilty of a felony.[2]

When things reach that stage, public service has collapsed into self-service, and little or no trustworthiness remains.

What can be done from within a department to prevent corruption from taking hold and to reduce it where it has a hold? And what can be done from outside? No remedies are likely to be effective unless they face both issues—how to avoid rotten apples and rotten structures in policing.

The general answers are not difficult. To avoid rotten apples, police need high standards for recruitment and selection, the capacity to attract candidates of high quality, and good educational programs both for new-comers and for experienced personnel. To avoid rotten structures, police need leadership that will not tolerate corruption, institutional procedures for accountability and for systematic investigation of complaints and of sus-picious circumstances, commonality of purpose and moral ideals among command and patrol personnel, and a decent political and governmental environment. Like most general answers, however, these provide scant practical counsel.

As administrators in all walks of life learn, reform of recruitment and selection, training, policy, practice, and attitude is never easy. Institutional habits run deep; they are often tied to uncritical acceptance of the inevitability of the way things have been done. People set in their ways resent efforts to change anything, not only in police work but also in edu-cation, business, and government. An old saw in education is: It is harder to reform a curriculum than to move a graveyard.

In police departments, as Jack Goldsmith suggested in *The Police Com-munity*, "a discernible *patrolman* subculture is found within the broader police subculture,"[3] but reform depends on initiative and commitment at the command level. In *An Anti-Corruption Manual for Administrators in Law Enforcement*, Richard H. Ward, professor emeritus at the University of Illinois, and Robert McCormack, formerly of the John Jay College of Criminal Justice, described analyses showing that "the level of misconduct or corruption is generally related to the quality and style of management . . . and the chief's commitment to eliminating such conduct."[4] Many patrol officers have told me that they care more how command personnel treat them—and speak publicly about them—than about public opinion or media coverage.

The Authority to Lead

To effect reform, administrators must be masters of the art of politics. No one can sustain reform who cannot survive in office, yet no one can stand for high principles who is not willing to lose a job over them. No person working alone—no matter in how high an office—can generate durable reform; and few administrators can implement reform unless they can generate pressure from outside the institution.

The strategy and tactics of reform must be built on those lessons. Failure to heed them leaves in place the fundamental obstacle cited by Lincoln Steffens in his *Autobiography*, the belief that "reformers are no better than others, that they lack the knowledge, efficiency, and machinery to establish permanent reforms,"[5] and that the prudent course is to wait until they move on. Ward and McCormack asserted:

> [T]he facts of political life cannot be ignored . . . and a chief must recognize the importance of developing a political climate in which an anticorruption campaign will not collapse and result in the chief's removal. Forces in political life and in organized crime support corruption, and they are frequently powerful enough to destroy an anticorruption campaign."[6]

Before accepting a position, top administrators should learn what they can of a department's history and present condition from federal and state officials, as well as others in nearby police departments, courts, and the media. They should review departmental policies, procedures, and budget and discuss pending lawsuits and related matters with departmental legal counsel, including consent decrees. The expectations of the mayor or governor in making the appointment ought to be discussed candidly.

Whether orally or in writing, top administrators need a clear sense of the nature and purpose of their appointment. The charge should make clear their authority to change structures without hindrance, since reform can seldom be achieved without structural revision, and it should give the authority to assign and reassign personnel. In some cases, prospective chiefs will want a guaranteed minimum term of office and an explicit account of causes sufficient for removal. They will want to know how many specific leadership positions in the department may be filled or vacated at their discretion and whether this is subject to revision.

Obviously, not all those items can be expected in some settings, but as many should be sought as possible. Too many candidates for executive positions in law enforcement try to get the job first and worry about management prerogatives later. They make themselves vulnerable to interference from politicians who will buy labor peace at any price. "The real bottom line of police reform," one chief said to me, "is control of personnel matters. The elected official who appoints you has a mandate and you have to be prepared to cooperate with him. But without authority for personnel decisions, you're finished before you start."

Longevity in office is not sufficient for reform, but it is almost surely necessary for it. When unconvinced that a chief or commissioner has staying power, the members of a civil service bureaucracy can resist by lying low and waiting for the next one. They can also commit sabotage without much fear of disciplinary action.

Because top administrators have many daily responsibilities that draw them away from close supervision of subordinates, they must have colleagues in the command structure they can trust, whether drawn from existing personnel or brought from outside. No administrator can accomplish much without them, especially in the chief's anticorruption program. As Ward and McCormack stressed:

> The sensitive and controversial nature of corruption makes it difficult to find administrators who are willing to assume responsibility for an anticorruption program. . . . [T]he individual selected to supervise an anticorruption program must have the complete trust of the chief. He must be willing to accept the "flak" that goes with the position, and he should be accepted by the rank-and-file as an individual who is fair but firm.[7]

The chief must make explicit that all command personnel—no matter who appointed them—are accountable for corruption and its control. Patrick V. Murphy insisted that "despite civil service restraints, the chief must find ways to make his subordinates in management actively participate, and hold them strictly accountable, for a positive approach to the control of corruption."[8]

Accountability is essential in all areas—lawfulness, conformity to institutional policy, prudent exercise of discretion, and fidelity to the best departmental traditions. To control corruption, a police department should be responsible to the public in direct and identifiable ways, subordinates should be responsible to their superiors, and command personnel to the honest members of the rank and file.

Accountability—like authority and power—depends on information. After informing the public and police about policy, the leadership should show that it means what it says by rewarding honesty and punishing corruption. Since information must be acquired from the public and from police about what is actually going on, command personnel at the highest levels must be accessible. Where the police leadership has established conversations among all ranks about problems and has done something about them, police performance is palpably improved, corruption minimal.

Policies and practices must appeal both to what moves the best people, their character and sense of public service, and to what moves the worst of them, fear. Fear alone cannot motivate all people. Command personnel must develop internal and external flows of information to appeal to motives of every kind.

Chiefs who take this counsel seriously must be willing to make dangerous and resolute enemies. Unless their own conduct is above reproach, those enemies will besmirch the chiefs' reputation to undermine their authority. At the same time, chiefs should keep in mind the adage, When you shoot at a king, you must kill him. When enemies attack, a chief is wise not to let things fester but to act to excise a cancer before it grows beyond control. Such action often forces hidden enemies to declare themselves; if the chief is in the right, enemies are better faced in the open.

Alliances

Although some anticorruption work is bound to be adversarial, enemies should not be made needlessly. Alliances should be sought in the department, the media, the broader political structure, and the general public.

Such alliances are more likely where people are genuinely disgusted with the corruption. A portion of the public wants corruption, whether graft for double-parking, gambling, or some other form. Whatever the jurisdiction, however, two fundamental points are on the side of reform and must be driven home in public and in the department: (1) the public always pays for corruption; and (2) corruption condemns honest and dedicated police to antipolice prejudice, harassment from colleagues, and dangers that can become life-threatening.

A significant number of people inside and outside government say that some corruption is part of the cost of doing business. Professor Herman Goldstein observed that some people "consider the problem of corruption unsolvable."[9]

The response should be, Which problems? Although no country, city, or sizable institution has ever entirely eliminated corruption, the issue is which specific problems can be addressed and solved. Recognizing this is one antidote to apathy about corruption. Countless instances prove that corrupt individuals can be weeded out: Law enforcement officers who have extorted money from defendants, for example, have been indicted or forced to resign. Police have been caught in the sale of drugs and in the use of illegal wiretaps in extortion schemes. Police who profited from scams have been convicted of income tax evasion. And police whose relations with informants were in violation of policy have been suspended or fired. Some departments have changed structures for the better. Even if some corruption is inevitable, specific problems of corruption can be identified, isolated, and solved.

The costs of corruption must be explained to the public and to the police themselves. When people are convinced that they are personally the victims of corruption, they are likely to be supportive, and when they sympathize with other victims, such as honest police, they can be made allies.

Former Police Commissioner Donald C. Pomerleau of Baltimore learned in 1972 from police officers of a "possible lack of integrity on the part of some members of the department."[10] For the first time in the history of the city, he sought assistance from the FBI and the U.S. attorney in undertaking an extensive investigation. In January 1973 eighteen civilians and six active and two former police detectives were indicted for violations of the Organized Crime Control Act of 1970. In the next six months, five detectives were convicted and other command and patrol personnel indicted. Pomerleau said at that time:

> Corruption is corruption, and like a cancer its malignancy spreads. . . . But one thing should be clear now: Baltimore is not permissive when it comes to paid winks at wrongdoing. The

lowliest patrolman on the beat should feel at this stage that he
can blow the whistle on payoffs, no matter who is involved, and
that he will be backed up. His badge is just as big as anyone
else's. . . . Members of the force . . . have been consistently reas-
sured, as I reassure you, of my wholehearted support of this
most important endeavor—the ferreting out of those few among
us who violate their public trust and solemn oath of office. It
is our individual and collective, moral and legal obligation to
do so.[11]

One of his former colleagues said:

Don Pomerleau witnessed many abuses by the police and many
abuses of the police. He felt he could make a meaningful contribution. He did, and many of us owe him a debt of gratitude.
He had a difficult job to do here. He did it well. He did it his
way. As others like him, he paid a price.

Although the chief must take local circumstances and history into
account, he can guarantee his honest subordinates that they are not alone
and that command personnel will initiate internal affairs investigations of
evidence that police, as in Miami, Florida, are living far beyond their means.
If political patronage or perversion of the civil service system has rendered
internal investigations impossible, assistance can be sought from the FBI
and other agencies.

A chief can provide command support and encouragement to honest
officers by seeing that reports of corruption are investigated. A chief cannot
necessarily guarantee confidentiality of disclosure of corruption by officers,
which may be limited in trials by the Sixth Amendment. If corruption runs
deep, the anonymity of informants may be difficult or impossible to protect. Chiefs should not falsely minimize the risks of breaking the code of
silence, but they can reduce these risks.

Annual in-service training should be required for every patrol and command officer, with special focus on the temptations of vice and narcotics
assignments. Supervisors in every department should know their subordinates thoroughly, so that they can detect any striking changes in cars,

houses, clothes, and so on. With today's higher police salaries and with the increase in employed spouses, those changes may be more difficult to detect than in the past. A strong disciplinary code is essential, even if it leads to high levels of attrition. Such measures can elevate the morale of the police who matter most—the honest ones. They are indispensable to penetrating what Goldstein and others have called "the most formidable barrier to eliminating corruption: the blue curtain—the conspiracy of silence among police."[12]

Conspiracies of Silence

The conspiracy of silence is not unique to police. Televangelists have apparently kept silent about corrupt practices for fear of reducing financial support. In education, faculty and administrators who know that others are taking sexual advantage of students turn away rather than risk criticism or public repercussions. The medical profession closes ranks against criticism, and in business and government, too, some choose silence rather than go out on a limb.

"Insider" groups that feel beleaguered in one way or another try to safeguard themselves by keeping outsiders ignorant of their practices. Some persons find strength in feeling that they have a special understanding of "how things really are." Ignoring the opinions and judgment of anyone outside the group is, however, a sign of weakness. If widespread, it lends support to all manner of corruption as fear always does.

Police studies, however, address the curtain of silence more frequently and extensively than any other field, perhaps because of the history of literature about police. In its monopoly on the use of force, undercover investigation, and so on, police work is distinctive but probably no more subject to corruption than other activities. Some police departments are corrupt to the core, and others are scarcely corrupt at all. Some individual police are corrupt; many are not. The same can be said of ministries, businesses, educational institutions, industries, retirement centers, hospitals, and government agencies.

Opportunities for corruption exist in all walks of life. Conspiracies of silence are different in policing only in degree, if at all.

Reform

Leadership seldom achieves much without a clear agenda, known within the institution and by key outsiders, that leaves no questions about the highest priorities. It cannot be effective if it is framed in platitudes or if it is vague.

In addressing corruption, commentators propose techniques after the pattern of guides to management. Ward and McCormack stressed that corruption in its various forms must be defined unambiguously. Borderline cases do not deserve emphasis in an agenda, which must make clear that even if day shades imperceptibly into night, noon can easily be distinguished from midnight.

They also urged that administrators "realistically consider community norms when defining corruption and formulating policy."[13] Some officials emphasize that indifference to conduct in the community establishes an untenable and self-defeating double standard for police. In Ward and McCormack's view, administrators must then identify the extent and level of corruption and develop manuals of procedure and guidelines for internal affairs investigations, all in the context of an anticorruption policy that is "realistic, manageable, and continually reinforced." The administrator can then "develop a program to implement and enforce his policy";[14] he may find it useful to establish "an ethics committee which is representative of the department. The committee should make recommendations about minor misconduct to the chief, but, ultimately, the chief must determine the policy."[15]

Although these are steps any competent administrator would plan, no one can responsibly allow community norms to dictate policies. Public opinion may have a bearing on enforcement of laws, for example, where strict enforcement of a law against drinking on a public street would cause immense disruption and antagonism and would be ineffective in any case. Although the standards of the community deserve serious attention, community expectations of police behavior may be so low as to be worthless. If the public expects police to accept gratuities, failure to set a higher standard would be tantamount to licensing corruption.

Police leadership should not leave a community in ignorance if it does not know how much can be accomplished by a truly fine police department. Teaching and showing what can be done, in an effort to raise community expectations, is better than taking community standards as immutable. If expectations are low, they may reflect dreadful past service and loss of confidence. Police can hardly achieve good community relations by concurring in that expectation.

A higher standard is sometimes the only means of improving a situation; great schools are built by discipline and aspiration that exceed the norm, and so are great athletic teams, great armies, great businesses, great countries, and great individuals.

Combating Mediocrity

No one remedy serves for all the varieties of corruption, as may be seen in the case of the Philadelphia Police Department, which according to the *New York Times* had "long been considered one of the worst in the country."[16]

On July 19, 1988, seven current or former narcotics officers were indicted for racketeering, drug dealing, and perjury after seven others had been indicted earlier.[17] Investigations also confirmed widespread judicial corruption, long known to the Philadelphia police and suspected by federal agencies. Where police corruption is widespread, internal reassignment, expanded powers for internal affairs investigations, improved recruiting and training, and so on are useful, but insufficient, to clean house. External investigative agencies that cannot be compromised by local political powers and departmental pressure are also needed.

Other kinds of corruption—petty graft, "cooping" (sleeping on duty in a secret place), trading favors with local merchants, and the like—can be signs of mediocrity in general, which may be susceptible to less direct treatment. In Philadelphia, efforts to improve policing through broad cooperation with citizen groups became the byword of reform under Commissioner Kevin Tucker.

William B. Eagleson Jr., the leader of a citizens' group overseeing improvement efforts, said that advances in 1987 had "proven wrong those who believed that the Philadelphia Police Department was so entrenched in its mediocrity that change was impossible to accomplish and would indeed be unwelcome."[18] An earlier panel appointed by Tucker confirmed that "years of complaints about mismanagement, corruption, and brutality were justified." Police cooperation with the two panels led to the establishment of foot patrols, programs to assist crime victims, and three "small satellite stations or precinct houses to 'provide a police presence that is different from the abstract links created by the 911 telephone system and patrolling automobiles.'"[19]

The *Philadelphia Inquirer* hailed the new alliance of "residents and cops" as "partners against crime." It described the effectiveness of foot patrols and satellite stations (community policing) in helping citizens and overcoming police-citizen animosity and pointed out that those advances had not come easily. As Thomas Bray, a ten-year police veteran, said:

> We were pessimistic and apprehensive . . . but at the same time we were eager because we knew it was going to be a challenge. . . . Initially community residents were suspicious. . . . Unfounded rumors spread of the existence of a jail cell in the ministation. Little by little, however, things changed. Children, lured to the ministation by games . . . returned to their homes talking not of jail cells but of the friendly officers. . . . Slowly, adults began to trickle in to meet the officers. . . . The trickle grew to a steady flow . . . as the officers proved adept at contacting city and state agencies to help residents with housing problems and other troubles.[20]

Not only are the citizens actually safer, but they feel safer. One resident observed, referring to Officers Brian Grievious and Martin Derbyshire, "I always feel better when I see those two guys." Another said, "They are really doing a good job. Before they came, it was like a revolution out there. . . . Now it's calmed down. You can really see the difference."[21]

Several officers described their renewed eagerness to go to work, their kinship with the citizens, and their satisfaction at "making a difference." Such progress shows that police-citizen efforts at improvement do not have to be adversarial and that even in departments where some police are corrupt or brutal, others are committed to high standards of faithful service.

Those advances in Philadelphia did not imply that everything had been done or that the future was entirely rosy. They had to be sustained and refined by assiduous leadership over many years that followed. Indeed, genuine reform never becomes secure by short-term progress. And within the Philadelphia Police Department, police reform was not without its critics. A spokesman for the police union, Rick Costello, accused the panels of "writing their own report card," since they were appointed by the commissioner; he dismissed their reports as "long on rhetoric."

Those criticisms were part of an internal struggle over new merit standards for promotion. Since merit promotion had been undermined by favoritism in the past, according to Costello, he asked, "Unless they can assure us that favoritism won't come back, how can we support it?"[22] The answer is for command personnel to establish rigorous criteria of merit and procedures for their application. Beyond that, only a growing record of command personnel's conscientious judgment within the standards has a chance to earn respect.

As Philadelphia has shown, police-citizen cooperation is especially important where street criminals have ravaged citizens in poverty. Barriers of secrecy are most likely to be penetrated by activities that join police and citizens in the common purposes that improve their daily lives. Temptations to corruption might be reduced for officers who find fulfillment in their work every day with citizens whose faces and names mean something positive rather than negative to them.

Will greater police responsiveness and neighborhood policing reduce corruption? Not necessarily. Close association between police and the citizens can be a force for good and a cause of corruption. Where the cooperation is for the public good, officers being rotated to new stations introduce their incoming colleagues to the community in hope of perpetuating good working relations and worthwhile projects. But where the cooperation serves illicit purposes, police may continue traditions of corruption and pass them along. Rotation is imperative to prevent bad habits from persisting unheeded.

No working relation between police and public, and no form of decentralization by itself, changes the need for close supervision of personnel by command and for performance in accord with departmental policy. Problems of favoritism, nonenforcement, bribery, and so on can be made worse rather than better by close association with members of the public. In Philadelphia as elsewhere, the issues of long-range improvement of services and reduction of corrupt activities remain in the balance.

Review and Advisory Boards

Experience in such programs has not established the rightful place of civilian boards in addressing problems of corruption. But it does suggest that citizen attention is wisely engaged in cooperation with police instead of being isolated with corruption as its only object. If citizens address only corruption, they are likely to be kept outside the barriers, but if they come with a cooperative attitude to a broader appreciation of policing, they can gain insight and trust.

That is an uphill path. As Chief Robert C. Wadman of the Omaha Police Department and Chief Robert K. Olson of the Corpus Christi Police Department wrote in 1991, "The commitment to past police practice is strongly felt and defended not only by police, but often by a public. . . . The same public . . . still reacts negatively to major changes in their police."[23] But if police teach citizens that "Neighborhood Watch groups, Senior Citizen Alert programs, and Career Criminal operations"[24] can increase safety and improve personal life, then bonds may develop that make citizen criticisms a bit more welcome. Most of us take criticism better when it is constructive. Wadman and Olson concluded that "the police should develop liaison with any and every organization in the community that is interested in enhancing the positive aspects of neighborhood life. . . . We must organize and encourage citizens to take an active part in their own well-being."[25]

Whatever the extent of citizen engagement, the chief or commissioner must in the end exercise authority in implementing anticorruption policy. Departmental committees, ethics committees, and civilian review may all be useful, but command must ultimately take the responsibility for problems of corruption. Command personnel should not have to stand alone, however, in combating corruption.

Two problems limit the effectiveness of civilian review boards. First, they often comprise representatives of many segments of society, without regard for understanding of law enforcement or institutional administration. Second, their members sometimes have political ambitions and betray confidences to the media when it is to their advantage. Working with already functioning citizen groups may be more useful in maintaining communication and improving services.

Many police administrators in major cities rely on civilian advisory boards, task forces, and blue-ribbon commissions. A police chief has much in common with business and other high-ranking executives, who also face problems of fraud, misconduct, union negotiation, budget, and discipline, so their experience can be instructive.

A task force or advisory board can give counsel on difficult issues. People in such positions generally respect confidentiality, especially with regard to the media, and can significantly expand the resources available to chiefs and commissioners without compromising their authority.

8

Leadership and the Character of a Department

This reminds me of a conversation which I once had with the Hon. Frederick Douglass. At one time Mr. Douglass was travelling in the state of Pennsylvania, and was forced, on account of his colour, to ride in the baggage car, in spite of the fact that he had paid the same price for his passage that the other passengers had paid. When some of the white passengers went into the baggage car to console Mr. Douglass, and one of them said to him: "I am sorry, Mr. Douglass, that you have been degraded in this manner," Mr. Douglass straightened himself up on the box upon which he was sitting, and replied: "They cannot degrade Frederick Douglass. The soul that is within me no man can degrade. I am not the one that is being degraded on account of this treatment, but those who are inflicting it upon me."

—Booker T. Washington[1]

Booker T. Washington and Frederick Douglass were heirs to the very old and wise moral insight that inflicting wrongs is worse than suffering them. That moral tradition does not suggest that a person should willingly suffer avoidable wrongs or should behave as though helpless. No self-respecting person will tolerate abuse when he can decently prevent it; the point is rather that if a person must choose between suffering and doing wrong (that is, if there is no alternative), suffering is better. The tradition does not imply that individuals should never use force in defense of themselves or others or in prevention of crimes and injustices. It is not a pacifist tradition. Many of its advocates—such as Socrates—were respected combat soldiers.

To find out where one stands on the matter, a person need only ask: Would I rather be in Frederick Douglass's shoes or in the shoes of the people who discriminated against him? Or, if that question seems to ignore the complexities of Douglass's times, a person can take a timeless—and therefore contemporary—example: If I had to choose between perjuring myself and having someone commit perjury against me, which would I choose? Few people want to be in either position; but if those are the only choices, which will it be?

No question of conviction in public life is more fundamental than that one. A police department whose members are not committed to that moral tradition is vulnerable to two corrosive flaws. First, officers who are more determined to avoid suffering wrongs than inflicting them may act preemptively—Do unto others before they do unto you! They may use force precipitously, act with prejudice toward suspects and others, and behave vengefully toward anyone they believe disrespectful. Second, officers who view suffering wrong as shameful may be unsettled by abuse that is best ignored; if it undermines their self-respect, it can make them cynical and subject to burnout. Public life requires a thick skin and an awareness that a person's honor is not besmirched by the misconduct of others.

The department's leadership should convey in word and deed its commitment to the Douglass lesson. Since mistreatment, failures, and disappointments cannot be entirely prevented in police work, that lesson is irreplaceable. Perpetrators may go undetected or escape punishment, and wickedness may appear unjustly rewarded, as when a drug dealer amasses immense profits and lives out his life in luxury and comfort. Police who prefer doing wrong to suffering it may use wrongful means to get at a suspect or known perpetrator. The Prince of the City, the Buddy Boys, and other cases show how dangerous and self-destructive that temptation can be and how yielding to it can breed disaster. Police must learn what is genuinely intolerable to do and to suffer.

Realistic Expectations

Policing unavoidably includes a significant level of failure. No society—and certainly no constitutional republic that pays heed to civil rights and liberties—can prevent all crime or apprehend all perpetrators. Command personnel must promote a realistic sense of what counts as success, what counts as failure, and how to live with both.

All of us want to succeed, but we often do not grasp what success is. Someone may believe that an internal affairs investigation succeeds only if it discloses wrongdoing, but its purpose is to discover the truth. If an investigation proves an accused person innocent, the investigation has succeeded.

People who succeed can fail at success. A basketball star is a considerable success, but not if the wealth and status of stardom lead to drugs and self-destruction. Similarly, those who become police officers in a department with serious recruiting and training standards have achieved a significant success. When they abuse authority and power, however, and do not live up to the trust of their office, they fail at success. Success can destroy a person whose character is not up to it.

So, too, with failure. Those who cannot live with the disappointments and failures of their job will be consumed by resentment, disgust, self-pity, and contempt for themselves and others. If they work diligently to reduce crime in a neighborhood and discover that the resources available are inadequate, they face partial failure and can respond in a variety of ways: by giving up; by becoming contemptuous of political leaders and police command personnel for having foolish expectations; by becoming indifferent to their own ideals; by resorting to more ruthless means of enforcing the law; by becoming corrupt themselves; and so on.

Or, they can adjust their expectations to the challenge, learn what the circumstances, the law, and departmental policies allow, and go on with endurance. If the expectations of politicians and police leaders are foolish, the officers' disregard may be warranted, but succeeding despite failure means enduring, with expectations that are in conformity with the facts.

Good character and wisdom allow a measure of equanimity in the presence of failure, and the lack of those qualities is a principal cause of burnout. A department should therefore recruit and sustain candidates who have achieved some moral and intellectual strength and teach them truthfully the hazards posed by both success and failure.

Burnout

Hillary Robinette, a supervisory special agent of the FBI, wrote in *Burnout in Blue*:

To elevate burnout to the lexicon of clinical terms, as if it were some new malevolent strain of Asian flu, is to deny the reality of human process. Lance Morrow is accurate when he says that the term "burnout" denies the human experience of "the ups and downs—even the really awful down to which all men and women, in all history, have been subject."[2]

Burnout is not a cause, but rather a description, of failure. Clinical studies treat burnout as "the debilitating malaise that affects people in the helping professions . . . like police officers, who initially have high expectations of personal contribution" but whose expectations, either of themselves or of their work, go basically unsatisfied.[3] As Morrow and Robinette pointed out, low times, sometimes of extended duration, are part of every human life. Although other accounts refer to burnout as a debilitating malaise, some people clearly have the fortitude to persist through terrible lows, without being debilitated by them. No one should be blamed for being so ground down by circumstances that counseling or medical treatment is needed. But those who consistently conduct themselves badly because they feel low show a failure of intellect or of character. In the same way, depression will inevitably come to many officers, but only those who do something about it reflect the character needed for police work.

Police officers may lack the self-knowledge to see that they have chosen the wrong line of work, or they may lack the resolve either to give it their best or to change to another kind of work. Or they may lose fortitude in the face of tedium, departmental shortcomings, the unavoidable inefficiency of government that respects both law and liberty, and the impossibility of completely succeeding at the police mission.

Work should contribute to meaning in life and help overcome feelings of pointlessness, as love, friendship, religious devotion, and avocational accomplishments do. But when a person's work seems futile, life itself may be cast into the balance. The only remedy is to pursue something else.

The challenge for departmental leadership is to try to prevent false expectations—and to find recruits whose backgrounds show fortitude. The leadership can try to build channels of information to reveal problems in the streets that may be addressed by changes of policy, of resources, of personnel, and so on. And the leadership can refuse to treat burnout as a given in policing.

That task should be a department's abiding priority, reflected in programs of peer counseling and in routine sessions of patrol and command personnel, with mutual candor and trustworthiness and without fear of reprisal. Since police work places stress on personnel at all levels, the leadership should work to reduce its effects. Ways to increase the durability of departmental personnel include good diet, healthy exercise, brief sabbaticals, assignment rotation, and confidential support services, including such professional counseling as its budget will permit. Baltimore County, Maryland, and other departments have made progress in those areas. When work is tedious and its purposes are blunted by persistent poverty, ignorance, helplessness, crime, and violence, some will stop thinking of success in terms of the institutional mission and purposes. Success is then reduced to matters within the departments: salary increases, promotions, approval from peers, and the like. As the emoluments of office cease to be marks of success and are transformed into success itself, the approval of peers becomes more important than performance that merits respect. If a person has given up on the work itself, then life inside the department becomes the antidote to futility.

Such dangerous confusion is the most debilitating feature of life in a subculture that looks only inward. The confusion can be squarely opposed by proven departmental respect for performance in the job—respect for merit. Since meritorious performance can take many forms in police work, each department must make its expectations clear and reward its best personnel.

Most command officers understand how difficult that is, given the power of unions, the faults of civil service, and the pressure of external political, legislative, judicial, and social agendas, especially in the tension between merit policies and affirmative action programs.

Merit and Affirmative Action

On Christmas Day 1987, Loyal Garner, a thirty-four-year-old black man from Florien, Louisiana, was arrested in Hemphill, Texas, for suspicion of driving while intoxicated. Two days after being beaten in jail, he died. A week later, Hemphill's police chief and two deputy sheriffs were indicted on charges of violating Garner's civil rights, and two months after that, they were indicted for murder.

In January 1988 a white candidate for sheriff of Sabine County, Texas, where Hemphill is located, said: "I don't know if you can blame the Loyal Garner death on there being no black law enforcement officials here. . . . It's hard for me to say whether it was a racial incident. But the time has come for blacks to be represented on the force. That's the least we can do."[4] The county never had a black deputy sheriff.

Philosopher Tom L. Beauchamp had written eight years earlier that "it is unrealistic to believe . . . that in contemporary society discriminating practices can be eradicated by legal measures which do not permit reverse discrimination."[5] Although he insisted that "all discrimination, including reverse discrimination, is prima facie immoral," he also asked, "What government policies are permissible and required in order to bring about a society where equal treatment is the rule rather than the exception?"[6] To establish a society where equal treatment is the rule, he concluded, "we ought to relax our . . . reservations against allowing any discriminatory practices whatever."[7] We ought to recognize that equal treatment in the short run is not an absolute duty, because past and present discrimination against minorities should be remedied. Affirmative action can provide the remedy.

By contrast, philosopher William T. Blackstone argued in 1975 against affirmative action policies:

> Such policies are simply self-destructive. In place of the ideal of equality and distributive justice based on relevant criteria, we would be left with the special pleading of self-interested power groups . . . who gear criteria for the distribution of goods, services, and opportunities to their special needs and situations. . . . Such policies would be those of special privilege, not the appeal to objective criteria which apply to all.[8]

On the one hand, it is argued, in a racially and ethnically diverse country the needs of the citizens can be met and their rights upheld only if their police departments represent the minorities. On the other hand, some argue that job opportunities and advancement should be based on past accomplishments and current performance irrespective of race or ethnic background.

The first position says, in effect, that institutions of power and authority cannot be fair if major portions of the citizenry are unrepresented. The second says that such institutions cannot be fair if they deprive the best qualified individuals of opportunity so that others may be represented. A complicating factor is the racial and ethnic discrimination that has denied equal opportunity in the past. Given our history, what is fair now?

In some situations, the tension largely eliminates itself. If the best candidates for deputy sheriff in Sabine County are black, then the community can achieve black representation by hiring them and thereby respecting both conceptions of fairness. But the tension in law and policy in America since 1970 has arisen partly from the fact that those conditions are not always satisfied.

Title VII. In 1970 Title VII of the Civil Rights Act established that it is:

> [U]nlawful employment practice for an employer (1) to fail or refuse to hire or to discharge any individual, or otherwise to discriminate against any individual with respect to his compensation, terms, conditions, or privileges of employment, because of such individual's race, color, religion, sex, or national origin; or (2) to limit, segregate, or classify his employees or applicants for employment in any way which would deprive or tend to deprive any individual of employment opportunities or otherwise adversely affect his status as an employee, because of such individual's race, color, religion, sex, or national origin.[9]

The legislation seemed straightforward: No one shall be deprived of opportunity on grounds of race, color, religion, sex, or national origin. Discrimination on those grounds is unjust and wrong, because those features of a person are separate from considerations of merit. Support of that law is natural for anyone opposed to bigotry and respectful of individual merit. The law stood in the tradition of the Constitution and the Fourteenth Amendment by guaranteeing rights to individuals—not to groups.

One response was that the legislation was fair in at last giving everyone an even chance. But others denied that it was fair to give even chances: Since some groups had been discriminated against for generations, fairness required that their past wrongs be redressed.

In 1978 Jesse Jackson asserted, "Equality can be measured. It can be turned into numbers."[10] Jackson stood with those who believed that if an ethnic group is not proportionately represented in, say, a police department, the group has suffered discrimination. Equality could then be turned into numbers by adopting policies that lead to proportionate representation. William J. Bennett and Terry Eastland wrote in *Counting by Race*: "By the middle 1970s, the idea of numerical equality . . . requiring no specific findings of discrimination . . . came to be, through the bureaucratic implementation of executive orders, government policy."[11]

Since proportionate representation could not be quickly achieved by equality of individual opportunity and selection by merit alone, it was to be achieved in practice by preferential treatment of groups that suffered discrimination. If the short-term goal was proportionality of representation, then the measures must include preference by race, sex, ethnicity, and so on.

On its face, preferential treatment by race seems to run counter to Title VII, but advocates of equality by numbers argue that it does not. Philosophy professor Carl Cohen explained that although preferential treatment "does of course distinguish by race, and does, admittedly, give favor by race," its proponents claim that it "does not 'discriminate' by race in the bad sense that the law condemns." Although some programs may adversely affect white workers, in this view they "are nevertheless justified by pressing societal needs" that make clear "what interpretation of the law is required by justice."[12]

That position was taken in 1974 by U.S. Representative Andrew Young of Georgia, when he said that affirmative action "is perhaps an individual injustice. But it might be necessary in order to overcome an historic group injustice or series of group injustices."[13] Professor Thomas Nagel argued that discrimination is warranted if it is "clearly contributing to the eradication of great social evils."[14] The same interpretation of justice and the law has been accepted in a number of judicial decisions. Despite assurances in Congress that the intention of Title VII was not to force racial balance or quotas on employers, events have often turned out otherwise.

When the bill was being debated, one of the sponsors, Representative Emanuel Celler of New York, said that under the law, "the court could not order that any preference be given to any particular race, religion or other group, but would be limited to ordering an end to discrimination." He added, "It is likewise not true that the Equal Employment Opportunity Commission [established by Title VII] would have power to rectify existing 'racial or religious imbalance' in employment by requiring the hiring of certain people . . . because they are of a given race or religion."[15] Representative John V. Lindsay of New York said: "This legislation . . . does not impose quotas or any special privileges of seniority or acceptance. There is nothing whatever in the bill about racial balance."[16] Senators Richard Clark and Clifford Case of New Jersey also said: "Any deliberate attempt to maintain a racial balance . . . would involve a violation of Title VII because maintaining such a balance would require an employer to hire or refuse to hire on the basis of race. It must be emphasized that discrimination is prohibited as to any individual."[17]

Nonetheless, in the 1979 case *United Steelworkers of America v. Weber*, the Supreme Court, by a vote of five to two, upheld the preferential treatment of racial groups. Justice William Brennan, writing for the majority, held that to promote racial balance an employer might have to "trammel the interests of the white employees."[18]

As the result of such rulings, Harvey C. Mansfield Jr., a professor of government at Harvard University, said that we and our institutions are now forced to accept an "immoral moralism," the principal tenet of which is that the end of racial balance justified means that rode roughshod over individuals and their right to equal treatment under the law. He held that proponents of affirmative action quotas "try to redefine merit. It no longer means the best, or the best available; it is made to mean acceptable, or beyond a certain minimum. Sometimes 'merit' is defined as what society needs."[19] "Affirmative action is obviously a way of helping people who are considered insufficiently capable of helping themselves. But just as obviously, this fact cannot be admitted. Or, if it is admitted in general . . . it must be denied in all particular cases."[20] Mansfield concluded that, in practice, we now have "government by consent decree" rather than "government by consent."[21]

In some police departments, consent decrees have required hiring of minorities by quota and promotion by quota—including promoting patrolmen to the rank of captain and skipping intermediate ranks. Minority members are sometimes promoted ahead of others with better test scores and field performance.

Individuals, Groups, and Rights. Is affirmative action a rightful means of redressing injustice or a wrongful form of "reverse discrimination"? No decent person can tolerate what happened to Loyal Garner or look on the history of racial discrimination with complacency. But are racially preferential schemes the answer to past discrimination? As Supreme Court Justice William O. Douglas wrote in 1974 in his dissent in *DeFunis v. Odegaard*, "There is no constitutional right for any race to be preferred. . . . There is no superior person by constitutional standards." A person "who is white is entitled to no advantage by reason of that fact; nor is he subject to any disability no matter his race or color. Whatever his race, he has a constitutional right to have his application considered on its individual merits in a racially neutral manner." Douglas, who was concerned for the quality of public service as well as for the rights of individuals, added, "Minorities in our midst who are to serve actively in our public affairs should be chosen on talent and character alone, not on cultural orientation or leanings."[22]

Although institutions refer to themselves in employment advertisements and on their stationery as "Affirmative Action/Equal Opportunity" employers, they can in no way adopt preferential hiring and stand for equality except by claiming that past discrimination against a group makes current discrimination in its favor "equal." Institutions that claim to be both types of employer may be trying to ignore hard questions, like those that follow.

How shall we think about history? Economist Thomas Sowell offered this perspective:

> The past is a great unchangeable fact. *Nothing* is going to undo its sufferings and injustices, whatever their magnitude. Statistical categories and historic labels may seem real to those inspired by words, but only living flesh-and-blood people can feel joy or pain. Neither the sins nor the suffering of those now dead are within our power to change.[23]

We can redress the wrongs suffered by those who are dead only by honoring them in our behavior and testaments. To have real regard for what befell them is to behave now so that they will not have suffered—or died—in vain. The decency of individuals as well as of families and of countries depends on a sense of history and of the importance of what has gone before. Admitting that past evils cannot be undone does not reduce those evils to insignificance.

On that principle, Mahatma Gandhi advised a repentant Hindu who had orphaned a Muslim child in a religiously inspired military action to adopt the child and raise him as a Muslim. Lyndon B. Johnson and others advocated affirmative action by pointing out that two runners are not fairly matched when one has had every advantage in training and opportunity and the other has been deprived. History matters.

Throughout history, savage bigotry over race, sex, or religion has always been directed against individual human beings. We should seek to redress the specific injustices suffered by those now living and to avoid visiting injustice on anyone. To treat each individual with the regard so often denied in the past, our laws and policies must be directed not to generalities of historical discrimination but rather to the specific effects of discrimination within institutions that are identifiable now. If an institution has discriminated against specific employees or candidates for employment on grounds of race and other identifiable individuals have benefited, however unintentionally, the wrong should be remedied. Those who have suffered discrimination deserve redress.

How should we think about representation of groups within institutions? When a group is underrepresented, is discrimination necessarily the cause? What does *underrepresentation* mean?

If specific discrimination against individuals can be redressed, but not general discrimination, we must question speculation about what "would have been" if our history had not included prejudice and favoritism. Can we say with confidence that except for discrimination, the proportion of any ethnic group in a given field would equal the proportion of that group in the general population?

Many factors besides discrimination influence people in their choice of a career and in achieving high positions. A group with a median age substantially lower than another will probably include fewer in high positions.[24] We cannot be sure, therefore, that underrepresentation in any occupation reflects discrimination. Only the facts of specific cases can prove discrimination. If a group seems underrepresented, we must define what we mean precisely.

In policing, the main appeal has been to community needs: If 60 percent of the population is Puerto Rican, for example, then 60 percent of the police force should be Puerto Rican, so that police who understand the culture, the language, and so on can respond to calls. Such an appeal is not to "what would have been" but to how the police mission can be best fulfilled. Perhaps the benchmark ought to be, not the number of people, but the number of calls for police services. If Puerto Ricans constitute 60 percent of the population but make 75 percent of the calls for police, then 75 percent of the personnel ought to be Puerto Rican.

Those suggestions have been buttressed by the argument that minority youngsters need role models in positions of authority who are of the same race, ethnic group, or sex. Such exposure to minority doctors, lawyers, police, business executives, and so on will encourage aspiration and high expectations, proponents say. If so, however, the police and the other role models must be good at their work. No one gains from exposing children to incompetence or from offering minorities worse services. Thus, arguments based on community needs are driven back to considerations of individual merit, rather than to preferential hiring of minorities at the expense of individual competence.

The Rev. Dr. Martin Luther King Jr. focused on the essential point in his famous speech in August 1963: "I have a dream that my four little children will one day live in a nation where they will not be judged by the color of their skin, but by the content of their character." Clearly, a role model must have good character. Human beings are not so different because of race or ethnicity or gender that they cannot admire, emulate, serve, and learn from those outside their own closed group. Counterexamples can be found throughout history and in our own lives. Boys learn from their mothers and sisters, as daughters do from their fathers and brothers; many people who are not black have learned from and emulated Frederick Douglass, Martin Luther King Jr., and Sojourner Truth. The Rev. Dr. King testified to his own indebtedness to Socrates, Thoreau, and Gandhi, just as many others of various minority groups have admired and emulated Eleanor Roosevelt.

Because we are not culturally impenetrable to each other, our ideas of excellence in character and other accomplishments are not utterly idiosyncratic by race, ethnicity, or gender. In 1988, Thomas Short, then associate professor of philosophy at Kenyon College, wrote: "The dogma of cultural separateness . . . incorporates the double lie that American minorities have a culture essentially different from that of other Americans and that Western civilization . . . exclude[s] women and minorities."[25]

Since history—and experience—teach otherwise, children deserve to learn as much. Ideals are shared across lines of race and gender: Parents of all backgrounds do not want their children to grow into bigots, cowards, drug addicts, and the like. Students of history understand the contributions of women and minorities to our own and other countries.

How should we think about rights? The Declaration of Rights, adopted by the Continental Congress on October 14, 1774, declares that individual inhabitants of the English Colonies in North America have rights to life, liberty, and property and that their ancestors were always entitled to the rights, liberties, and immunities of free and natural-born subjects of England. The Declaration of Independence similarly emphasizes individual rights, and the Articles of Confederation entitle individuals to "all privileges and immunities of free citizens." When the U.S. Constitution refers to the rights of the people, it clearly means each person. The First Amendment prohibits abridgement of the right of the people to assemble peaceably; the Third Amendment prohibits quartering of soldiers in anyone's house "without the consent of the owner"; the Fifth Amendment specifies that no person shall be "deprived of life, liberty, or property without due process of law"; and the Fourteenth Amendment says that no state "shall deny to any person within its jurisdiction the equal protection of the laws." In *Shelley v. Kraemer*, the Supreme Court explained:

> The rights created by the first section of the Fourteenth Amendment are, by its terms, guaranteed to the individual. The rights established are personal rights. . . . Equal protection of the laws is not advanced through indiscriminate imposition of inequalities. . . . Whatever else the framers sought to achieve, it is clear that the matter of primary concern was the establishment of equality in the enjoyment of basic civil and political rights and the preservation of those rights from discriminatory action on considerations of race or color.[26]

That tradition implies, as Carl Cohen wrote, that "individuals have rights, not races. . . . Rights do not and cannot inhere in skin-color groups." He added, "It is true, of course, that many persons have been cruelly deprived of rights simply because of their blackness. Whatsoever the remedy all such persons deserve, it is deserved by those injured and because of their injury; nothing is deserved because of the color of one's skin. . . . [T]he sacrifice of fundamental individual rights cannot be justified by the desire to advance the well-being of any ethnic group."[27]

On those grounds, we have a right to redress of injuries, not if we belong to a certain race or ethnic group, but only if we can show that our own rights have been violated—either by direct action or by policies that have adversely affected equal opportunity now. That is true for every individual, regardless of race, ethnicity, or sex. Otherwise, individuals who have suffered no injury for which anyone is identifiably responsible would be entitled to benefits at the expense of others who have done no wrong. Inflicting a wrong on innocent people in that way—in the name of social justice—underlies the resentment toward preferential employment and promotion.

But what of an institution that has in the past discriminated against candidates or employees who are no longer interested parties? Does it owe special consideration to present candidates because of its past wrongs against others? Do the rights of individuals who have suffered wrongs transfer to others? Do institutions that have committed wrongs in the past now owe preferential treatment to other individuals?

The argument offered above suggests that the answer is no. Because institutions always owe all of us equal treatment, injustice is an affront to us all. Those who have specifically suffered it gain a right to special treatment, but no one else does.

Even those who consider America a racist society oppose preferential hiring and admission to college. According to a Media General–Associated Press national poll of 1,223 adults conducted in 1988, 53 percent of whites said that "American society is racist overall, as did 68 percent of blacks." Yet 79 percent opposed preferential hiring, and 76 percent opposed preferential admission to schools; "large majorities of whites were opposed, and blacks were split evenly on the questions."[28]

In the words of Joseph Califano, former secretary of Health, Education, and Welfare and assistant for domestic affairs to President Johnson, affirmative action was an acceptable policy to the majority of Americans "only as a temporary expedient to speed blacks' entry into the social and economic mainstream. . . . Affirmative action has pried open some important doors for blacks, but it was never conceived as a permanent program and its time is running out. . . . More imaginative efforts to target talented blacks and open white networks to them can help ease the tension created by the across-the-board affirmative action programs that anger many whites and lead some blacks to question their own sense of achievement."[29]

What are the effects of racial and ethnic quotas, of "favor by race"? In a police department, comradeship is basic to performance. Since commonality of purpose and ideals must transcend race, ethnicity, and sex, police departments emphasize what their members share. Los Angeles Police Department brochures, for example, say, "Our cops only come in one color: Blue." Preferential treatment at the expense of those who have done no wrong can undermine comradeship and fragment a department. Resentment over matters as important as compensation and rank can have dangerous results.

Racial tension in police departments has many causes. I have never seen a department in which officers of one race feared that others of different races would fail to assist them in time of need—racial differences seem to stop there. But mistrust and lack of confidence may be revealed in unexpected ways. Some white officers hand dirty money to one another but pass it to black officers in unmarked envelopes delivered surreptitiously so that they cannot identify the white carrier. Racial tension is a problem that calls for forthright leadership, probity, mutual confidence, and trust.

Much more than bare justice is required for people to live and work well together. Mutual respect, not merely in general but for specific individual accomplishments, is basic. When individual performance is undervalued, professional standards are bound to decline.

The worst consequences of preferential treatment may be suffered by those who receive preference. As Charles Murray, currently the W. H. Brady Fellow at the American Enterprise Institute for Public Policy Research, wrote, such a person "has to put up with the knowledge that many of his coworkers believe he was hired because of his race; and he has to put up with the suspicion in his own mind that they might be right."[30] If that suspicion gnaws at those who were hired preferentially, they may conclude (perhaps accurately) that others expect low performance of them, and they may reject high standards of performance and become progressively more isolated, even from colleagues who are not racially prejudiced. They may fail to live up to the rightful ideals of policing.

Judicial Rulings, 1984–87. Under Section 1608.4, the Title VII Civil Rights Act of 1964 was amended in 1985 to read that reasonable affirmative action plans "may include goals and timetables . . . which recognize the race, sex, or national origin of applicants or employees . . . regardless of whether the persons benefited were themselves the victims of prior policies or procedures which produced the adverse impact or disparate treatment or which perpetuated past discrimination."

How this would be interpreted over time was as uncertain as the interpretation of Title VII was in 1970. Before that legislation, the courts had held, as in *Janoviak v. Corporate City of South Bend* in 1984, that "race-conscious programs do not, as a matter of law, violate either Title VII or the Equal Protection Clause of the Fourteenth Amendment." In that case, however, the Seventh Circuit Court held that statistical preference in employment by race could not be based solely on a "finding that a disparity existed between the percentage of minorities in the community and the percentage of minorities in the [police and fire] departments." The court rejected a two-to-one hiring plan designed to reach equivalent proportions and insisted that such a plan be warranted on evidence of past discrimination.[31] The case was appealed to the Supreme Court and certiorari was granted.

In *Williams v. City of New Orleans,* the Fifth Circuit Court held in 1984 that Title VII does not prohibit promotion quotas and does not require that only specific victims of prior discrimination may benefit from such programs. Although the court rejected a consent decree that required promotion of black and white officers in equal numbers until half the police at all ranks were blacks, it did so because it found the plan unfair to other minorities. Judge Thomas Gee cautioned in a separate opinion that quotas "are desperate measures, inherently invidious as calculated denials of the rights of one citizen in order to enhance those of another—both on the frank grounds of race." He described them as "a last resort . . . if ever appropriate."[32]

Municipal and state employment quotas were frequently upheld after the Williams decision. In 1987, in *United States v. Paradise*, the Supreme Court affirmed a court order "imposing an interim one-black-for-one-white promotion requirement for state troopers if qualified black candidates are available" on the Alabama Department of Public Safety.[33] Later that year, in *Johnson v. Transportation Agency*, the Supreme Court held that the "county agency did not violate Title VII by taking a female employee's sex into account and promoting her over a male employee with higher test scores." The Court held that the promotion was in accord with an affirmative action plan designed to remedy "underrepresentation of women and minorities in traditionally segregated job categories, and did not *unnecessarily* trammel the rights of male employees or create an *absolute* bar to their advancement [emphasis added]."[34]

As elsewhere, the idea of what is necessary is complicated by the question of the conditions and constitutionality of specific plans. In *United States v. Paradise*, the Court insisted that applicants be qualified. In *Wygant v. Jackson Board of Education*, the Supreme Court held in 1986 that preferential plans (as in protection against layoffs) must show prior discrimination by the employer and not just a history of social discrimination.[35]

The matter of qualifications was tested in *Davis v. City of Dallas* in 1985 by the Fifth Circuit Court, which held that the police department could legally require that candidates have forty-five semester hours of college credit with a C average; that no one would be eligible for candidacy who had been convicted of more than three hazardous traffic offenses in the past year; and that recent or excessive marijuana use was prohibitive of candidacy. Those standards were held to be job related and therefore legitimate, even if they reduced minority hiring. Citing earlier cases, the court was "unwilling" to require the city to "lower . . . its preemployment standards for such a job."[36] Denying the plausibility of requiring empirical proof of job-relatedness, the court relied largely on expert testimony. The job-relatedness of college education is probably not settled, and other court-recognized standards for employment may decline precipitously if marijuana is ever legalized.

Largeness of Spirit. Since the law is a living thing that grows, evolves, and changes, those rulings are neither comprehensive nor final. Litigation will continue, consent decrees will be entered and challenged, and few rulings will satisfy everyone—in terms either of principles or of methods and results. Because issues are complex, reasonable people will disagree about them. Scholars on opposite sides of affirmative action show sympathy for the concerns of their opponents, although they do not always do so in other legal and ethical disagreements.

When people of goodwill are defeated, they should try to find in themselves the largeness of spirit to make the best of things. They owe it to themselves and their professions to live as decently as they know how with rulings they believe to be wrong. When worthy persons are not promoted while someone else is promoted because of race, they can wallow in resentment and bitterness, or they can remind themselves that they chose to be police officers—and the best they could be. If they allow adversity to undermine their convictions and aspirations, they become their own worst enemy. No one should willingly be defeated by circumstance.

One reaction to that view has been, "That's easy for you to say—you are not the one who has been passed over by reverse discrimination, and you don't have to live with incompetent supervisors who have rank only because of race." Some add that it is unfair and unrealistic to expect people whose hopes have been dashed by affirmative action quotas not to be bitter.

Although all of us sometimes have to put up with incompetent supervisors, most of those set back by affirmative action will resent it. The issue is what to do about it. The task for the leadership is to ask everyone to try to make the best of the circumstances, to exercise self-control, to promote respect for fairness, and to oppose prejudice and its effects.

One important step is to minimize surprises about departmental policies and relevant laws and court rulings. When recruits are in training, the department should inform them of its methods of performance evaluation, of its goals for inclusion of minority members in the various ranks, and of binding consent decrees and related obligations. If persons with higher performance evaluations can be passed over while others are promoted because of quotas, the recruits should be told in the beginning so that expectations about merit and hard work will not be dashed later. The disgruntlement that may result from hearing the truth in the beginning is preferable to later resentment against department leaders and policies.

The leadership should be intolerant of bigotry in all its forms, whether it is displayed by members of minority groups or by others. The case of

Donald Rochan of the FBI illustrates behavior that should not be tolerated. Rochan, a black agent who joined the FBI in 1981, accused colleagues in Omaha of harassment; the *Washington Post* reported that "the face of an ape was pasted over a picture of his son in a family photograph on his desk. The message 'Don't come' was scrawled on invitations to office parties. A photograph of a black man who had been beaten was placed in his mail slot."[37] After he was transferred to Chicago in 1984, Rochan "received unsigned, typewritten letters threatening him with death and mutilation. . . . He received two letters requesting payment for death, dismemberment, and burial insurance that he had not purchased."[38]

The mistreatment was not denied by Rochan's FBI supervisors. According to remarks attributed to his Omaha supervisor, the incidents were "pranks," which were "healthy" marks of "esprit de corps" in the field office.[39] When an FBI agent in Chicago was proved to have forged the insurance documents, "he was simply suspended for fourteen days, and his colleagues chipped in to pay his salary."[40]

In the FBI, office personnel traditionally pay the salary of colleagues who are suspended or whose sick leave benefits are exhausted before they return to work. Although these are healthy signs of esprit de corps, the treatment of Rochan—no matter the reasons—is not. The leadership must insist upon that distinction and refuse absolutely to tolerate prejudice against others because of race or sex.

Racism and other forms of bigotry are often disclosed in the feel of a place. An institution may have an atmosphere of insidious bigotry that could never be proved in litigation. All levels of personnel ought to be alert to this, but the leadership should pay special heed, especially to subtle forms of bigotry, since the temptation to pass them off is likely to be greater.

Routine references to women by obscene anatomical terms or to minorities by racially derogatory epithets are signs of such an atmosphere even when it is denied. Casual acceptance of such behavior by ourselves and others is not harmless. We should put ourselves in the place of others and ask how we would feel in such an atmosphere in our own institution. We can preorder a kosher meal on an airline and see whether any change occurs in other passengers when the attendant delivers it. We can call a realtor and identify ourselves as black or Hispanic or pretend to be illiterate and ask for assistance with a government form. We can ask how we would feel if our own daughter worked in the atmosphere where we do.

Departmental planning should focus on recruitment, selection, and promotion plans that minimize the likelihood of incompetence at any rank. The adverse effects both of racial preference in hiring and of past discrimination may be limited if good candidates of all backgrounds are selected and every candidate is demonstrably qualified and motivated to do well. Those unjustly passed over are more likely to be magnanimous if they know that the promotions went to individuals who deserved them. High standards for recruiting, selection, and advancement may be the most important measures for combating internal friction over affirmative action or other discrimination. The courts have recognized that they are indispensable to faithful public service.

Recruiting, Selection, and Promotion

Between January and August 1988, more than twenty Detroit police officers were charged "with felonies ranging from assault and armed robbery to murder." At least one hundred others were "under investigation for ties to the drug underworld." Police officials denied that the corruption was systemic: "The department didn't commit those crimes. . . . People did, who happened to be wearing badges." One Wayne County prosecutor said that the department "needs to revise its recruiting standards very carefully."[41]

People do not just "happen" to wear the badge. They wear badges because they were hired by a police department, which is responsible for its employment and training policies and practices. What should be its criteria for recruitment and selection? In 1983 David C. Couper, former police chief of Madison, Wisconsin, answered that the skills and intelligence required for policing should be central, and not race and sex or size and strength. He added:

> Selection criteria must be demonstrably work-related. . . .
> Screening procedures for applicants should be structured to
> eliminate people who are clearly unsuited—psychologically,
> intellectually, physically, or morally—to do police work. . . . But

more important than eliminating unqualified applicants is identifying, through testing, medical and psychiatric examinations, personal interviews, and background investigations, the candidates with the necessary sensitivity, compassion, integrity, maturity, stability, intelligence, and ability to handle the complexity and stress involved in police work.[42]

As Couper pointed out, those standards are perfectly consistent with hiring minorities, whose representation in policing demonstrates to "minority communities that police authority is legitimate and should not be antagonistic." He added, "Women should be assigned to all fields according to their talents and skills." Couper appealed to research that showed women officers to be "particularly effective at defusing violent situations" and "less likely to use unnecessary force than men officers."[43] Good judgment and restraint are not, however, a function of sex or race; they are achievements of individuals, who should be assessed as such by a department.

Whether or not a department has been guilty of discrimination or has to hire more minority officers to provide good services, it can avoid errors in recruiting, especially if it does not make past residence in a specific locale a requirement. It is easier to teach police about an area and its residents than to make good police from unqualified applicants. *The Standards Manual of the Law Enforcement Agency Accreditation Program*, which favors affirmative action, recommends the following: (1) The department should advertise broadly for candidates and need not restrict recruiting to the area of its own jurisdiction. (2) The department should have trained personnel conduct a written background investigation of every eligible candidate, including verification of credentials, "a criminal record check, and verification of at least three personal references." In some cases, polygraphs may be used as "an investigative tool." (3) The department should have trained personnel conduct an oral interview of each candidate, and also test "general health, physical fitness and agility, emotional stability, and psychological fitness." (4) The department should require of all candidates a six-month probationary period and completion of entry-level training.[44]

Although a one-year probationary period for entry-level positions may be better, those procedures are effective if the standards and criteria are genuinely job related and are applied uniformly. To fill positions, a department should never forsake procedures and standards or lower its qualifications. Serious problems of unfitness of the kind encountered in Miami, Detroit, and New York may be prevented at the outset or addressed early in candidacy.

Police executives and federal law enforcement officials have asked how the use of polygraphs can be justified, since such tests are not admissible in court and some candidates for employment object to them. One answer is that a background investigation (or a departmental investigation of possible corruption or misconduct) is not a trial. A defendant in a trial is compelled to be a defendant, but a candidate for employment can terminate his candidacy if he does not wish to be examined, and an officer under investigation can resign. Therefore, the standards of a trial need not be treated as binding elsewhere.

The Employee Polygraph Protection Act enacted in 1988 does not apply to federal, state, or local government agencies. Although it specifies that private employers "are generally prohibited from requiring or requesting any employee or job applicant to take a lie detector test," it specifically "permits polygraph tests to be administered in the private sector, to certain prospective employees of security service firms (armored car, alarm, and guard), and of pharmaceutical manufacturers, distributors, and dispensers."[45] Thus, even in the private sector polygraph tests are legitimate if security and narcotics are involved.

Since rehabilitation and discipline are more difficult and expensive the longer a person is employed, supervisors should be alert to signs of trouble during training and probationary periods. If stress is a problem in police work, it can also be an asset in training, which should be sufficiently realistic, and therefore stressful, to discourage less dedicated and less able candidates. Rigorous training identifies people who are at their best when things are at their worst, the sort a police department needs.

Many departments maintain high standards while increasing the proportion of minority employees, without creating double standards for candidacy or promotion. In some, standards for candidacy and for performance evaluation are more rigorous now than they were even a few years ago, and the leadership remains stable without a rapid turnover of chiefs. As the chief of one such department observed, "Making progress takes courage and commitment to training. Getting the best people depends on widespread recruitment; state certification requirements help, and you can't live with double standards inside." He added, "It also takes a good bit of luck." Another emphasized that "skip" promotions are always a bad idea and that achieving proportionate representation of minorities is pointless if standards are compromised.

A comprehensive recruiting plan, developed in 1987 by the Personnel Department of the Police and Fire Selection Division in Los Angeles, contains many good ideas. Noting that the challenge "is to find previously untapped recruitment sources," the plan stresses

(1) mobilization of community resources, including the city council, mayor, community-based organizations, citizens, and LAPD personnel at all levels to reach qualified prospective female and minority candidates;

(2) establishment of a recruitment cadre of police officers to discuss careers at school career days, job fairs, church events, and athletic competitions;

(3) advertising on radio and television programs recorded in Spanish and Asian languages and whose audiences include bilingual members of ethnic communities;

(4) expansion of the recruitment program to include testing on more college campuses and military bases;

(5) greater LAPD involvement in activities of children and young adults in Boy Scouts, Girl Scouts, YMCA, YWCA, and ROTC, and expansion of departmental youth activity programs such as DARE (Drug Abuse Resistance Education);

(6) increased cooperation with magazines and newspapers to encourage feature stories about police and departmental career programs; and

(7) scholarships to students majoring in administration of justice.[46]

The program is expensive, and therefore prohibitive for some departments, but some of the activities may be implemented locally without great cost even by small departments.

The New York City Police Department has been experimenting with a police cadet corps, an effort to recruit college graduates. During the last two years of college, the city provides cadets with educational loans of $3,000, which are forgiven after two years of police service; students who do not choose police work have to repay the loans at 3 percent interest. For two summers, the cadets work full-time as observers with the Community Patrol Officers Program (CPOP) and are paid $7 an hour; they also work three days a month during their college years. Some cadets have seemed more interested in the loans and jobs than in police careers, but others have expressed enthusiasm about becoming police:

> CPOP is a fabulous program. We attended community board meetings, tenant association meetings, block parties. Sometimes we talk to crime victims and tell them about compensation that's available to them. . . . We also escorted senior citizens to the bank. . . . Now, there's no question that I will [become a police officer].[47]

Ordway P. Burden, president of the Law Enforcement Assistance Foundation, wrote that the New York Police Department believed "that college graduates may bring greater sensitivity to the officer's job."[48] He recalled a 1965 study in Los Angeles by B. E. Sanderson, which found that college graduates "did significantly better in the police academy, had fewer sick days and injured-on-duty days off, were less likely to be disciplined, and were much more likely to be promoted."[49]

Although the program is a worthwhile experiment that undoubtedly produces some favorable results, college-educated people should not be assumed to have better character than others, to be more resistant to stress, or to have better work habits. Some of the most notorious businessmen and officials in history have received fine educations. And as their professors know, many college students do not work very hard. Police departments everywhere have benefited from the excellence of personnel at all ranks whose formal education did not include college. A member of the Police Cadet Advisory Council said: "It's an open question . . . because whatever correlations are found between college education and performance . . . you're stuck with not being able to determine whether it's the college education that makes the difference . . . or the mix of personality, ambition, and talent that leads people to get a college education."[50]

According to some police officials, many recruits of the 1980s—regardless of their educational level—display troublesome characteristics that seem related to influences of the 1960s on their families. Some are undisciplined and have difficulty adapting to a police academy; some who are college graduates cannot read at the eighth-grade level; and some object to working nights and weekends. Some believe naïvely that they will rid the streets of crime, while others seem interested only in compensation and financial security, and not in performance.

Some of those characteristics are partly a function of youth, whatever the social and familial influences of the times may have been. Few of us have always been as self-disciplined, adaptable, skilled, realistic, or concerned about performance as we should have been. Some commentators infer that police should bring in older recruits, at least in their mid-twenties. While doing so may deal with part of a department's recruiting problems, it risks having more officers retire immediately after they complete twenty years of service, so that they can undertake second careers, as has happened in some federal agencies. Most important, all efforts to draw fine applicants to police work have to be combined with rigorous training and high performance standards.

9

Illegal Narcotics—Moral Issues
and Public Policy

Every reflecting man becomes daily more alarmed at our situation.

—James Madison[1]

Corruption of public officials by narcotics traffickers has become a subject of widespread concern among law enforcement agencies. Exposure of corrupt police has led many to suspect that the problems within law enforcement run deep. The U.S. Department of Justice awarded $375,000 to the International Association of Chiefs of Police to prepare a manual for command personnel on preventing and reducing such corruption.

As the public became more alarmed about drug use and increases in drug-related murders and other crimes, the media, a few scholars, and a handful of public officials sought to persuade Congress that legalization of narcotics should be debated. Most law enforcement executives have remained convinced that narcotics should not be legalized; many are developing more and better ways of combating the problems by employing high technology to gather and use information and by establishing procedures for greater accountability of their own personnel.

The moral issues raised in this public policy debate have been perplexing. Should police executives speak out, write editorials, and bring their knowledge and experience to the attention of the public and the makers of law and policy? Is legalizing dangerous and destructive substances moral, or is banning narcotics an immoral infringement of our freedom? How can we get a handle on the moral arguments in those public policy issues? Command officers have to answer the question I have heard put by officers about urban areas blighted by crack dealers and users: "What are we going to do?"

I have encouraged police leaders to speak publicly on policy issues and to set aside fears of being considered self-serving—of alarming the public to increase their own budgets. Just as many of them informed public attitudes and legislation on the sale of cheap handguns, they ought to help increase an understanding of narcotics issues.

To show how to move through the moral terrain of public policy arguments, a summary of the competing arguments in the case of narcotics follows, together with an analysis of them. Since public policy debates often resemble one another, this analysis has application to other disputes, such as those over easy and legal purchase of Saturday night specials.

The analysis may therefore be useful to police even if the current legalization controversy is short-lived.

Morality and Public Policy

In analyzing a policy dispute, the areas of agreement should be identified first. In this case, everyone agrees that no amount of diligence or expenditure on the supply and demand sides of narcotics can eliminate drug use. The issue is control of a problem, not eradication.

Furthermore, everyone wants policies and laws that promote public safety, reduce crime and corruption, respect individual liberties, limit profits to dealers, safeguard children, encourage productive adult lives, discourage criminal careers, and lower the levels of demand. All agree that greater emphasis on education, prevention, and treatment is imperative.

The issue—like most other public policy arguments—can be approached on four fronts. A set of policy and legislative recommendations can be offered, and it can be addressed by three kinds of arguments: assessments of the success and failure of current policies and laws; appeals to moral principles; and predictions of consequences. First, then, let us look at the basic proposals and arguments of the competing positions.

Arguments for Legalization of Narcotics

Proposals by Advocates. According to advocates of narcotics legalization, possession and use of many illegal drugs should be decriminalized so that the government can sell or distribute them to addicts and other adult users at low prices. Different substances are to be subject to different forms of government regulation: Low-intensity coca chewing gum might be marketed like other gum; high-intensity coca beverages would be sold in the same way as alcohol; and cocaine products, by contrast, could be purchased only with a prescription.

User taxes on some substances, like those on alcohol and tobacco, would generate income for drug treatment, rehabilitation, and education programs. Advocates of decriminalization propose the elimination not of all regulation and control by law, but rather of the profits in illegal drug dealing. The new laws and policies would undercut the market.

Assessment of Current Policies by Advocates. Proponents of legalization argue that current efforts to reduce supply and demand have failed. Although confiscation and arrest rates may be up, supplies of drugs have not been curtailed, nor have profits. Street crime is growing worse, as the demand in some sectors grows. Large sums of money—roughly $10 billion a year—are being poured into law enforcement efforts that fail, while inadequate funds are available for prevention and education.

The supply side of drug traffic cannot be controlled by the military, police, and other agencies, they say, because the flow of people and vehicles in and out of the United States is too massive. So many nations have climates favorable to cultivation of drug crops that international policies against production can never work for long. Within the United States, police sweeps have limited effectiveness against sellers and buyers of drugs who either avoid the sweeps or are freed soon after arrest. Some suburbanites now go to ghettos to buy drugs in inexpensive old cars, which would constitute a small loss if confiscated.

In sum, the flow of narcotics cannot be controlled by enforcement agencies.

Appeals to Moral Principles by Advocates. Advocates of legalization argue that the efforts of the criminal justice system to reduce drug supply—

and demand—threaten basic moral principles of our heritage. Government is obliged not to interfere in the lives of competent adults, they say, except when their behavior adversely affects others. Since the sale and purchase of drugs do not involve victims or complainants in the way a robbery does, illegal trafficking must be detected by undercover investigations that endanger agents, officers, and informants. Advocates say that such investigations involve deception and rough treatment of rights to privacy. Furthermore, drug testing to determine compliance with the law or to assess liability in accidents also jeopardizes rights to privacy. In addition, crimes without victims to report them invariably encourage citizens to become informants, as children in totalitarian countries are encouraged to betray their families. All that leads to erosion of civil liberties, to distrust among citizens, to the breakdown of families, and to a weakening of the social fabric.

Some proponents insist that illegal narcotics are not as dangerous as the media and some public officials say and that prohibition of drugs—as opposed to alcohol and tobacco—is therefore prejudiced. Except for drugs that pose a high danger of chronic dependency for all users, drug use is not a problem, although drug abuse is. Many people, the argument runs, live productive and healthy lives while using drugs, although others may have problems with drugs. Sometimes, the problems are connected to larger patterns of recklessness, aggressiveness, social isolation, low achievement, and bad habits in general. Social policy should therefore focus resources on controlling the supply of the most dangerous drugs and on educating the public on behavior generally.

Proponents also argue that the effects of efforts to control supply by criminal laws are immoral. Successful reduction of the supply drives up street prices and thereby increases crime and dealers' profits. High profits, in turn, enable subsequent corruption of criminal justice and other officials.

Prediction of Consequences by Advocates. Advocates predict, first, that legalization would immediately reduce criminal justice expenditures by several billion dollars and would thus free resources for expanded drug treatment, prevention, and education. Second, governmental control of sales and taxation would provide further revenues. Third, because drug prices would be controlled, the number of crimes committed by addicts to pay for their habits would drop. Fourth, legalization would largely force drug dealers out of business and would thus reduce crimes of violence among them and their victimization of users. Fifth, elimination of the enormous illegal profits would reduce susceptibility of law enforcement and other public officials to corruption. Sixth, police would have more time to prevent and solve crimes against life and property, and our prisons could hold more of the most dangerous criminals. Finally, although estimates of drug use and abuse after legalization are tentative, proponents doubt that drug use would increase significantly. Some proponents doubt especially that the use either of highly dangerous drugs or of shared needles that would increase the spread of AIDS would rise.

Proponents of legalization point to experiments with decriminalization of marijuana in California, Michigan, and other states. Studies indicate that prohibition of marijuana was a negligible deterrent and that use increased only slightly after sanctions were eased.[2] Many advocates liken current drug laws to those that prohibited alcohol in the United States from 1919 to 1933; they point to the failure of Prohibition and blame the rise of organized crime on it. We are making the same mistake again, they say; legalization can alleviate the worst consequences of that error.

Arguments against Legalization

Legislative and Policy Proposals by Opponents. Those who support criminal laws against narcotics favor international measures against the supply: military intervention to eradicate crops in countries that grow them or funding of local military and law enforcement efforts; economic and diplomatic pressure; increased resources for interdiction at sea and in the air; and greater control of our land borders.

They also advocate expanded law enforcement inside the United States: profile arrests, nationally computerized tracking of the movements of known and suspected dealers; zero-tolerance of illegal narcotics, with confiscation of property, arrest, prosecution, and heavy fines for possession; and the death penalty for drug-related murder. They also propose increased emphasis on the rest of the demand side, with more accessible programs in drug abuse prevention, treatment, and education.

Assessment of Current Policies by Opponents. Despite the gravity of the problems, opponents of legalization say the success of present policies can be seen in the increased arrests and punishment of major traffickers, in the seizure of hundreds of millions of dollars from traffickers, in the rising street prices in some areas, and in the apparent reductions in demand among some groups. Through the use of forfeiture funds, the technological capacity of law enforcement is expanding to deal with the flow of narcotics and the movement of dealers. Diligent patience is called for, therefore, rather than precipitous experiments with legalization.

According to many in law enforcement and public policy forums, Title 21 of the *U.S. Code*, section 881 (A) (7), can be applied more widely and effectively to obstruct supply. This law, as then–Houston Chief of Police Lee Brown explained in 1988, "provides for the forfeiture of real property that has been used to commit or to facilitate the commission of drug law violations."[3] It can be used to obstruct the operation of crack houses as long as the owner is notified that the property is subject to forfeiture.

Many acknowledge that local law enforcement by itself cannot control the supply but often only inconveniences the dealers, while stepping up arrests of users. Although organized crime units can infiltrate and "sting" drug operations, those forms of pressure, even with international interdiction, cannot eradicate the supply or the demand. Yet all of them are held to be necessary parts of a comprehensive effort that—even if it succeeds—will result in continuing drug use by some.

In 1988 Seattle local law enforcement cooperated with federal agencies so that suspects arrested for drug and gun violations that carried modest state penalties were turned over to federal authorities, who then applied federal drug possession and weapons laws that carried substantial mandatory sentences. Such cooperation, together with surveillance of airports, train stations, and bus depots, led to profile arrests and slowed the incursion of Los Angeles–based gangs in Seattle. Federal penalties can persuade suspects to become informants.[4] Although the traffickers may take countermeasures, including different patterns of dress for traveling, cooperation among law enforcement and other agencies is essential to success.

Appeals to Moral Principles by Opponents. Because drug use adversely affects families and the broader society, opponents say, government has a rightful interest in prohibition. A government that supplies dangerous substances, they add, not only suggests approval of them but gains enough power over those who are addicted to threaten their civil liberties. Many opponents see profound differences between the normal effects of alcohol and tobacco and those of Ecstasy, cocaine, crack, PCP, and "double-strength" marijuana (sinsemilla and high THC marijuana cultivated by hydroponics using dissolved inorganic materials). Opponents of legalization add that drug testing for accident liability would be necessary even if narcotics were legalized, just as it is for alcohol abuse. The law and the courts safeguard against wrongful invasion of privacy and illegal investigative techniques. Proper selection, supervision, education, and discipline of criminal justice personnel, they argue, are the best responses to the issue of public corruption.

Prediction of Consequences by Opponents. According to those who view experiments with the legalization of heroin and methadone as reckless, such legalization has never dramatically reduced illegal trafficking in England or the United States.[5] Unless the government legalizes the purchase of every drug in whatever quantity and potency every user wishes, illegal trafficking will be largely untouched—particularly in drugs with the most dangerous and bizarre effects such as cocaine, crack, PCP, and LSD. Government could not conscionably legalize a drug such as cocaine, which addicts use in binges that result in depression, paranoia, and violence. If cocaine were sold by prescription, users would buy quantities exceeding the prescription from illegal traffickers. Events in the Bahamas suggest that reduced prices lead to more widespread use: In 1982, no one sought treatment for cocaine-related problems in Nassau's only psychiatric clinic, but in 1984, after the price of cocaine had dropped by 80 percent, three hundred people did so.[6]

Even if drugs were available at lower prices through government regulation, opponents argue, addicts would still commit crimes for money to buy drugs and to pay other living expenses. Thus, law enforcement would still be forced to deal with illegal trafficking and related crimes.

Opponents of legalization point to marked differences between Prohibition of the 1920s and our present situation. Custom, habit, and public opinion favored legalization of alcohol, but, according to polls of both teenagers and adults, they oppose drug use and legalization. After thousands of years in which wine, beer, and hard liquor were accepted, Prohibition was opposed by such a weight of public desire that it was bound to fail. The current issue of drugs, however, remains in the balance. Legalization would disarm parents in their opposition to drugs; impair the efforts of businesses, schools, the military, and other institutions to become drug-free; and send a confusing signal to the young that might tip the balance toward widespread dependence on debilitating narcotics. Moreover, the end of Prohibition did not end organized crime but signaled more clearly its beginning. If drug dealers lost that enterprise, they would more likely engage in extortion, robbery, burglary, murder-for-hire, and the like than become law-abiding citizens.

Antilegalization arguments include the warning that experiments of this sort are extremely difficult to reverse. They conclude that the likelihood of adverse consequences is too great to risk.

Analyzing the Arguments

Disagreements over policies often stem from implicit differences about what counts as success and failure. In this case, certain facts are cited by both sides: that drug-related violence is increasing in some areas; that large amounts of money are spent on enforcement; that many dealers make high profits; that public corruption is often bought by narcotics money; that seizures and confiscations are on the rise; and so on. The disagreement is over how those should be understood and weighed.

Increases in seizures of money and drugs are a sign of progress against specific dealers, but the increases ought to be measured against the availability and price of drugs as well. If dealers are put out of business and incarcerated, then success is achieved in the apprehension and conviction of lawbreakers. If that has no effect on the volume of drug traffic, however, some goals of narcotics laws are not achieved. Since we have never had a comprehensive and cooperative supply-side program that included all appropriate agencies in cooperation with expanded demand-side programs, how much it could accomplish remains to be seen. The conclusion that we cannot control the supply of drugs is therefore untimely.

Disagreements can arise when different moral principles are considered of higher relevance or priority. One side in a dispute might consider justice paramount, another public safety. But in this case, the disagreements arise over matters of fact—and their bearing on the application of principles. Both sides are concerned for public safety, civil liberties, and so on; but they disagree about how dangerous various narcotics are, how far the rights of "competent" adults should go, and how adequate the legal safeguards of civil liberties are in the face of undercover investigations and the like.

My experience indicates that use of narcotics—even marijuana—is not healthy or harmless. Although people who use such narcotics may in some sense lead productive lives, it does not follow that those narcotics do not harm people. Students who use marijuana may get good grades, but their stamina, will power, and judgment are often diminished, and their sense of restraint and of self-respect is sometimes impaired. Clearly, narcotics like crack are immensely destructive, both of individuals and of entire communities. Addicts describe the drug as deadly; it kills individuals, and it ruins whole neighborhoods.

After a series of riots, Liberty City in Dade County, Florida, made progress in the early 1980s when widespread civic determination led to new investments by businesses and renewed concentration on schools. Some residents saw a promising future until the incursion of crack reversed much of the progress. In a few years Liberty City became a stagnant place as businesses closed and the sale and use of drugs became a dominant feature twenty-four hours a day.

Unfortunately, powdered cocaine and crack have become the drugs of choice among many users. The streets of our inner cities at night reveal the patterns of user dependency: "Hits" or dosages are repeated until the money, but not the desire, is gone. Young prostitutes take a hit of crack, turn a trick, take a hit, and so on, hoping to end the night with enough money for a hamburger and more crack. Because so many users are not adults, the concern of legalization advocates for the rights of adults is irrelevant.

More experience in the streets or more exposure to white-collar crime among narcotics users might settle some disagreements about the real dangers of narcotics but not about the rights of competent adults. As our laws concerning seat belts, motorcycle helmets, and Social Security taxes show, we do not entirely accept the argument that adults ought to be able to do what they please as long as they do not harm others. Although the legitimacy of such laws may be challenged, dependence on drugs clearly undermines a person's competence. Given that addiction almost always harms the family and others, the argument that laws against narcotics infringe on rightful freedoms remains unpersuasive.

Are the law and the rulings of courts inadequate to defense of civil liberties, privacy, and so on? To suppose that vigilant pursuit of narcotics traffickers must erode civil liberties implies a distrust of police, prosecutors, and judges and of the criminal justice system itself. To make a legitimate case against a suspect, police and prosecutors must overcome significant restraints and undertake rigorous procedures.

Because prediction in social matters can seldom approach exactness, disagreements over consequences often remain unsettled in public policy disputes. Conscientious and honest use of statistics and historical precedents is not necessarily conclusive. Crucial questions for both sides of the debate are: How much do we risk by this policy? What exactly do we risk? How much do we lose if the optimistic predictions do not come true and the pessimistic ones do?

The fundamental prediction at issue is whether legalization of narcotics will undercut profits and thereby reduce the black market and with it street crime, public corruption, and other adverse effects. How any of that would result from legalization is unclear. If narcotics dealers were indisposed to other illegal activities, we might infer that they would go straight when deprived of the profits in drugs, but we have no reason to think that. And we do have reason to doubt that legalization would destroy profits or reduce criminal activity.

First, legalization of drugs spawns its own variety of crime, like those that have become associated with drugs that can now be prescribed by a physician. Criminal diversion of Valium, Percodan, Oxycontin, and other prescription drugs is a huge enterprise, involving bribery, extortion, theft, hijacking, and counterfeiting.

Second, many in the narcotics traffic have little education and few skills to offer in the legitimate job market. They are as likely to pursue other criminal careers as to go straight. The major traffickers, accustomed to the profits of narcotics, are even more likely to behave as their predecessors in organized crime did when Prohibition was repealed. They entered other areas of crime, including loan-sharking, murder-for-hire, weapons smuggling, extortion, gambling, and prostitution.

Third, some traffickers might attempt to thwart legal sales by hijacking deliveries, underselling the government, using clever marketing schemes for high-potency drugs, investing more resources in marketing to children, corrupting public employees, and fomenting rumors that government drugs sterilize people, cause AIDS, or induce impotency. Some might continue to use violence for such purposes, since many drug dealers are criminals by habit and disposition.

Fourth, the markets in crack and other extremely dangerous—but preferred—drugs would be untouched by legalization. Criminal violence surrounds the marketing of those drugs, and legalization of other drugs offers no promise whatsoever of the reduction of such violence.

Both sides favor the reduction of traffic and profits on the supply side by expanding programs on the demand side. But even there, disagreements persist. Some officials doubt that the government or corporations can produce narcotics as cheaply as the cartels can. If drug production had to be subsidized by government revenues, they would yield nothing for demand-side programs. The costs of dealing with alcohol abuse and its effects in America alone exceed $100 billion a year—at least twice the estimated amount spent on all drug-related problems. Would legalization therefore result in any financial gain? Without much greater evidence of gain from legalization, even that rationale is too uncertain for such an "experiment."

The analysis remains incomplete without an assessment of the promise of expanded programs on the demand side, which bears on the extent of the risk of legalization.

Demand Reduction

The National Drug Policy Board, established in 1987, reported that drug education programs had an effect on both attitudes toward drugs and drug demand. In July 1988 the board's *Progress Report* reported that "only 54 percent of high school seniors in 1986 believed 'occasional' use of cocaine put one at 'great risk.' In 1987 that figure was 67 percent. During the same period, 'past month' use of cocaine by high school seniors dropped from 6.2 percent to 4.3 percent."[7] From February 1987 to March 1988, the Media-Advertising Partnership for a Drug Free America conducted two surveys involving 14,000 people—children aged nine to twelve, teenagers, college students, and adults. "While the study found an increase in antidrug attitudes in all groups, it was most pronounced among college students."[8]

Clearly, prevention and educational programs need to be expanded in schools, churches, businesses, the military, and youth organizations. Guides to family instruction about drugs are now available (through *Reader's Digest*, for example). The attitudes and behavior of adults and younger peers are especially important, because people are not necessarily constrained merely by learning how dangerous a form of behavior is. Drugs promise intense pleasure, and they often deliver on the promise. Even a person who knows the risks and understands that drug profits go to murderous drug traffickers may be too weak to resist the temptation. Persons of bad, weak, or unformed character may not have what it takes to "just say no." And bad judgment is possible for people who know that drugs are dangerous, just as corruption is possible for public officials who know that it is wrong and hazardous.

A reduction of demand throughout society probably cannot be achieved merely through education about the dangers of drugs. Many of those in school who have heard speakers tell horror stories about their ordeals from experiments with drugs are now asking for speakers who have never used drugs. Tired of stories of failure and recovery, they want to hear from people whose lives have never gone off track with drugs and are fruitful and productive. Exemplars of virtue can be every bit as compelling and informative as reformed failures.

Education and prevention programs hold their greatest promise for those reached by other forms of education, but they will not reach adults who naïvely believe they are exempt from the perils of addiction—the cocky and self-indulgent college-educated suburbanites who frequent ghettos to buy drugs. With youths deprived of a good family, school, or neighborhood, and without church influences and examples, programs are difficult to implement.

Columnist George F. Will argued that "not all Americans are equally open to teaching and there will be a class bias in the results of any policy that emphasizes teaching. . . . Drug abuse is disproportionately an inner-city problem. This will become increasingly so as public information campaigns become more effective at modifying the public's behavior."[9]

Although Will is correct that drug abuse is disproportionately present in inner cities, many advantaged youths and adults also depend on drugs for emotional or physical pleasure. At lunch hour or immediately after any workday, office workers can be seen visiting the inner city to buy drugs. Many have clearly convinced themselves, "It won't happen to me," and others probably will be similarly reckless in the future.

Many ghetto youths are extraordinarily ignorant of the dangers of their behavior. I have talked with teenage prostitutes who cannot read or write and who either are completely unaware of AIDS or believe that only homosexuals can be afflicted with the disease or transmit it. Many of those youths act as if they have nothing to lose in using drugs. The information that drugs debilitate and kill does not influence them because of the brutality they face every day. No quick or easy solutions can work with school-age and even younger children who prowl the streets day and night completely deprived of adult love and instruction, while their parents turn tricks or lie insensate on filthy blankets in crack houses.

Because of such facts, the demand side of narcotics cannot be viewed as an isolated problem. It is intertwined with problems in education at every level and with economic and social problems in families, schools, neighborhoods, corporations, and other institutions.

Such broad and complex social issues require resources far beyond any that might be gained from a reduction in law enforcement on the supply and demand sides. Furthermore, because of the disproportionate levels of drug abuse in our inner cities, legalization of narcotics could hurt those already disadvantaged most of all. Finally, some narcotics cannot be legalized because a single dose can addict a person virtually for life, despite repeated treatment; demand-side reductions will have to be combined with supply-side pressures.

Conclusion

The supply side may become manageable if more and more of the public resolutely oppose drug trafficking and use at home, on the job, and in the exercise of civic authority and civil liberty, and if peer pressure grows against purchase and use of drugs. If public opposition to narcotics becomes powerful enough, specific locales and neighborhoods have a good chance of improvement. We might witness effects resembling those of the campaign against smoking.

But this issue promises to remain forever in the balance. With each new generation, all the learning must be acquired anew, and all the habits of good character must be formed again by diligent practice and healthy instruction. The ability to bear the responsibilities of public and private life must be nurtured afresh, and opportunities for the fulfillment of worthy aspiration in school and at work must be provided for all. The question of drugs is inseparable from the question whether we have the character and will to give the best of ourselves to successor generations for their sake. If not, the country's resources will be exhausted in efforts to save the citizens from themselves, whether or not narcotics are legalized.

Police can improve conditions in the neighborhoods worst plagued by narcotics, but only briefly. Saturation policing works but has few lasting effects. Much broader civilian follow-up is required to achieve stability, including more individuals and facilities to provide drug treatment, counseling, tutoring in school, family assistance, and so on. Legalization seems unlikely to set the stage for such follow-up. Certainly, in the crack zones it would be irrelevant.

The arguments for the two positions suggest that legalization invites grave risks and offers few benefits. Therefore, I conclude that the public policy debate should be settled against the legalization of narcotics that are now illegal.

An important consideration in this conclusion is that legalization of gambling in Atlantic City and Las Vegas has been accompanied by increases, not reductions, in crime. In Atlantic City, where gambling has been legalized and taxed since 1977, Ovid Demaris reported that violent crimes in this "South Bronx by the Sea" have

> doubled, tripled, and quadrupled. Pacific Avenue, only a block away from the Boardwalk, is crawling with hookers, pimps, pickpockets, drug pushers, car strippers, and thieves. Loansharks are having a field day, and muggers attack people in broad daylight. . . . Slumlords . . . are burning down their buildings to collect the insurance. . . . Hotel rooms are broken into,

> guests assaulted, purses and wallets snatched, cars in the sub-
> terranean garages rifled. . . . Gambling is a game of fantasy . . .
> that involves greed and political corruption and organized crime
> and murder.[10]

Public officials, as I know from experience, privately lament the levels of public corruption.

Where off-track betting and state-run lotteries have been established, illegal bookies and numbers runners do enormous business, largely because they allow betting on credit and do not report bettor winnings for taxation. Many law enforcement officials believe that levels of criminal activity become worse where gambling has been legalized. Whether for gambling or narcotics, one law enforcement colleague observed, "Any system of legalization will require some set of rules, and there will be big money to be made in breaking those rules."

Advocates say that narcotics legalization is not a capitulation to drug traffickers but a means of destroying their profits, not a statement that drug use is perfectly all right but an expression of willingness to let people decide for themselves. Granting that advocates do not intend to capitulate to dealers, I believe that their recommendations would have little effect on black market profits, because we could not legalize every drug in the amount desired by every prospective purchaser.

I am not willing to see children raised in a climate where our opposition to dangerous narcotics is unsupported by criminal laws. Respect for liberty is not the same as legalized tolerance of socially destructive intemperance. Neither is government service to the public the same as producing and marketing substances that destroy the ability of citizens to govern themselves.

Some legalization advocates, who spurn such arguments, regard moral considerations as emotional and their own views as pragmatic. But morality should not be denigrated by those who profess a concern for civil rights and liberties and for the safety of police and other citizens. In any case, they are not being pragmatic if they forsake morality in policymaking, or if, in education and elsewhere, they ignore the cultivation of self-control and good judgment. Neither is it pragmatic to suppose that with legalization the drug dealers will quietly go away: The determination of ruthless people, who declare war on everyone who trifles with them, should not be underestimated. The streets, and their predators, are much meaner than most legalization proponents understand.

Many police officers recognize that their efforts and sacrifices in combating narcotics cannot completely solve any problem. The wisest among them also understand that their mission is not to reform society singlehandedly, but to do their best to enforce the law, keep the peace, and safeguard the public, with patience, honesty, courage, and fortitude, even when things are at their worst. Their good example is critically needed now.

10

The Fundamentals of Character and Training

Only thought can determine what course of action is best on any occasion; excellence of character has the sole but important role of making the agent willing to do what reason determines is the best course of action.

—J. O. Urmson[1]

In the training of police, four misleading views about ethics are best cleared away early.

First, if asked, many respond roughly this way: "Whenever I hear the word *morals*, I think of sex, and whenever I hear *ethics*, I think of money."

Second, many believe that realism—in belief, judgment, and action—and idealism are somehow incompatible. Some say that a realist is a person who cares only about "the facts," and an idealist is a pie-in-the-sky unrealist, a person who is naïve about "the way things really are."

Third, many believe that people concerned about ethics tend to be holier-than-thou goody-goodies, who disdain every pleasure, and purse-lipped prudes, who are, underneath it all, deeply unhappy.

Fourth, to a surprising number of people, including ethics teachers, the principal or sole subject matter of ethics is the treatment of moral problems, rather than the formation of habits of good character.

Both teachers and students in the academy program should be alert to those misleading views. They can be addressed without extensive theoretical baggage and with stories of police in action.

Sex and Money

That people think of morality and ethics in terms of sex and money is not surprising. Ethics scandals in government and business involve money, and morals scandals in the popular media usually involve sex. Sex and money get high billing because they titillate readers and viewers and because they are sources of great temptation.

They are not the causes of scandalous behavior but only two of many occasions for it. Sexual attraction and wealth are also occasions for much good and for behavior that is entirely honorable. The causes of bad conduct, by contrast, are character faults, bad judgment, and, infrequently, complex and even tragic circumstances.

Many philosophers, following the lead of Socrates, Plato, and Aristotle in ethics, have stressed the question, What is a person of good character? Answers to this question go far beyond matters of sex and money. Discussion of specific kinds of virtue—courage, for example—in the lives of police suggests that real examples that are not academically tedious are better than hypothetical ones.

Courage may be understood by contrasting it to both an excess and a deficiency—specifically, to recklessness and cowardice—which are deviations from true courage. A courageous person feels, judges, and acts differently from a reckless person or a coward. Those differences are appreciable by beginners and suggest analogies to other aspects of good character.

Most experienced police officers can describe what courage requires in specific instances and can distinguish it from recklessness and cowardice. For example, courageous officers understand that a domestic violence call poses dangers to everyone involved, including police. They will respond as quickly as they can, with such information about the situation and the parties as can be gathered from the dispatcher on the way and from bystanders at the scene. They are not likely to enter without adequate backup—indeed, department policies may disallow entering alone. They will carry the proper tools, including a radio and a nightstick. Since any combatant in a domestic fight may turn on the police, the officers will not ignore the risks; their purpose is to prevent the violence from continuing or growing worse.

By contrast, I have occasionally seen an officer who would rush into a scene, uninformed, without backup, and without nightstick or radio. Even if the motive is to end the violence as quickly as possible, such conduct is reckless and can lead to avoidable injuries that can end a police career.

Although outright physical cowardice is rare among the police known to me, I did witness one command officer who went to great lengths to avoid responding to domestic violence calls and gun calls. On his way to them, he would make sudden stops to break up harmless groups of idlers after radioing in that they were "hinky" and that "something was going down." Later he would try to save face by insisting that he was delayed by other problems, but his excuses wore thin. He had little credibility with his colleagues, who never counted on him for backup.

Neither sex nor money figures in any direct way in those illustrations. They highlight the moral importance of everyday conduct, as seen in realistic cases as opposed to hypothetical ones. Experience shows that courage is integral to the police function, with relevance to a range of specific issues, from the kind of colleagues an officer can depend on to the idea of aspiring to the best. Similar points about courage, recklessness, and cowardice can be made about high-speed pursuit, for example, and the handling of misguided peer pressure.

In 1975 Robert C. Wadman, chief of police in Omaha, and his coauthors Monroe J. Paxman and Marion T. Bentley, described the following case in *Law Enforcement Supervision: A Case Study Approach*:

> Chad Wilson has owned the Ranchero Steak House for the past twenty years. Formerly a reserve deputy in the county, he has always enjoyed the friendship of police officers. Wilson has arranged a table in his restaurant so police officers can come in and eat and not be bothered by other customers. For the past ten years Wilson has made it a practice to allow the uniformed officers working in his area to eat anything they want for "free." He states, "The police don't get paid enough, and I want them to have a good meal. They need a place where they can take a break and not be hassled by the public."
>
> Officer Harlow is working the night shift in an area several miles from the Ranchero Steak House. At approximately 2:30 a.m., he observes a vehicle weaving slightly and stops the car to see if the driver is under the influence. As he approaches

the driver's side of the car, he smells a strong alcoholic beverage. He asks the driver to step out of the car. The driver identifies himself as Chad Wilson and starts naming officers on the department who are his close friends.

Officer Harlow is a new police officer with approximately eight months on the job. He conducts a field test and determines that Mr. Wilson is under the influence of alcohol. After making this determination, he places Mr. Wilson in his police car and transports him to jail.

At the jail, one of the officers who eats regularly at the Ranchero Steak House sees Mr. Wilson in custody. This officer makes several comments about the quality of the arrest and states to Officer Harlow, "You have a lot to learn. This guy isn't drunk and has been a friend of the department for years."

Officer Harlow is concerned about the situation and two days later comes to you as his supervisor and states, "I arrested one of the best contacts of the department and guys are sure letting me know it."[2]

Officer Harlow might have let Chad Wilson go when he learned who his friends were, an act that would have shown reckless disregard for the safety of other citizens—and for Wilson himself. Or later, because of peer pressure, he could have canceled the citation, or failed to show up in court, or asked the prosecutor to dismiss the charges—all actions that suggest cowardice and some of which might constitute obstruction of justice. Instead, Wadman, Paxman, and Bentley explained what actually happened:

> Officer Harlow was put under extreme pressure to drop the case prior to trial. He refused to do so because it was a violation of department orders. Mr. Wilson became upset with the department and discontinued the free meals to officers. Many of the officers who had enjoyed the meals at the Ranchero Steak House continued to make sarcastic comments to Officer Harlow. No supervisory action of any consequence was ever taken in the matter, and Officer Harlow, after several months, was accepted as a good officer by his peers.[3]

In this case, money or money's worth is involved, but it is not as central as the character of the officer. This was reflected in his attitude toward violations of law and of departmental orders and in his courage in the face of peer pressure, just as the character of his peers was reflected in their treatment of him.

Realism and Idealism

The idea that realism and idealism are somehow opposed to each other—as though realism meant cynicism and idealism meant naïveté—needs to be corrected as well. This error suggests that ethics and morality are separate from real police work. Analysis of the actual experiences of officers will help make the correction:

> On a Saturday night, I was with two uniformed officers on patrol in an inner-city area. While we were waiting for detectives to arrive for investigation of a TV store armed robbery, an emergency call came about a shooting at a nearby address. The officers hurried to the home, where a woman in her early twenties stood screaming on the front porch. Two men were found in an upstairs bedroom, one pistol-whipped, the other shot in the wrist. Other officers and command personnel arrived, the two men were taken by ambulance to the hospital, the house was searched revealing ammunition and traces of drugs and no other people.
>
> One of the partners questioned the woman on the porch; it was about eight feet wide, screened on top with paneling to about waist level. The doorway was in the middle of the front of the house. Three steps led to it. Suddenly, the officer shouted to his partner, "There's somebody in the house!" pushed the woman into a chair, drew his sidearm and started into the house. As he did so, a command officer stepped hesitantly up nearly into the doorway onto the porch. The partner shoved him aside, saying, "Get the hell out of the way! My partner may need that door," made it onto the porch, preventing the woman from moving, and once the first officer had a protected position inside, followed him into the house.

A suspect was later apprehended, having fled through a basement window after successfully concealing himself in a cranny near the basement ceiling.

In his action, the second officer exhibited realism—awareness of facts, sensibility to potential danger, knowledge of how to safeguard his partner. He also showed regard for ideals—loyalty, personal responsibility, and courage. He was a realistic idealist, bringing respect for the facts and regard for standards and ideals into the union required for competent judgment, action, and life.

That combination of realism and idealism is required for the responsible exercise of command as well. A chief recently faced a situation in which eight hostages were taken by a gunman with a history of drug use and hospitalization. Police negotiated with him for twenty-four hours and secured release of seven hostages. Although they had several opportunities to shoot the gunman, the department persisted in negotiations in an attempt to save the remaining hostage and the perpetrator. When the hostage-taker demanded materials to build a time machine, the department provided all the specific items he requested.

Finally, however, after the gunman threatened to detonate a bomb, a police sniper shot and killed him. Patient negotiation had shown courage and respect for all the lives involved—high ideals in any setting—but when negotiations held no prospect of a better outcome, decisive action was realistic.

If realism and idealism are not joined in deliberations about what to do, our thinking may become useless or futile. When officers begin police work, they need to know that high ideals do not mean naïveté. When told by experienced police not to be naïve, they should see that this is good advice—unless it is taken to mean that they should stop taking their ideals seriously. Losing sight of this profound difference encourages cynicism, not realism.

Morality and Happiness

Those who think that morality runs against happiness, that it means forgoing every enjoyment, should be reminded that philosophers—and parents and teachers—encourage good character because they believe that decent people are better and happier than others. People who act reasonably rather than impulsively, and honorably rather than deviously, are better off for doing so. But many mistakenly believe that what is right will make them unhappy and what is wrong will make them happy. The Buddy Boys knew that they were doing wrong, rationalized that others profit from wrong-doing, and believed that the profits of drug dealing would make them happier. How wrong they were could be seen in their grinding awareness that they corrupted—and then betrayed—friends on the force in their desire to spare themselves the consequences of wrongdoing. Countless lives are ruined by misjudgments about happiness and by failures to understand the deep fulfillment that comes with peace of mind.

Everyday experience teaches us that a person can know the right way to behave and not follow it. At times we all know what is right but do not do it. Sometimes we are weak-willed, or we believe that doing right will interfere with our happiness, or we deceive ourselves for a while about what is right. Ashamed afterward, most of us who are honest with ourselves can admit not only that we should have known better but that we did know better.

Sometimes, of course, duty and happiness may be in conflict, as when a police officer imperils—and loses—his life. An officer who discloses the wrongdoing of a corrupt partner and is made an outcast by others may be made terribly unhappy.

But serious character faults cannot make anyone happy. Fair and decent people are far happier than cowards or unjust people who fear those they have wronged. People who cannot be trusted never enjoy the trustworthy companions who contribute so much to our lives.

Novelist Robertson Davies once said that happiness is like a cat. If you chase after it, the cat will never warm up to you. But if you go about your business, you will often find the cat rubbing up against your legs. Likewise, if you chase after happiness, it is likely to elude you. But if you pay attention to doing your best at work and in private life, happiness more often comes to you. In this respect, happiness is like fun—if we go out to have fun, we are unlikely to have a good time, because having fun is not a specific activity. If we go out with friends, however, and bowl our best while encouraging them, we are much more likely to have fun.

Happiness consists to a large degree of being able to offer ourselves as the very best people we can be to our colleagues, friends, and family; to this extent, morality, character excellence, and happiness are indivisible. When we understand this, we are unlikely to indulge moral shortcomings in ourselves that we can identify and prevent.

Moral Problems

Some police academy courses and in-service programs reduce the study of ethics to deliberation about moral problems. By ignoring the nature of basic character, this method may obscure the fundamentals of good and bad judgment in unproblematic situations.

Emphasis on character and the kinds of habits that form a good second nature is crucial. Only people who have acquired enough virtue to be ashamed of wrongdoing can appreciate the force of questions about right and wrong actions. What should we do? is a question for people who care to do what is right, but not for others. For them, ethics is only an academic pursuit, a matter of intellectual gymnastics. Education in ethics for police is not intended for that.

Good practical judgment means being able to tell what justice, courage, temperance, and other aspects of character excellence require in specific circumstances. It amounts to acting on an occasion with consideration for the right persons, in the right degree, in the right way, at the right time, for the right reason. Right action is conduct in accord with what reason requires in that case. Sometimes, of course, deciding what is right is terribly difficult, but often it is not.

Most of what matters in moral life does not involve difficult questions. Our lives are not filled with situations of the sort popular in ethics courses, such as what to do when not everyone can fit into the only available lifeboat. Giving such hypothetical problems the central place in ethics is highly misleading. Complicated hypothetical questions may refine our thinking, but only after we have given due importance to commonplace morality. We should not obscure the importance of the ordinary by preoccupying ourselves, our colleagues, or police recruits with the extraordinary.

Habits

Good character consists of good habits that are within our power to form, and most of us have formed some admirable habits. John Stuart Mill wrote that "a character is a completely fashioned will." Normal individuals can fashion their will by the daily behavior they make habitual. "The great thing . . . in all education," philosopher William James observed, is to make habitual, as early as possible, "as many useful actions as we can, and guard against the growing into ways that are likely to be disadvantageous to us."[4]

Police academy students can see that officers who respond to domestic violence calls should not sit in their cruisers agonizing over whether to take their nightstick and radio. They find them in their hands or on their belts because habit has put them where they belong. In the same way, habit safeguards officers from neglecting the possibility of danger posed by every combatant in a domestic battle.

The role of habit in character underscores the importance of learning by experience. Provided with opportunities to repeat actions, learners can see right and wrong ways to behave. With our support and encouragement, they can form the right habits. As we work with more mature students, we should make clear how much they can do for themselves in the same way.

When we teach youngsters to ride a bike by running alongside to give support, we enable them to feel and to learn by practice to correct a fall by turning the handlebars to that same side. When we teach marksmanship, we teach students by practice to raise or lower their aim in a crosswind, depending on the direction of the wind in relation to the rotation of the rifle bullet. When we teach billiards, students learn by practice that a lateral spin, or English, on a cue ball will "throw" an object ball in the direction of the spin and cause the cue ball to drift the opposite way. We encourage repeated practice to establish the right habits in all those activities.

By keeping a careful eye for the interests and curiosity of our students, we can teach them the reasons that specific habits may be trusted to work. We thereby encourage the habit of listening to reason, instead of acting on impulse or supposing that they can become good at anything without diligent practice. The more students grasp the connections between good habits and reason, the more they can do for themselves. They may be trusted with discretion, according to their ability to apply reason to novel situations, and in that way become good police officers. Good professionals understand the standards of their profession, sustain those standards by habit, and know how to use reason to make necessary decisions. For policing to become fully a profession, it should settle for no less.

Such training and education presuppose that careful background investigations have established that candidates are already disposed toward right action. Emphasis on the formation of good habits can scarcely be overdone. As William James observed, "Could the young but realize how soon they will become mere walking bundles of habits, they would give more heed to their conduct while in the plastic state." By our actions "we are spinning our own fates, good or evil." James added that because habits are formed by what we actually do each day, each student who learns to work diligently and well can "with perfect certainty count on waking up some fine morning, to find himself one of the competent ones of his generation."[5]

Particularly appropriate to police work is James's insight that the formation of powerful and reliable habits "alone prevents the hardest . . . walks of life from being deserted," just as it "keeps the fisherman and the deckhand at sea through the winter." Knowledge that the formation of good habits will serve them whatever their walk of life encourages the young. Ignorance of that fundamental fact of human life has probably, as James concluded, "engendered more discouragement and faint-heartedness in youths embarking on arduous careers than all other causes put together."[6]

Cultivation of habit and good judgment is very different from mere shrewdness and cunning. A shrewd intelligence that enables its possessor to do wrong with impunity is only a servant of the passions, however excessive or depraved they may be. A developed capacity to understand the reasons for behaving courageously is, by contrast, a guide to control of such feelings as overconfidence and fear. This is wisdom, which serves to govern a life, not to gratify desires slavishly.

Youngsters who live in homes where family members tell each other the truth learn by experience that trust makes a household warm and intimate. Even if children sometimes lie because they can find no other weapon to defend themselves, they learn how it feels to keep company with people whose love for each other is expressed in truthfulness. When habits of right action are formed, they help a person to want to achieve good character.

Anyone exposed to human beings who behave courageously, for example, can recognize, "That is the kind of person I want to be."

For that reason some police training has to be done by drills. They are essential, for instance, to the development of good judgment and reliable action in the use of force, including deadly force. Drills conducted in simulated conditions disclose personal weaknesses that must be overcome and strengths and talents that can be refined. They contribute to self-knowledge that makes an officer better able to use force rightly.

Also imperative are consideration and discussion of fairness, of inordinate force, and of the differences (and similarities) between a fast gun and a wise, just, courageous gun. Lectures, readings, writings, stories, testimonies of senior officers, explanations of departmental policies and the reasons for them, discussions of examples from the history of the department, careful criticism by teachers, and conscientious field training are all necessary to enable an officer to grasp the reasons for behaving in particular ways that make the judicious and wise use of force fully second nature—and that enable the officer to behave as quickly as the circumstances require without being precipitous.

Police training and instruction need, therefore, to include exercises for the formation of habits that make up such aspects of good character as courage, justice, temperance, and compassion. The formation of good habits is sometimes undertaken as well by initiative and by outspoken resolve—for example, when those who want to break a habit of intemperance say to their loved ones, "I will not do that any more." In this way resolve is distinguished from the mere good intentions that pave the road to hell.

Current Fashion in Ethics Education

Lawrence W. Sherman of the University of Pennsylvania asserted that many "ethics educators reject the idea of making people moral as naïve and unrealistic."[7] Surely, it is entirely true that no one can make another person moral. The will to do the right thing for the right reasons is, finally, up to each person; no one can acquire it for anyone else or force it upon another.

Each person must succeed or fail in this as an individual, but no one can achieve good character entirely alone. Excellent habits and excellent reasoning do not arise in a vacuum. Ethics education seeks to make people worthy to bear the public trust. It must provide them the opportunities to make the best of themselves.

Sherman, and many others, have said that "teaching the reasoning process for arriving at moral decisions"[8] is the fundamental purpose of education in ethics. For that reason, Sherman—with other members of the 1978 Police Foundation's National Advisory Commission on Higher Education for Police Officers—stressed that "every police education program should include in its required curriculum a thorough consideration of value choices and ethical dilemmas of police work."[9]

Their position resembles the view of the Institute of Society, Ethics, and the Life Sciences at Hastings-on-Hudson: "The primary purpose of courses in ethics ought to be to provide students with those concepts and analytical skills that will enable them to grapple with broad ethical theory in attempting to resolve both personal and professional dilemmas, as well as to reflect on the moral issues facing the larger society."[10] The Hastings Center identified five basic goals: "stimulating the moral imagination, recognizing ethical issues, developing analytical skills, eliciting a sense of moral obligation and personal responsibility, and tolerating—and resisting—disagreement and ambiguity." To those, Sherman added "understanding the morality of coercion, integrating technical and moral competence, and becoming familiar with the full range of moral issues specific to criminology and criminal justice."[11]

All that sounds well-intentioned enough, but is it realistic and theoretically and practically sound?

With respect to realism, I doubt that any program of instruction can acquaint students with the "full range of moral issues specific to criminology and criminal justice." The curriculum would have to be vast. Even "understanding the morality of coercion" takes a great deal of work. Immanuel Kant said in *The Metaphysical Elements of Justice* that coercion "is a hindrance or opposition to freedom. Consequently, if a certain use of freedom is itself a hindrance to freedom . . . then the use of coercion to counteract it . . . is just. It follows by the law of contradiction that justice [a right] is united with the authorization to use coercion against anyone who violates justice [or a right]."[12] Analyses of this sort are difficult, even for advanced students. In police training, it is enough to see that justice may require the forfeiture of the rights of those who aggressively violate the rights of others.

The same point holds for "grappling with broad ethical theory in attempting to resolve both personal and professional 'dilemmas.'" Even those educated in such theory seldom decide what is right or how to behave by grappling with broad ethical theory. Even if police academies or under-graduate courses could be sufficiently deep and thorough to make anyone a scholar of broad ethical theory, such scholars are not necessarily persons of good character. Instruction in ethics for police has to be more specific, precise, and respectful of time limits.

Undertaking a "thorough consideration of value choices and ethical dilemmas of police work" amounts to presenting students with problematic cases and asking what should be done. A teacher can show students "the reasoning process for arriving at moral decisions," but that process is point-less for a person who lacks the character to listen to reason or who simply does not give a damn about behaving rightly. The process may help weak-willed persons to avoid rationalization and self-deception, but only if they want it to. Only those already decent enough to care what is good and right can have a moral problem about what is good or right.

Few common moral failings and failures stem from inept reasoning about dilemmas. Many more arise from moral indifference, disregard for other people, weakness of will, and bad or self-indulgent habits. Otherwise, every philosopher who is good at moral reasoning and every student of ethics would be a person of excellent character. That is simply not the case.

Much of what is done in ethics instruction with value choices and eth-ical dilemmas is question-begging or misleading, and some of it discourages rather than promotes character excellence. Philosopher Matthew Lipman described the futility of basing ethics education on dilemmas:

> Dilemmas are constructed by arbitrarily ruling out meaningful options and by limiting those that remain to those that contradict either one another or themselves. In laboratory settings, the tech-nique is employed to determine how subjects will behave if their reasoning powers are neutralized and they are left to their instinc-tual or emotional devices. In a classroom, such a technique, if unaccompanied by the exploration of rational alternatives, can be of little educational value.[13]

Much more valuable is the study of specific situations with seasoned officers to learn how to bring one's best habits wisely to bear.

"Value" Choices and "Ethical Dilemmas"

Lawrence W. Sherman focused on decision-making about problems and dilemmas because he believed that the "primary question of normative ethics" is, "How should we discover what is morally right, what we ought to do?" Sherman rejected values clarification, values inquiry and analysis, and moral development techniques as irrelevant to ethics education. He was convinced that a vague treatment of ethics throughout the curriculum gives no assurance that this question will be treated explicitly. "If ethics is to be taken seriously," he said, "teaching it as a separate course seems to be the only viable option."[14]

Sherman was quite right to insist that moral instruction must not be a vague part of the curriculum, but if it is offered as a course, the rest of the curriculum must be consistent in its regard for moral standards. Otherwise, the course will be isolated, and it will be treated as an aside by the students.

Sherman was also right to reject values clarification and similar methods of moral instruction. Such methods are intended to enable people to discover what they already consider good and right, not to ask what we ought to consider good and right. They reduce the inquiry to questions of what individuals happen to like or want—a far different matter from what is worthy of our aspiration and respect.

Thus, by discovering that they enjoy seeing discrimination against a certain race, sex, or religion, they "clarify" their values. Many values-clarification strategies explicitly teach students that ethics and morality consist of no more than that. They teach that no value is better than any other—that everything is a matter of personal taste. In that view, the ideal is for those who like, for instance, racial discrimination or "kiddie porn" to discover that they like it. And since no form of character or conduct is better or worse than any other, that discovery concludes the educational program in ethics.

By contrast, true ethics is in part about justice, and justice is incompatible with bigotry; it is in part about temperance, and temperance and justice are both incompatible with sexual exploitation of anyone, let alone children.

Accordingly, values clarification cannot compose an ethics curriculum. It may help people discover that they like things they should not like, but ethically, it has no other purpose.

The place of dilemmas in the ethical education of police is suggested by the place of dilemmas in moral life generally. A moral dilemma is, by definition, a choice between two mutually exclusive courses of action, each of which has a serious claim to being morally right. To be torn between two arguably right but mutually exclusive actions, a person must already care about doing what is right.

Because a dilemma may be genuinely unresolvable, a person may be perfectly right in following either course of action. For example, a father who has important reasons for spending Father's Day with his father and other important ones for spending the day with his own children—and who cannot be with both—is faced with a dilemma. If he judges the reasons for each course to be equal, he cannot resolve the issue by further reasoning. Sometimes, the proper response is to recognize that more reasoning is futile and simply to do one thing or the other. Since endless effort to try to find—or fabricate—an overriding reason can be a fault, persisting in pointless deliberation is not a mark of character excellence for police or anyone else.

We should not assume that character excellence and decent behavior are based on skill at resolving dilemmas. A tremendous intellectual skill at diagnosing the elements of moral issues may be used only to maintain appearances and have no other effect on behavior.

Equally important, teaching police that moral life is one hard decision after another is both false and misleading. If that were the case, everyone who tried to be moral would burn out and grow weary of moral deliberation in a very short time. Moral decency and habits of character excellence in daily life are for the most part not fraught with problems of decision.

For twenty-five months during the Nazi occupation in World War II, the family of Anne Frank was hidden in the secret annex of a Dutch home in Amsterdam. Asked in 1987 how he and his wife found the courage to hide and feed the Franks—Jews in a city controlled by those who wanted to murder them—Jan Gies said, simply and eloquently, "It's not like one day you wake up and say to yourself, 'Let's be brave today.'"

Indeed, it is not. It is not a matter of painful deliberation but of character and therefore of habit. I do not mean to deny that we must learn to reason conscientiously in hard moral cases. But moral seriousness in daily life requires a firmer foundation than the habit of reasoning. Jan Gies and his wife did not reason through a dilemma, nor did they struggle toward some grueling decision about the relative advantages of courage and cowardice. They behaved as decent and courageous people behave. Given their conception of decency, they even denied (without false modesty, I might add) that they were heroic. I think that they were heroic, but I know no heroes who make a big point of it. They seem to know intuitively what Emerson said about a dinner guest who celebrated his own virtues: "The louder he talked of his honor, the faster we counted our spoons."

To take another instance, on February 22, 1988, four motorists stopped on a highway to help an Ohio trooper struggling with a man who was trying to take his gun. If no one had stopped, the outcome could have been tragic. One of the citizens who went to help, Jeff Stroud, a sales representative for a manufacturing firm, said later that he stopped "just because it seemed the right thing to do."[15]

Three conclusions can be drawn from those illustrations. First, good character exhibited in morally important acts frequently involves no difficult decision. Second, knowing how to make a decision is not itself a motive for decency. Third, those who are motivated to behave decently cannot necessarily explain how reliable decisions are made. We must address the issue of motivation and the fact that the normal circumstances of daily life do not require so many hard decisions. Only in that context can we fruitfully raise the levels of knowledge about how to deliberate in hard cases.

Many educators who wrongly treat dilemmas as the heart of moral life also wrongly elevate questions of choice to the status of moral dilemmas. That obliterates the distinction between temptations toward wrongdoing and conflicts between morally arguable courses of action.

I have encountered the following type of case in discussions with city government officials, businessmen and businesswomen, and police:

> You are a deputy police chief in a mid-Atlantic city where you have worked for eleven years. You accept an offer to become chief in a Western city within thirty days, but soon learn that your wife is pregnant. You decide that you do not want to move far and accept instead a chief's position in a nearby town. You then tell the

Western city manager you have decided not to come because of the baby. You point out that you gave him no acceptance in writing.

The question is what you should do when faced with the supposed dilemma of wanting to change plans after you accepted an offer.

As this hypothetical case is cast, is it a moral dilemma? It presents a tension between duty and desire, not between two obligatory courses of action. The case might be made into a moral dilemma if the facts were changed: if you and your wife have had great difficulty conceiving, if your wife's health is frail, if she needs to be near the doctors you have worked with for several years, and so on. Then the main question would be, Why did you accept a job so far away in the first place?

To see that the case as offered poses no dilemma, we can put ourselves in the place of the city manager. What would we say if we received such a call from a man who had accepted our offer to be police chief? My response would be to say that I was glad to learn of his wishes and to say goodbye. I would then tell my colleagues that we had misjudged the man, that he was immature or dishonorable or both, and that we were fortunate to learn it before he could take office. He was immature because he could not plan his personal life to accommodate perfectly normal events, let alone plan the future of a police department. He was dishonorable because he broke commitments when they interfered with his desires. And he implied that his word counted for nothing unless he gave it in writing. Imagine telling a child that you could break a promise because it was not in writing. Few of us want our sons and daughters to grow up that way.

The case illegitimately elevates a tension between duty and desire to the status of a dilemma. But even if that were a genuine dilemma rather than a problem for reflection, the exercise would still miss the point about many of the elements of moral life. Therefore, it cannot be the essence of education in ethics and morals.

Individual and Departmental Character

The purpose of developing moral habits is to learn from experience that it is better to be courageous than to be reckless or cowardly, better to be just than unjust, temperate than intemperate, charitable and compassionate than otherwise. And the purpose of developing intellectual competence is to learn that it is better to be wise than foolish, to reason well than badly, to be capable rather than inept.

With such a background, police can apply what they have learned to narcotics, drug enforcement, and drug use; to use of force; to racism, both among the public and inside law enforcement; to dealing with the ravages of poverty or with cynicism and corruption; to personal problems with alcohol, gluttony, and physical indolence; to preparing reports, serving warrants, and testifying in court; and to deception in undercover investigations and to the use of informants.

Some circumstances in police work call especially for justice and compassion. New officers, for example, are often assigned to ghettos or projects in inner cities, where they tend to be confrontational, especially with suspects. Newcomers may not realize that in any public meeting with police, citizen pride and "face" may be at stake. When officers are confrontational, citizens may see no way but violence to maintain self-respect or the respect of their peers. Learned in the streets, that lesson can be harsh or even deadly. A better way to learn it is from instruction in justice and compassion—and in listening to reason.

Justice is a complicated idea that cannot be contrasted to some simple excess or character deficiency. J. O. Urmson said that a just person is one who is "impartial, without fear or favor, eventempered and . . . clearheaded; in a word . . . of generally good character."[16] We could stress that justice is incompatible with prejudice, or with indifference to the rights of others, or with cheating, or with greed or selfishness. Sometimes we say that those who obey the law are just, but what is lawful is not always identical to what is just. If we contrast justice to forms of excess and deficiency, we might say that a person could be excessive in giving too much weight to the rights of others and deficient in giving too little weight to his own.[17] But sometimes we contrast the just person with one who is vengeful or takes the law into his own hands, doing on his own initiative what he judges the law ought to do. We also contrast being just with being tolerant of abuses of other people so long as we are not abused. Cicero made this point when he criticized his fellow citizens for believing that they did enough for their country by managing to avoid being killed by its political factions.

To the extent that those various ideas of justice overlap or share a common thread, they suggest that just persons do not play favorites and avoid exceeding their own authority or treating people in ways they do not deserve. They feel as indignant at the unfair treatment of others as of themselves. To decide whether to approve certain conduct, they may—as a matter of fairness—ask whether they would be willing for everyone to behave that way. In all that, a person of just character gives consideration to others—equal initial consideration, subsequently weighted by relevant facts. And even that relatively dispassionate regard for the rights and interests of others links justice to compassion.

A compassionate person is one who tries to understand how things look and feel to others. To be just in daily life, we must try to grasp the point of view of others, because their perception is an irreplaceable element in the overall facts. To decide what to do, just persons try to take into account how their conduct seems to others and how their actions affect them.

In the novel *To Kill a Mockingbird*, Atticus Finch, a lawyer in a small Southern town who is defending a black man falsely accused of attacking a white woman, expresses this to his six-year-old daughter, Scout:

> "If you can learn a simple trick, Scout, you'll get along a lot better with all kinds of folks. You never really understand a person until you consider things from his point of view—"
>
> "Sir?"
>
> "—until you climb into his skin and walk around in it."[18]

Police officers on the streets have to want to do this and to learn to ask, How would I feel if I were the other person? Without being able to "climb into the skin" of others, officers will be thwarted by differences of race, ethnic background, economic circumstances, and sex. With justice and compassion, they have a far better chance to enforce the law and keep the peace without unnecessary—and self-endangering—confrontations. Although they must not compromise their judgment or integrity, officers have to see things even from the point of view of informants to work effectively with them.

Such instruction should show newcomers that exposing their partners to the hazards of unnecessary confrontation is unfair and foolish. As one officer said to me of another, "When he gets into this 'macho' crap in the projects, it's not just his ass on the line. It's mine, and every other cop who comes in here."

Questions of justice and compassion naturally lead academy students to questions about departmental treatment of the police themselves and the rationale for specific policies. How does the department conduct its review of shootings by officers? How do seasoned officers review cases of accidental discharge of a weapon in a struggle with a suspect? What are the department's policies about recruitment, appointment, retention, promotion, and discipline? Where does the department stand on affirmative action and on merit? Does it hold that "if you wear a badge, you are supposed to be a cut above your environment"? How has it responded to the following situation described by another law enforcement official?

> Holding to a higher standard for police becomes more difficult each year as our nation has changed into one dealing with self-gratification, recreational use of drugs, and deterioration of home, family, and church associations. Continually, when it is necessary to discipline somebody for an infraction of rules, you do not find the support of the local government or the state labor board who hear grievances concerning those matters. More and more we are being told by others that a police officer is no longer different from any other worker.

What does the department expect of its members—who, unlike many workers, take an oath of office and say that they are members of a profession? In all those respects, why are the department's policies what they are?

A police officer is authorized to make decisions about the lives of others, an enormous power the rest do not have. Such power should be exercised only by those whose public and private behavior befits authority. A person who is hungover or weakened by other intemperance is more prone to errors of poor concentration, inattention to detail, and so on. The public cannot allow those who have special powers to indulge in excesses allowed others. The rights of police arise from their institutional mission.

Academy recruits should deal with such matters at the initiative of the department rather than wait for experience to tempt them toward cynicism.

Morals apply not only to how the officer behaves, but also to how the department behaves. Nothing lowers morale or undermines command personnel's concern for moral standards as much as discrimination and favoritism within a department. Injustice within it is ruinous to justice everywhere else. What of compassion for the families of officers subject to disciplinary action? One way to address this is to call departmental requirements to the attention of all personnel. Doing so places responsibility for adverse consequences squarely on them—and appeals to their own compassion for their families as a motive to refrain from conduct that could hurt them. Police candidates should learn that the consequences of misconduct may discredit fellow officers, endanger other police, disgrace the badge, and jeopardize the happiness of loved ones. No command officer can safeguard everyone else from a particular officer's wrongdoing. Officers can do so only by their own conduct.

Candid instruction about justice and compassion necessarily includes telling newcomers that as police they will be subjected to injustice, contempt, lack of respect, and abuse by some citizens. In some urban areas, an enormous network is involved in drug sales, all mobilized to prevent police effectiveness. In areas I have seen, when a police vehicle enters, three cars pull out in front of it and four or five behind, with their lights on and their radios blasting, to warn the dealers and buyers and to prevent free movement by police. Each car is occupied by two armed dealers, to intimidate and control the police. For two police officers in a vehicle to try to contend with that potentially lethal abuse would be reckless. Some dealers are also users, with a total disregard for life and a proclivity to violence. The wise and courageous alternative is to implement policies that thwart the dealers—such as using police in force, arresting buyers as well as sellers, and impounding vehicles—without needlessly jeopardizing the police or the general public. Provision must be made for immediate processing of arrests, or the drain on resources will be self-defeating.

To see such steps in progress is the best antidote to becoming resentful over injustice. A proper police response can forestall the frustration of officers and ill-advised or vengeful behavior in the streets. A department must show the officers that they are not alone, because the streets can, over time, tax the reserves of goodwill, hopefulness, and compassion of most officers.

Former police detective Dorothy Uhnak described in *Policewoman* a lecture to her academy class by a veteran command officer:

> Tomorrow, you will all graduate from the Police Academy. . . . But you don't know this city. . . . You don't know it because you haven't seen it, but you are going to see it now with policemen's eyes. . . . There is dirt and corruption and moral disease and agony and tragedy, and you are going to be a part of it. . . . You are going to touch and handle the living flesh and the dying blood. . . . You will deal with the vilest and the lowest and the most depraved forms of humanity . . . and what shocks you now will become merely routine. . . .
>
> This is not a job, it is a whole way of life, and if you decide to live it, you will have to live it twenty-four hours a day for as long as you are a police officer.[19]

Though true, this counsel should not be taken to mean that officers' lives must be directed solely to their job. Treated as a twenty-four-hour-a-day responsibility, the job can destroy the recreation and relaxation everyone needs. If the job obscures everything else, it invites an exaggerated sense of self-importance, a prescription for burnout.

The study of being an honorable person applies to private as well as public life. Someone who does not form habits of justice and compassion is unlikely to forge a durable marriage. And someone who does not fear drug habits or excesses of alcohol or food or a deficiency of physical stamina is unlikely to maintain the mental and physical conditioning needed to face each day, at home or at work.

11

Deliberation and Moral Problems in Training

There is no more contemptible type of human character than that of the nerveless sentimentalist and dreamer, who spends his life in a weltering sea of sensibility and emotion, but who never does a manly concrete deed. There is no more miserable human being than one in whom nothing is habitual but indecision.

—William James[1]

As officers develop good character by forging good habits, they learn to address hard questions productively. Deliberation about complex issues of right and wrong—or of which of several right actions should take precedence—becomes natural for a person of habitual moral seriousness. Responsible people learn to deliberate well and to be decisive and timely without being arbitrary or impulsive.

Officers also need a sense of which situations require no more than their habitual conduct and which ones call for careful—even if fast—decisions. Not every situation calls for deliberation. Officers who make everything a problem of deliberation are like the man philosopher Brand Blanshard wrote about "who is so anxious to cover all contingencies with insurance that he exhausts his income on it, and has nothing left to live on."[2] No reasonable person reasons consciously about every action. We waste ourselves, as Blanshard also observed, "in incessant deliberating over what should be matters of mere habit." The rational person "instead of perpetually questioning his habit and so check-mating his will, like the unhappy centipede that began to consider how it ran, will make habit his ally, turning over to it the larger part of his life so that he may bring his intelligence to bear freely on the rest."

We no more need to spend our first waking moments each day thinking about whether to behave honestly toward family and friends than we need to deliberate whether to brush our teeth. To paraphrase philosopher Alfred North Whitehead, thinking is like cavalry; it should be used only on special occasions.

The habit of deciding with care when circumstances require is, like other habits, acquired by practice. The rest of this chapter describes practical questions raised by police that offer opportunities to practice deliberation.

Moral Deliberation

Although they do not normally need to deliberate about whether to tell the truth, in discussions of ethics many police raise questions about honesty. On the one hand, they do not want to betray the truth by deceiving others to manipulate them for personal profit or to conceal their own failings. On the other, they do not suppose that being honest means spilling every piece of confidential information. Honorable people are neither deficient in truth telling by lying nor excessive by gossiping.

Honesty as a form of character excellence was described by Theodore Roosevelt in his 1904 Memorial Day tribute to those who fought at Gettysburg:

> The lessons they taught us are lessons as applicable in our every-day lives now as in the rare times of great stress. The men who made this field forever memorable did so because they combined the power of fealty to a lofty ideal with the power of showing that fealty in hard, practical, commonsense fashion. They stood for the life of effort, not the life of ease. They had that love of country, that love of justice, that love of their fellowmen without which power and resourceful efficiency but make a man a danger to his fellows. . . . Exactly as in time of war, courage is the cardinal virtue of the soldier, so in time of peace honesty, using the word in its deepest and broadest significance, is the essential basic virtue, without which all else avails nothing.

Clearly, honesty is directly connected to the courage of our convictions, to fairness or justice, and to compassion or fundamental respect for others.

But do not situations arise that allow exceptions to the general principle of truthfulness? Samuel Johnson replied this way, as his biographer, James Boswell, reported:

> We talked of the question . . . whether it was allowable at any time to depart from *Truth?*
>
> JOHNSON: "The general rule is that Truth should never be violated, because it is of the utmost importance to the comfort of life, that we should have a full security by mutual faith; and occasional inconveniences should be willingly suffered that we may preserve it. There must, however, be some exceptions. If, for instance, a murderer should ask you which way a man is gone, you may tell him what is not true, because you are under a previous obligation not to betray a man to a murderer."[3]

The lie Johnson calls legitimate involves a question initiated by a murderer. How does this apply to police work?

Such questions are pointless for anyone who has not established basic habits of honesty. But a person who aspires to behave honorably in both routine and difficult situations will take questions of honesty seriously. He can ask, What would an honorable person be likely to do in this situation? How would that conclusion be reached? What principles and possible consequences would be taken into account? And what should I do?

Police have presented various situations to me as problematic. Let us examine some of them with this question in mind: What would honorable persons (and hence honorable police officers) do?

Question 1. News reporters ask in an interview for information about an investigation that is confidential. Should police lie to protect confidentiality?

Question 2. Political superiors interfere in matters of police promotion and transfer. Should a command officer lie to them about what can legally be done to prevent them from manipulating the department?

Question 3. Adversarial relations between management and union threaten police performance. Should police lie to each other to gain advantage for one side or another?

Question 4. Political figures in a city vastly exaggerate what police can and should do for the public. Should police leaders remain silent for the sake of political survival?

Question 5. A suspect confesses to a number of crimes in addition to the one he is charged with. Police know it is unlikely that he committed all the others. Should they treat the confessions as true and clear the crimes to improve the record of the department?

Question 6. The truth about a series of crimes may panic the public or encourage it to take the law into its own hands. What should the police do?

Question 7. Routine burglaries are unlikely to be investigated, and homicides committed by strangers are extremely difficult to prevent or solve. Should police tell the truth, which may outrage the victims and the public?

Question 8. Several people suspected of committing a crime together are in custody. Should police lie to them individually to secure confessions?

In deliberating about such questions, honorable persons will consider truth telling obligatory in normal circumstances and will not lie for the sake of exploiting others. Nor will they lie simply to relieve short-term pressures. They reject opportunities for gain that betray duty and will not take advantage of their position at the expense of those who rely on them. What, then, might be included in classroom discussion as the sort of thing to be considered in these specific cases?

1. Lying to the media. Reporters asking for sensitive information about an investigation or a victim have no right to it; the police have a duty to safeguard confidentiality. Police must not be deceived by media protestations that "the public has a right to know." The media have neither the duty nor the authority to decide what the police should reveal and hence what the public may rightly know. Honorable persons will not break confidence, but they may preserve the truth by saying, "That is confidential" or "I am not at liberty to discuss the matter."

Such a reply might, however, suggest that the police have the information in question and that it might endanger an investigation by tipping a suspect. "No comment" might therefore be a better reply. In any case, only fools lie to people whose trust they need, as police need the future trust of the media. Prudence and morality join together against deliberate deceit. The answer to the question of when to lie to the media, according to most high administrative officers, is never. Even if journalists use policeband radios as a way of ambulance chasing and interfere with investigations, police should not lie to them. If they break the law in pursuit of stories, police may enforce the law.

These points hold even though police cooperation does not always result in complete media cooperation with police. In early 1988 a magazine in Charles Town, West Virginia, ran an article on drug sales in the county with emphasis on a Jamaican crack connection. ABC News then sent a crew to film street sales of crack. Law enforcement officials feared that if the film were broadcast, the suspects would go into hiding. U.S. Attorney William Kolibash told the Associated Press "that he had offered to let the crew tape from unmarked police vehicles, but that he had asked the network not to broadcast the footage until the suspects were arrested." He added that ABC officials "refused to hold off," and so the police raid had to be moved up several weeks. Police arrested only twenty-six of the forty people for whom they had warrants; one officer was shot in the foot, and two were injured in a car crash. ABC officials later insisted that the police "offered to move the date, they volunteered to do that."[4]

Police officials who conducted the raid confirmed that they did not want to change their timetable—having invested several months in the investigation. But they appreciated the problem facing ABC; the network needed to gather footage for an already scheduled national broadcast on narcotics in America. Except for the scheduling problems, mutual cooperation was very good, with ABC filming the day before the raid from police vans, and other television stations filming during the raid itself. The police set up a press conference at the command post that continued during the raid. Police spokesmen assured me that the change in timetable had nothing whatever to do with any officer injuries.

The cooperation of police with the media and their candor about their plans were both admirable and prudent. Open communication averted potentially worse consequences: If ABC had run the footage without prior police knowledge, the investigation would have been completely wasted, or if the television show and the arrests had overlapped, the police and the suspects would have been placed in graver danger. The media coverage may have alerted viewers to the seriousness of illegal narcotics trafficking in the United States.

2. Lying to political superiors who try to manipulate departmental affairs. If a mayor wants a crony in the police department promoted or transferred to a choice assignment, honorable police are unlikely to protect institutional autonomy through lies. Lies are a frail and temporary protection, too easily discovered in matters of this kind to be of much use. They also threaten to undermine trust and to invite reprisal. A conscientious person takes into account probable and possible long-term consequences, not just short-term.

A police executive appointed by a mayor has a twofold duty—to act in accordance with legitimate policies of the administration and to make clear when the mayor is overstepping his bounds. If that was not clarified when the job was offered, it should be when the problem surfaces. To do less is to invite progressively worse problems that cannot be solved by deceit.

To that the reply may be, But if I tell him to back off, he will fire me. A command officer who has lost authority over personnel assignments, however, has already been undermined in his ability to serve the public.

3. Lying to union or management adversaries. Where management-union relations are adversarial, morale at all levels suffers. The principal task of command—and of union—officers is to find areas of common purpose where trust may be built. Honorable people use imagination in such matters. For example, one urban police commissioner discovered soon after his appointment in the mid-1980s that when officers were killed in the line of duty, their families had to pay funeral expenses. Horrified, he informed the mayor that this practice would be ended immediately and that, if necessary, discretionary funds would be used until proper budgetary arrangements were made and an official policy formulated. Facing departmental tension over compensation, he did not pander to the fashionable but frequently false generalization that all police are underpaid. Instead, he appointed an independent task force to review compensation matters and, on the strength of their report, announced publicly that police in his city were underpaid in comparison with other police in similar cities. By taking such initiatives, which he believed obligatory, he took a step toward improved management-union relations and mutual trust.

Although such a step can do little without reciprocity, it is a mark of conscientious leadership and far superior to the deceit that clouds such issues in many cities. Mistrust undermines common purposes and commitment to mission within institutions. Even if representatives of different groups must hold in confidence the terms they would accept, they need not lie.

4. *Remaining silent to survive in office.* When politicians spout public nonsense about what police can and should do, silence is not a lie, but it is the deliberate toleration of falsehood, possibly at the expense of the public. According to the police executives I know, if you allow politicians to create unrealistic expectations, those expectations will come back to haunt you. You will be subject to unanswerable criticism, possibly at the price of your job. Police executives advocate forthrightness—either in cautioning political superiors that they are on the wrong track or in publicly denying their claims if no other method is effective. Police executives have a duty to subordinates to promote public understanding of the police mission and its limits. Silent toleration of political nonsense is a betrayal of those personnel, a basic failure of leadership. Many patrol personnel in my experience care more that their superiors defend them from unwarranted criticism and safeguard them from unrealistic expectations than they do about anything anyone else says. Here, honesty by command officers takes courage, but the moral issue is not complex.

5. *Clearing crimes by acceptance of confessions believed to be false.* This is an obviously dishonest means of manipulating political and public opinion. It closes the files on crimes by perpetrators who may remain at large. It may bury information useful in other investigations and prosecutions, thereby endangering the public. Certainly, it falsifies departmental data on accomplishment and makes a mockery of accountability.

In addition, dishonestly clearing crimes leads to false and unrealistic expectations among citizens about what officers can accomplish. Such deceit is an attack on the credibility of future officers. No officer who cares about them would falsify clearance rates at such a price.

6. Lying to avoid panicking the public or encouraging vigilantism. As in dealing with the media, the main question is whether judicious responses and regard for confidentiality serve the public interest. Honorable people in positions of responsibility do not assume that obligations to tell the truth entail obligations to tell the whole truth to the press or the public. Whether a lie is really necessary to protect the public from itself is a question likely to arise rarely and only in extreme cases. But if the fear of public panic or riot is genuine, then concern for public safety may legitimately override concern for honesty about a specific issue. Normally, if some morally overriding reason such as public safety obliges a person to lie, then it also requires an explanation or apology for the deception later, after the crisis has passed. The possible consequences of such an admission deserve consideration in the initial decision.

7. Lying to avoid enraging or depressing victims of crimes. Experienced police know, and newcomers soon learn, that crime victims feel violated—their homes, their bodies, or their freedom and security have been invaded. They want hope that their losses will be restored and the perpetrators punished. In many cases, both hopes will be disappointed. In my experience, good police listen patiently, express sympathy, take careful reports, and pass on information that may be useful to other police, but they do not make false promises or hold out false hopes. They may not explain that limits of personnel, time, and money prohibit investigation of many crimes, but they do not lie about this either. To force the truth on the victim would be cruel, and to lie would raise false hopes that will turn to cynicism.

8. Lying to suspects to secure confessions. In investigations, police sometimes tell suspects that they have been implicated in a confession, even if they have not been. The fear and distrust of the suspects are manipulated by deceit. That practice is highly questionable because even innocent suspects may have records that make them less than credible, and they may therefore feel that they cannot afford to stand on their genuine innocence. They may feel that lying is the only way of safeguarding their deepest interests and thus may confess to crimes and suffer punishments unjustly, while allowing the actual perpetrators to go undetected.

Police, however, have no overriding duty to sustain by their honesty a successful criminal conspiracy of silence. We sometimes agree to bargain for a lesser offense or grant immunity to break up such conspiracies—in hope of safeguarding the public. A consideration of relevant details is needed to determine whether an alternative is better than deceit: how dangerous are the suspects known to be and so on? Thus, I would ask for more details of the specific case and a review of possible alternatives to deceit.

Identifying Genuine Moral Problems

Obviously, such issues should be treated more thoroughly in police training by addressing questions and objections. But these general themes suggest the considerations that are relevant. And when personnel who are rising in rank understand how much is not morally problematic, they can identify real moral problems and distinguish them from other kinds of choices.

Let us take an extended example of the difference. First, a question of choice that does not involve a decision about conflicting moral goods: Would an honorable person whose duty includes enforcement of drug laws use drugs whose possession, sale, and purchase are illegal? The use of such illegal drugs violates the law the officer is sworn to uphold. Furthermore, use of drugs impairs human capacities, including strength and judgment. Finally, violating the laws the officers are sworn to uphold may generate feelings of hypocrisy in themselves and make them lax in enforcing those laws. Honorable persons do not force themselves into living a lie, because that is the most profound violation of the truth, not covered by any exceptions of the sort Samuel Johnson described.

Not every police officer who learns that will refrain from the use of drugs, because moral instruction cannot make people moral. But such instruction at least forewarns officers what they are letting themselves in for. That knowledge cannot entirely protect them from doing evil, but it does protect them from being deceived that what they do is not evil—for it is demonstrably a betrayal of duty and a self-inflicted harm. There is no dilemma—only a potential tension between temperance and duty on the one hand and desire for drug-induced delusion or euphoria on the other.

A moral choice does have to be made about working undercover, say, in narcotics. Undercover work is by nature deceptive; it is the adoption of a false persona for the purpose of gathering admissible evidence against suspected criminals whose covertness seldom provides obvious evidence. Undercover work requires being able to "get inside the skin" of others. As Malachi L. Harney and John C. Cross observed in *The Narcotic Officer's Notebook*: "Generally, the more readily the undercover man comprehends crime from the criminal's standpoint, the better. After all, he is now a figure in the world of crime, or so he pretends."[5] But the more successful undercover investigators are, the greater the trust narcotics traffickers will have in them, and the greater the capacity to exploit that trust. Although experienced undercover agents caution against being "too friendly with the suspect's wife or women friends," they do acknowledge that "an exception might extend to small courtesies to the suspect's mother or children."[6] Thus, undercover work may involve deception of innocent members of a private family.

Critics of undercover investigations argue that they are of questionable value and that they risk entrapment, misconduct by informants, psychological or moral damage to the agent and to the victims of deception, violations of civil liberties and democratic ideals, and erosion of trust within society. But even they generally agree that "certain types of crimes can be detected only by using deception and employing informants."[7] From the array of arguments on moral grounds for and against undercover investigations and use of informants in law enforcement, students should be aware of the following arguments.

Malachi L. Harney and John C. Cross served as undercover investigators for the Treasury Department and as superintendent and assistant superintendent, respectively, of the Illinois Division of Narcotics Control. They observed that the use of informants and undercover agents is necessary to solve crimes where the evidence is otherwise invisible and to prevent planned crimes:

- From the dawn of history, internal law and order has had to depend in greater or less measure on the informer.

- No modern policeman who properly uses informers needs to be apologetic about them. The apology should come from the officer who fails to use this device to protect his community.

- The citizen has a right and a duty to inform the government of violations of its laws. The fact that he recognizes this most readily only when his own person or property or his loved ones are involved does not invalidate the principle.

- The easily demonstrated fact is that the big cases usually are made by informers *and* undercover officers.[8]

Judge Learned Hand said, "Courts have countenanced the use of informers from time immemorial." Former Assistant Attorney General of the United States William F. Tompkins added: "*What our critics fail to, or will not, recognize is that those who are engaged in a criminal enterprise have no right to be free from such surveillances.* . . . It is not a question of informing on one's fellows, but of protecting society from those who would do us harm by their original conduct."[9]

Irwin B. Nathan, the Department of Justice lawyer who was in charge of the ABSCAM prosecutions, endorsed this view:

> Detractors of ABSCAM attempt to portray an image of high-level Justice Department officials engaged in a crusade against selected public officials or seeking to test the honesty or morality of randomly chosen politicians. The truth of the matter, as shown by the evidence developed in eight public trials, is far different. At critical junctures in the investigation, high-level officials in the Criminal Division and the FBI were faced with essentially only one simple choice: either ignore serious allegations of corruption by refusing to allow contacts with those represented to be ready and willing to engage in criminal conduct, or authorize FBI operatives to pursue the leads they had developed during their investigation, up to and including meeting and offering bribes to public officials identified by proven criminals. It would have been scandalous to have refused to explore fully these serious allegations.[10]

Nathan added that every person indicted or convicted in ABSCAM could have rejected bribes. In addition to that personal safeguard, access to appellate courts by defendants ensures that undercover operations are not unconstrained political attacks on targeted individuals.

Sissela Bok of Harvard University's Center for Population and Development Studies has argued against undercover investigations and use of informers: "Deceit and violence—these are the two forms of deliberate assault on human beings. Both can coerce people into acting against their will. Most harm that can befall victims through violence can come to them also through deceit. But deceit controls more subtly, for it works on belief as well as action."[11]

Sanford Levinson of the University of Texas College of Law added that undercover deception is a con game:

- Willingness on occasion . . . to identify with the con artist depends partly on dehumanizing the victim and being willing to ignore the implications of legitimating the con. Yet in all con games—no matter what the context—both victim and artist are diminished by the encounter. And in the case of the undercover agent . . . we lack both an ethical norm and a public policy that takes account of the damage done to the agent, the victim, and society.

- We are entitled to the belief that persons who present themselves to us will not actively be wishing us ill and using the encounter as a means of furthering their malevolence toward us.

- Neither warrant nor reasonableness seems necessary prior to a decision by a police department to attempt the infiltration of the life of a suspected criminal.[12]

Levinson feared as well that use of undercover investigations and informers undermines trust in society—among the citizens and between citizens and government.

These types of pro and con considerations should enable police to see, as Professor Mark H. Moore of Harvard University's Kennedy School of Government observed, that "[l]aw enforcement in a free society must strike a deliberate balance between protecting individual rights to privacy (especially from government-sponsored surveillance) and society's interest in detecting criminal offenses and punishing offenders."[13]

Those considerations also suggest the complexity of crime prevention and deterrence and of morally acceptable means to those worthwhile purposes.

Once exposed to such arguments, police students can ask, Would an honorable person work undercover, engage in systematic deception of suspects, and use informers? The obvious reply is that many honorable people have gone undercover, often at considerable personal risk, to gather evidence unobtainable otherwise. Many have used their wits rather than weapons and, by staring down threats and bluffs, preserved their false personas over long periods. They have waited out long delays designed to test their trustworthiness, without being able to communicate with any other law enforcement personnel.

Two measures of their honorability are their resolve not to commit any crimes of entrapment and their attitudes toward informants. Harney and Cross, both very successful and experienced undercover agents, insisted that the most important fact about entrapment is that it is immoral:

> In all his contact with underworld suspects the undercover man must avoid "entrapment," which is a good legal defense for the suspect and, more important, is . . . morally wrong and indefensible. A criminal in the unconscionable narcotic traffic . . . may be given an opportunity to complete a sale of contraband to the officer for the purpose of exposing evidence and it is the right and duty of the officer to afford him the opportunity, when advisable in obtaining evidence. But no officer, by word or deed, should lure into a wrongful act a person who, on his own initiative, had no intent to commit a crime. Brutal frankness should suggest that if anyone is to "do time" under these circumstances it should be the officer.[14]

Harney and Cross were equally straightforward about the treatment of informants:

> Obtaining and managing informers is a fine police art. . . .
> Important in this area is the reputation of the law enforcement

agency and the individual officer for integrity, fair dealing, and intelligent police operation. In many cases the informer takes a considerable personal risk. Like any of the rest of us, in danger he would want to be in the hands of competent people. The officer should be completely fair with the informer. He should not misrepresent nor hold out false promises. . . . He should not humiliate or degrade him. He should see that the full powers of all police agencies having jurisdiction are invoked if the informer is harmed or threatened.[15]

Their approach shows that the issues are not simple and that responsible advocates of undercover operations do not believe that they are free of moral restraints or of standards of decency.

Serious discussion should be welcomed on whether the various statements of proponents and critics are true. For example, does being deceptive toward a narcotics dealer diminish the agent? I do not see how, nor do I understand why deception should be by its nature coercive. Neither should deception and violence be lumped together as affronts to human decency. The movement of police away from brutality and toward more sophisticated investigations is a mark of professionalism and civility.

Good undercover work bears no resemblance to the deception of Shakespeare's character Iago, who convinces Othello that his wife is unfaithful. He takes advantage of Othello's free and open nature, which "thinks men honest that but seem to be so, and will as tenderly be led by th' nose as asses are."[16]

A jealous, vengeful man, Iago employs deceit to gratify his own passion to destroy two people. In such a person, one sees how deception and violence can be kindred instruments of evil, but not everyone who uses deception is as vile as Iago.

Some undercover operations go badly awry, as illustrated in Lawrence Lindeman's *Underground Agent*. After eighteen months working undercover with the Hell's Angels motorcycle gang and obtaining numerous arrests of high-level narcotics traffickers, a California police officer could not recover control of his life. He abused drugs and alcohol and was finally imprisoned for bank robbery.

Vanderick Desper, an exemplary police officer in Montgomery County, Pennsylvania, also went undercover and became a drug addict. His experience raises questions of how long officers should remain under-cover at a stretch, what they should be told never to do, and what sorts of supervision they should be guaranteed. Desper's downfall came from using drugs to win the confidence of dealers, a practice he described as "not infrequent among narcotics officers." When he went back to work, after treatment for addiction, he said, "I was treated like I had leprosy. . . . Nobody helped me. They let me down. They let me and my family suffer. It was hypocritical."[17]

Such examples illuminate the absolute necessity of departmental policy that refuses to compromise an officer for the sake of an investigation or to allow the use of drugs undercover except when threatened with death. Since many dealers do not use drugs, their confidence might be won by saying, "I don't put that in my body," or "I am a businessman, not a user." If not, the investigation should be sacrificed, not the officer.

The fundamental principle of undercover work and informant use is that the police officer must be in control, not the informer or the dealers. Because dealers and informers are in the business of selling things, officers must learn to use their advantage as buyers to control events.

At the same time, many informers are con men and con women who must be kept at a certain distance. Moreover, most of us do not have an entirely clean conscience and tend to resent informers, so care must be taken against prejudice toward them. Some informants are courageous in facing hard decisions and taking severe risks. Clean officers who work as informants in external investigations of narcotics corruption in police departments run great risks and merit our respect. Former Mafia enforcers who wear wires in racketeering and murder investigations also risk their lives.

Not every way of being in control is either decent or productive. Jonathan Rubinstein, the author of *City Police*, told of an officer who intended to turn a waitress at a lunch counter into an informant:

> She thinks I don't know she's hustlin' the truckdrivers. She'll find out tomorrow. I don't care if she makes a few bucks on her back, but she is gonna tell me what I want to know.[18]

That attitude may coerce an informant in the short run but will generate neither trustworthiness nor reliability. If the woman tells others, the officer may find difficulty in getting information on the street. Arrogance of power limits its own effectiveness.

The lesson to be learned is that one genuine good can conflict with another. Honesty and lawfulness in government officials and respect for privacy and friendship can be brought by circumstances into conflict with other goods, such as conviction of the guilty, protection of the public, and prevention of crime. Such conflicts are no trivial matter. The importance of the values in conflict must be recognized to appreciate the need for restraint, limits, and accountability, all of which are crucial for undercover investigations to be legitimate.

Sociologist Gary T. Marx said of undercover operations:

> [P]aradoxically, no matter what action is taken, there are moral costs. There are clear costs whenever the government uses deceit. . . . But not to use the tactics can have costs, too. . . . The danger of automatically applied technical, bureaucratic, or occupational subcultural formulas lies in their potential for generating the self-deluding and morally numbing conclusion that a cost-free solution is possible.[19]

At least some of those costs are paid by the undercover agents themselves. Those who go undercover voluntarily sacrifice the opportunity for wholeness that consists of being the same person in public and private. They engage in practices as part of a public persona that they reject in their private lives and their normal professional lives. Their undercover deception may not coerce, but it is intended to disarm and when successful may render those deceived easier to coerce.

The acceptance of extremely dangerous responsibilities, however, tends not to diminish but to ennoble us. We owe undercover officers of good character a special debt of gratitude that may increase if their duties require them to engage in authorized lawbreaking. And we owe them our assurance that while undercover they are not alone, that being out of sight does not take them out of mind. They must have colleagues and superiors with whom they can be the same person in public and private.

Identifying Relevant Reasons for Decisions

As Lon L. Fuller, then Carter Professor of Jurisprudence at Harvard Law School, observed in *The Morality of Law*, "Even if a man is answerable only to his own conscience, he will answer more responsibly if he is compelled to articulate the principles on which he acts."[20] A police officer should learn to ask, Is there a moral problem here, or is the problem answered by departmental regulations and policies, or by the law? Or is the answer morally obvious? If not, on what reasons is the issue to be decided? What principles and consequences should be taken into account?

Here are some cases that have been raised with me that invite those questions; I have suggested the lines of reasoning and the resources of the department to be used in facing those problematic situations. Since problems like them have been deliberated for centuries in law enforcement without arriving at any simple all-purpose solutions, readers should not expect to find them either in this book or in their discussions with fellow officers. To arrive at a solution, more of the specific circumstances of each case would have to be known than can be conveyed here. Some approaches, however, are clearly more fruitful than others. By considering the situations that follow, together with the suggested approaches to a solution, officers can improve their ability to address similar difficulties they will encounter on the job.

- While driving a new patrol car, you become suspicious of its speedometer. A check confirms that at fifty-five miles per hour, by the gauge, your speedometer reading is 25 percent above your actual speed. What should you do about the traffic citations for speeding that you have issued while driving that car? Why?

Officers should ask whether they would defend the citations in court while admitting that their equipment for speed detection was malfunctioning. Would they consider it fair for a driver to receive a ticket from an officer working with defective equipment—especially if the violation were borderline? Should some corrective measure be taken—such as a formal letter of remission and apology to unfairly cited motorists? These questions suggest consideration of possible consequences and call for the application of principles of consistency and justice.

- You are a team with Officer X, who drinks heavily or plays around with women on duty, or uses his position as an officer to take economic advantage of retailers and others, or accepts bribes from inefficient towing services with city contracts, or accepts bribes from criminal elements. What should you do in each case?

What other information, if any, do you need to deliberate responsibly? What principles should you apply in reaching a decision? Consider the following observation of Aristotle:

> Suppose . . . I have made a friend of a man in the belief that he is a person of good character, and he turns out—or one gets that impression—to be a scoundrel. Am I to go on treating him as a friend? Surely that is out of the question. . . . Should we then . . . break off the friendship on the spot? Not, I suggest, invariably but only when the friend is incurably bad. So long as he is capable of redemption our duty is to give him our support.[21]

The department's policies on conduct becoming an officer are clear for such misconduct. Is this counsel affected by that fact or by your being police officers who must bear the public trust?

Those approaches recall police to the nature of their mission and the kinds of conduct that impair its fulfillment. Normally, they lead to discussion of what it means to be compromised by bribes, sexual favors, and the like. They may be supplemented by stories or questions that disclose the potential consequences of such forms of misconduct.

At the same time, the questions provide an opportunity to discuss loyalty to friends—loyalty that does not allow you to stand idly by when your friend's career and happiness are at risk. The department's resources for helping officers with problems, such as peer counseling and medical care, can be examined. These resources also expand the alternatives available to their colleagues. How to report corruption, whom to approach, and how to follow up may then be discussed.

Questions of that kind lead to discussion of conflicting standards and ideals within police departments. Tell the truth, but maintain silence about other officers. Do not get involved, but be compassionate. Be faithful to your partner, but do not tolerate misbehavior. In many departments, such standards stand in a kind of rough and informal hierarchy: Confidentiality, even secrecy, between partners is more binding than silence about other officers; maintaining silence is more important than disclosing minor infractions but less important than disclosing major misconduct; and so on.

Such practices and unwritten codes of conduct suggest an underlying sense that to live and work effectively together, we must have some measure of give, some willingness to compromise. Compromise is not by its nature wrong, but some compromises are wrongful. The challenge is to discern which compromises are decent and which are not.

In this case, pleasure and profit on one side conflict with responsible behavior on the other. The pleasures of alcohol, sex, and extra money are the motives for misconduct. The behavior is wrong on its face, it is dangerous to self and partner, it is likely to grow worse, and it is a betrayal of the citizenry. Toleration of it is clearly unacceptable. Compromising with such forms of wrongdoing has no justification: It does not contribute to reliable partnership, dependable friendship, or good work. Given that such compromising must stop, the questions become: What should I do to stop it? And what should I do about what has already happened? The first question is one of proportionality and of means sufficient to the purpose. The second may be the harder, and for that reason, one should learn what can be done to stop such behavior as soon as it becomes known.

- Circumstances make it clear that enforcing the curfew in a city park can lead to violence, possibly on a wide scale. As the officer called to the scene by local residents who want the curfew enforced, what should you do?

An officer should learn beforehand not to tackle this kind of situation alone. Enforcement requires backup and a commitment of forces that may disrupt normal police services. If many arrests are contemplated, both jail and court officials may have to be warned. Accordingly, the situation calls for a command decision to risk a confrontation or to work with community groups to avoid one. Thus, the main questions about consequences involve the risk of taking steps that will lead to an uncontrolled situation. Such steps should be authorized and planned by command.

- Does a citizen who has made unique contributions to the community deserve special treatment when he is found to be driving while intoxicated? How should you treat a complaint against an apparently upstanding citizen by a complainant whose character is questionable?

Both questions invite discussion of the relevance of the given facts. Is the community service of the drunk driver relevant? Does the good citizen pose less of a risk to others—and to himself—when driving drunk than anyone else does? Is it fair to give special consideration? How does the department routinely treat first offenses? Are you serving the interests of the good citizen by overlooking his dangerous behavior?

In the second instance, is the character of the two individuals relevant? Is the complaint sufficiently implausible so that resources would be wasted pursuing it? Do the circumstances of the complaint suggest anything about the complainant's motives? Does the complainant waffle about having to testify in court?

By taking the inquiry in those directions, the discussion can emphasize that fear of the consequences of enforcing the law with a powerful citizen is no justification for failure of enforcement. Once, when the question of drunk driving was put to me in class, I learned that the violator was a powerful political figure who had influence on the police department's budget. After some officers criticized the inexperienced officer who had arrested him, we discussed the contempt the person might feel for police who were afraid to apply the law. Suspicion of their integrity in other matters might result.

- While investigating what is obviously the suicide of a young boy, you learn from his distraught mother that the boy's father had always been hard on him and she thinks the boy always viewed his younger brother as the favorite. The father fears that, too, and is suffering massive feelings of guilt. Continuing your investigation, you discover a note written by the dead boy. It says, "I have been a bother to you ever since Tommy was born. I no longer wish to be an embarrassment to you." You fear for the emotional well-being of the parents. What should you do with the note?

This is an issue of officer discretion. What do departmental policies allow? Within those limits, is there any obligation to disclose the note to the parents? If the officer has a right not to disclose it, should he exercise the right? The note must be made known to the medical examiner, of course, but what would be the point of disclosure to the parents?

The boy clearly intended his parents to see the note. It is his last testament, his last words to them. Normally, we honor the last wishes of the deceased, and our respect for their wishes has to be balanced against the consequences for the living. My sense is that the police should intrude on the relation between the boy and his parents with great caution. My own experience with student suicide suggests that at some point the parents should be made aware of the note.

- While working a stakeout, you discover $9,000 in a paper bag in a garbage can. Since you are utterly alone, no one would know if you kept the money. What should you do?

  Suppose, as actually happened, that you turn in the money, which an elderly man reclaims. He dumps the money on the desk, counts it, looks at you, and says, "You son of a bitch, it's a good thing it's all here." What should you do?

Here, departmental policies and the requirements of honesty are obvious. The main point is to remind inexperienced officers of the folly of expecting gratitude from every citizen for a job well done. Good officers do their duty because it is their duty, without expecting a reward. A story of this kind tends to generate both laughter and cynicism. The humor may be drawn upon as an antidote to the bitterness. The discussion of ethical issues should not be humorless.

- You and your partner stop a car that has been driven erratically through a red light. The intoxicated driver produces a license from another state and offers money to each of you. As you take him downtown, he increases his offer. After you cite him for DWI, do you also charge him with attempted bribery? Suppose the police are corrupt in his hometown where traffic violations are settled by passing money to them under the table. Does this make a difference?

This case provides opportunity to discuss actions people commit while incapacitated. Sometimes we treat drunkenness as an excuse for conduct we would not otherwise tolerate. By contrast, Aristotle described Athenian law that holds a man who commits wrong actions while drunk doubly responsible and calls for double punishment, because he has brought the incapacity on himself. The case also raises the question of the standards accepted elsewhere. When speeders say that drivers can go ten miles per hour over the speed limit in their home state, should you let them do so here as well? Obviously not. How is attempted bribery different? Or is the drunken driving citation enough?

- In addition to your regular duties as a police officer, you work in security at a local department store, where you see an old woman conceal several items of children's clothing. After apprehending her, you learn that her pension and Social Security benefits are insufficient to buy gifts for her grandchildren. What should you do? What factors go into the decision?

This problem can be used to highlight knowledge of local agencies that assist the poor. Where can the woman find inexpensive or free clothing and toys for her grandchildren? If the stolen items are returned, the merchant will probably decline to press charges, so the issue is whether the woman's circumstances can be improved.

- After working morals for some time, you have learned that certain gambling rooms in the city "have the blessing"—that is, political and administrative pressure is exerted on the police to refrain from inspection or arrests. To your knowledge, no police are on the pad; you conclude that political contributions are made to get this favorable treatment. Since you do close other gambling operations, you begin to feel like the agent of those interests. You realize you can do virtually nothing about this policy by yourself. What should you do? Why?

What are the differences between the duties of a patrol officer and a command officer in such a case? If the problem is reported and the command officers do nothing, is a patrol officer obligated to take further steps? If the Internal Affairs Division has been informed and does not act, should the officer then forget it? Should a chief who learns of the matter treat it as trivial compared with direct bribery?

Truthful accounts of past efforts of the department are needed here to ensure that an officer is never put in this lonely situation. If the department routinely allows such betrayals of its own officers, it is in a condition of moral disgrace. The increased levels of responsibility that attend increased authority can be discussed here, together with accounts of the usefulness of external agencies, such as the FBI. The emotionally charged issues of informing should be addressed, and with them the need for courage in the performance of duty.

The only way for a department to come clean in such a case is to reverse the administrative pressure. This fact invites discussion of honorable and dishonorable compromise with political interests.

- On a snowy December morning you are called to assist the court bailiff in an eviction of a family of nine, who insist that they have not been notified. All procedures required by the court have, however, been satisified, and the family is six months behind in rent. The property owner and the bailiff are insistent on eviction, even though the family has no place to go or to put the furniture. What can you do? What should you do? Do you want other facts?

Again, the issue is the officer's knowledge of available alternatives and services in the community. Caution in estimating the possible reactions of desperate people can also be discussed.

- As a captain, you are visited one morning by the wife of one of your officers, a good officer who does his work properly. She complains of his carousing, seeing another woman, spending money recklessly, and striking her during quarrels, and she wants you to talk with him. You know that locker room gossip supports her charges, but his private behavior appears not to affect his professional performance. Is his private life any of your business? What should you do?

Because problems in private life are often relevant to professional performance, a command officer may want to look into the officer's performance at work more carefully. Once the wife approached him, the matter was no longer private. If she does not want to press charges for assault, the issue becomes what counseling programs are available within the department. A confidential talk with the officer, or a request to a friend, priest, or other intermediary to encourage him to seek counseling inside or outside the department may be useful. An expression of concern that his problems may otherwise grow worse and end in disciplinary action would be appropriate. Given the extent to which marital problems affect police, a department should be prepared to address such matters.

- While off duty, you attend a meeting in your neighborhood of Little League Baseball managers, coaches, and umpires for the new season. You recognize a man introduced as a coach as someone who was taken downtown in connection with a sexual assault of a young boy. The man was released for lack of evidence—the boy was not sure he was the man. As a citizen and a police officer, what should you do?

Here departmental policies and the code of ethics on confidentiality may be reviewed. Although the man must be presumed innocent, he may have a record of convictions for sex offenses. Would that be part of the public record, and could it legitimately be brought to the attention of other league officials? How about a record of other arrests without conviction?

Can respect for confidentiality and presumption of innocence be squared with concern for the safety of the children? The conflict between those ideals may not yield any entirely satisfactory solution. The officer can review profiles of sex offenders and discuss the case confidentially with a departmental psychologist. That should result in a better judgment of the levels of risk and of possible actions.

- As the investigating detective in a serious felony case, you discover excellent physical evidence that a particular suspect is guilty. But you also discover information that, if made available to the defense, would increase the chances of acquittal. What are your obligations, and to whom?

This question suggests the wisdom of including a prosecuting attorney in some sessions. Like defense lawyers, prosecutors do not like surprises at trial or in plea bargaining. The question will probably be raised whether the defense could acquire the information for itself. Perhaps more important, the information may make the prosecutor doubt that the suspect should be held for trial. Laws about the rights of the defense to information disclosed by the investigation should be explained.

- After the brutal murder of your partner, who was very close to you, you frequently stop his wife for driving while intoxicated. She leaves her children untended and is becoming generally unstable in her grief. What should you do?

The initial question is why this has been allowed to become frequent before the problem is addressed. Does the department make provision for support and assistance to such spouses? If so, have they been called into play—or can they be? Clearly, the situation is likely to grow worse without intervention. The children could lose their mother to an accident or to imprisonment for an accident lethal to others. A friend cannot allow this to continue. The officer may seek advice within the department, from service agencies, and from groups that provide support in the face of grief and substance abuse and dependency.

- You are called to an average-income home by neighbors because of the sustained crying of a baby. Finding the house a shambles and four young children who have been beaten, you also learn that the father is away and the mother is a heavy drinker. The eldest child, who ran the household, has just run off with her boyfriend. As you are making arrangements for the children with a children's home, the mother returns drunk and threatens to kill herself if you take the children. What are your options? What should you do? Does the fact that the household is "average-income" make a difference?

The income is not relevant, but the nature of the neighborhood may be. In some ethnic areas, after neighbors call for assistance and learn of a problem, they say to police, "No report, no report," meaning that they will address the problem themselves. They are often more effective than the overburdened social service agencies. To decide what to do, officers have to know their beat and the sources of assistance that operate formally and informally within it.

Clearly, the children cannot be left to a mother who is not in control of her own life. Whether they must be moved—and whether the mother should be taken to a detoxification center or hospital—must be decided. If so, the mother's threats should be told to the medical personnel.

In general, a desperate person's threats should not deter an officer from safeguarding others. The mother cannot be allowed to determine the resolution of the problem.

- As a patrol officer with years of experience, you have come to know and trust (at least in certain contexts) several informants and have promised to keep their identities secret. One day you are ordered within the department to divulge the identity of an informant. What should you do?

Did you have a right to make the promise? Do you have a right—or a duty—to keep it? What are the department's policies about informants and about auditing officer-informant contacts and payments? Is command supervision of informant contacts standard practice? Should it be? If you have knowingly made a promise in violation of departmental practice to persuade the informant to cooperate, what are your subsequent duties?

Such questions may be used to introduce further consideration of obedience to orders. Suppose a superior gives an order you believe to be unwise or immoral or in violation of policy. How should you proceed? Suppose, for instance, that undercover narcotics officers are told, off the record, to make themselves credible to dealers by using drugs.

The inquiry may show that some disagreements are trivial and that obedience to an order is both right and obligatory, while other disagreements over principle must be faced. Compromise may be possible, but it is not likely to be easy. Such distinctions show that some compromises are decent and some are wrong. They also reveal that a person who repudiates a colleague over a trifle makes a serious error, just as an officer who compromises everything does.

- During an arrest of five suspects by you and three other officers, one of the officers is verbally abused by a suspect being escorted to a shield car. You do not see what else happens, except that the officer strikes the suspect on the arm with his nightstick. In his report, the officer does not mention that but says that the suspect bruised his arm while entering the vehicle. When internal affairs later asks you about the suspect's complaint that the officer struck him, you know that the allegation is true, but, for all you know, the officer may have been justified in striking him. What should you do? What if the record of this officer is outstanding?

A case like this can be used to show the importance of explicit expectations between partners. Although new partners would be unfriendly to announce in advance everything they will and will not tolerate, they owe it to themselves and to each other to make known any expectations that could not be taken for granted—for instance, not covering for a partner who brutalizes prisoners. Beyond that, officers should deal forthrightly with each case as it comes up. When their perception of an incident differs, or one has clearly omitted or concealed facts, the two had better sort out their duties to the public, the department, and each other. Although such conversations may be difficult, they are preferable to the development of habits that cause conflict or the erosion of standards.

In this case, the officer might feel obliged to encourage the other officer to tell the rest of the story to the Internal Affairs Department (IAD). Or the two officers might "stonewall" the IAD and agree not to get into such a situation again. Although such a course is clearly wrong with respect to the past, its long-term consequences might be good if their resolve is more than just words. Discussion of this fact can disclose that in moral deliberation, we are concerned for principles—such as that of honesty—and not only with consequences.

In many police departments, officers feel a strong sense of responsibility to a suspect in handcuffs. They understand the officer quoted by William Ker Muir Jr.: "When you've handcuffed a guy, you are taking care of his welfare and his rights, and you have to look out for them and not treat him as if he were in the ordinary situation where he can look out for himself."[22] Partners ought to have that much, at least, clear between them from the beginning. Finally, if a partner behaves badly, an officer can request a change. One officer who was exposed to the small-time corruption of a partner on his first day as a street cop opted for another partner. He was given one and went on to become one of the great police administrators and investigators of our time.

- Investigating a homicide, you become suspicious of the story told by the daughter and son-in-law of the victim. As you question the son-in-law, you point out the inconsistencies in his story, although you do not know what happened or who committed the crime, nor do you have reason to suspect that the son-in-law was involved. Nervously, he assures you that he did not do it, but he knows who did. He volunteers to tell what happened if you promise him immunity and promise to keep secret his identity as the informant. What should you do?

Officers cannot guarantee immunity and in well-run departments have no right to conceal the identity of an informant from specific supervisors. Once the son-in-law has gone this far, an effective interrogator can probably elicit the information, either by encouraging words or by reminders about legal penalties for concealing evidence and obstructing justice.

- You and your partner, and possibly other units, are called to a family disturbance in which a sixteen-year-old girl has badly hurt her mother with a knife. Since investigation reveals that the daughter was not defending herself, and the extent of the injuries makes her action felonious. Moreover, she has been in repeated fights at home and at school, though not charged previously, and she has been under psychiatric treatment for over six months.

  Both the girl's mother and the psychiatrist hired by the family object strongly to your charging the girl or involving juvenile court. The mother refuses consent for a second medical opinion. What are your alternatives? Which should you choose?

In this case, like others, the officer would show good judgment by using the department's resources, a police psychiatrist, for example. Obviously, judgment will have to be exercised as well in assessing the credibility of the mother and the family's doctor. Since the girl has proved that she is dangerous, should other considerations weigh as heavily as this one? Should you consult school officials?

Although it seems hazardous to allow the girl to go on without intervention, the normal procedures of the local juvenile court must be considered. Will the girl simply be released to the custody of her mother?

- As a uniformed patrol officer, you have found the information given to you by a voluntary informant reliable and instrumental in making cases against drug dealers. Later, you learn that his motives have been self-serving. He is a dealer seeking to eliminate competition. What should you do? What other information do you need, if any, to decide?

When this issue was raised in class, I was a little surprised that the officer had not suspected from the first that the informant was a dealer. Many of the best police tell informants that they will be arrested and prosecuted if they commit any secret crimes regardless of their informant status. In practice, this is no idle threat. Several questions apply to this issue: What is departmental policy on criminal activity by informants and on their previously concealed criminal actions? How serious are their crimes? If an informant is credible because he deals drugs, should he continue in that activity—but with the knowledge of the police? If the informant deliberately deceives the officer, should he be arrested and prosecuted? Police experienced with informants can offer guidance on such questions, especially on police control of the informant and the risks of tolerating deception by the informant.

- Working an office where complaints are received, you often get calls from intoxicated people reporting auto theft. Many of these complaints turn out to be untrue—the caller has misplaced the car, loaned it out, or abandoned it after an accident, or it was repossessed or towed for illegal parking. Theft reports cost time and effort, and so does removing them from the records. Should one have a policy about responding to such calls? If so, what? If not, how should one decide what to do?

This situation encourages discussion of discretion and policy as well as of limitations of available resources. No priority should be given to complainants who are obviously intoxicated or cannot say where a car was left. If they call after sobering up, they can be referred to the impound lot or elsewhere, and their complaints can be handled normally. If departmental policy says otherwise, then its rationale should be discussed.

- You work a district that has habitual drunkards. Arresting them is costly and time-consuming; it leaves your district unprotected; and it does no apparent good, because they are frequently back in the street soon after. But if left alone, they often do not care for themselves and bother others. What should you do? Has some other agency obligations on this score?

Attention to local details is imperative here. In some districts lack of funds has closed "detox" centers, jails are overflowing, and hospital services are unavailable. There is no place to take the helpless wino. In others, police and related services are well enough staffed to help take public drunkards off the streets.

The issue of the realism of departmental policies may be raised, and the procedures for review of policy discussed. In addition, any population of homeless or others who need help harbors a criminal element that preys on them. Even if homeless alcoholics cannot be taken off the streets, they can be protected by police who are alert to crimes perpetrated against them and who seek to apprehend the perpetrators. Departmental preparations to protect the helpless as severe weather approaches should also be raised.

- As a police officer, you have become thoroughly competent during several years of work, including patrol in several districts. Currently, you are assigned to the narcotics undercover unit; you have managed to get very near the top levels of a major drug-distributing organization.

  Accompanied by several members of the organization, you are on your way to a big drug transaction. Stopped at an intersection, you see two men violently, perhaps murderously, pistol whipping the owner of a local carry-out store as they rob it. The episode is noticed by your companions as well. What should you do? Why?

Many such questions can be answered by departmental policies and regulations or by moral principles that can be straightforwardly applied. The real usefulness of institutional policies and of well-established habits and clear principles is to show that such issues do not have to be approached alone or without guidance. Still, cases such as this one are likely to generate disagreement over the relevance and relative weight of reasons adduced.

In the case of the undercover officer who witnesses a life-threatening crime in progress, some police officers held in classroom discussion that

> officers should give priority to undercover assignments because: (a) they are assigned to them; (b) all the normal duties of police service are suspended for undercover officers, as they are for wartime spies; (c) a lot of money may have been spent on the undercover investigation that would be wasted if the cover were blown; and (d) in the circumstances described, the officer's life

would be placed at risk just by trying to get out of the car to aid the victim.

One officer asked, "Suppose the victim of the beating were a police officer. Would you go to his aid?" All who had given priority to the undercover assignment earlier replied that they would; if the victim were a police officer, the undercover assignment no longer came first. He then asked why the life of the officer mattered more than the life of the citizen.

A command officer in the class wrote this reply to the statement that the undercover assignment took priority:

> Whether the officer in question is assigned to an undercover role or any other role imaginable, I cannot conceive of a situation where he would be justified in allowing someone to be killed because he failed to act. I agree that one cannot be expected to do what is not possible, but the officer involved would be hard-pressed to satisfy his superiors that his action or lack of action was the only way to go. When any officer feels his assignment is more important than life itself, that officer's values have been misplaced. Police Division procedures are clear on this point as well as the law. If police procedures and the law as applied to criminal matters are not enough, the officer would be guilty of malfeasance, misfeasance, or nonfeasance in office.

Another officer expressed a similar opinion:

> This officer is, in my opinion, morally, legally, and professionally obliged to take whatever action is reasonably possible to prevent the death or serious injury to this victim regardless of his assignment at the time. The fact that he would, in all probability, blow his cover is certainly a consideration, but the life of a citizen is by any measure more important than the successful conclusion of a drug case. Another undercover agent or informant or some other operation might allow for the arrest of these individuals at some later date, but if that victim dies from these injuries, that cannot be corrected.

Both officers appealed to the section of the police manual that says the police department should protect all persons within its jurisdiction from criminal attack.

By such discussion, officers can see how reasons outweigh one another in arriving at sound decisions. The situations should be not only realistic but drawn from the actual experience of police if possible. Everyone should be forthcoming about what actually happened and where things went right or wrong. And everyone should understand that deliberation among colleagues who disagree is not a contest to see who wins. It is a shared pursuit of answers that can be reached by candid and knowledgeable use of intelligence. Deliberation is very different from the entertaining but usually unproductive telling of "war stories." If a class falls into mere exchanges of tales from the streets, practice at reasoning is forgotten.

The Fabric of a Life

Reasonable people deliberate about problematic cases because they understand that what they do matters. Some people who behave badly fail to grasp this. They seem to believe that a human life is made up of isolated actions that affect nothing else. Accordingly, an officer may believe that napping on duty, or "cooping," is all right because it affects nothing else; intemperance is all right because it affects nothing else; being needlessly confrontational is all right; and so on.

This kind of mistake has been made throughout history. It is the mistake of Macbeth and Lady Macbeth, who believe that, by committing murder, they will change only one isolated thing—who will become the next king and queen. They do not expect to be haunted by the blood they spill or to be changed in any way by their behavior. In the Bible, when King David sends Uriah the Hittite to certain death in battle, he believes that he will get Uriah's wife, Bathsheba, for himself and that everything else will remain the same. But as the Prophet Nathan shows David, everything changes when David makes himself into a ruler so unjust. People who make such mistakes are weakened, made worse, or destroyed because they fail to realize that our actions weave a tapestry of our life—beautiful, indifferent, or ugly.

Officers who sleep in a free hotel room while on duty require other officers to work and cover for them. They invite the contempt of hotel employees toward police, they risk returning to duty only half alert, and they steal from the public who pay their salary. In all this, their action reveals serious flaws of character and judgment. Similarly, officers who drink to excess privately are likely to be hungover on duty and more prone to errors of judgment and concentration than they have any right to be. They give less than their best to their colleagues and the public.

Neither does an officer who is needlessly confrontational commit some isolated action. As Aristotle observed more than two thousand years ago, by such rashness an individual

> gives the impression of overacting the part, and his courage is a little suspect. At all events, he would like people to believe that he is animated by the same feelings as the brave man when danger threatens. So he imitates him whenever he can. For this reason, most rash men are of the forcible feeble type. They swagger a good deal when things look bright, but make themselves scarce in the presence of actual danger. . . .
>
> We may add that the rash man is foolhardy, ready for anything before the danger arrives; but, when it does, shearing off. On the other hand, the brave man is gallant in action but undemonstrative beforehand.[23]

Police officers who unnecessarily make a situation confrontational do not fear the right things. They ought to fear needlessly endangering the public, their partners, and themselves, and they therefore ought to be firm but not swaggering. They ought to fear boastfulness that leaves others no room for flexibility and inspires feelings of hatred toward themselves and other police. They ought not to fear the use of force when nothing less will do, but they should fear hasty and precipitate force. They ought to fear in themselves weakness and lack of self-confidence that tempt them to confrontation for fear of losing their dignity. Fearing the right things and seeking to address them forthrightly is neither soft nor irresolute. What is at stake in a needless confrontation is not isolated but woven into the fabric of all of an officer's life.

When I asked a street cop how far officers go in interrogating suspects, she replied that they used phone books—that is, they hit suspects on the head with a telephone directory to intimidate them without leaving bruises. When I asked whether that was department policy, she asked how anyone could be interrogated without a phone book.

Qualified interrogators know more effective legal ways to elicit information from a suspect. That officer clearly took for granted, however, that brutalizing suspects is an isolated action that bears on nothing else. She did not understand that it necessarily involves officers in a conspiracy of silence, since it violates legal rights of citizens. It also violates "official" departmental policy, it requires the preparation of false reports, and it may involve perjury. Our actions have broad consequences, not least in the kinds of people they make of us.

What is taught by academies about ideals should be woven into the realities of the streets and the kinds of cases officers routinely encounter. Just as academy instructors need rich police experience, their instruction should be reinforced by field training officers, who show that it applies in practice. Ethics learned in an academy will be forgotten if field training officers tell new police officers that it is irrelevant to the streets and to real police work.

Police must learn in field training the truth of their academy lessons. Without coherence between academy preparation and field training, and cooperation between teachers and field training officers, even very good academy programs will soon be forgotten by officers in the field.

12

Tragedy and "Noble Cause" Corruption

Every rational being exists as an end in himself and not merely as a means to be arbitrarily used. Act so that you treat humanity, whether in your own person or in that of another, always as an end and never as a means only.

—Immanuel Kant[1]

Education directed to excellence of character and judgment is incomplete without some treatment of tragedy. The treatment is likely to be brief in criminal justice programs, since not all the features of general theory need be covered.

Tragedy may, but does not always, arise from a character flaw, as when blind ambition destroys a person of promise, or pride or hubris brings King Oedipus to grief in Sophocles' drama. Tragedy can also arise from the nature of the human condition itself.

Suppose that a doctor has two patients before him, both dying, but has the time and resources to save only one. The issue is not how he is to decide, but that he is to decide. If he cannot possibly save both—no matter what he does—he must decide. His deciding is not a case of "playing God"; it is a case of fulfilling the duties of a doctor.

That one patient dies, say, for lack of available blood, is tragic but not something the doctor could have prevented. By saving one—as many as he could—the doctor has done the right thing. In such circumstances, a doctor of fine character may feel regret bordering on remorse that he could not do more, even though he acted rightly in doing all he could. He faced the ordeal of judgment without shirking. Because he has behaved rightly and because only wrongful acts can logically be forgiven, we cannot respond to his regret or remorse with forgiveness. Instead, his friends and colleagues should offer comfort to him—and the humane reminder that sometimes the human condition causes tragedy, no matter how hard we try to prevent it.

Tragedy can also arise from the conflict of one undeniable good with another undeniable good, when no amount of effort, intelligence, or good-will can bring the two into harmony. Sometimes we cannot have things both ways. To make the public safe we must arrest and confine the criminally dangerous, but to make the public safe we must also restrain government from presumption of guilt and disregard for due process. Law enforcement officers sometimes know that someone is guilty of a serious crime but either lack evidence or have tainted evidence. The individual remains free to commit crimes against new victims. We are obliged to do everything in our power to safeguard the public and to make government just, but our best efforts cannot always prevent failure.

Despite the heartache, those who have to make practical decisions must acquire the fortitude to go on. They are obliged to give their best despite the stress that will otherwise grind down their aspirations. That is an irreducible element of taking the human condition seriously.

For those reasons, the possession of authority, discretion, and power leads reflective people from morally important but unproblematic cases to questions about extreme cases where tragedy may lurk. Often such cases are hypothetical, sometimes unrealistic. They are invariably extraordinary and distinct from commonplace decency in daily life. The principal value of examining them is that careful analysis can advance subtlety, good reasoning, and a sense of the tragic.

Although law enforcement officials do not always agree which cases are difficult, examples usually resemble the "lifeboat" type of problem. One question goes something like this:

> If you have a perpetrator in custody, and he has information that could save the life of an innocent victim, is it right to use extreme methods to get the information?

Such occurrences are removed from the daily realities of law enforcement. When the question comes up for discussion, I ask for more detail. Even hypothetical cases must be specific. Here is one response:

> Suppose that you have a perpetrator in custody who is known to have kidnapped a victim. The victim is known to be buried alive,

and the perpetrator is known to have the information sufficient to rescue the victim.

Time is short. The perpetrator will not divulge the information under ordinary legal interrogation, even though it is conducted very shrewdly. Is it morally right to exceed your authority and use physical coercion to get the information? Is saving the life of the innocent victim a sufficient end to justify such illegality? Does this noble cause justify a means we would normally consider wrong and evil?

Those types of questions are usually accompanied by others: Do ends justify means? Is there ever a cause so important that it justifies everything? Do noble causes justify illegality and immorality?

Many command personnel deny that this case is problematic or difficult. Police are sworn to uphold the law, they point out, and they have no right to violate it, certainly not by inflicting pain on a prisoner. The situation poses no ordeal, they argue, because the rules on prisoners are clear and unmistakable.

A smaller number admit that the rules are clear but still see a problem: What about the rights of the victim? They feel torn between a clear duty to obey the law and respect the rights of the suspect-perpetrator on the one hand and a sense of duty to try to save the life of an innocent victim on the other.

Some philosophers would direct the inquiry to another question. They say that mistreatment of the prisoner is wrong, but in such an instance—not as a rule—is it an excusable wrong? Should this person, who commits this wrong, under these conditions, this time, for the sake of this victim, be forgiven?

The questions raised by police can illuminate ways of thinking through such conflicts. Although character education would be incomplete without such illumination, hard cases cannot be the initial focus, and should not be the central focus, of academy programs in ethics.

Ends and Means

The meaning of the question, Do ends justify means? is neither simple nor clear. It might mean any or all of the following: (1) Do good ends make actions right? Do they contribute in part to the rightness of actions? (2) Should we take ends and consequences into account in deciding what to do? (3) Are a person's ends relevant to the quality of the person's character and to the praise or blame the person deserves for specific actions?

Clearly, having a good end contributes to the rightness of an act, just as having an evil purpose counts against it. And we do have to take consequences into account. A person's ends are relevant to the esteem the person deserves: One whose purpose is to benefit others deserves greater admiration than one whose purpose is to cause harm or than one utterly indifferent to everyone else.

But these answers do not lead to the conclusion that having a good end is sufficient to make an action right, or that ends and consequences are all we should consider in deciding what to do, or that having good ends is all that matters in a person's character. Furthermore, even if having good ends were the sole determinant of right action, we might still encounter conflicts about what we should do. Good ends can conflict with each other. They can pull us in contrary directions, just as worthwhile principles do.

Accordingly, the answer to the question is, Ends do justify means up to a point, and in certain ways, depending on what you mean, but not simply or unqualifiedly. Human life is just not so simple.

This is the lesson that French Algerian author Albert Camus tried, in July 1943, to teach to a former German friend who had become a Nazi. Camus wrote to him:

> You said to me: "The greatness of my country is beyond price. Anything is good that contributes to its greatness. And in a world where everything has lost its meaning, those who, like us young Germans, are lucky enough to find meaning in the destiny of our nation must sacrifice everything else."
>
> "No," I told you. "I cannot believe that everything must be subordinated to a single end. There are means that cannot be excused. And I should like to be able to love my country and still love justice."[2]

Camus' love of justice is akin to Kant's recognition that people deserve consideration, deserve not to be just used, simply because they are people.

A person is a repository of worth, of significance, even if that person appears without merit. This is the reason we oppose inordinate coercion; once we descend from reasoned persuasion—and respect for each other's freedom—to force, we deny the right to self-determination. Justice constrains us from going any further in this direction than we believe necessary.

American traditions affirm that principle. The right of due process and the prohibition against cruel and unusual punishment in the Eighth Amendment are based on the principle that human beings deserve to be treated as ends and never as mere means, never as objects, no matter how heinous their crimes. This moral tradition of America and other civilized nations contrasts with the gulags of the Soviet Union, where guilt was presumed, trials were a mockery, and cruel punishment routine. Where moral traditions are absent, the consequences are predictable.

Even in war, where enemy troops are often treated as mere obstacles to a nation's will, the Geneva Convention reflects the idea that nations still have an obligation to treat prisoners as human beings. Those standards prohibit torture because it is inexcusable brutality against a defenseless person. They should apply even to prisoners who refuse to divulge highly valuable information, but they are often violated. The North Vietnamese, for example, tortured American POWs to make them assist in their propaganda efforts. The Americans were routinely treated as mere means to their purposes.

American traditions stand squarely opposed to use of the third degree in interrogating suspects. Such methods violate at least the Fifth and Eighth Amendments, as well as *Miranda* and other judicial interpretations of those guarantees. Those amendments are not pieces of advice to law enforcement—they are fundamental law, the foundation of our way of life.

Yet in law enforcement as well as other national affairs, we are driven to the question whether illegal actions that violate the rights of citizens are ever morally right or excusable. I call that the question of "noble cause" corruption. Are police ever justified, or do they ever deserve to be excused, in breaking fundamental laws, not for personal gain, but for a purpose that appeals to our basic moral sensibilities? That is a question about extraordinary situations, when we cannot stand for all the goods we judge to be of the highest order, fulfill our highest principles, and respond to our most strongly felt duties in the treatment of all persons involved. The conflict between the rights of the innocent victim and the rights of the suspect-perpetrator is such a case.

Our response to that difficult question has crucial consequences. Since the literature about it leaves much to be desired, I have discussed it with philosophers and other scholars, lawyers, public officials, police chiefs, military officers, religious leaders, and corporate executives, whose counsel is paraphrased or quoted below. Sensible persons faced with hard problems should turn to the wisest people they know—the wisest friends, the best authors, and the historic figures and contemporaries they most admire. Their example is as precious as any moral precept and their judgment a powerful supplement to our own.

Three points are basic. First, since ends do not necessarily justify means, a good end cannot justify a means in a context that makes it wrong and evil. In a primitive setting where the law is nonexistent or ineffectual and where conditions of due process are not yet established, we might argue that physical coercion of a prisoner is at times justifiable. A lone champion of justice who behaves with regard for morality could be the only criminal justice system in existence. Or if a public official has thoroughly corrupted the system and become impervious to its sanctions, our main question might be one about what justice requires, not one about ends and means. But where civilizing law does have a hold, as in America, violations of fundamental civil liberties and laws, violations of oaths of office, abuses of authority and power—all betrayals of the public trust—are wrong and cannot be justified by any end.

Knowing this, however, does not help much in deciding what to do or tell us whether as decent people we should ever use evil means. It leaves open the question whether we should ever excuse the use of evil means because the end is undeniably good, lesser means are ineffective, and the motives of the agent are unquestionably noble.

Second, revising regulations and rules cannot eliminate tragedy and conflicts of ideals. Although revisions can alter the mechanics of accountability, they cannot change elements of the human condition. After the United States restricted the use of weapons by its ships defending tankers from attack by Iran, thirty-seven Americans died in an attack on the U.S.S. *Stark*. After the restrictions were relaxed, the U.S.S. *Vincennes* mistakenly shot down an Iranian civilian airliner and killed all aboard. Both events were tragic, despite efforts to establish the best policies.

Third, inflicting pain sadistically, with pleasure and without regret, can never be excused. Even in a conflict in which allegiances have been staked out and the pursuit of information has become brutal, thrilling to the torture of others, viewing them at most as containers of information, is wrong. It is depraved and inexcusable—even if the victim is loathsome.

Interrogators may pretend to be sadistic, however, and use fear rather than pain as their instrument. In Bertolt Brecht's play, the pope—who wants Galileo to recant his scientific discoveries—addresses the cardinal inquisitor:

> POPE (exhausted): It is clearly understood: he is not to be tortured. (Pauses.) At the very most, he may be shown the instruments.

> INQUISITOR: That will be adequate, Your Holiness. Mr. Galilei understands machinery.[3]

Who Is to Say (What to Do)?

To begin reflecting about a hard case, we should ask who should actually have to suffer the ordeal of making the decision. Asking whom we should trust differs from asking, What is the answer? Because hard cases must be approached with a knowledge both of particulars and of general principles, we must determine who in a police department should be faced with a moral issue so hard and of such profound consequence.

Most adults should reflect on and talk about painfully hard problems, which can contribute to the moral and intellectual maturation of younger people as well. Certainly, many police of all ranks can meet the challenge of demanding thought, but the issue here is, Who should actually have to make such a decision, not in thought, but in practice?

Not every moral question should require a decision by every officer, for some are beginners who are not qualified to decide problems of great magnitude. Beginners should not be asked to risk a career—for that may be at stake—in making decisions that go beyond their experience.

While citizens generally should try to develop informed opinions on public issues of all kinds, we would neither entrust policymaking to amateurs nor ask them to live with the trials of setting policy. As Walter Lippmann said, such decisions call for a kind of knowledge—not to speak of an experience and a seasoned judgment—which cannot be had by glancing at newspapers, listening to snatches of radio comment, watching politicians perform on television, hearing occasional lectures, and reading a few books. It would not be enough to make a man competent to decide whether to amputate a leg, and it is not enough to qualify him to choose war or peace, to arm or not to arm, to intervene or to withdraw, to fight or to negotiate.[4]

Although we may disagree with them, we want officials with "experience and a seasoned judgment" to have the authority to make such decisions.

As history teaches, the ordeal of judgment may be dreadful. When France fell to Germany in World War II, for example, the French government advocated alliance with Germany, not merely submission, so the French Navy seemed likely to become part of Germany's arsenal. Winston Churchill, as Britain's prime minister, had to decide whether to attack those ships, manned by former allies, to deny them to the enemy. He did so, thereby preventing German naval dominance. Although the decision was not compounded by any question of illegality, he described it as the most painful one of his life. Such hard decisions are part of the ordeal of command, not of lesser rank.

Police are the constituted authority for the use of force within society. They are uniformed as a mark of their authority and competence. Police departments have a structure of command just so that problems beyond the scope of junior personnel will not fall to them. Only in this way can the police live up to the public trust and safeguard against erosion of morale, which results when daily responsibilities simply cannot be met.

In many departments, policies on weaponry, ammunition, and the use of weapons other than sidearms are made by command rather than patrol personnel. In well-run departments, supportive and trustworthy authority flows from the top. The hardest issues should therefore be faced by officers with the most seniority and highest rank. Officers who have risen to command rank are probably better qualified than anyone else inside or outside law enforcement to identify the hardest moral questions. They know from experience the temptation to twist the law or manipulate the facts in routine matters in the streets. They know the common view that some excesses in the use of authority are necessary. They should therefore consider where such views lead when the stakes are life, death, and fundamental law, and they may then help the next generation of police grapple with such issues.

Every person I have consulted on this issue insists that only mature adults with considerable experience should ever contemplate actually practicing extreme and illegal conduct. The moral burden is simply too heavy for personnel inexperienced in policing, who are not competent or prepared to make such decisions. They lack experience and information, they are less able to identify and apply legal means, and they have not had the opportunity to reflect on hard cases. Those police would more likely guess than think their way to a decision.

My colleagues do not mean to suggest that patrol and midrank personnel are without deep moral insight and great personal maturity. The moral character of police forces often rests as much on the influence and training provided by sergeants as on higher officers, they say, and seasoned officers of all ranks can arrive at compelling conclusions about such issues. Considerations both of authority and of fairness, however, imply that the highest ranking personnel ought to make such decisions and live with the consequences.

The consequences of extreme illegality within law enforcement are so grave that only those in a position to appreciate their gravity should be involved. Police officers who step so far beyond their authority as to coerce a prisoner physically have ceased to function as legitimate enforcers of the laws under the Constitution. They must be prepared to lose their job, to see the courts dismiss all charges against the suspect, or to deny the admissibility of evidence and to stand trial themselves for assault and battery or more severe charges.

If the suspect-perpetrator goes free because the evidence becomes inadmissible, the police official who violated the rights of the prisoner in custody will have turned loose on society a murderous kidnapper, who can again prey on the innocent. If the victim dies despite the efforts of police, the crime for which the perpetrator can no longer be prosecuted is first-degree murder. Furthermore, no matter how brutal the official becomes, the prisoner may still lie. In that case, the police official has forsaken duty and all else for nothing.

No less important, command personnel are obliged never to permit officers under their command to employ third-degree interrogations. Even if they are willing to act *in extremis* as individuals and accept the consequences, they cannot as officers tolerate such conduct in the ranks. And if they are hypocrites, they cannot lead their subordinates effectively or deserve their confidence.

If senior personnel have a right to consider such action, how can they avoid hypocrisy and remain faithful to the central duties of command? Since any attempt to justify illegal behavior after the fact would come too late, the question is, How should they stand on the record in advance?

With respect to policymaking, command personnel should keep in mind that most of us tend to go a bit beyond the set limits. If the speed limit is fifty-five miles per hour, for example, ordinary traffic will go sixty or more. Since minor illegal infractions are likely to be commonplace, setting the limits a bit tighter than we intend to hold is prudent, so long as doing so does not make policing impossible or render the limits ridiculous or yield an appearance of indifference to infractions. Departmental limits should therefore be set slightly tighter than the legal treatment of suspects allows. Then, minor and predictable infractions will not violate the law.

If command personnel take a realistic view toward slight overstepping, they can specify some limits as absolute. They can make clear, for example, that prohibition of third-degree methods is absolute and that they delegate no authority whatsoever in that matter. They can say candidly that, should any discretion ever be exercised on that issue, it will be reserved to the highest authority only—with no exceptions. To follow this path, the command officers must be forthright and not hide from the decisions of high office. Although they would avoid hypocrisy, they would still have to answer why rank carries a right to consider lawbreaking.

The answer is that the hardest moral questions cannot be reduced to questions of legality. Reserving the right of decision to the highest authority exhibits respect for the law, and it discloses that no principle—including the law—is utterly inviolable by absolutely everyone under all possible circumstances.

Article I, section 9, of the Constitution says, "The Privilege of the Writ of Habeas Corpus shall not be suspended, unless when in Cases of Rebellion or Invasion the public Safety may require it." Yet, when Abraham Lincoln became president and feared that the Maryland legislature would vote to secede, he arrested many of its members and suspended habeas corpus. By that means, he preempted Maryland's possible secession and fulfilled his duty to preserve the Union. A state of rebellion may not yet have existed, however, and the danger to the public safety may not have "required" the action. And, certainly, there was no "invasion."

In practice, our moral sensibilities sometimes seem to call for things to be done, even though they are illegal. To make them legal would require too many specific details; otherwise, the law would be systematically abused. When we consider the morality of some illegal acts that we do not believe should be made legal, therefore, we recognize that no principle can be inviolable. Churchill and Lincoln perceived that inviolable principles can kill people. A refusal to fire on innocent French sailors in World War II might have enabled Germany to kill greater numbers with the French fleet and perhaps to win the war.

This ground is so slippery, especially in a nation that treats certain rights as inalienable, that only command personnel of the highest rank should ever step onto it. The complexity of human life seems to me to warrant their stepping onto it, to face the ordeal of judgment with all its consequences, rather than never to consider extreme measures. Not only does such a position foreclose future decisions; it also threatens command personnel in some future case with hypocrisy.

I understand why some in law enforcement say that no one ever has a right to consider illegal measures. They insist that command personnel should be told never and should be made to comply. They know the danger of a command officer's going beyond the law, and so do I. But I also believe that the human condition compels us to see that an unconditional position here is too strong.

Trying to Have It Both Ways

Since no one who can avoid it should ever step onto such dangerous ground, command personnel and departmental legal counsel must know the laws that may provide relief from a conflict between undeniable goods. The *Crimes Code of Pennsylvania*, for example, like many others, contains a section called General Principles of Justification:

In any prosecution based on conduct which is justifiable under this chapter, justification is a defense. . . .

(a) General rule. Conduct which the actor believes to be necessary to avoid a harm or evil to himself or to another is justifiable if

(1) the harm or evil sought to be avoided by such conduct is greater than that sought to be prevented by the law defining the offense charged.[5]

Such provisions may apply to command decisions in hard cases. Because such provisions may be overridden by other laws and by the Constitution, however, command personnel must use their intelligence, imagination, and experience to reduce the area of conflict.

A specific hypothetical case about physical coercion for information may help us test our suppositions to be sure that they do not draw us too hastily onto dangerous ground. In this case, the police know that the person in custody is the perpetrator, and not just a suspect. They know that the victim is buried and alive, and they know that the perpetrator knows where. They know that the perpetrator will not divulge the information under legal interrogation.

Are the police likely to *know* this much in the situations they face? Colleagues in domestic law enforcement and in military intelligence and interrogation say no. They stress the difficulty of knowing how much information a suspect has. Inexperienced officers often treat detainees disgracefully—and even commit atrocities—because they overestimate a prisoner's knowledge. Experienced officers would urge that the hypothetical situation be made more realistic by supposing that the suspect may have information on which a victim's life may depend. The victim may be alive, and whatever information is drawn from the prisoner by any means may be true and therefore may be useful in the preservation of life.

Those useful points show how the case becomes harder under plausible assumptions that call for intellectual humility. In such circumstances, a police command officer who is unsure of the facts contemplates the additional moral burden of wrongdoing, even while uncertain that the desired end can be achieved by any means. By contrast, he can be sure that a no-holds-barred interrogation is wrong.

This uncertainty of facts is quite different from the legal presumption of innocence. Police officers frequently know who committed a crime—they may even have apprehended someone in the act. Legally, however, the person remains a suspect entitled to due process of law and therefore to the presumption of innocence. Factual guilt and legal innocence are entirely compatible; if they were not, we could not bring evidence to a trial that proved beyond a reasonable doubt a suspect's legal guilt.

In the hypothetical case, my colleagues are not suggesting that the perpetrator be treated merely as a suspect. They are not saying that the conditions for admissible evidence at a trial must be satisfied here, although they want to preserve those conditions if possible. Rather, they are pointing to an uncertainty about what the perpetrator knows. Accomplices, for example, may have decided where to bury the victim. The officers are also uncertain whether the perpetrator under duress would be telling the truth and whether any information could save the life of the victim.

Several of those colleagues point to extreme measures within the law that can be tried to obtain the information the perpetrator has. And some observe that a perpetrator may lie, even in pain or under threat of death, especially a perpetrator who would bury a victim alive. One wrote:

> A number of reasons might account for not telling the truth: buying time for an accomplice, placing blame on another person, and—the most difficult to deal with—complete lack of conscience with regard to the crime. If the perpetrator lacks a conscience and the attendant guilt, he has no interest in saving the endangered life as an act of personal redemption. To that type of individual, whom we can refer to as sociopathic, outwitting the police officer is a far more appealing goal than a cleansing confession. This would be the type of personality that would thrive on burying a child alive in the first place.
>
> Sociopaths may understand that what they have done is perceived as wrong by society, but they have absolutely no sense that their behavior is wrong, and, as a result, they have no remorse. Misleading a bothersome police officer would be predictable behavior from a sociopath, and provoking the officer to act outside the law in order to extract information would give

the sociopath the last laugh that he seeks. Fooling the stupid officer and being very likely beyond prosecution *and* committing the original crime makes for the perfect sociopathic success.

The expertness of interrogators in such a case becomes a central issue. As one colleague noted, police must be "well enough trained in interrogation that they are not likely to rush into extreme measures." A poorly trained interrogator is more likely to panic under the pressure of trying to save a victim's life and ignore rules and policies. "The more urgent the need, the less rational a person is likely to be," one of my colleagues wrote. Although that may make us more tolerant of police behavior under pressure, it does not help the victim or achieve purposes within the law. Legal measures might have succeeded; at least they had as much potential as illegal ones.

Legal methods of interrogation may be distasteful, but they are preferable to illegal ones. If male perpetrators have kidnapped female victims, the interrogation may be more effectively conducted by women, so a department should have expert male and female interrogators.

As one colleague wrote:

> Scrupulous attention to detail, intelligent and practiced interrogation techniques based on an understanding of human psychology, and decisiveness . . . stand at least as good a chance of yielding the desired result [as physical coercion]. [T]hey do so without the risk of losing the admissibility of evidence. There are ways to flatter a suspect, gain his trust, convince him of his "rightness," enlist his assistance or enrage him, that yield information that can be acted upon. The lay person might very well be shocked by some of these techniques, and many police officers are uncomfortable using them because it requires their serious and convincing acting of roles which they find personally repugnant (such as telling a child molester that you understand perfectly how those little girls lead men on, and how they truly want to be screwed, and that you wish you had been screwed by someone strong and good-looking like the suspect when you were six years old), but they are not illegal, and they

are remarkably effective. The U.S. Supreme Court has consistently affirmed the legality of the police use of these techniques.

And another concluded:

The word "necessary" is slippery. It is often used merely for what appears efficient or expedient. "We had no choice" can be a lame and dishonest substitute for "It was the quickest way." There are many techniques for interrogation that are not violent.

In any deliberation about interrogation of great urgency, command personnel should be in close consultation with their legal personnel. A police department does not have to act alone in such a matter. A colleague wrote:

Historically, our courts have sought to resolve and adjust the conflict of legitimate rights and interests in our society. Were I representing law enforcement authorities in the case you pose, I would naturally consider an emergency application to a court of competent jurisdiction. A compelling factual presentation would have to be made as to the life-threatening consequences of a suspect's refusal to provide information. I would ask the court to consider ordering the supervised administration of sodium pentathol or the employment of some alternative practice which has gained a degree of acceptance in the medical community. For purposes of analogy, I would cite those instances where courts have ordered emergency medical intervention for minor children, despite the constitutionally protected religious scruples of their parents.

We should conclude that command officers who fail to exercise all the legal means at their disposal have failed in their duty. Those who proceed into flagrant illegality without doing so are neither justified nor excusable, and they thrust their departments into hazards of civil and criminal liability that might have been avoided.

Obviously, some illegal actions are more serious than others. Several of my colleagues point out that if they were questioning a suspect in a case of that sort in his home, they would listen illegally to a phone call from an accomplice if they could. Such a judgment would have to be made by an officer at the scene, without benefit of consultation or supervision. In my judgment, such an action, though illegal, would be morally appropriate; it is not a flagrant violation of the suspect's rights, and it seems less than extreme, given the peril to a life. Releasing a suspect to gain information by surveillance might be plausible in some cases, and it would be legal. An officer would be remiss, however, to spurn opportunities to secure information by intrusive but nonviolent means.

Thinking It Through

Given all those considerations, what should a conscientious high-ranking police official do in the extreme situation? Suppose that he is certain neither that the victim is alive nor that the suspect-perpetrator can be made to divulge what he does know. Suppose that the legal methods of interrogation have been tried, expertly (albeit quickly), and failed. The life of the victim may depend on information the suspect-perpetrator may have that physical coercion may yield.

Most thoughtful people will come down on one side of the issue with some feeling of respect and sympathy for those on the other. Even mature and experienced adults who agree with everything that has been said to this point will be divided on the issue. Certainly, my colleagues are. Some envision circumstances that would excuse the use of third-degree methods or drugs, but others do not. One wrote:

> If any end can justify all means, it would be the protection of innocent life. I would use all the instruments at my disposal to get information from someone who clearly possessed it to secure the safety of the blameless. And do so with the intention of taking the responsibility personally for such action. I would not consider putting such policy in writing; neither would I consider denying my actions afterward.

Another wrote:

I think that, for roughly utilitarian reasons, getting information from a suspect by hurting him could be justified . . . but I think that saying or writing to policemen that it could be justified is probably not itself justified. This is because policemen, being human, may fall short of their convictions about hurting suspects and hurt them more and more often than they really think they should.

Still another observed:

I think it unwise to offer a solution to this problem based on general principles. The problem for a real policeman is not so much what principles to apply but how to apply them. Much depends on the policeman's estimate of the suspect's knowledge, the urgency of the case, and the failure of successful interrogation by means less than physical coercion. . . . But I would want to make it clear that, when it is urgent to save human life, *any* rule is breakable.

Some who oppose those positions, including police, share the views of one colleague:

I see the violation of rights as an easy way out. . . . I want to be able to look at myself in the mirror every day and believe that I have done the best I could have under the circumstances. To do so, I proceed under the belief that there is no situation that I can predict in which I will meet the circumstances with a studied and purposeful decision to violate a suspect's constitutional rights as the best—or only—solution.

Another colleague was even more direct:

The rule of law requires all of us to submit to it. A cop who breaks the law, in order to enforce it more effectively, is a criminal. No one is above the law. If you can't live with it, quit. Anything else is a slope toward totalitarianism, and it is naïve to have faith that command personnel or anyone else can avoid sliding downward once they break the law, and it is hypocrisy to say that anyone in law enforcement has the right to do so. It is wrong to agree to the slightest compromise in these matters.

Another concluded with a reflection on the human condition itself:

> My position is a simple and plain acknowledgment of a conflict between official duty and an obligation of a person to do all he can to save the life of another. We must refuse to blur the distinctions between our official positions and our individual felt obligations. Thus, we should acknowledge on the one hand that using extreme measures to gain information from a "suspect" is never justified. On the other hand, as individuals we should be willing to consider acting in extremis and accepting the consequences of our actions. . . . In a sense my view is that this is one of the conflicts in the human condition (it is not a dilemma) for which there is no solution, even though individual human beings must, finally, decide. It is because the human condition can call for so much from the best of us that we should feel compassion for those who must face such conflicts.

When reasonable people of goodwill disagree about how to handle a complex problem, we can only hope that those who actually decide will do so with profound regard both for the status of the human beings involved as ends and for their own professional duties, including their duty not to bring the department into bad repute. They must not choose their methods in anger and passion, or in a vengeful or self-righteous spirit in the name of a supposedly all-justifying principle. They should recognize the moral peril of excess and take every measure to avoid it. Then, if they do choose to break the law and commit a wrongful act, they will at least not do so routinely or feel justified in cloaking their behavior in secrecy or perjury.

Terrorists and other extremists—in the name of justice—consider their murderous actions entirely justified. They are devoid of the humility that makes people trustworthy to bear authority or exercise power. Because they believe that they are entirely devoted to justice, they always believe themselves innocent as well. Human life is neither so easy, however, nor so simple.

The same tendency can be seen in law enforcement. In 1986 officers of the 106th Precinct in Queens, New York City, were convicted of assault in the second degree and coercion in the first degree for using stun guns to get confessions from misdemeanor suspects in custody. Also in 1986, in San Antonio, Patrolman Stephen Smith was shot to death by another officer, his closest friend, who believed that Smith was about to kill him. Smith was at the time suspected of a plot to assassinate city officials and of involvement in six vigilante murders. In an investigation by a local newspaper of what happens in a police department "when it has dangerous officers but cannot fire them because of union protection," City Manager Lou Fox had earlier declared, "I've got a killer cop I can't get rid of. . . . To know that there are renegade cops, dangerous people, on your force and to be unable for so long to do anything about it, that can scare hell out of you." Ballistics tests revealed that "bullets used in two unsolved murders matched slugs fired from one of Smith's AR15 rifles."[6]

This mentality of self-righteousness, which is absolutely incompatible with the public trust, was also exhibited by a Miami police officer on trial in 1988 for the murder of nine alleged drug dealers. According to the local press, his only regret was that he had not killed ninety-nine dealers before being caught. "I enjoyed what I was doing," he said, denying that he was a murderer because his victims were "not human beings." He acknowledged that he worshiped Hitler and said, "This is called absolute justice. . . . I took nine people with me. . . . They'll never sell drugs to your children." Prosecutors contended, however, that not all of his victims were involved with drugs.[7] Columnist William Safire put such behavior in perspective: "Toleration of the cop who deliberately kills a suspect threatens our way of life."[8]

A further problem, even for well-intentioned and normally restrained public officials, is the corrosive effect of extreme, illegal measures on restraint in future instances. Those who employ extreme measures may find it easier to do so the next time a hard case arises and perhaps easier in a case not quite so hard after that. Extreme measures can then become routine merely because they are convenient.

A point made in *A Man for All Seasons* applies here, because we are creatures of habit. After bribing someone to betray a trust, an official says, "There, that wasn't too painful, was it? . . . That's all there is. And you'll find it easier next time."[9] Once we go beyond the law for a noble purpose rather than a selfish one, we may feel that we have committed ourselves to illegal means, as further extremes become natural. As one of my colleagues observed, "When we violate a suspect's Constitutional rights, we deviate from fundamental principles. That can be the beginning of a substantial erosion. There's a fine line in these things, but once you step over it, you tend to justify subsequent acts by the former one." An intellectual and moral humility and an appreciation of the gravity of what we have done are the only bulwarks I know against such deterioration of character.

Dirty Harry

In a well-known article, Carl B. Klockars, professor of criminal justice at the University of Delaware, wrote, "The Dirty Harry problem asks when and to what extent the morally good end warrants or justifies an ethically, politically, or legally dangerous means to its achievement."[10] In the film *Dirty Harry*, a psychopathic killer, Scorpio, kidnaps a fourteen-year-old girl, buries her alive, demands a ransom, and reneges on the promise to provide information when the ransom is delivered. The main character, Inspector Harry Callahan, illegally searches the suspect's room, confirms that he is Scorpio, tracks him down, shoots him in the leg, and then "stands on Scorpio's bullet-mangled leg to torture the information out of him." Scorpio divulges the location of the girl, who is, as Callahan suspected, already dead. Since the physical evidence and the confession are inadmissible in court, Scorpio walks away a free man.

Klockars denied that the most difficult problem is what Dirty Harry ought to do:

> On the contrary, I suspect that most people would want Harry to do something dirty in the situation. I know I would want him to do what he did, and what is more, I would want anyone who policed for me to be prepared to do so. I want to have men and women of moral courage and sensitivity as police officers.

All of us want morally courageous and sensitive police officers, and many audiences seemed thoroughly satisfied with Callahan's behavior. In fact, many would no doubt approve of inflicting pain as punishment on Scorpio even if Harry knew that the victim was dead.

Yet we must not allow moral outrage to blind us to facts. The inspector's behavior is justified, Klockars said, by the goodness of the purpose, by his knowledge that Scorpio has the information, and by the "small possibility" that the victim is still alive. "There appears to be no reason for Scorpio to confess to the girl's location without being coerced to do so," he added. Although Scorpio would not divulge the information from any goodness in his heart, a shrewd interrogator might enrage or trick him or use deceptively sympathetic tactics to draw out the information. Harry Callahan does not try any such means, nor does he try to comfort Scorpio as a way of gaining his confidence, however offensive such false compassion might feel. Neither does he seek assistance from a court of competent jurisdiction. He goes from asking a direct question at gunpoint to torture.

Callahan's excesses are no more a mark of courage or sensitivity than calling on interrogation experts and deferring to higher authority are marks of cowardice or insensitivity. Trying to fulfill the purposes of law enforcement within the limits of the law takes as much courage as any other course. Command personnel can help by being forthright and resolute about departmental policy in training. Klockars acknowledged that "the department that trains its personnel well and supplies them with the resources—knowledge and material—to do their work will find that its policemen will not resort to dirty means unnecessarily." He should add that a multitude of inexcusable moral wrongs has sought, and found, refuge under the slippery argument that it was "necessary." As Shakespeare wrote, necessity is the plea of tyrants. "The troublesome issue in the Dirty Harry problem," Klockars wrote, "is not whether a right choice can be made, but that the choice must always be between two wrongs. And in choosing to do either wrong, the police officer inevitably taints or tarnishes himself."

In conversation with me, Professor Klockars has explained his position: The fundamental tenets of one moral theory may be irreducibly at odds with those of another moral theory; since an individual cannot satisfy both, he is bound to be tainted by one or the other. Thus, if one moral theory holds that you must always try to achieve the best immediate consequences (such as saving the life of the victim) and another holds that you must honor fully the status of a person as an end and not as a means to some goal (such as torturing a suspect for information), then a dilemma results.

The conclusion does not follow, however, because a person who subscribes only to one theory or the other has no moral problem at all, let alone a dilemma. The person simply acts in accordance with the theory. The real conflict arises for a person who sees a measure of rightness in each tenet, when circumstances force a decision between them. The incompatibility of some moral theories with others, by itself, taints no one. If it did, a vicious moral theory holding that might makes right or that white males are superior to everyone else and have a right to all positions of power and authority would taint everyone who rejected it. Theories have no such power, because they are sometimes wrong, simplistic, or overstated, and sometimes foolishly applied.

Furthermore, when we use coercion to prevent a person from self-determination, we do so either with or without restraint. The two differ profoundly.

Still, is it in some sense inevitable that police will be tainted by tensions between the limits of the law and moral constraint on the one hand and noble purposes on the other? Is this what we expect courageous and sensitive police to accept as their fate? Shall we tell students at police academies that they must "inevitably" become "dirty"?

The answer is no. Although the world has in it the makings of tragedy, not everyone who faces its most grueling demands need become dirty. Is it not still true, however, as suggested by the Klockars argument, that police officers who fail to use every means to achieve a high purpose are morally tainted? And are not officers who fail to abide by the law legally tainted or morally tainted by infidelity to their oath of office, to the Constitution, and to the public? I do not see why command officials would be morally tainted if they used all legal means at their disposal but declined to use illegal means that might be viewed by patrol personnel as a license for excess.

A more powerful consideration is that the suspect-perpetrator may go free if his rights are violated. The command officer may know that the prisoner is not suspected of other crimes that might lead to another arrest, that police surveillance of him will be prevented by charges of harassment, that no officers are available for surveillance, and that civic-minded private wealth cannot be enlisted to hire private surveillance. Moreover, the liberty of the suspect-perpetrator may be a murderous threat to other possible victims. The officer may imagine the eyes of the family of the next victim and hear their question, How could you have allowed the killer to walk away from his last murder?

That is, the command officer may see that using every conceivable means to save today's victim risks creating new victims tomorrow. What, then, is to be done? The slippery slope of physical coercion leads to the question whether false reports should be prepared to keep the perpetrator in custody and perjury should be committed to get a conviction. If the officer will do anything to save the victim and keep the suspect-perpetrator off the street, but he will not lie or commit perjury, then he cannot avoid the question whether he should murder the suspect-perpetrator.

I do not see how a person can be tainted by refusing to step onto this slope, toward which we are dragged by extreme illegal measures in law enforcement. Ignoring the slope, Klockars argued that the story of Dirty Harry is art, in the sense that at "all meaningful levels" it is "true." He meant that the Dirty Harry problem demands attention and analysis, not that all the particulars of the story are realistic.

After Scorpio goes free, Harry uses off-duty time to watch him until he is charged with harassment and ordered to stop. Scorpio then takes a bus full of elementary school children hostage. After Harry manages to force him away from the bus and they engage in a running gunfight, Scorpio takes yet another child hostage before Harry wounds him. When the child flees, the two at last confront each other. Now in a position to arrest Scorpio, Harry instead taunts him and dares him to try for the gun he has dropped. When Scorpio rises to the bait, Harry Callahan kills him. The shooting is calculated murder.

I do not know any police who would describe that denouement as realistic or "true" at "all meaningful levels" or describe Harry as a police officer of "courage and sensitivity." Klockars and others have said that Harry Callahan should be fired. After all, if arrested in those circumstances, Scorpio would almost certainly be prosecuted and convicted. For purposes of law enforcement or the safety of the public, murdering Scorpio is pointless. The murder offers delicious gratification to the appetite for revenge, and it satisfies moral outrage and hatred of the perpetrator. Such gratification has no place, however, in real law enforcement. It is not extreme action for the sake of high purpose, but raw self-indulgence.

If police officials are not tainted by refusing to step onto the slope of illegal action, neither are officials of demonstrated probity necessarily tainted by a last-ditch illegal step. Such an act may be unjustifiable by any unconditional principle, but it also may be excusable. Even if committed without regard to self-interest and at great personal sacrifice, inflicting pain is an undeniably evil act when committed by one who has no right to punish. Although it would constitute a betrayal of the duties of office, it would not necessarily be condemned in any subsequent legal proceeding. An enlightened governor could justifiably pardon the act. Still less does it follow that those who commit such acts are bad, that their character is besmirched, or that their honor is tainted.

I doubt that we would describe officials who act either way as "dirty." Some would say that they should have done more, and some less. We may condemn their judgment, but we would not therefore think them worthy of disrespect. Our respect for proven decency in service to the public is deeper, and more subtle, than that.

Persons cannot be held morally responsible because the human condition has cast them into situations where highly desirable ends are at least temporarily at odds with each other. Neither can they be held blameworthy when they have undeniably done their best. We can scarcely say that those who have done their best are tainted for failing to do better. To say otherwise is to be fundamentally wrong about the nature of moral life.

"Noble Cause" Corruption

What does taint us as moral agents is an arrogant appraisal of ourselves that concludes, "I am entirely justified in my means because my end was noble," or a cowardly response to demands, such as, "I'm damned if I do and damned if I don't, so it makes no difference." Giving everything we have when the issue is hardest does not taint us, but giving less suggests avoidable ignorance, weakness, or incompetence.

Such flattering self-appraisals and failures of nerve are the two forms of noble cause corruption. Arrogance and cowardice imperil the ideals of a constitutional republic because they are marks of individuals who despair of rising to the ordeal of command. In my experience, the republic has little to fear from officials who face up to ordeals and do not try to get off the hook by complacently justifying themselves or by whining that "the world isn't fair." What is fearful are the officials who believe that their ends always justify or excuse their means or who give up in despair but remain in office nonetheless. The greater the responsibilities and authority of those officials, the less the country can afford such flight from tension and conflict. They are the marks of a human spirit that has admitted defeat. In practice, they undermine the judgment required to bear the public trust faithfully. Arrogance corrupts by obscuring the need for thought, and cowardice corrupts by denying the point of thought, thus forsaking judgment to the whims of impulse.

Excusable Wrongdoing

At this point, we may wonder whether we should consider well-intentioned and remorseful wrongdoing in terribly hard cases to be excusable. That is a tempting way to handle the problem of tragedy because it invites us to make a rule for excusing (or not excusing) high-minded wrongdoing. Then, when faced with a tragically difficult case, we can appeal to the rule and spare ourselves the ordeal of judgment.

That way of proceeding is dangerous. If certain considerations excuse illegal conduct in one case, they do so in sufficiently similar cases too, but each case must be treated in all of its particularity. The specifics force us to be morally humble and intellectually thorough. We sacrifice doing our best if we lapse into the self-assurance that what we are about to do is wrong, but we deserve to be excused. That form of complacency can be as remorseless as any other.

Temptations of this kind are another reason to avoid making beginners in ethics courses focus on hard cases, which are not the mainstream of moral life. Beginners are likely to look for simple rules when they are taught, to paraphrase Edmund Burke, "to make the extreme medicine of human life its daily bread." When that happens, Burke observed, people tend to become weak, because they develop the bad habit of speaking and thinking lightly about profoundly demanding matters, both before and after the fact.[11] That is as true in law enforcement as elsewhere.

The conclusion to be drawn is that illegal conduct in a specific case may or may not be excusable—and I believe that it could be, depending on the particulars and even the minute details of the case.

Deciding

On more than one occasion, I have been asked whether I—as a command officer who believed that all legal means had been exhausted and that physical coercion was the only means of saving an innocent victim—would consider using the third degree.

My response is yes, in that I would not absolutely foreclose consideration. I would consider it in light of all the relevant facts available at the time: the condition and reputation of my department; the levels of respect for law among my subordinates and peers; recent episodes of brutality and corruption for profit within; the prospect of loss of departmental autonomy in any resultant political firestorm; the legal means available for subsequently keeping the suspect-perpetrator off the streets; and other matters considered relevant by any competent command officer.

Would I actually use the third degree? I would be unlikely to, but I might. I would certainly seek the advice of counsel about the outer limits of the permissible throughout the ordeal. I would use every form of psychological pressure on the suspect, while making sure that he would have a difficult burden of proof if he sought to suppress evidence on grounds that his rights had been violated.

If I actually crossed the line to physical coercion, I would then request or commence a departmental inquiry, along the lines recommended by counsel, to minimize the hazards to the department and to try to keep the suspect in custody. I would not participate in a cover-up because such conduct betrays the law itself, inspires conspiracies against the rule of law, and undermines by deceit the public trust. But I would avail myself of all my rights under the Constitution, on the grounds that I had never casually or routinely disregarded anyone else's rights. At the same time, I would resign from my position—not necessarily from the department—to make clear that no one who has violated the standards of a position of authority should continue in it.

I hope that I would be decisive but aware of the shiver that ought to be felt by anyone facing the moral demands of the grimmest realities. I would have at hand words of theologian Reinhold Niebuhr:

> The tragic element in a human situation is constituted of conscious choices of evil for the sake of good. . . . Tragedy elicits admiration as well as pity because it combines nobility with guilt. . . . Our idealists are divided between those who would renounce the responsibilities of power for the sake of preserving the purity of our soul and those who are ready to cover every ambiguity of good and evil in our actions by the frantic insistence that any measure taken in a good cause must be unequivocally virtuous: We take, and must continue to take, morally hazardous actions to preserve our civilization.[12]

I hope that I would remember that some actions are not just morally hazardous, but morally suicidal. And I would have in mind the deepest reservation: that some of those I respect most in the world have said to me that they could never physically abuse any person in custody.

13

Death and Bereavement, Deadly Force and Guilt

It is hard to have patience with people who say, "There is no death," or "Death doesn't matter." There is death. And whatever is matters. And whatever happens has consequences, and it and they are irrevocable and irreversible. You might as well say that birth doesn't matter. I look up at the night sky. Is anything more certain than that in all those vast times and spaces, if I were allowed to search them, I would nowhere find her face, her voice, her touch? She died. She is dead. Is the word so difficult to learn?

—C. S. Lewis[1]

The life of a police officer is more uncertain than most lives and frequently involves situations of danger and death. Violence, whether sudden and unexpected or anticipated and countered, is not part of the job for every sworn officer, but the potential for it is real. Many police officers lose colleagues, and even more are touched whenever a person in law enforcement dies in the line of duty.

Three ethical concerns are occasioned by these conditions and events that arise from them. All have to do with the role of character and wisdom in adversity. First is their place in facing the death of a beloved friend; second, in responding to the bereavement of others; third, in facing the future after using deadly force by which another person is killed. The third area embraces the worst case of all—where an officer has accidentally or mistakenly killed another officer or some other innocent person.

The Death of a Friend, Partner, or Loved One

When a beloved friend or partner dies in the line of duty, he or she is usually in the prime of life. This makes the death especially hard to bear, rather like the death of any young person with much life yet to be lived.

The agony that follows arises in part from love and affection and in part from the fact that we are creatures of habit. When a loved one with whom we share much dies—whether the death is sudden or expected—many of our deepest and dearest habits are shattered.

We are irrevocably deprived of the activities that have become habitual in daily life with that person. No more can that face and its many expressions be with us in person, no more the conversations, the daily excursions, the shared enjoyments and sufferings, the mutual trust, the feelings of contentment when that person was happy. The commonplace connections of heart and mind that made up perhaps substantial portions of each day are severed. The shock is so powerful that a person feels it physically. Heartache hurts all over.

Living Up to the Facts

Each individual death is a fact. We grieve because we know that it is a fact—hard, cold, and permanent. There are two ways to treat facts: A person can live up to them or seek ways to evade them.

Living up to the fact of a death—say, of a partner—begins with learning that when death takes someone you love, there is nothing to do but grieve with all your heart. However much anger, bitterness, guilt, or denial is involved, living up to the fact means learning to bear it, suffering what must be suffered, and learning to live in a world that is less because a specific person is forever gone from it.

Evasion of the fact of death takes many forms: numbing oneself with alcohol or drugs; giving way to flights of impulsive self-indulgence, to self-pity, or to the self-aggrandizing conviction that this love was so special that no one else ever suffered such sorrow, so great a loss; and failing to meet one's normal obligations to others, while expecting everyone else to show extraordinary consideration and generosity in this case.

The most fundamental evasion, of which many others may be only symptoms, is preoccupation with one's own grief. When the response to the fact of death is trying to "cope with grief," the object of focus becomes a psychological reaction to the fact, not the fact itself. This evasion is unrealistic; it is a failure to give reality its due. The real issue is what one should do about the fact, not how one copes with grief. A powerful response lies in the nature of good character and its relation to love and dignity.

Love

Poet William Butler Yeats observed that human beings are creatures who love what vanishes. We choose other people to love, in greater or lesser awareness that in time they and we will vanish into death. Many people deny this fact even to themselves, but the wisest among us do not.

When we take seriously that all of us are mortal, we may love not less but more, with greater rather than smaller consideration and attentiveness. We try to put the very best of ourselves into the lives of those we love. This is one of the spurs of morality: Knowing that death will one day part us all provides a powerful motive to treat each other's interests, concerns, well-being, and happiness with devotion.

Such devotion does not reflect a morbid preoccupation with death, but the courage to love with depth of heart despite death's heartbreak. Those who cannot or do not love fully and well may seem to risk less to death, but in fact lose more. For their days are emptier, and they are left in the end unable to say, "I tried to give the best of myself to you."

In this respect, habits of good character are habits of love; they make us most worthy and able to love others and to be loved. They give credibility to the words of love and friendship because our actions really do speak louder than words.

None of us ever becomes a perfect friend, any more than anyone achieves perfect character. Therefore, when death takes a dear friend, we are likely to feel guilt and remorse, as well as grief, over some of our past actions and words. But those will be less grinding if we have genuinely tried to be worthy friends.

Dignity

As we have seen earlier in the words of Frederick Douglass and others, our dignity does not turn on what others do to us, but on what we do ourselves. Neither does it turn on the circumstances of good fortune or adversity. Dignity rises or falls in our response to what befalls us.

Most of us think that our dignity is threatened by things we cannot control. When illness makes us dependent on others, helpless, perhaps forced to use a bedpan or rely on others to feed us, we are embarrassed, and our feelings of modesty and independence are offended. But dignity is much more at stake in matters we can control, particularly in the habits of feeling and acting we establish as aspects of our character.

When we have forged the habit of giving the best of ourselves to the people closest to us, the habit does not disappear when our hearts are breaking. Our dignity is never greater than when we can reach into ourselves, despite our own anguish, and find what it takes to comfort another. Such character emerges from firmly established habits of temperance, unselfishness, compassion, and courage.

Sometimes in face of the death of a person very dear to us, we seek consolation in the promise that "time heals all things—this, too, shall pass." Yet when John and Abigail Adams lost their daughter, they heard from Thomas Jefferson, who had lost five children and his wife, that the only ultimate relief from such losses is in one's own grave.

The power of time to heal us lies largely in our own power to control our lives by sustaining our best habits. We can direct ourselves to other friends and family with the constancy of character we brought to the friend who is gone. We do not need to form new habits of character, but rather to apply them faithfully to others.

The memories of the one who is dead never entirely fade away. Although our longing diminishes over time, we have not thereby forsaken the one who is gone, any more than the fading of that person's face in our mind means that we are forgetting.

We have seen that a person does not become happy by trying to be happy or have fun by trying to have fun. Neither does a person learn to live with the fact of death by trying to overcome or cope with grief, as so many current theorists assert. Just as happiness depends largely on doing and giving our best, we live best with loss when we bring our best habits of feeling and acting into our daily lives with others.

Sometimes the pain makes this very difficult, and the anguish may be made worse by feelings of lassitude, lethargy, and lack of willpower. If, in the past, we have practiced accomplishing difficult and disagreeable things by diligent application of our will, we will be able to call up willpower when we need it most and when others need it from us. Thus do habits of good character sustain us—and our family and friends.

The Bereavement of Others

When others lose someone they love, we may think that we can do little. We may avoid those who are suffering and confidently assure ourselves that they would rather be alone when, in fact, it is we who do not want to face death. Certainly, we should be respectful of the wishes of friends who truly do want to be alone in their heartache, but we should not generalize that everyone feels that way.

We say too easily that words cannot help. That is sometimes a way of sparing ourselves the effort of finding words that will help. Words make a difference, the right ones said in the right way. Words can become right by the manner of their delivery. Sometimes words comfort by their tenderness; they may evoke bittersweet memory; or they may simply express sympathy. Sometimes the right words recall something funny and cause laughter. The appropriate words and manner can be known only by careful, thoughtful, wise appraisal of the people and the circumstances. Sometimes silence is called for, but not because words do not make a difference.

Grieving people may believe that they will never smile again. They may even believe that they are somehow doing wrong if they smile. Friends who recall them to occasions for smiling can slowly erase such misunderstandings. Even the silent nearness of a friend serves to remind a bereaved person that not all love and caring are gone, not all intimacy and kinship are lost.

Responding to the needs of our friends in such circumstances is demanding. But if we are friends, we want most of all to respond when their needs are greatest. Practice at rising to those needs in ordinary circumstances gives us greater power to sense their feelings and to see things as they do. We learn not only to comfort but also to encourage them when they are suffering most deeply.

Deadly Force

A law enforcement colleague tells of an undercover episode in which he believed that his cover had been blown. Two things occupied his mind: how to get out without killing anyone and how to avoid being killed. No one of good character takes either question lightly.

In Phoenix an FBI agent on a fugitive arrest team is accidentally shot to death by other agents. In Dallas two elderly people call for police assistance and, in the ensuing confusion, both are mistakenly shot by police and die. In Prince George's County, Maryland, when a specially trained squad begins to break into an apartment suspected of containing weapons and drugs, the leader of the team is killed by police gunfire after a noise inside is mistaken for a shot. No weapons are found with the suspects.

Deadly force is deadly—and sometimes in the least intended ways. Because law enforcement can become chaotic and life-threatening and require immediate action, preparedness is fundamental.

Most people do not know exactly how they will behave in sudden danger, and most who take an innocent life—even when they acted with good judgment of what seemed necessary—are devastated by it. The guilt may be ineradicable.

The ability to perform must therefore be kept sharp. Weariness and stress take enough of a toll without the added burden of drugs, excessive alcohol, indolence, and the like. The most professional exercise of skill and judgment requires alertness. Not having been at one's best adds immeasurably to the anguish of taking a life.

Wisdom also cautions against unnecessary distractions, such as leaving home on a quarrelsome note, falling into excessive debt, complicating one's life with messy entanglements, living a lie of one form or another, or entering a fray after having had harsh words with a partner. They all distract and hamper alertness. After using deadly force, we would not want to face the ugly truth that our mind was elsewhere.

Guilt

Although a person who feels ashamed of avoidable errors is far better than one who does not, guilt can be corrosive. It may turn our minds so intensely to the past that we become indifferent to the present and the future. It can lead us to despair.

Thus, while a certain measure of character is required to feel guilt, greater character is required to avert its most pernicious effects. The first problem is the person who feels more guilt than is deserved. The second is the person who is to blame for a deadly error and suffers dreadful feelings of guilt and shame but must somehow turn to the future.

An officer may accept too much blame for the death of an innocent person or a fellow officer. Some deaths, especially in high-speed pursuits and in shootings, occur because departmental training standards are not good enough. If officers are not well taught how to work together in dangerous raids, levels of competence and expectation vary. A sudden and unpredictable movement by a suspect, bystander, or officer can cost a life. A department may find such factors hard, perhaps impossible, to admit, and so may a victim's family.

An officer whose action directly caused the death may believe that considering such facts is only a cowardly search for excuses. Those who feel guilty may be unable to give themselves the benefit of an honest appraisal of the facts. Their friends and colleagues may have to press such an appraisal upon them. For inordinate guilt, the antidote is truth.

In the worst cases of all, persons who really are to blame can lose their capacity to go on because of guilt. For those whose religious faith embraces the forgiveness of sins, repentance and confession may lift the burden of guilt. For others, various kinds of counseling and professional guidance may be helpful. In any case, humility is essential, and strength of character is irreplaceable—the strength to look in a mirror, acknowledge blame, bear guilt, perhaps always, and resolve not only to endure but to aspire. No evasions, no rationalizations, no attempt to escape the facts. That takes the honesty to face what one has done and the courage to recognize that it cannot be undone. It also takes the fortitude to exert effort despite suffering; it depends on habits—formed or yet to be formed—of applying oneself when doing so is most disagreeable.

Rising above the destructive effects of guilt—as opposed to rationalizing guilt away—is also a matter of wisdom. It consists of seeing that if we ever had reasons to aspire to do our best, we always have reasons for such aspiration. No failure, however massive, changes that.

We would be foolish to discount our past by celebrating today as the first day of the rest of our lives. Today has a past, which cannot be erased, because habits are not formed overnight. Today and tomorrow matter because we still have lives to live, however grievous our mistakes of yesterday may have been. Failure to grasp that is tantamount to self-annihilation; if it does not result in literal suicide, it may still destroy all purpose in life. And one mistake may thus become the basis for a host of further errors. We can at least begin to redeem ourselves by avoiding that.

14

Taking Our Lives Seriously

Moral performance begins in individual self-discipline on the part of officials, involving all that is meant by the word "character." But this is not enough. The official individually and organizationally must be concerned to go beyond simple honesty to a devoted guardianship of the continuing reality of democracy.

—Paul H. Appleby[1]

As we have seen throughout this book, living up to the highest ideals of policing calls for character and wisdom. Genuine professionalism always does. Technology may change, specific problems may become more or less severe, but this fact of life remains the same.

The Extra Mile

Police can live up to those ideals in a number of ways: by trying to inspire and deserve public confidence even when public expectations are inordinate; by exercising proper discretion on and off the job; by living up to higher standards of conduct than the general public; by acting with largeness of spirit in response to unfair personnel policies and laws; by behaving honorably undercover; by remaining compassionate and just despite exposure to human weakness and depravity; by bearing the ordeal of making judgments in complex circumstances; by sustaining one's best self despite disappointment and grief. To sum up, the police officer must often "go the extra mile."

Many police I know realize that and do not lament it. They understand that the rule of law is intended to promote the public good and that it cannot do so unless the guardians of that rule are devoted to it and willing to sacrifice for it. They share the realistic expectations expressed by columnist Walter Lippmann in 1930:

> The American ideal of government as a public trust to be carried on by disinterested men represents not the actuality but a long step ahead in the evolution of man. . . . . It is a very difficult ideal to attain, and I know of no man in America even in our time who has felt able to be completely loyal to it. . . . The campaign . . . on behalf of the idea of trust is no mere repairing of something perfect that has broken down, but the implanting of a new habit of acting in the ancient consciousness of man.[2]

The best law enforcement personnel aspire to acquire that habit of acting—the habit of going the extra mile.

The Morality of Aspiration

Legal scholar Lon L. Fuller wrote that the morality of aspiration consists of the will and resolve to become and behave as "a human being functioning at his best."[3] Fuller contrasted that high ground of morality with the lower ground of law and duty couched in terms of prohibitions of the form "Thou shalt not." Good law enforcement agencies reflect that distinction by stressing what police can do, not merely what they are not permitted to do. On the lower ground a person may respect the letter and limits of the law, while taking advantage of omissions and loopholes. That would require no aspiration to fulfill the spirit of the law or the purposes of law in a free country, and no sense of what behavior is worthy of oneself. A person who respects the prohibitions of law would not use illegal drugs but might indulge himself with them where they are legal. Such a person would refrain from gambling where it is prohibited but might gamble for high stakes where it is allowed. But a person who aspires to excellent character would not debilitate himself with drugs anywhere. Neither would he waste time on "deep play," as high stakes gambling is sometimes called. He would consider the action not as illegal but as beneath him. As Fuller explained:

> We are concerned not so much with the specific harms that may flow from gambling, but with the question whether it is an activity worthy of man's capacities. We would recognize that in human affairs risk attends all creative effort and that it is right and good that a man engaged in creative acts should not only accept the risks of his role, but rejoice in them. The gambler, on the other hand, cultivates risk for its own sake. Unable to face the broader responsibilities of the human role, he discovers a way of enjoying one of its satisfactions without accepting the burdens that usually accompany it. Gambling for high stakes becomes, in effect, a kind of fetishism. . . .
>
> The final judgment that the morality of aspiration might thus pass on gambling would not be an accusation, but an expression of disdain. For such a morality, gambling would not be the violation of a duty, but a form of conduct unbefitting a being with human capacities.[4]

A police officer must meet much more real risks and challenges: A command officer must decide whether to authorize subordinates to try to shoot a hostage-taker or try to save both the hostage and the perpetrator; a police officer must enter a dark hallway to answer the cries of a victim inside; an officer must resist the sapping of his alertness by boredom during a stakeout; an officer must remain cool in the midst of abusive citizens. Those are risks and challenges of reality, not fabricated, seldom enjoyable, and yet genuinely worth our best capacities.

Recognizing what is worth our best capacities—and devoting our lives to such activities—builds self-respect. Aspiring to make ourselves worthy of demanding responsibilities invests our lives with purpose and meaning. The ultimate power of moral aspiration is that it reduces the likelihood of using the failures or faults of others as an excuse for one's own. Genuine aspiration in a person tends to inspire sadness, pity, or disdain for the self-indulgence and corruption of others. Those who aspire to become the best they can be recognize that they are far from perfect. Their aspiration prevents them from becoming self-righteous, holier-than-thou, or permissive toward their own failings just because "others do it." Our most secure bulwark against moral weakness and wrongdoing is always the conviction that it is beneath us. It is inestimably more durable and reliable than the fear of being caught at wrongdoing, and it is therefore a guarantee of trustworthiness that no prohibition can ever provide.

Those who aspire to strength of character hold themselves answerable for their faults. Though accountable to others, perhaps in a chain of command, they become worthy of trust by being genuinely accountable to themselves. Surely the answer to the ancient question of Juvenal—Who guards the guardians?—lies partly in procedures for supervision and accountability; but it also lies partly within the levels of aspiration in each individual who is entrusted with authority, for, finally, the "unsleeping sentinels who guard the outposts of society," in Chesterton's words, must draw a fair portion of their vigilance and honorability from within.

In this crucial way, good character as well as the moral aspiration to become better is "the bottom line." Few people go the extra mile out of fear. They go because of devotion and self-respect and because it is second nature to them.

Taking Our Lives Seriously

In our actions and aspirations, we discover how seriously we take our lives. The idea of good character can be summed up in taking our lives seriously—not humorlessly, but seriously—in good fortune and in adversity. Each of us has a life to live. Although it will come to an end, it will remain always and indelibly that life that was lived.

That we cannot entirely accomplish our purposes—that the mission of the police cannot be fully realized—is no reason for despair or cynicism. That we fall short of our best expectations of ourselves is no reason to settle for less. That we and our loved ones are mortal is no reason for indifference or for preoccupation with short-term gratification.

Instead, all those facts of the human condition are reasons to do the best we can with what we have for as long as we have it. Doing so, becoming wise and forging habits of fine character, is success in the conduct of a life.

Morality, to paraphrase a philosopher of long ago, is the proper calling of human beings. It is not only the measure of whether we have any right to consider ourselves members of a profession dedicated to the service of others. It is also the measure, finally, of how we have sought to live.

15

Fatalism, Microcosms, and Therapeutic Reductions

Humility, on the one hand, and true, noble pride on the other, are elements of proper self-respect; shamelessness is its opposite. A low opinion of oneself in relation to others is no humility; it is a sign of a little spirit and of a servile character.

—Immanuel Kant[1]

Throughout *Character and Cops*, I have argued for the tradition that public servants are obliged to live up to higher ethical and intellectual standards than those expected of the general public. Obviously, the public cannot be morally bankrupt and still expect to draw individuals of high quality into public service; no one will make sacrifices for a public that is unworthy of personal sacrifice.

Although the United States, like the other nations of the world, leaves much to be desired in public dedication to justice, the people are not morally bankrupt. Huge numbers of people are law abiding, make commitments to ideals that transcend their own private desires, and invest their best efforts in their private and work lives. In more than twenty years of work on the streets with police, I have never seen a neighborhood, even where homicide and drug-trafficking are at their worst, that did not include substantial numbers of decent people. They may be frightened of their environment, suspicious of police, or reluctant to get involved, but they are not unworthy of fine public servants.

Since 1989, however, and especially since the widely publicized videotaped beating of Rodney King in 1991 by Los Angeles police officers, three developments have increased the difficulty of maintaining higher standards for public servants.

The first is a certain fatalism about institutions and individuals charged to bear the public trust. I call this fatalism the microcosm argument. The second is a progressive obliteration by political leaders of the distinction between higher standards for public servants and double standards within government itself (a problem discussed earlier, in chapter 6). The trend away from higher standards transcends all party politics and threatens excellence in public service to the core.

The third adverse development is the uncritical acceptance of a therapeutic vision of human beings, which sees human beings merely as victims of a host of diseases that require treatment and compassion. The therapeutic account of human nature dims the vision of human beings as agents largely responsible for their own fate. The notion that human beings are primarily objects of therapy underlies features of the Americans with Disabilities Act that threaten to impair policing. It is also implicit in unreliable forms of sensitivity training for police.

Fatalism and the Microcosm Argument

Responses to the police assault on Rodney King have varied among the police, the public, and academic circles. The most dangerous responses have been the most fatalistic; if widely accepted, they will tend to drive policing back to the situation described in chapter 6. As August Vollmer said in 1931: "In America, law enforcement is generally held in contempt, and policing is [taken as] one of our national jokes."

Fatalism insists that police departments are no more than microcosms of society itself. Since the general public includes a great range of excellence, mediocrity, and depravity, every police department must be expected to include the same characteristics. In the broad society are to be found brutality, incompetence, excessive consumption of alcohol and drugs, financial corruption and other forms of lawbreaking, and racism, sexism, and other forms of bigotry. Therefore, the argument runs, a roughly proportionate incidence of such attitudes, ineptitude, and misconduct will inevitably find its way into police departments. The brutal beating of King simply reflects this "fact."

The obvious flaws in the microcosm argument do not prevent it from being viewed favorably by some police, academics, citizens, and media figures. Fatalism always enjoys some popularity because it puts the solution to problems beyond our reach and thereby spares us responsibility for them.

The most obvious flaw in the microcosm argument is that most people become members of society, citizens or subjects, simply by being born. They do not select their society, and their society does not select them. Since 1957, it has been illegal in the United States to deprive a person of citizenship as punishment for a crime. In *Trop v. Dulles*, the Supreme Court ruled that deprivation of citizenship as punishment for a crime constituted cruel and unusual punishment and therefore violated the Eighth Amendment.[2] In a police department, however, no one has a right to membership by virtue of birth, and no one has a right to remain a police officer irrespective of criminal misconduct.

A police department is selective—the more selective, the better. People born into a society do not have to meet eligibility requirements and standards, submit to background investigations, complete instructional programs, undertake probationary terms and field training, learn and perform in accordance with departmental policies, cooperate with internal investigations, or, ultimately, retire from service. Police do. In every good department, such features elevate the department and its sworn and civilian personnel beyond the norms for society as a whole.

No selective institution can be a mere microcosm of any larger nonselective society. No flaw in a selective institution, therefore, can be excused on the grounds that it is a microcosm. Indeed, we establish principles for service in a selective institution, dedicated to the public trust, precisely because we know that mere membership in society is insufficient as a mark of fitness to serve the public. Selective institutions are designed so that they will *not* be microcosms.

Still, a police department cannot be impervious to the society around it. It cannot reasonably be expected to screen out all unfit candidates or to prevent all wrongdoing. The realistic goal is to minimize the adverse social influences through selective recruiting, rigorous training, able supervision, deft leadership, and so on. A police leader must make clear that the department is not intended to be a microcosm of society. The bigotry, brutality, corruption, and incompetence in the society at large are among the very facts that compel the department to live up to higher standards.

Every serious account of standards of ethical policing illuminates this point. In *Power and Restraint: The Moral Dimension of Police Work*, for example, Howard S. Cohen and Michael Feldberg argued for "five ethical standards against which police work can be judged":

Standard I: *Fair Access.* As a social resource, police must provide fair access to their services.

Standard II: *Public Trust.* Citizens, having limited their right to enforce their own rights, have made police work a public trust.

Standard III: *Safety and Security.* Police must undertake law enforcement within the framework of maintaining safety and security.

Standard IV: *Teamwork.* Police are part of a system that includes legislators, other law enforcers, prosecutors, and judges, so their behavior must meet the tests of teamwork: coordination, communication and cooperation.

Standard V: *Objectivity.* Police work is a social role that often requires the officer to set personality and feelings aside, and demonstrate objectivity.[3]

Those standards are drawn from ideals of justice expressed in the Constitution, such as impartiality of judgment and regard for domestic tranquillity. They cannot be met except by fidelity to the public trust and an understanding of the place of policing in the governmental framework designed to advance the public interest. Like other summaries of ethics in policing, this account shows that a department capable of responsible policing cannot be conceived as a mere microcosm of the general society.

The public has a right to expect police departments to try to live up to such ideals, despite the flaws in the general population. Neither police nor the public can afford to be fatalistic in matters of such consequence. Police who have a proper self-respect, which embraces humility toward the magnitude of their duties, will not consider themselves mere microcosms of society-at-large. By contrast, a complacent self-esteem—feeling good about oneself while thinking of the department as no more than a microcosm of society—is self-deception.

Rising above the Microcosm

In "Police Integrity and Public Expectations," my colleague, Scott R. Stripling, and I wrote:

> The public has a right to expect that police recruits will be chosen on the basis of moral, intellectual, psychological, and physical fitness to bear the public trust as established by thorough background investigations, rigorous testing, and professionally conducted personal interviews. Procedures for identifying suitable recruits should focus on the candidates' behavioral history—with emphasis on the question of whether they have displayed a settled disposition to act reasonably and with regard for others rather than impulsively and selfishly. That is, the criteria for fitness to serve should include the achievement of personal integrity, including established habits of justice, self-control, and trustworthiness.
>
> The public has a right to expect that police departments will provide excellent academy and field training for their recruits and ongoing inservice education and training for experienced personnel. Every aspect of policing deserves attention—not only peacekeeping, crime prevention and law enforcement, but also the delivery of social services, and the cooperative support of families and the business, civic, religious, educational, and medical institutions whose successful work is indispensable to neighborhood self-protection and the reduction of criminal predation.
>
> Police should be expected to achieve high levels of competence through training in communication and verbal skills, physical fitness, weapons, law, departmental procedures and policies, management of informants, conduct of interrogations, paramedical services, suicide prevention, domestic violence control, crowd and riot control, traffic enforcement, and preparation of reports. They should also be well-instructed about the nature of the communities they are to serve and about the public- and private-sector service agencies with

which they must work to advance public safety and the overall public good. And because the fulfillment of the mission of policing necessarily involves the exercise of discretion by police of all ranks, the public has a right to expect that police will be trained not only in the limits to their discretion, but also in the exercise of good judgment within those limits.

The public has a right to expect that the supervision and accountability of police will be rigorous and thorough, based on the same high standards and unequivocal policies that inform reliable training. By these dimensions of recruitment, training, and supervision, police departments have the best chance of providing wise and virtuous service of the sort Madison had in mind, and of safeguarding the public against betrayals of their trust.

Measures for fulfilling the public's rightful expectations continue to advance. Many police departments use psychological testing to screen candidates, and some are required to do so by state law. Drug testing and polygraph examinations have become part of the screening process in some agencies. Many states have instituted standards that require completion of some course work in postsecondary or higher education for police certification. Educational opportunities of the highest quality are offered for state and local police by the federal government through the programs of the FBI Academy and at the state level by a number of state police academies.

Some individual departments have established career development programs that link supervisory promotion to accomplishment in higher education. Because the number of open supervisory positions is always limited, and because many good officers do not want to be supervisors, some departments are also offering increased compensation and nonsupervisory promotion as incentives to pursue higher education. In these departments, police officers who do not desire the supervisory responsibilities of a sergeant are encouraged to continue their special training and education in order to be named, and receive the higher compensation of, a master police officer.

Few police leaders are so naïve as to suppose that higher education provides a guarantee of character excellence or professional performance. But they know that much of policing consists of talking with people—asking the right questions, listening diligently, giving people room to tell their stories—and keeping accurate records of the interviews. In the interest of professionalism most police leaders, therefore, take very seriously the habits of successful communication and systematic learning by study that higher education helps to inculcate.[4]

Various commission studies of police departments conducted in recent years have also stressed means by which the expectations of the public can be met. None of those studies seems to me to be very sophisticated—even about such straightforward matters as community policing, problem-solving policing, and their relation to other police practices in crime prevention and law enforcement. But some do contain instructive passages.

The Mollen Commission, a mayoral panel established to report on conditions in the New York City Police Department, issued an interim report at the end of 1993. Under the chairmanship of Milton Mollen, the commission asserted that the "police culture" of the New York Police Department tolerates corruption, brutality, and other forms of misconduct. The report alleged that the behavior of the Buddy Boys—robbing and brutalizing drug dealers—is copied by other groups of officers. The panel also claimed that command officers sustain a "code of silence" to protect their own careers from discovery of corruption in their units and that "a deep-rooted reluctance to uncover corruption" is to be found in all ranks.[5] Whether or not all these charges are confirmed, any pockets of officers in the department who behave as the commission claims draw it downward toward the mere microcosm—or worse.

Political and police corruption in any prominent city sets a bad example for the rest of the nation. For more than two hundred years, wise leaders in the United States have understood urban corruption as a threat to the vision, and therefore the quality, of public service everywhere. Endemic urban corruption lends persuasiveness to—and obscures the flaws in—the microcosm argument. As philosopher Francis E. Rourke explained in 1964, for over a century reformers have held a deep conviction that the corruption of urban politics reflected a very fundamental malaise in American life, the growth of a commercial spirit and a weakening in the moral fiber of the population that was endemic in society and the economy as well as government. "The boss is not a political, he is an American institution," wrote Lincoln Steffens, and this point of view was widely shared. What was needed from the reformer's perspective was a moral regeneration of American life—a "great awakening" which would cleanse and purify not only local but national politics as well, since the movement for urban reform was only part of a much larger reform effort directed at uplifting the tone of public life in every sector of the nation's business, including the practices of private institutions where they impinged on the public interest.[6]

In 1898 Josiah Strong, author of *The Twentieth Century City*, cautioned that "unless the reform of urban politics is successful, the boss will certainly rule the city when the city rules the nation." Strong reported that abolitionist and reformer Wendell Phillips, who died fourteen years earlier, had prophesied, "The time will come when our cities will strain our institutions as slavery never did."[7] Our contemporary urban crises may yet prove him right.

The magnitude of that strain may be even more evident in Los Angeles than in New York. Perhaps the most prominent of recent police department studies is the *Report of the Independent Commission on the Los Angeles Police Department*, published in July 1991. Warren Christopher, who later became U.S. secretary of state, was chairman of the commission. I have been told by public servants I trust thoroughly that the commission or members of its staff did not keep promises of confidentiality made during the preparation of the *Report*. Furthermore, although Los Angeles Mayor Tom Bradley's published charge to the commission promised the involvement of a distinguished scholar as a senior adviser to the commission, the scholar never served as an adviser. Because of those and other flaws in the *Report*, I do not assent to all the commission's practices, affirm all its findings, advocate all its recommendations, or encourage its use in academy training and criminal justice education. Nonetheless, the *Report* does stress important features of policy for background investigations, academy standards, field training, and supervisory accountability that merit the attention of police and their leaders.

While acknowledging that the Los Angeles Police Department has been admired for its professionalism in some dimensions of law enforcement and for its support of background investigations and field training, the commission reported:

> [T]he background investigation offers the best hope of screening out violence-prone applicants. Unfortunately, the background investigators are overworked and inadequately trained. . . . The training problem is magnified because a number of investigators have been selected with only patrol experience, despite the apparent policy of the Unit to select officers with significant investigative experience. . . . In a number of files, drug use and sexual background were marked for attention, but a candidate's discussion regarding losing his or her temper or engaging in fights was not.

To this potential source of departmental problems in policing generally, the commission added its concerns about reduced academy standards. For Los Angeles, the commission lamented the low numbers of "minority officers in management positions" but observed that "the LAPD has made substantial progress in hiring minorities and women since entry of the Blake Consent Decree in 1981." The commission insisted that neither the achievement of diversity in personnel composition nor any other consideration should be permitted to reduce academy standards:

> At present approximately 90–95% of each entering Academy class graduates. Less than ten years ago that rate was closer to 60%. Some of this difference undoubtedly is due to changes in teaching practices, the availability of remediation programs, improvement in prehiring screening efforts, and reduction in physical training requirements. A portion of this change, however, seems attributable to an unwillingness to terminate poorly performing recruits, especially those protected by the consent

decree or other similar mandate, for fear of civil liability or legal challenge or simply not meeting Departmental guidelines. The Commission urges that unqualified recruits not be retained for any reason. To do so only threatens the well-being of the public and the police force.

Background investigations and academy standards are as important today as they have ever been in policing. A few departments show signs of repeating the mistakes made by the Miami Police Department in the instance of the River Cops in 1980 (described in chapter 2), an entirely avoidable debacle that should never be allowed to happen again. The LAPD, according to the commission, also failed to select and train field training officers (FTOs) in accordance with reasonable standards:

> At present there are no formal eligibility or disqualification criteria for the FTO position based on an applicant's disciplinary records. Fourteen of the FTOs in the four divisions the Commission studied had been promoted to FTO despite having been disciplined for use of excessive force or use of improper tactics. There also appears to be little emphasis on selecting FTOs who have an interest in training junior officers, and an FTO's training ability is given little weight in his or her evaluation. . . .
>
> Twelve of the FTOs in the four divisions studied had been disciplined for dishonesty. For example, the officers had failed to report misconduct they witnessed, lied about their own involvement in an incident, or agreed to lie about other officers' involvement in an incident.

Similar problems were identified in supervision and discipline in direct testimony by one high-ranking LAPD official:

> In my judgment, we do a very poor job of management and supervisory accountability. . . . [H]igher command officers when learning of [incidents of excessive force] having occurred took no action or very indecisive action, very weak and slow

approach to doing something. Let me tell you that none of those people [the higher command officers], with rare exceptions, have been disciplined. And, in fact, I'm not even sure they've been counseled in many of these incidents. . . . And so, that's an area that I believe we have failed miserably in, is holding people accountable for the actions of their people.

The commission stressed few new problems in policing. But the importance of sound background investigations, high academy standards, good field training, and accountability at all ranks cannot be prudently neglected anywhere. All are fundamental to the integrity of a department and its personnel and indispensable to any effort to rise above the microcosm.

More on Higher Standards and Double Standards

Nothing stands more in the way of rising above the microcosm than the collapse of higher standards into double standards. Double standards generate not aspiration to excellence in public service but rather cynicism among public servants and within the public.

Such problems persist in government at all levels. The nomination of Zoe Baird as attorney general of the United States showed how government leaders had either forgotten or never understood the differences between a higher standard and a double standard. After her nomination in 1992, Baird admitted that she and her husband had hired two illegal aliens from Peru to serve as their chauffeur and nanny. Baird, a corporate lawyer, and her husband, a Yale Law School professor, had paid no Social Security taxes for those employees. Although Baird paid $12,000 in back taxes and a $2,900 fine after her nomination, opposition to her confirmation led her to request, on January 22, 1993, that the president withdraw her nomination. The president agreed to Baird's request and, on the same day, wrote the following letter to her:

Dear Zoe:

I have received your letter asking that I withdraw your nomination as Attorney General of the United States from further consideration by the Senate. With sadness, I accept your request that the nomination be withdrawn.

You are an exceptionally gifted attorney and a person of great decency and integrity. You have responded to the call of public service with energy and a firm dedication to the mission of the Justice Department. *I realize that it was your candid disclosure of the child care matter that led to the circumstances we face today. I believe that the concerns raised about your child care situation were unique to the position of Attorney General* [emphasis added].

You are highly qualified to be Attorney General. Your stated goals for a nonpartisan, independent and strongly managed Department of Justice were fully in accord with my own. I believe you would have been a fine Attorney General.

Hillary and I value your and Paul's friendship. We look forward to seeing you often. I hope that you will be available for other assignments for your country in my administration.

Sincerely,
Bill Clinton[8]

Significantly, the president said that Baird's confirmation problems came from her "candid disclosure" of her lawbreaking, rather than from her lawbreaking itself and her indifference to law. Then he asserted that such lawbreaking was relevant only to "the position of Attorney General"—a declaration of a double standard as pronounced as those that had been made about the position of secretary of defense during the confirmation hearings for John Tower.

In reaction to the withdrawal of Baird's nomination, some academics and government officials insisted that opposition to her was really a sign of a higher standard for women than for men nominated for high office. The president fueled that view and the concerns about justice that it raised by his later nomination of Bobby Ray Inman as secretary of defense. Like Baird, Inman failed to pay the required taxes for employees in his household but was nominated all the same. Had he not withdrawn, his confirmation would have shown that there is a lower standard for men than for women, that there is a lower standard for one cabinet position than for another, or that in the aftermath of the Baird controversy the president, Congress, and the media lowered their standards for everyone.

All those alternatives threaten further erosion of the tradition of higher standards for public servants than for the general public. Justice Leah Sears-Collins of the Georgia Supreme Court said: "If [Baird] had been up for environmental secretary, this probably would not have been as big an issue and would not have axed her appointment. But above all, an attorney general needs to have absolute integrity and be very tough."[9] If this view dominates thinking about public service in American life, no public servants except law enforcement personnel will be expected to have integrity. That is an ominous prospect for all of our institutions, for the status of obligations to the public trust, and for the way police view public service.

The Therapeutic Vision of Human Beings

Double standards and their erosion of higher standards take on staggering proportions with the rising popularity of a therapeutic vision of human beings, which views human beings not as Homo sapiens (man the thinker) but as Homo victus (man the victim). A credulous public seems to be accepting the social science ideology that human beings are neither free nor responsible for their actions. Instead, an article of faith in many academic circles holds that adults and children are merely victims of genetic or environmental circumstances beyond their control.

When people misbehave, according to that ideology, they do so because they are ill, or because of needs for which they are not responsible, or because of suffering that could have been counseled away, or because of externally inflicted damage to their psychological health—their self-esteem. Those who criticize "lifestyles" different from their own merely disclose their own illness, their own phobias.

This therapeutic reduction of all human misconduct to illness differs dramatically from the obvious truth that some wrongful human actions do spring from afflictions. Some people, after all, are sick. The therapeutic reduction, however, denies that persons are ever moral agents, responsible for their actions, and implies instead that they can never be understood and reasoned with as autonomous equals. People are only patients under therapy in an endless state of either recovering from their afflictions or suffering relapses.

No one familiar with the quasi-metaphysical pronouncements of social science for the past several decades will find such unsupported claims for determinism unusual. For years, one school of thought on policing has contended that people thrust into corrupt institutions have no choice but to become corrupt. The many police in corrupt environments who remain entirely honorable and morally upright do not shake proponents of this dogma.

The therapeutic vision is equally indifferent to evidence from other walks of life. In our lifetime, we have witnessed unprecedented progress in medical research, medical treatment, medical technology, and health care. Advocates of therapy want to treat everything in human life as a medical issue, as if we are beset by daunting new diseases unknown in former times. This range of putative diseases continues to expand, in ways that border on the ridiculous, but are, in practice, very dangerous. In 1990 the Health and Environment Department of New Mexico released a report, *Let Peace Begin with Us: The Problem of Violence in New Mexico*, by Dr. Victor LaCerva, who said, "[T]he most important aspect of the report is to realize that violent behavior is a disease."[10]

Attempts to classify dispositions to violence as a disease disclose an ignorance of the many forms of violence and dispositions to it. Dante in the *Inferno* was right that "wrath, lust, and the will to dominate" are fundamental causes of violence. All of them are integral features of human nature at some times, but not always, and none is a disease. The therapeutic vision also ignores the times and circumstances in which violence, unlike disease, is justifiable and even obligatory.

The therapeutic vision threatens both liberty and justice because it lends itself to the tyrannical subjection of individuals to "treatment" in disregard of due process, of individual responsibilities, and of individual rights. Such diminution of human beings offers only the illusion of mercy, at the expense of respect for achievement and contempt for depravity.

The therapeutic vision is, however, gaining momentum worldwide. When South Africa's antiapartheid religious leader Allan Boesak resigned his ministry amid charges of adultery, his wife told the media, "I think it is just a sickness among men over 40."[11] Stephanie Jefferis, serving as student coordinator in Pennsylvania State University's peer sensitivity and diversity training program, routinely told students: "I consider myself a recovering racist, sexist, and homophobic. It's ridiculous for anyone to say they're not."[12] Mary Abowd, a senior at Notre Dame, explained at a "conference on women's ordination" that "a lot of feminists, former Catholic feminists, call themselves 'recovering Catholics,' like it's an ailment that they're getting over."[13]

Frank Riessman, codirector of the National Self-Help Clearinghouse, said that addiction "is becoming a major problem—not just alcohol and drug addiction, but gambling, overeating, sex certainly, money," and added, "I would be hard-pressed to find anyone I know who doesn't have one kind of addiction or another."[14] Describing herself as a "recovering psychotherapist," Anne Wilson Schaef said that she had "never met anyone who only has one addiction." When she told "a national conference of female Lutheran ministers in Los Angeles" that "they are all addicts of . . . some kind," the ministers gave "her a standing ovation."[15]

In 1990, responding to charges of ethical misconduct, Senator Dave Durenberger described his immersion in work after the death of his wife as his "grief counseling" and lamented the difficulty of his life at that time, when "ethics, like beauty, is in the eye of the beholder."[16] He spoke in the words of health professionals, funeral directors, and other counselors, who view grief as an illness and offer therapy for it. In the same way, dependency on drugs, narcotics, or alcohol is considered a disease. "Drug addiction isn't an issue of morality," said one such professional. "It isn't an issue of willpower—it's a disease."[17] Not to be outdone, sex therapists have written of promiscuity as an illness called sexual addiction. Sexaholics Anonymous, with 20,000 members in America, has joined the growing list of "Anons" for putative victims of their own genetic make-up.[18]

A popular rock 'n' roll song blared, "Might as well face it, you're addicted to love." Newsweek defined rape as men's "preempting of another person's body for the gratification of their own *needs* [emphasis added]."[19] A talk show host trumpeted the question, "Are you a hostage of your own emotions?"

New Age retreats and spas offer treatment to "destress" customers they call guests and provide therapy to promote "mind-fitness."[20] A Beverly Hills "psychiatric script consultant" for television dramas and situation comedies announced that "a psychological consultant should be part of the crew for each show." The *New York Times*, oblivious to distinctions between the subject matter of psychiatry and psychology and that of ethics, mistakenly identified the consultant as a "connoisseur of character."[21]

A movie idol referred to videotaping his own sex acts with teenage females not as something he did, but as something that "happened" to him and his career. Similarly, the convict who masterminded the primary cocaine-trafficking organization in Washington, D.C., said, "I'm a good guy, and just something bad happened to me."[22]

New heights in the popularity of the ideology of illness may have been reached by the aggrandizement of celebrity addicts. Glorification of celebrities who tell all as if doing so were heroic, courageous, honest, and inspirational tells more about America's love affair with addiction than about anything else, including the nature of good character. We should, after all, scarcely want to identify the limit of human aspiration as recovering one day at a time. Neither should lust for the limelight rank high among credentials for admiration and self-respect.

In keeping with the therapeutic vision, a California task force on education advocated "*healthy* self-esteem" as a "*social vaccine*" to inoculate us "against the lures of crime and violence, alcohol and drug abuse, premature pregnancy, child abuse, chronic dependence on welfare, and educational failure." It recommended that "training in [promoting self-esteem] be a part of the teacher credentialing process and a part of all in-service training."[23] It also urged that courses in raising children with self-esteem be given in all schools, which should appreciate the "uniqueness . . . and address the special needs . . . of each child" by "serving to liberate rather than domesticate" all children and to prepare every student "to become fully competent in . . . Relationships"—one of the six Rs.[24]

As teachers were taught not to be critical of their students' performance for fear of impairing their self-esteem, students were to learn to feel good about themselves, no matter how shabby their work or disgraceful their behavior. The report asserted: "Ultimately, we also need to learn to accept and treasure ourselves. . . . The point is not to become acceptable or worthy but to acknowledge the worthiness that already exists . . . [to] accept, appreciate, and celebrate ourselves as we are . . . unique."[25] Furthermore, the task force insisted that "as a result of cultural conditioning . . . most of us feel some shame when we honestly express our innermost feelings," so we must always create an environment for healthy self-esteem, "an atmosphere in which honest expressions are in fact encouraged, accepted and affirmed."[26] Presumably, that included affirmation of even the most depraved forms of self-indulgence.

At no other time in history has self-esteem been vaunted as the social vaccine against grave problems at the very time it was practiced so self-indulgently by so many people. Of America's high school seniors in 1988, only 5 percent could read well enough to do college-level work. Seventy-four percent could not write "an adequate persuasive letter, and a third did not know that the Mississippi River flows into the Gulf of Mexico."[27] Yet, of these same students, "eighty percent 'take a positive attitude' toward themselves, eighty-three percent judge themselves to be 'person(s) of worth,' seventy-nine percent claim to be generally satisfied with themselves, and . . . only fifteen percent agree with the statement 'I feel I do not have much to be proud of.'"[28]

Rather than self-esteem, in the sense of feeling good about themselves no matter what, people, including children, need to acquire a proper self-respect, a respect for *selves* that involves taking others seriously by considering the effects our actions will have on them. We also need to learn that we deserve our own esteem and the esteem of others because of our achievements. Self-confidence should be acquired from activity that brings intellectual and moral powers to life, as in good schoolwork and acceptance of daily responsibility at home and with friends. To lead responsible lives, all of us must learn to discipline our emotions, including our feelings of self-love and pride.

Some advocates of the therapeutic vision even go beyond the effort to promote self-esteem and inordinate self-love. They claim that particular groups of people are exempt from the fallibilities and weaknesses of others because they were *born* exempt. Academics and political figures define some human failings as a disease and then insist that only certain groups of people can catch it. In an article in the influential *Phi Delta Kappan*, two professors of education declared, "Racism is a mental illness." It "may be thought of as a sick belief system," a "stubborn disease . . . characterized by perceptual distortion, a denial of reality, delusions of grandeur (belief in white supremacism), the projection of blame (on the victim), and phobic reactions to differences."[29]

Since only white supremacism counted as a delusion of grandeur, only some groups identifiable by race could be afflicted with the illness. "A colonizer may be a racist, but a victim cannot be so,"[30] announced the professors.

Their message echoed the declaration of U.S. Representative Gus Savage of Illinois: "Racism is white. There is no black racism."[31] And despite the obvious capacity of some members of every racial, ethnic, gender, and economic group to discriminate against others, these educationists subscribe implicitly to the dogmatism of Detroit's former mayor Coleman Young: "I think racism is a system of oppression. I don't think black folks are oppressive to anybody, so I don't consider that blacks are capable of racism."[32] Perhaps Mayor Young never noted the sexist bigotry of the black activist Stokely Carmichael, a member of the Student Nonviolent Coordinating Committee (SNCC), who said, "The only position for women in SNCC is prone."[33] Similarly, the anti-Semitism of Louis Farrakhan and Khalid Abdul Muhammad, black leaders of the Nation of Islam, and the murder of a black civil rights leader by the white racist Byron de la Beckwith prove that a person's color tells nothing about his character.

Such alleged exemptions by birth of groups of people from specific forms of human fallibility demean them. All of us are fallible and flawed because we are human. To exempt any group is to claim that its members are more than human or less than human—a grotesque falsehood.

Similar difficulties emerge in discussions of homosexuality. Some religious fundamentalists call homosexuality an addiction, sometimes "demonic oppression."[34] Gay rights activists classify all objections to homosexual conduct as "homophobia," an irrational fear and hatred of homosexuality, which they call a "lifestyle." Neither homosexuality nor heterosexuality, however, is a lifestyle. The lives of homosexuals differ as much from one another in substance as do the lives of heterosexuals. Some of each group are honorable persons; some are not. Some are courageous, fair-minded, and trustworthy; others are not. Some are promiscuous; others are not. Some of each group indulge sexual tastes that involve predation on children and commit acts of domestic violence against their partners. Homosexuals no more think alike on every issue than heterosexuals do; and many homosexuals and heterosexuals agree on some issues. Opposition is widespread to the North American Man/Boy Love Association (NAMBLA), an association of pedophiles that asserts their right to respect as a minority and the right of children to the alleged benefits of sexual involvement with adults. In NAMBLA we see how the popular doctrine that all "lifestyles" are morally equivalent ends in nihilism. Failure to take individuals into account is bigoted, no matter where it occurs: in exempting black people from racial prejudice, in indicting all religious people as prejudiced, or in claiming that all homosexuals are bad or that all homosexuals are good.

The therapeutic vision also implies an assault on the traditional family. Self-help guru John Bradshaw, the author of *Healing the Shame That Binds You*, estimated that "there are 131 million addicts in the U.S. of various stripes." Almost all of them, he said, can blame their illness on what he described as the fundamental premise of his work: "All families are dysfunctional . . . distorted by the addictions and compulsions of one or more members, usually to the detriment of each individual."[35]

The movement against the family, for the therapeutic agenda, and against personal responsibility depends on what journalist and psychiatrist Charles Krauthammer called "defining deviancy up." This means, for example, generating or inventing data to show that the traditional family is so riddled with child abuse that the "middle class lifestyle" is deviant. Then, illegitimacy can be viewed as perfectly normal, even though it results in unwed teenagers' bearing children who will be destroyed by neglect, abandonment, and exploitation in the streets.[36]

The description of all families as dysfunctional, together with the insistence of the "self-esteem" movement that we must "liberate rather than domesticate" children, recalls earlier ideological claims that the family is an instrument of repressive power, "the factory of reactionary ideology and structure," as Freudian Marxist Wilhelm Reich called it.[37] Some educational traditions have treated society, culture, and the institutions of both as affronts to freedom and self-fulfillment, which fraudulently sustain themselves by pretending to advance the formation of character in the young and to safeguard morality. Today, the bitter fruit of such indefensible practices is the decline of schooling and the family—with 1.2 million children born annually in the United States out of wedlock and frequently abandoned to their own devices.

At the same time, the movement for moral equivalence depended on what Daniel Patrick Moynihan called "defining deviancy down."[38] One example was the view of staggering levels of homicide as normal rather than as deviant; another was the assertion of psychoanalyst R. D. Laing and psychiatrist Thomas Szasz that mental illness is a myth and a coercive instrument of political and social control. Since the late 1960s that view has contributed to the dramatic increase of homeless people in the United States and to criminal predation within the homeless population. In this and other respects, the therapeutic agenda has become highly politicized.

Krauthammer graphically identified still another instance of the therapeutic vision:

> Consider this advice from one of the more popular self-help books on sex abuse, *Courage to Heal*: "If you are unable to remember any specific instances [of childhood sex abuse] . . . but still have a feeling that something abusive happened to you, it probably did." And "if you think you were abused and your life shows the symptoms, then you were." . . . Whenever a patient complains of depression, low self-esteem, or any of the common ailments of modern life, the search begins for the underlying childhood sexual abuse. As the book says, if your life shows the symptoms, then you were abused. This new psychology is rooted in and reinforces current notions about the pathology of ordinary family life. . . . So much for the family.[39]

Police will recognize the illogic of those claims in *Courage to Heal* and the spectacular contempt for evidence and due process they convey.

Police and law enforcement leaders should recognize the threat to their standards in the therapeutic agenda, which holds that human beings are bundles of addictions who cannot be genuinely responsible for their actions. All of us are victims except those born into groups of victimizers, who are identifiable by color or sex. Those tenets influence social and criminal justice policy at the federal, state, and local levels. A surgeon general, urban mayors, and other public servants have suggested that crime and violence should be viewed as *health* issues; that their "root causes" are illnesses bred in perpetrators by their victimization at the hands of a perverse society; that law enforcement is not central to policy on drug trafficking and consumption; that minimum sentences for drug and firearm violations should be eliminated; and that public policy in those areas should focus on the expansion of health and social services.

Many of those positions reveal a startling incoherence. On December 7, 1993, for example, Joycelyn Elders, then the surgeon general of the United States, recommended that the government consider studying the legalization of drugs as a means of reducing violent crime. Given the popularity of the therapeutic agenda, her recommendation was surprising not in itself but only in conjunction with a pronouncement of the surgeon general a week earlier, when she was asked whether it was immoral for people to have children out of wedlock. She replied, "No. Everyone has different moral standards. You can't impose your standards on someone else."

Why, then, should the surgeon general be concerned about violence? If you cannot impose your standards about anything, all moral standards fall. By denying moral standards that transcend the individual, Joycelyn Elders denied that violence against the innocent is wrong. Neither are drug consumption, murder, abandonment and neglect and abuse of children, sexual harassment, rape, discrimination, and injustice.

In one broad sweep, the surgeon general rejected both morality and law—the two principal instruments of civilized life—as means of safeguarding the public. In rejecting moral standards, she denied that individuals are responsible for their behavior: We must not "impose" standards of responsibility on anyone, even in their treatment of helpless children.

Is drug legalization worthy of consideration? Would it reduce violent crime and illegal drug trafficking? No. Drug users would still commit crimes of violence for money to buy other things—food, clothes, liquor, entertainment, and the like. And they would commit violent acts because they would be on mind-altering drugs. Drug traffickers would market drugs to children who could not buy them legally and would wage war over market share. They would introduce new free-based drugs that have not been legalized. They would sell the drugs in any quantity to anyone who wished to buy. And they would use murder, hijacking, extortion, and bribery to secure shipments of legal drugs to sell cheaply, just as they have been operating a multibillion dollar industry in the criminal diversion of legal prescription drugs. Can drug legalization reduce the consumption of harmful drugs? It is not likely.

In 1994 Dr. Herbert Kleber of Columbia University's Center on Addiction and Substance Abuse explained, "There are 50 million nicotine addicts, 18 million alcoholics or problem drinkers, and fewer than 2 million cocaine addicts in the United States. Cocaine is a much more addictive drug than alcohol. If cocaine were legally available, as alcohol and nicotine are now, the number of cocaine addicts would probably rise to . . . perhaps 20 to 25 million."[40]

Even if all those arguments were invalid, drug legalization could succeed only if education, peer pressure, family influence, and drug treatment were geared to dissuade people against using harmful drugs. But former Surgeon General Elders's assertion that we should never "impose" our standards on anyone else suggested that teachers, peers, parents, and health care providers should not be allowed to say that use of harmful drugs is wrong.

Anyone who wonders about the logical consequences of the therapeutic vision of humanity for our institutions need only ask, What would be the consequences for the Americans with Disabilities Act if every human failing were treated as a disability and thus outlawed as a reason for denying employment just as the law now prohibits institutions from treating a history of illegal drug consumption as a reason for denying employment? One therapeutically inclined federal official once told me, "Within ten years, we will have everything classified as a disease, and then we can hope for justice and the end of discrimination in this country." Insofar as his goal has already been achieved, the idea that we are normally responsible for our lives is dimmed. There can be no greater threat to the dignity of human beings or to the ideals of constitutional government than this slippery slope.

The Americans with Disabilities Act

Although the therapeutic vision threatens integrity in all human institutions, its most immediate adverse consequences for policing may lie in features of the Americans with Disabilities Act and of multicultural sensitivity training for police. The Americans with Disabilities Act, signed into law in July 1990, became effective in July 1992 for all institutions with twenty-five or more members and in July 1994 for smaller institutions. In many respects, the law is wise and should be welcome; it prohibits employment discrimination for a variety of disabilities that should never have led to disadvantage for the people who suffer them.

But according to the Bureau of National Affairs, the act provides that "individuals who have successfully completed a supervised drug rehabilitation program and who are no longer engaging in the illegal use of drugs, or who have otherwise been successfully rehabilitated, or who are participating in supervised programs and are not using, or who are erroneously regarded as engaging in such use, are protected by the statute."[41] Police department policies that disqualify candidates because of a history of illegal drug consumption are threatened by this feature of the act. Although federal officials say that this is not the intention of the law, few laws are applied and enforced over time only in accordance with their original intent. The act not only ignores the limits to our knowledge of how to treat drug habituation but also neglects the failures of personal responsibility, the weaknesses of character, the disregard for other people, and the contempt for the law that often accompany such habituation.

Some police departments will find deficiencies of character related to illegal drug consumption compelling reasons for disqualification and will do their best to maintain standards without violating the law. Others will be intimidated by the possibility of lawsuits, just as they feel constrained by possible lawsuits from establishing policies of zero tolerance for lying in internal investigations. If those departments discard standards related to prior drug consumption, they are likely to deteriorate.

My experience confirms that some police departments are already lowering standards to avoid difficulties with the Americans with Disabilities Act. In some large urban departments, physical standards—strength, endurance, stamina, agility, fitness, weight in relation to height—are being entirely set aside, and background investigations either are not being conducted at all or are being ignored for fear of diminishing applicant pools. The result is not only that drug users are becoming police, but also that drug traffickers are entering police departments. A crisis of corruption, brutality, and incompetence looms in those departments. Drastic problems are appearing, as officers steal weapons held in evidence, traffic in illegal substances, threaten the lives of other police, commit acts of grievous incompetence, and commit rape, murder, and kidnapping. This crisis deepens where departments disregard records of serious juvenile crimes, as some departments now do.

Many police leaders are utterly opposed to suspension of high standards and high expectations, but there are exceptions. A few police executives have told me that they consider the use of juvenile records and background investigations an instrument of racist efforts to minimize the diversity of departments. One prominent police executive told me—in the presence of other command officers—that the idea of "competence" is purely subjective, that there actually is no such thing as competence in policing or any other walk of life. Police training for the sake of competence, he said, only establishes racially biased ideas of how to do a job.

Academy and field training can surely fuel racial, gender, and other biases and do other harm. But assertions that literacy is irrelevant, that deftness of communication is unnecessary, that the powers of observation police sometimes call street eyes make no difference, that acting in accordance with the law and with departmental policy is unnecessary, and that knowledge of the languages, customs, and habits of the public to be served can be neglected with impunity are as dangerous. Police leaders who spurn rigorous standards of candidate fitness and training because some are ill-conceived bring ruin to their own departments and heartache to the public.

Therapy and Multicultural Sensitivity Training

While many police departments understand themselves to serve a diverse population in terms of color, gender, ethnicity, cultural heritage, religion, and economic condition, the more crucial fact is that all police departments serve a diverse population. All police departments serve the individuals who make up the public, and no two individuals are alike in every respect. This fact must be heeded if police are to avoid thinking of people merely as members of one group or another. Real sensitivity to human beings consists of taking them seriously as individuals.

When police departments help their officers become competent in the native languages of residents or to understand their customs and traditions, they take a step toward excellent police service. If they treat their officers as students who need such training to do their jobs ably, they advance their departmental missions.

But the therapeutic vision leads to multicultural sensitivity training that treats police as if they were patients rather than students—patients who have an affliction that calls for treatment. Such a view of police is demeaning, ignores aspirations to excellence, and tends to be discriminatory. Author Ralph Ellison was right to insist that "our task is that of making ourselves individuals. The conscience of a race is the gift of its individuals."[42]

Some programs of multicultural sensitivity training arbitrarily treat police officers as if they were disposed toward racism, sexism, xenophobia, homophobia, and the like. The claim that all white people are racists and that only white people are racists is no less malign than any other form of racism. Yet textbooks used for sensitivity training often make that claim. In *Counseling the Culturally Different*, multiculturalist ideologues Derald Wing Sue and David Sue asserted:

> First, racism is a basic and integral part of U.S. life and permeates all aspects of our culture and institutions. Second, Whites are socialized into U.S. society and, therefore, inherit the biases, stereotypes, and racist attitudes, beliefs, and behaviors of the society. In other words, all Whites are racist whether knowingly or unknowingly.[43]

The same textbook charges that America is utterly intolerant of diversity:

> Many of the Asian immigrants to the United States tend to hold very positive and favorable views of their own culture. What happens when they encounter a society that views cultural differences as being deviant?[44]

The proposition that all and only white people are racists refutes itself, since it is itself racist, and not everyone who asserts it is white.

Any intelligent police officer, regardless of background, will recognize the perniciousness of such assertions and will resent them. Educational programs designed on this model impair the mission of the department. Nothing is more certain to undermine real integrity in a department than the attempt to make officers feel guilty for harboring prejudices that they do not actually harbor.

Such sensitivity training is designed not to increase knowledge or competence but to spread the view that all lifestyles must be accepted as morally equivalent. Such programs celebrate differences as if every difference were good, and they sentimentalize other cultures as if all were models of justice and respect for human dignity. Celebration of all differences denies that even the worst forms of human depravity are wrong. Serial killers, after all, are different. Sentimentalization of all cultures amounts to falsification, since no culture can be wise and just in every respect. Today, various regions of the world are plagued by problems of corruption, discrimination, bigotry, sweat shops, de facto slavery, genital mutilation of girls and women, ethnic cleansing, and genocide. No population in history has been exempt from flaws or fallibility, but programs of sensitivity training often lie about that. Education about cultures and cultural differences should be educational, not therapeutic. It should be reliable, rather than sentimental, and should never uncritically celebrate differences. Training should advance competence rather than instill guilt or treat putative afflictions. It should teach that cultural differences provide no warrant for indifference to basic decency and lawfulness.

Police executives must show more wisdom and circumspection than federal lawmakers did when they adopted the "Declaration of Findings and Purposes" for the National Foundation on the Arts and the Humanities that provided:

> The arts and the humanities reflect the high place accorded by the American people to the nation's rich cultural heritage and to the fostering of mutual respect for the diverse beliefs and values of all persons and groups.[45]

The United States and other nations have police departments precisely because the diverse "beliefs and values of all persons and groups" do not merit respect. Predatory gangs and their members, for instance, believe that they have a perfect right to behave violently and ruthlessly in pursuit of their own pleasure or profit.

Finally, educational programs should not be perceived as reactions to misconduct by individual officers. Police resent it as much as anyone else when they are presumed to be insensitive or bigoted because someone else happens to be. Judiciousness and freedom from prejudice are as essential to educational programs as to other matters of policy.

If educational programs about cultures and differences are conducted without attributing character flaws to the members of the department—if police are treated as students—such programs can be assets in a department's efforts to rise above the microcosm. If they presume that police should be treated as patients, they will drive wedges within the department and solidify us-against-them attitudes toward the public.

16

Ethical Ideals, Youth Violence, and Gang Enforcement

If we heedlessly trash the minds, indeed the very souls, of our children; if through reiterated models of violence and the false promise of endless instant gratification we produce generations incapable of self-discipline and restraint; if we encourage the development of insatiable men and women who put the pursuit of pleasure before the pursuit of happiness; if by shortening the attention span we create persons incapable of complex analysis and responsible judgment; if we distort events of the day, garble the words of our leaders, simplify the character of nations, positing a false equivalence between democratic and totalitarian governments—there can be only one result. A dictatorship may survive by virtue of the strength of one man and an army that stands behind him, but the survival of democracy depends upon the moral virtue and reasoning power of all its people and on their participation in government as responsible, understanding citizens.

—John Silber[1]

When state and local police executives, sheriffs, and other leaders of federal law enforcement agencies ask me for a thumbnail sketch of an ethically ideal law enforcement agency, I offer one with the strong caveat that such an institution is impossible to forge. Moreover, unrealistic expectations breed cynicism, and ignoring human limitations invites tyranny. Unrealistic expectations lead to the idea that a powerful government—fascist, socialist, or communist— could make life perfect. Tyrannies always betray justice as their inevitable failures become more desperate. Any sketch of an ideal department is at best a rough template of what to strive for in policing and law enforcement.

Conversations about the difficulties of approximating the template sometimes focus on gangs, juvenile career criminals, and youth violence. Ruthless and violent antisocial behavior by girls and boys and youths who grow up without adult supervision has reached intolerable levels. Juvenile justice systems are inadequate because they were never designed for such staggering levels of depravity in the young.

Violence is on the rise even in the elementary, middle, and junior high school grades. In New York City, nine hundred elementary and junior high school students were suspended for carrying illegal weapons in school in 1992 alone.[2] Many states showed dramatic increases in juvenile crime from 1983 through 1992. In 1992, in Florida, which has at times suffered the highest crime and violent crime rates in the country, "149 juveniles were charged with murder or manslaughter . . . compared with 69 a decade earlier. During the same period, attempted murder cases involving juveniles rose to 249 from 13, armed robbery cases to 1,972 from 645, and aggravated assault and battery cases to 7,083 from 2,688."[3]

In 1993 William J. Bennett, the former U.S. secretary of education, pointed out in his *Index of Leading Cultural Indicators* that since 1960 there had been

> a 560 percent increase in violent crime; more than a 400 percent increase in illegitimate births; a quadrupling in divorces; a tripling of the percentage of children living in single-parent homes; more than a 200 percent increase in the teenage suicide rate; and a drop of 75 points in the average S.A.T. scores of high school students. . . . [In 1993] 30 percent of all births and 68 percent of black births [were] illegitimate. By the end of the decade, according to the most reliable projections, *40 percent* of all American births and *80 percent* of minority births will occur out of wedlock. . . . And then there are the results of an ongoing teacher survey. Over the years teachers have been asked to identify the top problems in America's schools. In 1940 teachers identified them as talking out of turn; chewing gum; making noise; running in the hall; cutting in line; dress code infractions; and littering. When asked the same question in 1990, teachers identified drug use; alcohol abuse; pregnancy; suicide; rape; robbery; and assault.[4]

Surely, no greater crisis faces us than the spawning of generations of young bereft of regard for civility, restraint, and law. And because large segments of the public are inclined to think of that as a crisis only for police, no social phenomenon is likely to cause deeper or more persistent ethical problems in policing. How, then, should ethical ideals be brought to life in relation to youth violence and gang enforcement?

A Sketch of the Ethically Ideal Institution

Foremost, an ethically ideal organization would be one with integrity, in which policies and practices were forged for moral reasons—such as the dignity of human beings—rather than from impulse, whim, desire for personal gratification, and the like. There would be no us-against-them attitudes against the public and no disrespect for the limits of the law. Everything done in private would be done exactly as if the public were watching.

Conduct would be informed by considerations of justice, not only in dealing with the public but also in all reward and accountability structures. Merit would be recognized, and mistakes made in good faith would be treated as opportunities for instruction rather than for punishment. By definition, there would be no bad-faith errors or misconduct, but everyone would be fully aware that bad-faith errors should be punished and treated differently from good-faith mistakes. There would be no bigotry of any kind.

Members of the organization would draw upon deep reservoirs of temperance and courage; no one would sacrifice duty to personal desire and gratification or show cowardice or rashness. Accordingly, they would show probity rather than financial corruption, restraint in use of force rather than brutality, and healthful personal habits, without problems of drug consumption or excesses with alcohol.

Since integrity embraces honesty, the leaders would be faithful to sworn and civilian personnel by giving them clear policies and acting in accord with stated policies. There would be no falsified reports, no perjury, no covert uses of the badge for private gain of any kind, and no acceptance of gratuities. In such an organization, there would be no peer pressure against the faithful fulfillment of the police mission, so no one would be unsuited to be police. Recruitment programs would have to be flawless.

Because in ethics we recognize that people have a duty to be competent at their work, in an ideally ethical institution there would be no crucial weaknesses in academy or in-service training and no acceptance of personnel who were unable or unwilling to perform well and honorably. And the institution would give its personnel whatever resources they need to perform the work required by their mission.

Finally, inexperienced personnel would not be left to their own devices without guidance in the field, and no one would be deprived of ample supervision. Because the leaders would recognize the pressing need to know what their personnel must contend with, open lines of communication would be routinely used throughout the ranks, upward, downward, and laterally. This same level of communication would be maintained with the public and the media; police policies and actions would generate few surprises.

That is, roughly, what an ethically ideal organization would be like. Obviously, no human being or group of human beings, no matter how ethical or wise, could create or maintain such an institution. It would have to be exempt from all the contingencies of the world in which we live and be made up of angels, not human beings. So it is, when we describe the ideal. Nothing real is ever utterly ideal; the challenge is to make intelligent use of the ideal as a standard of judgment.

Youth Violence and Gang Enforcement

How, exactly, are these ethical ideals to be realized in contending with youth violence and gangs? The answer begins with courage—the courage to tell unpleasant truths.

School officials sometimes manipulate data to show student performance as better than it really is (for example, by excluding various groups of students from the data samples) or to show that everyone in school is learning well (by making tests so trivial as to be meaningless or by graduating students on the basis of accumulated credits rather than on scholastic performance). School officials also downplay violence and pressure school police to deny the existence of gangs. Political leaders also may minimize reports of violent crime and gang predation to mollify prospective tourists and local residents. Broad segments of the public commonly regard crime as someone else's problem—a problem only for those whose neighborhoods are hardest hit or whose children are imperiled.

Since such matters become politically volatile, police candor on youth violence and gang activity may be unwelcome. Many political leaders even call gang enforcement units by some euphemism to obscure gang problems. Nonetheless, it seems to me obligatory for police leaders to be forthright in alerting the mayors, city managers, governors, or others to whom they are accountable. Police leaders should also issue warnings about gang activity likely to have an impact on youth organizations, drug treatment centers, and hospitals, as well as on the streets and in schools. Disputes about whether a pack of youths who cruise in search of racial confrontations is properly called a gang should not delay or prevent proactive steps by police.

If youth violence and gang activity are ignored or denied, gangs acquire a head start in recruitment and criminality that is difficult to overcome. A city that believes that it has no problems will not mount unified opposition to gang incursion and recruitment by schools, youth organizations, civic groups, corporations, the media, police, prison and probation officials, prosecutors, judges, private foundations, and health and other social service agencies. Without such a unified front, the odds against reversing gang activity can become overwhelming.

Enlisting the help of the media may be difficult but must be attempted. Publishers and editors must learn that gang activity resembles guerrilla theater in that gangs use publicity to aggrandize themselves and to promote recruitment. Public visibility, like conviction for violent crimes, is a mark of success and honor.

I have seen local police plead with television reporters not to interview a gang member because they knew that he would declare war on rivals and, once publicly committed, could not back down. Yet the television reporters interviewed the gang member on camera and precipitated the violence.

Some reporters who write feature stories are susceptible to manipulation by gangs that present a false picture of themselves as civic-minded youth organizations. Such well-organized criminal conspiracies as the Latin Kings, also known as the Almighty Latin King Nation or the Almighty Latin Charter Nation, and the Latin Queens have become skilled at manipulating community leaders, youths, and the media. Concealing their ruthlessness and violence, they sought 100,000 members by the year 2000 to control large markets in drugs and weapons smuggling, while professing to be dedicated to education, good citizenship, ethnic pride, and the self-esteem of the young. Not even the most convincing evidence the police can provide persuades reporters to acknowledge the facts. Reporters who get a voyeuristic thrill from being around violent criminals may slant their stories to extend their access to a gang.

Despite such difficulties, police have to try to work with the media for the sake of the public interest, without pandering to their every desire. Police leaders must have their own agenda for media interviewers. They should think of themselves as teachers of the public whenever they speak for the record, rather than as objects of media interviews. No matter what questions are asked, police spokesmen and spokeswomen should say the things the public most deserves to know and not be diverted by the reporter. Police departments should videotape extended interviews in full so that they can respond if sound bite editing misrepresents the department or jeopardizes the public.

At the same time, police should resist the temptation to inform the media of search and arrest warrants to be served and the like. Some departments yield to that temptation in the hope of currying media favor and showing the public that police are effective. When camera crews arrive, however, crowds—including many police and police command officers—follow them, and confusion reigns. I have seen episodes where warrants served on the wrong address or the wrong person made the police a laughingstock on the next day's news. The work of policing is hard enough without courting such unnecessary impairments.

To the courage of telling unpleasant truths and the wisdom of trying to work with the media in the public interest should be added the virtues of wise planning and preparedness. In gang enforcement and the prevention of youth violence, the most essential of all resources is the capacity to gather intelligence and to use it effectively. Departments should also make a commitment to the education of nonpolice organizations in their own areas and of neighboring police departments. If local police alone know what needs to be anticipated and opposed, their efforts will be isolated and less than effective. Officers who learn to read gang graffiti can teach others that graffiti are not harmless art work or trifling vandalism.

Gang graffiti are declarations of terror that mean, "If you can see this, you are under our dominion. Here you have no rights, no public space. This space belongs to us, and you live only at our sufferance and with our permission."

Police teach school officials and city officials that to lose the graffiti wars is to lose immeasurable ground, so they stress graffiti eradication every day, before school starts. Although we spend several billion dollars on graffiti eradication annually in the United States and succeed only about 20 percent of the time, this form of opposition to gang power remains imperative. The basic idea is James Q. Wilson and George L. Kelling's "broken window" principle: Leave a broken window unrepaired, and other forms of neighborhood decline will follow.[5] So, too, with graffiti.

Gathering gang intelligence and keeping it current are always crucial. This includes information about recruitment, weaponry, agendas, graffiti, tattoos, codes, signs, mobility, affiliations and enmities, prison associations, wealth, vehicles, patterns of criminality, and gang colors, dress, jewelry, and paraphernalia. Some departments assign pregnant officers and officers who are temporarily disabled for patrol duty to update computer records daily. Informing patrol personnel, detectives, gang enforcement units, and other personnel of the most current information is essential to proactive enforcement.

Some gangs use computers in gathering intelligence on police. I have seen raids of gang houses, some of them fortified, where police discovered computer records of police assignments, patterns of patrol for marked and unmarked vehicles, movements of the spouses and children of police officers, and the activities of rival gangs. Police departments have been forced to relocate spouses and children under names that conceal their ties with gang intelligence or enforcement officers. Departments must know what the gangs know and are capable of discovering to protect their own people.

It has never been unusual for prostitutes and other lawbreakers to keep careful track of police. As one Chicago officer put it:

> Streetwalkers organize their lives around cops' schedules. They keep close watch on the vice cops and the district tac teams. They know the guys they can outrun and outfox. They know when we're out there and when the watch changes. Their peak times are shift changes. They can do a lotta, lotta stuff in half an hour. Sometimes we switch shift times to confuse them. They get real perturbed at us— "What you doing out here? You're not supposed to be here now. You're not playing by the rules."[6]

But the stakes are dramatically higher now, and underestimating them can be deadly.

Unfortunately, some departments are inept at gathering and using gang intelligence, and some create gang enforcement units in name only—as a sop to the community or to the media. I have worked with departments that assigned officers to gang enforcement who had no training in managing informants or in gang activities. Where gangs are involved in drug trafficking—and, of course, not all of them are—I have seen narcotics and gang enforcement officers who had no real knowledge of drugs or narcotics and who would not have recognized them had they encountered them. I have also seen weak officers assigned to drug and gang education programs in schools and youth organizations, officers who were not very good on the streets and were even worse in classrooms. Such imprudent steps by police thwart their own investment in gang and drug enforcement and undermine their credibility, especially with the young.

Departments that deal well with youth violence and gangs assign to those units very good people who teach leaders in civic, educational, foundation, and corporate affairs what they need to know, and those trainers formulate plans for coordinated activities. If officials want to rely on youth curfews and related measures, the police are straightforward about the resources and personnel needed to make them useful. Police leaders stress the risks of enacting policies and laws that cannot or will not be enforced and that parents will not support, especially if they have given up hope of controlling their children. Those police explain that isolated measures without a comprehensive plan accomplish little.

Abilene, Tex., has a well-conceived and coordinated plan that reduced known gang members from 650 to seventy-five from 1988 to 1993. Boys and girls club gymnasiums and youth centers, built adjacent to lower-level schools in high-crime areas, led in each area to at least a 46 percent reduction in reported crimes. Those facilities served as gyms for schools during the day and as accommodations for youth recreation and entertainment at night. A local foundation bought a motel, restored it, and underwrote its operations to prevent the erosion of a neighborhood; other business leaders, encouraged by that anchor, succeeded in reversing the decline of the area. Schools have fought graffiti daily. Police have focused on prevention of prostitution, in cooperation with health officials, to avert a rise in drug addiction and the market for crack that prostitution brings. The city has eliminated buildings that provided haven for drug trafficking and other gang activities, and the police have concentrated patrols in areas beset by drive-by shootings. They have made drug and other criminal business sufficiently difficult that gangs have looked for more promising markets elsewhere.

Nothing of such magnitude can be accomplished in a city that views youth violence and gang predation as police problems or problems of a specific area or group of residents. In my experience, it is unusual for anyone except police to provide the initial leadership in educating the community and advising investments of money and time. Excellent personnel must therefore be assigned to those tasks. Their work may not appear as exciting as kicking down doors, but it reduces the dangers to the community, including the officers who have to kick down doors.

Gathering intelligence can be especially difficult where language barriers interfere, as with some Jamaican posses and Asian gangs. Immigrants frequently come to the United States from parts of the world where governmental corruption is the norm and police are only another gang to be feared. Securing the trust of those newcomers is time consuming and may yield only modest success. Large, diverse populations of immigrants who speak little or no English may resist all police efforts to be of service, particularly if they fear prompt and fatal gang reprisals. I know of no remedies except persistence, making and keeping promises faithfully, recruiting officers whose backgrounds give them access to the public, maintaining high visibility, and working with prosecutors to ensure mutually supportive agendas. Even those efforts may take years to produce results, and the results may be disheartening.

Wise police and sheriffs' departments establish close ties with state and federal agencies. They look for opportunities to have violators prosecuted under the statutes with the stiffest penalties and thereby dissuade outside gangs from incursion. Although joint law enforcement task forces can be effective, their operations call for care. When agencies with different standards work together, the lower standards may dominate the task force and impair the better departments. When officers supervise personnel from other agencies, they do not always take accountability seriously. Officers may be faced with temptations without benefit of supervision or clear policy.

A chief, sheriff, or agency head cannot afford to assign personnel to a task force and expect it to run smoothly by itself. Vigilant maintenance of institutional standards is as crucial here as in undercover work within the department.

Noble cause temptations can be as dangerous as temptations for private gain, especially if asset forfeiture is involved. When departments imprudently suggest that they seek to acquire assets, perhaps to sustain a portion of the operating budget, officers may be tempted to skim. Some of the worst corruption cases involve skimming to "cut out the middle man" in asset forfeiture and to buy equipment for the department or the task force with the stolen money. Inevitably, it seems, the noble cause theft becomes plain theft by the members of the unit as they begin taking money for themselves.

Falsification of reports, planting of evidence, and perjury can also become tempting, especially in departments or task forces that reward outcomes too heavily and conscientious performance too weakly. Supervisors too much concerned with outcomes may turn the other way when officers cut corners in violation of policy or law and thus undermine their ability to enforce any other policy and to stand for integrity in any respect. Poorly trained officers may also be tempted to gratify the wishes of area residents who ask them to beat up gang members and drive them out of the neighborhood. Officers who yield to that temptation may not learn until too late that the person they assaulted is someone's son, nephew, cousin, or lover. Friends and relatives of gang members will file complaints, and the public will turn on brutal police. A disregard for policy and law by officers turns into a source of tension between police and the public and makes their cooperation virtually impossible.

As gangs turn from territorial organizations concerned principally with turf and reputation into criminal conspiracies for profit resembling organized crime, they learn the advantages of bribery and the value of "friends in high places." When a willingness to take violent reprisal against adversaries and competitors is joined with a sophistication in co-opting public servants, the result is an institution capable of profoundly undercutting the public interest.

Some gangs, rich enough to hire prestigious lawyers and shrewd enough to enlist the sympathy of civil rights groups, persuade the media or the public that police investigations and arrests are motivated by racism. Mere denials by police count little. Here, only a deserved reputation for fairness can safeguard a department. Such a reputation can be secured only by the high quality of daily performance, by great care in classifying individuals as gang members, and by due restraint in the use of force.

Perhaps prompted by suspicion of racism among police, several mayors proposed that all police data and crime statistics should be colorblind, although they are unlikely to opt for colorblindness in such matters as personnel recruitment, employment opportunities, departmental composition, and the proportion of complaints filed against police departments by members of minority groups.[7] The mayors may argue that crime statistics that are not colorblind fuel racial bigotry and prejudicial stereotyping. But colorblindness of crime data seems unlikely to advance the safety of the public, including the minorities that are disproportionately the victims of violent crimes, nor will colorblindness in data reporting prevent the perpetuation of racism. Instead, the proposal will be seen as special pleading, an effort to cover up facts about crime. The proposal risks solidifying racism among those who are tempted to believe the vicious falsehood that a person's color indicates character or criminality.

Some youth violence and gang activity are racist. Wild packs of youths of one color do look for individuals of another color to assault or kill. The disgusting history of racist violence shows that no one is exempt from racist feelings by virtue of color or other accident of birth, and we must be willing to acknowledge the facts of history to improve the future. Disputes about presentation of statistics will not advance education against prejudice, encourage contempt for racism and other forms of bigotry, or further the prosecution of racially motivated crimes of violence.

The very real challenges of safeguarding the public become more grim when juries decide that individuals have less responsibility for their own violent acts if they are part of a mob. That proposition demeans us, because it implicitly denies that we are free and therefore accountable. Denial of personal responsibility threatens to dim public perceptions of the savagery of wild crimes and gang-inspired riots. That makes prevention of youth violence and gang predation more difficult for police, schools, and other institutions of civility and civilization. Toleration of excuses for violence adds to the already powerful influences that corrupt the young.[8]

Gangs, Education, and the Heroism of Cowards

Although police have no hope of combating these corrupting influences without the help of schools, parents, and other public- and private-sector institutions, police know more about gangs and the threat they pose than anyone else does. Their educational programs—about the malevolence of criminal conspiracies, about the signs of gang membership, and about constraints against gang involvement—can be central to crime prevention and gang enforcement.

Police must therefore know thoroughly the criminal conspiracies their communities face. They must be prepared to make concrete proposals for community and parental action. The basic points to follow would be the same whether a city suffers an incursion by a white supremacist motorcycle gang trafficking in amphetamines or some other type of criminal conspiracy, but Jamaican posses are so spectacularly dangerous that they provide a good illustration. Originally formed as strong-arm political street gangs in Kingston, Jamaica, they took their name from the cowboy posses in western movies.

In 1984 federal agencies estimated that at least forty posses, with between 10,000 and 20,000 members, operate in Jamaica, Great Britain, and the United States. The most infamous were Jungle, Spangler, and Shower Posses, based in, but not restricted to, America's eastern seaboard. Most members are black Jamaicans, but Chinese, white, and Indian Jamaicans are also members. The human capacity for evil has no racial boundaries.

Those posses are beneficiaries of the demand for crack in the United States. Incredibly brutal (some of their members were trained by Cuban guerrilla warfare specialists), by 1985, the posses had been implicated in more than two thousand drug-related murders. The posses are so powerful in the United States that they buy and fortify crack houses for retail distribution of drugs and other houses for wholesale distribution to their retail outlets, with local juveniles running the supplies. Sometimes they buy whole sections of neighborhoods to shelter their facilities. They control almost half the crack marketed in America.

Confidential law enforcement documents confirm that the posses launder drug money through the purchase of record stores, supermarkets, and car dealerships. For a steady supply of vehicles altered to conceal narcotics, they purchase and operate automobile repair shops. To divert law enforcement agencies, they use women as assassins. They can also be extremely effective in recruiting and exploiting girls and boys. They are utterly indifferent to the fate of those they recruit.

Late one night in a chilling fog outside the main entrance to a tenement, I stood with several uniformed and plainclothes police as they prepared to execute a warrant to search an apartment that they believed was a stopover place for a leading Jamaican posse. Police went up the stairs quickly and pounded on the apartment door, which was quickly opened. But a fast search of the three rooms revealed only two women, both high on crack. The high did not last through the fifteen minutes of questioning that revealed that the apartment had been used by Jamaican gang members transporting drugs.

Although crumbling plaster, garbage, urine, and vomit were pervasive throughout this tenement, a staggering odor of filth and decay rose and assaulted our senses when we entered this apartment. The bathroom had not worked for many days; the sink, the toilet, the floor, and the bathtub were covered with excrement and befouled paper towels. The floor was a soggy swamp of waste that no one was willing to search by hand. The living room, littered with drug paraphernalia and broken-down furniture, was dimly lit by two bare light bulbs. Oilcloth covered a window, and rotting food, fist-size piles of roach droppings, and crusted stains of semen covered the bed and the sofa. The kitchen sink and counter were piled with dirty dishes that were wedged all the way up to the cupboards overhead and might have tumbled down at a touch. The freezer, running constantly with a door that would not close, was filled with one huge block of ice dripping blackened icicles. Everywhere—on the table and counters, refrigerator and floor—roaches fed on garbage and cast-off chunks of fast food. There were ratholes in the walls, and the noises of rats close-by.

One of the women sat crying; the other flopped, limp, against the wall. Still young girls, they were prostitutes whose lives revolved around drugs. Although they were paid to let posse members stay in their apartment, the police would not arrest them. The one being questioned could not conceal that she was calculating how much she must say to satisfy the police without risking gang reprisal against herself. After she struck a deal for information with an officer, and a threat and a promise were exchanged, we left. A tenement hallway never smelled so clean.

Those girls resembled many used by Jamaican posses. Their business is the betrayal of our children. Despite their contempt for the lives they manipulate, criminals such as posse members often achieve hero status in the eyes of inner-city youths. By acquiring wealth and power through ruthlessness, those criminals seem to possess a shortcut to fame, fortune, and pleasure. The shortcut, the quick fix, has enormous appeal for youths who have failed in school and are bereft of decent adult companionship. Like adults, youths who want shortcuts often band together to commit wrongs in greater security and safety. Not surprisingly, the levels of behavior of urban gangs seldom rise above the depravity of their meanest members. "Mobocracy," wrote columnist Sidney J. Harris, "is the heroism of cowards."[9] That point should be emphasized in educational programs on gangs, at the same time that the record of the specific gang is made clear.

According to long-time gang enforcement officers Robert Jackson and Wesley McBride, the tendency toward remorseless wrongdoing rises in part from the belief that the youths are themselves victims of an evil society. When mothers of delinquents meet law enforcement authorities, they often make excuses for the children in "the form of accusations against society in general. Thus, children are taught early that they are not responsible for their actions. . . . By the time the youngsters reach their mid-teens . . . they truly believe that they are victims and that they have the absolute right, if not the duty, to do whatever they want, whenever they want."[10]

Nothing worse in the way of education can befall girls and boys than to be taught that they are mere victims of society. Such teaching, however well intentioned or grounded in desperation it may be, diminishes children in their own eyes to such a degree that a hopeful sense of their own real possibilities for achievement, decency, and happiness may be forever obscured to them. The consequences of thwarting youthful aspiration in this way threaten always to be dreadful; as C. S. Lewis said, "Famished nature will be avenged."[11] Police and schoolteachers should emphasize those points with parents.

Like police departments, school districts around the country lack lines of systematic communication with one another, so they learn little from the experience of others. Addressing problems alone is staggeringly inefficient and slow. Much of the readily available literature about gangs lacks analytical power and offers recommendations that are banal, unrealistic, or utopian.

Many writers on gangs simply follow the media, which in turn chase ambulances in accordance with the maxim of many local television stations, "If it bleeds, it leads" (the news broadcast of the day). Because those writers ignore the emergence of gangs in suburbs and rural areas, they identify the "root causes" of gangs with inner-city social conditions. They overlook human nature, the fact that all of us are creatures of habit and imitation, and cannot say how to try to bring out the best in the young. Police and school teachers and administrators need to know how to do so.

The most experienced police I have worked with offer advice along these lines:

> What my work with gangs and schools has taught me is that school officials must control the walls; they must paint out all graffiti every morning, preferably before the students arrive. The worst possible mistake is to legitimize the gangs by setting special walls aside for graffiti.
>
> There has to be a strict dress code: no gangbanger or wannabe clothes allowed, no colors, no caps. Administrators must not kow-tow to kids. When a kid does something wrong, do something; get the parents involved. If they won't get involved, discipline the kid yourself. And the kid who won't stop must be put out of school.
>
> You cannot be heavy handed, and you must not destroy face, or try to make object lessons of gang members. You must treat them like men, since that is what they insist they are. If you humiliate them, they will commit not only vandalism, but arson and murder. Every gang member is a potential death wish, an absolute advocate of "vengeance is mine."
>
> Give your attention to the good kids. And, believe me, there are a lot of gang kids you cannot reach or rescue. Give them a steady diet of the cops.

Instructive, generous, and patient school officials and teachers echo those views; here is a distillation of the counsel I have gathered from the most experienced of them:

Much of the time, parents, teachers, and administrators don't understand about gangs. They don't even know the meaning of colors. Parents will deny gang, alcohol, and drug problems and insist, "Not my kid!" You have to bring in experts to talk with teachers, parents, and student assistants about what to look for. Everybody has to learn that education is impossible unless there is peace and order everywhere on school property and in the streets adjacent to campus.

In some schools, we brought in Hispanic police officers, who had been raised in the neighborhood and could communicate, and introduced them to everybody, including gang members, as our "Homeboys." And we quietly brought parents in so they could see the gang members their kids were actually hanging around with.

The police who work in and with your schools have to be in agreement with your administrative philosophy. Once they're working in the schools, they're more than cops; they're really school administrators, too.

Once kids are in the gangs, there's not much you can do for them. We told them, "You follow your rules out there on the streets. You follow our rules in here." Some of us had school police bring each gang leader into the boiler room to meet privately with the principal to establish the schools as neutral ground: "No gang wars on campus, no hanging around after school." After a while, the gangbangers saw the advantage to schools as "islands of safety" just as we did.

We faced graffiti everywhere, and we learned to read it on the kids' notebooks, on the underside of their baseball cap visors, on the soles of their tennis and basketball shoes. Parents, grandparents, and cops helped us paint over graffiti on the walls every morning. It took us six months to win, but eventually we had clean doors, tables, elevators, water coolers, everything. We proved that the schools were our turf, and the more determined we were, the more the decent kids rallied to the cause.

Top administrators went door to door, to everyone who lived near the schools, and personally gave them telephone numbers to call anonymously if they saw anything bad happening. Principals rode perimeter blocks to get kids to school on time, and police moved loiterers out of the area after the morning bells had rung. We locked the gates and the doors all day, and we covered the tops of our exterior fences with printer's ink, so that anyone who climbed over and managed to get in would be easily identifiable.

We made police welcome on our campuses all the time. They had to be there often—not just to arrest people, but to make communication easy and natural. We trusted each other. If something went down over a weekend between the gangs, the police told us before school started on Monday who to keep an eye on and what to look out for.

The police constructed two curriculum units on gangs for us as part of their DARE (Drug Abuse Resistance Education) program. We had many kids who couldn't read or write, and they would make all kinds of trouble in class to hide their illiteracy. We had to keep them out of the gangs while we taught them to read.

We supervised our hallways closely. There were always adults available and visible everywhere. Principals visited every classroom at least once a week, and many classrooms once a day. Every nonclassroom staff member had to supervise activities before, during, and after school.

We couldn't have made it without gaining the support of the parents. We told them the truth: "Move away. Your son's going to be killed if he stays here. If you stay, fight him now, or bury him soon."

With the support of parents and community advisory councils we were able to enforce a dress code. No colors. No gang jewelry or paraphernalia. No caps indoors, including the baseball caps and watch caps the gangbangers fancied. No suspenders left hanging down in back. No canes. No bandannas, no shoelaces in gang colors. And no blasters. The only things you bring to school are books, pencils, and tablets. Many kids changed clothes when they got to school and again when they left. We let them keep straight clothes in their lockers overnight and gang clothes during the day.

We also got a lot of mileage from "opportunity rooms," where we sent trouble-makers. They had to stay in the rooms, closely supervised, do all their assignments, eat all their meals, with all their privileges suspended. Sometimes this worked better than sending them home or throwing them out. If they straightened out, they got the same chances for extracurricular activities as everybody else. We tried to treat everybody as an individual, and we required all school activities and school organizations to be integrated—cheerleaders, teams, student councils. At dances, nobody's favorite music got all the play.

We became friends with parents and colleagues, police and community leaders, alumni. We looked out for each other and for our students.

In some of our schools, levels of achievement and pride are now so high that enrollments have risen dramatically, drop-out rates have declined, and faculty and staff retention and continuity exceed 90 percent over periods of several years. It was hard and exhausting, but we stuck to it. And, in the end, it became fun.

Police departments may also benefit from instructional programs on gangs such as the Gang Resistance Education and Training (GREAT) program of the Bureau of Alcohol, Tobacco, and Firearms. First mounted in 1991 in cooperation with the Phoenix Police Department, GREAT is designed to teach "middle school children to set goals for themselves, resist pressures, and resolve conflicts without violence. GREAT provides at-risk teenagers with the necessary skills and information to say no to gangs. In 1992 the Federal Law Enforcement Training Center joined the partnership to assist with the national expansion of the program." The program rightly focuses on educating "teachers, parents, and the community about precrisis indicators showing that gang involvement or activity is in their geographical area." More than four hundred police from thirty-six states have been trained in GREAT. Eligibility for participation requires a formal agreement of mutual cooperation between local police and schools and on the local selection of highly able officers.[12]

The GREAT program is well designed in many respects. But in the program's emphases on cultural sensitivity and self-esteem, trainers and trainees will need to be alert to the problems described in chapter 15. Similarly, GREAT instructors charged to prepare officers to teach the young skills of conflict resolution will need to avoid conceptual errors rife in such programs in higher education. Many of those programs teach that the way to resolve conflict is to "acknowledge [the] other person's position as legitimate."[13] Clearly, not all positions are legitimate, and students should not be taught that they are—or that all beliefs and actions are tolerable or excusable. Learning resistance to gangs necessarily includes learning that much of what they do is grievously wrong. Making that clear becomes imperative where gangs hold sway. As Evan Simpson observed in his writings on violence, "In a hostile environment one may become inured to almost anything, including injury, and it is to be expected that what from a more favored standpoint is violent may fail to be so regarded by one raised in the midst of turbulence or social decay."[14]

Neither the police departments nor the ATF can advance the interests of children and youths on the ideological premises accepted by many conflict resolution specialists. The National Institute for Dispute Resolution in Washington, D.C., for example, provides instruction about "Alternative Dispute Resolution" in *Peaceful Persuasion: A Guide to Creating Mediation Resolution Programs on College Campuses*:

> Mediation requires acceptance of certain assumptions about human nature and human beings: that there is a genuine desire to cooperate; that disputants know best how to resolve their own disputes; and that people can be trusted to negotiate in good faith. In educational settings, the goals and language speaking to trust, cooperation, learning, and growth as applied to students are often at variance with individual and institutional ways of actually dealing with students. A dispute resolution process that assumes a high level of trust in students may be consonant with rhetoric, but not with actual assumptions and institutional practice. When the institutional norm is to prescribe for students, to intervene, direct, solve, and discipline— mediation requires a major reorientation.
>
> It is important to realize that mediation is not a total substitute for conventional conflict resolution mechanisms. It is not appropriate for all conflicts. Some disputes need to be dealt with publicly in order to develop or reinforce community standards

on issues or behavior patterns. Others, by their nature, require a response that will deter others from similar action. However, mediation is useful when there is a need for a conflict resolution approach that may be less intimidating than the Dean of Students Office, when greater sensitivity to disputants' concerns than that afforded by evidentiary proceedings is sought, when one seeks to produce the feeling that grievances are actually heard, or when one wishes to empower disputants by enabling them to retain more control over the resolution of problems.[15]

Mediation programs could be dramatically improved if they were designed to produce not merely "the feeling that grievances are actually heard," but the fact that they are actually heard. Programs would be strengthened if they showed disputants that respect for evidence and for truthfulness is irreplaceable in genuine sensitivity to the concerns of our fellows. We need not be misologists to care about each other—and we cannot care about each other responsibly if we disregard the real effects of our intentions and actions. The *Guide* continues:

> Mediation can be used in a variety of ways to handle a wide range of individual and social problems and needs as is illustrated in the case studies found in this manual. It can be incorporated into disciplinary codes as an option for handling specified code violations or it can be structured to handle student conflicts in which no code violations are involved. It's a useful intervention tool for short-term crises that over the long-term may require therapy. Or conversely, in a violent dispute, arrest may be used to control the immediate situation while mediation might be part of the longer range solution. *In a broad context, mediation provides a forum for resolving any conflict involving personal, institutional, or policy difference* [emphasis added].[16]

In the event that the reader does not find this account persuasive, the authors offer an ad hominem argument, disguised as benevolent therapy, and attack the background of the reader. Instead of offering reasons for accepting what they say, they disparage individual judgment of evidence in pursuit of the truth. All forms of inquiry intended to discover the truth and enable responsible evaluation are illogically equated with the imposition of punishment:

> It is difficult to overestimate the importance of acquiring a full and deep understanding of mediation whether one is preparing to become a mediator or preparing to initiate a program. It is not easy to readjust one's inner assumptions about how a dispute should be settled. Growing up with the idea that breaking the rules results in punishment makes it very difficult to accept the notion that rule breaking can be resolved without punishment. If punishment for misdeeds is fair, then how can it be fair for there to be no punishment? *If one is socialized to believe that disputes are settled by obtaining evidence that points to the truth of a situation, it is very difficult to accept fully a process in which evidence and objective truth are not the focus. In order to embrace mediation, one must give up judging. Giving up the notion of analyzing a dispute in terms of who is right and who is wrong is hard* [emphasis added].[17]

No one should be taught "to give up judging." Resistance to gangs depends on judging. Neither should people be taught to spurn the relevance of right and wrong. Some conflict resolution programs, however, demand not only this but also that participants must surrender facts. In its Human Resources Leadership Strategies, the Program on Negotiation at Harvard Law School provides "stop-action video analysis [to] help you learn the six key lessons of successful fact-finding." The first is, "There is no such thing as a 'fact.' . . . [F]act finding is really a process of documenting differing perceptions." In addition, "Each person presents information according to the outcome she/he desires." Therefore, the human resources leader must learn "how to separate 'facts' from reactions to facts—while being sure to validate the feelings of each person being interviewed." Not surprisingly, once the very idea of fact has been undercut, the reader is cautioned, "After fact finding, your recommendations will be subjective and value-laden."[18]

This skepticism about the capacity of human beings for intellectual honesty is self-refuting. In political theory, it is well to establish the safeguard that no person shall be a judge in his or her own cause. Indeed, this is one element in the genius of the United States as a constitutional republic. But political safeguards do not make epistemological theories, especially not when the advocates' description of conflict resolution implies that everything they say is only their own "presentation of information according to the outcome [they] desire." On such a premise, no distinction can be drawn between truth and falsity within conflict resolution theory itself. Validation is reduced to making people feel good; it no longer has anything to do with being reasonable or thinking rationally. This marks the intellectual bankruptcy of the theory.

Children and youths deserve better than this. They need better instruction if they are to acquire the backbone necessary for real resistance to gangs and other corrupters of the young. Many conflict resolution programs misinform by downplaying resistance and giving the impression that the avoidance of conflict is easy.

I know of no place where efforts to combat youth violence and gang activity have gone easily. Most school and police policies generate disputes, and parents may be the last to cooperate. Accordingly, efforts to get the various institutions to work hand in hand call for great levels of fortitude. They usually draw encouragement from their cooperation and reciprocity. Otherwise, resistance to cynicism and despair would be much more difficult.

Unconditional Obligations

Even if legislators and others admit publicly the gravity of youth violence and gang activity, they may remain unwilling to combat them. When drug trafficking is disrupted by arrests and successful prosecution, the short-term homicide rate tends to rise in turf and market wars. Politicians who understand that reform of juvenile justice systems costs real money may be reluctant to propose anything requiring new taxes.

Politicians must expect to draw fire if they advocate the establishment of orphanages for dispossessed children, boot camps for juvenile criminals, prosecution of juveniles as adults, expulsion of convicted felons from schools, and prohibition of increased welfare payments to unwed mothers who have additional children. Only those who care more about the public interest than their own political survival or advancement will risk it. Jacques Barzun, the great cultural historian, was right to caution that "there are few statesmen or good politicians who can govern."[19] Accordingly, police are unwise to expect rationality and courage in legislation and public policy. They are obliged to do their best even when officials fail to take the most obvious steps.

A group of political leaders abroad who faced a massive scandal of noble cause police corruption proposed to announce that the public had a right to trustworthy police and that the police had a right to a trustworthy criminal justice system. Those leaders could not have been more wrong or less informed about the obligations to the public trust when they implied that police lawfulness and integrity depended on whether the criminal justice system convicted and punished every guilty suspect. Fortunately, with the benefit of outside consultation, those leaders ultimately took the correct position when they went public: Police lawfulness and integrity are unconditional obligations. The force of the obligation does not depend on the effectiveness of anything else, including the criminal justice system as a whole. Many political leaders will, however, continue to bungle the most important issues involving gangs and juvenile crime.

That is a hard lesson; it can be difficult to teach police that their obligations remain unconditional despite it. But it lies at the heart of ethics in policing, as it does in every other walk of life that involves the public trust. In my experience, no area of police work makes the ideal of principled conduct harder to live up to than work on juvenile crime, gang activity, and drug trafficking, particularly when they involve murder. Pursuit of serial killers also dramatically tests the fortitude and mettle of police, but there the police have the citizens and political leaders on their side. They do not always have either the public or the politicians on their side on juvenile crime, youth violence, and gang predation—far from it.

Accordingly, my police and law enforcement colleagues seem to me to be exactly right to raise questions about how to live up to ethical ideals as they try to bring policing to bear on grim realities of contemporary life. Our future as a people rests in the balance.[20] When I am with police leaders, and our discussions of ethical ideals in policing draw toward a close, I remind them how very much will be asked of police in the years to come. The magnitude of public expectation should serve to remind all who bear the public trust, all police: *Nothing is incorruptible except personal character that will not be corrupted.*

17

Police, the O. J. Simpson Trial, and Race

You know, the skins of those thin-legged little girls who faced the mob in Little Rock marked them as Negro, but the spirit which directed their feet is the old universal urge toward freedom.

—Ralph Ellison[1]

On November 20, 1995, six-year-old Elisa Izquierdo suffered a brain hemorrhage when her mother, Awilda Lopez, hit her with such force that she crashed headfirst into a cement wall. Elisa died on November 22, the day before Thanksgiving.

Elisa had been born in 1989 addicted to crack, of a mother who was evidently deranged. Her earliest years were spent with her father, Gustavo Izquierdo. She was described by adults as a "well-adjusted, lively, intelligent child."[2] Before her father died of cancer in 1994, he requested that Elisa be placed in custody of his aunt. A court, however, placed her in custody of her mother.

There, she suffered terrible beatings, genital torture with a hairbrush, solitary confinement in a small room where she was forced to relieve herself into an overflowing pot, and being held upside down while her hair was used to mop the floor. Her mother claimed to have stuffed snakes down Elisa's throat to exorcise demons.

Before she was killed, the little finger of her right hand had been broken, the bone exposed through the skin. Her body was marked with red welts and large scars, bruises, and wounds. At the scene of Elisa's death, Lieutenant Luis Gonzalez of the New York City Police Department said, "In my twenty-two years of service, this is the worst case of child abuse I have ever seen."[3]

While Elisa was with her mother, members of Mr. Izquierdo's family and Elisa's school teachers repeatedly reported their suspicions about her suffering and abuse. But government agencies and courts refused to separate her from her mother, even after Elisa was withdrawn from school. And so, with her repeated cries for relief—"Mommy, please stop! I'm sorry"— unanswered, Elisa Izquierdo died, terrified and violently brutalized.

No one of any sensibility can imagine the suffering of that child without feeling heartache and anguish, without feeling enraged by the snarl of laws, regulations, and bad judgment that abandoned her to the mercy of a demented mother who terrorized, tortured, and finally killed her. Our pain and indignation may resemble those of New York Police Department Detective Nancy Farrell, who led the investigation of Elisa's death: "I'm very angry that this was allowed to happen in the greatest city in the world, and nothing in my job makes me angry. I've been wanting to hug and kiss every child that walks past me just because of how I've spent the last few days."[4] As with Detective Farrell, our feelings and our judgment spring from empathy with this lonely, helpless child and from our sense of the wasteful and avoidable injustice of innocent suffering.

What color was Elisa? What race was Elisa? What were the ethnic elements of Elisa's makeup? All these questions are starkly irrelevant to our feelings for her and to the horror she endured. She was murdered after subjection to treatment that no person should ever have to suffer. Elisa's color, race, and ethnicity make no difference. They do not alter the enormity of her agony. They mitigate nothing. They have no bearing on our sense of her pain, her fear, her dread and desperation. What befell Elisa Izquierdo is intolerable for each and every human being.

Individuality and Group Identity

The O. J. Simpson murder trial has suggested that we risk losing sight of human beings as individuals. Many in the media, in polling, in education, and in other positions of influence portray us as if we are mere members of racial, color, ethnic, or gender groups—as if our color or gender defines us.

It should not take the suffering of an Elisa Izquierdo to make us realize that no individual is reducible to membership in any group. No person— not Elisa, not her mother, not any police officer—is just a member of a group. Martin Luther King Jr., had this in mind when he spoke of his dream that one day his children would be judged by the content of their character—as individuals—rather than by the color of their skin. To judge otherwise is to give impetus to bigotry.

The great divide in the public reaction to the Simpson verdict has revealed the peril of our present situation. Although this peril is not new, the trial disclosed it with renewed clarity. Historian Gertrude Himmelfarb, author of *The De-Moralization of Society*, wrote:

> With the Simpson trial, we can no longer ignore the extent to which race and gender have infiltrated into the public consciousness and, more fatally, into the legal process. After decades of the most strenuous efforts to overcome racial and sexual stereotypes, to judge people as individuals rather than as members of groups, we have regressed to the concept of group identity. And precisely those who have most to lose by it have embraced it most enthusiastically.
>
> The overwhelming support of Simpson by blacks throughout the trial and their jubilation at its outcome have nothing to do with the individual defendant and the murder of two other individuals, and everything to do with the fact of race. Those on both sides of the racial divide must now confront the true dimensions of racism in this country—a racism revealed as much in the final appeal of the defense attorney as in the abhorrent prejudices of one of the prosecution witnesses.[5]

That witness, a homicide detective of the Los Angeles Police Department, Mark Fuhrman, showed where the reduction of individuals to membership in groups leads. In taped interviews with screenwriter Laura McKinny, recorded through July 28, 1994,

> Fuhrman used the word "nigger" 41 times in his hate-filled discourse about his life as a policeman. In explaining his opposition to building a new headquarters in a minority district, Fuhrman said, "Leave that old station. Man, it has the smell of niggers that have been beaten and killed in there for years." Fuhrman also told of viciously beating suspects after the shooting of two police

officers. "We basically tortured them," Fuhrman said matter-of-factly. "We broke 'em. Their faces were just mush. They had pictures of the walls with blood all the way to the ceiling and finger marks from trying to crawl out of the room."[6]

Yet on March 15, 1995, Mark Fuhrman was asked by an O. J. Simpson defense attorney, F. Lee Bailey, "Do you use the word 'nigger' in describing people?" Fuhrman said, "No, sir." The cross-examination proceeded:

Mr. Bailey:	Have you used that word in the past ten years?
Det. Fuhrman:	Not that I recall, no.
Mr. Bailey:	You mean if you called someone a nigger you have forgotten it?
Det. Fuhrman:	I'm not sure I can answer the question the way you phrased it, sir.
Mr. Bailey:	You have difficulty understanding the question?
Det. Fuhrman:	Yes.
Mr. Bailey:	I will rephrase it. I want you to assume that perhaps at some time, since 1985 or 6, you addressed a member of the African American race as a nigger. Is it possible that you have forgotten that act on your part?
Det. Fuhrman:	No, it is not possible.
Mr. Bailey:	Are you therefore saying that you have not used that word in the past ten years, Detective Fuhrman?
Det. Fuhrman:	Yes, that is what I am saying.
Mr. Bailey:	And you say under oath that you have not addressed any black person as a nigger or any black people as niggers in the past ten years, Detective Fuhrman?
Det. Fuhrman:	That's what I'm saying, sir.[7]

In response to questions whether he had "ever falsified a police report" or "planted or manufactured evidence" in the murders of Nicole Brown Simpson and Ronald Goldman, Fuhrman asserted his Fifth Amendment privilege.[8]

Fuhrman seemed completely at ease with lying and abusing his authority as a police officer. He told the screenwriter, "In twelve years on the department, I have never felt guilty one day, one split second. . . . Because all the people out there deserve exactly what they get and probably 20,000 times more. . . . That's the thing I've always said too. Even if you get the wrong guy, this guy's done something before or he's thought about doing something."[9] The presumption of innocence meant nothing to Fuhrman. He betrayed a fundamental principle of the American way of life, that no one should be punished for what he or she "thought about doing." On March 14, 1995, Deputy District Attorney Marcia Clark told the court, "Whatever anyone may ultimately decide about Mark Fuhrman's personal life or personal views of the world has nothing to do with whether or not he is credible as an officer and with the issues that relate to his honesty and veracity."[10] She could not have been more wrong. Personal integrity has everything to do with credibility—and with being morally fit to wear a badge.

Detective Fuhrman seemed to take both pride and satisfaction in his own racism and brutishness, despite his lying to conceal them. Because racists have difficulty seeing individuals or individuality, they often do not respect individual rights. The moral status of individuals is invisible to them—only skin color is perceptible to them. Because they are so benighted, they can commit egregious wrongs without shame, compunction, remorse, guilt, or hesitation.

As for the defense, Attorney Johnnie Cochran exhorted the jurors to ignore the individuals in the case—to ignore the questions of individual guilt or innocence and the brute fact of two murders. Instead, he encouraged the jurors to make a public statement against racism. Cochran told the jurors to "continue to fight to expose hate and genocidal racism." He urged them, "If you don't do what's right, this kind of conduct will continue forever."[11] He compared Fuhrman to Adolf Hitler, thereby grotesquely trivializing the bigoted, systematic murder of 6 million human beings and the deadly ravages of unrestrained tyranny.

Experienced police will have seen this defense ploy in other trials. It has a conspicuous place in the history of racism in the United States. Abigail Thernstrom and Henry D. Fetter, coauthors of "From Scottsdale to Simpson," drew a striking parallel:

Cochran's closing statement eerily echoed a defense attorney's final argument on behalf of two white men accused of the brutal murder of a 14-year-old black youngster, Emmett Till, after he "wolf-whistled" at a white woman in 1955: "I am sure that every last Anglo-Saxon one of you has the courage to acquit these men."[12]

Mark Fuhrman was a bigot, a liar, and a brute. For years he was utterly unfit—and known to be unfit—to be a police officer and a homicide investigator. But he was no Adolf Hitler, just as Johnnie Cochran was no Mark Fuhrman. In the O. J. Simpson trial, however, Cochran betrayed his obligation to recognize individuals as individuals. He defended Fuhrman by racist means, because he rejected the idea of individual accountability—not least by seeking to reduce every individual police officer to membership in a racist group. Another lawyer for the defense, Alan Dershowitz, also lumped all police into a group by alleging that police academies teach police to lie in the performance of duty. Although he later recanted, he unfairly and irresponsibly damaged the reputation of police.

Police must shun any behavior that denies the identity of individuals or that reduces them to mere group identity. To be faithful to their mission of service to the public, police must keep in mind the rights of each member of the public as an individual.

This is not to say that individual human beings are completely self-sufficient or "self-made." We do not come to be who we are in isolation from others. We are social beings, dependent on one another, and we form our habits by imitation, under guidance from others. Environment and circumstance form individuals, just as our biology and genetic makeup play a part in what we do and become.

I have learned from others, for example, most of what I know about running in marathons. Although I try to imitate better athletes in my training and diet, I never had the build—and I no longer have the youth—to be a great runner. I train and run with friends and family members. In marathons we give each other encouragement. No doubt, we do better because of our shared sense of purpose. But none of us can do the running for anyone else. We depend on one another, but each of us must expend the *individual* effort of striding through the twenty-six miles.

Everyone belongs to many different groups by accident of birth or circumstance or by choice. Elisa Izquierdo was one of a group of children born of Awilda Lopez. Police are members of departments. School children are classmates. Some criminals belong to syndicates and gangs. None of those facts implies that anyone is *no more* than a member of a group. Whatever groups we belong to, each of us is still an individual and deserves to be treated as one.

The Lessons of the O. J. Simpson Trial for Police

What lessons should police draw from the O. J. Simpson trial, its verdict, and its aftermath? *There are no new lessons to be learned, but only old ones to be remembered.*

The principles of ethics in policing, the ideals of worthiness to bear the public trust, the dispositions and habits of good character that befit police officers, and the standards of good judgment in performing police duties remain exactly the same after the trial as they were before it.

Nothing fundamental was changed by the trial and verdict, anymore than anything fundamental was changed by other controversial trials. Similar disquiet followed the fabrication of racist victimization by Tawana Brawley; the acquittal of Lemrick Nelson after he confessed and was identified by his dying victim in Crown Heights, New York; the conviction of LAPD Sergeant Stacey Koon and Officer Laurence Powell for violating the civil rights of Rodney King and the acquittal of those officers in a prior trial held in Simi Valley; and the conviction for rape of heavyweight boxing champion Mike Tyson. Professor John J. DiIulio Jr., now of the University of Pennsylvania explained, "What is so extraordinary about the outcome of the O. J. case is how ordinary it was. . . . In 61 percent of all murder cases, the defendant pleads not guilty. And in four or five out of 10 cases, the accused murderer who doesn't plead guilty walks free." DiIulio added that "about two-thirds of all murder trials involving defendants accused of murdering a family member drag on for more than six months."[13]

Media Attention. The notion that much is changed by the O. J. Simpson trial arises not from the case itself, or its outcome, but from the intensive and ubiquitous publicity and from the intensity of the reaction to the verdict. Public fixation on the fate of a defendant, who (though never a hero) was a great athlete and a celebrity, became confused with our desperate desire to be entertained—a conclusion that is verified by the popularity of mindless television talk shows in which guests debase themselves before credulous, vacuous, and voyeuristic viewers. Although the relentless pursuit of gratification is as old as human history, and while there is nothing new about lust, our popular media now give unprecedented public exposure to vulgarity, shamelessness, and vice. The promotion of lowest-common-denominator entertainment in the United States is not new. What is new is its proliferation following the collapse of barriers to permissiveness.

Every local television news team in the country now mingles news with entertainment—reducing the news to such pap that only personalities make a difference in ratings, and subscribes in some measure to the shallow policy that "if it bleeds, it leads." Radio talk shows are becoming not only increasingly obscene but also more virulent. While nothing is fundamentally new about the popularity of yellow journalism or ambulance chasing in America, television bombardment of the public with trash is unprecedented.

The media displayed their intellectual bankruptcy by referring to the O. J. Simpson trial as the "trial of the century." If there were any "trial of the century," it was the trial of Nazi war criminals at Nuremberg, which affirmed the principle that "I was following orders" is no defense against charges of barbaric slaughter of the innocent. The media have not even reported widely that the public divide over the O. J. Simpson trial verdict is not drawn on exclusively racial lines. Accounts of polling data vary. Rolando V. del Carmen, a Sam Houston State University professor of criminal justice, and doctoral student Craig Hemmens reported in *Law Enforcement News* that "opinion polls" show that "roughly 70 percent of white Americans" believed Simpson guilty and "70 percent of black Americans" believed him innocent.[14] But Thernstrom and Fetter reported in the *Public Interest* with much greater precision: "At the end of the trial, 83 percent of blacks agreed with the verdict, while only 37 percent of whites did."[15] That meant that 17 percent of blacks agreed with 63 percent of whites in rejecting the verdict—a significant overlap.

Analyzing the Simpson trial, syndicated columnist George F. Will identified the most important problems with the media and their rightful place in coverage of criminal trials:

At least there should now be sober reconsideration of the presence of television cameras in courtrooms. One question is
whether it is good for society to treat the criminal justice system
as a source of entertainment. It simply will not do to chant the
mantra about "the public's right to know." The impulse often
behind that is just voyeurism tarted up in rights talk. The public's "right" to whatever entertains it is not sovereign over considerations of the moral standing and proper functioning of the
criminal justice system.

Regarding the latter, Cochran himself says that he believes
some of Judge Ito's rulings during the trial were made as they
were because the world was watching. If so—if cameras are
not a passive presence, if the act of observing alters that which
is observed—then the case against cameras in courtrooms
is irrefutable.[16]

Even though Norfolk, Massachusetts, Superior Court Judge Barbara
Dortch Okara disallowed television cameras at the 1996 trial of John Salvi III
for allegedly killing two abortion clinic employees, police should not
expect the media to lower their shrill and indiscriminate insistence on "the
public's right to know." My own experience in media interviews confirms
what police leaders say: When reporters are told that considerations of
privacy or confidentiality prevent an answer to a question, many of them
unhesitatingly respond that the media and the public have "a right to
know." Even when the reasons for confidentiality in a specific matter are
explained, they persist. The conduct of many in the media in that and other
celebrity cases illuminates their profound indifference to the rightful
privacy of victims, and their loved ones and friends who suffer when their
privacy is invaded.

The persistence of thoughtless reporters in the claim that they and the
public always have a right to know seems to me more than mere stubbornness
and crass self-interest. Anyone who is frequently interviewed by the media
soon learns that many reporters in the print, audio, and video media are poorly
educated. They have no command of logic; they do not read the work of good
writers (including journalists); they know little of history, principles of government, law, and ethics; and they do not appreciate the value of firsthand

experience. As a result, they do not *report* stories, so much as they gather comments from supposed experts and string them together. Their work is therefore inevitably superficial. Many of them think that objectivity and balance in reporting require no more than gathering quotations from people who disagree; they make no real effort to discover the truth of the matter. Such intellectual weaknesses make reporters susceptible to the idea that disagreement and conflict of opinion make the story; that susceptibility undercuts journalism as pursuit of the truth and pushes it down a slope toward mere amusement and entertainment. Thus do popular news magazines, for example, come to look more and more like gossip publications and tabloids that pander to prurient interest in the name of the public's right to know.

Reporters have a duty to think carefully about the question of what the public genuinely has the right to know and about the adverse effects on the public interest caused by media debasement of serious news coverage into shallow entertainment. But many reporters do not know how to think about such questions, and neither have they been taught nor have they learned for themselves their obligations as journalists.

For such reasons, the popular media cannot be trusted as guardians of the public interest. That is, however, the sole justification for their rights under the First Amendment. Police who deal with them should act with overriding respect for confidentiality and privacy; they should never allow the media to dictate the "rights" of the public and should keep in mind that many in the media are unwilling or incompetent to pursue, much less report, evidence that bears on complex issues.

Problems in the Judicial System. Neither incompetent judges nor careless prosecutors are anything new. The judge in the O. J. Simpson trial failed even to require the defense to provide evidence of a police conspiracy against O. J. Simpson. Instead, he allowed the defense extensive rein in conspiracy speculation. Similarly unsettling were the failures of prosecutors to look scrupulously into the backgrounds of their own witnesses, to exercise all their peremptory challenges to prospective jurors, and to challenge the behavior of a jury that reached its verdict in less than four hours. That verdict suggested intimidation within the jury.

Some judges make rulings that are at least as inimical to the mission of policing and the safety of the public as any in the Simpson trial. And over a century ago, Justice Oliver Wendell Holmes, then of the Massachusetts Supreme Court, wrote in a letter, "I think there is a growing disbelief in the jury as an instrument for the discovery of truth."[17]

Early in 1996, for example, Judge Harold Baer Jr., of the U.S. Court for the Southern District of New York, presided in a case involving two narcotics officers from drug-ridden Washington Heights. The officers saw four men put two duffel bags into the trunk of a double-parked car at five o'clock in the morning. The officers stopped the car. When they did, the bag men ran away. The officers then searched the trunk and found that the bags contained ninety pounds of crack cocaine and heroin. The driver confessed, and the confession was filmed.

At a pretrial hearing, Baer ruled that the officers had no reasonable grounds for a search and pronounced the evidence inadmissible. He accounted for the flight of the bag carriers by saying, "Residents in this neighborhood tend to regard police officers as corrupt, abusive and violent. . . . [H]ad the men not run when the cops began to stare at them, it would have been unusual."[18]

Baer's acceptance of the prejudicial lumping together of police as just members of an untrustworthy group without regard for the individual officers in that case did not befit anyone, let alone a public servant. Such prejudice against others is exactly what police should refuse to allow in themselves and in the performance of their duties. Most police very much dislike being second-guessed by outsiders. But if they behave in bigoted ways, outsiders will be as likely to second-guess them as police themselves were likely to second-guess Judge Baer. Baer subsequently reversed his decision. It is not clear that his reversal was based on recognition that he had demeaned both residents and police in Washington Heights. His change of mind may have been only a matter of political expedience, given pressure brought to bear on him by the White House and members of the U.S. Senate.

The quality of judgment in juries may well be declining, and Justice Holmes's skepticism has surely been confirmed. But the O. J. Simpson trial has not been the cause. Hiller B. Zobel of the Massachusetts Superior Court cautioned:

> Nowadays we are not content merely to know that a jury candidate has formed no opinion about the case or its underlying

facts; we want our jurors' minds to be even purer. Our desire to ensure the jury's absolute impartiality causes us to hunt for and enlist only those citizens who, as in the trial of Oliver North, do not read newspapers, watch television, or even discuss the events of the day. Claiming to pursue the ideal impartial juror, we actually seek the impartiality of complete ignorance.

Zobel went on to say that "despite pious protestations to the contrary, modern lawyers and their clients (including in a criminal case, the government) do not want impartial jurors; they want jurors who will return a favorable verdict."[19] Through the use of psychologists and polling specialists to identify sympathetic jurors, legal procedure has become a "form of extrajudicial competition, a contest to produce the jury group most likely to bring in the right verdict."[20] The very possibility of justice is threatened when ignorance is substituted for impartiality and when competing counsel deliberately seek partiality. Since such practices have become commonplace, however, police should expect to see their effects routinely.

Police and the Public. The denigration of police everywhere by the exposure of Mark Fuhrman as a bigot and a liar may tempt some police to become bitter toward the public. Public ingratitude for sacrifices by good officers may fuel an "us against them" attitude, a sense that policing is not only thankless but pointless in a compromised criminal justice system.

Wiser police understand that the mission of policing cannot be accomplished without the cooperation of the general public. They will not allow us-against-them attitudes to undermine their efforts to serve the public interest. They will remember the many outpourings of public support for the families of police who have been hurt or killed in the line of duty. Even if popular opinion is sometimes fickle, most citizens consistently support the police and understand that the Mark Fuhrmans are the contemptible exception rather than the rule.

In sum, the lessons for police in the O. J. Simpson trial are old ones. It is true that tabloid entertainment sells, that some judges are inept and prosecutors careless and defense attorneys cynically indifferent to truth and justice in jury selection, that the media can be vulgar and exploitative and disrespectful of confidentiality, that criminals walk free to perpetrate further crimes against the innocent, that police are often subjected to prejudice, that their best work may be futile, and that they cannot save the public from itself.

Regardless of those facts, every police officer has chosen to be a police officer. All law enforcement officers have voluntarily affirmed a duty to uphold the Constitution and the laws; they have willingly entered a life in which service to the public is fundamental. They have voluntarily accepted an obligation to be worthy of the public trust even under adverse conditions, including public ingratitude.

Anyone who decides to be a police officer forfeits the right to say, "Well, I'm not going to do my best to be a good police officer, because other officers are corrupt, the rest of the system is broken, and the citizens don't appreciate me." Elisa Izquierdo did not have to suffer and die at the age of six. Her needless death gives us no right to stop safeguarding other children from such depredation. Exactly the opposite is true: Her death cries out for better *child* protection. Indeed, her death is a police officer's call to service.

Police may be encouraged by the agreement of distinguished former prosecutor and Knapp Commission member Nicholas Scoppetta to leave his law practice to head the Administration for Children's Services, an organization formed in 1996 in New York City. Scoppetta, who lived in a city orphanage for seven years as a child while his mother was too poor to raise him and his brother, promised to teach caseworkers in his agency to work cooperatively with police, doctors, and teachers to safeguard children from abuse. As with police, he has faced political obstacles, a biased media, entrenched bad habits, and the inertia of a large bureaucracy as he has tried to protect children who have been abused under shelter of the private home. But he has provided for police and other public servants a splendid example of willingness to reenter demanding, even daunting, public service precisely because present conditions—in this instance, in child welfare—are intolerable.

However great their disillusionment or dismay over any event or pattern of events, when officers can no longer give their best in public service, they are obliged to leave it. It is not dishonorable to choose a less demanding walk of life: It is dishonorable to remain in public service after losing respect for the public. In seminars or in private, I am sometimes told that I am being unrealistic. The most candid of my critics say, "I don't believe in the job anymore, but I can't afford to leave." They sometimes add, "I'm no worse than anybody else. You just expect too much." Those critics are either kidding themselves or they're kidding me.

Some of them, I suspect, give more of themselves to their work than they admit, lest they be thought naïve. But others seem genuinely past caring about policing, and some are bitterly cynical. Some reject the tradition that public servants must live up to higher standards than the public they serve. I do not expect policing to be free of people who are no longer worthy of their jobs. No walk of life consists entirely of dedicated people. When I affirm a duty to one's best, I do not expect that everyone will live up to it—only that everyone *should*.

Nothing in the O. J. Simpson trial provides an excuse for lowering standards of individual police or any law enforcement agency. The disclosure of bigotry, brutishness, and mendacity in police officers like Mark Fuhrman— or like those implicated in disclosures of corruption and brutality in New York City, Atlanta, Philadelphia, and New Orleans—may even provide opportunities to elevate policing. The future of policing rests on the standards police bring to their work.

Policing and Prejudice

Most of the officers I have come to know since 1975 feel even more than others revulsion toward corrupt or brutal police. Still, I have never worked with a police or sheriff's department of any size that had no Mark Fuhrmans in it. Edward A. Flynn, former chief of police in Chelsea, Massachusetts, said:

> Mark Fuhrman is a jerk. A racist jerk. His racism makes his jerkiness more offensive. Most disturbing, he was, for twenty years, a racist jerk with the power of arrest and the authority to use force lawfully. His racist jerkiness, coupled with his authority, made him a dangerous man. . . . There is no defending the things Mark Fuhrman said about black people, about women, about police misconduct, about the violation of suspects' rights. There is no defending the things Mark Fuhrman

said he did to people. I haven't heard any police officer try to defend him. I have heard many officers repudiate his remarks and disavow his tactics.[21]

Flynn added that the O. J. Simpson trial made Mark Fuhrman more than dangerous: "He has become notorious. And in doing so he has tarnished the image of all police."[22]

It is dramatically unfair for police to be sullied by the unconscionable behavior of a Mark Fuhrman. Flynn was right that police "deserve a nation that is above stereotyping them."[23] Stereotypes are, by definition, oversimplified ideas that do not distinguish in any way among individuals. A stereotype such as "All police resemble Mark Fuhrman" is demonstrably false and differs from an accurate generalization such as "The Gestapo are cruel."

When asked to comment on criticisms of the jury in the O. J. Simpson trial, Johnnie Cochran said, "It's not the jury system they ought to get rid of. It's lying policemen."[24] He should have stressed the need to get rid of corrupt and racist trial lawyers. But whatever the merits of Cochran's opinion of juries, he is right about the obligation of police. In its October 23, 1995, cover story, "Why O. J. Simpson Was Found Not Guilty," *Jet* magazine reported that "the defense case partly centered on sloppy police work and the racism of Mark Fuhrman."[25] Los Angeles Police Chief Willie Williams told *Jet*, "The verdict is not an indictment of my department. I hope the decision wasn't based on the race card that was played." Williams "pointed out that most of the men and women of the LAPD are hard-working and honest people who should not be painted with the same brush as Fuhrman."[26]

Certainly they should not. But police departments cannot live up to the public trust when officers like Fuhrman remain police for many years after their bigotry is well known. The public confidence essential to fulfillment of the police mission is fragile, and throughout history, Americans, including many police, have had reservations about authority.

Living up to the public trust and inspiring public confidence in police are not simply a matter of overcoming bigotry in policing and law enforcement. They depend as well on the competence of individual police and the rigor of departmental policy in gathering and handling evidence, securing necessary warrants, timely involvement of personnel—including coroners—in investigations, and scrupulous adherence to reliable procedures in crime laboratories. In a number of those respects, including Detective Fuhrman's entry into the O. J. Simpson property without a warrant, the investigation of the murders of Nicole Brown Simpson and Ronald Goldman left much to be desired. Commander James T. McBride of the LAPD said, "On the topic of evidence collection, there are certainly areas that can be improved upon. . . . [W]e can expect improvements in identifying, categorizing, care and collection of evidence in future cases."[27]

Achieving high levels of competence and rigor in policy and procedures depends, in turn, on the recruitment and training of very good personnel who are free of bigotry. In addition, it depends on ridding departments of bigots who have already been hired. I am familiar with LAPD Chief Willie Williams's view that Mark Fuhrman's long-term employment by the LAPD is attributable to cracks and inadequacies in departmental bureaucratic structures and procedures. To the extent that this explanation is true, there is a desperate need to eliminate those cracks. I suspect that the problem is not merely bureaucratic. Retired LAPD Assistant Chief David D. Dotson, who is widely respected among police leaders, cautioned, "The Department got to where it is over the last 50 years, and I suspect it will take a generation of police officers to change attitudes." He has "viewed the Simpson verdict as a strong repudiation of the department, and particularly its past and present leadership."[28]

In an *Essence* magazine article, "The Other Side of Johnnie Cochran," Diane Weathers referred to the "notorious LAPD":

> The Law Offices of Johnnie L. Cochran, with 11 staff attorneys, has secured a string of precedent-setting police-brutality victories, forcing California taxpayers to fork over more than $40 million in jury awards and settlements. . . . If there's any topic that gets Johnnie Cochran fired up and flustered, it's police brutality and the lengths to which the system will go to hide what he calls "society's dirty little secret."[29]

Although not all court judgments against police departments are justified, some settlements are clearly warranted. Bigoted officers are visible to anyone who works closely in or with police departments, and some of them are resolutely protected by their unions.

Police and Bigotry. How deep does the "Fuhrman problem" run? Writing for the Police Executive Research Forum, Captain Larry C. Plummer of the Mountain View, California, Police Department claimed:

> Behavior motivated by bigotry and hate is endemic to the law enforcement profession. It persists not so much because we fall victim to basic "human" shortcomings, but rather because we—police professionals—have not taken the very deliberate individual and collective actions required to eliminate, or at least control, the problem. . . . Bigotry is fueled by many things, but the most critical and overriding factor in our bigotry problem is our failure—individually, organizationally, and collectively—to expose, confront and address it. . . . Many people who have witnessed or experienced repeated police bigotry understandably view us as a foreign entity designed to force compliance to the law and maintain the status quo rather than as a public service entity focused on collaborative efforts and enhancement of public safety and quality of life.[30]

Police departments cannot eliminate bigotry. They are no more perfectible than other selective human institutions. But Plummer was exactly right to insist that they are obligated to reduce and control it—to do everything in their power to root it out. I think that Plummer was wrong, however, to claim that motivations of bigotry and hatred are endemic to law enforcement. *Endemic* means *prevalent*. I have seen departments where bigotry is prevalent, in the sense that bigoted views and behavior stemming from them go uncriticized and that considerable peer pressure exists to conform to those prejudices and to bad, often illegal, practices. But I have seen many more departments where bigotry, with the peer pressure that supports it, is not prevalent. I have also come to know many more police at all ranks who are intolerant of bigotry in themselves and others than police who are complacently bigoted. Still, bigotry does not have to be endemic to poison and destroy public confidence and the morale of police departments.

In my experience, the depth and breadth of departmental vigilance and intolerance for bigotry and brutality vary dramatically within the

United States and in other countries. Some departments are perceptibly worse than others. But no department can honorably spare itself the obligation to design recruitment, training, supervision, accountability, discipline, and overall institutional policy so as to minimize the admission to policing, and the opportunity to remain in policing, of people whose dispositions and habits of speech and action disclose bigotry. Perhaps it is largely true that criminal trials are to some extent trials of the credibility of police themselves. But as long as bigoted, hateful, and brutal officers are known and feared by the public, criminal trials will focus inordinately on police credibility rather than on the guilt or innocence of the defendants. That diversion from the cases being tried undermines justice itself—one more bitter legacy of bigotry and its corrosion of institutions intended to sustain civilized life.

Some police leaders believe incorrectly that because of First Amendment rights they can do almost nothing to prevent or take action against bigoted speech by their personnel. If they consult departmental or other governmental legal counsel, they will find that First Amendment case law provides virtually no protection for bigoted speech by police and law enforcement personnel. Police leaders should not suppose that the First Amendment prevents them from taking action against bigoted speech by sworn or civilian personnel.[31]

Need for Screening and Training. Law enforcement agencies must reject the view expressed by John Warner, the former director of foreign operations in the Drug Enforcement Administration: "One of the reasons that law enforcement corruption exists and has proliferated is that the perpetrators are representative of a cross-section of the general population. As such, a certain percentage of them will be as sleazy, cruel, racist and corrupt as the public at large."[32] Certainly, representatives of such a cross-section will appear in every applicant pool for police positions, but few will hold police jobs if departments do systematic background investigations and maintain rigorous accountability. Warner agreed: He said that the only way to eliminate bigoted and incompetent candidates is to be highly selective in recruiting, with "a full background investigation, psychological testing and written entrance exams."[33]

Circumstances in Chicago show the importance of that point:

Some of the city's most notorious street gangs are infiltrating the police department, and officials can't do much about it. Until gang members in blue break a law, they are protected by their union contract and the right to associate with whomever they please. In the last three years, at least 15 police officers have been charged with crimes, forced to resign or investigated for membership in a street gang, the *Chicago Sun-Times* said. . . . Seven officers in one police district are under investigation for gang ties, the newspaper reported. Harold Kunz, a trustee with the Fraternal Order of Police, said the department should not blame the union for the problem and should instead perform better background checks. The union has a responsibility to defend the right of officers to associate with anyone they want, Kunz said.[34]

Kunz's claim of absolutely unconditional rights of association for police is ridiculous and dangerous. He pitted the union squarely against the public interest and against every officer who opposes low standards and bigotry in policing. As experienced police officials know, it is harder to rid a department of personnel who are unfit than to prevent their being hired in the first place. Union policies, civil service regulations, the mind-set of arbitrators, and the unwillingness of city officials to risk adverse legal rulings exacerbate the problem. High standards and rigorous recruitment procedures are the first line of defense against unacceptable behavior, and dismissal of officers who do not measure up during their probationary term is the second.

In addition to the most determined and conscientious frontline leadership, counseling and training in what the department will and will not stand for are indispensable. Although vapid training in "cultural awareness" and "sensitivity" will not eliminate bigotry, brutality, and corruption, teaching officers to listen carefully and to express themselves will reduce excessive uses of force that arise from ineptitude, fear, and incompetence. Training alone, however, would probably not have set straight the six former Philadelphia police officers who confessed to falsifying reports, committing perjury, planting evidence, and brutalizing people in their custody. Neither would it have been effective against the fifty officers in New Orleans who were arrested on charges of robbery, rape, narcotics trafficking, and murder, nor against six officers in Atlanta who ran extortion and protection rackets.

In Philadelphia, according to a *New York Times* editorial, "the rogue cops
. . . might still be on the street had they not beaten and kidnapped a college student who filed a claim and doggedly pursued it. The criminals in
blue were apparently known as such, both among fellow officers and on the
street."[35] The Atlanta Police Department offered an encouraging counter-
point to any department where police silently tolerate wrongdoing. There,
"the current case began when other Atlanta police officers, angered that
their reputations would be sullied by corrupt colleagues, came forward to
initiate the investigation."[36] Atlanta chief Beverly Harvard, while lamenting
the actions of the corrupt officers, rightly celebrated "officers who felt so
compelled and moved by what they were hearing going on that they came
forward and spoke out."[37]

Steven Bishop, former chief of police in Kansas City, Missouri, won a
reputation for his dedication to the highest standards in policing. He came
to be known as the "Terminator," because in his tenure of just under six
years he forced more than one hundred people out of his department. In
my experience, at the local, state, and federal levels, many law enforcement
officers share Bishop's high standards. They understand that the only way
to demonstrate what you will not tolerate is not to tolerate it. Eighteenth-
century statesman Edmund Burke said: "Those who are habitually
employed in finding and displaying faults are unqualified for the work of
reformation. . . . By hating vices too much, they come to love men too
little."[38] The police leaders I have in mind are exceptions to this frequently
quoted claim. They are vigilant in rooting out bigotry, brutality, and corruption because of their esteem for human dignity and public service, not
because of their preoccupation with human frailty.

Thinking about "Race"

It is not at all clear that any scientific basis exists for the concept of "race."
The idea of race is vague, seems to have greater standing in social policy and
political agendas than in science, and lends itself to the prejudiced over-
simplifications of stereotyping and other forms of bigotry. In its vagueness,
the notion of race leads easily to the idea of "racial purity," despite the fact
that none of us can trace his or her ancestry all the way through the mists

of ancient time to ascertain the ultimate beginnings of our genetic makeup. A child can see that people differ in color, but that fact is not the basis for a scientific theory of race.

Racial Categories. In 1977 the U.S. Office of Management and Budget (OMB) established Race and Ethnic Standards for Federal Statistics and Administrative Reporting. As set out in Statistical Policy Directive No. 15, the racial and ethnic categories for official statistics and reporting are American Indian or Alaskan Native; Asian or Pacific Islander; Hispanic; White, not of Hispanic Origin; and Black, not of Hispanic Origin. In 1995 in its Interim Notice of Review and Possible Revision of OMB's Statistical Policy Directive No. 15,[39] the agency said, "For purposes of collecting data in the United States, race and ethnicity are cultural concepts and social constructs. As stated in the current version of Directive No. 15, the racial and ethnic categories are not intended to reflect scientific or anthropological definitions."[40] The fact that the categories are not anchored in science or scientific taxonomy is further disclosed by their utter inadequacy to provide an answer to the question, Which race is a person whose known ancestry includes a white person, a black person, an Asian person, and an Alaskan Native? Historically, many individuals and nations have used such categories as instruments of racism. Was it ever anything but racism and racial supremacism that denied a person known to have any black ancestry the social benefits and "status" of being "white"?

Ironically, while supposedly distinct racial categories have been used for centuries to deprive people of equal human rights, controversy abounds now about the idea of a "multiracial" category. People of mixed ancestry who wish to identify themselves as "multiracial" in background claim that governmental categories compel them to "deny a part of [their] identity."[41] They meet opposition from political leaders and constituency group representatives who fear that statutes designed to protect minorities, including desegregation and affirmative action laws, would be made difficult to enforce by introduction of a multiracial category. The idea of race, poisonous for so long, is now a lever of power for people, some of whose forebearers have been treated most disgracefully in the past in the name of race.

We must not allow ourselves to suppose that categories designed to facilitate social and legal policy are entirely adequate to capture reality. No matter who prevails in political and social controversy, they will not thereby provide any scientific or moral legitimacy for the idea of race. It will remain true that human beings differ in many ways; we would not otherwise be the individuals we are. Skin color is among our differences, within as well as across supposed racial lines. But skin color does not define us, any more than eye color or hair color does, and geneticists such as Luigi Cavalli-Sforza have explained that beneath the skin, "the remainder of our genetic makeup hardly differs at all."[42]

Historian Lewis Hanke, who is in agreement with a number of other distinguished historians, wrote, "Generally speaking, there was no true racial prejudice before the fifteenth century."[43] Still, most of modern world history has been affected by conceptions of race, and more than a little of that history exhibits patterns of racial supremacism, subspeciation (the claim that some people, because of color or gender or ethnicity, are a subspecies and less than fully human), and racial injustice. The history of the United States contains all three of these, from slavery and racial lynchings to racially motivated abuses of police authority.

Racial Nullification. Largely because of those features of our own history, which reach into the present in such persons as Mark Fuhrman, we face the possibility of a "racial nullification" movement within the criminal justice system. In law schools, as columnist John Leo observed, "'critical race theory' spreads the notion that law is nothing more than a politicized expression of whites."[44] Leo recounted

> that what appears to be a racial nullification movement is humming right along. The journal found that some black jurors "are choosing to disregard the evidence, however powerful, because they seek to protest racial injustice and to refrain from adding to the already large numbers of blacks behind bars."
>
> If so, that's a very ominous development indeed. An explicit attempt to politicize jury verdicts along racial lines would clearly put the whole, faltering criminal justice system at risk, with many unforeseen consequences. . . .
>
> Some racial division on juries is simply the result of different people bringing different life experiences into court and viewing

evidence through different lenses. And some is based on the fact that many blacks are less likely than whites to believe the unsupported testimony of a police officer, even if the officer is not Mark Fuhrman. That's well within the normal functioning of juries.

But now we are starting to hear various racial pleas to ignore evidence and free black defendants either as a political protest against a system perceived as oppressive and racist, or as a way of reducing the high number of black males in the prison system.[45]

Thernstrom and Fetter observed that "post-verdict letters and statements (by jurors) in a number of cases draw a clear picture of jury nullification." But they cautioned that no one knows how often jury racial nullification occurs, partly because "courts do not keep records indicating the breakdown of jurors by race."[46]

What seems to contain the greatest danger as the legacy of racism and the preoccupation with "racial identity" take new forms is that group identification may blind many of us to our common humanity and to our shared and indivisible interests. If racial nullification becomes habitual with juries—a far different matter from perfectly justifiable nullification in specific cases—we face a dreadful risk that police will self-righteously and cynically exceed their authority and mete out brutal "street justice." Some police are likely to draw more deeply into the shell of belief that they have obligations to no one except other police, and some may become brutal because they believe that they can protect the public in no other way.

Racial nullification means refusal to convict a defendant because of the person's skin color, even if it is proved beyond a reasonable doubt that the defendant committed the crime. A jury might nullify the law and due process if members see the criminal justice system as biased, are prejudiced against people different in color from themselves, or believe that the law is unjustly enforced. That is different from jury nullification grounded not in race but in the belief that a specific law is unjust and that no one, irrespective of color, should be punished for breaking it or from belief that circumstances were sufficiently extenuating that any defendant should, under such circumstances, be excused from sanction.

Nonracial nullification resembles civil disobedience in the sense that it amounts to rejection on conscientious grounds of the justice or application of a specific law. It is not a rejection of the system of laws itself, while racial nullification is precisely that. A jury could not, for example, responsibly refuse to convict a proven murderer on the grounds that there should be no law against murder. But a jury could racially nullify the law against murder by refusing to convict a defendant because of his or her race. Such an act by a jury has the effect of nullifying the legal prohibition of murder, provided that the defendant is of the favored race, no matter what race the defendant (or the victim) happens to be in any specific case. The profound moral and legal wrongness of murder makes such nullification indefensible.

If juries routinely acquit defendants because of their skin color and because of a singular political allegiance to identity of color or ethnicity or gender, we face a legal system that confuses, as news producer Kurt Mack wrote, "power with justice":

> I had the opportunity to see Los Angeles in all its post–O. J. glory. I interviewed O. J. supporters—many of whom were white— outside his tony Brentwood home. They were "carrying on," drunk with happiness. One woman said she prayed so hard for O. J. it hurt her. Another sat quietly, flowers and a love note for O. J. in hand. At Bundy—the scene of the crime—flowers and condolences covered the ground where Nicole's and Ron's bloodied bodies once lay. . . . One black woman there mumbled at me, "We gotta stop this denial . . . protecting these crazy fools . . . O. J., Tupac, Tyson, Michael. . . . [C]hild this is a mess." Precisely.
>
> Fear and anger and denial had turned my people into a cynical mob. I watched as blacks from Los Angeles to Times Square to prestigious Howard University Law School cackled at the Goldmans. That day everyone drank from the same 40-ounce beer bottle of bitterness, cynicism and rage. It was no longer about murder but about beating the system that had worked against them for so long. It was not a moment to "say it loud and clear I'm black and I'm proud."
>
> Some postulate that maybe now "my" people will get treated fairly—that in the end race relations will be better. They are wrong. Race relations are worse, and it's worse for blacks than it is whites. Sadly, the cheering hordes of black sympathizers have

confused power with justice, and while this victory may feel
good now, it's a battle percentages alone tell us we can't win.[47]

Nobody wins when either the public or the police lose sight of the differences between justice and power, when the idea of race or racial identity
blinds people to our individuality and our shared humanity and makes us
indifferent to the behavior and character of individuals.

It is nonetheless entirely possible that a portion of the public will
remain sympathetic with racial nullification because of belief that the
criminal justice system and law enforcement are racially biased. That
belief may be fueled by the fact that one of three black men now in their
twenties is under supervision by one arm or another of the criminal justice system. By the end of 1993, as reported by the Bureau of Justice
Statistics, "[n]early two-thirds of all sentenced prison inmates were black,
Asian, Native American, or Hispanic. . . . Between 1980 and 1993, the latest data available, the percentage of sentenced inmates who were black
rose from 46.5% to 50.8%. Relative to the number of residents in the U.S.
population, blacks at year-end were 7 times more likely than whites to
have been incarcerated in a State or Federal prison." During that period,
the percentage of federal prison inmates incarcerated for drug-related
offenses rose from 25 percent to 60 percent; in state prisons, the percentage of inmates incarcerated for drug offenses rose from 6 percent to 22
percent, but the increase in prisoners incarcerated for violent crimes was
even higher.[48]

To combat the perception of racial injustice in the criminal justice system,
some scholars and social critics have recommended legalization of drugs as a
remedy for high rates of incarceration for drug-related offenses; others have
recommended that no crimes of drug consumption or possession, but only
drug-trafficking crimes, should carry a penalty of imprisonment.

As I have argued in chapter 9, I believe that a compelling argument for
the general legalization of drugs and narcotics cannot be given. Neither can
we combat the scourge of drugs without the pressure of legal sanctions
against users. Demand-side arrests, fines, and public exposure are essential.
Imprisonment as a penalty for drug consumption (as opposed to property
and violent crimes committed to support habits of drug use), however, may
not be in the best interest of individuals or the country. Clogging the courts

with drug-user cases, subjecting drug users to the dangers of victimization by rapacious and violent inmates, and exposing drug users in prison to patterns of criminal behavior that they may copy after release seem clearly undesirable. It is not clear that the adverse consequences of current law and policy are counterbalanced by advancement of public safety or reductions in demand for drugs. Perhaps changes in law and policy would benefit the public and give police departments freedom to allocate their resources somewhat differently from present practices.

But it will not do to suppose that the facts of minority crime and punishment are nothing but symptoms of a racially biased criminal justice system. Orlando Patterson, John Cowles Professor of Sociology at Harvard University, rightly cautioned, "The high rate of arrests and jailings afflicting the bottom third of blacks is not just racism in the criminal justice system, but criminal behavior and its roots in disintegrating families and neighborhoods."[49] We will not protect the victims of crime, many of them members of our minority population, or improve the lives of children by ignoring the social conditions to which Patterson pointed.

Harvard Law School Professor Randall Kennedy stressed the great resentments to which the O. J. Simpson trial and verdict gave renewed visibility and asked, "What are we going to do to drain this reservoir of distrust and cynicism?"[50] That is a question for police, too, because whatever changes in law or policy may come to pass, police are obligated to do their part to avoid contributing to cynicism and distrust in the future by behaving honorably in their treatment of all the public.

The magnitude of that duty is suggested by John Ellis, a consultant at Rasby and Company, who foresaw dreadful consequences from the Simpson verdict. In the context of O. J. Simpson attorney Robert Shapiro's statement in an interview with Barbara Walters, "Not only did we play the race card, we played it from the bottom of the deck." Ellis predicted:

> That card will be played back now in the political arena. It won't affect Johnnie Cochran. It won't affect O. J. Simpson. But it will do damage to black America and to the country as a whole.
>
> The verdict freed a guilty man. Its aftermath will punish millions of people whose only "sin" is the color of their skin.

> It will get worse before it gets better. The trial of O. J. Simpson
> is over now. The politics of O. J. Simpson are just beginning.[51]

If, as a people, we do not have what it takes to reject the reprisals Ellis describes as "the politics of O. J. Simpson," our future as a nation is dim. The lust for "payback," if unchecked, could destroy us. But even if Ellis's pessimism about the country turns out to be warranted, police must rise above every temptation toward prejudice and reprisal.

Thinking about Human Beings

If I were to recommend one object of study for police and police executives who are asking, with Randall Kennedy, what we can do about "this reservoir of distrust and cynicism," I would recommend that they read the writings of distinguished American author Ralph Ellison. His novel, *Invisible Man*, is powerfully instructive, and the thoughtful commentaries in his autobiographical essays published as *Shadow and Act* seem to me even more so.[52] Police will find great rewards in reading both.

In the introduction to *Shadow and Act*, Ellison told of his "slow and blundering discovery" of his own voice as a writer. He described straightforwardly his "struggle to stare down the deadly and hypnotic temptation to interpret the world and all its devices in terms of race."[53] In an interview, "That Same Pain, That Same Pleasure," which appears as the first chapter of *Shadow and Act*, Ellison spoke of an experience in boyhood that enabled him to prevail in that struggle. Asked by interviewer Richard G. Stern about the sources of his strength as a writer, Ellison replied:

> Well, to the extent that one cannot ever escape what is given I
> suppose it had less to do with writing per se than with my
> desire, beginning at a very early age, to be more fully a part of
> that larger world which surrounded the Negro world into which
> I was born. It was a matter of attitude. Then there were the acci-
> dents through which so much of that world beyond the Negro
> community became available to me. . . . Like so many kids of
> the twenties, I played around with the radio-building crystal sets

and circuits consisting of a few tubes, which I found published in the radio magazines. At the same time we were living in a white middle-class neighborhood, where my mother was a custodian for some apartments, and it was while searching the trash for cylindrical ice-cream cartons which were used by amateurs for winding tuning coils that I met a white boy [nicknamed Hoolie] who was looking for the same thing. I gave him some of those I'd found and we became friends. . . . Due to a rheumatic heart Hoolie was tutored at home and spent a great deal of time playing by himself and in taking his parents' elaborate radio apart and putting it back together again, and in building circuits of his own. . . . [K]nowing this white boy was a very meaningful experience. It had little to do with the race question as such, but with our mutual loneliness (I had no other playmates in that community) and a great curiosity about the growing science of radio. It was important for me to know a boy who could approach the intricacies of electronics with such daring and whose mind was intellectually aggressive. Knowing him led me to expect much more of myself and of the world.[54]

In the same interview, recounting further formative experiences, Ellison said:

I knew Jimmy Rushing, the blues singer, who then was not quite the hero of the middle-class people whom I knew, that he is today after years of popular success. But for us, even when he was a very young man, a singer who came home to the city once in a while, Jimmy represented, gave voice to, something which was very affirming of Negro life, feelings which you couldn't really put into words. Of course, beyond jazz there was all the boasting, and bragging that went on when no one but ourselves was supposed to be listening, when you weren't really being judged by the white world. At least when you thought you weren't being judged and didn't care if you were. For instance, there is no place like a Negro barbershop for hearing what Negroes really think. There is more unselfconscious affirmation to be found here on a Saturday than you can find in a Negro college in a month, or so it seems to me.[55]

In summing up the core of the lessons of his youth, he said, "Put it this way: I learned very early that in the realm of the imagination all people and their ambitions and interests could meet."[56] In his youth, Ellison grasped a fundamental truth about us as human beings that Kwame Anthony Appiah, African American studies professor at Harvard, emphasized in 1995. In "Beware of Race-Pride" Appiah wrote:

When people organize around their own separate groups the result is not just difficulty in understanding across cultures but that we end up preferring our own kind. And if we prefer our own kind, it is easy enough to slip into preferring to vote for our own kind, to employ our own kind, and so on. These loyalties will be mobilized in politics unless a civic culture can be created that explicitly seeks to exclude them. And that is why real multiculturalism—pluralism, to use an older word—is so necessary: it is the only way to build bridges of loyalty across the ethnicities that have so often divided us.[57]

Police, who sometimes socialize almost exclusively with each other and may be tempted to think only of other police as "their own kind," should take particular note of Appiah's words. The fundamental moral principle here is that it is wrong to confine our sense of duty, of justice, of compassion, to people with whom we feel some sort of personal kinship. All human beings are entitled to moral consideration, simply because they are human.

Concluding the interview in Shadow and Act with a perceptiveness that compels the intellectually honest reader to recognize each person, regardless of color, gender, or ethnicity, as an individual who shares in a common humanity—and with a poignancy that should call us back to the tragically unacceptable fate of Elisa Izquierdo—Ellison said: "You know, the skins of those thin-legged little girls who faced the mob in Little Rock marked them as Negro, but the spirit which directed their feet is the old universal urge toward freedom."[58] No one who genuinely understands what it means to love a child can be diverted from that insight by the color of any child's skin.

Conclusion

The future of the United States as a nation and the future of policing in the democracies of the world turn on whether in law, policy, and daily practice we see beyond color and gender and ethnicity into that spirit of which Ellison wrote, that universality of human feeling and yearning within each one of us.

No matter what color, ethnicity, or gender we are, if we are prejudiced against others because of their color, ethnicity, or gender, we fail in our understanding of humanity. Inability to grasp this, to *see* that people are not reducible to mere members of groups, is the pitiable squalor of the bigot. The bigot evokes not only our contempt but also, by his self-abasement, our disdainful pity. How can we fail to pity a person so divorced from a trustworthy perception of reality about human beings, human feelings, and human life?

On March 4, 1865, Abraham Lincoln delivered his second inaugural address. Speaking for many Americans, he said, "Fondly do we hope—fervently do we pray—that this mighty scourge of war may speedily pass away." And then, using words to draw stark and dreadful pictures of both slavery and war, he spoke of the possibility of retribution "until all the wealth piled up by the bondsman's two hundred and fifty years of unrequited toil shall be sunk, and until every drop of blood drawn with the lash, shall be paid by another drawn with the sword."[59]

Slavery was ended by force of superior arms. But the ravages of its legacy, racism and bigotry, are far from past and continue to limit the course of justice.

Police cannot save the public from racism and other varieties of prejudice that treat people solely as members of groups. But police can do a great deal, institutionally and individually, to ensure that policing and law enforcement are hostile territory for bigotry. The thoughts, words, and actions of every single officer—regardless of color, gender, ethnicity—count; each and all must resist the temptations of prejudice and the bad habits that follow. This goal is within the power of each officer. The intellectual and moral standards of policing as a profession demand no less.

18

The Spirit of Public Service and Individual Conscience

Conscience, Socrates thought, must be educated by reflective criticism into clearness and coherence; otherwise the ideals in terms of which we must pass judgment on the actual will themselves be confused.

—Brand Blanshard[1]

Police leaders refer to "a spirit of service" as a particularly desirable trait in officers, even those whose mission lies primarily in law enforcement rather than in other domains of policing. Good policing depends on a willingness to make sacrifices for others, most conspicuously for the innocent, the needy, and the helpless.

Experienced police will be able to think of countless examples of the power of a spirit of service in practice, not only in their own lives but in the lives of other police with whom they have worked. In the summer of 1995, I encountered a particularly memorable instance of that spirit.

A high, black, rusted steel fence marks the border between the United States and Mexico from east of Tijuana and south of San Ysidro to the Pacific Ocean. White and amber lights are positioned on high towers to reveal people coming over the fence to make a run into the undergrowth behind the lights. Helicopters outfitted with infrared scopes adapted from army tanks fly overhead in search of illegal immigrants hiding in the darkness. The stretch of land is grim. Although the lights make it difficult for bandits to rob, rape, or kill, people trying to enter the United States illegally can still take a long and dangerous fall into the canyons. The brush, taller than a person, is home to poisonous snakes and insects.

At this border, the Tijuana River is a sluggish mass of untreated toxic and human waste. When you get near it, it burns your eyes, its nasty odors assault your nose, its acrid filth makes your face and hands tingle. The river is no place for human beings or for other living things, except the bacteria that feed on it. More than two hundred Border Patrol agents in the sector filed suit against the Border Patrol in pursuit of hazardous duty pay.[2]

As adviser to the U.S. attorney general and to the Immigration and Naturalization Service and the Border Patrol, I spent time there in 1995. To conduct programs for Border Patrol agents and for their teachers at the Federal Law Enforcement Training Center in Georgia, I had to know at first hand what is demanded of agents in the field.

For a long time, people crossing the border illegally would take refuge in the Tijuana River to avoid being arrested by the Border Patrol. Knowing that no agent would come in after them, they would stand in the river— looking for a chance to cross it—until they neared collapse from hypothermia. In 1995 at least fifteen people drowned in the river, probably victims of sinkholes: A person can go from ankle-deep to water ten feet deep in a single step. Now, however, fewer people go into the river, partly because of Border Patrol agents, including one man in particular.

Because he used to work for a pharmaceutical company, he was asked to serve as an adviser to U.S. customs agents trying to reduce smuggling of criminally diverted prescription drugs. During his work with customs, he realized that he really wanted to work full-time in federal law enforcement. After he became a Border Patrol agent, he saw the people trying to cross the border in the Tijuana River.

Thinking about that horror, he told his supervisor that he believed that the dangers to those people were unacceptable. If caught, they would be returned to Mexico. Some of them made two, three, or even four attempts to cross the border in a single night. The agent proposed to stop them from endangering themselves and their children in the river by showing them that the Border Patrol would go in after them. He proposed to make that his job.

He got the job, but he no longer goes in as often as he did in the beginning because the word is out. People know that the river will not protect them from the agents anymore. He does not brag about what he does, and he does not complain. With a wry smile, he says that he does not like running after someone in the river, because he cannot keep the splash out of his face. He is exactly the kind of person who is suited to the serious responsibilities of law enforcement, as surely as Mark Fuhrman of the Los Angeles Police Department was not.

I have met many police officers, sheriff's deputies, federal agents, and others in law enforcement, including support staff, who give their best day after day with a real determination "to protect and to serve." In some departments, the most dedicated personnel do not get the benefit of very much peer encouragement and support. In other departments and agencies, the majority of members leave no doubt about their dissatisfactions with peers who are short on the spirit of service. In that respect, as in others, the weight and direction of peer pressure make a great difference—perhaps the greatest difference of all—in the quality and the spirit of the department.

Reciprocity and the Spirit of Service

No one can reasonably expect the spirit of service to take root in a police department or law enforcement agency unless the leadership embodies the same spirit in its treatment of departmental personnel. Leaders must be prepared to stand up for their subordinates when they perform admirably or make good-faith mistakes, as surely as they must refuse to tolerate bad-faith betrayals of the law and departmental policies and ideals.

Too often in law enforcement, reciprocity—application of the golden rule within a department and mutual faithfulness of all ranks to high ethical standards—is absent or weak. Sometimes leaders expect much but give little; sometimes leaders are faithful to their personnel, but their subordinates are cynically indifferent to high standards of service.

In the aftermath of the crisis with the Branch Davidians at Waco, I witnessed a disappointing lack of reciprocity by high-ranking officials in the U.S. Department of the Treasury. And since the confrontation with the Weaver family at Ruby Ridge, I have seen dramatically egregious failures of reciprocity by high officials in the U.S. Department of Justice.

My extended conversations with members of law enforcement agencies in positions of authority at Waco and Ruby Ridge have convinced me that everyone understands that good-faith mistakes were made in both cases. Although I have been unpersuaded that the mistakes of greatest importance resembled anything routinely emphasized by the popular media or elected officials, I met no one with authority in Waco and Ruby Ridge who would repeat all the decisions made there. I think, for example, that critics have not concentrated sufficiently on the circumstances that led to the initial involvement of the Bureau of Alcohol, Tobacco, and Firearms at the Branch Davidian compound. Neither have they been very instructive about weaknesses in preliminary ATF surveillance of the movements of David Koresh and in other means of gathering and assessing intelligence before the decision to attempt to serve search and arrest warrants with a great show of force.

Commentators similarly disregarded the dangers to law enforcement personnel at Waco as negotiations continued. Many made the mistake I made when I wrote the preface to the second edition of *Character and Cops*: that of believing that the FBI intended to enter the compound following the use of tear gas. There was in fact no such intention, and supposing otherwise obscures the details and the relevant lessons of that last heartbreaking day. For all that, all the law enforcement officials involved with the initial assault at Waco, and the standoff that followed, with whom I talked agreed: In retrospect, none would have mounted the initial assault on the Waco compound in attempting to serve warrants.

Some of the law enforcement leaders who were involved in those cases are among the most admirable and conscientious people I have ever known in any walk of life. A number of them have devoted their entire adult lives to the public interest with a rare spirit of service and willingness to make personal sacrifices for the sake of departmental mission and the public good.

After Ruby Ridge, some of those men were accused of participation in a conspiratorial coverup of events there. Following those allegations, several were summarily suspended from the FBI, and their careers are now in tatters.

When I inquired, in August 1995, of high-ranking Justice Department officials how those career-shattering suspensions could possibly have been justified, particularly in the case of one man of whom the U.S. attorney's office had said there was no evidence of wrongdoing, I was sent a letter saying that the overriding consideration was "the need for the FBI and its employees to avoid even the perception of corruption." I objected that when, for a period of over twenty years, a person has shown integrity, has been above reproach in matters of honesty and professionalism, no appearance or "perception" is more important than that history and those facts.

The decision of Justice Department officials to place somebody's "perception" above everything else—and the dreadful failure of reciprocity that such a decision embodied—seemed to me a case of slavish devotion to political expediency at the price of justice. In hope of persuading those officials that appearance and "perception" should not be allowed to ride roughshod over known facts and realities, I wrote a letter in October 1995:

> Years ago, when I first began to serve on various federal boards in education and related fields, an experienced Washington veteran in high office said privately to me, "Ed, the only thing you have to remember is that, in this town, appearance is the only reality." Knowing him as I did, I was not surprised by his cynicism, but I was pretty sure he was wrong. My experience in the years since has proved that he was wrong—there are too many serious people in our nation's capital . . . for the government to collapse completely into adoration of appearances. I do not deny that appearances, including appearances of wrongdoing, matter, and I do not deny the presence in Washington of a widespread lust for the appearance of rightdoing when the reality belies it, but neither of those reduces reality to appearances. In ethics, as you know, the distinction between reality and appearance is fundamental.
>
> Accordingly, when there is "perception of corruption," I want to know as much about the condition of the perceiver as of the perceived, and I want to know the historical context of both. I share your view that full investigations are imperative, but I do not believe that the suspension, with or without pay, of a public servant . . . whose moral and intellectual distinction have been proved over the life of a career can be justified by a momentary perception or allegation which even the officials empowered to investigate publicly acknowledge to be unsupported by evidence. A temporary shift in duties is no doubt absolutely essential while an investigation proceeds, but a peremptory suspension is punitive—in some respects, irreversibly so—and may inexcusably alter for the worse the entire career future of the person so treated.

> I understand, of course, that some readings of considerations of law or policy or politics might be adduced against my view. But where law or policy, let alone politics, comes into conflict with considerations of justice, ethics always favors justice.

Although my letter was passed along from the Justice Department to members of the U.S. Senate, and I made it known to other public officials, it had no effect whatsoever. Some politicians were even so outrageously hypocritical as to castigate law enforcement officials with responsibilities at Waco and Ruby Ridge in public while speaking in private of their admiration and support. When a police department or law enforcement agency—or any other kind of institution—shows its honorable personnel that it will not stand by them publicly in the face of political and media pressure, that agency sows the seeds of its own internal decline. All police have seen officers who, convinced that they cannot trust their own leaders, will go to great lengths to avoid involvement in any situation on the streets that might become politically volatile. The spirit of service withers wherever officers have reason to believe that if they make a good-faith mistake in a difficult situation—or if things go badly despite their having done everything conscientiously and responsibly—their leaders will abandon them. The spirit of service is overrun by a concern to survive, followed by a self-defensive refusal to take risks even for the sake of public safety.

My colleagues in policing are right to emphasize the desirability of a spirit of service in officers. In practice, that spirit can be undermined by recruiting the wrong people, by training and supervising them badly, and by other obvious departmental weaknesses. But in my experience, nothing so drastically undercuts willingness to be of service in the most demanding circumstances than a demonstrated failure of departmental nerve under political pressure.

Ultimately, when the spirit of service in the members of a department withers, the overall mission of the institution withers with it. Internal failures of reciprocity reduce the power of an institution to rise to hard challenges. They undermine traditions of peer pressure in favor of excellence, thereby threatening the future of the institution. That consequence is virtually inevitable, because without reciprocity, there can be no mutual trust, and where mutual trust fails, individuals put self-protection first. Few of us are willing to take responsible risks for the sake of others unless we are confident that our leaders will not abandon us.

Individual Conscience

The very habits of character that inspire good policing—a spirit of service, integrity, moral seriousness, devotion in friendship, intolerance for betrayals of the public trust—may also lead to questions of conscience. Officers may find themselves torn between their loyalty to a partner who mistreats suspects and their duty to refuse to tolerate such wrongdoing. Although such tensions can be extreme, they cannot justify allowing a friend to violate the trust of public office. It is not betrayal to expect a friend to live up to the known duties of office. Still, decent people are seldom free of conflict when they face questions of conscience.

Conscience and Police Assignments

Officers sometimes ask not to be assigned to patrol parades conducted by Nazis or the Ku Klux Klan or not to have to safeguard abortion clinics or arrest protesters. What should supervisors do when faced with such requests—or demands? What departmental policy should they establish to anticipate them? And what should police do when they are given an assignment contrary to their religious or moral principles?

First, not every appeal to conscience deserves moral approval. Human beings are capable of believing anything whatsoever. They may think that their conscience tells them to commit appalling acts. Terrorists and assassins sometimes say that they are following the orders of God; fanatics carry out racist lynchings and terrorist bombings in the name of conscience; parents announce themselves bound by principle to deny their children desperately needed medical treatment; and police commit acts of "noble cause corruption" because they believe that their mission raises them above the law. We do not grant the rightness of such appeals in ethics, law, or policy, even when the beliefs are sincerely held. Sincerity in itself does not justify any belief or action, and self-righteousness exempts no one from the law. As philosophers have long noted, deciding the right thing to do in complicated circumstances often calls for deliberation. Conscience may be insufficient to serve as a guide to conduct.

While conscience may be sovereign—in the sense that we have the right to act as we think right, without interference, as long as we do not tread on the rights of others—it does not follow that our conscience is always right. In the privacy of the home, parents have a right to teach a child a falsehood—for example, that foreigners are inferior—although they would be wrong to do so. Because we can be confused and adhere to such erroneous beliefs, Socrates called for reflective criticism in conversation as a means of educating our conscience and refining our moral judgment. Aware of that need, police routinely discuss what they ought to do in real or hypothetical cases. If conscience were enough, we could tell recruits just to follow it on the job. Clearly, we would be courting disaster if we educated police in that way.

No one should blithely assume that, once the voice of conscience speaks, the matter is settled. An officer who believes, for example, that homosexuality is wrong and therefore ignores abuses of homosexuals by police and others has reached an indefensible conclusion. Any officer who has not given rigorous thought to the nature of homosexuality is likely to be prejudiced. Furthermore, quality of character cannot be judged simply by knowing whether a person is heterosexual or homosexual. It is wrong to identify a person merely as a member of a group and to ignore that person's individuality. And even if a compelling argument against homosexuality could be articulated, it would not show in the slightest that the rights of homosexuals are therefore forfeit. No responsible supervisor can tolerate such prejudice in the performance of duty, and no appeal to conscience can change that fact. Accordingly, when questions of conscience are raised, supervisors are not obliged to regard any individual's conscience as necessarily right or reasonable.

That caveat does not indicate what to do, however, when questions of conscience are supported by good reasons. Nor does it indicate what individual police should do about duty assignments that seem to conflict with their well-considered religious or moral convictions.

We have conclusive reasons, after all, for judging the conduct of fascists, racists, and other bigots to be reprehensible. How, then, are we to understand the obligations of police to them? And what of abortion? The decision to have an abortion is not considered trivial even by those who believe that abortion should be legal and that every woman has the right to decide whether or not to have an abortion. What, then, are we to do about police who believe abortion to be wrong and object to safeguarding abortion clinics?

Those questions may be made more pressing for police departments by First Amendment protections of the free exercise of religion, by Title VII of the Civil Rights Act of 1964, and by the Religious Freedom Restoration Act of 1993. As FBI attorney Daniel L. Schofield explained, Title VII "makes it unlawful to discriminate on the basis of religion," and the Religious Freedom Restoration Act of 1993 "restores . . . the requirement that governmental actions that substantially burden freedom of religion be justified by a compelling interest."[3] Local statutes may likewise affect police departments, as with Section 2-160-050 of the Municipal Code of Chicago:

> No employer shall refuse to make all reasonable efforts to accommodate the religious beliefs, observances and practices of employees or prospective employees unless the employer demonstrates that he is unable to reasonably accommodate an employee's or prospective employee's religious observance or practice without undue hardship on the conduct of the employer's business.

Such statutes contribute to a community's definition of its ideals and character. Community respect for religious accommodation, especially where populations are heterogeneous, may be linked to respect for both liberty and civility. Those ideals are not to be taken lightly, even though living up to them may involve inconvenience for employers, including police departments.

Recruitment, Training, and Departmental Policy

In recruiting for police positions, departments should look for evidence that the candidate is a person of conscience—a person whose habits show a trustworthy sense of right and wrong and a regard for the golden rule. Questions should be designed to disclose the candidate's thoughts about our form of government, the mission of police, and the human rights that anchor our Declaration of Independence and our Constitution. Ignorance of the constitutional heritage of the United States is so commonplace in schools, colleges, and universities that police departments should expect it in their applicant pools. Academy and field training should be designed to address such ignorance in otherwise promising candidates.

Interviewers may find it useful to explore with candidates specific constitutional guarantees to see how the candidates think. Academy instructors should certainly do so. In training, at least three lessons must be taught.

First, the Fourteenth Amendment to the Constitution explicitly denies to government the power to "deprive any person of life, liberty, or property, without due process of law." Neither is government allowed to "deny to any person within its jurisdiction the equal protection of the laws." *Any person.* Even advocates of racist and ethnic hatred who are acting lawfully should be able to exercise their right to assemble or parade. It may fall to police to provide them with protection. The police oath to uphold the Constitution implies an obligation to people whose beliefs are contemptible. That obligation is inescapable for police departments, even if specific officers are sometimes spared assignments that are particularly offensive to them.

The second lesson is that all of us have faults. If police deny civil rights to persons they consider flawed—or allow citizens to trample the rights of those they disrespect—none of us can be sure of our rights. Those who would unilaterally deprive others of their rights because of real or alleged imperfections thereby breed tyranny or even genocide. All police should learn unequivocally that an individual's standing before the law is not impaired by adherence to beliefs that are repugnant to decent people.

Perhaps most of us feel the temptation, from time to time, to think that it would be all right to abandon the constitutional safeguards of despicable people. Yielding to that temptation, however, is morally wrong, a violation of a police officer's oath. It brings injustice and arbitrariness into law enforcement. Such actions begin a pattern of behavior that threatens the rights of everyone. There is no end to it. Vigilantism—taking law enforcement into one's own hands—poses a grim threat to the public safety.

The third lesson, an echo of the first two, concerns the way of life intended by the Constitution—a way of life in which justice and securing "the blessings of liberty to ourselves and our posterity" are fundamental. When police take their oath to uphold the Constitution, they should understand that rights are not *given* by the Constitution; rather, rights are *guaranteed* by it. Government is intended to secure those rights, and rights are not reserved solely for people we admire. An officer pledges to safeguard the rights of all people, not just those who merit approbation or share our own beliefs.

There is no room for ambiguity in departmental policy about these matters. When departments waffle, they open the way for officers to abuse suspects and look the other way when others do so. Such officers may then yield to the temptation to steal from drug dealers, behave vengefully toward segments of the public, and conduct lax investigations of crimes against people of whom they disapprove.

Supervision and Leadership

In departments that teach the real meaning of the oath to uphold the Constitution and that clearly frame their obligations to the public, officers may be less inclined to request exemptions from assignments. Even where instruction is good and policy clear, however, much remains for leaders to do in practical management.

If an officer raises a serious question of conscience or makes an appeal to conscience in relation to an assignment, supervisors should never dismiss it summarily. A supervisor sets a callous example by replying abruptly, "If I give you a break, everybody will want one, and then we can't do the job." The last thing that a leader should want to teach subordinates is that a serious conscience is an intrusion, a bother to be gotten out of the way of normal operations as quickly as possible.

It is one thing to understand that conscience is not infallible. It is something entirely different to mock a person's conscience or give it short shrift. The proper response to a morally serious person is attentiveness, responsiveness, and possibly instruction. Policing is made worse, not better, by a supervisor's indifference to achievements of good character among those who hold offices of public trust.

One of my colleagues in the field of ethics has made that point nicely: "As a general rule, police departments, especially as places already committed to enforcement of moral order, should take steps to make certain that respect for conscience prevails *as far as is consistent with the demands of effective policing.*" Obviously, respect for conscience does not require a supervisor to grant every request. If the request is made on religious grounds, a supervisor can show respect by encouraging the officer to talk to a rabbi, priest, minister, imam, or other congregation leader. Religious teachers may help officers decide where to draw the line about assignments.

Some religions distinguish between formal and material cooperation with actions believed to be wrong. An officer who directs traffic to keep it moving smoothly, for example, may cooperate *formally* with someone making a getaway from a crime or surreptitiously transporting illegal drugs. But that officer is not cooperating *materially* and is in no way responsible for such law-breaking. That distinction might apply, say, in an assignment to help stop a violent clash outside an abortion clinic, where the public safety is at risk, even if the officer believes abortion to be wrong. The same officer might find it morally intolerable to remove nonviolent protesters near the same clinic. No officer should claim an exemption from all duties to abortion providers. Officers who drew no distinctions at all, and would not intervene to prevent the murder of an abortion clinic employee, cannot in good faith remain in policing. A departmental chaplain or teacher from an officer's congregation may assist police in working through questions of conscience.

Supervisors can demonstrate their respect for conscience in a variety of other ways. I know thoughtful watch commanders who do not assign certain officers to abortion clinic patrol to avoid compromising their religious convictions. But those commanders tell the officers that they may have to assist in emergencies. If they concur in the overriding significance of public safety, the matter of conscience is resolved compatibly with departmental needs. In practice, however, such principled compromises cannot always be achieved.

Sergeants and watch commanders occasionally refuse to make adjustments in assignments to accommodate conscience or religious convictions or to abide by agreements made by previous supervisors. Some supervisors are professional and evenhanded in taking such positions, some are not as respectful of expectations as they might be, and some are unnecessarily blunt and dismissive. And sometimes officers are so intransigent—and expansive—in their demands that no department could reasonably meet them.

In such matters, moral obligation cuts both ways: Supervisors cannot reasonably be called upon to forfeit the lawful mission of the department or their own dedication to that mission; and officers cannot reasonably be required to ignore their conscience. No formula can provide an honorable compromise in every case, but meeting the demands of effective policing should be the goal of deliberation between supervisors and their personnel. Nothing can take the place of shared goodwill and mutual respect.

Trying to be responsive to an officer's conscience is not the same as sharing the officer's beliefs. A department that takes the moral convictions of its members seriously is not advocating those convictions or affirming their truth. Searching for compromise in abortion clinic assignments in no way implies that legal abortions are morally wrong.

Some officers are offended by efforts to stop women from exercising their lawful rights in having abortions. Some are offended that the rich have had greater access than the poor to safe abortions. Some are moved by the misery of children who are born and live unwanted, neglected, unloved. And everyone should be appalled by violence against abortion clinic personnel, as in the 1994 murders of two abortion clinic employees in Brookline, Massachusetts. I have met police who earnestly want to patrol abortion clinics to secure the rights of women who seek abortions. It would be unfair to regard the moral sensibilities of these officers as any less worthy than those of officers who oppose legal abortions.

A supervisor must disallow police lawbreaking in the name of conscience—beating up drug dealers because they ruin the lives of children, for example, or committing perjury to secure conviction of a dangerous person. In the same way, a supervisor must refuse to tolerate police laxity or abusiveness toward people of whom they disapprove. It is no more the province of police to decide that one view on abortion deserves respect and another does not than to decide that one religion deserves respect and not another. People of goodwill and admirable character disagree on such complex matters: That is one of the fruits of liberty, of freedom of religion and conscience. A supervisor may find it more difficult to be responsive to one view than to another, but duty calls for evenhandedness.

Nevertheless, supervisors have a right to convictions of their own. Their rights are undiminished by the requirements of justice in professionalism.

In my philosophic and scholarly studies, I have worked extensively on the questions about abortion. Many of the faculty, staff, and students in my university differ deeply with my conclusions. When I review their grades or their fitness for promotion, tenure, or salary increases, I would commit a serious wrong against them if I were to take into account whether they agree with me. Neither I nor a police supervisor should bring personal convictions on such a subject into an assessment of the performance of others.

Supervisors may also face conflicts of conscience between officers that make it difficult for them to work together. There, too, if neither officer is the sort of bigot who does not belong in policing, supervisors must be even-handed. If they separate the officers, they should not act as if one is morally superior to the other.

Neither should police consider religious proselytizing while on duty a rightful part of their work. As Daniel L. Schofield wrote:

> Religious neutrality especially is threatened when a supervisor proselytizes to subordinates in the workplace or when a law enforcement officer proselytizes to a private citizen during duty hours. The government's duty of neutrality in its role as public employer is to protect the religious beliefs of all employees by not encouraging or promoting one religion over other religions or any religion over nonreligion.[4]

Unchecked proselytizing can polarize officers, undermine attention to police mission, harm departmental morale, and erode mutual cooperation in the field. Mockery of religious beliefs is no more acceptable than proselytizing.

Law and Policy

Those considerations, however, do not require police departments to sacrifice their mission to the dictates of conscience or to the religious convictions of their personnel. Schofield wrote, "A law enforcement agency is not obliged under Title VII or the Constitution to accommodate the religious beliefs of its employees by permitting them to refuse a lawful assignment."[5] Neither does the law require departments to arrange shift assignments to relieve officers from working on their Sabbaths. Rather, under Title VII, "employers have the burden of demonstrating they are unable to *reasonably accommodate* an employee's religious practices without *undue hardship* on the conduct of business."[6]

Legal counsel should, of course, keep departmental leaders and officials of the union and patrolmen's association abreast of developments in the law. But law has its justification in the moral force behind it, not the reverse. The moral authority of individual conscience underlies the laws that safeguard religious freedom from the impositions of government. Human beings should be self-determining unless they interfere with equal rights to self-determination of others.

If police departments can "reasonably accommodate" the convictions of their personnel, they should do so. Indifference to the beliefs of officers and support staff is self-defeating. Respect for the dignity of every citizen is the basis of the tradition of high standards for public servants. It is hardly appropriate to show less respect for the dignity of officers who bear the public trust. The overriding consideration, however, must be to fulfill the mission of the department in policing and law enforcement. It is wrong to sacrifice the essential work of the department to anyone's individual convictions; doing so is neither reasonable nor compatible with the public interest. An ordained minister put this point to me succinctly: "Personal conviction, even if religiously based, is not trumps in every situation."

Policies That Aid Conscience

Since the bombing of the Murrah Federal Building in Oklahoma City on April 19, 1995, a number of police and law enforcement officers have described to me what is for them a new question of conscience. Specifically, they are encountering people in traffic stops who identify themselves as "freemen" or "militia" and insist that the government and police have no rightful authority over them. They may refuse to display a license plate or to produce a driver's license. Such traffic stops can involve vehicles with several passengers; it may be reasonable to assume—or it may be obvious—that they are armed; backup may be far away.

These officers tell me that they know full well that they are supposed to enforce the law and that the rightful authority of government and police cannot be left to every member of the public to decide. Nonetheless, they fear that if they insist on immediate compliance, some of those encounters will escalate into avoidable violence. I have asked what their departments said they should do; on a number of occasions, the reply was a shrug or a complaint that the department said no more than to exercise discretion and use good judgment.

Those officers are right about their duty to enforce the law. If every individual decides the extent of government authority, the result is anarchy. They are also right to want to prevent, and certainly not to cause, avoidable violence. But merely telling them to apply basic dictates of conscience and use good judgment is insufficient. In such matters, formulation of clear and instructive departmental policy is essential and can serve as a guide to the officer's conscience.

This is one more opportunity for leaders, supervisors, and instructors to explain what good judgment and wise exercise of discretion are in practice. I have corresponded with nearly sixty police and law enforcement leaders about those traffic stop encounters and have asked them the questions, "What should be the policies of the department, and what should officers be taught about how to behave in the variety of circumstances where the problems they describe may arise?"

Every letter of counsel to me affirms that the law must be enforced, and nearly every one explains that the law need not always be fully enforced immediately, irrespective of the risk of escalation into violence. Officers should be taught not to force the issue without regard for consequences where they are alone and outnumbered and backup is distant, but rather to identify license numbers where possible and take careful note of the vehicle and its driver. The matter can be rejoined later with a summons—as long as the department and the courts take each summons seriously—at a time when the officer is not alone and the balance favors the police. That balance alone is likely to reduce the likelihood of violence. If backup is readily at hand, the matter may admit of earlier peaceful resolution. Extreme cases where, for example, a driver is drunk and must not be permitted to proceed may make violence simply unavoidable, despite best efforts.

Many of the letters stress the importance of teaching officers that in potentially violent traffic stops where the best efforts at communication get nowhere and where the officer is at an overwhelming disadvantage, temporary retreat may be the right action. Such a temporary retreat is neither a betrayal of law enforcement nor an act of cowardice. But these same letters caution that if police allow themselves to be bullied, if the department does not follow up with later arrests, and if prosecutors do not take seriously refusal to comply with police authority, then the ability of police to perform their duties will be dangerously undermined. If the reputation of police is compromised, more people will be tempted to behave confrontationally when stopped by police; the law will fall into contempt; and the public will be put at risk.

As one letter explained, "In serious situations, officers can use their discretion at the instant and follow up later." *But there must be follow-up*. The letter continued:

> For example, a Sheriff's Deputy pulls over a violation that clearly needs to be attended to and finds him/herself in a sticky situation—several people, a lot of guns, they're on a lonely road, whatever the case might be, and that maybe they have to back up a little bit and do enforcement later. If the situation starts to escalate and they see that this relatively minor infraction is going to turn into a more serious confrontation, they then just back off and obtain a summons or take other actions which ultimately bring the person to court or justice on the matter. Cops have to learn that in those situations, they need to tuck their ego back in their pocket and be creative with the problem.

Note the emphasis on "ultimately bringing the person to court or to justice." If that is not part of the equation, then failure to enforce the law at the scene amounts to giving license to anarchy. The letters to me emphasize several themes for the formulation of policy, education, and training:

- Guidelines should be sought from the state attorney general, local prosecutors, and department legal counsel. Police and prosecutors need to know each other's expectations, so that the matters will be resolved ultimately without allowing individuals or groups to place themselves above the law or outside its jurisdiction. Each officer should learn thoroughly the laws of arrest.

- Officers must be trained to exercise authority without losing control of themselves under stress. Officers should also be

instructed in the ideology and tactics of opposition and resistance used by extremist groups, cults, and gangs they are likely
to encounter.

- Officers should be taught skills of tactical communication and
  told not to debate their authority at the scene. They must also
  be thoroughly educated in self-defense and officer safety as well
  as the best methods for traffic stops: how to stop, where to park,
  how to approach, and so forth.

Above all, if officers do their best to act conscientiously at the scene,
with due regard for the instruction of the department in the exercise of discretion, then the leadership is obligated to stand by them. If an officer had
reason to decide that allowing the offender to proceed without arrest would
place the public in harm's way and the offender became so violent that the
officer had to use deadly force, the department has no excuse for abandoning the officer in the face of political, media, or public pressure.

Furthermore, where extremist groups are involved, departments may
have to protect their personnel from threats of reprisal. As one letter
explained:

> A recent case in Eastern Ohio is exactly on point. A city police
> officer stopped an individual for no license plates. Instead the
> vehicle displayed a piece of cardboard with "Freeman" printed
> on it. The driver exited the vehicle holding a firearm. The driver
> refused to drop the weapon, claiming that he feared for his life.
> The police officer continued to demand that the driver drop the
> weapon, and after several refusals by the driver, the police offi-
> cer fired his weapon and fatally injured the driver. Associates of
> the deceased made public statements that they witnessed the
> shooting and contradicted the officer's account. Later when
> these witnesses were offered an opportunity to testify before a
> grand jury, they declined, choosing instead to testify before their
> own "Court." The grand jury declined to indict the officer. The
> "Freeman Court" did indict the officer, and there was a period of
> concern about retaliation.

Under such circumstances, where extremism of various stripes threatens civil society itself, police and law enforcement officers need more than ever departmental commitment to their safety. Police should be expected to possess a spirit of service and a willingness to make sacrifices. But they should not be expected to serve the public at risk to themselves without the faithful promise of departmental regard for them.

Conclusion

Professionalism in policing includes both a spirit of service and a respect for the public order and civility. Police must have both if we all are to enjoy the free exercise of judgment, conscience, and religion guaranteed by the Constitution. An oath to uphold and defend the Constitution is an expression of this spirit and this respect. Living up to the oath inevitably involves some assignments that are odious and some situations that are dangerous. Police should be forewarned of this fact of life in policing when they apply to become recruits and while they are trained.

In the United States, we are becoming a highly litigious people. Many among us seem to have lost faith in the possibility of mutual respect, tolerance, reasoned compromise, and goodwill in our dealings with others. Some of us suppose that only intervention by the courts can enable us to live together. Because police departments are not exempt from this tendency, lawsuits can tear them apart.

Police, of all people, should know from experience the dangers that follow when people go to the courts to settle every conflict, complaint, grievance, or disappointment. A shared awareness of the mission of a department will minimize the acrimony that can undercut its efforts to serve the public and enforce the law. At the same time, as threats to the rule of law and to civility within the public grow worse, police leaders should be vigilant in framing policy, education, training, and supervision to equip their personnel for the demands of public service. In this, they should keep always in mind—and teach their subordinates by words and deeds—the ideal of reciprocity.

19

Ethics in the Future of Policing

It is now orthodox to regard social stigma as a form of oppression, to be discarded on our collective quest for inner freedom. But the political philosophers and novelists of former times would have been horrified by such a view. In almost all matters that touched upon the core requirements of social order, they believed that the genial pressure of manners, morals, and customs—enforced by the various forms of disapproval, stigma, shame, and reproach—was a more powerful guarantor of civilized and lawful behavior than the laws themselves. Inner sanctions, they argued, more dependably maintain society than such external ones as policemen and courts.

—Roger Scruton[1]

By early 1999, the Florida Criminal Justice Standards and Training Commission was considering revisions to its "Moral Character Rule" prescribing decertification of officers for "failure to maintain 'good moral character'":

According to Section 943.13 (7), *Florida Statutes*, a criminal justice officer must, "Have a good moral character as determined by a background investigation under procedures established by the Commission." Once certified, a criminal justice officer is subject to discipline by the Commission if he/she fails to maintain good moral character.

Specifically under review was the question of decertification of officers found guilty of lying under oath in any official proceedings. The Florida Police Benevolent Association, under the leadership of President Ernest W. George, opposed the revisions under consideration to strengthen the rule.

On March 23, 1999, Florida Police Benevolent Association General Counsel G. "Hal" Johnson sent the following letter to Richard Coffey and Patrick M. Kelly, then chairman and vice chairman, respectively, of the Florida Criminal Justice Standards and Training Commission:

> Re: Revisions in CJSTC Moral Character Rule
>
> Dear Chairman Coffey and Vice-Chairman Kelly:
>
> The Florida Police Benevolent Association would like the opportunity to address the Criminal Justice Standards and Training Commission at its upcoming Key West meeting on the issue of its revised moral character rule. We are requesting that we be granted fifteen minutes on the agenda in order that we can explain our concerns with the proposed rule and the standards set forth therein.
>
> The Association feels it is important we address these issues on behalf of our members in light of recent events on the national level. At the time when the Commission is moving toward ever more stringent standards of conduct which will result in "automatic" decertification of an officer, the public appears to be sanctioning similar conduct so long as the individual is doing "a good overall job." Simply put, our members are confused as to why this nation's chief law enforcement officer can engage in misconduct without penalty, while the same (or lesser) conduct results in the loss of an officer's professional career.
>
> Please advise the undersigned as to the scheduling of the matter on the Commission agenda. We thank you in advance for your cooperation.

Ethics and Rules

Some police ask, "Why, if President Clinton can lie under oath with impunity, should police be disciplined for doing so? President Clinton lies to protect himself, even under oath, and gets away with it. He has high public approval ratings, even though everybody knows he lies. If it's all right for him, why do you say it's wrong for other people who hold positions of public trust to do as he has done? He's the president. Is it fair for us to have to live up to a higher standard than the president of the United States?"

Many police at all ranks know how to think about such questions and how best to explain the answers to them. The answers are straightforward and not very complicated. Lying under oath is wrong. The fact that someone gets away with lying under oath does not make doing so right. When public servants lie under oath, they violate the public trust. Their being allowed to do so with impunity is not fair to the people they are obligated to serve.

We might add that "approval ratings" are different from respect. Historian Paul Johnson, author of *A History of the American People*, has pointed out the paradox that despite high approval ratings, "Clinton is a despised figure, held in contempt and largely rejected."[2] Ultimately, of course, President Clinton did not go entirely unpunished. He was the first elected president in U.S. history to be impeached (when Abraham Lincoln was assassinated, Vice President Andrew Johnson became president and was later impeached); and, in January 2001, on his last day as president, Clinton suffered the humiliation of being suspended for five years from practicing law in Arkansas and of having to pay a fine for making false statements under oath.

It is surprising to see the leadership of a police union authorize a letter claiming that "our members are confused" about an elementary matter of right and wrong. After all, asserting that if a high-ranking official escapes sanction for serious misconduct in office, then everyone else in public service should be exempt from sanction as well, is no different in principle from asserting that if someone gets away with murder or rape or theft, then everyone else who commits murder or rape or theft should be exempt from prosecution.

The Florida Police Benevolent Association letter is disingenuous. If the leadership of the union had been honestly concerned about the putative confusion of its members, its letter would have requested an explanation from the commission to alleviate the confusion. It asks no such thing. The letter asks only for time to present the position of the union leadership in opposition to revisions to the rule and standards. By sending that letter, the union leadership insulted the intelligence and compromised the integrity of its own members.

Experienced police understand that the criminal justice system is imperfect. Police frequently know who committed a specific crime but cannot secure sufficient evidence for a prosecutor to win a conviction, and criminals proven guilty beyond a reasonable doubt sometimes go free on technicalities. Individuals who commit crimes sometimes escape sanction because public officials are intimidated by their status, wealth, or political power. Jury nullification can thwart the law and allow the guilty to escape conviction and sanction. Guilty parties may make their escape to countries where they are safe from extradition and prosecution. Fugitives can sometimes secure executive pardons from a corrupt governor or president in return for political favors and financial campaign contributions. Unwise plea bargains exempt criminals from the punishment they deserve. Terrorists may be shielded from prosecution by political regimes that secretly finance and abet their crimes. And, worst of all, some innocent people are convicted of crimes they did not commit and suffer punishment they do not deserve.

We live with imperfection and injustice every day. Even when we do our best, neither we nor our institutions are perfectible. But no one of any sense concludes that imperfections in the criminal justice system imply that we should abandon the pursuit of justice. Yet, exactly such abandonment is implied by the claim, "If somebody else gets away with something, then I should be allowed to get away with it, too." The fact that injustice prevails in one case cannot logically yield the conclusion that injustice should prevail in every case.

To its credit, the Florida Criminal Justice Standards and Training Commission was undeterred by Florida Police Benevolent Association leadership opposition to revisions in the Moral Character Rule. The commission not only adopted the rule of decertification for lying in official proceedings; it also expanded the rule to cover discipline for police officers who are proven to have cheated on promotional examinations. Today, the commission's rule, "Failure to Maintain 'Good Moral Character,'" includes the following provisions:

> The Commission defines failure to maintain good moral character as:
>
> a. Any act constituting a felony offense regardless of criminal prosecution;
>
> b. Any act constituting any of a specified group of serious misdemeanor offenses regardless of criminal prosecution;

c. Any principal, accessory, attempt, solicitation, or conspiracy, pursuant to Chapter 777, *Florida Statutes*, where there would have been a felony offense had the crime been committed or completed;

d. Any act in any jurisdiction other than the State of Florida, which if committed in the State of Florida, would constitute a felony, any of the specified serious misdemeanors, or violation of Chapter 777;

e. The following noncriminal acts or conduct:

- excessive use of force;
- sexual harassment involving physical contact or misuse of official position;
- misuse of official position, as defined in Section 112.313(6), *Florida Statutes*;
- engaging in sex while on duty;
- unprofessional relationship with an inmate, detainee, probationer or parolee, or community controllee: having written or oral communication that is intended to facilitate conduct which is prohibited by Commission Rule; or engaging in physical contact not required in the performance of official duties, defined as kissing, fondling of the genital area, buttocks, and/or breasts, massaging or similar touching, holding hands, any other physical contact normally associated with the demonstration of affection, or sexual misconduct as applied to all certifications and defined in Section 944.35(3), *Florida Statutes*;
- false statements during the employment application process;
- conduct that subverts or attempts to subvert the Officer Certification Examination process pursuant to Rule 11B-30.009(3), F.A.C.;
- conduct that subverts or attempts to subvert the Criminal Justice Standards and Training Commission

approved training examination process, or an employing agency promotional examination process pursuant
to, but not limited to acts described in Rule 11B-
30.009(3), F.A.C.

f. Testing positive for controlled substances by a urine or
blood test, in accordance with the requirements for testing reliability and integrity set forth in Rule 11B-27.00225, F.A.C. (For
additional information refer to Rule 11B-27.0011(4)(a–d), F.A.C.)

Title 46, chapter 837, of the *Florida Statutes* identifies perjury—
knowingly making false statements in an official proceeding—as a felony.
Thus, police who make false statements in official proceedings fail to maintain
good moral character as specified in section a of the commission's definition.

For police to deserve the public trust and earn public confidence, we
need such rules, just as we need officers who understand and respect them.
Rules clearly have greater effectiveness with people who respect them and
understand the reasons for them than with people who merely fear the consequences of being caught breaking them. Respect and understanding
internalize a rule and make it part of our way of seeing matters of right and
wrong. Fear of consequences does not, for the rule remains alien to us, and
the consequences for violating it take the form of an external threat. The
person who respects a rule understands that it has moral authority and
therefore does not seek ways to violate it with impunity; but the person to
whom the rule is alien sees it only as an assertion of power without moral
authority and may break it when the risk of being caught is small. External
constraints on wrongdoing tend to carry far less weight with persons of
good moral habits than the internal constraints of their own conscience. But
no institution can take for granted that all of its personnel are people of
good conscience, so attaching sanctions to rules of accountability remains
essential. Institutions have a duty to explain the reasons for each specific
rule, so that all personnel have the opportunity to understand why the rule
deserves to be followed, why the rule has moral authority. Good explanations encourage persons to internalize the standard of conduct.

No matter how many police are men and women of conscience, and no
matter how well conceived and explained are the rules of honorable

performance, I fear that we have not heard the last in policing and other walks of life of the narcissistic and childish idea that if someone else gets away with wrongdoing, then we also have the right to get away with it.

Narcissism and Childishness

In mythology, Narcissus was a youth so physically beautiful that everyone who saw him fell in love with him. The son of a god and a nymph, he loved no one in return, until he saw his own reflection in a pool of water and fell hopelessly in love with himself. Unable to tear himself away from adoration of his own reflected image and achingly frustrated that every time he reached into the water to embrace his image he destroyed it, Narcissus lay gazing upon himself until he died.

Narcissism means loving ourselves so much that we are indifferent to others and therefore indifferent to our moral obligations. Narcissists are preoccupied with themselves and the gratification of their own desires, no matter what their pursuit of self-gratification may cost anyone else. Such self-indulgence is characteristic of those who insist that they are not obligated to live up to professional and private obligations simply because someone else does not do so. In contrast, a mature readiness for any position of trust—police officer, teacher, nurse, parent, spouse—includes voluntary submission to a sense of obligation that does not fade away whenever others fall short of fulfilling similar obligations.

It is perhaps inevitable that narcissism should be on the increase in a country that permits high levels of freedom and provides widespread luxury. Many adolescents have money to spend and time to kill. Purveyors of vulgar entertainment and fashion bombard adolescents with the false promise that physical beauty and self-indulgence are the keys to happiness. Teenagers remain infantile when no one expects them to accept serious responsibilities at home or in school.

Such conditions tend to perpetuate childishness among youths and adults. All of us are familiar with the proclivity of children to try to overcome parental resistance to the gratification of their desires by saying, usually in exaggeration, "But all the other kids' parents let them do it. Why can't I?" Properly guided and taught by conscientious and loving adults, children and youths learn the answer to their question: The fact that parents permit their children to do something does not make it right, worth doing, deserving of our approval, or even tolerable. Deciding how we should conduct our lives is not a matter of looking for and imitating the lowest common denominator of human behavior.

With the toxic social conditions that prevail in some sectors of contemporary culture in the United States, that is not an easy lesson to teach or to learn. Yet the future of trustworthy policing depends on the recruitment and retention of sworn personnel and support staff who have learned the lesson and made it fundamental to their way of life.

Morality and Social Conditions

Many recent books and articles describe and offer analyses of morally dangerous social conditions in the United States. Some of the authors see only bleakness on the horizon, the decay of civilization in our country. Others pay greater attention to the vast complexity of the American people. They observe that hedonism and selfishness dominate many lives, but moral decency, devout religious faith, piety, and intellectual refinement are also evident in significant portions of the population. Authors of those more subtle and nuanced writings rightly caution against imagining the public to be monolithic.

Most books and articles give evidence of trends toward the coarsening of life in the United States. They describe a decline in morals and manners reflected in obscene language in entertainment and daily life; sleaziness and tastelessness in dress, body ornamentation, and general appearance; sexual promiscuity; vulgarity; incivility, and what sociologist Charles Murray calls the "thug code": "Take what you want, respond violently to anyone who antagonizes you, gloat when you win, despise courtesy as weakness, treat women as receptacles, take pride in cheating, deceiving, or exploiting successfully."[3]

Those trends cross economic and educational lines as well as lines of color and gender. Rich or poor, college educated or not, some mothers and fathers raise their children devotedly and steer them away from vulgarity and thuggery. Others irresponsibly abandon the formation of their children's character to the most vulgar and corrupting influences of our time.

Some parents in humble homes provide fertile ground for children to grow up well, while some children in the lap of luxury desperately need parental instruction and guidance they never get. Some inner-city schools have a well-established culture of civility and decency where teachers and students are mutually respectful and considerate. Other urban schools are chaotic and dangerous. Prestigious universities harbor young men and women who have had abundant educational opportunities and advantages and are nonetheless foul-mouthed, loutish, dishonest, overtly licentious, and amused by the licentiousness of their peers. Many of those students flout the law in social lives that revolve around illegal drugs. At the same time, there are university students who are mature beyond their years, take their studies seriously, and live up to high moral standards in public and private. So, too, with police. Some subscribe in their daily lives to something resembling Murray's "thug code," while others embrace a sense of professional and private obligation deserving the greatest respect and admiration.

Philosopher Roger Scruton has perceptively and persuasively argued that our social conditions are growing progressively worse because many among us, including especially intellectual elites, have rejected traditional forms of social stigma necessary for the formation of individual conscience and the maintenance of a wholesome social environment:

> It is now orthodox to regard social stigma as a form of oppression to be discarded on our collective quest for inner freedom. But the political philosophers and novelists of former times would have been horrified by such a view. In almost all matters that touched upon the core requirements of social order, they believed that the genial pressure of manners, morals, and customs—enforced by the various forms of disapproval, stigma, shame, and reproach—was a more powerful guarantor of civilized and lawful behavior than the laws themselves. Inner sanctions, they argued, more dependably maintain society than such external ones as policemen and courts. That is the reason the moralists of the eighteenth century, for example, rarely

touched upon murder, theft, rape, or criminal deception; instead, they were passionately interested in the small-scale mores on which social order depends and that, properly adhered to, make such crimes unthinkable.[4]

A community whose members neither respect nor fear moral reproach from their peers cannot regulate behavior for itself. Individual self-control withers, and with it regard for the public good. Incivility grows, as with road rage and other similar excesses. Government enacts more laws, but without active support of law by the moral pressure of social stigma, individuals break the law when they believe that they can get away with doing so. Scruton averred:

> In addition, the law increasingly distinguishes the "public" realm, where the law is the sole objective authority, from the "private" realm, where the law cannot intrude, and leaves the private realm less and less regulated, despite the fact that it contains most of the matters on which the future of society depends: sexual conduct, the rearing of children, honest dealing, and self-respect.[5]

Scruton has argued that under those conditions the demands on police become ever greater, ever more complex and difficult, while the possibility of fulfilling the police mission dwindles. Where social stigma declines, where the sense of shame within a people withers, laws and law enforcement cannot replace them:

> The law combats crime not by eliminating criminal schemes but by increasing the risk attached to them; stigma combats crime by creating people who have no criminal schemes in the first place. The steady replacement of stigma by law, therefore, is a key cause of the constant increase in the number and severity of crimes. . . .
>
> The evidence from modern societies suggests that where the community ceases to respond to moral faults with public sanctions, individuals cease to feel guilty about them, and

conscience weakens. If we wish for inner sanctions to exist, we must back them up with sanctions of a more public and outward-going kind. Moral norms, generated collectively, must also be collectively imposed.[6]

Because "statistical studies of American prisoners show that illegitimacy is by far the greatest factor in disposing children to a life of crime" and because societies have long "recognized that they could not make adultery and out-of-wedlock childbearing into crimes without opening the way to intolerable injustices,"[7] Scruton has emphasized the crucial importance of social stigma in the case of sexual morality. Only when sexual feelings are governed by conscience, self-control, and social disapproval of promiscuity and its consequences do they lead to love, solid marriages, devoted parenthood, sound education of children, happiness, and a good society. Without the constraints of conscience and social stigma, wanton pursuit of sexual gratification prevents us from forming lasting attachments and mutual trust. Promiscuity free of social stigma becomes predatory and aggressive and leads to shallow lives and vulgar social conditions, just as we see in the United States.

Social opprobrium in a society, public disdain for irresponsible conduct, does not have punishment as its purpose but deterrence. Properly applied, social opprobrium nurtures conscience:

> Stigma is not an act of aggression but a sign that we care about our neighbors' lives and actions. It expresses the consciousness of other people, the desire for their good opinion, and the impetus to uphold the social norms that make judgment possible. It is the outward expression of an inner orderliness—and a declaration of faith in human nature.[8]

This implicit declaration of "faith in human nature"—the faith that most of us, if properly educated and treated by others, have the capacity to acquire a sense of shame and a self-controlling conscience—lies at the heart of constitutional government. It is an expression of faith that with the opportunity to mature beyond narcissism and childishness, to form the habits of civic virtue and regard for others, men and women can sustain a way of life in which liberty is not license and reciprocity prevails over selfishness. Where social stigma is lacking, we have little chance to form an enlightened conscience, and all of us become less fit to live with one another. No police presence, no criminal justice system, can overcome the precipitous deterioration of our mutual fitness to live together.

Where such faith in human nature is absent, however, social stigma becomes perverse, as it did in Nazi Germany. With deadly and evil intent, Hitler and the Nazis stigmatized individuals by virtue of race, religion, ethnicity, nationality, and disability. Tyrants and bigots do not respect human dignity. They aggressively stigmatize human beings to destroy them, not to encourage enlightened conscience.

Social stigma has other risks, as has long been evident, because every society has in it inordinately censorious busybodies who eagerly intrude on the privacy of others and indulge themselves in cruel gossip. They are nasty and self-serving people whose intention is not to nurture conscience and protect us from the worst in ourselves, but to cause hurt and enjoy feelings of superiority while doing so. They, too, must be checked by social stigma—by public contempt for rumor mongering, by visible disdain for gossips, by outrage at invasions of privacy, and by outspoken intolerance of meanness.

In addition, benighted individuals and groups can bring social stigma to bear unjustly and foolishly against other individuals who merit admiration and praise rather than blame. Such was the case when Perry Duncan, a former constable in the Cornwall, Ontario, Police Service, was harassed and ostracized in both his police agency and his hometown. Duncan's supposed offense? Acting against department rules that he could not in good conscience obey, Duncan reported "a case of child sexual abuse to the Children's Aid Society." He also spoke out "against official silence and inertia. . . . On October 14, 2000, Mr. Perry Duncan accepted the Annual Ethical Courage Award . . . for his display of moral courage" from the Center for Law Enforcement Ethics of the Southwestern Legal Foundation in Richardson, Texas. During the ceremony, Duncan received two standing ovations from police attending the conference on ethics.[9] Right was on Duncan's side, not the side of those who sought to shame him.

As with any other social practice, social stigma is imperfect; but the coarsening and thuggery of social life without it are undeniable facts. Clearly, the "genial pressure" of morals and manners is a vital presence in some of our lives. We expect it and depend on it in our homes, in the class-rooms and schools of our children, in our places of worship, workplaces, restaurants, amusement parks, athletic and fitness facilities, shopping areas, and in the print, audio, and video media we allow into our homes. Sometimes, that "genial pressure" is conspicuously absent in the places we go, or have to go, in our daily lives—and all of us who work in grim and dangerous social environments see the effects of the withering away of social stigma. To the extent that we care about the safety and well-being of our families and friends, and to the extent that we are concerned to live together with some sense of mutual respect and reciprocity, we will not ignore the irreplaceable authority of that "genial pressure" in its various appropriate forms.

"Broken Windows" and Social Stigma

James Q. Wilson and George L. Kelling described the necessity for social stigma as "an informal control mechanism of the community" when they first articulated their "broken-window" theory. Not all police departments that mount programs in community policing, problem-solving policing, and zero-tolerance order-maintenance policing pay ample attention to that fact.

In March 1982 the *Atlantic Monthly* published the Wilson and Kelling article, "Broken Windows: The Police and Neighborhood Safety."[10] The article described the conduct of foot patrols in one rundown Newark neighborhood. At the time, foot patrols were part of a New Jersey experiment in twenty-eight cities, the "Safe and Clean Neighborhoods Program." Foot patrols made that particular neighborhood safer, a better place to live, not by reducing crime but by increasing order on the streets. Officers distinguished "regulars" from strangers. Strangers without evidence of legitimate reasons to be on the streets were sent away or arrested for vagrancy. "Regulars" were the "decent folk," the gainfully employed and law-abiding residents, and also "some drunks and derelicts who were always there 'but knew their place.'"

The work of the foot patrol officer "was to keep an eye on strangers, and make certain that the disreputable regulars observed some informal but widely understood rules": where drunks and addicts could sit, where they could not lie down; where people were allowed to drink in public and where not; which parts of the neighborhood were off limits to panhandling and annoying "decent folk," along with the rule that where conflicts arose, the police would side with the "decent folk" who operated businesses or were waiting at the local bus stop or otherwise occupied in the neighborhood. Wilson and Kelling noted:

> These rules were defined and enforced in collaboration with the "regulars" on the street. Another neighborhood might have different rules, but these, everybody understood, were the rules for this neighborhood. *If someone violated them, the regulars not only turned to [the foot patrol officer] for help, but also ridiculed the violator.* [Emphasis added.][11]

Here, then, was community enforcement, with help from police, of informal neighborhood rules and expectations for conduct by the social stigma of ridicule—one form of shaming. The broken-window thesis that has had such a profound effect on community and order-maintenance policing depended from the very beginning on the imposition of social stigma by the "regulars" of the neighborhood.

The broken-window thesis is that "untended property becomes fair game for people out for fun or plunder" and that "vandalism can occur anywhere once communal barriers—the sense of mutual regard and the obligations of civility—are lowered by actions that seem to signal that 'no one cares.'" Wilson and Kelling went on to say:

> We suggest that "untended" behavior also leads to the breakdown of community controls. A stable neighborhood of families who care for their homes, mind each other's children, and confidently frown on unwanted intruders can change, in a few years or even a few months, to an inhospitable jungle. A piece of property is abandoned, weeds grow up, a window is smashed. Adults stop scolding rowdy children; the children, emboldened, become more rowdy. . . . Teenagers gather in front of the corner store. The merchant asks them to move; they refuse. Fights occur. Litter accumulates. . . . Such an area is vulnerable to criminal invasion.[12]

Quality of life deteriorates because harmful behavior goes "untended": unchecked by social stigma from residents who care enough and have the courage to maintain community controls. Wilson and Kelling insisted: "*The essence of the police role in maintaining order is to reinforce the informal control mechanisms of the community itself.* [Emphasis added.] The police cannot, without committing extraordinary resources, provide a substitute for that informal control."[13]

Wilson and Kelling thus identified social stigma as essential to "civilized and lawful behavior," just as Scruton did. In their article, Wilson and Kelling likened the policing done by those foot patrol officers in the neighborhood to the work done by much earlier police who served essentially as night watchmen. A night watchman does not solve crimes; his "function" is "to maintain order against the chief threats to order—fire, wild animals, and disreputable behavior."[14] Community policing reflects the night watchman tradition.

Community policing throughout the United States relies on the insight of Wilson and Kelling that "the police role in maintaining order is to reinforce the informal control mechanisms of the community itself." In fact, the work of many police departments is to help people who live in proximity but are in every other respect fragmented by linguistic and other barriers to create and implement the informal social controls that turn fragmented residency into community.

The 60,000 residents of City Heights in San Diego have been estranged from one another by "language barriers, cultural differences, lack of knowledge of community resources," and the fact that many residents are illegal aliens. The City Heights Neighborhood Alliance joins a team of police officers with community organizers "to solve drug-related crimes in a partnership with community residents" and "to provide residents with the knowledge and skills to solve their own problems related to quality of life." Police base their work on three elements of community policing—neighborhood cooperation, shared learning, and social control—all of them traceable to "Broken Windows."

In "'Mind Your Own Business' Is Bad Advice," Recheal Stewart-Brown of the Mid-City Division of the San Diego Police Department reported that the alliance tries to form a community by helping residents to trust one another sufficiently "to intervene for the common good." Police bring residents together to make common cause, learn how to interact with police, and mobilize efforts to control vandalism, litter, prostitution, loitering, drug dealing, and related problems. Stewart-Brown reported that "community support of police was directly related to the arrest of more than 320 drug dealers" and that disreputable behavior is declining. Property owners have been held accountable for the condition of their properties.[15] In San Diego, as elsewhere, informal social controls are essential to civilized life, just as Roger Scruton emphasized. Mounted in cooperation with police, such controls can and do improve social environments, just as Wilson and Kelling saw in 1982.

In the balance of their article, Wilson and Kelling addressed the tension, even conflict, police must face between maintaining order by reinforcing local informal controls and scrupulously following the letter of every law and rule of the state. They explained that police have to be carefully trained and supervised in the limits to responsible discretion, and they admitted that they did not know an entirely satisfactory solution to the problem.[16] Policing involves endless exercises of judgment in applying rules, without the possibility of further rules for applying rules.

Because of the unlimited variety of situations in which laws and rules must be applied, I doubt that we can find an entirely satisfactory solution. The needs of the public and the demands on police are too complicated. The impossibility of framing such an answer may explain why many departmental policies on discretion in community, problem-solving, and order-maintenance policing remain somewhat vague and why principles of supervision differ so considerably from place to place.

Today, there is a great academic dispute among sociologists, criminologists, and political scientists over whether empirical evidence confirms that police applications of the broken-window theory actually reduce crime. Much of the dispute arises from fear among scholars that zero-tolerance order-maintenance policing rides roughshod over civil rights. Wilson and Kelling nowhere advocated zero-tolerance order maintenance or draconian paramilitary police tactics. Those were not elements of the broken-window theory.

Some police departments have, in fact, invoked "broken windows" as the rationale for zero-tolerance order-maintenance policing and have claimed to reduce crime by those police practices. But does zero tolerance of disreputable behavior actually reduce serious crimes against property and persons? Are specific forms of disreputable behavior correlated with specific serious crimes? Whether systematic research will ever yield a preponderance of evidence on such questions remains to be seen. Despite the obvious fact that where disreputable behavior goes unchecked, it becomes the norm, police departments will have to be very careful about the degree of discretion they allow their personnel in maintaining order.

In many of the worst urban areas, social conditions are so bleak and fear within the public so great that no prospect remains of local residents' trying to improve matters through social stigmatization of disreputable individuals and behavior. Where gangs control the streets and terrorize the public, police must frequently act alone, without community assistance. There, it is not windows that are broken, but the entire fabric of social existence that is shredded.

Conditions in those areas are far worse than in the neighborhood Wilson and Kelling described in 1982. Such conditions may be more effectively improved by major law enforcement and prosecutorial task force projects designed to overcome criminal gang dominance than by draconian and legally questionable order maintenance. Law enforcement investigations conjoined with effective prosecution over time enable police and "decent folk" to restore some measure of civilized life in a neighborhood. In contrast, trying to "take back the streets" by zero tolerance, without adequate departmental constraints, can lead to ghastly wrongdoing, as in the Rampart Division of the Los Angeles Police Department (described below).

Social Stigma within Policing

On August 9, 1997, New York City Police Officer Justin Volpe beat Abner Louima and sodomized him with a broken broom handle in the restroom of the Seventieth Precinct station house. Louima required multiple surgeries to repair the injuries Volpe inflicted on him. When Volpe confessed to committing six federal crimes against Louima, he admitted that Louima had been handcuffed while sodomized and told the court that after sodomizing Louima, he held the feces-covered stick in front of Louima's mouth and said, "If you tell anybody about this, I'll find you and kill you."

When asked by Judge Eugene H. Nickerson if he had intended to humiliate Louima by putting the stick in his face, "Volpe responded, 'I was in shock at the time, Your Honor. . . . I couldn't believe what had happened. . . . I was mad.'" The judge repeated his question twice more. Volpe finally said, "Yes." Other NYPD officers said Volpe later bragged about what he had done to Louima.[17]

Before Volpe was sentenced to thirty years in prison, defense attorneys filed a defense psychologist's report in which Volpe had said he was a victim, that Abner Louima had punched him in the head on the street, that he had believed he was going to die, and that he responded in the restroom with "animal rage." Prosecutors said that Volpe was punched by Louima's cousin. Volpe denied that he had ever boasted about torturing Louima.[18]

The torture of Abner Louima is not something that happened. It is what Justin Volpe did. Volpe could not have believed himself to be at risk of his life when he committed the crimes against Louima. However much Volpe may have feared for his life in the altercation on the street, he tortured Louima later—after he had been brought into the station house and after he had been handcuffed. Volpe's rage was not so uncontrollable that he could not think to protect himself by threatening to kill Louima if he talked. Volpe knew that he was breaking major laws, violating Louima's civil rights, inflicting painful and dangerous injuries, and trampling departmental regulations and policies. His knowledge did not constrain him in the least.

I do not know whether Justin Volpe's fellow officers could have deterred him by preventive moral reproach from his assault on Abner Louima, or whether they were in a position to prevent him physically from isolating Louima in the restroom. What is clear is that those forms of deterrence did not come sufficiently into play to provide any chance of saving Abner Louima from Justin Volpe, or Justin Volpe from himself.

In August 2000 the U.S. Commission on Civil Rights issued a report, *Police Practices and Civil Rights in New York City*. In her cover letter, Chairperson Mary Frances Berry stressed the "significant impact" of the "publicized" torture of Abner Louima "on police-community relations in New York City." She added, "In previous studies by the Commission on police practices, it has been established that most properly trained, culturally sensitive officers handle the difficult and life-risking challenges of policing with the level of professionalism required to protect lives, civil rights, and property within the boundaries of the law."[19]

It is certainly true that the commission has frequently *claimed* that to be the case, but the commission has never *established* its truth. Officers can be properly trained and culturally sensitive but go wrong because they are poorly supervised and subjected to corrupting peer pressure or because they have weak or bad character. Mere sensitivity is no substitute for the settled dispositions of justice, courage, and temperance constitutive of good character. Sensitivity is not integrity. Sensitivity is not sufficient for self-control—control of ourselves when we feel fear or rage or other powerful emotions and passions.

Justin Volpe did not need "cultural sensitivity." He did not need to be "sensitive to cultural diversity" to know and fully respect Abner Louima's civil rights. There is no diversity among cultures on the subject of the violent sodomization of a handcuffed suspect in custody. Every civilized culture on the planet explicitly abhors any such act. Justin Volpe needed character good enough not to have sadistic impulses, or strong enough to resist them, and to control himself in the face of his own rage, if that is the emotion he felt after he reached the precinct station. He needed fellow officers who had the character to protect Abner Louima from Volpe's assault either by moral suasion or physical force. And so did Abner Louima.

In 1996 Los Angeles police officers in the Rampart station's Community Resources against Street Hoodlums (CRASH) unit shot, permanently crippled, and framed Javier Francis Ovando. By police falsification of evidence and perjury, Ovando, who had no prior criminal record and had commited no crime, was convicted and sentenced to twenty-three years in prison. In the same year Rampart CRASH officers murdered Juan Saldana. They shot Saldana in the back and the chest, then planted a gun on him and cooked up their story of the shooting while Saldana lay dying. Officer Rafael Perez of Rampart CRASH said of those and other crimes he committed: "When I planted a case on someone, did I feel bad? Not once. I felt good. I felt, you know, I'm taking this guy off the streets."[20] Other Rampart CRASH officers choked and beat suspects until they vomited blood and broke bones of suspects whose hands were tied behind their backs. An array of police officers in the United States from New York to Los Angeles have taken "thug code" all the way to torture and murder.

"Thug code" is a way of life in some police precincts and units. The distinguished former assistant chief of the Los Angeles Police Department, David Dotson, wrote: "[A]t bottom, the problems at the Los Angeles Police Department's Rampart Division are cultural in nature, the result of an institutional mind-set first conceived in the 1950s. Unless this police culture is overthrown, future Rampart scandals are inevitable."[21] Were that not true, Rampart Division personnel could not possibly have covered up their depravity for as long as they did.

The "culture" to which Dotson referred lacks every form of moral restraint. In the Rampart CRASH unit, police were not accountable to law, regulation, or department policy. They did as they pleased, without disciplined and trustworthy supervision. They encountered no peer pressure on the side of law or morality—no "disapproval, stigma, shame, and reproach," in Scruton's words—not even peer intolerance of the absolutely intolerable. The police who commited crimes were "cowboy cops" who wore patches depicting a skull and a "dead man's" poker hand. They were without personal conscience, respect for law, and regard for human dignity and civil rights. They self-righteously granted themselves "inner freedom" to do whatever they wanted, whenever they chose, to whomever they targeted.

Those cops told implausible lies about probable cause. Their supervisors either tolerated or encouraged such lies, and judges who should have known better swallowed the lies without question. Such a "culture" kills morality completely. Los Angeles County Supervisor Zev Yaroslavsky rightly insists that the Rampart depredations are "a dagger aimed at the heart of constitutional democracy."[22]

The Rampart outrage is certainly the worst police scandal in the history of Los Angeles. After being framed by police, Javier Ovando served two years in prison and has since been paid a $15 million settlement by the Los Angeles government. So heinous and widespread was police wrongdoing that by September 2000, Beth Shuster and Vincent J. Schodolski could report that "approximately 100 convictions have been overturned. It is estimated that 3,000 cases need to be reviewed. Five officers, thus far, have been arrested and are facing criminal charges. Seventy officers, at this point, face disciplinary proceedings."[23] I have never encountered a worse police scandal anywhere in the country. In Los Angeles the Police Department Board of Inquiry compounded the outrage by issuing on March 1, 2000, a report titled "Rampart Area Corruption Incident." What police did in the Rampart Division was not mere corruption, and it was no incident. It was murderous tyranny inside the boundaries of the United States.[24]

Los Angeles Chief of Police Bernard Parks has disbanded the CRASH units. Gangs still dominate the Rampart area, terrorizing residents. Years have been lost during which good policing and judicious prosecution could have reduced gang power and predation. Now police and residents have to start over.

Ethical problems continue to surface in many departments. Some problems are grave, others serious, some large-scale, some smaller scale, some systemic, and some of the "rotten-apple" variety. Officers have abandoned their precincts while on duty in pursuit of sexual adventure or corruption opportunities. Officers have brutalized suspects, submitted false reports, lied in official proceedings. Some officers, fired for egregious misconduct, have been returned to their jobs by politicized urban personnel boards that review police disciplinary actions.

Many departments conduct the work of policing competently but are to some extent thwarted by political intrusions. When political interference undermines moral and professional standards in a department, a certain cynicism arises among police who know that some of their colleagues have been proven unfit to hold positions of public trust. In such a situation, peer pressure supporting moral and legal conduct becomes more essential as it becomes more difficult to sustain. Officers who have done wrong and escaped police discipline through the stupidity or bias of external personnel boards, or through the cowardice of police supervisors, may simply smirk disdainfully at social stigma within the department. Other decent and honorable police may conclude that exerting peer pressure for better performance is simply not worth the trouble or the hassle. Where police give up, their departments tend to slide down the slippery slope to ethical and professional mediocrity—or worse. Without the active support of officers in the field and front-line supervisors, top officials often labor in vain to prevent that descent.

Those phenomena have their parallels in institutions other than policing. Edward Albert Shils, the most knowledgeable scholar of the twentieth century on the nature of fine universities and the ethical obligations of those who work in them, wrote the extraordinarily illuminating book,

The Calling of Education. Shils understood that without "the genial pressure of manners, morals, and customs—enforced by the various forms of disapproval, stigma, shame, and reproach" of which Scruton wrote, a university can neither become great nor stay great.

Shils cast the point in terms of the need for a university to have an "invisible senate":

> A university needs an "invisible senate," a stiffening spine which, outside the formal and official committees and boards, spreads its concern for the university beyond the boundaries of departments and up to the boundaries of the university. This "invisible senate" cannot be planned; it must emerge from the relationship of colleagues throughout the university. It arises from a sense of obligation to the university as an intellectual institution. This is not the same as being an "academic politician"; it means acting in a patently disinterested manner in a way which gains the general acknowledgment of colleagues.[25]

"A stiffening spine," arising from a sense of obligation to the mission of the institution and provided by the mutual commitment of those who do its essential work: Every police department and law enforcement agency—every institution with obligations of public trust—needs such spine—an "invisible senate" comprising colleagues throughout the ranks who perceptibly stand for the highest ideals of the profession and will not bear in silence their being betrayed or forsaken. That is leadership from within that refuses to be ground down by external politics or internal cynicism. I have never seen a great institution of any kind that is without some form of "invisible senate."

Recruiting Problems

Recruitment and promotion of personnel are the arts of destiny. The standards and procedures by which the leadership of an institution selects and promotes personnel in the present determine who will hold the fate of the institution in their hands in the future. Whether a police department, a university, a corporation will rise, stagnate, or decline in years to come—

whether a police department will comprise personnel at all ranks who can rise to the obligations of an invisible senate—depends on today's recruiting.

Police departments are in many instances encountering greater difficulty in attracting strong applicants and filling recruit classes with qualified candidates. Some departments are handcuffed by residency requirements, others by deficient compensation packages, and some by comparatively grim working conditions. Too many recruits drop out of academy training as soon as they encounter the intellectual and physical demands of training or the character expectations of the department. At least some recruits leave because they have been habituated to laxity and resent authority.

Residency requirements exacerbate the problem. The U.S. Commission on Civil Rights has misguidedly recommended that the New York City Police Department "should require all police officers to live in New York City, or at least give preference points to applicants from the city."[26] The commission itself acknowledges that "a strict residency requirement could weaken the field of qualified candidates" and that "another possibility is that a residency requirement would cause the NYPD to lose good officers who want to move out of the city into the suburbs." The commission went on to say:

> [T]here is no evidence that city residents make better police officers. In fact, resident officers have been slightly *more* likely to be suspended or dismissed from the police force for misconduct and are disproportionately the subject of civilian complaints.[27]

Flying in the face of its own evidence, the commission nonetheless concluded, "Despite these reservations, a residence requirement that is part of a larger scheme tied to an affirmative action plan may positively affect police-community relations and increase effective policing."[28] There is no discernible connection between higher levels of police professionalism and competence on the one hand and police residency on the other. Major city departments with residency requirements—Miami, New Orleans, and Washington, D.C., among others—have been harmed by those requirements. Departments subscribing to the policy that only police who reside within a department's jurisdiction are eligible to be considered for promotion have lost all cohesion and sense of common purpose.

The commission also advocated that all candidates and active police in the NYPD should have a four-year college degree: "[A] college degree requirement would help restore public confidence in the police by producing smarter and more mature police professional [sic] with proper training and who are less likely to succumb to the temptations of deviant behavior."[29] If the NYPD and other departments can fill recent classes with otherwise qualified candidates who have earned baccalaureate degrees, all to the good. That prospect, however, seems slim for many departments, given already existing problems in recruiting.

Patrick M. Kelly, chairman of the Florida Criminal Justice Standards and Training Commission and chief of the Medley, Florida, Police Department, has compiled a very useful summary of evidence that policing can be improved by requiring all recruits to be college graduates. His report, "College Education as an Entry Level Requirement for Law Enforcement," cites commission data for 1987 showing that officers with "less than 2 years of college were 4 times more likely than officers with 2 years or more of college to face discipline by the Commission for moral character violations."[30] A 1999 commission study showed that "police officers with a High School/GED level of education were approximately 3 times more likely" to face commission discipline than those with an associate or baccalaureate degree.[31] In correspondence Chief Kelly added that since the average high school graduate in Florida now reads at the fifth-grade level, a postsecondary education requirement is necessary for basic competence in policing.

Academic standards and behavioral expectations have declined in many public school districts. So have standards and expectations in many colleges and universities. Police departments should seek to attract recruits with postsecondary and higher education backgrounds, but they should not assume that a college graduate will automatically be trustworthy. Some college students become very shrewd at cheating and plagiarism. Neither should police departments suppose that a college degree inevitably makes individuals "smarter." Many college graduates cannot read a significant fiction or nonfiction book with comprehension, write a literate paragraph, or exercise reliable judgment in the conduct of daily vocational and private life. Graduates from very good high schools can be, and sometimes are, better educated than many college graduates. Establishing postsecondary and higher education entry requirements for police will improve policing only if police carefully scrutinize the achievements of candidates.

A college degree does not necessarily make a person less vulnerable to "the temptations of deviant behavior." All corrupt judges are college graduates, as are all corrupt lawyers. Politicians who raise campaign funds illegally, engage in conflict of interest schemes, and prey sexually on subordinates are college graduates. Almost all corrupt personnel in federal bureaucracies and federal law enforcement agencies are college graduates. Most white-collar crime—including financial fraud, insider trading, money laundering, income tax evasion, and price-fixing schemes—involves college graduates. All schoolteachers, academics, and ordained clergy found guilty of sexual misconduct against and predation on children and students are college graduates. Everyone involved in the Watergate cover-up, including the president and the attorney general, was a college graduate. High-ranking police officials caught up in corruption scandals have been college graduates.

Neither does being college educated guarantee intellectual honesty or objectivity—even within the U.S. Commission on Civil Rights. Two members of the commission, Carl A. Anderson and Russell G. Redenbaugh, persuasively dissented from the commission report, *Police Practices and Civil Rights in New York City*, on the grounds that the commission's "findings and recommendations are not the product of careful consideration or rigorous analysis of how the NYPD can improve, which is what the people of New York City deserve. Rather, they appear to be the result of the Commission's own biases and predispositions. . . . Instead of providing a 'meaningful discourse' on police–community relations in New York City (the stated intent of our hearing), the report is, itself, an exercise in profiling. The attack it makes is based not on evidence, but on conjecture, opinion, and 'perception of reality.'" Anderson and Redenbaugh documented their criticisms and also cited an April 28, 2000, letter to the commission in which New York County District Attorney Robert M. Morgenthau wrote:

> [I]t is disheartening that no one from the Commission ever bothered to speak to representatives of this Office, or other prosecutors' offices, prior to the Commission reaching its conclusions. . . . [I]t is hard to avoid the conclusion that the

Commission is more interested in publicizing and politicizing its views than it is in solving real problems.[32]

A careful reading of the report and appendixes confirms that the commission summarily dismissed evidence, including expert testimony by Dr. Robert Louden of John Jay College, that did not support positions the majority was determined in advance to advocate.

College students routinely graduate without learning right from wrong. A 1999 cheating scandal at San Diego State University illuminates this point. The cheating incident received fairly wide media attention because of the irony that the twenty-four students cheated on a test in an ethics course in the business and management program. Asked what he had learned, one student said, "Don't cheat. It isn't worth it." He had not learned that cheating is *wrong*, only that cheating is not worth the risk of paying the price if one is caught. That is the kind of thinking that leads people to risk corruption, brutality, perjury, and the like, if they believe that they can avoid being found out. Ethics is about right and wrong, not about cost-benefit analysis; and police departments will not do themselves one bit of good by hiring candidates with college degrees who do not know the difference.

Both the history of deviant behavior among college graduates and tests of intellectual accomplishment among college graduates belie the claim that police departments will automatically improve themselves by hiring only college graduates. If they hire the *right* college graduates, they will be well served; but exactly the same is true if they hire the *right* candidates who have not graduated from college.

Will hiring only college graduates lead to the "restoration of public confidence" in police, as the U.S. Commission on Civil Rights has asserted? In some abstract sense, perhaps, but not in practice. Practically speaking, trust in police on a daily basis in the neighborhoods where they work depends on professionalism, competence, decency, and manners, not on academic credentials. Not diplomas but how police conduct themselves on and off duty, what they tolerate among themselves, and their moral expectations of one another determine whether police deserve to be trusted and, in most cases, whether they are in fact trusted.

Police departments will find some candidates without college degrees, even without postsecondary education, who show great promise because they are literate and have a history of good judgment and good character and of responsible behavior in the workplace. Such candidates should not be summarily excluded from policing.

Police departments should certainly provide opportunities for their sworn and support personnel to acquire further postsecondary or higher education, but only in college programs they know to be sound and serious. Some college curricula and courses are so badly designed and taught that they do students harm, not good; others are too intellectually vapid to make any difference. That problem will grow worse as distance education college degree programs on the Internet proliferate, because standards of accreditation are, and will continue to be, lax.

Specialized degree programs for police in colleges and universities have also been exempt from rigorous accreditation standards. In Massachusetts, under the 1970 Quinn Bill, police officers receive a 10 percent salary increase for associate degrees in criminal justice, 20 percent for baccalaureate degrees, and 25 percent for graduate degrees. In 2001 those salary increases cost the state $385 million—despite the fact that, except for one small college graduate program, the courses police take for degrees have never been evaluated or approved by the Board of Higher Education. None of the programs has been reviewed by the Academy of Criminal Justice Sciences in Virginia. Samuel L. Tyler, president of the Boston Municipal Bureau, observed, "The graduation standards for high school seniors are tougher than the standards for police officers in these programs."[33]

College "degrees" from such programs are not likely to elevate policing, despite their high cost to the taxpayers. Those programs have not shown themselves to be educationally strong enough to help police develop the intellectual capacities or to form the good character essential to trustworthy policing. Our social conditions threaten to complicate the challenges for police. The capacities of police will have to rise to meet those challenges.

Essential Capacities

What capacities must police develop? What must they be capable of learning and what must they be capable of doing? How should education, training, and supervision be designed to enable police to develop or refine the essential capacities?

Of capacities, philosopher John Passmore wrote:

> In the course of life, whether as a result of experience, imitation, or of deliberate teaching, every human being acquires a number of capacities for action. . . . [H]e will learn to walk, to run, to speak, to feed and clothe himself; in literate societies he will learn to read, to write, to add; particular individuals will learn to drive a car, to play the piano, to repair diesel engines, to titrate, to dissect. . . . [S]uch other objectives as the development of tastes, the inculcation of habits, the arousing of interests, the imparting of information, all rest on capacities. To form the habit of quoting accurately, one must first learn how to copy a sentence; to develop a taste for poetry, one must first learn how to understand a language; an interest in mathematics grows out of a capacity to solve mathematical problems; to acquire information one must be capable of listening, reading, observing.[34]

Information. A good cop has a capacity for acquiring information. In policing, a well-developed capacity for acquiring information depends not only on being good at "listening, reading, observing," but also on asking relevant questions, gathering evidence, conducting surveillance, effecting access to computerized databases and other Web-based material, and maintaining communication with other police and law enforcement agencies. A more fully developed capacity for acquiring information includes in addition fluency in more than one language and specialized knowledge, as in forensics, homicide, narcotics, community policing, or the thickets of politics and law. The most fully developed capacity for acquiring information includes also the sensitivity, "feel," savvy, "street smarts," and refined judgment necessary to assess the reliability of witnesses and informants, read the responses and body language of a suspect in an interview or interrogation, reconstruct a crime, appraise the volatility of a situation, and establish a psychological profile of a serial killer.

A good cop also needs a well-developed capacity for imparting information. Such a capacity depends on being accomplished at writing, drawing, speaking, showing, and, in its more refined forms, translating, demonstrating, explaining, instructing, correcting, and exemplifying. In many specialized police assignments, both acquiring and imparting information require advanced capacity to use computers, along with communications, informational, instructional, and surveillance technology, and therefore the capacity to use a keyboard accurately and efficiently.

Thinking. Acquiring and imparting information, and all the capacities on which they depend, must be conjoined in police with the capacity to reason logically, draw inferences reliably, think comprehensively through problems with imagination and foresight, anticipate the consequences of one course of action rather than another, and imagine in the mind's eye the perceptions of police that they invite by their treatment of the public.

For each kind of capacity needed in the future of policing, police leaders need to ask how and where the capacity can best be taught and developed, how capable police need to be, and which personnel most need to develop specific capacities. Every good cop should be able to read with comprehension, discuss and write intelligently, and discern the practical applications of an article like "Broken Windows." Not all police can do so, and not all police academies are equipped to develop those necessary capacities. That is a case where a department should avail itself of instruction by local high school or college teachers of reading and composition. The same points apply to clear speaking, effective uses of language, and study of the native languages of local residents who do not speak English. Selective employment of qualified school and college personnel or enrollment of police in specifically relevant courses can yield far more gain to police departments in the development of such capacities than undifferentiated college degree programs.

Formal and informal logic can best be learned from books and from written exercises that are reviewed and if necessary corrected by a qualified teacher. With a command of logic, learning to think through problems is both a solitary and a cooperative undertaking—sitting alone with a description of a problem and figuring out just what the problem is, and unpacking it in conversation with others, especially experienced police. While logic itself can be taught effectively in a school or college course, few academics can provide guidance in thinking logically through the de facto problems and difficulties police face. Lectures, seminars, and simulations provided by police departments for their own new and experienced personnel will be superior to most college courses.

Departmental education and training should emphasize the difference between a problem and a difficulty: A problem can be solved; a difficulty can only be ameliorated.[35] If police in a precinct do not know the social service agencies to which residents should be referred, teaching police about the agencies and introducing them to agency personnel could solve the problem. But no matter how adequately and persuasively police communicate the information to residents in a complex neighborhood, they will always face the difficulty that some residents will neither help themselves nor seek the help they need. The difficulty inevitably leads to further problems and difficulties in the future that police must learn to anticipate.

Police can learn to anticipate consequences by becoming familiar with a broad range of departmental successes and failures of the past. Films taken from cameras in cruisers and other vantage points have proved useful. Working as an apprentice to a good field training officer who explains what he or she can see and foresee in a developing situation or incident may be the most effective of all.

Academic and scientific models of capacity development may be otherwise useful in academy and field training that police and law enforcement agencies can best conduct for themselves. Police need the capacity for scrupulous and concentrated observation in almost everything they do. The great naturalist Louis Agassiz taught one student to become an observant laboratory scientist by giving him a small, dead fish in a tray and telling him to discover everything he could about the fish by observation and thought, without discussing it, dissecting it, or reading about fish. The student thought that he had completed the assignment in an hour, but Agassiz left him to the task for a week. The student stayed at it, ten hours a day. At the end of the week, Agassiz asked for a report. The student's report did not satisfy Agassiz, so the student spent seventy more hours in observation. After he had invested those 140 hours in detailed scrutiny, the student gave a report acceptable to Agassiz; and the student was astounded by the amount he had been able to learn by thorough, sustained observation and thought.[36]

We may think to ourselves that such an exercise would be hopelessly tedious and boring, especially if we have no interest in fish. But police need just such a capacity for sustained attention to detail over long periods of time and in much more difficult settings than a scientific laboratory. They cannot develop that capacity sufficiently without extended practice, or without the conscientious instruction from experienced police that shows the less experienced observer what he or she has missed. Such practice and instruction are indispensable, for instance, to acquiring the patience and attentiveness and the sustained and perceptible interest that a police officer has to muster to bring community policing to life with frightened and suspicious residents. Listening for hours at a time, especially when people are repeating themselves and each other, can be far more difficult than examining a dead fish—in part, because the fish is not observing the observer.

Local residents *do* observe the police—in countless venues, including community policing meetings and forums. Seeing ourselves as others see us, taking the place and point of view of others in discerning how they are likely to perceive us, is an exercise in moral imagination best undertaken by applying the golden rule. "How would I feel, what would I think, if I were out there listening and a cop was over here saying what I am saying? Am I behaving in a way that shows these people I am truly listening? Do I need to take notes, not only so I will remember, but so they will see that I am taking them seriously? Am I interrupting anyone because I am tired and impatient? Am I pandering to anyone, patronizing anyone? Do I think of these people condescendingly? Am I giving encouragement where it is needed? Do I need a better command of language for them to understand what I am trying to say? Am I dressed in a way that shows respect? What will the residents think of sloppy police with scruffy shoes?"[37]

Observational power and the capacity to see things from the point of view of others figure in virtually everything police education and training cover, including maintenance of officer safety. Specialized assignments require those capacities and many others: driving under extreme conditions, negotiating with hostage takers and rescuing hostages, coordinating rescue operations, controlling riots, breaking up criminal conspiracies, managing informants, preserving chains of evidence, using weapons, making legitimate traffic stops, formulating and implementing departmental policies, working effectively with the media. All those depend on detailed training conjoined with thorough explanation. The most complex of them require assessment of student learning by performance tests, simulation exercises, and written examinations.

Driving. With respect to training and explanation, take the case of driving: The capacity to drive well under extreme conditions takes observational acuity. It also takes great deftness in handling an automobile and sensing the machine's limits, most of which can be acquired only by experience under supervised conditions. It usually helps, however, to be taught directly that the fundamental principle of all extreme and hazardous driving is to make the very most of the purchase on the road, the traction, of the small portion of each tire that is at any instant in contact with the pavement. Thinking in terms of maximum traction is more illuminating than any other way of approaching extreme driving. Some police do not learn to think that way and cannot make the most of their automobiles, because they tend to overpower the tires with the engine, the brakes, and the steering gear. Others have cruisers that are too worn out to be driven safely under extreme conditions.

To develop more complex specialized capacities, such as making legitimate traffic stops properly, conducting hostage negotiations, or working with the media under pressure, police have to practice under the most realistic simulated conditions. Police instructors who can describe their own experience and explain why traffic stops or hostage negotiations should be conducted in one way rather than another bring irreplaceable credibility to the lessons. No such training is complete until students can give a coherent account in writing of relevant laws, policies, and procedures and the reasons for them.

Traffic Stops and Profiling. In learning how, when, and why to make traffic stops, police must be taught how to separate proactive enforcement entirely from racial or ethnic profiling. Police trainers should be unambiguous in distinguishing legitimate from illegitimate profiling, and they should make certain that their students understand and can explain the distinction.

The International Association of Chiefs of Police (IACP) draws the distinction by equating proactive enforcement with (1) selective enforcement of traffic and criminal laws at times and locations where statistical data show that accidents and crimes frequently occur; and (2) criminal interdiction based on reasonable suspicion rather than race or ethnicity. In "Recommendations from the First IACP Forum on Professional Traffic Stops" and "Sample Professional Traffic Stop Policy and Procedure," the IACP equates "reasonable suspicion" with "articulable suspicion"— suspicion for which an officer can give explicit and relevant reasons and facts. Reasonable suspicion is

> more than a mere hunch, but is based on a set of articulable facts and circumstances that would warrant a person of reasonable caution in believing that an infraction of the law has been committed, is about to be committed, or is in the process of being committed, by the person or persons under suspicion. This can be based on the observations of a police officer combined with his or her training and experience, and/or reliable information received from credible outside sources.[38]

In those documents, the IACP defines "racial profiling" as "the detention, interdiction, or other disparate treatment of any person on the basis of their [sic] racial or ethnic status or characteristics."[39] The IACP also offers a comprehensive description of the elements of sound academy and field training and supervision for making "professional" traffic stops, including proper officer conduct toward the occupants of stopped vehicles.

IACP traffic stop recommendations on policy, best practices, and community relations include the provision that officers be trained initially and during regular inservice programs in "proactive enforcement tactics . . . officer safety, courtesy, . . . the laws governing search and seizure, and interpersonal communications skills." Department policy should be unambiguous:

> Motorists and pedestrians shall only be subjected to stops, seizures or detentions upon reasonable suspicion that they

have committed, are committing, or are about to commit an infraction. Each time a motorist is stopped, the officer shall radio to the dispatcher the location of the stop, the description of the person or vehicle being detained, and the statute number violated or other reason for the stop, and this information shall be logged.[40]

In the absence of a specific, credible report containing a physical description, a person's race, ethnicity, gender, or sexual orientation, or any combination of those shall not be a factor in determining probable cause for an arrest or reasonable suspicion for a stop.[41]

The IACP rightly emphasizes the responsibilities of supervisors, insisting that traffic enforcement should be conducted with "consistent, ongoing supervisory oversight to ensure that officers do not go beyond the parameters of reasonableness in conducting such activities."[42]

Police departments should follow the IACP recommendations, but they should not adopt the jargon of "professional" traffic stops. The words *professional* and *unprofessional* do not carry enough weight to cover racial profiling or to distinguish legitimate from illegitimate traffic stops. Traffic stops based on racial profiling are not merely unprofessional. They are indefensibly wrong. An officer may behave unprofessionally by being discourteous to the occupants of a stopped vehicle; but the officer who makes a traffic stop because of race or ethnicity commits a grave offense.

Even with the best policies and practices for traffic stops, police departments will face difficulties. Some critics of police believe that all profiling is racial or ethnic profiling and that profiling as such is therefore illegal and immoral. They will not listen to explanations that *racial profiling* is not one word, that legitimate profiling is not racism, and that legitimate profiling is fully respectful of civil rights.

The sticking point is that under certain circumstances police may legitimately look for suspects of a particular color, ethnicity, gender, or age. Police are not committing wrongful acts of discrimination when they *know* (1) that a crime has been committed nearby; and (2) that witness descriptions of the perpetrator(s) include "racial or ethnic characteristics" or references to gender or age, and police therefore take the descriptions into account in seeking, identifying, and stopping possible suspects.

If witnesses say that a bank was robbed by a white man with gray hair in a red shirt, police should look for men who fit that description. So, too, if witnesses have described a black man with gray hair in a red shirt. Neither is a case of racial profiling; both are cases of taking relevant facts into account. If police see a motorist who reasonably fits the description, they should make the stop. The traffic stops do not constitute "disparate treatment on the basis of racial or ethnic characteristics." *Disparate* means "markedly distinct in quality, fundamentally different, made up of incongruous elements." But in these hypothetical cases, the police apply the same principle to everyone: They make each stop because the person reasonably fits the description. Police thus satisfy the basic requirement of justice by uniform application of the principle.

The crucial issue is why the police make the stop. It would be a good idea to change the IACP definition of *racial profiling* from "disparate treatment *on the basis* of racial and ethnic status or characteristics" to "disparate treatment *because* of racial or ethnic status or characteristics." Explaining a justifiable traffic stop succinctly adds lucidity: "I did not stop the person *because* he was black (or because she was white). I made the stop *because* the person reasonably fit the description of the perpetrator given by witnesses at the scene."

The best way for police to provide evidence that they have made legitimate traffic stops and behaved professionally toward vehicle occupants is to film all traffic stops with video cameras in police cruisers. Videotaping traffic stops protects officers from false complaints, protects the public from officer misconduct, and can show whether the person police stopped reasonably fit witness descriptions. Videotapes can also be used in training to improve officer safety. Departments can exchange videotapes that show the danger to police in the "kill zone" between a cruiser and a stopped vehicle with numerous occupants. Police can learn from such tapes how best to protect themselves. Putting $3,500 video cameras in all police cruisers taxes the budget of many departments, but the cameras, along with microphones worn by the officers, earn their keep in providing a record of the truth—at least the truth that is visible and audible.

Self-Examination. How we act and what we say are visible and audible. How we think and feel may not be. Watching a videotape can tell us how we performed at a traffic stop. It cannot replace the moral self-scrutiny of the conscientious person. That requires asking ourselves hard questions and trying to answer them honestly: "Are my thoughts, feelings, attitudes toward individuals 'disparate' because of race or ethnicity? Do I want to enforce laws more or less rigorously because of race or ethnicity? Do I cast a more or less suspicious eye on motorists because of race or ethnicity? Do I let some traffic stops I should make slide because of race or ethnicity?"

The answers to such questions may be yes, without that fact's ever being perceptible to anyone but ourselves. The inner dialogue with the soul, the moral examination of our heart of hearts, is nobody else's business. But if we find in ourselves "disparate" feelings, thoughts, attitudes, and dispositions because of race or ethnicity, we should try to overcome them. Private contemplation of the nature of integrity—reminding ourselves that injustice in thought and feeling is unworthy of us—and trying to think of others in the light of the Golden Rule can be helpful. Humility—as in praying for deliverance from our faults—may help as well.

Hostage Rescue and the Media. Crisis situations, especially those where hostages have been taken and are held at length, require police who have developed the capacities necessary for hostage negotiation and rescue, tactical intervention, and media relations. The purposes of police are to rescue hostages without loss of life; protect others in the vicinity; enforce law and policy by negotiation if possible, by force if necessary; and inform the public through the media while preventing the media from interfering with negotiations or tactical measures.

Bill Toohey, media relations director for the Baltimore County Police Department (BCPD), describes the conduct of media relations during the March 2000 hostage negotiations with murderer Joseph Palczynski, who was finally killed by tactical officers before he could shoot a twelve-year-old boy. Toohey and Corporal Vickie Warehime were the only departmental personnel who spoke with the media during the standoff:

> We set up a command post in a firehouse and asked the media
> to gather in a parking lot across the street. Commanders

> allowed no one—including reporters—inside the secure
> perimeter. The department also contacted the Federal Aviation
> Agency, which imposed a temporary flight restriction over the
> area so no news helicopters could hover noisily overhead. . . .
> During the opening hours of the incident we briefed the
> media frequently, sometimes as often as every 45 minutes. . . .
> We were not going to discuss the content or tone of the
> negotiations, and were not going to discuss our operations. . . .
> Those stressful and frustrating briefings required us to weigh
> every word we said, and put up with reporters who could
> be aggressive and rude. But the process had advantages. We
> dispelled rumors and released facts when we needed to
> do so.[43]

Toohey described the admirable restraint of the general manager of
television station WJZ during the crisis. WJZ filmed one of its reporters
talking on the telephone to Palczynski, who had reached the station by
cellular telephone after the BCPD had closed off regular telephones in the
hostage site. At the request of the police chief, WJZ did not run its footage
until the standoff had ended. Toohey attributed such restraint to media
trust of the police department established over a period of years.

Other departments will do well to emulate the policies and practices
of Baltimore County and to train their personnel accordingly. But media
relations may nonetheless be strained by a department's refusal to provide
information on negotiations in progress or tactical plans. The media may
also unfairly criticize and stigmatize police after the fact, if hostage negotiators and tactical personnel have deceived and manipulated hostage takers during the crisis or used potentially deadly force as a last resort. Few
media officials and journalists are competent to appraise negotiations
with hostage takers and uses of force by tactical teams. No police department should ever bow to media pressure to divulge information about
negotiations in progress or possible tactical measures. Neither should
departments permit transparently self-aggrandizing media pronouncements to influence police policy.

On May 30, 2000, an armed gunman in Luxembourg, Neji Bejaoui,
took twenty-five children and three adults hostage in a day-care center.

On June 1 Bejaoui demanded television airtime. Negotiators agreed. Luxembourg tactical police officers then posed as a television crew. When Bejaoui came out for the interview, with a grenade in one hand and a child on his other arm, two tactical officers posing as television cameramen shot him in the head, but not fatally. All the hostages were freed without injury.

After the rescue, the 450,000-member International Federation of Journalists, headquartered in Brussels, Belgium, strenuously objected to the police deception and demanded an investigation. Adrian White, general secretary of the federation, said:

> Cameramen are always potential targets when filming in dangerous conditions. Incidents like this may put them even more at risk from trigger-happy criminals. . . . Each year many journalists die reporting on incidents of violence. . . . Their life is dangerous enough without adding to the difficulties.[44]

Media in the United States followed the federation's lead by featuring the media criticism of police and not the rescue of the hostages. The June 3, 2000, *New York Times* headline read, "Criticism for a Police Rescue in Luxembourg." The Portland, Maine *Press Herald* carried the same story with the headline, "Tactics Questioned in Hostage Standoff." On June 12, *Time*'s European edition ran the headline, "Lights, Camera, Shoot!" *Newsweek*'s international edition for Europe ran the headline, "Neutralizing the Bad Guys." One column published in Europe criticized the Luxembourg police for using potentially deadly force, on the preposterous grounds that deadly force in a crisis is no different from capital punishment and should therefore be prohibited by law. I could not find any newspaper or magazine headlines that said, "Police Rescue Children in Luxembourg" or "Luxembourg Police Rescue Hostages from Gunman."

The strident indignation of the International Federation of Journalists in Brussels and the diversionary coverage of the Luxembourg rescue in the U.S. media have shown that the media shamefully inflate their prerogatives and importance, underestimate the plight of hostages, and denigrate the responsibilities of police. Hostages are taken against their will. Police have to go to the rescue. But as in Baltimore County, absolutely no reason exists for media personnel to be inside a secure police perimeter, or in danger, unless asked for assistance by police. Even then, the media people can decline.

Journalists and media representatives insist that "the public has a right to know." The television industry has changed that claim into, "The public has a right to see events up close as they happen," which is a fancy way of saying, "If it bleeds, it leads, and we want to be able to broadcast it." The public's right to know is seldom unconditional; it is limited by overriding considerations, including rights to privacy, confidentiality, and safety. The public does not have the right to "see events up close as they happen" in a crisis. To the contrary, police have an obligation to bar media personnel from dangerous ground, because they may jeopardize negotiations and cause greater danger to hostages and police. If media crews decide that they must go into dangerous places to get stories, without police or military protection, they are responsible for their own actions. Their decisions have no bearing on what police may rightly do in resolving crises. If qualified hostage negotiators are convinced that tactical measures must be used to end a hostage crisis and that the best means is for tactical police to impersonate a television crew, then that is the method the police should employ.

The International Federation of Journalists might as well have claimed that police have no right to put an officer undercover in the guise of a journalist or that a nation's intelligence agencies have no right in a cold or hot war to give an agent the persona of a journalist. If the federation wants to disallow impersonation of media personnel, who will they allow tactical police and undercover agents to pretend to be? If a policeman enters a hostage scene disguised as a milkman, does he violate the rights of milkmen? If a policewoman enters disguised as a doctor, does she violate the rights of doctors? The question cannot be whether police have the right in crises to use deception; to deny police that right would cost the lives of countless hostages.

Media stigmatization of the Luxembourg police resembles the stigmatization of Constable Duncan by his department and hometown for refusing to keep silent about a case of child sexual abuse. The Luxembourg police deserve gratitude and praise for ending the hostage crisis with no loss of life and no injury to hostages. The International Federation of

Journalists and the media who assailed the Luxembourg police deserve moral reproach. They should be ashamed of themselves.

Character and Capacities

The development of capacities can never be prudently separated from respect for ethics and the formation of good character. This is so because all know-how cuts two ways. The journalist who learns to write effectively learns to manipulate the public by telling only one side of the story. The counterintelligence agent who learns tradecraft learns how to sell state secrets. So, too, with all the capacities police develop. The cop who learns how to investigate narcotics trafficking learns how to deal drugs. The cop who investigates burglaries learns how to commit them. The cop who learns how to conduct surveillance learns how to invade privacy. The cop who learns how to lift a latent print learns how to plant evidence. The cop who learns how to investigate corruption learns how to solicit bribes.

All human capacities and skills in every walk of life can be both rightly and wrongly applied. How good we become at doing something is distinct from whether it is a good thing to do. Thus, when we help police develop and refine the capacities essential to their work, we are entrusting them with enormous new powers. If we choose the wrong people, the more diligently and thoroughly we educate and train them, the more dangerous they will become.

Recruits who are not smart enough or disciplined enough to develop the capacities essential to good policing in the future and who make it through the probationary period will be dangerous because incompetent. The more complex their assignments, the more glaring their incompetence and the greater the likelihood of public mistrust—not only of them, but also of other police because of them. Furthermore, incompetent police needlessly put the public, other officers, and themselves in danger. Police departments cannot simultaneously tolerate incompetence and stand on the side of officer safety.

These two facts—that all capacities can be used either ethically or unethically and that both intelligence and self-discipline are required to develop our capacities—should be the beacons by which the ranking personnel and the "invisible senate" of a police department pilot policing into the future. They shed light on everything that matters in recruitment, training, supervision, and accountability. They show that integrating ethical considerations into all training and supervision is imperative and that offering only isolated academy training units on ethics is folly. They illuminate the obligations of police departments to their own personnel and to the public and the rationale for "the genial pressure of manners, morals, and customs"—enforced by social stigma and reproach—among police. Police who steer by those beacons have the best chance of rising to the challenges of their duties, no matter how complex those duties may yet become.

20

Terrorism and Policing

Bargaining by outrage is an old game.

—Jacques Barzun[1]

On September 11, 2001, militant fundamentalist Islamic terrorists hijacked four transcontinental commercial aircraft flying west from Logan Airport in Boston, Newark Airport in New Jersey, and Dulles Airport near Washington, D.C. They used box-cutting knives to take control. On a suicidal mission of mass murder, they flew two of the planes into the World Trade Center towers in New York City and a third into the Pentagon in Northern Virginia. Heroic passengers and members of the crew attempted to wrest control of the fourth plane from the terrorists and prevented them from attacking their intended target in Washington, D.C., but the plane crashed in rural Pennsylvania with no survivors.

Immediately after the initial terrorist attacks, U.S. Secretary of Transportation Norman Mineta ordered the Federal Aviation Administration to cancel all commercial flights still on the ground inside the United States and to instruct domestic flights in the air to land as soon as possible. Within two hours, domestic commercial air traffic had shut down. Subsequent federal investigations have confirmed that terrorists had made their way aboard several additional flights scheduled for departure from other airports on the Atlantic seaboard. In the enormity of the catastrophes and the confusion of the morning, most of those terrorists managed to escape detection and apprehension. Two of them, however, still carrying box-cutters, were apprehended aboard a train and remain in custody.

Within an hour of being struck by the two Boeing 767 passenger airplanes—United Airlines Flight 175 and American Airlines Flight 11, with a total of 135 passengers and twenty-two crew members aboard—carrying up to twenty thousand gallons of aviation fuel apiece, the World Trade Center towers collapsed. The third plane destroyed a section of the Pentagon on impact. Twenty-three New York City police officers, thirty-seven Port Authority police, and 343 firefighters engaged in rescue operations perished in the collapse of the towers, along with thousands of people who worked or were visiting in the World Trade Center, nearly two hundred Pentagon personnel, and all passengers and crew aboard the fourth aircraft. Days later, as search, rescue, and recovery operations reached what the father of one missing son called "the last innings of hope," the nation knew that by their attacks, the terrorists had murdered some three thousand people, including hundreds in the World Trade Center from eighty different nations. Exaggerated and careless reports by some popular media led to widespread belief that the terrorist attacks deprived some fifteen thousand children of at least one parent. The most reliably documented estimate, provided by the *New York Times*, is that at least 2,830 children lost a parent.

Fewer than two weeks after those atrocities, letters contaminated with powder containing anthrax spores reached a newsman in Florida and the offices of NBC anchorman Tom Brokaw and U.S. Senator Tom Daschle. A small number of anthrax-laced letters may have "cross-contaminated" other mail and thereby exposed postal workers to the disease and fouled mailrooms and federal buildings. By the end of October, medical tests had confirmed seventeen cases of anthrax, four of them fatal. Doctors prescribed prophylactic antibiotics for twenty thousand employees of the postal service and other institutions who might have been exposed. Terrorist copycats, wannabes, or full-fledged terrorists mailed envelopes containing similar-looking but harmless powder. Exposure to that powder has nonetheless necessitated building inspections and evacuations and medical tests for children and adults.

The perpetrators of the anthrax terrorism remain unknown at this writing, with the investigations complicated by the anthrax deaths of a New York City hospital worker and a ninety-four-year-old Oxford, Connecticut, widow not known to have been exposed to contaminated mail. Vincent Cannistraro, former head of CIA counterterrorism, said that the letters looked like the work of "either a lone psycho in the U.S. or a small cell of one of the hate groups like Aryan Nations or Christian Identity." A number of other experts have agreed.[2] Several scholars have doubted that the perpetrators are Islamic, since the contaminated letters invoke Allah at the end, rather than in the beginning as is Islamic custom. Other analysts have identified clues that suggest production of the anthrax "by a state-sponsored bioweapons program": the expense and expertise required to produce "aerosol forms" of anthrax; the fact that "no radical groups in the United States are known to have the capability" of such production; and the proof of long-standing connections between the terrorist network behind the atrocities of September 11 and the bioweapons program of Iraq.[3]

For several years, a number of U.S. scientists have conducted research to trace the origins of different strains of anthrax. Their analysis ties the anthrax spores in the recent terrorist mailings to the "Ames strain" first taken from a dead cow near Ames, Iowa, possibly as long ago as the 1930s. This very strong resemblance may help investigators to identify the perpetrators, but record keeping and security in anthrax research over that long period have, unfortunately, been sketchy at best. No one can be certain which individuals or governments have come into possession of various anthrax strains, including the Ames strain.[4] In early November 2001 the Federal Bureau of Investigation released a psychological profile of the "anthrax terrorist" as an adult male, a vengeful and socially inept loner who probably has scientific training and may work in a laboratory. Profilers suggested that the man may have shown signs of anxiety, withdrawal, and preoccupation since September 11, along with unusual absenteeism.[5]

Anita Barry, director of communicable disease control at the Boston Public Health Commission, and other public health officials have tried to convey a sense of proportion to the public by urging that we face greater danger from the new forms of influenza that occur naturally every thirty years or so than we do from the current anthrax bioterrorism. Various strains of flu kill 20,000 people a year in the United States, more when a new form surfaces.[6] At the same time, public health and safety agencies have to design responses to bioterrorism, because we face the dread possibility of international biological warfare mounted by such terrorist states as Iraq that have germ warfare capacity. Madeline Drexler, author of a book on "bacteriological warfare agents," wrote, "During the Gulf War, Iraq's germ warfare facilities were believed to have had bombs and warheads packed with botulinum toxin, anthrax bacteria, and aflatoxins [highly toxic compounds that cause cancer and liver damage]."[7] U.S. Senator Joseph I. Lieberman added that Iraq's dictator Saddam Hussein had "developed weapons of mass destruction and used them, firing missiles at American soldiers and Israeli cities, using poison gas on Iranians, and employing chemical warfare against his own citizens."[8]

With the long history of research into biological warfare conducted by Japan, the United States, and the former Soviet Union (which in the late 1980s worked on "2,000 strains of anthrax and produced twenty tons of smallpox virus annually"[9]), terrorist states may have been able to secure or produce and stockpile deadly chemical and biological substances (called agents), including anthrax, smallpox, and bubonic plague. Iraq stands out, because several of the leading bioweapons scientists from the former Soviet Union are now on the Iraqi payroll.[10] During the 1990s, the U.S. Department of State identified Iran, Iraq, Sudan, Libya, Syria, North Korea, and Cuba as terrorist states—states that use "terrorism as a tool of foreign policy." On August 20, 1998, the United States launched ineffective missile strikes against suspected terrorist facilities in both Sudan and Afghanistan.[11]

How soon and to what extent terrorists can deliver throughout the world weapons of mass murder and destruction are less clear. "Agroterrorism"—the use of biological or chemical substances to destroy crops and livestock—may be less complicated and more feasible for terrorist networks. Terrorists may be able to buy or build nuclear devices, attack nuclear power plants, or pollute water and air by dispersion of radioactive material, but germ warfare seems to remain the greater threat. Many states that support and harbor terrorists also employ highly educated and trained specialists in advanced technology who can invent and deliver what philosopher and columnist George F. Will calls "weapons of mass disruption"—"cyberattacks" on the computerized systems of developed nations, industry, and commerce.[12]

What is clear is that terrorists with whom we must contend will stop at nothing. They prey on Muslims as well as infidels, skim money from charities for Muslim orphans to finance terrorist activities, and murder children they suspect of being informants.[13] Their malevolence and self-righteousness trample all limits historically associated with human decency and with restraint in the conduct of war. With all the weapons they can acquire and deliver against civilian populations, such terrorists hope to enlist us in our own destruction by sowing among us insurmountable feelings of vulnerability, fear, and helplessness.

Islamic zealots write gleefully of the anthrax terrorism. They preposterously claim that the will and resistance to terror of the people and the government of the United States are already falling apart. On November 7, 2001, Dr. Atallah Abu Al-Subh, a columnist for *Al-Risala*—published weekly by Hamas—celebrated the release of anthrax into the U.S. population:

> Oh Anthrax, despite your wretchedness you have sown horror in the heart of the lady of arrogance, of boastfulness! Your gentle touch has made the US's life rough and pointless. . . . In sound mind, I thank you and confess that I like you, I like you very much. May you continue to advance, to permeate, and to spread . . . enter the air . . . the water faucets from which they drink. . . . Turn the bodies of the tyrants into matches burning slowly and gradually, so that they understand that the truth belongs to Allah. . . . Then, and only then, will you return to your place.

Five days earlier, the United States had added Hamas to Executive Order 13224, which "provides the [United States the] authority to act against individuals and organizations that associate with the named [Hamas] terrorist groups."[14]

On the basis of credible intelligence reports, John D. Ashcroft, the U.S. attorney general, three times since early October 2001 asked the American people, 18,000 police departments, and 27,000 corporate security agencies to be on highest alert for possible terrorist attacks, their specific nature unknown. On November 1, 2001, California's Governor Gray Davis issued an alert based on uncorroborated information acquired by the U.S. Customs Service and the FBI of possible terrorist plans to bomb four suspension bridges, including the Golden Gate Bridge, between November 2 and November 9.

On November 6, the FBI judged the uncorroborated information not to be credible. No doubt, both government and the private sector will have to act from time to time on information about possible terrorist plans that turns out to be unreliable. Corroborated threats of terrorism—as well as uncorroborated but plausible raw intelligence—by weapons of mass murder and mass destruction compel police departments and law enforcement agencies to take on new investigative and security tasks. Anthrax scares, bomb threats, and heightened security measures raise departmental expenses dramatically, while antiterrorism priorities may divert personnel from community policing, "broken-windows" policing, and tested crime prevention measures. Some major city chiefs fear that reductions in violent crime in recent years will be reversed by deployment of officers to new duties.

Throughout these trying times, experienced police and law enforcement, military, and political leaders have, for the most part, given the citizenry good preliminary information, instruction, and counsel. But police and other local authorities have not themselves always had enough information and intelligence from federal agencies to determine how best to apply their assets to instruction and protection of the public. And deciding how thoroughly to inform the public can be difficult, since law enforcement leaders should not release to the media information on investigations in progress or possible locations of suspects that might be used by perpetrators of terrorism to escape apprehension.

Some academics, media commentators, broadcast journalists, social pundits, bureaucrats, politicians, educators, and a variety of other self-appointed and media-appointed "experts" exercise no comparable restraint. They have filled the airwaves with instant analyses, simplistic explanations, and endless speculation about terrorism and the future. Many citizens, perhaps even a majority according to recent polling data, rely primarily on entertainment media for news. Like others who do not read serious news coverage and who follow the news mainly on television talk shows and "tabloid" channels, they watch and listen to a procession of those supposed sages, many of them no more than celebrities, who have presumed since that horrible sunlit morning of September 11 to make pronouncements about our nation, the situation for our children and ourselves, and the future. By uninformed speculation about matters in which they have no competence and by excited reports of their own feelings of terror, no matter how irrational, many of those media personalities do nothing but stir up unhealthy fear in credulous audiences.

Such people repeatedly make five pronouncements—and then they confidently echo one another in assuring us that those pronouncements are not only true but also momentous: First, that the terrorist mass murders were acts of "senseless violence."[15] Second, that suicide bombers are cowards. Third, that the "events" of September 11 were unimaginable, beyond belief, outside the realm of comprehension. Fourth, that we live now in a whole new world, a world so fundamentally changed that nothing will ever again be the same. And fifth, that the people of the United States are united as never before in a spirit of patriotism and of compassion for those who were murdered and those who are in mourning.

None of those pronouncements is true. Most of the police and law enforcement executives with whom I have been in contact since September 11 understand that those pronouncements are false and that basing any police policies or practices on them can only thrust the public and police themselves into danger.

Before turning to the evidence that those five pronouncements are false, we should address a sixth view, important enough to be singled out because of its popularity in some media, academic, and political circles. That is the view that, in reality, there is no such thing as a terrorist, because "One person's terrorist is another person's freedom fighter."

What Is a Terrorist?

Distinguished columnist William Safire has written that a terrorist is "a person who murders even one innocent civilian to send a political message. . . . The evil purpose of modern barbaric murder is to carry out a blindly worshiped leader's desire to shock, horrify and ultimately intimidate the target's civilized compatriots."[16] In a September 20, 2001, speech to the U.S. Congress, former prime minister of Israel Benjamin Netanyahu said, "Terrorists do not *unintentionally* harm civilians. They *deliberately* murder, maim, and menace civilians—as many as possible."[17]

Steven Jukes, global head of news for the Reuters News Service, rejected those definitions and the use of the word *terrorist* as pure, subjective bias. In September 2001 he wrote to his staff: "We all know that one person's 'terrorist' is another man's freedom fighter and that Reuters upholds the principle that we do not use the word 'terrorist.'" He later added, "We're trying to treat everyone on a level playing field, however tragic it's been and however awful and cataclysmic for the American people . . . [and] we don't want to jeopardize the safety of our staff . . . in Gaza, the West Bank, and Afghanistan."[18]

The two pieces of Jukes's position contradict each other. On the one hand, he has eschewed the word terrorist so as to achieve a "level playing field"—that is, to imply that every belief, every way of acting, is the moral equivalent of any other. In that view, nothing is really right or wrong, and there is no such thing as a real terrorist, or a real freedom fighter, but only rival factions and nations whose members love their side and hate everyone else's. The logical conclusion of that view is that the people who hijacked the airplanes on September 11 and piloted them as guided missiles into civilian targets cannot be criticized in any rational way, because accusing them of wrongdoing makes the playing field uneven. On the other hand, Jukes has wanted to protect the personnel of Reuters from murderous reprisal against freedom of speech in places like Gaza and Afghanistan.

The incoherence in his position shows in the fact that every day all sorts of people—academics, political critics, media commentators, college students—openly call the government and the people of the United States terrorists. But they do not have to fear that the government will kill them when they do so, because their speech is protected both by the First Amendment to the Constitution and by the customs and traditions of the people. If the playing field were truly even—if moral neutrality were intellectually justifiable—so-called freedom fighters would not kill people for speaking freely, and freedom of speech would be as safe from terrorist reprisal in Afghanistan as it is in nations that respect human dignity and civil liberties.

Neither does the United States prevent Muslims from speaking freely or punish them for doing so. The civil liberties of the large portion of the U.S. Muslim population and Muslim leaders who share, according to Daniel Pipes of the Middle Eastern Forum, "a hatred of the United States and the desire, ultimately, to transform it into a nation living under the strictures of militant Islam," have been kept secure. Pipes quoted the late Ismail Al-Faruqi, founder of the Institute of Islamic Thought at Temple University, as "the first contemporary theorist of a United States made Muslim." Said Al-Faruqi, "Nothing could be greater than this youthful, vigorous, and rich continent [of North America] turning away from its past evil and marching forward under the banner of Allahu Akbar [God is great]." Other Muslim leaders take the same position. Zaid Shakir, formerly Yale University's Muslim chaplain, stated that "Muslims cannot accept the legitimacy of the American secular system, which is 'against the orders and ordainments of Allah. . . . The orientation of the Qur'an [Koran] pushes us in the exact opposite direction.'"[19] Hatred of the United States, speech that condemns the United States, and efforts within the law to turn the United States into an Islamic theocracy are permitted. Nothing comparable is possible for Muslims in countries where terror rules.

The playing field is not level when we compare life under tyranny with life where popular sovereignty—government of, by, and for the people—prevents tyranny. And when zealots violently attack civilian populations to overthrow popular sovereignty and replace it with their own brand of tyranny, or use weapons of mass destruction to keep their own people under the yoke of tyranny, we properly call them terrorists. Terrorists are, as philosopher John Silber has explained, "individuals or groups who aim to undermine the confidence of a people that the government is capable of ensuring that level of security which every citizen in civil society has the right to expect. Terrorism is in effect a determined effort to convince the people of a country that their government is impotent and that in reality they live in a state of nature in which life, as Thomas Hobbes said, is 'solitary, poor, nasty, brutish, and short.'"[20] Terrorists seek to bring down governments and nations by destroying the faith of the public in their own institutions.

It is important for police and law enforcement personnel to understand that Jukes's position is incoherent. His attempt to avoid facing up to the reality of terrorism fails miserably, because terrorism is undeniably real. Safire, Netanyahu, and Silber all shed light on the nature and purposes of terrorism, and history testifies to the perpetration of terrorist atrocities.

In daily practice, police can also rely on the applicable definitions of terrorism in the law. The federal law of the United States, a nation with genuine popular sovereignty where the public is not in bondage, asserts, "The term 'Federal crime of terrorism' means an offense that (A) is calculated to influence or affect the conduct of government by intimidation or coercion, or to retaliate against government conduct; and (B) is a violation of. . . ." (There follows here a long list of laws prohibiting violent crimes against persons and property, including homicide, assassination, kidnapping, torture, assault, hostage taking, piracy, arson, destruction of aircraft and ships, use

of weapons of mass destruction, conspiracy; and also a list of laws that prohibit harboring or providing material support to those who conspire
to commit or commit "Federal crimes of terrorism.")[21] The law continues,
"(1) [T]he term 'international terrorism' means activities that (A) involve
violent acts or acts dangerous to human life that are a violation of the criminal laws of the United States or of any State, or that would be a criminal
violation if committed within the jurisdiction of the United States or of any
State; (B) appear to be intended (i) to intimidate or coerce a civilian population; (ii) to influence the policy of a government by intimidation or
coercion."[22] By law, terrorists are individuals who commit or conspire to
commit such crimes on American soil or against Americans, guests of
Americans, or American facilities anywhere in the world with the intent to
affect government conduct or policy.

Bargaining by Outrage

We did not witness on September 11 mad, insane, mindless, senseless, or
cowardly terrorist acts. We witnessed the willful, relentless, carefully
planned murder of thousands of innocent civilians by calculating men
whose mission and methods are identified in a terrorist training manual,
Military Studies in the Jihad against the Tyrants:

> The main mission . . . is the overthrow of the godless regimes
> and their replacement with an Islamic regime. Other missions
> consist of . . . assassinating enemy personnel as well as foreign
> tourists . . . spreading rumors and writing statements that insti-
> gate people against the enemy . . . blasting and destroying the
> embassies and attacking vital economic centers . . . blasting and
> destroying bridges leading into and out of cities.

The manual gives detailed instructions for "living among the enemy,"
including maintenance of multiple false identities and sets of identification
papers, use of reliable methods for secure communications, and establishment of "cell or cluster methods" of operation in which the members of different cells do not know or know of one another and leaders never disclose

their real names. Undercover terrorists are told to "have a general appearance that does not indicate Islamic orientation (beard, toothpick, book, long shirt, small Koran)." The manual contains 180 pages of specific instructions for mounting terrorist attacks and declares the religious legitimacy of torturing and killing hostages.[23]

On July 7, 1984, then–U.S. Secretary of State George Shultz warned against thinking of terrorism as senseless:

> Many countries have joined the ranks of what we might call "The League of Terror" as full-fledged sponsors and supporters of indiscriminate, and not so indiscriminate, murder. . . . The epidemic is spreading, and the civilized world is still looking for remedies. . . . What we have learned about terrorism is, first, that it is not random, undirected, purposeless violence. It is not, like an earthquake or a hurricane, an act of nature before which we are helpless. Terrorists and those who support them have definite goals; terrorist violence is the means of attaining those goals. . . . With rare exceptions, they are trying to impose their will by force, a special kind of force designated to create an atmosphere of fear. And their efforts are directed at destroying what we are trying to build.[24]

The terrorists who hijacked the airplanes on September 11 were bent on the annihilation of a country they believed to be an affront to all that is holy, and a way of life they viewed as irredeemably despicable. The terrorist leaders on whose orders they acted moved them with either a perverse and indefensible interpretation of classical Islamic religious doctrine or an extremist strain of imperialism deep within it. In either case, the hijackers went forward with a murderous and evil arrogance. But whether flying an airplane into a heavily populated building or binding the wrists and then slashing the throat of a cabin attendant in hijacking the plane (as the terrorists did), the hijackers committed sacrificial mass murder for their own glorification and the expansion of the already substantial worldwide political, economic, and military power of their terrorist organizations.

Among the principal terrorist leaders is Osama bin Laden, head of the terrorist organization called al Qaeda. Thorough investigations have proved

398 CHARACTER AND COPS

that bin Laden and al Qaeda are primarily to blame for terrorist mass murders in the bombing of U.S. embassies in Nairobi, Kenya, and Dar es Salaam, Tanzania, in 1998 and for the 1993 bombing of the World Trade Center as well as the September 11, 2001, catastrophe. On November 4, 1998, U.S. "federal prosecutors unsealed a 238-count indictment charging bin Laden and his suspected top operational commander Muhammed Atef with conspiracy and murder in connection to the bombings of the U.S. embassies." In 1999 the U.S. State Department offered "a reward of up to five million dollars for information leading to bin Laden's arrest and conviction."[25] In November 2001 the department increased the reward to "up to $25 million." On May 1, 2011, President Obama announced that bin Laden had been killed after resisting arrest by U.S. forces during a raid in Pakistan.

Osama bin Laden declared his purposes many times. In 1998, he signed a decree mandating "holy war" against all possible U.S. military and civilian targets and clearly expressed his determination to bargain by outrage:

> For more than seven years the United States is occupying the lands of Islam in the holiest of its territories, Arabia, plundering its riches, overwhelming its rulers, humiliating its people, threatening its neighbors, and using its bases in the peninsula as a spearhead to fight against the neighboring Islamic peoples. . . . To kill Americans and their allies, both civil and military, is an individual duty of every Muslim who can, in any country where this is possible, until the Aqsa mosque and the Haram mosque are freed from their grip, and until their armies, shattered and broken-winged, depart from all the lands of Islam, incapable of threatening any Muslim.[26]

The threat is to murder Americans indiscriminately—children, women, men who are noncombatants—whenever and wherever possible. The bargain bin Laden offered is the implicit promise to stop committing the outrage of mass murder against Americans as soon as the United States abandons its allies in the Middle East and the terrorist network linked to bin Laden and al Qaeda.

Of necessity, bin Laden's offer of a bargain was a lie. He could not draw political legitimacy from any religious authority, for he was not an Islamic cleric and therefore had no religious standing to declare holy war. His power came from hatred. Nothing less than the destruction of all traditions of civilization that revere individual human dignity, hold that human beings are created equal, respect religious freedom and toleration, and treat justice as inseparable from liberty can appease the militant funda-mentalist Islamic zealotry bin Laden's followers continue to fuel as the engine of his power and "legitimacy." Mass murder and mass destruction are means by which terrorist organizations and states rule by force and seek the power to make their brand of Islamic zealotry compulsory worldwide. The United States, a constitutional republic that avoids both religious tyranny and political tyranny over religion by separating church and state, stands to those zealots as the embodiment of evil. They can strike no bargain they will keep with the United States and its allies.

President George W. Bush described the agenda of bin Laden and al Qaeda in his September 20, 2001, "Address to a Joint Session of Congress and the American People":

> Al Qaeda is to terror what the mafia is to crime. But its goal is not making money; its goal is remaking the world—and imposing its radical beliefs on people everywhere. . . . This group and its leader—a person named Osama bin Laden—are linked to many other organizations in different countries, including the Egyptian Islamic Jihad and the Islamic Movement in Uzbekistan. There are thousands of these terrorists in more than 60 countries. They are recruited from their own nations . . . trained in the tactics of terror . . . sent back to their homes or sent to hide in countries around the world to plot evil and destruction. . . . They want to overthrow existing governments in many Muslim countries, such as Egypt, Saudi Arabia, and Jordan. They want to drive Israel out of the Middle East. They want to drive Christians and Jews out of vast regions of Asia and Africa.[27]

Organized crime has been big business worldwide for most of a century, a quest for power and wealth. Militant fundamentalist Islamic terrorism seeks by all available means to rule the entire world as an Islamic empire. Dr. Farouk El-Baz, director of the Boston University Center for Remote Sensing and former science adviser to President Anwar Sadat of Egypt, has described the basic terrorist goal as political control: "[T]he main objective of bin Laden and those like him remains the political control of Saudi Arabia and Egypt, the two most influential countries among Islamic and Arab countries. They believe that only one thing stands in their way: U.S. support in the form of military presence in Saudi Arabia, and economic assistance in the case of Egypt." El-Baz explained further that bin Laden and his allies became convinced that the United States could be driven from any part of the world by the loss of American lives at home or abroad. Because the United States retreated from Lebanon after the terrorist bombing of a U.S. Marine barracks and retreated from peacekeeping in Somalia after "the brutal ambush of a few American soldiers," those terrorists concluded that "the attacks of September 11 would surely clear the way for them to gain political control of any country they would target in North Africa or the Arabian Peninsula—the source of much of the world's oil."[28]

The lessons driven into youths in thousands of madrassas—institutions where terrorist advocates prepare Muslim boys and young men, by indoctrination, propaganda, and the preaching of hatred, for holy war against the United States and other democracies—confirm that terrorist agenda and reveal the ruthless political ambition of bin Laden and his closest associates in terrorist networks around the world. The elders of the madrassas in Pakistan and elsewhere, like the leaders of the terrorist networks that the madrassas support and populate, offer no plan for the amelioration of the poverty and repression of Muslims, except the destruction of the United States and the annihilation of Jews. They teach "a drumbeat of American injustice . . . [that] Americans kill only innocents" and that America prevents all humanitarian aid to Muslims in poverty and desperate circumstances. They identify repressive and tyrannical terrorist governments such as the Taliban in Afghanistan as saviors of Muslims from the tyranny of the United States and the United Nations. Madrassa elder Al-Sheikh Rahat Gul is typical of those who prepare the young to become terrorists. He "condemns the World Trade Center attack" and teaches that it was not Islamic terrorists who committed those mass murders and acts of destruction: "'The Jews have done this,' he said, calling the attacks a plot by Israel to draw the world into war. 'And the Hindus are just like them.'" The madrassas allow no dissent, prevent access to indisputable evidence that flatly contradicts the disinformation by which they exploit the young, and teach deception of infidels as a basic ethical tenet.[29]

One measure of the expansion of terrorist power is the proliferation of madrassas. In 1978 Pakistan had 3,000 madrassas. By 2001 there were 39,000 madrassas in Pakistan, with the largest of them—Darul Uloom Haqqania—training 2,800 youths at one time and awarding honorary degrees to terrorist leaders.[30]

Some of the media in the Middle East, sympathetic to terrorism against the West, fuel hatred with their own deceitful propaganda. On October 11, 2001, New York City Mayor Rudy Giuliani rejected a $10 million charitable donation to the Twin Towers Fund from Saudi Prince Al-Walid bin Talal bin Abdul Aziz Al-Saud. The prince's letter of condolence condemned all terrorism. But Giuliani would not accept the check, because the prince's publicist added to the letter a press release in which the prince laid blame for the attack on American foreign policy: "However, at times like this one, we must address some of the issues that led to such a criminal attack. I believe the government of the United States of America should reexamine its policies in the Middle East and adopt a more balanced stance towards the Palestinian cause."[31]

In reporting those events in the Saudi newspaper *Al-Riyadh*, columnist Mahmoud bin Abd Al-Ghani Sabbagh referred to Giuliani as "the homosexual governor [sic] of New York" and said, "Because the governor [sic] of the Big Apple is a Jew, he refused [to accept the donation] and caused a storm." The columnist falsely attributed to Giuliani the statement: "The Prince's declarations are grievous and irresponsible; these Arabs have lost the right to dictate [to us what to do]. What we (America) must do is kill 6,000 innocent people." He then addressed Giuliani directly, "By Allah, I am amazed at your act, you Jew; everything Prince Al-Walid said was true."[32] The editor of the Palestinian Authority media outlet *Al-Hayat Al-Jadida*, Hafez Al-Barghouthi, added, "New York mayor Rudolph Giuliani was obsessed by his hatred of Arabs even before the attacks on New York. He hides his first name, chosen for him by his Italian father, so as not to remind the Jewish voters of the infamous Rudolph Hitler [sic]. This is why he prefers to shorten it to Rudy."[33]

The madrassas deny obvious facts, spread false accounts of conspiracy against Islam, and prevent the young from learning of American efforts to save Muslims by intervention in Somalia, Kuwait, and parts of Europe. Biased media deceive the public and spread hatred and vituperation. By the lights of some widely respected scholars, the terrorist networks also twist Islamic doctrine to satisfy their own reach for power. Bernard Lewis, professor emeritus of Near Eastern Studies at Princeton University, explained:

> [C]lassical Islam in all its different forms and versions has never permitted suicide. This is seen as a mortal sin, and brings eternal punishment in the form of the unending repetition of the act by which the suicide killed himself. The classical jurists, in discussing the laws of war, distinguish clearly between the soldier who faces certain death at the hands of the enemy, and one who kills himself by his own hand. . . . Similarly, the laws of jihad [holy war] categorically preclude wanton and indiscriminate slaughter. The warriors in the holy war are urged not to harm noncombatants, women and children, "unless they attack you first."

Lewis concluded that for the "unprovoked, unannounced mass slaughter of uninvolved civil populations that we saw in New York two weeks ago [September 11] . . . there is no precedent and no authority in Islam. Indeed, it is difficult to find precedents even in the rich annals of human wickedness."[34]

Repressive and deadly religious intolerance; the use of religious dogma to "justify" oppression, mass murder, and terror; and vilification of individuals because of religion are despicable. But there is nothing mindless or senseless or crazy about them. Throughout history, deadly prejudice and hatred have been shrewd instruments of the lust for power, for vengeance, for personal salvation, for martyrdom. Today's international terrorists bargain by outrage in hope of gratifying the very same lusts.

Suicide Bombers and Cowardice

I understand our inclination to identify anyone who preys on the innocent and helpless by treacherous and deadly stealth as a coward who lacks the guts for a fair fight. The terrorists who send the spores of deadly diseases through the mails and their copycats, all of whom try to conceal their identity, behave as cowards. But we need to resist the temptation to think of suicide bombers as cowards lest we misunderstand their motives and underestimate their resolve. Violent terrorist zealots who believe that deliberately dying in a sacrificial mass murder of "infidels" gives ultimate meaning to life, confers martyrdom, and makes death a portal to paradise are far more dangerous than any coward. Their beliefs may be sufficient to make them fearless in committing suicidal mass murder. The genuinely committed suicide bomber is beyond compromise and beyond remorse.

Fearlessness is not, however, the same as bravery, courage, or heroism. A person who commits a suicide bombing in the belief that he has nothing to fear, nothing to lose, and everything to gain acts with confidence. The confidence rests on delusions of holiness and a sense of exemption from danger. Such confidence may look like courage, but it is not. Individuals who perform courageous acts, such as firefighters and police who attempt to rescue victims from burning buildings, know that they are going in harm's way and risking pain, injury, and death. They act despite danger, not by believing that there is none.

The terrorists who committed the atrocities on September 11 died expecting to be revered as heroic martyrs by the families, comrades, and advocates they left behind. They may have expected their families to be handsomely compensated by terrorist organizations. They certainly expected to be welcomed immediately to an eternal life of sensual pleasure. They buttressed their confidence with a document later released by the FBI and published by the *New York Times*: "When the confrontation begins, strike like champions who do not want to go back to this world. . . . Know that the gardens of paradise are waiting for you in all their beauty, and the women of paradise are waiting, calling out, 'Come hither, friend of God.' They have dressed in their most beautiful clothing."[35]

Why did the September 11 hijackers die with those expectations? Because terrorist organizations have given substantial sums of money to the families of some suicide bombers. And because terrorists who commit atrocities by suicide are the supreme egotists. They believe themselves anointed as agents of holiness with the mission of annihilating their enemies, all of whom—even children—they hate as "embodiments of undifferentiated evil" who are never worthy of humane consideration. Imagine the self-satisfaction of the suicide bomber: He is an "avenging angel" whose "ego expands in direct proportion as his bigotry increases." He can feel no qualm at plotting the destruction of his subhuman adversaries, imagine no remorse for killing what are to him essentially vermin, the scourge of the earth. The suicide bomber expects rewards for his family, adoration on earth, and entry to paradise, because of his conviction that he slaughters the enemies of God.[36]

As Aristotle explained, even drunken men can act with confidence when they believe that they are immune to adverse consequences.[37] We do not mistake their drunken confidence for courage. Neither should we do so in the case of mass murderers besotted with zealous hatred and egotistical confidence in their personal invulnerability as men of divine destiny.

Imagination, Horror, and History

Talk show celebrities and other highly visible commentators tell us that the death and destruction of September 11 were unimaginable, unbelievable, beyond comprehension, and that we now live in an entirely new, fundamentally changed world. As I stood in front of a television and watched the terrorists pilot the hijacked passenger jets as bombs into the towers of the World Trade Center, I felt shock and revulsion, but I did not find what I saw to be unimaginable. After all, the porousness of airport security in the United States has been obvious, and there is nothing new about suicide bombers or kamikazes, except for the use of passenger jets as the explosive devices.

The planes and their passengers disintegrating in explosions of aviation fuel were images of a nightmare come true. I had, since 1991, heard federal law enforcement and intelligence personnel describe the vulnerability of the United States to catastrophic violence from terrorist groups already operating in our country with international support. In June 1997 I had read the speech of my friend John P. O'Neill, of whom I write near the end of this chapter, to the National Strategy Forum in Chicago. He was then chief of International Terrorism Operations in the FBI. He said of militant terrorist cells covertly at work in the United States, "A lot of these groups now have the capability and the support infrastructure in the United States to attack us here if they choose to." He spoke of many rogue states that harbor and support terrorists; cautioned against underestimating the fanaticism of foreign and domestic groups, including militant Islamic terrorists, who seek the destruction of the United States; and described a very large number of lethal acts successfully carried out in the 1990s by many different kinds of terrorist cells and networks throughout the world. His speech has been available to the media, the public, and elected and appointed government officials at all levels for more than three years.[38]

American historical documents have cautioned us for centuries of our vulnerability to horrific acts. As early as January 1788, James Madison described the exposure of New York City to attack, in words that resonate anew now. Arguing the need for naval protection of the Atlantic seaboard, Madison wrote that only good luck had thus far saved our coastal cities from being "compelled to ransom themselves from the terrors of conflagration, by yielding to the exactions of daring and sudden invaders. . . . [N]o part of the Union ought to feel more anxiety on this subject than New York [state]. . . . The great emporium of its commerce, the great reservoir of its wealth [New York City], lies every moment at the mercy of events, and may almost be regarded as a hostage, for ignominious compliances with the dictates of a foreign enemy, or even with the rapacious demands of pirates and barbarians."[39]

Nothing Will Ever Be the Same?

The pundits who tell us that the horrors of September 11 were unimaginable also say that they felt safe before those terrorist acts because they believed that the United States was secure and not vulnerable. Several of them have told me, "Nothing will ever be the same." Because they are strangers to the past, to human history, they do not realize that the horrors inflicted on us now have been inflicted on others before—those and worse—so they now find themselves in a world that seems to them altogether new. It is not.

The horrific acts committed against the innocent and helpless on September 11 did not change either human nature or the most fundamental elements of human existence. History itself is premonitory. Consider the

following passage by C. S. Lewis, the great scholar of medieval and renais-
sance literature and author of *The Chronicles of Narnia*:

> I think it important to try to see the present calamity in a true
> perspective. The war creates no absolutely new situation: it sim-
> ply aggravates the permanent human situation so that we can no
> longer ignore it. Human life has always been lived on the edge
> of a precipice. Human culture has always had to exist under the
> shadow of something infinitely more important than itself. If
> men had postponed the search for knowledge and beauty until
> they were secure, the search would never have begun. We are
> mistaken when we compare war with "normal life." Life has
> never been normal. Even those periods which we think most
> tranquil, like the nineteenth century, turn out, on closer inspec-
> tion, to be full of crises, alarms, difficulties, emergencies.
> Plausible reasons have never been lacking for putting off all
> merely cultural activities until some imminent danger has been
> averted or some crying injustice put right. But humanity long
> ago chose to neglect those plausible reasons. They wanted
> knowledge and beauty now, and would not wait for the suitable
> moment that never comes. Periclean Athens leaves us not only
> the Parthenon but, significantly, the Funeral Oration. The
> insects have chosen a different line: they have sought first the
> material welfare and security of the hive, and presumably they
> have their reward. Men are different. They propound mathe-
> matical theorems in beleaguered cities, conduct metaphysical
> arguments in condemned cells, make jokes on scaffolds, discuss
> the latest new poem while advancing to the walls of Quebec,
> and comb their hair at Thermopylae. This is not panache: it is
> our nature.[40]

Lewis was not writing about *our* "present calamity." He was born in
1898, fought in World War I, and died on the day John Kennedy was assassinated in 1963. The words above come from a sermon he delivered in
England at Oxford's Church of St. Mary the Virgin in 1939, after Hitler's
military forces invaded Poland on September 1. The Nazi invasion was a

secretly calculated act of war and of terror against civilian populations and was followed by genocide.

No contemporary terrorist has shown us anything about human nature or ruthlessness, or about indiscriminate mass murder, that we cannot find in Vladimir I. Lenin, Joseph Stalin, Adolph Hitler, Mao Tse-Tung, Idi Amin, Pol Pot, or any number of other tyrants, ancient and modern. Such ruthless terrorists always hold human nature in contempt. They cynically believe that all people can be terrorized by mass murder of noncombatants and other atrocities into betraying and forsaking everything they hold dear. If those tyrants had been right about us, the entire world would be in chains today. Liberty would be everywhere dead. But campaigns of terror have failed again and again to achieve their goals, because the human spirit—courage and resolve—does not simply cave in to horror, or even to horrific persecution. We are better and stronger than that. We live with, try to prevent, and witness all sorts of losses—the accidental death of loved ones, dread afflictions, crimes against the innocent, chronic pain, war, famine, pestilence, genocide. Many of us need help and support to go on with our lives, but most of us do not give up. Neither has humanity given up to the old or the new terrorists who want to enslave us all.

The words of Lewis were true when they were first uttered, they were true on September 11, and they are true today. The cynicism of tyrants and terrorists has always been erroneous, just as it is erroneous now. The fundamentals of human suffering and the human potential for virtue as well as the human capacity for evil do not change.

In response to the attacks on the United States on September 11, 2001, the International Association of Chiefs of Police has issued a very good report, "Leading from the Front: Law Enforcement's Role in Combating and Preparing for Domestic Terrorism."[41] The report begins, unfortunately, with the sentence, "On September 11, 2001, everything changed." All the rest of the report, well conceived and clearly written—with the promise to police that the report will be "a living document," regularly revised, refined, updated—belies that sentence.

Throughout, the report draws on lessons learned in the history of policing and law enforcement that apply directly to preparedness to deal with both terrorist attacks and the threat of terrorist attacks by weapons of mass murder and mass destruction. The association very intelligently invokes principles, recommends practices, and adduces facts that have been understood in policing for a great many years and certainly have not changed since September 11:

> [W]hile we strengthen our efforts to thwart future terrorist attacks, democratic nations must maintain their founding principles of freedom, civil liberties, and individual rights. . . . No matter how the future unfolds, local law enforcement will be on the front lines. . . . [L]ocal police will often be the first responders to any and all incidents. . . . Their first priority is to protect the public and secure the scene. . . . Leadership in planning and preparation before an incident occurs highlights the ongoing responsibilities of police chiefs. . . . Part of any chief's preparation should include thinking strategically about how to gather and process intelligence. . . . Reducing a community's vulnerability to attack requires, among other things, analyzing a locality to identify likely targets and working to improve the security at these locations. . . . All communications systems should be inventoried, serviced, and tested on a regular basis. . . . In an emergency, the public looks to law enforcement to respond and mobilize staff, equipment, and resources to deal with it. . . . Without adequate resources to fulfill missions or assignments, the commander of an operation may not be able to take appropriate steps to properly manage the situation. . . . One of the central marks of well-commanded critical incidents is that people knew what had to be done and in what order and how their portion of the operation linked with others. . . . As the events of an attack unfold and suspects are identified, the chief must be prepared to respond. A major focus of the chief's response will be preventing backlash against any segments of the community that some consider responsible. . . . Law enforcement needs to be aware that a crisis in the community or country will inevitably result in some illegal activity directed against people, groups, or organizations believed to be associated with the act(s) of

terror. . . . The primary goal of law enforcement is to ensure public safety. . . . A well-maintained and trained department will be prepared to respond to any type of situation and implement with skill and efficiency the policies and procedures that are in place, thus saving lives, maintaining safety, and calming fears—the true goal of the front line of any emergency situation.[42]

Those principles, practices, and facts of life in policing and law enforcement have not changed. They will not change in future editions of the International Association of Chiefs of Police's report. The current version provides a very good summary of types of weapons of mass destruction and methods by which they can be delivered. Then, the report provides chronologically "an overview of critical elements that need attention at the three stages of an event: before, during, and after an incident." The report is valuable, because it is attentive to detail. It provides specific guidance for intelligence gathering and sharing and other operational priorities. The report includes a carefully designed six-step incident response plan and addresses police obligations comprehensively. The report covers, for example, support for police on the front lines who may suffer stress-related afflictions and provisions for the release of victims' remains to families. The report should be very useful to police at all ranks, not just to chiefs. Experienced police will apply the principles of the report precisely because its recommendations are drawn from knowledge of the most challenging ordeals in the history of policing and from tested and reliable practices that do not change.

Perhaps we will see over time that because of the attacks of September 11, some among us who had been cynical toward public service in general and policing in particular, toward noble ambition and sacrifice for the sake of others, toward patriotism, toward the ideals of liberty and justice, and toward trustworthiness in public and private life have shed those prejudices. We may find that some young people have sensed the futility of spending our lives on trivial amusements and shallow relationships and have begun to take more seriously the questions of what is worth living for and what is worth dying for. Reflection on the horrors of September 11 may eventually lead some among us to a better understanding of self-reliance and the terms of self-respect. Those would be welcome changes, not in the nature of the world but in ourselves.

Disagreement and Conflict within the United States

In store windows, on magazine pages and billboards, and at sports events, we see the words "United We Stand." Our American flag flies proudly from homes, businesses, schools, automobiles, trucks, and bicycles. The U.S. Post Office issued a new stamp of our flag waving above a "United We Stand" inscription. Many of us wear flag pins. We want to express our love for our country, our patriotism, our faith in the ideals of the Declaration of Independence and the Constitution. Bumper stickers say "Proud to Be an American." These expressions of solidarity and allegiance tell us that the terrorists have attacked all of us, not only the men, women, and children they murdered. Symbols of unity give us encouragement and hope. They remind us that we are in this together and that we should try to do our best by one another. Those are perfectly appropriate sentiments for adults to feel and express and convey to their children, integral to the obligation to instruct our children in the long but unfinished human history of struggle to secure liberty and justice.

Not everyone agrees. An administrator and a resident adviser at Central Michigan University told students that their dormitory display of posters of an American flag and an eagle was offensive and had to be removed. The chairman of the Sociology Department at the College of Holy Cross ordered a department secretary to take down an American flag she had put on her wall in memory of a friend who died in the crash of the hijacked plane in Pennsylvania. The secretary refused, so the professor took it down. The college later apologized, under pressure of adverse publicity, but there is no flag in the Sociology Department today. At Lehigh University the vice provost of student affairs insisted on removal of an American flag from a campus bus. The dean of library services at Florida Gulf Coast University ordered library employees to "remove from their workspace 'Proud to be an American' stickers." She said that she feared offending international students. Public pressure forced those two universities to relent.[43] At the University of Massachusetts at Amherst, one professor said that the

American flag is a "symbol of terrorism and death and fear and destruction and oppression." Shocked witnesses put her home and e-mail addresses on the Internet. Then she received many "harassing" and intimidating messages and calls.[44] The professor's contemptuous hyperbole makes a mockery of objectivity, regard for the truth, and respect for honorable sacrifices under our flag; but her lack of intellectual self-control gives no one the right to threaten to harm her.

The American people and American institutions are diverse and complex. We are never altogether of one mind about anything, never fully united in thought, belief, and readiness for action. We do not *have* to conform to what others think or say or want. Police must remember that we greatly exaggerate when we claim that because of September 11 we stand shoulder to shoulder in the United States, resolute in wanting terrorism rooted out, joined anew in a sense of mutual civility and patriotic duty, and brought together in shared grief for the dead and sympathy with their loved ones.

On our highways we still encounter rudeness and incivility, drunken driving, and foolish endangerment. In our workplaces we still find laziness and laxness, nasty gossip, simmering resentments, clawing ambition, and incompetence. The public and police must still contend with crime and predation. Since September 11, con artists have bilked the public with charitable contribution scams. Members of the U.S. Senate have made deals behind the scenes that allow trial lawyers to gain punitive damage fees against institutions that could not possibly have prevented the terrorist acts in September. Texas Senator Phil Gramm calls such greed "piracy aboard a hospital ship."[45] Both the con artists and the trial lawyers are war profiteers—parasitic opportunists who line their pockets by exploiting both civilians and military personnel. Racist leaders of the Aryan Nations have celebrated the September 11 bombings as exactly what America deserves, and supremacists in the American Nazi Party have extolled the terrorists as heroes to be imitated.[46] Many of us are trying to be better citizens, better family members, better friends, colleagues, and neighbors. Not all of us.

Disagreements proliferate among us about the meaning and causes of the terrorist atrocities and about what we should do in response. Two days after the terrorist atrocities, the Reverend Jerry Falwell said on a television broadcast of *The 700 Club*:

The abortionists have got to bear some burden for this, because God will not be mocked. And when we destroy 40 million little babies, we make God mad. I really believe that the pagans, and the abortionists, and feminists, and the gays and the lesbians who are actively trying to make that an alternative lifestyle, the ACLU, People for the American Way—all of them have tried to secularize America—I point the finger in their face and say, "You helped this happen."

Falwell retracted his impassioned and nasty attack on other Americans a week later. His retraction was too little and too late.[47]

Hollywood celebrity Richard Gere, interviewed by *ABC News Radio* on October 10, after being booed by members of the New York Police and Fire Departments for remarks he made at a concert in honor and memory of those who died in the September 11 atrocities, repeated his position:

In a situation like this, of course, you identify with everyone who's suffering [but we must also think about] the terrorists who are creating such horrible karma. . . . It's all of our jobs to keep our minds as expansive as possible. If you can see the terrorists as a relative who's dangerously sick and we have to give them medicine, the medicine is love and compassion. There's nothing better.[48]

Other entertainers and celebrities have made similar claims. They are not likely, with such confused rambling, to persuade public servants who go in harm's way to protect or rescue victims of terrorist violence.

"The initial response of left-wing intellectuals to Sept. 11," wrote *New Republic*'s senior editor Andrew Sullivan, was insistence on one point:

This was America's fault. From Susan Sontag to Michael Moore, from Noam Chomsky to Edward Said, there was no question that, however awful the attack on the World Trade Center, it was vital to keep attention fixed on the real culprit: the United States. Of the massacre, a Rutgers professor summed up the consensus by informing her students that "We should be aware that, whatever its proximate cause, the ultimate cause is the fascism of U.S. foreign policy over the past many decades."[49]

How starkly the Falwell, Gere, and professorial pronouncements conflict with the "message of resolve" issued by the NAACP: "These tragedies and acts of evil must not go unpunished. Justice must be served."[50]

On October 1, 2001, the *Washington Post* quoted Judith Rizzo, deputy chancellor for instruction in the New York City school system, who placed the blame for terrorist atrocities on failure to teach multiculturalism in American schools: "Those people who said we don't need multiculturalism, that it's too touchy-feely, a pox on them. . . . I think they've learned their lesson. We have to do more to teach habits of tolerance, knowledge and awareness of other cultures."[51] On October 5, 2001, Lynne Cheney, wife of the vice president and formerly chairman of the National Endowment for the Humanities, rejected Rizzo's imputation of blame. She said, "It was manifestly not the United States that acted out of religious prejudice on September 11." She added, "If there were one aspect of schooling from kindergarten through college to which I would give added emphasis today it would be American history."[52]

In fact, students in most American schools need far more and better instruction in U.S. history, world history, physical and political geography, literature, sciences and mathematics, and the comparative study of religions. Until schools meet those obligations, students will continue to be subjected to what distinguished scholar and author George Steiner calls "the organized amnesia of present primary and secondary education" and "the debilitation of genuine literacy."[53] We should remember, however, that not even the best education is any guarantee that the student will become a decent person; and there is not the slightest evidence that better education for the American people would have altered the hatred, lust for power, and religious bigotry among the terrorists responsible for the atrocities of September 11.

Disagreements within Law Enforcement

Disagreements persist inside law enforcement as well. Since mid-September, many police chiefs, mayors, and city managers have criticized the FBI for being too secretive about its counterterrorism investigations. They say that to make the best use of their manpower and local knowledge in safeguarding the public, police need much more information from the FBI about terrorist suspects and networks, potential local targets, and likely forms of attack. Not only terrorism prevention depends on mutual candor and cooperation among local, state, and federal agencies. So do well-designed and coordinated first responses to terrorist attacks by thoroughly trained local police, firefighters, hazardous materials experts, and hospital and other emergency personnel. A number of police chiefs stress the importance of acquiring security clearances to give qualified local police access to classified information. FBI spokesmen point out that in some investigations the bureau is prohibited by federal grand jury rules of secrecy from sharing information.

New federal antiterrorism legislation has been enacted that expands law enforcement authority. The legislation includes a "sunset" provision that will eliminate some of the new law enforcement powers after four years, on December 31, 2005. The sunset provision is a compromise among lawmakers who disagree about the nature of adequate legal protections of civil liberties on the one hand and public safety on the other and therefore about the rightful limits to governmental powers.

Those disagreements reach far back in time. On November 20, 1787, Alexander Hamilton wrote to the American people:

> Safety from external danger is the most powerful director of national conduct. Even the ardent love of liberty will, after a time, give way to its dictates. The violent destruction of life and property incident to war—the continual effort and alarm attendant on a state of continual danger, will compel nations the most attached to liberty, to resort for repose and security, to institutions, which have a tendency to destroy their civil and political rights. To be more safe they, at length, become willing to run the risk of becoming less free.[54]

Twenty-eight days later, Hamilton wrote the people again, this time warning, "The circumstances that endanger the safety of nations are infinite; and for this reason no constitutional shackles can wisely be imposed on the power to which the care of it is committed."[55] In both instances Hamilton was writing about the establishment of military forces; but the history of criminal justice cannot be told without focus on the tension between individual liberty and public safety.

Political and educational policy disagreements emerging from September 11 will within a very few years have profound effects on schools and curricula and therefore on the competence of the individuals in police applicant pools. Disagreements about what our antiterrorism laws should be, how much intelligence federal agencies can and should share with state and local police, how our immigration policies should be framed, and the extent to which the terrorist peril we face must be combated with military forces and tribunals rather than by the criminal justice system will have even greater immediate effects. Unless we can handle—I do not say resolve—those disagreements more wisely than we have in the past, we will squander potential opportunities to protect the public from terrorists.

A common enemy—terrorism itself—can bring us together as a people only partially. Who would expect anything else where liberty flourishes? Disagreements over the rightful extent of police authority and powers will continue among us. But however divisive those disagreements may become, lawmakers, political leaders, and police executives should keep two points firmly in mind. First, when the mission of an institution expands, resources to fulfill the mission should expand proportionately. Second, when legislation enlarges the authority and powers of police and law enforcement personnel, the moral obligations of police grow. With enlarged powers to seek to prevent and combat terrorism come expanded obligations of preparation, vigilance, expertise, communication, training, supervision, accountability—and restraint.

All who hold positions of public trust need especially now moral clarity and moral humility. We need to be clear that terrorism is always wrong, always intolerable, never justifiable or excusable. At the same time, we need to be clear that fighting against terrorism does not endow us with the right to trample the Constitution or to take the law into our own hands. Neither does our personal engagement in the fight against terrorism wash away our faults and weaknesses or exempt us from every other duty of professional and private life. The fight against terrorism is a noble cause. We have to remember that serving noble causes does not make us angels.[56]

Terrorism and the Police Mission

Survivors of the World Trade Center atrocity speak in awe of the police and firefighters who went to the rescue of victims stranded in the towers. Again and again survivors have said, "They were going up the stairs when we were coming down." At the Central Virginia Criminal Justice Training Academy, executive director and former FBI special agent Edward Sulzbach now teaches academy students, "This is your mission: to go up the stairs when everyone else is going down."

We cannot ethically ask men and women in police and fire departments and other public service agencies or in the military to go in harm's way against terrorism without enacting the laws and policies—and providing the resources—necessary for them to be effective. Neither should we expect them to do so without providing them with adequate life insurance and education benefits for their families. The September 11 terrorist atrocities committed on American soil, against our citizens and guests in our country, have forced the U.S. Congress to take seriously at last much earlier proof that we have been targets of militant fundamentalist Islamic terrorists worldwide. By 1999 ten of the twenty-eight groups on the U.S. Department of State's "Designated Foreign Terrorist Organization List" were classified as "Islamic Extremist."[57]

The United States has been under attack for more than twenty years. The public, Congress, and the executive branch of the government have too often responded irresolutely and thus have invited and encouraged further terrorist attacks against our people and institutions. Attacks committed by and attacks planned by militant Islamic terrorists include the 1979 assault on the American Embassy in Iran under the dictatorship of the Ayatollah Khomeini, with 66 Americans taken hostage; the 1983 bombing of the U.S. Embassy in Beirut, with 63 murdered; the 1983 bombing of the U.S. Marine barracks in Lebanon, with 241 Marines killed; the 1984 bombing of the U.S. Embassy Annex in Beirut, with 14 deaths; the 1988 murder of 271 Americans in the bombing of Pan Am Flight 103 over Lockerbie, Scotland; the 1993 bombing of the World Trade Center, with 6 murdered, 1,000 injured, and $500 million dollars in damage; the discovery and conviction of terrorists in the 1993 plot to bomb bridges, tunnels, and landmarks in New York City; the 1998 U.S. Embassy bombings in Africa, with 12 Americans included in the 224 murder victims, and 4,500 people injured; and the 1999 prevention of Ahmed Ressam from perpetrating millennium bombings inside the United States.

Militant Islamic extremism is not the only terrorist threat, but it is by far the largest and most dangerous. In 1995 the Aum Shinrikyo cult murdered 12 people and injured 5,000 more by releasing sarin gas into the Tokyo subway. On April 19 of the same year, Timothy McVeigh and Terry Nichols slaughtered 168 people by bombing the Murrah Federal Building in Oklahoma City. Drug cartel narcoterrorism has plagued countries all over the world for decades.

Distinguished scholars, international statesmen, military strategists and leaders, and law enforcement and intelligence executives have insisted for nearly twenty years that the United States could not "passively" defend itself and its citizens from international or domestic terrorists. It is impossible for a large country to safeguard in advance, from all possible weapons of mass destruction, all the targets terrorists of every stripe might attack. Government must take active measures of defense—including proactive law enforcement. As Uri Ra'anan, director of the Boston University Center for the Study of Conflict, Ideology, and Policy explained in 1986, we must take active measures, because "terrorism exploits cruelly the vulnerabilities of the open society." The challenge is not merely to react, but to preempt terrorist attacks, a possibility only for a nation "able and willing to move toward 'active defense' in the place of a purely reactive and essentially passive posture."[58]

In 1995 Benjamin Netanyahu prophetically warned of U.S. immigration and surveillance laws and policies that allowed international terrorists to make their way easily into our country, to plot in secret, and then to perpetrate large-scale violence inside the United States:

> [T]hese subversive or terrorist groups can operate far more freely in the United States than in their home states. While the United States is certainly not a sponsor of state terror, it has nonetheless become an incubator of terror. And it can only be a matter of time before this terror is turned *inward* against the United States, the leader of the hated West.[59]

In 1999 the FBI predicted that in the future, terrorists would concentrate on "more destructive and high-profile attacks . . . to maximize media attention, fear, and public anxiety"; noted "increased interest among terrorists in weapons of mass destruction"; and described "massive destruction and casualties" as "an ominous security challenge as the world enters the twenty-first century." The FBI also warned that bin Laden's al Qaeda "has a presence in dozens of countries, including the United States." Describing bin Laden as a financier of Islamic extremism and terrorist ideology whose wealth and standing "have established him as a type of de facto state sponsor of terrorism," the FBI cautioned that bin Laden "does not control or direct all such extremism. Should either he or al Qaeda cease to exist, this international movement would, in all likelihood, continue."[60]

Speaking in Poland on November 6, 2001, President Bush reaffirmed that fact. In describing international coalition steps against al Qaeda and the Taliban, he said:

> We are at the beginning of our efforts in Afghanistan. And Afghanistan is the beginning of our efforts in the world. No group or nation should mistake America's intentions: We will not rest until terrorist groups of global reach have been found, have been stopped, and have been defeated.[61]

On October 26, 2001, President Bush signed into law the Uniting and Strengthening America by Providing Appropriate Tools Required to Intercept and Obstruct Terrorism Act of 2001 (U.S.A. Patriot Act).[62] The act covers 131 pages, too much to be summarized in any detail here. But several provisions of the law stand out.

The law enlarges the surveillance and search powers of federal agencies and expands their authority to share among themselves intelligence and information, including previously secret grand jury information. It enables greater sharing of intelligence with foreign governments. When permitted by a court, federal agencies are enabled to notify state officials of otherwise secret grand jury information that discloses a violation of state law. The law grants the Department of State and the Immigration and Naturalization Service access to criminal history records and other materials maintained by the National Crime Information Center and expands federal authority to deny admission to any alien "who has been associated with a terrorist organization and intends while in the United States to engage solely, principally, or incidentally in activities that could endanger the welfare, safety, or security of the United States" (section 411). The law also makes provision for holding in custody for seven days without criminal charges any immigrant suspected of involvement in terrorism and holding in custody for consecutive periods of six months any alien when "the Attorney General has reason to believe that the alien . . . is engaged in . . . activity that endangers the national security of the United States" (section 412). The law greatly expands federal authority to penetrate money-laundering operations and outlaws bulk cash smuggling.

The law amends the Omnibus Crime Control and Safe Streets Act of 1968 by appropriating to the Bureau of Justice Assistance $50 million for fiscal year 2002 and $100 million for fiscal year 2003 for "establishing and operating secure information sharing systems to enhance the investigation and prosecution abilities of participating [federal, state, and local] enforcement agencies in addressing multijurisdictional terrorist conspiracies and activities" (section 701). The law authorizes $50 million per year to expand training and cooperation among federal, state, and local law enforcement agencies in rooting out computer-related crime (section 806). The law also authorizes $25 million per year from fiscal year 2003 through fiscal year 2007 to fund grants that will "improve the ability of State and local law enforcement, fire department and first responders to respond to and prevent acts of terrorism" and "technical assistance programs that emphasize coordination among neighboring law enforcement agencies for sharing resources, and resources coordination among law enforcement agencies for combining intelligence gathering and analysis functions, and the development of policy, procedures, memorandums of understanding, and other best practices," as well as training grants in "critical incident management for all forms of terrorist attack" (section 1005). Each state will receive a federal block grant to be used to prepare jurisdictions to respond to terrorist use of "biological, nuclear, radiological, incendiary, chemical, and explosive devices" (section 1014). The federal government will also provide the states with background records checks of persons seeking state licenses to transport hazardous materials (section 1012).

Congress made explicit in enacting the law its opposition to racial and ethnic profiling by "finding" that "the concept of individual responsibility for wrongdoing is sacrosanct in American society, and applies equally to all religious, racial, and ethnic groups." Congress expressed its sense that "the civil rights and civil liberties of all Americans, including Arab Americans, Muslim Americans, and Americans from South Asia, must be protected, and every effort must be taken to preserve their safety" (section 102).

The U.S.A. Patriot Act will help law enforcement and police agencies to safeguard the public from terrorist attack and to respond effectively to terrorist acts. To protect the public and the infrastructure of our society to the fullest extent reasonably possible, legislators will have to do considerably more. Any active and comprehensive defense of the public from terrorism has five principal domains: military action; diplomacy; economic sanctions and disruption of terrorist finances; intelligence gathering, analysis, and use; and first-responder protection of the public from terrorist attacks and other forms of criminal predation and threats to the public safety. Police and law enforcement agencies have responsibilities at the federal, state, and local level in the last three of those, including dramatically expanded duties in safeguarding potential terrorist targets. In addition, as federal agencies such as the FBI, the Immigration and Naturalization Service, the Border Patrol, the Coast Guard, the Federal Emergency Management Agency, the Bureau of Alcohol, Tobacco, and Firearms, the Secret Service, and others allocate more of their personnel and investigative resources to terrorism, state and local police will have to pick up some of the work those agencies have traditionally performed.

"Homeland defense" from terrorism requires police to undertake a larger mission. Where police departments have to commit their personnel and budgets to new antiterrorism assignments, at the cost of other priorities, the public interest suffers. In Philadelphia, since narcotics detectives were reassigned to patrol duties to safeguard historic buildings in the center city, drug-related homicides have risen by 50 percent. Similarly, nearly half of the sixty bank robberies in Richmond, Virginia, in 2001—a record high— were committed in the eight weeks following September 11. Most cities will not be able to enlarge police and law enforcement budgets sufficiently to combat both terrorism and other predation on the public, so those agencies will need larger and more regular federal and state financial support for personnel, overtime expenses, equipment, training, and coordination with other agencies than ever before.[63]

The provisions of the U.S.A. Patriot Act do not adequately address funding to combat computer-related crime. Neither does the law even begin to provide for necessary intelligence sharing by federal agencies with state and local law enforcement. The Police Executive Research Forum has reported that for prevention of and response to terrorism, police chiefs say that their departments need above all assistance with and funding for intelligence-gathering capabilities, technological equipment and training in its use, and federal sharing of intelligence.[64] The International Association of Chiefs of Police has promised, "Our legislative effort, concentrated in the United States, will be directed toward making intelligence gathering easier for law enforcement."[65]

In implementing the provisions of the U.S.A. Patriot Act, Attorney General John D. Ashcroft announced on November 8, 2001, that "defending our nation and the citizens of America against terrorist attacks is now our first and overriding priority. . . . We are engaged in an aggressive arrest and detention campaign of lawbreakers [over 1,000 arrests and detentions] with a single objective: to get terrorists off the streets before they can harm more Americans." He then described "ten new initiatives for the systematic reform and restructuring of the Department of Justice . . . a wartime reorganization and mobilization of the nation's justice and law enforcement resources." Those initiatives include reorganizing the Immigration and Naturalization Service into a bureau of immigration services and a bureau of immigration enforcement and making the prevention of terrorism the highest priority of the FBI in all of its law enforcement and national security mission. In the fifth of the ten initiatives, the attorney general insisted, "We must develop a seamless relation with state and local law-enforcement agencies." He then stressed the importance of information and intelligence sharing, *but only among federal criminal justice and counterintelligence personnel and operations and without any reference to state and local agencies and police.*[66]

It will be a great defeat for the public safety if we cannot find means beyond those in the U.S.A. Patriot Act and the initiatives of the Justice Department for federal agencies to make known to state and local agencies all intelligence that bears on the most effective allocation of their personnel and resources for prevention of terrorism and apprehension of suspects. Most jurisdictions have far more police than federal personnel. The public safety depends on the vigilance of police in the performance of their duties in all respects, including the community-oriented and problem-solving policing that are basic elements of domestic security. Their vigilance has the greatest effect when they know what to look and listen and search for. At the same time, the acquisition and use of intelligence depend on strict confidentiality and secrecy. Inadvertent betrayal of confidence can compromise informants, who may be tortured and murdered in reprisal, and can render useless irreplaceable methods of gathering intelligence. Intelligence sharing among federal, state, and local agencies can, therefore, best be undertaken by selected personnel with proper security clearances who work with a clear mutual understanding of how intelligence is to be conveyed and applied in practice.

How coordination is to be achieved among mayors, city managers, police chiefs, fire chiefs, and other local and state officials, with the Office of Homeland Defense, remains to be determined by legislation or executive order covering the authority and powers of that federal office. The directors of newly formed state-level offices of homeland security or public security, as well as state lieutenant governors and adjutant generals with similar responsibilities, should be qualified for the security clearances necessary to do their jobs. If they are not, antiterrorism responsibilities should be reassigned. The U.S. Congress should give high priority to measures that will make for reliable sharing of intelligence.

Congress should also repeal the McDade Act of 1999.[67] The amendment, named for Congressman Joseph M. McDade of Pennsylvania, compels federal agents and federal prosecutors to abide by state ethics laws, as in Oregon, that disallow dishonesty, deceit, and misrepresentation by public servants. The McDade Act makes undercover investigations, stings, covert operations, and some internal affairs investigations illegal. The McDade Act was a foolish law from the time of its enactment, because it obviously prohibited rightful forms of investigative procedure essential to the public safety. With respect to the threat of terrorism, the act blatantly jeopardizes the public interest. States such as Oregon need to refine their own ethics laws so that they prohibit dishonesty for private gain but do not make legitimate law enforcement practices illegal.

Active defense against terrorism should, if possible, include a trustworthy international police and law enforcement agency through which information on suspected and known terrorists can be shared. Interpol has never been that agency, because some of its 178 member nations, such as Iran, have been havens and sponsors of terrorism. Some member nations have been represented by law enforcement professionals, others by unqualified politicians. And some member nations subject individuals to criminal sanctions without due process and impose cruel and unusual punishments. Interpol's recently appointed secretary general, Ronald K. Noble—a former U.S. Treasury Department undersecretary—poses three questions:

- At what point do we begin to share information internationally about people we suspect of being engaged in planning to engage in terrorist activity?

- Is the world ready for an international criminal database accessible by the public sector and the private sector?

- Is the world prepared to have an international database where people not convicted of crimes but under suspicion are listed?[68]

In addressing those questions, police and law enforcement leaders should protect the security of intelligence-gathering methods and operations. They should also distinguish between people who are known to have committed terrorist acts but have never been convicted of crimes and those who are suspected but not known to be involved in terrorist activities. Many terrorists commit atrocities and then flee to safe havens in sponsor nations. They may be indicted by the nations where they have perpetrated those atrocities without being subject to apprehension, extradition, or conviction. Treating such terrorists as if we do not know whether they have committed terrorist acts is irresponsible and self-destructive. It is also self-destructive to rely on law enforcement and criminal justice agencies to do what should be done by military means.

Due regard for protection of the security of intelligence-gathering methods and operations should remind us, therefore, that it is not always in the public interest to prosecute terrorists in criminal courts. Frequently, it would be catastrophic to prosecute in U.S. courts international terrorists captured overseas. As Public Service Fellow Duncan Deville of Harvard University's John F. Kennedy School of Government and a former federal prosecutor has asserted, U.S. law provides:

[All] informants who are witnesses to events are subject to having their identities disclosed. . . . [A]ll payments made to witnesses must be reported to the court and to defendants during trial. . . . "[C]hain of custody" rules . . . demand that everyone (including U.S. operatives overseas) who comes into contact with evidence be prepared to testify openly in court. . . . The public record produced in any trial of terrorists is an intelligence bonanza for our enemies, revealing in detail all of our surveillance and infiltration techniques.[69]

Accordingly, if police learn through an international law enforcement information clearinghouse the location of a specific known terrorist, whether or not previously convicted of any crime, their knowledge may be of greater use to intelligence agencies and the military than to law enforcement and criminal justice personnel. Thus, Deville has recommended:

For foreign terrorists found overseas, when the president is satisfied by a preponderance of the evidence (not the "beyond a reasonable doubt" standard used in courts) that an individual is guilty of committing or planning large-scale violence in order to intimidate the U.S. government into granting his demands, he should make a very specific "lethal finding" and order U.S. military forces to kill this individual. In wartime such a policy would not appear to violate explicitly Executive Order 12333 (the prohibition against assassinations).[70]

That recommendation takes into account that the president as commander in chief has authority to counter foreign terrorism by means that law enforcement officials, including the attorney general, do not have either inside or outside the United States. Former U.S. Attorney General Griffin Bell has observed that "every recent president . . . has asserted the right to protect the country from foreign terrorists, even when doing so required covert domestic searches and electronic surveillance of U.S. citizens without any prior court approval."[71] Within the United States, in terrorism prevention and response involving suspects who are citizens or legal aliens, police and law enforcement personnel are bound by the Bill of Rights. The extent to which illegal aliens are protected by the Fourth Amendment is questionable, but until the Supreme Court rules definitively on the question, police should not exceed normal Fourth Amendment limits unless called upon to act under presidential counterterrorism authority.

On November 13, 2001, President Bush issued a military order covering "detention, treatment, and trial of certain noncitizens in the war against terrorism." The military order applies to any person not a U.S. citizen of whom there is reason to believe that the individual

> (i) is or was a member of the organization known as al Qaida; (ii) has engaged in, aided or abetted, or conspired to commit acts of international terrorism, or acts in preparation therefor, that have caused, threaten to cause, or have as their aim to cause, injury to or adverse effects on the United States, its citizens, national security, foreign policy, or economy; or (iii) has knowingly harbored one or more individuals described in subparagraphs (i) and (ii).[72]

The president's order directs that such individuals are to be placed under the control of the secretary of defense and to "be tried by military commission . . . with the military commission sitting as the triers of both fact and law . . . [and] conviction [and sentencing] only upon the concurrence of two-thirds of the members of the commission present at the time of the vote, a majority being present."[73] The president's order explicitly does not "authorize the disclosure of state secrets to any person not otherwise authorized to have access to them."[74] It gives military tribunals exclusive jurisdiction over offenses by any individual to whom the president's order applies:

> [T]he individual shall not be privileged to seek any remedy or maintain any proceeding, directly or indirectly, or to have any such remedy or proceeding sought on the individual's behalf, in (i) any court of the United States, or any State thereof, (ii) any court of any foreign nation, or (iii) any international tribunal.[75]

Understandably, the president's order has stirred great controversy over the protection of civil rights and civil liberties. Harold Hongju Koh, professor of international law at Yale and assistant secretary of state for human rights during the Clinton administration, wrote, "I hope never to see Osama bin Laden alive in the dock," but he insisted that if we do capture known or suspected al Qaeda terrorists, we should try them in our federal courts. Only then will we show "the world that American courts can give universal justice."[76] William Safire described the president's order as a case of "seizing dictatorial power" that will "corrupt our judicial tradition." The better way to proceed is to "turn [bin Laden's] cave into his crypt." To prevent terrorists like bin Laden from surrendering and making their trials into bully pulpits for worldwide publicity and propaganda, Safire urged President Bush to establish a policy of "'universal surrender': all of al Qaeda or none," no selective surrender by individual leaders.[77] Ultimately, the circumstances of bin Laden's death and sea burial raised objections from terrorist and Islamist groups. But his body was treated with respect and no one offered a serious alternative for ending his atrocities.

Safire argued further that the president's military order violates the *Uniform Code of Military Justice*, which "demands a public trial, proof beyond a reasonable doubt, an accused's voice in the selection of juries and right to choose counsel, unanimity in death sentencing and above all appellate review by civilians confirmed by the Senate." He concluded that in abandoning those provisions of the *Uniform Code*, President Bush had undermined the war on terrorism by committing an injustice that will cause foreign nations to refuse extradition of terrorist suspects to the United States.[78]

In contrast, Neal A. Richardson, a deputy district attorney in Denver, and Denver lawyer Spencer J. Crona have argued since 1996 that "it is illogical and unjust to bring the criminal justice system to bear on" terrorist attacks that threaten national security and assail the public with weapons of mass murder and destruction—weapons of war:

> After first being subjected to the immediate impact of the incident itself, the victims—including the American people generally—must then agonize over whether justice will be served while the usual judicial process goes forward at its incremental pace. Then, if the process achieves a conviction against the defendants, the jurors must endure the enraged threats hurled at them by the convicted enemy agents. This constitutes further terrorism against ordinary Americans doing a difficult civic duty.

Afterward, the arduous and expensive appellate process of reevaluation of the entire pretrial and trial proceedings begins. Thus the final terrorist act is committed on our collective bank account to fund the assurance of more-than-due process, with the ultimate outcome uncertain for perhaps decades.

Neither justice nor reason can survive such procedural abuse. It is legally and intellectually disingenuous to provide terrorists the same rights as persons accused of ordinary crimes against society. Our Bill of Rights was designed to protect individuals in society against the arbitrary exercise of government power. It is not meant to protect commando groups warring on society through arbitrary acts of mass violence.[79]

I agree with Safire and Koh that it is not the purpose of war measures against terrorists to take prisoners. I do not understand, though, how we would implement and verify a policy of "universal surrender." Al Qaeda has terrorist network cells inside the United States and throughout the world. Not all of the members are known to us, and, because of falsified identifications and the deliberate separation of terrorist cells from each other, the entire membership may not be known to anyone. Whose surrender would we demand before allowing anyone else to surrender? What would we do with terrorist leaders who laid down their arms and walked into the open?

Even if we could offer satisfactory answers to such questions, no matter how we conduct the war against terrorism, we will inevitably take into custody certain individuals to whom the president's military order applies. Therefore, we cannot evade two ethical questions: Is it in principle wrong to deny specific noncitizens access to normal due process in the criminal justice system? Can military tribunals as described in the president's military order in fact serve justice?

With respect to the first question, there are good, prudential reasons for preferring military tribunals to civilian criminal courts for the trials of specific terrorist suspects. I have described in chapter 17 above, "Police, the O. J. Simpson Trial, and Race," some of the severe flaws that now plague criminal trials and criminal justice procedures. We have at times gone beyond the presumption of innocence by requiring unreasonable standards of proof to dispel reasonable doubt, and we have corrupted jury composition by conflating the distinction between a prospective juror who can be objective and impartial and a prospective juror who is instead only ignorant and manipulable. Such patterns of excess undermine due process, and they do not serve either justice or public safety in normal criminal trials. Neither would they do so in trials of individuals to whom the president's military order applies.

But those prudential considerations do not answer our ethical question about the justice of trying specific suspected terrorists in military tribunals. Rather, the justification for doing so is that the provisions of the *Uniform Code of Military Justice* definitely apply to trials of foreign nationals who are not members of armed forces and to suspected spies and agents of espionage.[80] No one can legitimately question the president's authority to issue a military order directing that specific terrorist suspects be tried in military tribunals. Much of the current controversy about the president's military order is therefore beside the point. The real question, as Safire has understood, is the extent to which the president's military order must comply with the provisions of the *Uniform Code of Military Justice*.

To what extent does the president have discretion in a war against terrorism to set the terms for the conduct of those tribunals? During the Civil War, Abraham Lincoln unilaterally suspended rights of habeas corpus. During World War II, Franklin D. Roosevelt exercised extrajudicial power in having suspected German saboteurs tried in a secret military court. The court was convened at FBI headquarters. Ultimately, the Supreme Court upheld the president. Disagreements about the rightness of Lincoln's and Roosevelt's acts have raged ever since among political theorists, philosophers, political scientists, and legal scholars. Has President Bush the right to follow in the steps of Lincoln and Roosevelt?

The *Uniform Code*, section 836, article 36, establishes that, within limits, the "president may prescribe rules" for the conduct of military tribunals:

> (a) Pretrial, trial, and posttrial procedures, including modes of proof, for cases arising under this chapter triable in courts-martial, military commissions and other military tribunals, and procedures for courts of inquiry, may be prescribed by the President by regulations which shall, so far as he considers practicable, apply the principles of law and the rules of evidence generally

recognized in the trial of criminal cases in the United States district courts, but which may not be contrary to or inconsistent with this chapter.[81]

The *Uniform Code* guarantees defendants the opportunity to cross-examine witnesses "if they are available" and establishes that "if there is a reasonable doubt as to the guilt of the accused, the doubt must be resolved in favor of the accused."[82] The *Uniform Code* also establishes procedures for appellate review through the U.S. Court of Military Appeals and to the U.S. Supreme Court.[83] Must the president's military order conform to those provisions? How much latitude is given the president by the phrase "so far as he considers practicable"?

As Richardson and Crona have argued, noncitizens suspected of affiliation with specific terrorist groups and of engagement in acts of war against the United States have no constitutional grounds for claiming all of the constitutional rights of citizens, including citizens who commit crimes. If the president's military order falls under the *Uniform Code*, what rights *must* be secured for those noncitizens? The president's military order secures specific rights by requiring that detainees be accorded humane treatment and be provided with adequate sustenance and water as well as needed medical care. The order guarantees the free exercise of religion within the limits of custody and prohibits adverse discrimination.[84] Are those sufficient?

With respect to the second question, whether military tribunals can in fact serve justice, the president's order leaves much in the way of implementation and procedure to the authority of the secretary of defense, but within specific limits. Respect for those limits; respect for the fundamental purposes of the attendant requirement that the secretary of defense establish "rules for the conduct of proceedings of military commissions, including pretrial, trial, and posttrial procedures, modes of proof, issuance of process, and qualifications of attorneys"; and respect for human dignity itself contribute to the possibility of both procedural justice and just verdicts in military tribunals. By the terms of the order, it is also true that the ruling of a military commission in a specific tribunal may not be the last word. Although the order prohibits appeal to other tribunals, it does not prohibit review and final decision by the secretary of defense or the president, and it does not limit the authority of the president to grant reprieves and pardons.[85]

Ultimately, therefore, the answer to our first ethical question is no. It is not wrong in principle to deny specific noncitizens the right to normal due process in the criminal justice system. Ample moral justification exists for trying them in military tribunals. The answer to our second question, whether the military tribunals conducted under the president's order can serve justice, depends on the pretrial, trial, and posttrial rules and procedures established by the secretary of defense and the president. If those rules and procedures depart from the provisions of the *Uniform Code*, the executive branch will be obligated to show that the departures are compatible with the achievement of justice and due protection of the civil rights of the accused.

Racial Profiling and the Public Trust

Some legal experts criticize the U.S.A. Patriot Act as discriminatory against immigrants. Georgetown University law professor David Cole said in an interview on *The NewsHour*, "Under this law, we impose guilt by association on immigrants. We make them deportable, not for their acts but for their associations, wholly innocent associations with any proscribed organization, you're deportable."[86] His criticism seems unwarranted since, as I have noted above, the law applies *only* to any "immigrant who has been associated with a terrorist organization and intends while in the United States to engage . . . in activities that could endanger the welfare, safety, or security of the United States." Association alone is insufficient.

A September 23, 2001, *New York Times* headline said, "Americans Give in to Race Profiling: Once Appalled by the Practice, Many Say They Now Do It." The article reported, "A CNN/*USA Today*/Gallup poll taken a few days after the attacks showed that Americans were supporting special measures intended for those of Arab descent. In the survey, 58 percent backed more intensive security checks for Arabs, including those who are United States citizens, compared with other travelers; 49 percent favored special identification cards for such people, and 32 percent backed 'special surveillance' for them."[87]

In the column "'Racial Profiling' and Terrorism," *Wall Street Journal* senior editorial writer Jason L. Riley reported:

Two respected pollsters have reported that blacks, the frequent target of profiling, are now more likely than other racial groups to favor it. Seventy-one percent of black respondents to a Gallup poll, and 54% in a Zogby poll, said they want Arab-looking travelers singled out for extra scrutiny at airports. And when the *Detroit News*, whose readership includes one of the nation's largest Arab-American enclaves, conducted its own survey last month, it found that even Arabs want lookalikes checked.[88]

Riley claimed that extra surveillance and closer inspections for Arabs, now that "the nation is at war," are not pernicious in the way of random traffic stops because of race:

Of the 19 hijackers responsible for last month's calamity, all were Arabic, all were practitioners of Islam and all came from known state incubators of terrorism in the Middle East. Of the 22 suspects on the FBI's "most wanted" list of international terrorists, all are Arabic, all are practitioners of Islam and all come from known state incubators of terrorism in the Middle East. Not "some" of them, or a "disproportionate number" of them. All of them.

Those numbers dictate that any sensible domestic effort to expose terrorist cells would include concentrating on particular groups in particular communities associated with a particular culture. To ignore the fact that America's enemies in this war share a faith and ethnicity—and that their actions, by their own reckoning, are ethnically and religiously inspired—would be self-deluding and foolish.[89]

Should police conclude that because of changes in public attitudes and in our circumstances since September 11, racial and ethnic profiling are no longer wrong? No, they should not. They should familiarize themselves with the suspects on the FBI's "most wanted" list and with others suspected of terrorist activity and be prepared to act, should they see anyone who resembles any of those suspects. They should cultivate sources, and use existing sources, of information in the neighborhoods and precincts where they work. They should establish regular procedures for using to the fullest criminal investigation databases and information systems, including the El Paso Intelligence Center and Regional Information Sharing Systems. They should work as closely as possible with federal counterterrorism agencies and with law enforcement and police agencies in their region by sharing relevant information regularly and promptly. Police and law enforcement agencies should also be linked to corporate security agencies and to the National Infrastructure Protection Center and the FBI's InfraGard network for the security of business, industry, academic institutions, and other elements of our national infrastructure.

Police departments and law enforcement agencies should train their personnel in the patterns of behavior that might disclose terrorist intent and establish the habit of looking for and keeping track of unusual as well as suspicious behavior, irrespective of a person's ethnicity or color. Preoccupation with color and ethnicity can divert police and law enforcement personnel from noticing unusual behavior. Working in cooperation, agencies can identify behavior that merits attention, especially when they are allowed to share intelligence across local, state, and federal lines. Proper training and interagency cooperation will deepen understanding of the circumstances under which it is reasonable to be suspicious that terrorist acts have been, will be, or are being committed. Surveillance conducted by federal agencies within the limits imposed by the U.S.A. Patriot Act, provided that information can be shared with state and local agencies, should be far more effective in combating terrorism than any form of profiling based solely on racial or ethnic characteristics could be.[90]

On October 29, 2001, Los Angeles County Sheriff Leroy Baca described a model of such interagency cooperation to the U.S. House Subcommittee on Domestic Preparedness for Terrorist Attacks. He explained that several of his deputies have security clearances that facilitate their work with the FBI as members of a joint antiterrorism task force. The task force also includes representatives from the Los Angeles Police Department, forty-five Los Angeles County police agencies, the district attorney's office, the coroner's office, the Department of Health Services, the California Highway Patrol, the Los Angeles Airport Police, the National Guard, the U.S. Coast Guard, the Federal Aviation Administration, and private-sector security agencies. Properly managed, with the right security clearances and adequate technology, those agencies should be able to share a great deal of information and intelligence relevant to coordinated efforts to safeguard the public from potential terrorists and terrorist cells—and certainly without any practices that border on racial profiling.

It was wrong before September 11 for police to stop, interdict, or detain a person solely because of color or ethnicity. It is still wrong. That constraint does not diminish the capacity of police and law enforcement agencies to impose rigorous identification standards in airports, since everyone who flies should be subject to careful inspection. Neither does it foreclose rigorous inspections of people traveling by other means, including rental trucks and cars, if their behavior bears a resemblance to behavior identified in intelligence reports.

The public interest would be dangerously threatened, however, if Congress were to enact S. 989, "The End Racial Profiling Act of 2001." That piece of legislation presumes the guilt of police departments by making "proof that the routine investigatory activities of law enforcement agents in a jurisdiction have had a disparate impact on racial or ethnic minorities" stand as "prima facie evidence of a violation of this title." But statistical proof of "disparate impact" does not provide any evidence at all of disparate treatment in any instance or any collection of instances. The legislation rests on the grave but elementary logical mistake of supposing that a gross statistic reveals the nature of individual cases. The logical flaw of S. 989 leads to completely indefensible consequences: Because police departments are presumed guilty on the basis of a statistic that proves nothing relevant to guilt, plaintiffs who prevail can recover attorney's fees, but police departments found not guilty cannot.[91] If enacted, the law will do nothing to safeguard the public, but it will harm the public by undermining police departments and responsible policing. Fortunately, no action has been taken on "The End Racial Profiling Act" since August 2001.

As the nation and its police and law enforcement agencies expand efforts to prevent and combat terrorism, new questions about legitimate and illegitimate practices will inevitably arise. On November 9, 2001, Attorney General Ashcroft set in motion a plan to interview five thousand men between the ages of eighteen and thirty-three who have since January 2000 come into the United States from countries where terrorist acts against the United States have originated. Federal officials have requested assistance from local police departments in finding and questioning those men, whom the Justice Department identifies not as suspects but as "potential witnesses 'who may have information'" that would contribute to the investigation of the September 11 attacks.[92]

A spokeswoman for the Justice Department, Mindy Tucker, "compared the interview project to a neighborhood canvass after a murder. 'This is a preventive effort, focused on information gathering. The instructions are clear. These are voluntary interviews, and anyone who doesn't want to answer questions doesn't have to.'"[93]

The interviews, which are to be done in homes rather than in police stations, are therefore different from racial profiling stops, interdictions, and detentions. Still, some police leaders have declined to provide assistance to federal agencies for one or more of three reasons: that the project smacks of racial profiling and would undercut hard-won gains and mutual trust and reliance between police and public; that questioning immigrants who are not suspected of crimes violates state laws or constitutions; and that such interviews are an offense to the fundamental rights of individuals. Other chiefs accept the analogy to a postmurder canvass and have expressed their willingness to cooperate in the interview project. Some of those chiefs have arranged meetings with local Arab and Muslim leaders to affirm that all the interviews are voluntary and to promise that the police will twist no arms of individuals who prefer not to be interviewed.[94]

The great majority of the five thousand young men sought for interviews are Middle Eastern, even though national origin is irrelevant to their inclusion on the federal list of possible witnesses. Identifying individuals as possible sources of information because of where they have been immediately before entering the United States is not a case of racial or ethnic profiling. Requesting that individuals voluntarily answer questions is no abridgement of their right to say no.

Nonetheless, many of those men may be unfamiliar with their rights inside the United States. Police are obligated not to exploit their ignorance. Police and law enforcement personnel may undertake interviews well or badly, respectfully or abusively. Police who have successfully built trust with the populations in the jurisdictions they serve will already know how to conduct voluntary interviews properly, and they are not likely to squander trust they have worked hard to build. There, too, individual integrity—

dedication to justice in practice—provides the greatest assurance that the rights and concerns of immigrants will be accorded the respect and consideration they are due.

Integrity and Professionalism: John P. O'Neill

As the public and public servants, including police and law enforcement personnel, strive to prevent the depredations of terrorists, all of us should remember that the nature of integrity never changes. Twenty-four hundred years ago, Greek historian Xenophon said this about two Greek generals who, along with others, had been tricked and then executed by the treacherous Tissaphernes of Persia: "No one ever scorned them for any cowardice in war or complained about any fault in their friendships."[95]

On September 11, 2001, my friend John P. O'Neill died in the treacherous mass murder at the World Trade Center. He, too, was a man of unflinching bravery, unfailing friendship, and probity in professional life.

I met O'Neill in Baltimore in 1980, when I first began to work at the FBI Academy and in FBI field offices. He had been a special agent since 1976 in the Baltimore field office, after he had started as a clerk in 1970 when he was a teenager. We became friends, and over the years, dear friends.

During his distinguished career in the FBI, he led investigations of organized crime, white-collar crime, governmental fraud, violent crime, and terrorism. In 1993 he participated in the investigation of the World Trade Center bombing and was instrumental in the arrest of the perpetrators. In 1995 he became chief of the FBI's Counterterrorism Section at FBI headquarters. Responsible for the leadership of FBI investigations of domestic and international terrorism, including the 1998 bombings of U.S. embassies in Kenya and Tanzania and the 2000 bombing of the U.S.S. *Cole* off the coast of Yemen, O'Neill documented the terrorist aims and deeds of bin Laden and al Qaeda. In 1997 he was named special agent in charge of the National Security Division of the New York City field office.

As the most accomplished counterterrorism investigator in FBI history, O'Neill helped to thwart terrorist plots against our country as early as the mid-1980s. In August 2001 he retired from the FBI to become director of security for the World Trade Center. On the morning of September 11, he made his way from his thirty-fourth-floor offices to the street to assess damage from the first terrorist attack. Then, he returned to the building to help rescue others and died when the building collapsed.

John P. O'Neill taught me a very great deal about law enforcement, crime, and terrorism. I relied heavily on his counsel in drafting my lectures, articles, and books. He took me on the streets with him, as did members of the Chicago Police Department Narcotics, Gang Enforcement, and Homicide units, when he was assistant special agent in charge of the Chicago Violent Crimes Task Force. The thousands of hours I have spent on the streets with police in the United States, the Caribbean, and in foreign countries where narcotics trafficking and homicide are most out of control have been essential to my competence, and I owe John P. O'Neill, as I owe many others, for all I have learned from them.

In his conduct of professional life, O'Neill embodied the ideals of the FBI seal: Fidelity, Bravery, Integrity. In a friendship lasting more than twenty years, I never saw him flinch—not from ambitious bureaucrats and politicians whose invincible ignorance has been a blight on federal law enforcement and antiterrorism, not from incompetent political appointees in the Justice Department and the White House who have done enormous damage to the FBI and the DEA, and not from physical danger in the field. *Of course* he walked back into the tower to help others. Anything else would have been utterly out of character for him.

Conclusion

The perpetration of horrific acts cannot change human nature or the nature of integrity. Confrontation with terrorism cannot yield total unity of resolve and conviction in a complex society. Exposure to horror does not inspire everyone to be a better person, a better citizen. The world does not stop when terrorists strike and then reopen as an entirely new world afterward. Today, as on September 12, 2001, and likewise on September 10, 2001, the United States is an experiment in ordered liberty that cannot succeed without trustworthy and dedicated police who know what they are doing. The rest of the free world and all those who yearn to breathe free deserve the same.

Some of us are learning what Winston Churchill meant when he described the cast of mind and heart among Londoners subjected to Hitler's Nazi bombings during the blitz as "defiant mourning": adamantine resolve forged in grief. Freedom has always depended on resolve and vigilance despite adversity and grief. Today is no different.

If we have courage as adults, we will protect our young from emotional ruin by terrorism. When Abraham Lincoln's friend, the father of Fanny McCullough, was slain in battle, Lincoln wrote the girl:

> In this sad world of ours, sorrow comes to all; and to the young, it comes with bitterest agony, because it takes them unawares. The older have learned ever to expect it. I am anxious to afford some alleviation of your present distress. . . . [W]ith time . . . the memory of your dear Father, instead of an agony, will yet be a sad sweet feeling in your heart, of a purer, and holier sort than you have known before.[96]

Our children deserve the same compassionate instruction—and the same truthfulness about the inevitability of sorrow.

I will remember the words of a little boy in an elementary school within sight of the World Trade Center that were reported to my Boston University colleagues and me by a school superintendent who is one of our graduates. The little boy's comprehension did not reach to the idea of people in flames leaping in desperation, beyond all hope except that of choosing their manner of death, from buildings a quarter of a mile high. After staring through a window toward the conflagration and witnessing death unawares, the child fled toward his teacher, crying aloud, "Teacher, teacher, the birds are on fire." Civilized countries use their powers to prevent terrorists from forcing such horror on children.

I do not share the consolations of those who find solace in saying that the atrocities of September 11 have this or that silver lining. I do have questions: Will the visibility of New York's Finest—in the unflinching and unassuming heroism of police and firefighters—affect for the better the capacity of police departments to attract and retain larger numbers of very good recruits? Will the heroism of those police teach a broad public that the NYPD as a whole is not accurately characterized by the susceptibility to panic that caused

Amadou Diallo's death or by the perversity and sadism in Justin Volpe's sodomization of Abner Louima? Will public attitudes toward police nation-wide, and of police toward the public, grow wiser, or will there be a short period of rosy feeling without a gain in more durable mutual reliance and respect? Will a significant portion of the population ask more of itself in civic responsibility, and thus reach greater cooperation with police? Will new fund-ing for police and law enforcement training and coordination be applied without compromise to the achievement of the highest standards of perform-ance and to overcoming old habits and jealousies of turf?

Over one hundred years ago, philosopher William James wrote that "no one sees farther into a generalization than his own knowledge of details extends."[97] Will we teach the newcomers to policing and law enforcement how to learn, and continue to gain access to, all the details of terrorism and terrorists they need to know to uphold and defend the Constitution in daily practice? Will we demonstrate to them that they cannot responsibly base profiles on generalizations about skin color and ethnicity that collapse as soon as we examine the relevant details?

The moment is upon us when we must decide whether we will yield to the coercion of those who would force us by outrage to bargain with them. That is a moral decision of fateful proportion to be made once and then lived with forever. It has no sunset clause. This, too, we must teach our children. Our experiment in ordered liberty—"securing the blessings of liberty to ourselves and our posterity"—depends for its maintenance on our decision.

21

Ethics in Action: Case Studies of Professional Excellence in Policing

Tell me, who it was who first declared . . . that a man does evil only because he does not know his real interests, and if he is enlightened and has his eyes opened to his best and normal interests, man will cease to do evil and at once become virtuous and noble . . . and since it is well known that no man can knowingly act against his best interests, consequently he will inevitably, so to speak, begin to do good. Oh, what a baby!

—Fyodor Dostoyevsky[1]

During more than thirty years of working with police and law enforcement personnel (and in the associated fields of prosecutions and corrections), I have been deeply impressed by the outstanding character and thorough competence of many of the public servants I've known. These two traits are not unrelated. Good character and competence are the principal criteria of fitness to bear the public trust. The future of policing and law enforcement as a profession depends on the women and men who meet them.

In this final chapter, it is important to emphasize the future of policing as a profession and the level of work and standards—ethical and professional—that are required for policing to achieve the level of professional excellence necessary to prevent crime effectively and protect the public. Key to understanding this is an in-depth examination of law enforcement agencies, as well as the work of individual police officers, who may be seen as exemplars of what is best in policing today, and the attributes that make them so.

While policing has not everywhere achieved professional excellence, there are certainly agencies and individuals who have made tremendous progress in this regard, and who serve as outstanding examples for everyone concerned with issues related to character and cops. The police I have come to know who embody professional excellence, whether in uniform or in different specialized assignments, are conscientious learners, acute observers, and rigorous thinkers. With penetrating insight, they see beyond superficial first impressions. They know what to look and listen for, what to ask, what to tell one another, what to hold in confidence. They talk to criminals in jails and prisons and on the streets, because, as one very able cop in gang intelligence and enforcement recently said to me, "If you want to understand gangs, you talk with gangsters." Many of them travel at their own expense to learn all they can from more experienced colleagues in distant jurisdictions. They also travel to teach police in other jurisdictions, from coast to coast, how to do difficult jobs more effectively.

Despite the din of media "experts" chattering about every social problem, the best police and law enforcement personnel concentrate tirelessly on details, and dismiss simplistic explanations and quick fixes. They are relentless in their pursuit of the truth. Mindful of both strategic and tactical planning, some of them foresee social dangers and criminal trends far better than celebrated pundits. And, of course, all of them live and work by the ethical standards that are the subject of this book. In fact, adherence to and belief in these standards by departments and individual officers likely go hand in hand with achievement of professional excellence. It is doubtful that the unethical officer or police department would go the extra mile to improve the quality of work they do.

Among those officers I've worked with who embodied professional excellence, I have found these men and women to be resolute in trying to prevent and reduce criminal predation, unravel criminal conspiracies, identify and apprehend criminal suspects, and understand the ideas and motives behind heinous crimes of fraud and violence. Day after day, many of them deal with extreme evils of criminal malice. They do their duty, without complaint. They go out of their way to help one another, and they don't give up. Working with them has been one of the greatest satisfactions of my career.

The future of policing as a profession depends upon police departments throughout the country emulating the ideals of competence, service, courage, integrity, and other hallmarks of ethical behavior demonstrated by these people, and upon the creation of policy that will enable their furtherance and allow policing to come fully into its own as a profession.

In this chapter, I present case studies of law enforcement personnel and agencies that are currently demonstrating how professional excellence can be attained in police work based upon the ethical principles this book has discussed. In the first section, "Pursuit of Truth," I look at the work of clinical psychologist and former FBI special agent Dwayne Fuselier and Michigan State University psychiatrist Dr. Frank Ochberg. In their investigation and analysis of the mass murder at Columbine High School in 1999, they persisted relentlessly in debunking a well-established conventional wisdom about the killers' motivations, revealing some very unpopular truths, and in so doing identified profound differences from typical school shootings, with important implications for effectively dealing with such crimes in the future.

Also demonstrating "ethics in action" is the Los Angeles Police Department. In "Ethics Restored," I describe the reforms the Rampart Division of the LAPD undertook in the wake of the corruption scandals of the 1990s, as mentioned in chapter 19 of this book. Police authorities in Los Angeles have demonstrated not only how professionalism based on ethics and integrity can transform a division of a large police department that has been harmed by the shameful malfeasance and ignominy of some of its sworn personnel, but also how the effectiveness of that department can be improved by it.

"Competence and Cooperation" showcases the Fairfax County Police Department in northern Virginia. Through professional excellence based upon the highest levels of competence, interagency cooperation, and community involvement, they have kept at bay in Fairfax County the gang problems that are threatening so many other parts of the country.

Finally, in an examination of one agency's response to new demands on police professionalism in a post-9/11 world, I review the outstanding efforts of the New York State Office of Homeland Security in working against terrorism while safeguarding civil liberties and privacy.

In Pursuit of Truth: Investigating Mass Murder at Columbine

One of the ethical obligations of a true professional is to reject easy answers and conventional wisdom and persistently pursue the truth. In Fuselier and

Ochberg's investigation and analysis of the mass murder at Columbine High School in 1999, they identified profound differences from typical school shootings and provided important insights into such shootings that could help us prevent them in the future.

In the aftermath of the Columbine mass murder, much was published in the popular media that was not true. Media reports continually portrayed shooters Eric Harris and Dylan Klebold as outcasts who were repeatedly bullied in school, and suggested that this was what drove them to commit their heinous crime—similar to the motivation in many other recent school shootings. However, there is no evidence that Harris and Klebold had been victimized by high school bullies. They had not been ridiculed, isolated, or intimidated by athletes or other students. They were not friendless loners and outcasts. And they were not actually members of a group at the high school called "The Trench Coat Mafia," as media reports led people to believe.

While the characterization of Harris and Klebold as mere school shooters who acted in reprisal for being bullied outcasts seems inconsequential on the surface, such supposed knowledge that is actually false can cause a great deal of harm. Where is the harm in this misconception? It lies in the potential misdirection of valuable resources to strategies for preventing future school shootings that will ultimately prove ineffective. Following the Columbine massacre, tracing mass murders in schools to explosive rage over having been bullied and humiliated became fashionable, far beyond what the evidence would support. Antibullying legislation was passed and government funding devoted to research on bullying, neither having anything perceptible to do with the Columbine tragedy.

It is only because of the efforts of individuals who understood their ethical obligation to seek out the truth and not settle for the easy and popular answers that we know this now. Once the killers had been identified and the conventional explanations for their actions generally accepted, law enforcement officials and other agencies involved in the case could easily have stopped the investigation. After all, that motive was widely portrayed in the media, and there were no living suspects to be prosecuted in this case. But a group of investigators didn't stop here. An FBI summit on Columbine consisting of highly regarded mental health personnel showed that the killers at Columbine, especially Harris, were not after revenge. Further analysis by Fuselier and Ochberg has shown that the shootings were but a small part of the overall agenda Harris and Klebold had set for themselves.

On April 20, 2004, the fifth anniversary of Columbine, Fuselier, who led the FBI investigation of the murders and served on the FBI summit panel, and Ochberg, his summit colleague, released their analysis and findings on Harris.[2] They identified him as a remorseless, monomaniacal killer, a psychopath with a huge superiority complex who felt contempt for the entire human species. In their documented account, Harris sought to commit indiscriminate murder on a scale unprecedented in the United States.

In his journal, Harris elevated pet peeves to self-glorifying, monumental disdain for everyone. He ranted arrogantly about his disgust with humanity, even though he knew very little about human history and accomplishment. He persistently lied for the pleasure and self-aggrandizement of getting away with it and feigned remorse to avoid punishment for wrongdoing. Once, after apprehension for breaking into a vehicle to steal property, he sent a written expression of regret and empathy to his victims, but he wrote in his journal,

> Isn't America supposed to be the land of the free? How come, if I'm free, I can't deprive a stupid, f...ing, dumbshit from his possessions if he leaves them sitting on the front seat of his f...ing van out in plain sight and in the middle of f...ing nowhere on a Frif...ing night? NATURAL SELECTION. F...er should be shot.

Harris was shrewd enough to be regarded by some as "nice." Yet in a videotape, he and Klebold boasted that at Columbine they would eclipse the death count of the McVeigh/Nichols Oklahoma City bombing. Klebold, a depressed, impulsive boy, seems not to have blamed others for his troubles. Although different from Harris in that he might have been steered away from violent predation by insightful professional intervention, he was a willing partner during the year they planned the Columbine massacre.

From Harris's journal and videotape and from the murders he committed, Fuselier and Ochberg inferred that he had not targeted any specific victims. He chose the school as his crime scene because the large number of people gathered there would give him the chance to commit mass murder with the highest body count in American history.

Columbine was supposed to be a massive massacre by bombs. According to law enforcement estimates, if the twenty-pound pipe bombs surrounded by propane cylinders Harris and Klebold had rigged in the Columbine school cafeteria had exploded at 11:16 in the morning as planned, more than six hundred of the nine hundred students and faculty present would have been killed. At 11:25, Harris and Klebold entered the cafeteria and tried unsuccessfully to detonate the bombs with gunfire. Although fewer than five hundred people were still there, hundreds would have died in the structural collapse triggered by the explosions.

Harris and Klebold also rigged bombs in their cars in the school parking lot to explode at noon. Had they gone off, they would have killed untold numbers of students, school personnel, deputies, police, firefighters, rescue workers, emergency medical technicians, doctors, nurses, and rescue workers, as well as casualties carried from the school. Clearly, Harris and Klebold wanted their planned carnage in the parking lot to be broadcast on live television. And by noon, they would have been positioned to shoot the fleeing survivors of that carnage, as the last of their mass murder strategy.

Harris knew just what he was doing. He freely chose to do evil for evil's sake and for the fame (or infamy) he thought his actions would bring him. I think he took pleasure in imagining others, all supposedly inferior to himself and with no right to exist, dying at his hands. As Fuselier and Ochberg rightly observed, there is no telling how great a massacre Harris might have achieved had he waited until he had acquired greater expertise in the use of explosives or found his way into circles with access to more powerful weapons.

We may be tempted to think that such a person must have suffered some abuse or mistreatment or humiliation in childhood or youth against which he could not defend himself and over which he had no opportunity to express his anger, resentment, and outrage. This is the thesis of the Swiss psychotherapist, Alice Miller, who attempted to analyze violent conduct and explain why Hitler and other genocidal tyrants became who they were.[3] But I think insistence on the perpetrator's prior victimization neglects undeniable elements of human nature and facts of individual behavior.

In my conversations and correspondence with those involved in and close to the Columbine investigations, I have learned that no one has found evidence of any such abuse in Eric Harris's home or school life and background. They found no references to abuse in Harris's journal or videotape. The thoroughness and depth of the investigations do not absolutely prove that there never was any abuse; but they suggest that the likelihood of any kind of serious abuse is extremely small. It is dangerous to suppose that everyone who might be resolutely determined to slaughter innocent people, as Harris was, can be identified and helped by antibullying programs, or that all school massacres have a single, easily identified and predictable underlying cause in prior victimization.

Human nature and human life are more complex than that, not least in our capacity to imagine that we have been wronged or humiliated by others. We blame self-caused troubles on others in no way responsible; we hate the world instead of hating our own vices. Because human nature is so complex, securing the public safety as fully as possible takes greater insight into human nature than popular accounts of the causes of violence provide. This is why the principled excellence demonstrated by Fuselier and Ochberg in seeking out the truth in this case, rather than accepting the readily available media explanation for the killings, is so important. Without this kind of work, the root causes of various types of criminal events will never be discovered, and countless resources will be wasted on intervention efforts that will ultimately prove ineffective as they target the wrong individuals and the wrong problems.

The kind of professional excellence found in the work of Fuselier and Ochberg will become ever more important in policing and law enforcement. They remind us that a person can know actions to be evil and nonetheless commit them. Their analysis of Harris depicts a quite extraordinary, but entirely human, malice capable of deliberately producing massive misery with relish. Many of those making public policy and educating the young seem blind to these possibilities in human thought, feeling, and action. It is easier to believe the readily available explanations of being driven to commit such atrocious acts by some form of abuse than to accept that some people simply have the capacity to do such grievous harm to other human beings through their own, unprovoked free will.

Human history is no stranger to endless varieties of misanthropy. Pascal seems wisely to have grasped something of the vast range of evil motives and actions, observing that "evil is easy, and has infinite forms."[4] The insights gained by Fuselier and Ochberg from their investigation of Eric Harris and Columbine help us to grapple with daunting facts about human nature that will be increasingly salient in policing and law enforcement in the post-9/11 landscape.

However, it is clear that most of us still have problems accepting this notion of people who are simply evil. Dwayne Fuselier has written to me,

> When I have spoken to groups about what happened at Columbine High School, and offered my opinion of the motives of Eric Harris and Dylan Klebold, I have found that listeners can more readily accept and understand Dylan's depression and suicidality, but in general, have a difficult time accepting that Eric Harris wanted to hurt people he had never met; and that he simply didn't care how his actions would affect their lives and moreover, the lives of his own family. I have found that since most people have internalized the mores of their society and developed a "conscience" (although not always perfect), and haven't had the opportunity (thankfully) to repeatedly deal with those who haven't, they have a difficult time accepting that "people could feel and act that way toward others."[5]

Many of us do, indeed, find it hard to accept the possibility that there are among us conscienceless predators filled with malice. As a teacher of philosophy, I regularly encounter such difficulty among students. Their innocence is touching in its trust in a benign human nature. But it is also dangerous in its blindness to the threat posed by remorseless predators. The safety of the public depends on police who stand day and night in harm's way with both the wisdom to understand how gravely dangerous human malice can be and the courage to remain steadfast.

Fuselier and Ochberg tackled the horrors of Columbine without flinching, knowing that respect for the truth is no impediment to compassion.

Their commitment to their profession's ethical obligation to seek out the truth led them to take steps to inform both the public and others in law enforcement about the real "why" behind the Columbine tragedy, rather than accepting the widespread, and more easily acceptable, belief that the horror resulted from abuse and bullying. That is professionalism at its best.

Dwayne Fuselier and Frank Ochberg undertook their work with the intellectual humility of true scientists who understand that new evidence uncovered in the future may require refinement of current analyses and conclusions drawn from the past preponderance of evidence. Their work, and the manner in which they did it, added to the experience of police and other public servants who deal with murderers of every kind.

Fuselier's intellectual probity and courage in the investigation are all the more striking because his son, then fifteen years old, was in the school cafeteria at the beginning of the Harris/Klebold rampage. He was not harmed. "My involvement with the Columbine High School shootings was one of the most emotional matters I was involved in during my FBI career," Fuselier told me. Yet his being a parent as well as an FBI supervisor added to his determination: "The dual perspective as the FBI's investigative supervisor and as a Columbine parent was one of the many aspects of this incident that continuously drove me to understand the 'why.'"6

Fuselier's sense of proportion about his own work further exemplifies the highest standards of ethics in police and law enforcement. "I don't think I did anything during the investigation that any other FBI supervisor wouldn't have done," he told me. "I was just doing my job." My account of his professionalism in the Columbine investigation is, he says, "even more reflective of the character of thousands of cops around the U.S. and the world."

Ethics Restored: Reform in the Los Angeles Police Department

In chapter 19 of this book, I described the dreadful moral problems—scandalous betrayals of the public trust—that occurred among some police in the Rampart area of Los Angeles in 1996 and 1997. So extreme were these catastrophes of brutality and corruption that it was not until March 31, 2005, that city officials announced the settlement of almost all civil lawsuits stemming from the Rampart Division police scandal, at a total cost of $70 million. Even so, police chief William Bratton has said that he suspects "that some officers who committed misconduct related to the scandal remained on the job." Nevertheless, "knowing is not necessarily proving." Two hundred and fourteen claims were resolved, with 179 of them settled in payouts averaging $400,000.[7]

In the summer of 2004, I was invited to Los Angeles by LAPD captains Deborah McCarthy and Charlie Beck, with whom I had worked while teaching in the Senior Management Institute for Police offered in Boston by the Police Executive Research Forum, to review the reform of Rampart policing since the crisis. I was eager to see what the LAPD had accomplished.

Spectacular Transformation. In Rampart, I saw a spectacular transformation, demonstrating the profound effectiveness of fine leadership and splendid recruitment and training. I saw wise supervision and thorough accountability, a shared sense of purpose among colleagues of all ranks, and very sound strategic and tactical thinking about the police mission. Cooperation with city and county attorneys and state and federal law enforcement had also become a powerful asset in fulfillment of the police mission, easing in some measure a longstanding shortage of police personnel in Rampart.

Bratton may be right that some officers involved in the Rampart scandal of the mid-1990s remain in the Los Angeles Police Department. I cannot remember ever participating in a police or law enforcement investigation of large-scale brutality and corruption where we succeeded in acquiring legally admissible proof of wrongdoing against everyone we knew to be involved. But, regardless of this possibility, police in the Rampart Division now work in a place with powerful peer pressure against corruption and with exemplary standards of leadership and procedures for accountability at all ranks. Any corrupt officer in Rampart would now be surrounded by both uniformed and plainclothes personnel who have no tolerance for police wrongdoing and criminality. In short, the restoration of ethical standards into the police culture of the LAPD has created formal and informal barriers to the types of corruption that plagued the Rampart Division a decade ago.

Furthermore, as Mariana Vasquez of the Rampart Division explained to me, there are very good cops and staff members there who have stayed on since the scandal. They were outstanding at their work then, and they still are. They kept doing their work through thick and thin. They persisted undaunted by daily media pressures exerted outside Rampart Station by reporters eager to assume the worst. They remember what can be lost, and they rightly take pride in the resolute integrity and professionalism within the Rampart Division.

In its Professional Standards Bureau, the LAPD now has one of the best internal affairs divisions in the world. It is proactive not only because of consent decree provisions spawned by the scandal, but also as a matter of principle. I have cautioned elsewhere and often that neither human beings nor human institutions can be made perfect, and no institution can afford to be complacent about its hard-won achievements. But a great deal of honorable and effective effort has been spent in Rampart to bring policing to the highest possible levels of integrity and professional excellence.

The Professional Standards Bureau of the LAPD. Technology is vital to gathering evidence in internal affairs investigations, especially where testimonies conflict. Whether the outcome is guilt or innocence, investigations, due process, and resolution should be timely, for the sake of both the police and the public. Where guilt is established, sanctions should be imposed without delay. If a termination offense by a member of a department has been proved, that person should be dismissed immediately, instead of awaiting the result of a criminal prosecution. Such standards elevate the department's reputation, protect other departmental personnel from subjection to or suspicion of wrongdoing, and safeguard the public from further misuse of official power by a person who has betrayed the public trust. The Professional Standards Bureau of the LAPD holds to these ethical standards. Its leaders emphasize the importance of assuring members of the department and the public that no one proved unworthy will any longer wear the badge. Every time a fired officer is identified in the media as "formerly of the LAPD," this assurance is reaffirmed.

A case I observed in Los Angeles shows how these policies are applied. Two women in separate domestic violence incidents accused a uniformed officer of sexual assault. Each woman said the officer and his partner responded to her 911 call for assistance, entered the residence, and arrested and handcuffed the man she lived with. Then, they said, the officer ordered his partner to remove the man from the apartment and take him to their cruiser, locked the door behind him, and fondled her. Both women said the officer's partner had not witnessed the assaults. The officer denied the allegations.

The two women's descriptions of the assaults were so nearly identical that Professional Standards Bureau (PSB) investigators could not in good conscience merely dismiss them as unsubstantiated allegations. Instead, they put surveillance cameras in an apartment and staged a 911 call from a woman who said she was being attacked by her husband. Both the woman and the "husband" were undercover officers, who feigned drunkenness when the police arrived. The tape showed the officer doing exactly what he had been accused of doing. He and his partner separated the man from the woman and handcuffed him. The officer then directed his partner to remove the man from the apartment, locked the door behind him, and began to fondle the woman before telling her to sit down. The undercover officer turned to one of the cameras, unbeknownst to the officer under investigation, made a gagging face, and sat down. The evidence against the officer under investigation was irrefutable.

Acting in accordance with due process, the department found the officer guilty and dismissed him without further delay. Without awaiting a decision by the district attorney to prosecute the officer, the department rightly separated its work from the question of a criminal prosecution.

Based on instructive accounts given to me by Deborah McCarthy, and having worked on internal affairs in both Boston and New York with William Bratton and in other venues with Los Angeles deputy chief Michael Berkow, I believe this investigation was typical of the work of the LAPD Professional Standards Bureau. The fifteen-month restructuring of the Bureau in the light of a consent decree has also contributed to the department's overall effectiveness. The internal organization sensibly divides personnel responsibilities and assignments so as to enable both criminal and administrative investigations to be conducted and administrative complaints to be adequately reviewed. Current policies also provide for a wide variety of random and targeted means of encouraging, testing, and securing integrity and professional excellence.

Reform Increases Effectiveness. When I visited the Rampart Division in 2004, Captain Charlie Beck described to me the crisis in infrastructure and procedures that resulted in the collapse of trustworthy policing there in the 1990s, and the widespread impact this had on the ability of the police to perform their duties effectively. We discussed also the steps taken in Rampart to prevent any repetition of outrageous acts such as those committed by Rafael Perez and other lawbreaking police.

At that time, the police worked out of two separate buildings, but the police who worked in one of them were able to act largely without supervision. The division also suffered from the institutional breakdowns that have afflicted policing elsewhere: not enough sworn and support personnel; failures in personnel selection and training; inadequate dissemination of intelligence on gangs and organized crime because of insularity of units; and shortcomings in oversight, review, and accountability. Breakdowns in cooperation were endemic with corrections, parole, and probations; with the Los Angeles City Attorney's Office, the Los Angeles County District Attorney's Office, and the Los Angeles Sheriff's Department; with the California State Attorneys and the California Highway Patrol; and, on the federal level, with Immigration and Customs Enforcement (ICE), the U.S. Attorneys, the FBI, the Drug Enforcement Administration (DEA), and the Bureau of Alcohol, Tobacco, and Firearms (ATF). Discretion, leadership, strategic focus, tactical direction—all were weak or absent.

All of these occurring together invited catastrophe, in an area already beleaguered by illegal narcotics, very high crime rates, and, especially, gangs.

In reorganizing, the Rampart leadership established a Gang Impact Team with a single command structure for gang and narcotics intelligence and enforcement. This structure draws vitality from the selection of extremely able cops at all ranks who work together splendidly in the field. Their work includes effective gathering and analysis of information and dissemination of intelligence, trustworthy management and payment of informants, wise use of limited resources in gang and narcotics enforcement, and thorough cooperation with the city attorney, county district attorney, and state and federal agencies.

Such coordination expands the capacities of the police, an improvement in effectiveness that may be seen in Rampart in the application of civil gang injunctions, both preliminary and permanent. In close cooperation with police, deputy city attorneys in the Gang Unit of the Los Angeles City

Attorney's Office prepare these injunctions. In a conversation with me in October 2004, Deputy City Attorney Jim McDougal explained that the injunctions prohibit such gang activity as public association, trespassing, loitering, and curfew violations in specific locations; witness and victim intimidation; and having or using weapons, narcotics, and alcoholic beverages. Enforcing the injunctions against the gangs, McDougal says—18th Street, MS, and others—allows the people in a neighborhood some room to breathe. By naming a gang itself as the defendant in an injunction, you can stop the members of the gang from constantly gathering together in public as an intimidating street presence.

When gang members violate the civil injunction, their behavior may provide probable cause for arrest. The attorneys also conduct "gang injunction symposia," which instruct police and criminal justice personnel far beyond Rampart in the nature, preparation, and use of gang abatement actions and civil gang injunctions.

In June 2005, after months of preparation, McDougal and the Rampart Gang Unit secured an unprecedented preliminary injunction against ten gangs at once: 18th Street, Crazy Riders, DIA (also known as Down in Action), KTO (also known as Krazy Town), La Raza Loca, Orphans, Rockwood Street Locos, V Arrio Vista Rifa, Wanderers, and Witmer Street Locos. In a letter to me, McDougal described the injunction as "another victory for the community and another innovation for Rampart," adding, "We hope to get a permanent injunction by the end of the summer. The preliminary [injunction] is in effect, though, and has already resulted in local gang members becoming scarce on the street."

Although such injunctions require painstaking work, they add powerfully to effective gang intelligence and enforcement. Police and city attorneys working in close association are drawn into common purpose and friendship. Failures of communication and understanding become rare, and prosecutions of gang suspects go much more smoothly.

The repertoire of gang and narcotics enforcement grows from this close cooperation in many other ways. In Rampart, as elsewhere, police seek to discourage suburbanites and others from coming into the neighborhood to buy illegal drugs. The buyers' money increases gang power, including the power to buy sophisticated weapons and to pay for high-priced lawyers. Reducing that cash flow is a crucial strategic measure that makes streets safer.

In Rampart, buyers may be apprehended in "macadamia nut stings," conducted by narcotics detectives or officers posing as drug dealers. The stings, which are carefully structured to avoid any hint of entrapment, work like this:

In Los Angeles, crack cocaine comes in slivers that look like small, translucent, whitish slices of macadamia nut or almond. Rampart narcotics officers put slivers of nut into tiny bags of the kind used by dealers to sell crack in twenty-dollar amounts. Four officers posing as dealers set up at a prime location for dealing, with the approval of the property owner and also owners of nearby properties from which surveillance of dealers can, from time to time, be conducted. The four officers working together can protect each other, ensuring their collective safety. They prefer corner locations with fenced yards, so buyers have to leave their vehicles to make a purchase. A narcotics supervisor positioned nearby in an unmarked vehicle coordinates the operation and further protects the officers conducting the sting. Uniformed officers in marked cruisers are stationed out of sight but close at hand.

Prospective buyers attempting to purchase one of the bags of slivered nut often say something like, "Give me a twenty," to which the plainclothes officer will reply, "A twenty of what?" A prospective buyer who identifies the drug he wants and then pays for it is arrested for attempting to purchase a controlled substance, a felony in California. After arrest, the buyer is taken to jail and the evidence is logged. Bail for this offense is automatically set at $10,000. Usually, the buyer spends the night in jail. Then, a deputy city attorney experienced in the procedure offers the buyer release without jail time or a fine but with a sentence of extended probation. Most buyers accept the offer, but a second offense invites prosecution and a hefty fine or prison time.

These stings, made effective by expert police and prosecutors working hand-in-glove, provide a strong deterrent to repeat buying in Rampart by suburbanites. Although I have observed well-executed narcotics operations in many different places in the United States and other countries, I have never seen them done better than in Rampart. Police and other law enforcement agencies there work ably together, make arrests carefully and properly, and have good reason to rely on one another for their safety—in short, their work illustrates the ethical standards and professional excellence emphasized in this volume.

Many of the police in Rampart have a good college education, and all I met are well-trained and supervised. Some have very substantial experience in a wide range of police assignments, but almost all started policing in uniform. Some have international experience, and some have seen military combat. Some have spouses who have served or are serving in the military overseas. A large number are bilingual, some with first languages other than English, and quite a few are literate and experienced in more than one culture, either by birth or by marriage. Some come from generations of cops.

Good cops in Rampart have a history of attending to cultural matters. In the early 1980s, when many Salvadorans were arriving in California, LAPD arresting officers routinely ordered suspects considered dangerous to drop to their knees and place their hands behind their heads. When Salvadorans panicked at the order to kneel, LAPD officers talked with them and learned that in the Salvadoran civil war, government murder squads forced people to kneel before killing them. The LAPD changed its arrest policy. Gang members and cops in Rampart have also taught one another how to avoid and prevent confrontation and violence that could spring from language barriers, confusion, misunderstanding, misperception, unintended affront or insult, and unwarranted fear. Gangsters are gangsters, many of them very dangerous; but neither they nor the police deserve to be drawn into fatal misunderstandings.

My observations in Rampart confirmed the maturity, professionalism, and teaching of frontline supervisors in gang and narcotics intelligence and enforcement. Sergeant Curtis Woodle, officer-in-charge of the Gang Enforcement Detail; Senior Detective Ricky Ramos, officer-in-charge of Gang Detectives; and Senior Detective Jerry Ruffin, officer-in-charge of the Narcotics Enforcement Detail, all within the Gang Impact Team, set very high standards of learning, performance, and expectation. Very good top leadership in Rampart, including Lieutenant Justin Eisenberg, then officer-in-charge of the Gang Impact Team as a whole, enables and supports their work. Mutual trust and reciprocity across ranks lead to "directed freedom" in daily operations at the street level; that freedom, legal resources, and strong staff support make up, to some extent, for the need for more police in Rampart. Police in Rampart know the price of bad leadership and the benefits of good leadership, having seen both. Their unspoken determination to do their best is palpable.

In the Gang Impact Team, I sensed a willingness to learn, to do difficult and dangerous work, and to do it right with real impact, even when short-handed. New people are carefully chosen. They find a strong work ethic, working with highly competent police who want to do what they are doing and have stayed at it. That kind of work environment is hard to establish in policing or any other walk of life. Anyone who gets to work in such a place is fortunate indeed, especially when the work is so desperately needed by the public.

"Leveraging the impact" is the watchword of Rampart police on gang and narcotics crime. Interagency cooperation maximizes the effect of injunctions, stings, surveillance, and other special operations. So do targeting gang leaders and members for surveillance, tracking their activities, and maintaining updated and purged data bases by using a local version of Compstat and the California Gang Data System. Detailed PowerPoint presentations deliver crime alerts in citywide roll calls. Arrest warrants are served whenever possible; purveyors of fraudulent identifications are pursued. Police emphasize homicide prevention and seek federal prosecutions. They work jointly with ATF on a Violent Crime Impact Team. Operations in conjunction with Immigration and Customs Enforcement use immigration laws that prohibit weapons possession and related behavior. Rampart police learn from experiments that fail. They don't repeat many mistakes. Above all, they stay faithful to one specific, central strategic principle.

That principle, first articulated to me in Rampart by Lieutenant Eisenberg, follows a centuries-old military strategy of bringing all one's resources to bear on the central goal. In the words of Frederick the Great, "To defend everything is to defend nothing." This philosophy can be seen in law enforcement with the development of "hot spots" policing over the past decade. Hot spots policing focuses police efforts on troublesome areas that generate a large amount of crime and disorder. Such efforts have received a great deal of support in the criminological literature for being an effective way to reduce crime and disorder.[8]

During my stay in Rampart, police of different ranks referred to the principle of selective defense in explaining how they made their individual assignments according to the priorities of the strategic plan. Rampart police concluded that they could have the greatest impact on crime in general and on gang activity and narcotics trafficking in particular by reclaiming thirty-two-acre MacArthur Park and its surrounding neighborhood. Their purpose, of course, was to seize the initiative; not just to respond to crime, but to prevent it.

Gangs had made the large park and bordering streets into an open-air drug market, selling night and day. Dealers were so brazen they offered to sell drugs to uniformed officers in unmarked cars. The park was the center of gravity for other crime, too. Gangs vied for territory in shootouts and other violent confrontations. They extorted protection payments from all the businesses and street vendors in the area, except for one delicatessen owner who resolutely refused. Crime of every kind was committed openly—vandalism, robbery, burglary, prostitution. Gangs intimidated victims and witnesses. No one was safe from crimes against property and persons.

During my visit, the only remaining criminal activity I saw was the sale of illegal documents, ironically within yards of the restaurant whose owner had been the only businessman refusing to pay protection. Thirteen different kinds were available. Illegal social security cards for $40 to $60 could be prepared in thirty minutes; passports for $500 in an hour. Fraudulent drivers' licenses from other states are in demand among parolees, illegal immigrants, students under the legal drinking age, ex-convicts, and drivers whose licenses have been suspended. Obviously they would be useful to terrorists too, so Rampart police and federal agencies focusing on terrorism are working together to end the illegal documents business. Too much progress has been made in reclaiming MacArthur Park to suppose that sale of fraudulent identification will continue at this pace much longer.

Police elsewhere are encountering similar fraudulent identification operations, some quite sophisticated. In Rampart, buyers give money and a photograph to a street runner who promises to return with the product on time to a designated spot. The street runners do as they promise. Buyers can also arrange for documents to be mailed to other locations.

Surveillance cameras provided by General Electric and integrated by Hamilton Pacific played (and continue to play) a major part in reclaiming MacArthur Park. Well-lit and well-patrolled, the park area now allowed the filming of gang members. They learned that they would be filmed and that crime was no longer tolerated. Merchants and the general public learned they would be protected. When crimes were committed, police made follow-up arrests and worked very effectively with prosecutors. The price of doing business in the park drove the gangs out.

It took years of efforts to restore ethics and increase professional excellence to enable the agency to accomplish this, but the results have been impressive. Anyone can now walk safely through the park, day or night, without fear. Protection rackets are no more. In the mid-1990s, Rampart saw one hundred and fifty murders a year. In the first nine months of 2004, there were seventeen. Even after significant reductions in the crime rate were well underway, other single-year reductions were still impressive in 2004: 8 percent in total crimes; 21 percent in violent crimes; 39 percent in homicides; 37 percent in shooting victims; 22 percent in gang crimes. Gang enforcement arrests were up by 33 percent, narcotics enforcement arrests by 13 percent.

Street gangs often evolve into more sophisticated versions of organized crime. The immense successes of Rampart Area police, including the Major Offenders Unit, in cooperation with such law enforcement agencies as the FBI and ATF, in penetrating this veil testify to their professional excellence. Seeking out and targeting top gang leaders and focusing on drugs sold every day in Rampart paid off. These measures taught gang leaders to expect serious consequences for doing business in Rampart. There are progressively stronger deterrents against gang crime in the area. The Rampart Division enables its personnel to travel to other jurisdictions to teach about MS-13 and its criminal operations and the measures being taken in Rampart in gang and narcotics enforcement. Rampart's Damien Levesque has been especially helpful to police in eastern Massachusetts. All of this splendid work advances the larger effort of the City of Los Angeles to rebuild Rampart, to build more schools, and to attract more businesses and apartment construction.

Competence and Cooperation: Combating Gangs in Fairfax County, Virginia

From 1986 until 1990, while my daughter attended high school, my family and I lived about two miles from the Fairfax County Police Department, in northern Virginia. I wrote *Character and Cops* while I lived there, working at the American Enterprise Institute in Washington, D.C. The public high school in Fairfax was unusual. It offered an exceptional four-year program in Latin, a language our daughter had already studied for three years and was eager to continue. So we bought a house across the street from the school and lived there until she left for college in 1990. Thus, when I returned in 2004 to learn about the current work of the police department, I already knew something of their history and accomplishments in policing.

Previous work in Los Angeles had taught me about the expansion of gangs, Latin American in origin, to the East Coast. In particular, recent federal and state antigang initiatives had focused on MS-13, or Mara Salvatrucha, a dominant gang power. I knew that some Boston area jurisdictions were playing catch-up in gang enforcement. I had also heard from a number of public officials outside of Virginia that Fairfax County and northern Virginia police departments, which were especially hard hit, were far behind the curve of MS-13 incursion. That seemed to me unlikely, given my experience in Fairfax. Media accounts of congressional and Justice Department measures to combat gang activity in northern Virginia led some to infer that local police were in trouble. But while most forms of federal involvement had been welcome in Fairfax and other parts of Virginia, it is not true that the Fairfax County Police Department had been unprepared for and overtaken by gang problems.

Even though much of Fairfax is a well-to-do suburb where the general public of a million people might be inclined, through ignorance, inexperience, or suburban complacency, to deny any gang problem, the police had no such inclination. Police at all ranks in a variety of assignments with whom I spent time had clearly resolved that no such complacency should impair their mission. They were not behind the curve with MS-13; they took the initiative. They had gone far beyond reacting and were taking expansive steps to prevent both area MS-13 cliques and MS-13 leaders elsewhere in the United States and Central America from judging Fairfax to be an attractive target of opportunity for gang recruitment and criminal predation.

Competence. Becoming thoroughly competent in gang enforcement takes years of study and hard work on the streets, in prisons, at conferences, and among qualified police and law enforcement and corrections personnel. Professional excellence in police work on gangs includes coming to know gang members first hand and in depth, trying to understand them as individuals and not as mere members of groups, and engaging in extended communication with them and those who are close to them without forgetting the dangers of the work.

The Fairfax County Police Department engages in this work with the benefit of its splendid reputation, which derives from the quality and constancy of a great many of its sworn and staff personnel. The department's longstanding policy in recruitment is: When in doubt, do not hire. Police in a variety of assignments and ranks told me they would rather work short-handed than work with someone they were not sure they could trust.

Fairfax County attracts well-educated and able recruits and richly experienced senior candidates for police positions. The department seeks diversity, but in combination with good character, and it teaches the imperative to safeguard civil rights and privacy. Leaders urge police to initiate communication with immigrants who need to learn how to reach and take advantage of police assistance and other agency services. This is essential, as Fairfax County has the fifth most rapidly expanding Muslim population in the United States. To secure personnel who share a first language with one of the county's many immigrant populations, the department will consider, and even assist, applicants who are legal residents and have applied for but not yet gained citizenship. Should this effort bear fruit, the department would rely, as it does uniformly, on careful background investigations and rigorous training and supervision.

Preparing immigrants for police duties in the United States when they have little or no experience with secular traditions of public service can be complicated or impossible, especially if their religious obligations override all others. Still, Fairfax County demographics require the department to recruit speakers of Arabic and Farsi, the languages of a growing segment of the population. Not only is such language capability essential to providing comprehensive police services; it is also necessary for counter-terrorism operations. The leadership of the department has implemented an intensive language-acquisition program in Spanish for sworn personnel and hopes to introduce Korean, too, as these are first languages of growing area populations.

The work of addressing widespread gang problems can be grim and exhausting at all levels. It can be very difficult to keep uniformed patrol officers adequately informed of all relevant developments in local gang activity, but doing so merits high priority in daily operations. At the same time, police must anticipate the directions gangs are likely to take as they evolve into more advanced criminal enterprises. In Fairfax, surveillance and investigative steps are being taken as dominant gangs, such as MS-13, move toward greater involvement in prostitution, drug trafficking, and extortion of businesses as sources of profit. Police take seriously the likelihood of greater MS-13 violence in defense of their expanding criminal operations.

The best antigang police in the United States and other countries that I have come to know in the past twenty-five years speak, not of how much they know, but of how much they must learn to keep pace with the rapid evolution of gangs and specific gang cliques, and the behavior of individual gang members. That is exactly right.

Newcomers to gang assignments may overestimate what they know, underestimate what they need to know, and find themselves lacking the stamina and perseverance required to become really good at the work. Fairfax pays attention to these facts of life. The vigilance of its police department leads to its choosing promising people for difficult assignments and offering them long, steep learning curves. I have found widespread understanding at all ranks that dangerous assignments should be offered only to police who have very good reason to trust one another in adverse conditions. They recognize competence, good judgment, and courage as irreplaceable elements of professional excellence.

Cooperation. MS-13 in northern Virginia is not a major power in drug trafficking, but MS-13 leaders in the Washington metropolitan area and elsewhere want it to be. There may be five thousand members of MS-13 in the metropolitan area and the northernmost parts of the Shenandoah Valley. Membership stretches into the agricultural regions of western North Carolina and affects Charlotte, Raleigh, and Durham. A long and difficult contest of wills between those who are sworn to protect the public and those who want ruthlessly to exploit it threatens the region. In addition, federal, state, and local cooperation in criminal justice, law enforcement, policing, and corrections is essential to combating MS-13 and other gangs.

Fortunately, gangs do not exercise great power in Virginia prisons, and Fairfax police and parole officers are well-coordinated. In fighting gang predation, relevant government agencies need to share gang intelligence

comprehensively, both internally and across institutional lines, and mutually allocate resources to the greatest effect. Accomplishing that will take
patience and resiliency—and the efforts will tax good will here as much as
elsewhere. But MS-13 members have shown their ruthlessness, as in the
murder of witnesses in the United States and the mass murder of bus passengers to threaten the Honduran government. Combating them with anything less than the full authority and power of the law weakens everyone,
so the authority, resources, and powers of agencies must be combined at all
levels. Fairfax recognizes the urgency: School resource officers have reported
MS-13 recruiting efforts in schools as early as kindergarten.

We have already seen the benefits of the interagency cooperation established in the wake of reforms of the Los Angeles Police Department. The
Fairfax County Police Department also understands the imperative of cooperative policing and law enforcement, and implements it on an even larger
scale. Despite disappointments about some promised external funding and
operational support, it has risen above rivalries to become what has been
lauded as "a model of federal, state, and local information sharing."[9]

To date, the department and its partners in the area's antigang efforts have
achieved great success. The likelihood of apprehension and conviction for
crimes in Fairfax County has driven some gang members out of the jurisdiction and has kept the gang problem from becoming as serious as in other
areas of the country. Central to this success has been a task force started over
a decade ago, before the effectiveness of this strategy had been widely shown
in anticrime efforts around the country. This task force has steadily grown and
involved more personnel and more agencies over the years.[10]

Fairfax County police began their gang unit in 1994 with three members, expanded it in 1997 to twelve, and made the unit permanent in 1998,
well ahead of the curve on gang incursion into the suburbs. Each police
station in the department has a gang coordinator, an organizational arrangement shared by police in Alexandria and Arlington, Virginia. In 2003,
the department became the original supervising agency for the establishment, with federal funding initiated by Congressman Frank Wolfe, of the
Northern Virginia Gang Task Force. The task force also includes police
departments from Herndon, Manassas, Manassas Park, Prince William
County, Leesburg, and Loudoun County, plus the Virginia State Police, with
support from the FBI, ATF, ICE, and DEA.

The mission of the task force includes educating the public about gang predation and types of criminal activity, gang graffiti, tattoos, and hand signs. It gathers information and disseminates gang intelligence, the latter consisting of information that has been carefully reviewed and analyzed for its meaning and implications. With its staff of twenty, the task force shares case investigations and tries to establish practices of mutual institutional support. It is especially effective in providing training and support for the personnel in police departments who are conducting gang-crime investigations and in communicating with commonwealth attorneys prosecuting gang crimes. These prosecutions are aggressive, and, for serious crimes, they seek sentencing that denies the possibility of parole. As both legal and illegal immigration affect gang growth and membership, the task force works closely on both political and criminal matters with Immigration and Customs Enforcement officials.

In short, the cooperative work by the agencies involved in this task force has enabled them to study and respond proactively to the gang issue and attempt to prevent it from worsening, rather than simply responding to problems as they arise. This strategy includes many elements of the problem-oriented policing model that is centered on studying crime problems, finding underlying causes, and developing the ability to combat crime in a proactive manner.

By the time the task force was initiated, Fairfax County police had gathered information and prepared intelligence on some four hundred gangs in northern Virginia. They had identified a hundred gangs with a total of about three thousand members in Fairfax County itself. During its first year, the department worked 837 gang-related cases, with 78 of them involving the Fairfax County public schools; there were 203 gang-related cases in northern Virginia schools overall. By January 2004, the Fairfax County Police Department had classified MS-13 as the dominant gang, with 760 identified members divided into twenty-two cliques.

The Fairfax County department has a history of teaching the public the differences among gang graffiti, hate crime graffiti, and graffiti painted by taggers. Instructional programs continue to focus on graffiti spread by Latin Kings, Latin Queens, Cholos, Cholas, MS-13, Playboys, Asian Gangster Disciples, Tiny Rascal Gangsters, Folk Nation, Crips, Central Killers, and Vatos Locos, among others, with attention to such despicable threats as

"187 All Cops" (187 is the California penal code designation for murder). Instruction on tattoos addresses those specific to particular gangs, as well as those worn by gang members generally, such as the three-dot tattoo forming the points of a triangle that identify gang membership as "Mi Vida Loca" ("my crazy life"). An especially arresting explanation of ties between popular fashion and culture on the one hand and gang life on the other relies on a photograph of a group of Central Killers throwing hand signs signifying cK while standing beneath a large billboard advertising a Calvin Klein line of clothing with its identical cK logo.

Public instruction is uncompromising in denouncing the ruthless "live today, die tomorrow" mindset of many gangsters, to prevent any naïve glorification of gang life as benign and lovingly familial. During a recent three-year period, Fairfax police conducted public and police gang-awareness programs on a large scale—over 125 sessions attended by more than five thousand people. They included more than three dozen school resource officers who teach school personnel and neighborhood watch groups. Civic groups, Latino and other business leaders, hospital personnel, and church groups also attended. Fairfax police, and not only those in gang enforcement, have learned that teaching about gangs expands the domain of police allies and reduces that of gangs. Fairfax police have gone to other cities for instruction and brought to Fairfax such widely respected gang experts as Wes McBride of the Los Angeles Sheriff's Department.

Intelligence materials disseminated among police and police agencies include the precise identification of members of particular gang cliques through tattoos, aliases, associates, and criminal records. The establishment in Fairfax of a Regional Gang Database has proved to be more effective than drug tracking and gang books. It has facilitated the work of other departments, especially those of sufficient size and resources to dedicate personnel to gang assignments. Operation of this database is coordinated with databases on narcotics and vice, and with those of the region's Joint Terrorism Task Force, headed by the FBI. Criminals and suspects often show up in more than one database. Accessibility by patrol officers and special-assignment personnel reduces the risk of overlooking information relevant to investigations in progress.

Senior informants, having witnessed gang meetings and initiation rites, enrich the data with information about the imposition of discipline among gangs and assassination threats against undercover officers. Important additions to gang information and intelligence come from data ports at booking desks, where suspects in custody unhesitatingly answer questions such as, "Who do you want us to contact in case of an emergency?" Close cooperation among police, corrections personnel, and immigration and customs agents reaps much information useful in combating gang crime.

Partnerships with public services agencies have also played a key role in fighting the infiltration of gangs in Fairfax. The police department is represented on the Fairfax County Workforce Investment Board Youth Council. Collaboration in comprehensive antigang efforts led to the establishment of the Youth Employment Center, which has moved more than two hundred young people between the ages of sixteen and twenty-one away from gang influence and juvenile delinquency and into the adult work force. Police cooperate with a wide variety of public service agencies that support families and draw the young away from criminality and into more fulfilling ways of life.

Continuing Challenges. In Fairfax, police encounter obstacles encountered by police elsewhere. Gangsters escape detection by using fraudulent identification. Counterfeit drivers' licenses ostensibly from faraway states pass muster with local police, because there is no national database and no uniformity in state drivers' licenses. Until the states agree on a form of license common to them all, terrorists and criminals of all kinds will continue to exploit this weakness. Fraudulent immigration papers and other forms of identification facilitate criminal mobility as well; Fairfax police have found deported members of MS-13 making their way back into the United States under new aliases within three weeks. MS-13 leaders returning illegally are now exploring the potential for criminal activity in West Virginia.

Gangsters from distant jurisdictions travel and meet surreptitiously with local gangsters to guide them into more sophisticated and lucrative forms of crime, teaching them how to use weapons and escape from crime scenes. This poses severe threats. Mobility and communication by telephone and email enable MS-13 gangsters to control the lives of immigrants to the United States, intimidate witnesses, and exploit the helpless. They can quite plausibly threaten to harm or kill family members still in El Salvador or elsewhere in the Americas.

Witness intimidation by gangs in the United States seems to be reaching epidemic proportions. Daniel Conley, the district attorney of Suffolk County, Massachusetts (which contains Boston), estimated in 2005 "that witness intimidation applies to 90 percent of the roughly 450 of his active cases involving gangs and guns."[11] In one case in Boston in January 2005, "a witness to a shooting by a member of a street gang found copies of his grand jury testimony taped to all the doors of the housing project where he lives."[12] Prosecutors in many major eastern cities give equally distressing accounts.

To control this epidemic, legislators, judges, and executive branch officials have to devise more comprehensive and straightforward means of safeguarding the capacities and purposes of the Constitution and the criminal justice system. The public safety cannot be remotely secured when criminals can routinely use violence and threats of violence to thwart prosecutions. City, state, and federal attorneys must expand their means of protecting witnesses, taking preemptive steps to prevent intimidation, and prosecuting and punishing those who threaten witnesses, so that constitutional safeguards of individual liberties are not perverted into shelters for the perpetration of crime with impunity. If the nation does not face up to this crisis, it can slip into the condition of countries where criminals escape justice by terrorizing the public and assassinating investigative reporters, police, prosecutors, judges, and witnesses.

The principle that justice can be achieved if, and only if, criminal defendants are guaranteed the right to know and face their accusers seems to me to merit reconsideration. If being known as a witness amounts to putting yourself and your family in mortal peril, you cannot justifiably be compelled to be a witness. We make exceptions to rules of criminal procedure when doing otherwise defeats the very purposes of the criminal justice system. We should never do so lightly; but justice sometimes requires witness testimony, and justice cannot be separated from witness safety.

States should consider witness protection programs, as with California, Colorado, and Ohio. The Leroy Brown Jr. and Karen Clark Witness Protection Program in Connecticut has provided a model for safeguarding witnesses and the interests of justice since 1999. State programs should be adequately funded for extended protection and relocation, and they should be designed so that prosecutors and police take the initiative in offering protection. Witness intimidation should be a felony carrying a substantial prison sentence, and leaking grand jury testimony should be illegal. Some legislators and prosecutors advocate a "hearsay exception." Its purpose is to "allow past statements by witnesses to be admitted at a trial if the witness disappeared or was unwilling to testify."[13] But these remedies do not protect witnesses (and thus their families) from being identified by gang defendants in pretrial discovery. That problem merits further consideration. The names of witnesses should be held in confidence in plea bargains, if the law allows; and if the law prohibits such confidentiality, it should be changed. Further measures should be considered by state and local executives and legislators in consultation with prosecutors, defense attorneys, police, and law enforcement and corrections personnel about the means necessary to safeguard both witnesses and the criminal justice system.

Fairfax County is not exempt from the witness intimidation crisis. Gang crime prosecutions are not uniformly well-managed, and prospective witnesses cannot always be protected from risk of gang reprisal. No remedy for this crisis is likely to be found anywhere at the local level alone; local, state, and federal cooperation and resources seem essential to protecting the public and the Constitution from the ruthless determination of gang members. A nation that offers no protection against their ruthlessness cannot preserve the basic elements of civilization itself: liberty, order, and justice.

The ignorance of judges about gangs and gang crimes can also thwart justice in prosecutions and sentencing and make gangsters progressively more contemptuous of laws and law enforcement. In a case in the Washington metropolitan area that is not unique, when MS-13 gang defendants stood together to form the number thirteen while flashing MS-13 hand signs, the judge was oblivious to the fact. Unfortunately, gang injunctions are not yet possible in the region.

Finally, even the highest level of vigilance and the most effective witness protection program cannot protect witnesses whose ties to gangs remain strong. On May 17, 2005, "a federal jury in Alexandria [Virginia] convicted two members of the violent Mara Salvatrucha street gang . . . in the slaying of a 17-year-old government witness but acquitted two others, including a convicted killer accused of plotting the murder from his jail cell."[14] The convicted killer, Denis Rivera, is believed by police to have given the murder order by mobile telephone from his prison cell. The witness,

Brenda "Smiley" Paz, was sixteen weeks pregnant when she was repeatedly stabbed in the chest and throat and nearly beheaded by her killers. They followed the MS-13 "green light" to murder her, an order that came to MS-13 cliques throughout the country from as nearby as northern Virginia and as far away as El Salvador. Herself a member of MS-13, Paz had been in the Federal Witness Protection Program, but she had been persuaded to rejoin the gang by members plotting her murder.

Paz's decomposing body was discovered four days after the murder lying near a river in the Shenandoah Valley. She had been unknown to local law enforcement personnel who could not identify her remains. Mike Porter, a Fairfax County Gang Unit member whose expert witness testimony has been decisive in several gang crime trials, knew Brenda Paz well, having cultivated her as an informant. He was able to tell Shenandoah County deputies the identity of the body as soon as he learned the description of her still visible tattoos. I asked Porter, whose knowledge of gangs and individual gangsters both inside and outside of prisons is encyclopedic, how Brenda Paz could possibly have been so fatally foolish as to return from witness protection to MS-13. Surely, I said, she must have known that there would be a gang green light to kill her. He replied without hesitating, "You can take the gangster out of the gang, but you can't take the gang out of the gangster." Bad habits die hard, and sometimes, they kill you.

Beyond Antigang Enforcement. The professionalism of the Fairfax County Police Department is not limited to gang intelligence and enforcement; it is to be found widely in its other operations as well. Soon after 9/11, the department established a Criminal Intelligence Unit "to address not only traditional criminal intelligence, but also the real possibility of domestic and international terrorists" in the Fairfax area. Staffed by "personnel handpicked for their experience, interpersonal skills, and ability to establish and maintain effective working relationships," this unit exercises administrative responsibility for "detectives assigned to the Joint Terrorism Task Force." Through this unit, the department dramatically enlarged its cooperation with federal agencies.

Subsequently, the department became home to and manager of the National Capital Regional Intelligence Center, which is federally funded and staffed by personnel from several intelligence and law enforcement agencies.[15] Under the leadership of Fairfax County Lieutenant Roger Kelly, the NCRIC is a model organization. The Terrorism Research Center focuses on vulnerability assessments and training. The Counter Terrorism Center provides detailed analysis of information. Center personnel have wide experience in the United States and abroad, including firsthand knowledge of radical Islamism, which provides a huge asset in center operations that other departments would welcome. Here, concerted attempts are made to prevent terrorist atrocities and to develop first-response capabilities.

Center personnel are experienced in the forms of association and use of multiple identifications typical of terrorists. The center has had extraordinary success in interagency communication and cooperation, and it makes use of retired members of the intelligence community and law enforcement. Nevertheless, like other centers throughout the country, it has personnel shortages. But I have heard no excuses; instead, I see a resolve to do the best possible work, no matter the obstacles or limited resources. In Fairfax, as in Rampart, many police are doing the work they want to do, where they want to do it, with humility about the magnitude of the work but not fear of it.

Regaining Public Trust: Corruption and Reform in the Greece, New York, Police Department

Every police officer in America affirms or takes an oath to uphold and defend the U.S. Constitution and therefore its Bill of Rights. The New York State Constitution begins with an extensive Bill of Rights consistent with the Bill of Rights in the U.S. Constitution. The town code of Greece, New York, begins with a code of ethics intended to secure the rights of the people from abuses of power and authority by Greece public servants, including every member of the police department, whether sworn or civilian.

All of these explicit commitments and safeguards mean to make clear that public servants are obligated to serve the public and not to reap illicit profit or enjoy exemption from the law at public expense. They are not charged merely to possess the public trust and confidence; rather, they are charged to behave so as to deserve it.

The special authority and powers with which public servants are entrusted in order to fulfill their duties carry with them the obligation to live up to higher intellectual and ethical—and, where relevant to work requirements, physical—standards than are incumbent on the public they serve. Maintenance of such standards of competence, judgment, and integrity in the daily work of government officials and their institutions and agencies depends on:

(1) Electing and appointing persons with the intellectual capacity, willingness to learn, and decency of character to exercise their authority responsibly and within the limits of the letter and spirit of the law; and

(2) Holding every individual public servant, institution, and agency accountable for its policies, procedures, practices, overall performance, and individual conduct.

Where these essentials of trustworthiness break down or are forsaken, the security, rights, and safety of the public are at best put at risk and at worst betrayed and violated. Concerted efforts to fulfill their duties by competent and honorable public servants such as members of a police department—and to do so in spite of the incompetence, misconduct, corruption, or lawbreaking of others—face severe and unnecessary impediments.

When the citizenry learns that some in government, including those in positions of leadership and high office, have betrayed their trust, allowed accountability to wither, or covered up serious wrongdoing, citizen confidence in public servants in general and in government itself may be shaken. This is a profound disservice to all who have never strayed from the path of duty and faithful service. But confidence in government, including police, can be fragile, susceptible to erosion by even the appearance of wrongdoing or exploitation of authority for private gain.

Accordingly, where reasonable grounds for concern cannot responsibly be ignored that failures of performance, integrity, and accountability have been committed in government; the public interest demands that an institutional review, inquiry, or investigation be undertaken to discover the truth. If the ability of the institution to conduct a conscientious, thorough, unblinking, and trustworthy investigation is itself in question, then the matters ought to be referred to duly authorized and qualified personnel from outside the agency.

By the middle of 2008, events and actions that had come to light within the Greece Police Department demanded such an investigation. In March 2009, many of these concerns were confirmed by the conviction of a Greece police sergeant of five felonies and two misdemeanors. He had crashed into a stopped vehicle containing a pregnant woman while he was impaired by alcohol and cocaine. Testimony at his trial by the police supervisor at the scene of the accident supported the allegation that a proper investigation was not undertaken. The supervisor asserted he had judged the accident not serious enough to warrant an investigation despite the fact that the driver who caused the accident fled the scene of the crash and the pregnant woman sustained serious personal injuries. Other incidents of serious wrongdoing by police also came to light, including accusations by several women that a member of the department attempted to extort sexual favors. In April, several senior members of the department were suspected of shredding documents under subpoena by the district attorney. Local media reported that "a few police officers have made the [police] department look like an above-the-law posse of cowboys" from which "residents cannot feel secure."[16]

Faced with a worsening situation and evidence of a breakdown of accountability in the police department, in April 2009, the town supervisor appointed a new director of public safety. His initial charge was to investigate internally the police handling of the hit-and-run accident, the allegations that an officer extorted sex from women in the town, and the question of document shredding by senior officers of the department. On April 27, the new director, with a team of investigators he selected as staff for his office— all of them, like himself, former investigators with the New York State Police—initiated these investigations.

This beginning led to thirty-eight internal investigations in which investigators alleged widespread operational failures, lack of adequate rules and regulations essential to competent policing, reckless disregard of internal orders and procedures, poor training, outsourcing of background investigations without oversight by the department, and countless other severe obstacles to trustworthy policing. Based on the results of the investigation, the director proposed to the town supervisor a "spot procedural audit" of key department divisions so he and his team could recommend policies, procedures, regulations, and operational changes designed to prevent as much as possible the continuation or recurrence of these affronts to the public interest. These steps to restore accountability where it was absent would begin the task of helping the honorable police within the department make it worthy of the public trust and confidence throughout its operations.

Based on the results of the internal investigations and audit, several senior officers of the department and subordinate officers were alleged to have been involved in serious misconduct and incompetence. By successfully deceiving town officials and holding them at arm's length, fabricating background investigation materials, nurturing a culture of cronyism at the top, and intimidating subordinates who were willing to go along to get along, the leadership of the department was allegedly able to establish and perpetuate a fiefdom in which accountability was a fiction and contempt for policy and law a fact of life.

Beyond the problems described above, the Greece police department was accredited, a status that is supposed to be enjoyed only by departments whose operations conform to high standards of performance. The director of public safety's investigation showed that, in reality, the department was out of compliance with numerous standards of accreditation, all of which had to be remedied for accreditation to be legitimate. These conditions had widespread adverse consequences in the department.

The much-needed audit covered the range of operations and practices in the criminal-investigation division and a special review of the availability of sufficient personnel to accomplish the work; all aspects of property management, custody of evidence, and maintenance of reliable records; processes for background investigations and selection of new personnel; all policies and practices in the internal-affairs and personnel-complaint systems; procedures and methods of accountability for approval of travel and expenses; management and control of overtime permissions and costs; and maintenance of military equipment in the care of the department.

The investigating team found deficiencies of profound practical consequence in every area. Some of the deficiencies arose from inadequate staffing, some from an atmosphere and ingrained habits of nonaccountability at the highest levels of the department, and others from careless outsourcing of vital department responsibilities. Neglect, inexperience, shoddy training and preparation for assignments, and mismanagement and intimidation of subordinates by top leaders compounded other critical faults. No police department could possibly be expected to fulfill its mission and most basic purposes with so much of its internal structure and content in desperate need of reform. Thus, the director of public safety prepared sustained recommendations for each operational domain requiring detailed and specific responses from the newly appointed chief of police.

In addition, the director of public safety and his team established criteria for identifying qualified recruits and other personnel, conducting background investigations, and conducting searches for senior command staff. Implementation of the recommendations and application of the criteria will be needed throughout the department to bring it up to acceptable standards of professionalism, accountability, and trustworthiness.

In thirty-five years of working with federal, state, and local law enforcement and police in the United States and other countries, often dealing with grave crises, I have never seen a better investigation of conditions within a police department or articulation of imperatives for overcoming the worst of those conditions and securing a responsible future. Such is the thoroughness and precision of the work and the report issuing from it that it could serve as a splendid textbook or instructional manual for training in institutional investigations and audits. If the town and the police department of Greece follow through resolutely on the recommendations for reform and the establishment of reliable procedures, policies, regulations, personnel allotments, and conscientious reports, they should succeed in greatly reducing or preventing altogether the excesses and deficiencies of the past. The Greece Police Department now stands at the threshold of opportunity to take full advantage of the service of their police personnel who have remained always faithful to their oath, their colleagues, and the public. Thanks to them, and to the expertise and conscientiousness of the office of the director of public safety, the police department has an excellent chance to earn and deserve in every facet of its work the trust and confidence of the people of Greece.

Ethics and Professionalism in a Post-9/11 World

The case studies above illustrate how the ethical ideals espoused repeatedly in this book are crucial for achieving professional excellence in police agencies. They also showed how these combine to increase the effectiveness of police and allow them to adopt more proactive strategies. The experience of the Fairfax County antigang task force, and the collaborative efforts in Rampart, showed the utility of law enforcement agencies working together to fight the problems plaguing their jurisdictions. As I have noted, it has long been clear that isolation of police and law enforcement agencies from one another does not serve the public interest. Failure to share information and intelligence, within appropriate limits of security, can enable criminals to evade the law. The threat of terrorism makes the problem more urgent, and interagency collaboration even more crucial, to the work of police in the post-9/11 world.

In addition to fostering simple cooperation among themselves, therefore, law enforcement and antiterrorist institutions need to avoid institutional "stovepipes." They cannot afford to be sealed off from other institutions with overlapping missions, like stovepipes that admit entry of nothing except from within. And they cannot afford for action recommendations to go directly to top authority without undergoing thorough evaluation of the data along the way. Stovepipes work like blinders: they treat raw data as analyzed intelligence, and they invite mistaken decisions. They prevent adequate focus on contingencies, especially on what can go wrong, if a recommendation is implemented. They cause, and they result from, inevitably wasteful turf jealousies and battles inimical to the public safety.

If policing is to come into its own as a profession, such stovepipes must become a thing of the past. Law enforcement agencies have an ethical obligation to relinquish territoriality and work together as effectively as they possibly can. A model of such professional excellence, established in the wake of the terrorist atrocities of September 11, is the New York State Office of Homeland Security.

The OHS was established by Governor George Pataki in early October 2001. In a 2003 letter to the citizens of New York, Senior Advisor to Governor Pataki for Counter-Terrorism James Kallstrom described the office as "a professional homeland security team who are dedicated to coordinating and directing state efforts to prevent another terrorist attack in New York State" and "a national leader in defining the pivotal role state and local authorities play in homeland security." He added that homeland security is not just a federal responsibility: The Office of Homeland Security has "begun to empower the 70,000 law enforcement officers, thousands of fire and emergency personnel, hundreds of public health officials, the corporate community, and the public" in New York to combat terrorism. In his introduction to its 2003 annual report, Public Security Director James McMahon, former Superintendent of the New York State Police, explained that the OHS (then called the Office of Public Security),

> has the critical responsibility of overseeing, directing and coor-
> dinating the public security resources and reviewing the public
> security policies, protocols, and strategies of state agencies. The
> Office facilitates information sharing among local, state and
> federal law enforcement agencies and acts as the primary state
> liaison to the federal Department of Homeland Security . . .
> [It fulfills its mission] by working with state agencies and the
> federal and local governments, and through the use of tech-
> nology, intelligence analysis, supporting legislation, providing
> terrorism-related training to law enforcement, and encouraging
> citizen involvement.

Late in 2004, McMahon told me, "We're trying to do away with stovepipes—while protecting civil rights, privacy, and essential confiden-tiality." As with most accomplished police leaders, McMahon knows that those who are sworn to defend the Constitution can do it enormous harm if they abuse their powers and authority. He and his colleagues maintain careful vigilance in defense of civil liberties during the performance of their duties. They are not tempted by the idea that ends justify means, or that the threat of terrorist atrocities gives them license to ride roughshod over the public's constitutional rights.

Their mission is enormous. Their staff is not. The office oversees, directs, coordinates, and reviews "public security policies, protocols and strategies of state agencies including, but not limited to, the Division of State Police, Division of Military and Naval Affairs, State Emergency Management Office, Department of Health, Department of Environmental Conservation, Division of Criminal Justice Services, Department of State, Office of Technology and the Department of Transportation." The staff coordinates "state agency resources for the collection and analysis of information regarding terrorist threats and activities of terrorists throughout the State." They assess health system preparedness at all levels, early-warning systems, available supplies of vaccines and other pharmaceutical products, institutional vulnerability, and communication systems, and they are responsible for formulating plans to enable recovery from terrorist attacks. They do all of this comprehensively and see to its integration throughout New York state in both policy and practice. Under the aegis of the office, task forces address cyber-crime, border security, aviation and maritime security, public transportation, weapons of mass destruction, intelligence officer training, law enforcement executive counterterrorism training, and the security of food supplies.

Among members of the staff, these are not mere words on paper. Their mutual sense of purpose is palpable, their trust in one another's competence and integrity compelling. In some institutions with responsibilities that affect millions of people and thousands of public servants, bureaucrats and others lose sight of everything but statistics. Cost-benefit analyses inordinately dominate institutional policy. The humanity of the individual citizen, resident, or public servant becomes morally invisible. Not here.

McMahon sets the tone. In the New York State Police, he rose from trooper to superintendent, earning respect throughout the wide range of assignments he undertook. As a police executive, he did not bow to pressures from within the agency or from outside that could damage it. As superintendent, he was a worthy successor to Thomas Constantine, who went on to serve as administrator of the Drug Enforcement Administration and later as oversight commissioner of the Independent Commission on Policing for Northern Ireland (the Patten Commission).[17]

McMahon is determined that first-responders not be mere "blue canaries"—cops, firefighters, and emergency medical personnel who are unnecessarily exposed to deadly biological or chemical agents, or die in the immediate aftermath of terrorist attacks because they are ill-equipped or poorly trained. He also wants to improve our ability to model the spread of contaminated air and water in emergency situations, and develop better quarantine policies to safeguard the public.

Alert to avoiding waste, he supports incentives for police trained in antiterrorist responsibilities to stay in their assignments rather than exercise seniority rights to leave them. He advocates comprehensive training to prepare personnel in security forensics for professional testimony, the development of university graduate study on institutional information- and intelligence-sharing, recruitment of law enforcement personnel from a wide range of linguistic and cultural backgrounds, language-acquisition programs, and study of the history of radical fundamentalist Islamic terrorism. In the interest of public safety and civil liberties, he supports access by antiterrorism personnel to information and intelligence on crime and violence acquired from police and law enforcement agencies by the New York State Intelligence Center and the Upstate New York Regional Intelligence Center, but not the inclusion of antiterrorist intelligence in criminal databases without regard for security and privacy.

McMahon insists that antiterrorist funding be distributed on the basis of demonstrated need rather than presumed entitlement. He takes the heat and stands behind his staff, all of whom are well-prepared for their duties. No federal funds are accepted by the office, a policy that safeguards autonomy, independence, and standards. But the office has established a comprehensive range of partnerships with local, state, and federal agencies, including unemployment and corrections offices, and operates as the principal contact agency with the U.S. Department of Homeland Security, while McMahon serves as chairman of the State Disaster Preparedness Commission and, with his staff, coordinates work with the National Incident Management System. Of special importance is the Office of Homeland Security's establishment of the Counter-Terrorism Network, in the vanguard of state-level operations in the United States. As annual reports emphasize, this network enables the dissemination of highly sensitive material to over 340 police and law enforcement agencies. To enable regional information- and intelligence-sharing, the Office of Home-land Security cooperated in establishing the Northeast Regional Homeland Security Agreement. New York personnel work directly with counterparts in Delaware, Pennsylvania, New Jersey, Connecticut, Rhode Island, Massachusetts, Vermont, New Hampshire, and Maine.

Also of particular importance is cooperation with the state's Department of Motor Vehicles, because verifying identity is so crucial to the proper issuing of drivers' licenses and nondriver identification cards. The fraudulent use of Social Security numbers to acquire other identifications enables insurance scams, flight from child support and other court orders, and many forms of white collar fraud, and allows criminals, gangsters, and terrorists to escape detection and apprehension. The Office of Homeland Security therefore "fully endorsed the acceleration of the Department of Motor Vehicles' Social Security number verification program," which uses the Social Security Administration's electronic system for immediate determination of whether a Social Security number is valid. To date, the department has checked more than ten million records and applications. Fraudulent applications are down, arrests are up.

The work of the DMV is essential to the overall mission of the Office of Homeland Security, because it thwarts precursor crimes by terrorists and is essential to public safety. The cooperation of the two agencies provides a model for other states. New York State has been a leader in this field for years, initially through the establishment of the Governor's Fraudulent Documents Task Force in Queens, which, in cooperation with a growing group of agencies, has had great success in rooting out and closing down producers of fraudulent documents.

Concerns about the broad accumulation of confidential information about individuals by both the private sector and government led New York State to focus on the question of how to protect individual privacy and simultaneously prevent terrorist atrocities. Part of its answer has been to establish a position for an "intelligence privacy officer" within the Office of Homeland Security, whose job is to ensure the implementation of the state's overall counterterrorism strategy while also protecting, as much as possible, individual privacy. Working with senior command personnel of the state police, the privacy officer assists the gathering and dissemination of counterterrorism information, and assesses the methods of collecting, storing, and sharing that information. The officer is also involved in conducting a complete review of information policies and procedures, a study of relevant privacy law and Freedom of Information law, and planning for a comprehensive privacy training program for Office of Homeland Security and counter terrorism personnel. This focus on individual privacy is an important element of law enforcement's efforts to protect the public from the very real threat of terrorism while also respecting the ethical and constitutional principles that we all hold dear.[18]

Conclusion

A great many police departments and law enforcement agencies beyond those I have described in the case studies in this chapter embody comparable ideals of professional excellence. Their work promises a bright future for policing as a profession. Despite the social ills that beset modern societies, many police departments continue to ratchet up their already high standards of recruitment, training, supervision, promotion, and service to the public.

I noted in chapter 3 that in 1931, the great police leader and reformer August Vollmer wrote, "In America, law enforcement is generally held in contempt, and policing is [taken as] one of our national jokes." Such has been the progress in policing in the last seventy-five years, that any such claim made today would be taken as utterly uninformed and indefensible, indeed preposterous.

Obviously, some departments have been left behind in the progress toward professionalism and remain urgently in need of profound reform. Police in some departments do the bidding of corrupt elected officials and follow orders that violate the civil rights of the citizenry. No police department is flawless. But on the whole, I take great encouragement for the future of Western democracies from the moral, scientific, and intellectual advances in policing I have witnessed at first hand during my career.

22

From War Veterans to Peace Officers

Few of us ever know how far fear and violence can transform us into creatures at bay, ready with tooth and claw. If the war taught me anything at all, it convinced me that people are not what they seem or even think themselves to be. Nothing is more tempting than to yield oneself, when fear comes, to the dominance of necessity and to act irresponsibly at the behest of another. Freedom and responsibility we speak of easily, nearly always without recognition of the iron courage required to make them effective in our lives.

—J. Glenn Gray[1]

Fulfillment of the mission of every police department and law enforcement agency depends on the competence, good judgment, and integrity of its individual members; the wisdom, clarity, and fairness of its regulations, policies, and practices; and the effectiveness of its measures for recruiting good people and ensuring their accountability. In the best places to work, one finds across ranks a spirit of mutual respect, cooperation, and common purpose.

The Challenge

Institutions rise and fall with their standards of personnel recruitment, fitness for duty, and work performance during initial training and probationary periods and thereafter. Whenever employees of police departments take a leave of absence and have a legal right to return, the institutions, their leaders, and the returning employees face a challenge: how best to reintegrate the employees without relaxing institutional standards and without complicating return with unnecessary red tape and thereby causing impatience and resentment.

479

The challenge is even greater with respect to civilian employees who take leaves of absence to perform military service because of very specific and strict federal legal requirements and veteran entitlements. Of the relevant laws, the most important and potentially problematic is the Uniformed Services Employment and Reemployment Rights Act (USERRA) of 1994.

USERRA. All private- and public-sector employers, except a small number of federal agencies, must comply with the provisions of USERRA. The U.S. Supreme Court has ruled that no state or local employment law, regulation, or institutional policy may supersede USERRA or abridge the rights it establishes and guarantees for veterans.

> The statute itself:
>
> USERRA is a federal statute that protects service members' and veterans' civilian rights. Among other things, under certain conditions, USERRA also protects service members from discrimination in the workplace based on their military service or affiliation.[2]
>
> The explicit purposes of USERRA are:
>
> (1) to encourage noncareer service in the uniformed services by eliminating or minimizing the disadvantages to civilian careers and employment that can result from such service;
>
> (2) to minimize the disruption to the lives of persons performing service in the uniformed services as well as to their employers, their fellow employees, and their communities, by providing for the prompt reemployment of such persons upon their completion of such service; and
>
> (3) to prohibit discrimination against persons because of their service in the uniformed services.[3]

USERRA is a complex statute, filled with qualifications and restrictions. Police and law enforcement leaders may need guidance from local, state, or federal legal counsel to understand relevant case law and ensure compliance. But the essence of the statute has been very well described—for the most part—by the International Association of Chiefs of Police (IACP)/Bureau of Justice Assistance publication *Law Enforcement Leader's Guide on Combat Veterans: A Transition Guide for Veterans Beginning or Continuing Careers in Law Enforcement*, prepared under the leadership of project manager Arnold Daxe Jr., certified protection professional:

> The Uniformed Services Employment and Reemployment Rights Act of 1994 (USERRA) is administered by the U.S. Department of Labor through the Veteran's Employment and Training Service (VETS). USERRA covers every person who has served in the military and applies to all employers in the public, private and federal sectors. Federal, state, and local law enforcement departments must adhere to USERRA.
>
> USERRA mandates that returning service members are to be re-employed in the position that they would have attained had they not been absent for military service, with their seniority, status, and pay as well as other rights and benefits determined by their seniority. USERRA also requires [that] employers make reasonable efforts, such as training and retraining, to enable returning service members to refresh or upgrade their skills and help them quality for re-employment or continued employment. The law provides for alternative re-employment positions if the service member is not able to qualify for their [sic] previous position or the position to which they would have been promoted. If an officer returns from deployment and is unable to return to duty, the department will usually be required to find an alternative position.[4]

Daxe's only error here is in saying that the law applies to all employers, including all employers in the federal sector. A Sixth Circuit Appellate Court ruling upheld by the Supreme Court on March 2, 2011, in the case of *Petty v. Metropolitan Government of Nashville–Davidson County* affirmed that a small number of federal agencies have the discretion to decide for themselves whether the provisions of USERRA are binding on them. No other public- or private-sector employer enjoys this exemption. In fairness, I should note that IACP published its "Transition Guide" over a year before the Supreme Court ruled in the *Petty* case.

Petty v. Metropolitan Government of Nashville–Davidson County. Brian Petty, a captain in the Army Reserve and sergeant in the Nashville–Davidson County Police Department, "was charged with violations of the Uniform Code of Military Justice" while serving in Kuwait. "CPT Petty appeared before a military judge for arraignment . . . and then he agreed to resign his commission 'for the good of the service' in lieu of court martial. He received a general discharge under honorable conditions, and he was sent home, his military career over."[5]

Petty applied for reinstatement to his police position, but the police department, suspecting misconduct during his military service, postponed reinstatement while conducting an internal investigation. Petty sued under USERRA. While a district court upheld the Metropolitan Government of Nashville–Davidson County, that decision was overturned on appeal and the ruling in Petty's favor was upheld in March 2011 by the U.S. Supreme Court.

That Petty had behaved irresponsibly and against regulations in Kuwait was not at issue. The issue was whether any of the events that could disqualify Petty from the benefits of USERRA had taken place. Specifically, under Section 4304 of USERRA:

> A person's entitlement to the benefits of this chapter by reason of the service of such person in one of the uniformed services terminates upon the occurrence of any of the following events: (1) A separation of such person from such uniformed service with a dishonorable discharge or bad conduct charge. (2) A separation of such person from such uniformed service under other than honorable conditions, as characterized pursuant to regulations prescribed by the secretary concerned [a service secretary, such as the secretary of the Army]. (3) A dismissal of such person permitted under section 1161(a) of title 10. (4) A dropping of such person from the rolls pursuant to section 1161(b) of title 10. 38 U.S.C. 4304.[6]

Sections 1161(a) and (b) of title 10 cover dismissal of commissioned officers from the armed forces who have been convicted by court martial or have been absent without leave for a period of at least three months.

None of the disqualifying events had taken place during Petty's military service or discharge. Petty's appeal was upheld on these grounds, with the court denying that the city government, including the police department, had any right to subject Petty to any employment or reemployment policy or practice that would supersede the overriding authority of USERRA. In fact, the Sixth Circuit Court of Appeals ruling read: "It is of no consequence here that Metro believes it is obligated to 'ensure that each and every individual entrusted with the responsibility of being a Metropolitan Police Officer is still physically, emotionally, and temperamentally qualified to be a police officer after having been absent from the department.' In USERRA, Congress clearly expressed its view that a returning veteran's reemployment rights take precedence over such concerns."[7]

The Court of Appeals ruling in Petty's favor emphasized further that Congress has given only a small group of federal agencies discretion in determining the applicability of USERRA: "In certain circumstances, Congress altered this general rule [that USERRA would 'limit the ability of employers to screen returning veterans'] to allow vetting of veterans before full rehiring. Section 4315 allows the heads of agencies listed under 5 U.S.C. 2302(a)(2)(C)(ii)—e.g., FBI, CIA, NSA—'to prescribe procedures for ensuring that the rights under [USERRA] apply to employees of such agency.' 38 U.S.C. 4315(a). Congress did not grant similar discretion to local police departments."[8]

The Supreme Court decision in Petty's favor shows that private- and public-sector employers—including police departments, sheriffs' offices, and some federal law enforcement and other types of federal agencies—cannot impose conditions on the reemployment of veterans that supersede USERRA. Civilian employers should not infringe on this legal principle. They should work cooperatively with returning veterans to avoid litigious disputes whose outcome can reliably be predicted and which inevitably waste money and cause widespread antagonism.

USERRA limitations do not apply, however, to the misconduct of anyone, including a veteran, who is actively serving as a civilian police officer or law enforcement agent. Local law, regulation, policy, and exercise of discretion by police executives and supervisors apply to the actions of actively serving civilian employees, including those in civilian policing.

It is worth looking again at the troubling passage in the *Petty* decision where the ruling states that "it is of no consequence" that the local government believed it had a duty to ensure the physical, mental, and emotional qualifications of its police officers and that instead, under USERRA, "a returning veteran's rights take precedence over such concerns." The law, as enacted by Congress, interpreted by the Sixth Circuit Court of Appeals, and upheld by the Supreme Court, may imply that a local government's effort to maintain high standards of fitness for duty is of "no consequence." But it is of enormous consequence in providing competent and trustworthy police services, living up to the police oath of office, earning public confidence, and protecting the well-being, safety, and morale of police and civilians.

How, then, are police departments to maintain their high departmental standards, do their best by returning veterans, and comply fully with USERRA?

Training and Retraining Provisions

Fortunately, USERRA authorizes, and in some cases requires, training and retraining provisions for veterans returning from military deployment to civilian employers. Often, police departments have training and retraining protocols in place that resemble those of the Kansas City, Missouri, or Topeka, Kansas, police departments. In Kansas City,

> if the employee has been on leave for six months or longer: 1. The employee will be assigned to the Training Division for a period of time to be determined by the Training Division Commander. The training period will vary depending on the requirements of the employee's duties and how many changes have been implemented since their departure. The Training Division is responsible for making sure the officer is brought up to date on changes since their departure. 2. In addition to

the training the employee will receive, the Training Division will also coordinate the employee's reacclimation process, which is designed to provide an incremental and staged re-entry process. This may include, but is not limited to, the following components: a. Short-term assignment with an FTO [field training officer] to allow the employee to serve in the capacity as a back-up officer and re-familiarize with current procedures. b. Participation in the Ride Along program to allow familiarization with the employee's reporting assignment area and other areas of the city, including identification of persons of interest, trends, etc. c. Reintroduction to reporting procedures, if applicable.[9]

In nearby Topeka, Kansas, the police department lists as postdeployment protocol:

mandatory training requirements for every officer returning from a military deployment of 365 days or more. When possible, this reentry training will be conducted one-on-one or in a small group setting: Mandatory psychological evaluation with Dr. Claiborne. Retraining on critical skills, that is, CPR/First Aid, Taser refresher, One on One Control Techniques etc. General Orders and SOP updates. Use of Force review. Weapons re-familiarization and qualification to include less lethal methods. A judgmental shoot/don't shoot refresher course utilizing FATS [Firearms Training System]. EVOC [Emergency Vehicle Operation Course] refresher course. Legal and search and seizure updates. Any mandatory training as required by KLETC [Kansas Law Enforcement Training Center]. Assignment to a field training officer of equal or higher rank when possible.[10]

A number of departments whose policies I have reviewed require psychological screening for all employees who have been on leave, for any reason, for a year or more. None that I have seen explicitly exempts returning veterans from this requirement—regardless of whether the requirement is placed under the heading of "retraining." Some add to this requirement a demonstrated capacity to meet all department standards and to qualify for certification under state standards. A few departments stipulate that no one will be reinstated after an extended leave of absence until the appropriate professional standards bureau has conducted a background investigation on the employee's behavior while on leave.

Because of the March 2, 2011, Supreme Court ruling on the strength of USERRA in the *Petty* case, I believe departments may have legal difficulty maintaining such requirements should they be put to the test under lawsuits. It is possible, though uncertain, that providing for one or more meetings with a therapist who does not conduct official fitness-for-duty evaluations could ease potential legal tension. In any case, it is difficult at this time to predict where USERRA and *Petty* will lead in terms of postdeployment policy. Likewise, it is unknown whether Congress will consider any alteration of the law to accommodate the obligation of police departments, for the sake both of the public and of returning veterans, to protect their highest standards of fitness and performance from subordination to federal law. Congress could, with knowledge and good judgment, have enacted legislation that protects veterans from arbitrary injustice and discrimination *without* reducing legitimate and necessary law enforcement standards to matters of "no consequence." Regrettably, there is no reason to believe Congress will revisit USERRA.

USERRA as it stands exposes police departments and law enforcement agencies to legal liabilities. It can also be a cause of internal personnel tensions over questions of fairness stemming from any failure to maintain uniform standards of performance and accountability for everyone. It also holds dangers for returning veterans. Hasty return to predeployment duties in civilian policing, without adequate retraining (including updated information about dangerous suspects at large, changes in gang behavior and weaponry, and so forth), can thrust a veteran into harm's way without warning.

Several veterans have told me they felt put at risk by departmental haste in reassigning them to predeployment duties. Some said they felt unprepared for changes, not so much in departmental policies and practices, but rather in changes in the field, including new sources and places of danger. Some said they still felt themselves to be in military combat mode when they resumed active police duty and feared they might react badly to people, situations, or circumstances (fortunately, none have done so). Others said they felt mentally and physically fit upon return from deployment but needed—and wanted—retraining, which they did not receive. Invariably, they opposed being forced to meet with psychologists or psychiatrists—some said even required sessions were "career wreckers"—although some were quite willing to see therapists on the grounds that therapists do not carry the same ruinous stigma as psychologists or psychiatrists.

Other veterans have told me how well they were treated upon return to their departments, and how their departments lived up to every obligation and more during military deployment and thereafter, from assisting officers' families while they were deployed to welcome-home celebrations, retraining, and return to predeployment assignments. Everyone who spoke positively about their return to civilian duty had received retraining from their police departments before resuming or taking on new assignments.

Without question, retraining of returning veterans is unconditionally obligatory for departments. That much is clear. USERRA constraints in other respects in no way conflict with or abridge that obligation.

One more thing is certain: averting legal conflict has depended on and will continue to depend on building mutual trust between departments and their individual members, including returning veterans.

Building Mutual Trust

Wherever conditions permit, able leaders, supervisors, and their subordinates try to build a reservoir of mutual trust within their agencies or departments. Where personnel across ranks and assignments can tap such a reservoir, it becomes easier to put the interests of the department as a whole and the interests of individual members on the same side of the ledger. The possibility of reasonable compromise increases.

Sometimes a history of conflict, a deeply embedded "us-against-them" culture of conflict between union and management, thwarts the formation of mutual trust. At times, too, the formation of trust is obstructed by suspicion, warranted or unwarranted, that an incoming police or law enforcement executive has a threatening hidden agenda. And sometimes the interests of the department and those of an individual or group of individuals genuinely—and irreducibly—conflict.

But even if mutual trust across the board in an institution is difficult or impossible to achieve, personnel at all ranks should still try to deserve the trust of others. And leaders should do their best to invite trust in their handling of every specific issue, problem, difficulty, and question where the interests of departmental personnel—even if only one person—are at stake.

Certainly the potential for conflict exists whenever personnel on leave have a legally guaranteed right of return that supersedes institutional standards—as in the case of USERRA. It is folly to wait for that potential to ripen into real problems and conflicts, and then try to resolve or ameliorate them after the fact. Forcing people to play catch-up gives tension, ill will, and resentment a chance to fester and obstruct cooperation and compromise.

Good leaders, in contrast, anticipate conflict; when they see the potential for serious problems, they take early action to overcome or solve them. In matters involving USERRA and the *Petty* decision, such action should demonstrate their commitment to the rights, opportunities, safety, and job security (even if an alternative assignment is necessitated by injury or disability) of employees on or returning from military leave. Department leaders should also confirm their desire to be helpful to soldiers' or veterans' families and provide assurance that budget constraints will not prevent a veteran's return to work. Active-duty military personnel should not be distracted from immediate matters by worry that they may not have a job back home.

In the case of reintegrating returning veterans (and by extension, in the initial recruitment and hiring of veterans), the actions and policies of the department need to cover not only the point of return and transition to civilian policing, but also the periods before and during deployment. These measures should be known throughout the department to forestall suspicion or rumors of favoritism.

Departments can build trust among employees leaving for military service by putting in place the right kind of "go-to" person, what IACP and some others call a military liaison officer and Colorado Springs and other departments call a military-support officer (MSO). This officer should assist and instruct police officers throughout the stages of preparation for departure, deployment, return, and reintegration, in coordination with others who are part of an overall military-support team. Small departments that cannot afford to hire a full-time MSO may be able to handle such matters informally using volunteers who have substantial experience in both policing and military service, or share such a position or turn to larger departments for assistance.

But thorough support for veterans returning to civilian policing requires more than a single MSO; it requires a team. Local department leadership should determine the division of labor among the various personnel on the team. Obviously, this determination will depend on the resources, structure, composition, and needs of each department or agency. The overall job descriptions of team members will probably include veteran-related assignments in addition to other broader, perhaps primary, duties. An average military-support team might include an MSO, training-division commander, chaplain, employee-assistance program director, therapist, psychologist, volunteer peer-support team paraprofessional, department human resource officer, field-training officer, front-line supervisor, department legal counsel, contact person for spouses, deputy chief, chief, and possibly others.

A Sketch of the Ideal Military-Support Team

As I have done elsewhere in *Character and Cops*, as with "A Sketch of the Ethically Ideal Institution" in chapter 16, I sketch here what I believe to be the qualifications, experience, capacities, and duties of the ideal military-support team. The practical utility of such a sketch is to give us a model to follow in designing a team and choosing employees to staff it, while taking local circumstances into account. Ideals reach beyond realities: we know that they can seldom be fully realized and that even coming close to reaching them is a tremendous achievement.

Still, some departments may have several people whose qualifications, experience, and capacities taken together meet this ideal or come very close to it; and, if properly coordinated, they may successfully implement very effective ways to help fellow employees leaving for military duty or returning from it, along with their families. Other employees, acting informally and on their own, can also be enormously helpful.

Some veterans who have returned to civilian policing positions have told me that nothing at work has mattered so much as being requested for reassignment to their predeployment positions; being enthusiastically welcomed back by their partners, friends, colleagues, and supervisors; and having those people help them grasp all the changes that have taken place in their absence. A good military-support team can help weave that welcoming fabric of comradeship and common purpose.

The Colorado Springs Police Department provides a good model for designing the MSO position, often the key position in the military-support team:

> The health and welfare of military employees who are deployed and their immediate family is important to the Colorado Springs Police Department. The department has designated a single point of contact to effectively manage communication and support to the deployed employee's family and serve as a liaison during the employee's deployment. The Military Support Officer (MSO) is a department employee of the rank of sergeant or above who has been identified to serve as a liaison between the deployed employee and the department during his/her absence. The MSO is designated based on his/her military experience and reserve affiliation and is uniquely suited to frequently interact with the deployed employee, their family, the department, and, if necessary, local military components. This is a collateral duty in addition to the normal responsibilities of a sergeant or above. The selection of a MSO must be approved in writing by the [relevant] Deputy Chief.[11]

In Colorado Springs, the MSO is also required to check on the well-being of each deployed employee's family every month and report "up the chain-of-command."

Colorado Springs requires the MSO to "be familiar with [USERRA] when communicating with a deployed employee throughout all phases of his/her deployment cycle." It prohibits the MSO, however, from giving counsel on USERRA rights. "Only employees of City [human resources] and Colorado Springs Police Department [human resources] staff may give advice or guidance to a department employee or their family concerning their USERRA rights."[12]

This is a wise regulation, indeed an essential one, because it eliminates from the outset any possible conflict or tension between the MSO and a veteran over USERRA rights, and it eliminates a potential source of distrust. Other departments will find it wise to limit similarly the authority of their own MSO.

Equally crucial is making certain periodically—and with regularity—that human resources personnel are completely competent and up-to-date on the USERRA statute and all relevant case law that may have an impact on personnel or the institution. In some departments with which I have worked, and in colleges, universities, and corporations where I have had responsibilities, human resources officers have usually been very well versed in matters of institutional policy and regulation and at least narrowly competent in regulatory employment statutes. But their competence has not always reached to broad coverage of legal matters, especially involving evolving federal statutes and case law. If a department or agency learns that its human resources personnel are not best qualified to handle USERRA and other statutes of great importance to active-duty military personnel, veterans, and families, it should determine whether its own or its city's legal counsel could better perform that work.

Whoever has responsibility for advising employees about USERRA rights should also be entirely qualified to teach and advise them about other federal and state laws that guarantee rights and benefits. While this ground may be covered by outside agencies as well, making sure employees know how to avail themselves of such benefits can advance mutual trust within a department, inspire confidence, and serve employee well-being. Besides, a department is likely to be able to offer more individual or small-group attention than a huge federal or state bureaucracy in whose maze of regulations individuals, especially inexperienced ones, can too easily lose their way.

Crucial laws include the updated versions of the G.I. Bill—specifically, the revised Montgomery G.I. Bill of 2008 and the Post-9/11 G.I. Bill of 2009—that provide for education opportunities, tuition benefits, and home loans. Of profound importance is the Servicemembers Civil Relief Act (SCRA) of 2003. This law provides financial protections to armed services personnel on active duty and their families. It is "intended to postpone or suspend certain civil obligations to enable servicemembers to devote full attention to duty and relieve family members."[13] Among the civil obligations the act postpones or suspends are "outstanding credit card debt, mortgage payments, pending trials, taxes, termination of lease, eviction."[14] The law also insulates up to $250,000 in life insurance against default for nonpayment.

I emphasize the special importance of SCRA because of alarming data on suicides and attempted suicides in the military, including those among personnel on active duty. Hypotheses about causes and reasons point to dangerous levels of depression and stress that derive in part from a service member learning of severe problems at home about which he or she can do nothing. The stress of military deployment and combat can combine with domestic stress to produce conditions that seem unbearable. But data show that service members not currently serving in combat or combat zones who have ample opportunity to communicate with their families may be at the greatest risk of suicide.

In 2009, 164 U.S. Marines attempted suicide, and 52 killed themselves. Navy Commander Aaron Werbel is the Marine Corps suicide-prevention officer and a psychologist. He reported a 2009 Marine suicide rate of 24 per 100,000, compared with the latest available civilian rate of 20 per 100,000. In the first five months of 2010, 89 made suicide attempts; 21 died.[15] Journalist Gregg Zoroya reports: "Much attention has been focused on the active-duty Army, which is more than twice the size of the Marine Corps. It suffered a record 163 soldier suicides in 2009, Army records show . . . a rate of 2.2 per 100,000."[16] The Marines are teaching sergeants and corporals in a suicide-prevention program to learn more about the troops they command and look for at-risk behavior, "with plans to place civilian suicide-prevention coordinators at each Marine installation and to provide a distress hotline."[17] More than half the Marines who killed themselves in 2010 "were or had been in combat."[18]

But General Peter Chiarelli, "the vice-chief of staff of the Army who led the effort to reduce suicides . . . said it wasn't just the stress of war that weighed heavily on soldiers, but also stresses from back home. 'For us to blame this just on the war would be wrong,' he said."[19] A higher percentage of soldiers kill themselves who are working in "forward-operating bases [with] easy access to phones and computers with which to call home" than in "more primitive outposts." Chiarelli emphasized the need to teach families to "understand the importance when their soldiers are deployed of not dragging them back into a life at home that they have very little ability to try and fix."[20] He also said the Army is teaching officers suicide-intervention practices.

Obviously, anything the military-support team can do to alleviate domestic stress, including ensuring that deployed service members and their families know and take advantage of their rights under SCRA, may lessen suicidal temptations or feelings of despair among police colleagues on active military duty. These matters should be brought to the attention of families before deployment.

A department-sponsored spouses association consisting of volunteers who work in cooperation with the MSO and other team members and who contribute to a solid and positive environment for families can be very helpful as well. Spouses may be better positioned than anyone else to counsel friends and family members against burdening deployed husbands or wives with bad domestic news. If I were a volunteer in such an association, and I encountered a family doing very badly—say, financially—in the absence of husband or wife, I would advise the MSO of the need for prompt assistance, including, where relevant, immediate application for benefits available under SCRA. If the department or agency had established any sort of emergency discretionary fund for temporary assistance to families, I would recommend its use pending SCRA action. Depending on relevant facts and circumstances, I would also consider reminding the head of the family at home of the risks of informing absent spouses of domestic problems about which they can do nothing.

Other measures are underway to lessen the stresses that accompany veterans' transition back to civilian life. In addition to federal statutes and court rulings designed to protect and assist armed forces personnel and veterans, some state governments are working wisely in cooperation with the federal government to expand veterans' benefits. In Wisconsin, a proposal under consideration from the Veterans Affairs Committee of the Legislative Assembly would grant veterans 128 university credit hours tuition-free, once their federal tuition benefits have been used in full.

Montana, Colorado, Washington, and California are helping veterans take advantage of eligibility under Department of Defense and Department of Veterans Affairs (VA) provisions for "health care, long-term care benefits, or pensions." These provide benefits that are financially superior to Medicaid—both for veterans who have not previously applied for a specific benefit under Medicaid and for veterans who have already been receiving financial assistance from Medicaid, including sometimes the "full cost of [a] nursing home." Veterans of service during and since World War II are benefiting from such steps by states. These steps should also be made known to deployed police and returning veterans who might benefit from them.[21]

Qualifications for the Ideal Military-Support or Liaison Officer. The Colorado Springs Police Department's requirement that an MSO hold supervisory or command rank and be respected in the police department confirms the seriousness of the department's dedication to the well-being of its personnel. I recommend that other departments follow this model, as without the MSO's having such standing, some police personnel will almost surely conclude that the position is not very important.

The requirement that the MSO have a background of military service carries comparable weight. A department cannot expect the MSO to be viewed as credible and trustworthy by police colleagues and their families before, during, and after deployment without this combination of stature and experience.

My colleague Captain Paul Ciesinski of the Hartford, Connecticut police department wrote me a very insightful letter that bears on this point: "While only a few percentage points of the general population are veterans, much less war veterans, this is in my experience not the case with police officers. There appears to be more overlap between the two populations (veterans and police officers) than in the general population. It seems reasonable that the same personality type self-selects into both professions."

Ciesinski observes:

> My training and experience as a police officer was a significant ben-
> efit to me in Iraq due to the psychological conditioning that comes
> with the job. Police officers are emotionally tolerant of the idea that
> other people will try to hurt and kill them. This is not always true of
> soldiers from other walks of life, and soldiers I served with had a
> hard time addressing that their lives would be in danger. . . . The
> restraint in the uses of force I was taught as a police officer was
> simultaneously a potential detriment and an experienced benefit to
> me in Iraq. It was a detriment because I had to suppress use-of-force
> rules I learned and internalized for a decade and a half as a police
> officer (for example, in combat it is allowable and indeed necessary
> to shoot fleeing enemy personnel in the back, even if they pose no
> imminent threat to anyone; this is illegal for a police officer). It was
> a benefit because the type of war we were fighting, a counter-
> insurgency, inherently called for restraint in the use of force com-
> pared to other types of wars. I was able to explain these constraints
> to my men in a coherent manner, and obtain willing compliance, by
> using concepts and verbiage I had internalized as a police officer.
> Returning to "the job" is difficult after a combat tour. People ask you
> if you killed anyone, if you were shot at, but there is an implicit, and
> sometimes explicit, assumption that something is or could be wrong
> with you psychologically due to your combat experience. Offers of
> psychological counseling from your agency upon your return, meant
> with the best of intentions and necessary at a minimum to defend
> the agency from liability, can be interpreted by the returning soldier
> as a vote of no confidence or suspicion that you are now less capa-
> ble of being a police officer than before your combat deployment.
> Considerable tact must be exercised in these issues. Every
> soldier/police officer had a different combat experience, depending
> on the time and place he served. My experience as a lieutenant
> colonel and advisor to an Iraqi Army brigadier general and infantry
> brigade commander in 2005–2006 would be different in many ways
> from a sergeant in a well drilling unit in Afghanistan in 2010 or a
> tank gunman corporal in the initial invasion of Iraq in 2003.[22]

These are the sorts of insights that only a person with civilian police experience and military service can gain firsthand and apply in assisting others and in considering best policies and practices. Ciesinski's warning that offering, let alone requiring, psychological counseling to returning veterans may be interpreted as suspicion or a vote of no confidence echoes what returning veterans have told me. His comments also suggest a point that medical personnel have emphasized about the circumstances of veterans reaching home: they will encounter people, perhaps in leadership positions in their institutions, who do not know the difference between perfectly normal reactions to trauma and post-traumatic stress disorder (PTSD). The veterans may be adversely prejudged by people who confuse the former with the latter.

Normal Reactions to Trauma versus Post-Traumatic Stress Disorder. Andrea Elkon is a clinical psychologist in the Atlanta, Georgia, Veterans Administration Medical Center. David Glick is a Drug Enforcement Administration area clinician, licensed clinical social worker, and employee-assistance professional who has worked extensively in police and law enforcement agencies. Both Elkon and Glick have explained to me that post-traumatic stress, including combat stress reaction, is perfectly normal following traumatic experiences. It is distinct from PTSD and should not be identified as or confused with any sort of *disorder* at all. Yet, institutions often mistakenly rush to judgment. Police departments and law enforcement agencies are not exempt from this serious error.

In her presentations to police departments, Elkon explains that "nearly all troops who serve in a combat zone experience some type of combat stress reaction in the early days and weeks of returning home. If these reactive symptoms persist beyond one month, the condition is referred to as . . . PTSD. Current estimates of PTSD among returning Operation Enduring Freedom/Operation Iraqi Freedom veterans: 10 to 20 percent."[23]

Glick, who has assisted law enforcement personnel suffering stress reactions from traumatic experience in the line of duty, explained that unless the traumatic experience is continuous over time—as with an innocent person who becomes the subject of an extended internal affairs investigation or a criminal prosecution—many police recover from post-traumatic stress within the thirty-day window identified by Elkon. Obviously, physical injuries, healing, rehabilitation, and the stress they cause may take longer to overcome without being indicative of any disorder.

Dr. Jonathan Shay is a psychiatrist who treats Vietnam combat veterans with severe, chronic, post-traumatic stress disorder. He works in a VA outpatient clinic. Shay is the author of *Achilles in Vietnam: Combat Trauma and the Undoing of Character.*[24] It is a book of powerfully instructive insights that all police leaders oughtto read.

Shay explains that many of the victims of PTSD have suffered a combination of "betrayal and bereavement" that makes recovery extremely difficult. This combination, which gained momentum in Vietnam after civilian and military officials established "body count" as the criterion of success in troop missions, has affected many of Shay's patients. They returned from Vietnam having had no chance to mourn the deaths of comrades and with deep feelings of betrayal that were intensified at home by media and public disapprobation, contempt, and indifference—and also by being blamed for "losing" the Vietnam War by veterans of previous wars. They felt that civilian defense leaders, manufacturers of weapons, rear echelon officers, and some of their own officers "betrayed" them by failing to do "what's right."[25]

They describe betrayal by officers who lied to them and lied about what they had accomplished. In one instance, told by officers that Viet Cong nearby were offloading weapons from boats, U.S. troops moved into position at night and opened massive firepower:

> It was just a constant, constant firepower. It seemed like no one ever ran out of ammo. Daylight came [long pause], and we found out we killed a lot of fishermen and kids. What got us thoroughly f— –ing confused is, at that time you say to the team, "Don't worry about it. Everything's f— –ing fine." Because that's what you're getting from upstairs. The f— –ing colonel says, "Don't worry about it. We'll take care of it. . . . We got body count! We have body count!". . . . So we packed up and we moved out. They wanted to give us a f— –ing Unit Citation—them f— –ing maggots. A lot of medals came down

from it. The lieutenants got medals, and I know the f– –ing colonel got his f– –ing medal. And they would have award ceremonies, y'know, I'd be standing like a f– –ing jerk and they'd be handing out f– –ing medals for killing civilians.[26]

Vietnam veterans felt betrayed by six-month rotations of officers that repeatedly left troops under the command of new leaders who had no idea what they were doing or how to protect their troops from ambush and other deadly hazards. They felt betrayed by "the military officers, civilian defense officials, and civilian contractors . . . involved in the specification, design, prototyping, testing, manufacture, field testing, and acceptance of the M-16 [rifle]."[27] The weapon was unreliable and subject to "stoppages" in the middle of close combat; soldiers called it a "Mattel toy" whose stock shattered when used in hand-to-hand combat. Troops whose lives were held in trust by their officers and whose survival depended on their weapons viewed their officers' distribution of the M-16 "as a gross betrayal of the duties of care and of loyalty."[28]

Veterans of the Vietnam War feel that "what is right" was betrayed, that the men who died were betrayed, and that they were betrayed by being denied the chance to mourn dead comrades: "[M]ourning was dreaded, perfunctory, delayed, devalued, mocked, fragmented, minimized, deflected, disregarded, and sedated."[29] One narrative among many about officers dismissing death and dead comrades as if they did not matter comes from a veteran who said: "The battalion commander droned through the names of the men who had died since the last 'debriefing' and then, without pausing for breath, concluded with, 'The mess tent is open.'"[30]

Shay is often asked why so many more veterans of Vietnam suffer long-term psychological injuries compared with veterans of World War II. Data for World War II are sketchy at best, but Shay notes:

Most World War II soldiers trained together, went overseas together, fought together, had R&R together, and came home together. The typical Vietnam soldier went over alone, integrated himself as the "f– –ing new guy" in an already formed and highly stressed unit to the extent that luck and his personal traits permitted, went on R&R alone, and came home alone, often leaving behind a unit that was still in combat. He had no chance to "debrief," to talk about what had happened with people he trusted who understood his experience. What a returning soldier needs most when leaving war is not a mental health professional but a living community to whom his experience matters. There is usually such a community close at hand: his or her surviving comrades.[31]

A police department is also a living community. Its military-support team and MSO are key members of a smaller community designed to assist veterans and their families—not least by being people to whom the veteran's experience and that of his loved ones "matter." Most of the members of the team, as well as partners, colleagues with parallel or associated assignments, friends, and supervisors, do not have medical or clinical expertise. They can invite conversation without asking intrusive and possibly prejudicial questions of the sort Ciesinski rightly warns against. They should avoid hasty suspicion or skepticism about the fitness of veterans for duty. But if they observe lasting problematic changes in behavior after return from deployment—anxiety around other people, hypervigilance, actions essential in combat but seldom seen in civilian policing, inordinate and chronic anger, or problems concentrating—they cannot responsibly turn a blind eye. That, too, can be a form of betrayal that risks doing a disservice to the very people they are trying to help. Instead of ignoring the behavior, they should suggest conversation, the possibility of visiting a therapist, or a talk with a supervisor. But neither should the members of the team be left to their own devices in reaching out to a veteran.

Each department's leadership needs to make clear what it expects of front-line supervisors, the MSO, and military-support team members under such circumstances. This question of "what to do" when veterans or family members exhibit potentially dangerous behavior should not be left entirely to individual discretion, and neglect of it may lead to danger for the veteran, families, other police, and the public. Knowing that many returning veterans have suffered bereavement while deployed, and perhaps have encountered one sort of betrayal or another, we can see

from Shay's account that we should do nothing sudden or surprising that
they could easily perceive as betrayal. Obviously, this implies that the
answer to the question of what to do has to be made public from the outset: no surprises. The same is true of requiring a veteran to see a qualified
therapist or doctor immediately upon return to civilian duty. Therapy has
to be arranged in such a way that no one could reasonably believe the
meeting to be secretly a fitness-for-duty examination.

But to repeat an earlier point: if the problematic behavior occurs
during active service in civilian policing, USERRA no longer constrains
the department from applying institutional standards, protocols, and
regulations, including fitness-for-duty evaluations. Indeed, doing so is
obligatory, not a matter to be left to anyone's discretion.

Here, as elsewhere, family members, friends, colleagues, partners at
work, and a trusted MSO can be helpful by suggesting to a veteran
just returned from deployment the wisdom of not rushing back to
work and of allowing time for patient adjustment to being home. IACP's
publication *Combat Veterans and Law Enforcement: A Transition Guide for
Veterans Beginning or Continuing Careers in Law Enforcement* delivers this
advice very well:

> Don't jump into work too soon. Take some time off, relax, and
> enjoy being back in the United States. . . . Take the time to
> decompress, get reacquainted with family and friends, and
> adjust to family life and normal daily activities. This adjust-
> ment period before returning to work will help you cope with
> the normal challenges that occur after serving in combat. . . .
> If your department's in-service training officer provides or
> requires training to support your transition from combat to
> policing your community, be willing to accept the additional
> training. If your department does not automatically offer or
> require transitional training, ask for the training or assistance
> as you readjust [your] skill sets.[32]

Heeding this advice can prevent problems that spring from a hasty
return to work and attendant denial or avoidance of the need for patience
during transition. A chief who delivers this message while presiding over

a celebration of veterans' returning home from deployment may be most helpful of all.

Can an MSO Be Effective without Combat Experience? In addition to command rank in the civilian department or agency and military experience, is it necessary for an MSO to have had *combat* experience (as opposed to peacetime service or noncombat positions)? If not necessary, is it desirable? It is a commonplace belief among combat veterans that no one except other veterans can understand their experience—and even then, possibly only veterans of the same type of combat or in the same zone or theater of battle. Having had combat experience may elevate the credibility of an MSO among returning veterans. But desirable as such experience may be, I do not believe it should be a requirement for the position. In the first place, such a requirement would exclude many well-respected civilian police with military but not combat experience who would make fine MSOs.

Beyond that, I am not convinced that the experience of combat veterans is absolutely, unqualifiedly, and without exception unobtainable through vicarious learning. Such learning, certainly, cannot be altogether an armchair project in understanding; acquiring any grasp at all requires enormous patience, humility, and hard work—and may depend on the desire of one or more combat veterans to lead those without combat experience to some level of understanding.

Whether we can apprehend something of combat experience vicariously is a question of great ethical, practical, and philosophical importance, so I do not want to pass over it lightly here. It is ethically important because so much of moral life turns on our trying diligently to see things from the place and point of view of others—to take the place and point of view of others in deciding which kinds of thoughts, feelings, and actions toward them are morally worthy of us. It is of practical importance because gaining insight into combat experience can bring new wisdom and a refined sense of proportion to deliberations about the fairness and likely effectiveness of institutional expectations, standards, practices, policies, regulations, and procedures—and to the exercise of leadership itself. (These two dimensions of understanding have as much to do with successful family life as with professional life.) Finally, the question of the efficacy of vicarious learning is philosophically important because it addresses the limits of human knowledge—specifically, knowledge of minds other than one's own.

While conversation, correspondence, reading, watching documentaries, and pursuing other forms of study may further the possibility of vicarious learning about combat experience, policing offers a unique foundation. As Ciesinski and many others have observed, there are differences and similarities between policing and active military duty, and considerable sameness in the experience of going into harm's way, whether to protect police colleagues, military comrades, or strangers. When civilian police and law enforcement personnel confront or are attacked by criminal gangs, narcoterrorists, or mass murderers armed with automatic weapons and explosives, or are fired upon without warning during traffic stops or the service of warrants, they are engaged in a form of combat, albeit under different orders and regulations than those of military personnel. Military combat usually lasts longer and the terror may grind harder over time against soldiers, but the supposition that combat is utterly or even mainly beyond the understanding of police seems to me mistaken.

I have never served in any of the armed services or witnessed military combat firsthand. My work for more than thirty-five years with police and law enforcement personnel has brought me into the presence of criminal violence and its often-deadly consequences. I have watched SWAT teams perform brilliantly coordinated—choreographed—operations in which everyone functioned with one mind and purpose, each alert to the safety of hostages, other innocents involved or nearby, and colleagues. I have also witnessed inadequately trained SWAT teams do very badly under pressure. I have observed gang enforcement teams do well in situations for which there is no accurate description but combat; I have watched partners and teams in uniform and partners and teams in plain clothes do their work effectively while in danger, each member constantly aware of and protective of the others. In these respects, the ways of thinking, feeling, and acting that typify such outstanding police and law enforcement personnel very deeply resemble the experience described by combat soldiers.

Some veterans of combat have talked with me extensively about their experience in battle. All of them have been my friends. They knew that they could trust me, that I cared about them, that I would never be judgmental, and that I would never betray a confidence. They knew that I would willingly sit through long silences without interrupting and that I would also try to learn about their experiences through formal study, such as reading, that might inform my perspective in our conversations. In some cases, these veterans talked about their broader military experience away from combat. On occasion, they spoke about injury, hospitalization, and rehabilitation; about capture, imprisonment, and torture; and about returning to civilian life. Some of these friends requested that I help them learn about writing letters, essays, or memoirs to enable them to communicate with comrades at a distance or with family members or close police friends, or possibly with a broader readership. What they described to me resembles in many respects the insights and emphases of very instructive published military memoirs. I have concluded from our conversations and related study over time that their combat experience is not utterly impenetrable to and completely beyond the understanding of a trusted friend, a loved one, a dedicated civilian police partner.

In all these conversations, the centrality of comradeship in combat is a common theme. Combat veterans talk about comradeship as the reason for braving dangers and comrades as those who matter most of all. This is largely the case in published memoirs of combat veterans as well.

Learning from memoirs and war reporting. J. Glenn Gray received his Ph.D. in philosophy from Columbia University on the same day in 1941 that he received his draft notice. Gray served as a combat infantryman and subsequently as an intelligence officer during assignments in Africa, Italy, and France from 1941 until 1945. In *The Warriors: Reflections on Men in Battle*, Gray explains:

> [C]omradeship at first develops through the consciousness of an obstacle to be overcome through common effort. A fighting unit with morale is one in which many are of like mind and determination, agreed on the suppression of individual desires in the interest of a shared purpose. . . . The impulse to self-sacrifice is an intrinsic element in the association of organized men in pursuit of a difficult and dangerous goal.[33]

No one who has served in or witnessed firsthand a truly accomplished SWAT team can miss the applicability of Gray's description of comradeship and morale. Gray further emphasized comradeship in his reflections on "the secret attractions of war . . . of the emotional environment of warfare, more specifically, the atmosphere of violence." He wrote, "I believe that they [the attractions] are: the delight in seeing [lust of the eye], the delight in comradeship, the delight in destruction."[34] Comradeship alone, unadulterated mutual loyalty under extreme peril, is what motivates soldiers in deadly combat situations—not abstractions. Police who face extreme peril together experience this sense of comradeship. It is likely that some police experience the other two attractions as well. Who among us has never felt the "lust of the eye" amidst the gore of a terrible accident or catastrophe?

Gray continues:

> The soldier who has yielded himself to the fortunes of war, has sought to kill and to escape being killed, or who has even lived long enough in the disordered landscape of battle, is no longer what he was. He becomes in some sense a fighter, whether he wills it or not—at least most men do. His moods and dispositions are affected by the presence of others and the encompassing environment of threat and fear. He must surrender in a measure to the will of others and to superior force. In a real sense he becomes a fighting man, a Homo furens . . . a subspecies of Homo sapiens. . . . Man as warrior is only partly a man, yet, fatefully enough, this aspect of him is capable of transforming the whole.[35]

Civilian police and law enforcement agents know as well as anyone that the phenomenon Gray points out is not unique to men and women in military service or military combat. The responsibility for prevention of the most violent crimes and apprehension of the most deadly criminals can have the same effects. Gray concludes that "any fighting unit must have a limited and specific objective, and the more defined and bounded it is, the greater the willingness, as a rule, on the part of soldiers to abandon their natural desire for self-preservation. . . . Men are true comrades only when each is ready to give up his life for the other, without reflection and without thought of personal loss."[36] The best police and law enforcement members—as well as the most devoted parents—I have ever known meet this description.

I find in Gray also an explanation of a soldier's attachment to his weapons that further illuminates the feelings of betrayal that can accompany defective weapons, as we saw in Shay's account of Vietnam soldiers and the M-16. "The intimate relation of the soldier to his weapons involves more than any love of possessions." Joined with the impulse to survival, "often the vehicles and implements of war come to be a replacement for home . . . not only an extension of the soldier's own power, but . . . a link with past and future."[37] Many of us who have worked extensively in or with the criminal justice system know police officers or law enforcement personnel who, when wrongly abandoned by self-righteous and irresponsible police executives, have been forced by considerations of prudence and devotion to family to plead guilty to a crime they did not commit. They do so to avoid the severe sentence that could arise from conviction by a prejudiced jury manipulated by a ruthlessly ambitious prosecutor. When the crime is a felony, the officer loses both his or her job and the right to bear arms. This combination can tear to pieces a person's belief in his or her ability to protect loved ones in the worst of times; undermine a family's history and culture of hunting as part of raising children; and permanently sever normal ties between past, present, and future.

Gray also tells of the spirit-rending tension a soldier may face between conscience and obedience to orders. The example he provides does not take place in combat, but it has so much to do with the emerging character of a person who has seen combat that I include it here. It also bears on the emerging character of people I have known in policing. Gray describes a situation where he and a comrade decided that being court-martialed, punished, and dishonorably discharged were better than obeying a specific order.

For several months, Gray and his comrade, a fellow intelligence officer, were attached to an infantry division in France. The divisional intelligence officer, a colonel, was "an insensitive military tyrant . . . who liked to meddle with our somewhat specialized job of interrogating the civilian populace in the search for spies and saboteurs the retreating Germans might have left behind or sent over the front."[38] When the division reached Alsace, they found a number of young Alsatian men who had been forced into the German army when France fell in 1940. These men, many of whom had been conscripted as boys, deserted as soon as they could and returned to Alsace, where civilians, at the risk of their own lives, hid them from the Gestapo.

The division colonel insisted that unless these youths could show discharge papers from the German army, they must be treated as German prisoners of war and sent away to prison camps. He reached this "breathtaking" conclusion and gave the order to send young men away in trucks with captured Germans, despite knowing that the Germans never gave discharge papers to deserters. Gray and his comrade refused to obey the order because it was hideously unjust and obeying it would alienate the Alsatian people. The young men and the rest of the civilian population were doing everything possible to help the Americans. The colonel then for a second time ordered Gray and his "fair-minded, profane, and intelligent" comrade to obey, "and was this time insulting and insistent."[39]

The third time, the colonel threatened them "with court martial and worse for disobeying a direct order." Gray recalls:

> The two of us talked it over and decided to continue to refuse. It was not so much courage on my part as physical weariness and moral disgust at the injustices of warfare. In the most obscene language, my associate declared that the army could court-martial him a hundred times and he would not obey such a stupid, senseless command. . . . He had been much longer in the war than I, having served with distinction in Africa and Sicily as well as Italy and France. If his concern with the injustice of the order was not as great as mine, his resoluteness was greater, and fortified me.[40]

Here again, we see the power of comradeship, and the kind of moral fortification with which many police and their partners on the job are entirely familiar. And what decent person has never felt the tension and faced a grueling decision between conscience and orders—whether in military or civilian life?

Gray knew that his court-martial, dishonorable discharge, and disgrace would break his father's heart. "Still, I knew that if I did not draw the line here, I would be unable to draw it anywhere." The two men prepared for the worst. The colonel reported their insubordination to Army headquarters. "He chanced to reach an intelligent officer who knew us both slightly." That officer asked the colonel why they had disobeyed. The colonel had never asked, "but when he did communicate the cause, Army Intelligence found our reasons good and within a day or two sent through an order that all Alsatian deserters were to be left with their families and in no case to be transported anywhere with German prisoners of war." Gray wrote that this experience had profoundly furthered his self-knowledge and his conclusion that "survival without integrity is worse than perishing outright."[41] This is no different from the creed of exceptional individuals everywhere and large numbers of people who bear the public trust faithfully in policing and law enforcement.

Throughout memoirs of combat soldiers, as in conversations and correspondence with veterans of combat, comradeship comes to the fore. Matt Gallagher, who led troops in Iraq, says of his comrades: "Soldiers were trained to be loyal, and the type of loyalty we learned in Iraq could not be conveyed to them [civilians] at home, whether they stayed true or not [true to returning veterans]. We relied on one another to survive, trusting each other with our very lives, under the most trying of circumstances."[42]

Bing West, a decorated former combat Marine officer and author of *The Wrong War: Grit, Strategy, and the Way Out of Afghanistan*,[43] has embedded twice with members of the Third Platoon of Kilo Company, Fifth Marine Regiment, in Afghanistan. West recalled: "Over the past six months, two members of the Third Platoon have been killed, two have lost limbs and eight have suffered shrapnel or bullet wounds. A quarter of the original platoon is now gone. . . . Lieutenant Vic Garcia . . . the platoon commander now in his third combat tour, has infused his platoon with an aggressive instinct, but he's not foolhardy. 'We're looking for a fight,' he said. 'But we think before we move.'" Between September 2010 and March 2011, "the third platoon has shot somewhere between 125 and 208 Taliban . . . The cumulative effect has been crushing."[44]

Troops in the platoon objected that soldiers like Sergeant Matthew Abate, their hero and a comrade of the highest order, have gone unrecognized in the United States for their courage and sacrifice. "When a patrol hit a minefield in late October, Sgt. Abate had left his safe position and run to apply tourniquets and carry out the screaming, grievously wounded men. He was killed in action five weeks later, but only the platoon remembers his name."[45] His valor and sacrifice for his comrades made him their hero.

Describing the motives of these soldiers, West wrote: "The members of the platoon do not care about bringing freedom and development to Afghanistan. They are here because they believe they are defending America. . . . They endure the mud, heat, stench, blood, fatigue and terror of lost limbs and lost lives. There is hard bark on these men. . . . The grunts chose their profession and they draw satisfaction from their Spartan existence. . . . These soldiers have not lost their devotion to the mission or their country."[46]

The journalist Sebastian Junger made five trips into the Korengal Valley of Afghanistan over a fifteen-month period in 2007 and 2008. While there, Junger was embedded with combat troops in "axle-breaking, helicopter-crashing, mind-bending terrain" where "few military plans survive intact for even an hour." He came to think of comradeship as learning to play by "big-boy rules": "making your interests secondary to those of the group no matter how much it costs you." Soldiers understand that war is "about winning" and to win, every soldier has to "make decisions based not on what's best for him but on what's best for the group. If everyone does that, most of the group survives. If no one does, most of the group dies."[47]

Big-boy rules cover virtually everything in the behavior of comrades in a combat unit: "Once I watched a private accost another private whose bootlaces were trailing on the ground. Not that he cared what it looked like, but if something happened suddenly—and out there everything happened suddenly—the guy with the loose laces couldn't be counted on to keep his feet at a crucial moment. It was the other guy's life he was risking, not just his own." Junger tells, too, of an instance where the odor of a man's urine meant he was not drinking enough water. "If you're not hydrated you're that much closer to becoming a heat casualty, and that could slow a unit down long enough to get cornered and overrun. There was no such thing as personal safety out there; what happened to you happened to everyone. . . . Frankly, after you got used to living that way it was hard to go home."[48]

Many civilians, Junger notes, can live carelessly and get away with it. Not so in combat or in readiness for combat. And not so for civilian police who, day after day, fill dangerous assignments. I have never seen truly accomplished, exemplary police, including hostage-rescue team and SWAT members, who played by anything except "big-boy rules" in training, preparation, and subsequent action. I also know men and women who head police departments and play by "big-boy rules" in the sense that they invariably put the interests of the department and the people who work for them ahead of their own.

Shay, too, describes the singular bonds of loyalty among comrades: "Men fight mainly for their comrades; this has become conventional wisdom even among civilians. Prolonged exposure to danger and the profound strain of battle compel this contraction of loyalty to some degree in every war. . . . The veteran speaks of his training in an elite unit: 'We were down in Kentucky, and you got to care about people there, everyone in that outfit. . . . You grew like [fingers on] a hand.'"[49] I believe comradeship in the face of extreme peril—the unity of purpose, mutual trust, loyalty, and reciprocal reliance that bind soldiers together in united commitment to "big-boy rules"—deters suicide. Killing oneself betrays one's comrades; it weakens the unit and imperils everyone.

Gender differences in combat experience. Everything we can learn about the experience of combat, the capacity to play by "big-boy rules," and the "iron courage"[50] of which Gray writes (see the epigraph to this chapter) transcends gender differences. Narratives of women in military service, and in combat, reveal the continuity of their experience with that of their male comrades.

Officially, of course, U.S. female troops are prohibited from serving in combat. But it is disingenuous to claim that none of them serve in combat areas or in combat conditions. Many drive vehicles in convoys in Iraq and Afghanistan that come under attack from insurgents; some are explosive ordinance disposal (EOD) technicians. In plain language, an

EOD technician is a member of a bomb squad. This and other assignments thrust female troops into harm's way just as much as combat or
immediate combat-support assignments that may be restricted to men.

The way the public conceives of women's duties and achievements in
the military, however, is very different from the way it conceives of the
duties and achievements of men. Genevieve Chase, founder of the
American Women Veterans organization, says: "The VA has diagnosed
some female veterans of Iraq and Afghanistan with depression instead of
post-traumatic stress disorder, because of the mind-set that they didn't
serve in combat." The Army's 10th Mountain Division awarded Chase
both a Purple Heart and a Combat Action Badge because she was injured
when her vehicle was attacked in Afghanistan by a suicide bomber.
Chase adds that many civilians at home, and even some VA hospital staff
members, take for granted that women veterans have not served in or
been exposed to combat. "There is nothing worse than having gone
through everything your buddies did when you were there and to come
home and have people treat you as an afterthought or arm candy."[51]
Would the feelings of any civilian police officer, or anyone at all, whose
true work was ignored or prejudicially dismissed feel any differently?

Many narratives of women's military service and duties in Iraq and
Afghanistan confirm our obligation to understand what women actually
experience during military service. This is especially true for any member
of a police department's military-support team. No kind of prejudice
toward or avoidable ignorance about veterans—male or female—has any
place there.

Sergeant Michelle Barefield, an EOD technician and squad leader, was
awarded the Bronze Star for her actions in a five-hundred-square-mile
area that included Baghdad International Airport:

> Her leadership contributed to the safe resolution of 828 EOD
> emergency-response missions, including 583 IEDs (Improvised
> Explosive Devices), 119 unexploded ordnance responses, 81
> post-blast analyses, 72 weapons caches, and 9 vehicle-borne
> IED missions. The destruction of 11,883 ordnance items,
> 78,750 rounds of small-arms ammunition, 448 IED compo-
> nents, and 1,100 pounds of homemade explosives significantly

hindered insurgent groups in conducting attacks against coalition forces. Barefield personally led eighty missions.[52]

The fatality rate among EOD technicians since September 11, 2001, has risen to unprecedented levels in both Iraq and Afghanistan. The stress of the work, especially for leaders such as Barefield who are responsible for other troops, has lasting effects. On returning from Iraq to Seymour Johnson Air Force Base in North Carolina, Barefield—like all other Air Force veterans returning from Iraq and Afghanistan—was "required to see a Global War on Terrorism deployment specialist at the base before [she] integrated back into society. Then airmen are required to follow up three, six, and nine months later."[53] Barefield feared for her health because she was preoccupied, even obsessed, with the deaths of EOD technician comrades who mattered deeply to her, and she was suffering grim dreams. When she sought help, VA doctors diagnosed and treated her for post-traumatic stress disorder; later, medical personnel at Fort Bragg successfully treated her for traumatic brain injury.

Learning from "the other side." Three other valuable sources of vicarious learning about the experience of others in extreme combat conditions are documentaries, films, and war memoirs of foreign and even enemy troops. A prime example is *The Anderson Platoon*. It is a 1968 Academy Award–winning documentary made by Pierre Schoendoerffer, a veteran of France's First Indochina War. To complete the documentary, Schoendoerffer spent a year in Vietnam with members of a thirty-three-man platoon within the U.S. 1st Air Cavalry Division. *The Anderson Platoon* draws the viewer into the intense fighting in Vietnam in 1966; warfare and combat injuries from enemy booby traps; injuries inflicted by accident; comrades comforting and evacuating the wounded; comradeship itself in exhausting, stressful jungle-combat conditions; the lives of men fighting and risking death far from home; and even delivering a baby in a battlefield.

The leader of the Anderson Platoon was Lieutenant Joseph B. Anderson, a West Point graduate. Twenty years later, Schoendoerffer met with survivors of the platoon and released a sequel in 1989, *Reminiscence*. Joe Anderson and I have served together for many years on the Quaker Chemical

Corporation Board of Directors. I admire the soldier he was and the veteran he has become.

Even war memoirs of enemy veterans can give us some intellectual, moral, and emotional access to life in combat. One such memoir is *The Forgotten Soldier* by Guy Sajer. Sajer was an Alsatian boy of mixed French and German parentage who entered the German army at the age of sixteen in 1942. Sajer believed the lie told by his superiors that France and Germany were allies in the fight against communism. He thought he was being loyal to both his French and his German heritage. Trained as a truck driver, he drove in convoys ordered to relieve the German 6th Army at Stalingrad. The convoys never made it. German field marshall Friedrich Paulus was forced to surrender the army to the Russians. As the tide turned against the Germans on the Eastern Front, retreat became a nightmare of exposure to deadly freezing conditions and attacks from overwhelmingly superior Russian ground and air power. As desperation grew, German officers asked for volunteers to transfer to the infantry. When too few volunteered, the officers forced troops, including Sajer's closest comrade, to transfer. So they could stay together, Sajer then volunteered. Such is the power of comradeship.

Sajer's memoir is a chronicle over four hundred pages long that describes three years of suffering, chronic illness, betrayal by rear echelon bureaucrats who hoarded food while troops went hungry, combat against relentless enemy troops, carnage, bereavement in the death of comrades, and the slaughter of civilians. The book depicts page after page of horror and despair. As the troops were driven into the besieged town of Memel near the Baltic Sea, Sajer describes "an island of courage in an infinite sea of anguish."[54]

Though almost unimaginably ghastly, is such experience really entirely beyond our own moral sensibilities and heartache, our own capacity for vicarious understanding? The feelings of any patient reader when immersed in such accounts of combat say no; nothing human is utterly beyond comprehension. In a review of *The Forgotten Soldier* published shortly after the book appeared in English, J. Glenn Gray wrote that Sajer "succeeded uncommonly well in describing the details of action and feeling of suffering and terror that fell to his lot as a private. . . . Those who have never known war at first hand will be unable to grasp more than a fraction of the reality he describes." A fraction, perhaps—but not nothing at all.[55]

I conclude that combat experience is, in some degree, knowable to noncombatants who have the right opportunities to learn, the desire and determination to understand as much as they can, the right teachers, and the right kinds of overlapping or analogous experience. Anyone on a military-support team should make at least some effort in this direction with the intention and hope of becoming as qualified as possible to work with veterans returning to or entering their departments. I infer as well that, all other things being equal, combat experience in an MSO would be desirable. But civilian police and veterans who have not seen military combat and serve as MSOs or other members of military-support teams can keep faith with and deserve credibility from veterans through a suitable admixture of humility, willingness to learn, and outstanding professionalism. This conclusion is confirmed by the actual experience of departments whose very effective MSOs have not previously served in combat.

It may also be possible for one or more members of a military-support team to elevate their service by working directly with and learning from a transition assistance adviser (TAA) at their local National Guard headquarters. The TAA serves as "the statewide point of contact to assist members in accessing Veterans Affairs benefits and healthcare services."[56] The linkage with the VA, as IACP rightly observes, has to be maintained to provide the best service to veterans, but working conscientiously with an able TAA may provide other benefits to the team.

Unintended Consequences

Sadly, the practice of honoring veterans can be accompanied by painful challenges. MSOs, military-support teams, and friends and colleagues of veterans in the police force should be aware of these challenges and prepared to address them.

The Prodigal Effect. Readers will remember the biblical parable of the Prodigal Son told in Luke 15:11–32. The younger of two sons asks his father to give him his inheritance in advance. He takes his share of the estate, goes far away, and squanders all that he has in sinful and dissipated living. Dissolute and desperate, he struggles home to beg for forgiveness and mercy and for menial labor so he can avoid starvation. When the father sees the lost son, he rejoices, has the son clad in fine robes, and orders a fatted calf to be slain and a feast to be prepared. The older brother, who has stayed at home and faithfully done all the work required of him by his father, has never received such special treatment, rejoicing, or celebration. He deeply resents the selfish behavior of his younger brother and their father's rejoicing in his return. The older brother feels that he has been taken for granted, badly used, and subjected to grievous injustice.

In the course of writing this chapter, I have met a few—a very few—police officers who resemble the older brother in the parable. They resent public events honoring departing and returning veterans for their military service because they feel they receive no gratitude or honor for doing additional work in the department during the veteran's absence. Their typical grievance is as follows: "A guy leaves for a year. For all I know, he's taking it easy on an extended vacation in some rear echelon country club. When he comes back, he's a hero. What about us? We did his job for a year and didn't even get paid overtime. Nobody thanks us for taking up the slack."

We probably think to ourselves, "That's petty and small-minded. Cops ought to rise above that." And so they should. But fair is fair; police do sometimes take on additional work while colleagues are on leave, without public acknowledgment, gratitude, or extra compensation. In celebratory events for returning veterans, police leaders should stress to the public that their safety during a veteran's absence depends increasingly on every officer who does more than his or her share to sustain the highest levels of police protection and service. Those officers' praises, too, deserve to be sung. The message should be that service members, cops, and citizens are all in this together. Reciprocal helpfulness and cooperation make life better for everyone.

Neither the prodigal effect nor any other reservations should deter us from publicly honoring every service member who departs for and returns from active duty. We have made the unconscionable mistake in the past—as with veterans of the Vietnam War—of ignoring or visiting contempt and opprobrium on returning veterans. There can be no excuse for repeating that cruel mistake.

But for many people, the atrocities of September 11 have faded into the past, and wars against terrorism are no longer the highest priorities. Times have changed. A global economic crisis starting in 2007 has shifted public concern. By January 2011, a CBS News/*New York Times* poll found that only 12 percent of adults nationwide considered wars in Afghanistan and Iraq "the most important thing for Congress to concentrate on right now."[57] Confirming this trend, in March 2011 a Bloomberg national poll found that only 7 percent of adults nationwide considered war in Afghanistan "the most important issue facing the country right now."[58] In the following month, a CBS News/*New York Times* poll found that only 4 percent of adults nationwide identified wars in Iraq and Afghanistan as "the most important problem facing this country today."[59]

Nonetheless, many adults and children turn out to honor returning veterans and to memorialize and support the families of those who have died. Police departments are among the most faithful in doing so. They set a good example for the citizenry; their practice of honoring veterans prevents them from being ignored or forgotten.

Our failure to honor veterans of Vietnam guides philosopher Charles Griswold's poignant interpretation of the Vietnam Veterans Memorial. In *Forgiveness: A Philosophical Exploration*, he tells us of its distinctiveness and importance. The memorial bears two inscriptions. The first says: "In honor of the men and women of the armed forces of the United States who served in the Vietnam War. The names of those who gave their lives and of those who remain missing are inscribed in the order they were taken from us." The second inscription reads: "Our nation honors the courage, sacrifice, and devotion to duty and country of its Vietnam veterans. The Memorial was built with private contributions from the American people."

"Normally," Griswold explains, "war memorials honor those who died, not all who fought, and normally, they honor the cause, as well. . . . The point is emphasized even by the monument's title: it is a memorial to the Vietnam veterans, not the Vietnam War. That it honors everyone who fought there without qualification suggests that they had not previously been honored by the American people. . . . Public recognition of the sacrifice [of Vietnam veterans] rights the wrong of earlier official oblivion."[60]

Police and public alike who honor active-duty service members and veterans in a timely way banish that "official oblivion" to which no veterans who have served honorably deserve to be exiled.

Social and Criminal Justice Problems Involving Veterans. Of the roughly 23 million living U.S. veterans, government officials estimate that over 100,000 are homeless. By 2008, the Bureau of Justice Statistics estimated that "229,000 veterans were in local jails and state and federal prisons, with 400,000 on probation and 75,000 on parole."[61] I have found no firm estimates of the number of veterans of Iraq and Afghanistan who abuse prescription drugs and illegal narcotics, but experts agree that percentages are rising, especially among younger veterans.

Unemployment figures for young veterans returning to civilian life consistently run high. Early in 2011, the *Washington Post* reported: "Concerns that Guard and Reserve Troops will be gone for long stretches and that veterans might have mental health issues or lack civilian work skills appear to be factors in keeping the unemployment rate for Iraq and Afghanistan veterans at 20.9 percent . . . well over the 17.3 percent for non-veterans in the same age group, 18–24."[62] These figures suggest that local police may encounter a significant number of veterans in their jurisdictions who cannot care for themselves, run afoul of the law, or try to do themselves harm.

Judges, prosecutors, defense attorneys, advocates, and others in the criminal justice system are addressing questions about fair sentencing of veterans convicted of crimes who appear to be suffering from service-related cognitive, emotional, or other injuries. Questions are thorny—veterans should not have a "get-out-of-jail-free card," but some judges have suggested less prison time, longer probation, or more medical treatment, or have imposed lighter sentences in specific cases. Some jurisdictions require that judges and prosecutors agree on sentencing, a provision designed to prevent judges from exercising altogether unconstrained discretion in sentencing. Strong disagreements persist within the criminal justice system and advocacy groups. Federal sentencing guidelines "tend to punish the crime while giving little weight to the specific sentences of the defendant. The guidelines explicitly state that 'good works' like military service 'are not ordinarily relevant,'" but in several rulings, the Supreme Court has held that guidelines are just that: "advisory, not mandatory."[63]

Leniency for veterans, though perhaps nobly motivated, can be a strain on police departments and communities. Many police departments have had to adjust to severe budget cuts in recent years and are trying valiantly to maintain services that they had earlier hoped to expand. Personnel complements often fall far short of needs. Where sentencing varies from judge to judge and defendant to defendant and medical facilities are unavailable or overcrowded, the workload of police and probation and parole officers is likely to rise, perhaps substantially. Where judges go beyond reasonable leniency and ignore the risks of excessive or misdirected compassion, they may expose other civilians to new dangers, further taxing police and probationary resources. Heightened levels of communication and cooperation among these departments and prosecutors—as well as such medical facilities as exist—will be essential to maintaining current levels of public safety, let alone improving them.

Adverse Attitudes in Higher Education. Many college and university faculty members are fair-minded, intellectually honest, and competent. They give their best to their students in designing and teaching courses and assigning and evaluating student work. They do not politicize their classrooms and, for the most part, they have no animus against veterans or police.

Other faculty do not have these virtues. Throughout my career, I have seen faculty who do not like to teach and do a lousy job of it, faculty who are lazy and ask far too little of themselves and their students, faculty who want to convert colleges and universities into political institutions at the expense of education, and faculty who use their classrooms to advocate their own political views and biases—positions that have nothing whatever to do with the subject matter they were hired to teach.

Like everyone else, faculty members are entitled to their opinions. This gives them no right to parade those opinions in class, squandering the educational opportunities and time for which students have paid. Some veterans and police pursuing higher education will encounter such infringements from faculty on their chances to learn.

They will also encounter some faculty whose opposition to many U.S. policies, especially defense and military policies, runs very deep. Some of these faculty make no secret of their resentment of both military and law enforcement institutions as well as military veterans and police. Much of the time, what they know or believe about war and policing comes from the media, rather than from working experience.

Veterans will find in some universities strong and vocal opposition to Reserve Officers' Training Corps (ROTC) programs. Columbia University is such a place. The distinguished intellectual historian Jacques Barzun, 2003 recipient of the Medal of Freedom, who served as a professor and provost at Columbia University, writes of the university's "ROTC Shame." Barzun explains that in 1969, "spurred by anti-war riots," Columbia canceled its ROTC program. ROTC at Columbia had grown out of the Columbia Midshipmen's School that trained over 23,000 naval officers in World War II.[64] Twenty years later, Columbia faculty members and administrators refused to return ROTC to campus. Their reason was that they judged the military's "Don't Ask, Don't Tell" (DADT) policy toward homosexuals to be morally offensive and discriminatory.

Congress repealed DADT in 2010. But still, Columbia faculty rejected ROTC programs. Barzun describes the current faculty reasoning against ROTC: the military is a "discriminatory institution" in terms of "physical disability and age." Barzun notes wryly that "the basketball team discriminates too." A faculty petition warns "that a few students wearing uniforms around campus would be a harbinger of 'militarization.'" To this ridiculous warning, Barzun replies: "They ignore the Eisenhower Leadership Development Program, a joint endeavor with West Point that sends dozens of commissioned and uniformed officers each year to Columbia's sacrosanct campus. They also ignore Columbia's law and medical schools, which commission students directly into the Armed Forces Judge Advocate General's Corps as well as medical residencies, and count among their faculties several active-duty military officers."[65]

Having shown that the reasons faculty currently give for opposing the return of ROTC are spurious and fly in the face of undeniable facts,

Barzun points to the irony that in the "core curriculum" of Columbia University, "students read Pericles on the virtue of citizen-soldiers. Too bad the college doesn't encourage that virtue in practice." He concludes by calling on Columbia's president and trustees to "restore the university's long-estranged relationship with the armed forces."

On April 22, 2011, the president of Columbia and Navy Secretary Ray Mabus jointly announced the return of ROTC to Columbia as a way of "strengthening the relationship between our military and civil society."[66] Faculty opposition, including assertions that the U.S. military is committing acts that "may be considered immoral and illegal by international law" and that faculty "have a moral obligation to do everything we can to prevent people from thinking [military practices are] natural and normal," did not prevail. "The student-run Coalition Opposed to ROTC immediately issued a statement declaring the resolution to be 'flawed and politically biased' and decrying 'the highly undemocratic process'" leading to the decision.[67] It has long been fashionable in academic circles to insist that universities must be run as democracies. Fortunately, trustees at some colleges and universities have refused to cede their fiduciary authority and responsibility to that insistence.

And it is not the place of universities and colleges to "prevent" people by whatever means possible from thinking for themselves. A good teacher helps students cultivate their intelligence to be able to pursue the truth conscientiously and with intellectual honesty, not do their thinking for them. After all, how would you prevent students from thinking differently from yourself? Prohibit them from studying any book or author who disagreed with you?

Unfortunately, veterans should be prepared to experience this anti–armed forces sentiment upon pursuing the higher education that is their due under VA benefits. Family, friends, colleagues, and the military-support team can assist by affirming to veterans the importance of their service.

Self-Righteous Cruelty against Veterans and Their Families. We find in the United States a small number of people who will use any means possible to gain publicity for their political or religious views. To get media and public attention, one group pickets funerals of veterans for the purpose of spewing venom, condemnation, and hatred.

Members of the Westboro Baptist Church in Topeka, Kansas self-righteously commit despicable offenses against service members, veterans, and family members of troops who have made the ultimate sacrifice. Fred Phelps heads the church, which is entirely separate from other Baptist churches and organizations. Phelps's children and his many grand-children make up a large portion of the congregation. Phelps proclaims his church the guardian of God's law and declares that "God's hatred is one of His holy attributes." The church proclaims toleration of homo-sexuality by the United States to be unqualifiedly evil. The members are also virulently anti-Semitic.

Members of the church travel long distances to reach the funerals of veterans who have died in Iraq and Afghanistan. According to Phelps and his followers, service members' deaths are God's vengeance against U.S. toleration of homosexuality and other sins. They picket the funerals with cruel signs, songs, and speech. In March 2006, church members traveled to the funeral of Lance Corporal Matthew Snyder in Westminster, Maryland. They carried "signs saying things like, 'You're going to hell,' 'God hates fags,' 'Thank God for dead soldiers,' and 'Thank God for 9/11.'"[68] As it happens, Lance Corporal Snyder was not homosexual.

To Westboro Baptist Church, nothing about Snyder's life, character, or service made the slightest difference. What mattered was that they could exploit his death supposedly in "celebration" of "God's judgments." Members of the church picketing a Marine's funeral in the summer of 2010 included "a 6-year-old girl, wearing gray shorts dotted with pink hearts and yellow stars, who held a 'You're going to hell' sign and sang 'God Hates the World.'"[69]

Corporal Snyder's father sued Phelps and the Westboro Baptist Church for damages because of the emotional distress he suffered from their picketing his son's funeral. On March 2, 2011, the U.S. Supreme Court ruled by a vote of eight to one in favor of the church, saying that under the First Amendment, members of the Westboro Baptist Church have a right to picket funerals, including the funerals of veterans, with hateful and cruel signs and speech. Writing for the majority, Chief Justice John G. Roberts said the speech of the church protesters "cannot be restricted simply because it is upsetting or arouses contempt," even though the "funeral picketing is cer-tainly hurtful and its contribution to public discourse may be negligible."[70]

Only Justice Samuel A. Alito dissented from the majority opinion. He wrote: "In order to have a society in which public issues can be openly and vigorously debated, it is not necessary to allow the brutalization of innocent victims."[71] The *New York Times* reported that "the Reporters Committee for Freedom of the Press and 21 news organizations, including the *New York Times* Company, filed a brief supporting the church."[72]

Massachusetts attorney general Martha Coakley sharply criticized the Supreme Court's decision and announced that the commonwealth would enforce its law prohibiting picketers from coming closer to a funeral than five hundred feet. Coakley said: "We respect the First Amendment rights of our citizens, but we also believe that, consistent with those principles, families have rights to honor their loved ones free from disruptive and harmful protests."[73] In this, she echoed Justice Alito's words: "Mr. Snyder wanted what is surely the right of any parent who experiences such an incalculable loss: to bury his son in peace. . . . But respondents, members of the Westboro Baptist Church, deprived him of that elementary right."[74]

More than forty states have laws that restrict funeral picketing and will no doubt consider further restrictions to safeguard mourners within the limits of the *Snyder v. Phelps* decision. Richard E. Eubank, national commander of the Veterans of Foreign Wars (VFW) of the United States, wrote upon learning the decision: "The [VFW] now urges all state legislatures to strengthen their laws to help protect military families from future protests and great emotional pain that can be just as debilitating as any physical injury."[75]

Others are doing their part to combat the hatred shown by the Westboro Baptist Church. The Patriot Guard Riders honor fallen veterans by attending funerals whenever invited by family. They have pledged to continue their practice of running their motorcycle engines loudly enough to drown out cruel and hateful songs and speech by picketers. Police assigned to maintain order and keep the peace at veterans' funerals have told me of their respect for the Patriot Guard Riders, who have, in every case with which they are familiar, acted legally, nonviolently, and very effectively to protect mourners. American Legion Riders intend to provide comparable service at the funerals of veterans wherever they are held.

The Supreme Court ruling in *Snyder v. Phelps* illuminates the difference between having a legal right and being morally right to exercise it. Even if we were to agree with the majority ruling in favor of the Westboro Baptist Church (I do not), we need not concede that the behavior of the church members is morally right or even minimally decent. Deliberately inflicting pain on innocent mourners is morally reprehensible. No First Amendment guarantee of freedom of speech provides any moral justification or excuse for the specific content of speech—in this case, the despicable speech and behavior of Westboro Baptist Church members.

Conclusion

In the course of writing "From War Veterans to Peace Officers," I have learned that many departments and agencies have taken no steps to prepare for the absence of police during military deployment and their return as veterans. I hope that this sixth edition of *Character and Cops* will lead them toward policies and measures valuable to their personnel and appropriate to their circumstances. For departments that have made progress in this direction, I trust that the chapter will suggest refinements.

Finally, I hope that police departments and law enforcement agencies will avail themselves of the knowledge of active-duty personnel by having veterans offer instruction in such areas as recognition of suspicious, furtive, or anxious behavior (also called behavioral profiling); tactical driving where necessary for police or law enforcement safety; effective use of firearms and applicable self-defense techniques; teamwork; self-discipline and respect for orders and policies; and ways of managing high levels of stress for extended periods. Just as departments and agencies can be of enormous assistance to veterans, veterans have much to offer their colleagues.

Appendix A

A Guide to the Further Study of Ethics in Policing

Those who read *Character and Cops* will see that the opening paragraph of chapter 2 speaks of "being a good person and doing what is right." Ethics is the branch of philosophy that asks such questions as: What is a good person? What is good character? What makes actions right or wrong? What are the principles for deciding how individuals and human institutions should behave? How can we identify our obligations and our rights?

Those questions are universal. They do not ask what a good person is according to one society or another, or how different individuals behave in fact. Rather, they seek answers that apply to all of us, because we are all human beings capable of rational thought, capable of giving and appreciating reasons for and against specific ways of behaving. Answers to such philosophical questions must also be universal. Ethical standards and principles cannot be one thing for public servants and another for business executives, one thing for farmers and another for coaches, one thing for parents and another for police. Any answer that is relevant to the questions must hold for all of us. This is the reason *Character and Cops* refers to ethics in policing and never to police ethics.

Still, fundamental ethical principles must be applied in specific circumstances. Accordingly, police instructors should know both the fundamentals of ethics and how to apply them in policing. They must know the departmental policies, the codes of ethics, and the laws that establish the context and boundaries for applying fundamental ethical principles in policing. Since the moral obligations of policing or any other profession depend on professional competence, officers with a strong record of professional achievement will gain the most from the study of ethics.

Instructors should have taken an ethics course at the college level. Most courses involve reading either classics and masterpieces in ethics, or an anthology or survey textbook, or both. The more that can be gained from philosophical sources, the better. Even studying a textbook for an introductory course is better than nothing.

Some ethics courses, however, focus only on real or imagined dilemmas and do not advance knowledge of ethics. Reading the sections on "Moral Problems," "Habits," and "Current Fashion in Ethics Education" in chapter 10 of *Character and Cops*, along with the introductory section of chapter 11, will safeguard against the conceptual weakness of such courses.

Whether through a formal course or through a program of reading on their own, officers will want to address questions about the nature of good character, the criteria for identifying right and wrong actions, and the principles for deciding what we should do. Officers should be familiar with portions of *Character and Cops* that deal with character, integrity, and the formation of dispositions and habits that make up our character for better or worse—especially chapters 2, 4, 10, 13, 14, and pages 109–113 of chapter 8. They should reflect on the nature of moral deliberation by thinking about fundamental principles and deciding what we should do—as presented in chapters 8, 9, 11, 12, and 18. And they should concentrate on the context for policing provided by the law and by the Constitution as presented in chapters 3, 5, 19, and 20.

They should be thinking about contemporary challenges to the proper mission of policing described in chapters 15–18. And as they look toward the complexities of policing in the twenty-first century outlined in chapter 19, police leaders should consider the prime importance of recruiting well-educated men and women of strong character and of the means to sustain those capacities through competent leadership—that will be challenged still further by the imperatives of policing and law enforcement in the face of terrorist atrocities.

For further background, *Plato's Apology* and *Crito* provide a valuable introduction to principled conduct and careful ethical reasoning as Socrates embodied them. Aristotle's *Nicomachean Ethics*, accompanied by J. O. Urmson's little book *Aristotle's Ethics,* captures much about character and decency.

Nonphilosophers find a number of short essays by American philosopher William James very readable. They include "Habit," especially the sections on the practical effects of habit and on the ethical and pedagogical importance of the principle of habit. "On a Certain Blindness in Human Beings" and "What Makes a Life Significant" are instructive about justice and compassion.

John Stuart Mill's *Utilitarianism* deliberates on the identification of right actions as those that produce the best results, by one standard or another of "best." Such ethical theories are called teleological—from the Greek words *telos* (end, goal, or desired result) and *logos* (account), in the sense of giving an account from the perspective of the goal or end result.

Immanuel Kant's *Foundations of the Metaphysics of Morals* is irreplaceable for grasping moral life as self-directed actions performed because of the justifiable belief that they are right or obligatory. To behave rightfully, we must "treat all persons as ends in themselves and never as means merely"; we must act on principles that rational beings can universalize and therefore respect, whether these principles are applied in the treatment of other persons or in their treatment of oneself. Such ethical theories, called deontological, hold that some ways of behaving are obligatory because they are required by fundamental principles of rationality and justice, and others are wrong because they violate such principles and not because of actual consequences. The term *deontological* comes from the Greek words *deon* (duty, that which is binding or right) and *logos* (account), in the sense of giving an account from the perspective of duty.

Kant's account of rightness denies that mere consideration of consequences is adequate to responsible moral deliberation. Martin Luther King Jr.'s "Letter from the Birmingham City Jail" shows how respect for justice involves more than producing good consequences. *Ecclesiastes* 3:1–9 suggests the importance of learning how to decide when specific conduct is justified:

> For everything there is a season, and a time for every matter under heaven: a time to be born, and a time to die; . . . a time to kill, and a time to heal; . . . a time to love, and a time to hate; a time for war, and a time for peace.

Those who find this difficult to cover on their own may want to study some secondary sources. Introductory books on ethics that have served undergraduates for many years include William K. Frankena's *Ethics* and Richard B. Brandt's *Ethical Theory*. More recently, such books as Edmund Pincoffs's *Quandaries and Virtues*, David Falk's *Ought, Reasons, and Morality*, Christina Sommers and Fred Sommers's *Vice and Virtue in Everyday Life*, James Rachels's *The Elements of Moral Philosophy*, Louis P. Pojman's *Ethics*, and John Silber's essays "The Ethics of the Sword" and "The Gods of the Copybook Headings" in *Straight Shooting* have served readers well.

Chapter 3 of *Character and Cops*, "The Mission of Police," should be read with direct attention to the constitutional and ethical heritage and traditions of America. Papers from *The Federalist* are especially useful, particularly those written by James Madison, including numbers 10, 51, 55, and 57, and numbers 1, 6, and 78 by Alexander Hamilton. Boston University's National Center for America's Founding Documents produces a fine manual for teachers on The Declaration of Independence and *The Annotated Federalist* for *Federalist Papers* Nos. 1, 10, 39, 47, 51, 78, and 84. Both volumes were written by Steven S. Tigner. The Declaration of Independence is must reading:

> We hold these truths to be self-evident, that all men are created equal, that they are endowed by their creator with certain unalienable rights, that among these are life, liberty, and the pursuit of happiness—that to secure these rights, governments are instituted among men, deriving their just powers from the consent of the governed.

That is the philosophy of government declared in the founding of the United States to which every police officer should be committed. It is enriched by the statement of purposes of the preamble to the Constitution:

> We, the people of the United States, in order to form a more perfect Union, establish justice, insure domestic tranquility, provide for the common defense, promote the general welfare, and secure the blessings of liberty to ourselves and our posterity do ordain and establish this Constitution for the United States of America.

Police ought to learn from the outset that the Constitution is not advice but the fundamental law of the land. The existence and authority of police are justified by that philosophy and those purposes. Although no country or institution ever fully achieves the highest purposes for which it is established and although we fall short in our pursuit of justice and public safety, police never have any right to exceed the limits of the law to achieve their goals.

The philosophy of government declared here stresses the equality of human beings. In providing services to the public and enforcing the law, police should understand that all discrimination on grounds of race, sex, ethnic background, religious affiliation, or economic condition is wrong. The philosophy of government to which we as a nation are committed confirms that no form of prejudice or bigotry is tolerable within the work of police.

A Short Bibliography

To supplement *Character and Cops: Ethics in Policing*, the following books are recommended:

Aristotle. *The Nicomachean Ethics*. Translated by David Ross, revised by J. L. Ackrill and J. O. Urmson. New York: Oxford University Press, 1988.

Baier, Kurt. *The Moral Point of View: A Rational Basis of Ethics*. New York: Random House, 1965.

Bennett, William J. *The Book of Virtues*. New York: Simon and Schuster, 1993.

Brandt, Richard B. *Ethical Theory*. Englewood Cliffs, N.J.: Prentice-Hall, 1959.

Cohen, Howard S., and Michael Feldberg. *Power and Restraint: The Moral Dimension of Police Work*. New York: Praeger, 1991.

Cooke, Jacob E., ed. *The Federalist*. Middletown, Conn.: Wesleyan University Press, 1961.

Delattre, Edwin J. *Against Brutality and Corruption: Integrity, Wisdom, and Professionalism*. Tallahassee, Fla.: Florida Criminal Justice Executive Institute, Florida Department of Law Enforcement, 1991. For information on cost and to order, contact Florida Criminal Justice Executive Institute, Florida Department of Law Enforcement, P.O. Box 1489, Tallahassee, FL 32302; tel. (904) 488-1340.

Falk, David. *Ought, Reasons, and Morality*. Ithaca: Cornell University Press, 1986. See especially, "Morality, Self and Others."

Frankena, William K. *Ethics*, 2d ed. Englewood Cliffs, N.J.: Prentice-Hall, 1973.

Fuller, Lon L. *The Morality of Law*, rev. ed. New Haven: Yale University Press, 1975.

James, William. *The Writings of William James: A Comprehensive Edition*. Edited by Jefferson, Thomas. The Declaration of Independence. 1776.

Kant, Immanuel. *Foundations of the Metaphysics of Morals*, 2d ed. Lewis White Beck, trans. New York: Macmillan, 1990.

———. *Lectures on Ethics*. Translated by Louis Infield. New York: Harper Torch-books, 1963.

King, Martin Luther, Jr. *A Testament of Hope: The Essential Writings of Martin Luther King Jr.* ed. James Melvin Washington. San Francisco: Harper and Row, 1986. See especially, "Letter from the Birmingham City Jail."

McDermott, John J. Chicago: University of Chicago Press, 1977.

Mill, John Stuart. *Utilitarianism*. ed. Samuel Gorovitz. Indianapolis: Bobbs-Merrill, 1971.

Pincoffs, Edmund. *Quandaries and Virtues*. Lawrence: University of Kansas Press, 1986.

Plato. *The Trial and Death of Socrates*, 2d ed. Translated by G. M. A. Grube. Indianapolis: Hackett Publishing, 1988.

Pojman, Louis P. *Ethics: Discovering Right and Wrong*. Belmont, Calif.: Wadsworth, 1990.

Rachels, James. *The Elements of Moral Philosophy*. New York: Random House, 1986.

Silber, John R. *Straight Shooting: What's Wrong with America and How to Fix It*. New York: Harper and Row, 1989. See especially, "The Gods of the Copybook Headings" and "The Ethics of the Sword."

Sommers, Christina, and Fred Sommers, eds. *Vice and Virtue in Everyday Life: Introductory Readings in Ethics*, 2d ed. New York: Harcourt Brace Jovanovitch, 1989.

Story, Joseph. *A Familiar Exposition of the Constitution of the United States*. Lake Bluff, Ill.: Regnery Gateway, 1986.

Tigner, Steven S. *The Declaration of Independence: A Manual for Teachers*. Boston: National Center for America's Founding Documents at Boston University, 1989. To order, contact the National Center for America's Founding Documents, Boston University School of Education, 605 Commonwealth Avenue, Boston, MA 02215; tel. (617) 353-2950. ($7.50, plus $2.00 shipping and handling.)

———. *The Annotated Federalist*, Nos. 1, 10, 39, 47, 51, 78, 84. Boston: National Center for America's Founding Documents at Boston University, 1990. To order, see above.

Ulich, Robert, ed. *Three Thousand Years of Educational Wisdom*, 2d ed. Cambridge: Harvard University Press, 1954.

Urmson, J. O. *Aristotle's Ethics*. Oxford: Basil Blackwell, 1988.

The U.S. Constitution, preamble.

The following periodicals are also useful:

Criminal Justice Ethics. Published semiannually by the Institute for Criminal Justice Ethics in association with the Department of Law, Police Science, and Criminal Justice Administration, John Jay College of Criminal Justice/CUNY, N.Y.

FBI Law Enforcement Bulletin. Published monthly by the U.S. Department of Justice, Federal Bureau of Investigation, Washington, D.C.

Law Enforcement News. Published bimonthly by John Jay College of Criminal Justice/CUNY, N.Y.

Appendix B

Internal Affairs and Integrity

To me, integrity—in a person or an institution, in a police officer or a police department—means the settled disposition, the resolve and determination, the established habit "of doing right where there is no one to make you do it but yourself." Those words were spoken early in the twentieth century by the distinguished English judge Lord Moulton, who went on to say, "The real greatness of a nation, its true civilization, is measured by the extent of this land of obedience to the unenforceable . . . the extent to which individuals composing that nation can be trusted to obey self-imposed law"—trusted to behave rightly when no one is in a position to make them do so or to impose sanctions on them if they behave badly.[1]

Thus understood, integrity is the highest achievement there can be in a human life. Philosophers who have understood morality as the vocation, the proper calling, of human beings have explained that living a successful life—being a genuine success and fulfilling the purpose of human existence—means achieving integrity. Acquiring integrity of character, becoming the kind of person who behaves rightly when not externally forced to do so, is what makes a person thoroughly and profoundly worthy of trust in public and private life. For this reason, integrity properly understood is irreplaceable as the foundation of good friendships, good marriages, good parenthood, good sportsmanship, good citizenship, and good public service.

Integrity is not only the highest of achievements but also among the most difficult—and it is not achieved by accident or mere good fortune. Achieving the disposition and habit of behaving rightly depends on being able to control our own natural passions, being willing to deny ourselves things we may powerfully desire, being prepared to make sacrifices we have strong inclinations not to make. Without such habits of control, we may yield to the temptation to behave unjustly, to indulge prejudices or to gain advantage; to behave dishonestly when doing so promises pleasure or profit; to behave cravenly when acting with moral or physical courage may risk pain or loss or death; to behave selfishly in general; to exploit and manipulate others when we want something from them; to abuse power and authority to gratify our impulses.

When Integrity Suffers

In a country where the family is in disarray; where children are routinely abandoned to their own devices and allowed to form bad habits in the company of peers, youths, and adults who do not love them or care what becomes of them; where the entertainment and advertising media extol violence and parade sexual promiscuity and wantonness as desirable features of the good life, the news media forsake all aspiration to intellectual honesty and objectivity, and the docudrama slaughters the distinction between news and entertainment; where many of the most advantaged people in all the world flout the law by consuming illegal drugs; and where formal education has become academically shallow and indifferent to the formation of good character—in such a country, integrity becomes an object of neglect, or even of ridicule and derision. Such a country loses purchase on the fact that as the general public loses respect for self-imposed obedience to moral principle, what is worst in human nature takes free rein; left long unchecked, such free rein of impulse and selfish gratification makes for a public that cannot be safeguarded from its own destruction.

Even in the best of times and in the best of circumstances, achieving integrity is a struggle, and our times and circumstances are very far from ideal. It is hard to live up to the golden rule of doing unto others as we would have them do unto us, even when we are raised by parents and benefit from the encouragement of companions who teach us by word and deed of their respect for this formulation of integrity. Think, then, of the countless numbers of children—and adults—in our country who have never even heard of the golden rule and who, odds are, never will.

These simple truths about us, our condition, our nature, our frailties, and our achievements are not new. Alexander Hamilton warned the American people in 1787, "Has it not . . . invariably been found that momentary passions and immediate interests have a more active and imperious control over human conduct than general or remote considerations of policy, utility or justice?"[2] The answer to Hamilton's question, in general, is yes. This fact is revealed in policing just as it is in other walks of life.

The Dark Side of the Force

It is revealed in the "blue cocoon," the "blue veil," the "us-versus-them mentality," the haven for corruption that springs from the explicit belief among police, as the Mollen Commission put it, "that nothing is more important than the unswerving loyalty of officers to one another—not even stopping the most serious forms of corruption."[3] What are these if not confirmation that "passions and interests" can and sometimes do influence human behavior more powerfully than do ideals of justice and honesty, respect for law and policy, and concern for fidelity to the public interest? What does the existence of such a corrosive and bankrupt idea of loyalty prove if not that even pretty good people may forsake their own integrity if they are sufficiently afraid of being left out in the cold, ostracized, labeled as rats, or expected to oppose corruption and brutality all alone? We live in a country where more than 90 percent of all students in schools of management and business identify themselves as cheaters—and say that they cheat because they believe that they can get ahead, serve their self-interest, by cheating. Why should we expect, then, that the darker, and weaker, elements of human nature will not show themselves in policing as well?

The passion for secrecy—the lust to conceal actions inside a blue cocoon or behind a blue veil among police who want to commit acts of corruption or brutality—amounts to a desire to draw police work away from the constraints of law and policy and into the domain of the unenforceable. Once that is accomplished, then bad police can behave without integrity, at will, and with impunity. The intimidation of otherwise decent officers is but an instrument of that passion for secrecy, and where it succeeds, it confirms the insistence of nineteenth-century British historian

Lord Acton that "everything secret degenerates, even the administration of justice; nothing is safe that does not show it can bear discussion and publicity."[4] Secrecy, as Lord Acton knew, is far different from legitimate confidentiality.

If bad cops cannot drive out or destroy good cops, they will be content to corrupt them by entanglement in a web of secrecy, whether it is woven of fear and a related willingness to go along to get along or supported by cynicism about the department itself and by contempt for the general public. And if supervisors are concerned not about corruption and brutality but rather about public scandal in the discovery and disclosure of corruption and brutality, they become either active or unwitting allies of the worst police among them—at the expense of the public and of every decent cop. But some supervisors do just that. Loath to have corruption or brutality discovered on their watch, they place appearance above reality; they place reputation above actuality; they sacrifice good police and good police work to the dictates of their own narrow ambition, to the impulses of their own cowardice, or to pressure from subordinates they have unwisely made into their social intimates.

None of that should come as a surprise to anyone. No walk of life is exempt from the frailties of human nature, and no institution ever achieved integrity by supposing that the integrity of its individual members could be relied upon to take care of itself. The alternative to such a naive supposition is not the cynical belief that "everyone has a price"; that no one can ultimately be trusted; that all human motivation is finally selfish and contemptible and that behind every noble deed there is an ulterior purpose; that police must be intimidated or cowed into behaving decently; that no one has integrity. Cynicism is the view that human beings are capable of feeling and being motivated by fear but that none of them is capable of feeling shame. History and personal experience prove conclusively that many of us are capable of feeling shame and of doing what is right even when we are afraid. It is equally cynical, and therefore equally mistaken, to presume that the need for police to achieve the disposition and habit of "doing what is right where there is no one to make you do it but yourself" can be entirely replaced by sufficiently rigorous policies, sufficiently proactive internal affairs and inspections operations, sufficiently draconian sanctions for misconduct.

Toward a Higher Standard

Neither innocence nor cynicism about human beings and institutions can elevate the achievement of integrity and trustworthiness in policing. The proper alternative to innocence and cynicism—the achievement of integrity in a police department—involves doing a great many sensible things, doing them all at once, and doing them regularly and permanently rather than episodically. That has not just recently become true. It has always been true, but it has not always been heeded, nor is it everywhere heeded now.

What are the sensible things to be done simultaneously and permanently? James Madison captured the idea for us in his framing of the ideal of higher intellectual and moral standards for public servants in our country than for the general public:

> The aim of every political Constitution is or ought to be first to obtain for rulers, men who possess most wisdom to discern, and most virtue to pursue the common good of the society; and in the next place, to take the most effectual precautions for keeping them virtuous, whilst they continue to hold their public trust.[5]

What Madison's words mean for police departments, in the most succinct terms, is that they should do everything possible to recruit people who show evidence of intellectual competence, good judgment, and integrity. They should seek candidates for sworn and civilian positions who, even if they are young, have shown a disposition to think and behave responsibly even when no one makes them do so. And police departments should then take what Madison called "effectual precautions for keeping them virtuous"; that is, departments should establish reliable policies and procedures to secure the accountability of their personnel. In sum, get the right kinds of people in the first place and take steps to achieve accountability at all levels. Those are more easily said than done. Both the history of policing in the United States in the twentieth century and current events confirm the difficulty.

In 1931 August Vollmer, the most respected police leader of his time, wrote that in the United States "law enforcement agencies are usually held in contempt and policing is [taken as] one of our national jokes."[6] Then, as now, competent and honorable police served the public, while inept, corrupt, and brutal police betrayed the public and their fellow officers.

Rising above Ridicule

In the years since Vollmer's commentary, many police departments in the United States have risen far above contempt and ridicule. They have improved themselves by greater selectivity in recruitment of new officers; more refined background investigations and recruitment interviews, including the use of the polygraph where the right of polygraph inquiries has not been bargained away or otherwise prohibited; better and more demanding academy and field training and in-service education of experienced officers, including real coherence between academy and field training and greater selectivity in choosing field training officers; more rigorous limitations on use of force; more instructive and diligent supervision; greater accountability at all levels; more effective uses of better technology; more thorough internal investigations of allegations of police misconduct, including proactive internal affairs divisions or bureaus concentrated on the systematic gathering of intelligence, on random and targeted integrity testing, and on the inclusion of command personnel in investigative efforts; more sustained communication with the public; and expansion of opportunities in policing for members of minority groups and women.

Those improvements have been achieved by police and law enforcement leaders who understand that a police department is not supposed to be a microcosm of the society in general with all of its ills—racism, sexism, drunkenness, illegal drug consumption, dishonesty and corruption, promiscuity and sexual predation, domestic and street violence, indifference to the law, cowardice and rashness, illiteracy and other forms of incompetence, and disregard for the safety and well-being of other people. Police departments, like all other institutions and individuals that bear the public trust, are supposed to be *better* than the public they serve.

Fidelity of a police department to the rightful expectations of the public therefore depends above all on the selection of officers who are intellectually, morally, and physically fit for positions of public trust and on personal and institutional accountability for their performance behind the badge. Everywhere in America, and conspicuously in Washington, D.C., the greatest threat to honorable, professional, trustworthy policing is the interference of politicians who understand neither the nature of police work nor the tradition of higher standards for public servants than for the general public.

The High Price of Meddling

Political meddling in police departments takes many forms, but the most dangerous to the public interest is forcing police departments to undertake massive and rapid hiring of new officers, especially where residency requirements limit the pool of eligible applicants. Everywhere that such a mandate is forced upon police by politicians, as by Congress and the city government in Washington, D.C., in 1989 and 1990, disaster follows.

In 1980 Miami, Florida, adopted a policy requiring that 200 new police be recruited immediately, with 80 percent to be minority residents of Miami. The debacle that followed has nothing to do with the fact that minorities were involved; the same results would have followed for any group of recruits who were selected so carelessly, trained so badly, and supervised so negligently. Many of the recruits were utterly unsuited to be police, as background investigations and the warnings of academy instructors confirmed at the time. Sloppy field training, inadequate supervision, and an ineffective Internal Affairs Division permitted them to behave with contempt for the law. By 1988 more than a third of them had been fired. Twelve members of a group known as the River Cops had been convicted of crimes ranging from drug trafficking to murder. Many of those recruits became police to profit from illegal activity with drugs.

Every mistake that was made in Miami was repeated in Washington, D.C., ten years later, with utterly predictable and even more disastrous results. Faced with a congressional threat to withhold $430 million unless 1,800 new officers already in residence in the city were rapidly hired, the Metropolitan Police Department hired 1,471 new officers in 1989 and 1990. Normal procedures for application were suspended in haste; and the passing grade on the entrance examination was reduced to 50 percent, because, I think, the city government wanted to avoid a high failure rate that would embarrass the District's public schools. Background investigations were conducted by telephone and abbreviated to the point of worthlessness; FBI criminal records checks were ignored; academy and field training were dramatically shortened to put new officers on the streets; personnel policies and regulations were overlooked; and some recruits were subjected to training by incompetent and dishonorable field training officers. So trifling were the background checks that some applicants who were incarcerated at the time received letters denying them parole at the same time that they were admitted to recruit classes.

By 1994, five years after the rapid hiring and suspension of policies intended to safeguard the public *and* the department, more than one hundred of the police who entered the department in 1989 and 1990 had been arrested. Their crimes included drug trafficking, rape, and murder. Nearly as many officers from those recruit classes were included in the 185 Metro officers who had such bad records that they could not be used as credible trial witnesses. They were but a fraction of the 256 District police officers who had escaped discipline or termination because the department failed to live up to its own rule requiring adjudication of disciplinary action within forty-five days of the discovery of misconduct. All of them were an affront to good police officers in Washington and elsewhere and to the interests of the public.

The part that Congress and top elected officials in the Washington, D.C., city government played in that debacle was a disgrace. But they do not bear the blame alone. Many police leaders are better educated and more attuned to respect for the public trust than elected officials, and every good police executive in the country knows that forsaking high standards of selection and accountability in policing is the surest way to return to the days when law enforcement was held in contempt and ridicule.

Sacrificing Selectivity

Everywhere that police leaders silently sacrifice selectivity to political pressure for rapid expansion conjoined with residency requirements, they become instruments of the reduction of their departments to mere microcosms of society, unworthy of the public trust. *Police departments are authorized to be selective precisely so that they will not be microcosms of everything that is morally worst in society.* And the worse the shortcomings and deficiencies in the general public become—as in widespread cheating by students in schools and colleges, neglect of intellectual and moral seriousness in the raising of children, bad schools, gang recruitment and predation, public cynicism—the more carefully selective police departments ought to be.

No large and complex human institution can be made perfect. No program of recruitment, education, accountability, and supervision can eliminate *all* bigotry, brutality, or corruption from a police department or from any other selective institution. But political meddling in departmental hiring and training policies, conjoined with tacit police compliance with the reduction of standards, maximizes the entry of police who are unfit to wear the badge. That is the ordeal that was visited on the many fine police officers in Washington, D.C., and on the residents of our nation's capital.

Congress ran the risk of making exactly the same mistakes by insisting on the rapid expansion of the U.S. Border Patrol. I was deeply hopeful that Attorney General Janet Reno would have been able to persuade Congress of the perils of inordinate expansion that would have resulted in too many agents having less than five years experience by 1998, with many underprepared and inexperienced frontline supervisors in the bargain—a prescription for disaster even in conditions much less difficult than those that face us in matters of immigration and our borders. Federal, state, and local law enforcement and policing can be elevated only by great scrupulousness in selection, training, and supervision of personnel, both sworn and civilian.

Many other departments have undergone massive hiring programs—including the New York Police Department, which hired 11,000 new officers from 1993 to 1996—and I feared that those departments would not be entirely spared the problems that attend such rapid expansion or replacement of personnel. In 1994 the Mollen Commission reported, "Of over four hundred officers that were dismissed or suspended for corruption over the past five years, we found that a large number of them should never have been admitted to the Department based solely on information in the officer's personnel file at the time of the application."[7]

Safe Havens for Misconduct

This source of weakness in a department is doubly dangerous when new officers are drawn into a culture where corruption and brutality may already have found at least localized safe havens. The NYPD has risen to that challenge in its investigation of the severe problems in the Thirtieth and Forty-eighth precincts and its resolute response to the debacles of moronic self-indulgence by NYPD officers, at risk of the public safety, in Washington, D.C., and in New Jersey. Those episodes bordered on the staggering acts of misconduct, drunkenness, and vandalism committed a number of years ago by police at an annual conference of the California Narcotics Officers Association, but the California misconduct was not so widely reported.

In the NYPD both random and targeted integrity testing are being made into linchpins of internal accountability. Notably in 1994, in 115 tests, most of them targeted, 151 police passed, while 35 failed—a failure rate of almost 19 percent.

That condition must be addressed and remedied to establish a cultural environment that will draw new personnel toward integrity in policing. Anything less, in any department, would be disastrous. I have explained why in chapter 6:

> The hypothesis of structural deviance and the attendant perplexity about remedies are not complex: (1) If a young person of high ideals but little exposure to realities that challenge naive expectations of human decency (2) enters a world that exposes the worst in people and (3) is trained and influenced by senior colleagues who have lost faith in police work, and (4) if the young person must establish some mutual trust and reliance with colleagues who use their work to line their own pockets and to get their share of what all others are grabbing as fast as they can, and (5) if their superiors are unlikely to support efforts to behave honorably, and (6) the likelihood of sanction for corruption is negligible, (7) *then* the young person will probably accept the status quo and join in corrupt practices, perhaps with initial feelings of shame, but ultimately without remorse. The

difficulty of remedy is equally transparent: When cynical persons on both sides of the law profit from an alliance, and when the ability of police command to force the issue is constrained, those persons will use any means to preserve the status quo and to prevent reform from outside.

No one has to conduct massive studies to know those things. They are amply demonstrated in history and political theory and in daily experience.[8]

Asking Too Little

The cultural environment for the prospective newcomer begins, obviously, in the way applicants are screened and interviewed, in the sense they acquire of the department's seriousness about standards, as exhibited in the rigor of background investigations and the focus of questions in interviews. The operating culture and the ethos or character of the department come more fully to life in the academy and overlapping or subsequent field training and supervision.

My sense is that many academies ask too little of their students; study materials are routinely pitched at the seventh-grade level, hardly a level of intellectual maturity and judgment that befits the authority of a badge and a gun; and in some academies, such as that of the LAPD, the recruit pass rate approaches 95 percent. I doubt that any department is good enough at recruiting to offer a demanding and stressful course of academy education and training that 95 percent of recruits are likely to pass; certainly, no college or university has ever done so. If I am right that recruiting standards in some departments are conspicuously low, that extraordinarily high pass rates suggest a certain intellectual, and perhaps moral and physical, laxity in academies, and, as affirmed by the Mollen Commission and others, that recruits may be exposed to corrupt practices and expectations while still in police academies, then it is transparent that the battle for integrity can be lost from the start.

If the best work of the academies is betrayed and undermined by field training officers who teach that academy lessons have nothing to do with reality, and by supervisors who are not utterly determined to make the standards, expectations, and policies of academy training, field training, and daily supervision of personnel entirely coherent, unambiguous, and free of hypocrisy, the battle will frequently be lost soon thereafter.

The very heart of the avoidance of supervisory hypocrisy is to be found in the integrity of the leadership of the department, because there alone can the commitment to accountability at *all* levels be proved. Such integrity is nowhere exhibited with greater effect than by defense of honorable police work in the face of unwarranted media or public criticism. In that regard, I admire particularly the work of Kevin Tucker while he served as superintendent of police in Philadelphia. When police were subjected to unjustified criticism of their work in an area near the center of the city, rife with highly organized drug trafficking and the threat of violence against police who made any effort to intervene, Kevin had videotapes surreptitiously made showing the actual conditions. The videotapes proved that as police entered the area—often announced in advance by street children serving as lookouts (Philadelphia then, as now, had no truant officers)—their cars, marked or unmarked, were routinely led and followed by hatchback vehicles containing heavily armed drug dealers and their enforcers who warned white-collar drug buyers of the police presence by playing blasters at top volume. The superintendent then held a press conference at which he showed the videotapes and spoke in defense of police working the area. He was right—and the media had little choice but to admit it.

Two-Edged Imperative

Accountability and the avoidance of hypocrisy thus have two edges: praise and support and reward for excellence, and intolerance for bad-faith mistakes, including, in my view, the imperative recognized by Bill Bratton in New York City for zero tolerance of illegal drug use by sworn and civilian personnel. In addition, supervisors must be sufficiently wise and subtle to distinguish bad-faith misconduct from errors of judgment made in good faith because of inexperience, to which the proper response is not discipline, but rather instruction and guidance. I have in mind here, for example, the sorts of mistakes that gang-enforcement unit members sometimes make because they have never been trained in the gathering of intelligence and the proper management of informants. That inadequacy in training is not unusual in contemporary policing, and it is departments, not individual officers, that are most often to blame. Departmental integrity depends on improving training and admitting the shortcomings of past practices.

I like very much the emphasis on those points in the Statement of Principles and Values, prepared by police leaders in New South Wales, Australia. Their "leadership principles" instruct supervisors, managers, and commanders to:

- Properly prepare their people for roles and responsibilities, in recognition that they are [the department's] most valuable resource.

- Provide appropriate training and development because of its crucial importance to the future development of the Service.

And the document adds:

- Though incompetence is not acceptable, [leaders should] support those people who act in accordance with the Statement of Principles and Values and in good faith, even if they make mistakes.

The Role of Internal Affairs

The highest levels of integrity in a department clearly cannot be achieved without a splendid internal affairs division or bureau, one that is a part of the operations and ethos of the department and not an isolated and secretive entity. The NYPD's reforms in internal affairs promise elevation of integrity in the department. The reforms include application internally of the same strategy employed to reduce crime externally: the systematic gathering of accurate and timely intelligence; rapid deployment of resources; tested tactics of investigation; and "relentless follow-up and assessment." The strategy of departmental reform overall is not mere words; it embraces superb measures by the Internal Affairs Bureau's Training Unit, including both in-service and advanced training furthered by a ten-day course in methods of internal investigations. I hope that this course is open to internal affairs personnel from other departments, just as the Colonel Henry F. Williams Homicide Seminar of the New York State Police Department is made widely available to homicide investigators.

The NYPD reform strategy also includes an Executive Review Board of top police officials who are to monitor Internal Affairs Bureau investigations and thereby shows commitment to systematic advancement of integrity throughout the department's leadership; a Liaison Unit to work hand-in-glove with city, county, state, and federal agencies in securing an early warning system; an Excessive Force Unit with responsibility for teaching systematically about the principle of human dignity and its implications for use of force, including deadly force; provisions for genuine cooperation with a Civilian Complaint Review Board; and commitment to a philosophy within the Internal Affairs Bureau and the department itself of including precinct and unit commanders in the process of internal investigations.[9] Conjoined with the elevation of recruitment, training, and supervision overall, those reforms have the potential to make the department most faithful to its honorable personnel and to the public and to support individual integrity against the "blue cocoon."

At best, the reforms will help to reduce "us against them" attitudes, not only within the department but also between the department and the public. It has long been recognized, as James Madison explained, that only when laws are as binding on public servants as on the general public can we bring to life that "communion of interests and sympathy of sentiments . . . without which every government degenerates into tyranny."[10] Corruption and brutality are mainstays of tyranny, expressions of a tyrannical spirit that thrives on disdain for the very idea that authority is granted to government for the sake of faithful service to the public.

Virtue and Self-Interest

Another very old truth about human nature is embodied in one of the NYPD's most significant reforms. Specifically, all students of political theory know that integrity—virtue—has the best chance of prevailing where people see that behaving well is not only right but also advantageous. That is, if virtue and fertile ambition, integrity and legitimate self-interest, can be made to weigh on the same side of the balance, be entered on the same side of the ledger, then the likelihood of good conduct is increased. Much of the time all of us have mixed motives for our actions, usually more mixed than even the most honest and self-knowledgeable of us fully recognize. Accordingly, the disposition to do "right when there is no one to make [us] do it but [ourselves]" may be strengthened by awareness that we are not making some permanent sacrifice in behaving rightly. I therefore think that it is very wise for the NYPD to be making the Internal Affairs Bureau into an appealing career track, where a two-year assignment will provide a path toward assignment in the Detective Bureau or the Organized Crime Control Bureau.

The obstacles to achieving individual and institutional integrity cannot be entirely eliminated; for this reason, it is always foolish to suppose that sustaining integrity is a one-time project. Integrity must be encouraged, and betrayals of it must be rooted out, with persistent and enduring vigilance. Many of the most deeply ingrained individual and institutional habits in human life militate against integrity, as Walter Lippmann observed in 1930:

> The American ideal of government as a public trust to be carried on by disinterested men represents not the actuality but a long step ahead in the evolution of man. . . . It is a very difficult ideal to attain, and I know of no man in America even in our time who has felt able to be completely loyal to it. . . . The campaign . . . on behalf of the idea of trust is no mere repairing of something perfect that has broken down, but the implanting of a new habit of acting in the ancient consciousness of man.[11]

This habit cannot be acquired wholesale or at a discount; it can be acquired only by individuals and institutions who give it their highest allegiance in the routine affairs of daily life. Institutional policies and practices are indispensable to its achievement and survival. But finally, the disposition and habit "of doing right when there is no one to make you do it but yourself" live or die in the conduct of individual life. Thus it is that I concluded the second edition of *Character and Cops* by reminding all who bear the public trust, all police: "*Nothing is incorruptible except personal character that will not be corrupted.*"[12]

Notes

Chapter 1: Introduction

1. G. K. Chesterton, *The Defendant*, Essay Index Reprint Series (North Stratford, N.H.: Ayer, 1977).

Chapter 2: Excellence of Character

1. J. A. K. Thomson, trans., *The Ethics of Aristotle: The Nicomachean Ethics Translated* 2.1 (Hammondsworth, Middlesex, Eng.: Penguin Books, 1958).

2. J. O. Urmson, *Aristotle's Ethics* (Oxford: Basil Blackwell, 1988), 25.

3. M. F. Burnyeat, "Aristotle on Learning to Be Good," in *Essays on Aristotle's Ethics*, Amelie Oksenberg Rorty, ed. (Berkeley: University of California Press, 1980), 86.

4. *The Ethics of Aristotle* 3.5.

5. Urmson, *Aristotle's Ethics*, 26.

6. Immanuel Kant, *Education* 1.4, 1.5, Annette Churton, trans. (Ann Arbor, Mich.: University of Michigan Press, 1960), 3, 4.

7. John Stuart Mill, "Moral Influences in Early Youth," in *Autobiography* (Indianapolis, Ind.: Bobbs-Merrill, 1957), 35.

8. Alasdair MacIntyre, *After Virtue*, 2d ed. (Notre Dame, Ind.: University of Notre Dame Press, 1984), 3, 4.

9. Urmson, *Aristotle's Ethics*, 22.

10. William Ker Muir Jr., *Police: Streetcorner Politicians* (Chicago: University of Chicago Press, 1977), 3, 4.

11. I am grateful to personnel from the Miami Police Department and other law enforcement agencies in Florida who have shared their knowledge of the River Cops with me. See Morris S. Thompson, "Miami Vice: Police Trafficking in Drugs," *Washington Post*, February 7, 1988; and "Miami Jury Convicts Two in Drug Ripoffs," *Washington Post*, February 10, 1988.

12. I appreciate the assistance of personnel from the New York Police Department in my review of the Buddy Boys. See Mike McAlary, *The Buddy Boys:*

When Good Cops Turn Bad (New York: G. P. Putnam's Sons, 1987); CBS News transcript of *60 Minutes*, February 14, 1988, vol. 20, no. 22.

13. This position can be drawn from experience and is articulated by Aristotle in the *Nicomachean Ethics*. It is described in detail by J. O. Urmson in "Aristotle's Doctrine of the Mean," in *Essays on Aristotle's Ethics*, Amelie Oksenberg Rorty, ed. (Berkeley: University of California Press, 1980, 157–64).

14. Muir, *Police: Streetcorner Politicians*, 4.

15. Don L. Kooken, *Ethics in Police Service* (Springfield, Ill.: Charles C. Thomas, 1957), 21, 23.

Chapter 3: The Mission of Police

1. Aleksandr Solzhenitsyn, *The Gulag Archipelago*, 2 vols., Thomas B. Whitney, trans. (New York: Harper and Row, 1973), 163.

2. Alexander Hamilton, James Madison, and John Jay, *The Federalist Papers*, no. 47 (New York: Mentor Books, 1961), 301.

3. Ibid., No. 51, 322.

4. Ibid., 324.

5. "Continentalist No. 1," July 12, 1781, in *The Papers of Alexander Hamilton*, vol. 2, Harold C. Syrett et al., ed. (New York: Columbia University Press, 1961–1979).

6. Benjamin Rush, "An Address," Philadelphia, 1787, in *Principles and Acts of the Revolution in America*, Hezekiah Niles, ed. (New York: A. S. Barnes and Company, 1876), 234.

7. Robert Goldwin, "Of Men and Angels: A Search for Morality in the Constitution," in *The Moral Foundations of the American Republic*, Robert H. Horwitz, ed. (Charlottesville: University Press of Virginia, 1979), 11.

8. Ibid., 4, 5, 12.

9. Charles E. Silberman, *Criminal Violence, Criminal Justice* (New York: Random House, 1978), 4, 5.

10. Adam Walinsky, "What It's Like to Be in Hell," *New York Times*, December 4, 1987.

11. "Frontier Justice," *Wall Street Journal*, June 16, 1988.

12. Julia Preston, "Letter from Nicaragua: Deterioration Is Now a Way of Life," *Washington Post*, December 16, 1988.

13. Ibid.

14. Jack Anderson and Dale Van Atta, "Fearful Khomeni Turns on Own," *Washington Post*, December 19, 1988.

15. Solzhenitsyn, *The Gulag Archipelago*, 173.

16. O. W. Wilson, ed., *Parker on Police* (Springfield, Ill.: Charles C. Thomas, 1957), 13. Psychologist Stanton E. Samenow wrote in *Inside the Criminal Mind* (New York: Time Books, 1984), 204–5: "The criminal has long stood apart from

the community, contemptuous of people who lived responsibly. . . . It is not his self-esteem that needs building. . . . Rather, he thinks of himself as an exceptional person who is superior to others."

17. Solzhenitsyn, *The Gulag Archipelago*, 307.

18. Ibid., 309.

19. Leon Radzinowicz and Joan King, *The Growth of Crime* (New York: Basic Books, 1977), 3.

20. "A Look at Crime Statistics," *Soviet Life* 8, no. 383 (1988): 24, 25.

21. *Experiments in Police Improvement: A Progress Report* (Washington, D.C.: Police Foundation, 1972), 9.

22. David A. Hansen, *Police Ethics* (Springfield, Ill.: Charles C. Thomas, 1973), xiii.

23. Lee W. Potts, *Responsible Police Administration: Issues and Approaches* (Tuscaloosa: University of Alabama Press, 1983), 8.

24. Ibid., 8, 9.

25. August Vollmer, *The Police and Modern Society* (College Park, Md.: McGrath Publishing, 1969), 1, 3.

26. Silberman, *Criminal Violence, Criminal Justice*, 203, 204.

27. Egon Bittner, *The Functions of the Police in Modern Society* (Rockville, Md.: National Institute of Mental Health Center for Studies of Crime and Delinquency, 1970), 7. See also my essay, "The Police: From Slaying Dragons to Rescuing Cats," *FBI Law Enforcement Bulletin* 50, no. 11 (1981): 16–19.

28. See, for example, Lawrence W. Sherman and Richard A. Berk, "The Minneapolis Domestic Violence Experiment," *Police Foundation Reports* (April 1984): 1–8.

29. The President's Commission on Law Enforcement and Administration of Justice, *Task Force Report: The Police* (Washington, D.C.: Government Printing Office, 1967), 120.

30. Elijah Adlow, *Policemen and People* (Boston: William P. Rochfort, 1947), 13.

31. Vollmer, *The Police and Modern Society*, 237.

32. Ibid., 81.

33. Joseph Story, *A Familiar Exposition of the Constitution of the United States* (Lake Bluff, Ill.: Regnery Gateway, 1986), 326.

34. Silberman, *Criminal Violence, Criminal Justice*, 46, 47.

35. Quoted in United States National Commission on Law Observance and Enforcement, *Report on Police*, no. 14 (Washington, D.C.: Government Printing Office, 1931), 17. This study is also known as the Wickersham Report, after the commission's chairman.

36. Leonard V. Harrison, *Police Administration in Boston* (Cambridge: Harvard University Press, 1934), 28, 29.

37. William J. Bopp, *"O. W.": O. W. Wilson and the Search for a Police Profession* (Port Washington, N.Y.: Kennikat Press, 1977), 138, 139.

Chapter 4: The Public Trust and Probity

1. George Washington, "Farewell Address," in *A Collection of Orations from Homer to McKinley*, vol. 6, Mayo W. Hazeltine, ed. (New York: P. F. Collier and Sons, 1902), 2511, 2513.

2. Quoted in Philip Greven, *The Protestant Temperament: Patterns of Childrearing, Religious Experience, and the Self in Early America* (New York: Alfred A. Knopf, 1977), 346.

3. B. C. Brymer, *Abraham Lincoln in Peoria, Illinois* (Peoria, Ill.: Edward J. Jacob, 1926), 103.

4. Marvin Meyers, ed., *The Mind of the Founder: Sources of the Political Thought of James Madison*, rev. ed. (Hanover, N.H.: University Press of New England, 1981), 158.

5. Dan Meyers, "Roofers Jury Hears Parade of Officials Get Cash," *Philadelphia Inquirer*, October 27, 1987.

6. Lynne Duke, "Operation Clean Sweep Net Snares Atlanta DEA Agent," *Washington Post*, March 13, 1988.

7. Jeff Barker, "Sen. Specter Calls for Appointment of Judges," *Philadelphia Inquirer*, March 21, 1988.

8. Howard Kurtz, "28 New York City Restaurant Inspectors Accused of Extortion," *Washington Post*, March 25, 1988.

9. Philip Shenon, "Enemy Within: Drug Money Is Corrupting the Enforcers," *New York Times*, April 11, 1988.

10. Robert E. Shalhope, *John Taylor of Caroline: Pastoral Republican* (Columbia: University of South Carolina Press, 1980), 160.

11. John Adams to Mercy Warren, January 8, 1776, in *Warren-Adams Letters, Being Chiefly a Correspondence among John Adams and James Warren, 1743–1814*, vol. 1 (Boston: Massachusetts Historical Society, 1917–1925), 201, 202.

12. Francis Hutcheson, *A System of Moral Philosophy in Three Books* (New York: August M. Kelley, 1968), 285.

13. Ibid.

14. Ibid., 335.

15. Joanne Giza, "A Policeman's Lot," *Newsweek* (November 24, 1980): 31.

16. Ibid.

17. Forrest McDonald, *Novus Ordo Seclorum: The Intellectual Origins of the Constitution* (Lawrence: University Press of Kansas, 1985), 93.

18. Marvin Meyers, ed., *The Mind of the Founder: Sources of the Political Thought of James Madison*, xxix.

19. Alexander Hamilton, James Madison, and John Jay, *The Federalist Papers*, No. 49 (New York: Mentor Books, 1961), 315.

20. Albert A. Seedman and Peter Hellman, *Chief!* (New York: Avon Books, 1974), 43, 44.

21. Elijah Adlow, *Policemen and People* (Boston: William P. Rochfort, 1947), 71.

22. Quoted in Ralph Lee Smith, *The Tarnished Badge* (New York: Arno Press, 1974), 227.

23. Seedman and Hellman, *Chief!* 44.

24. Patrick V. Murphy and Thomas Plate, *Commissioner: A View from the Top of American Law Enforcement* (New York: Simon and Schuster, 1977), 184.

25. Thomas Hardy, *The Return of the Native* (New York: Washington Square Books, 1959), 34.

26. Cicero, *On Duties* 2.12.42, in *Cicero: On the Good Life*, trans. Michael Grant (Baltimore, Md.: Penguin Books, 1971), 142.

27. Xenophon, *Memoirs of Socrates* 2.6.39, in *Xenophon: Memoirs of Socrates and the Symposium*, Hugh Tredennick, trans. (Baltimore, Md.: Penguin Books, 1970), 104.

28. James Madison to Ambrose Madison, October 11, 1787, in *The Papers of James Madison*, vol. 10, Robert A. Rutland et al., eds. (Chicago: University of Chicago Press, 1977), 192.

Chapter 5: Discretion

1. T. H. White, *The Once and Future King* (New York: Berkeley Books, 1958), 247.

2. Herman Goldstein, *Policing a Free Society* (Cambridge, Mass.: Ballinger Publishing, 1977), 107.

3. *Standards for Law Enforcement Agencies: The Standards Manual of the Law Enforcement Agency Accreditation Program* (Fairfax, Va.: Commission on Accreditation of Law Enforcement Agencies, 1984), 1-1, 1-2.

4. Goldstein, *Policing a Free Society*, 106, 107.

5. Philadelphia Police Study Task Force, *Philadelphia and Its Police: Toward a New Partnership* (Philadelphia: City of Philadelphia, 1987), 130, 131.

6. Kenneth Culp Davis, *Police Discretion* (St. Paul, Minn.: West Publishing, 1975), 171.

7. Ibid., 93.

8. Ibid., 65.

9. Reinhold Niebuhr, *The Children of Light and the Children of Darkness* (New York: Scribner, 1944).

10. "New York Racial Tensions Run High since Verdict in Howard Beach Case," *Washington Post*, January 18, 1988.

11. Dick Dahl, "Mean Streets," *Twin Cities* (November 1984): 69, 70.

12. Ibid., 61.

13. Ibid., 61, 62.

14. "Police Probers Say Two Officials Gave False Data," *Washington Post*, January 17, 1988.

15. "Strengthen Kidnap Laws," *News Tribune* (Woodbridge, N.J.) January 15, 1988.

16. Patricia M. Wald, "The Unreasonable Reasonableness Test for Fourth Amendment Searches," *Criminal Justice Ethics* 4, no. 1 (Winter/Spring 1985): 2, 88–90.

17. Ibid.

18. Ibid.

19. *United States v. Place*, 462 U.S. 696, 703 (1983).

20. Wald, "The Unreasonable Reasonableness Test for Fourth Amendment Searches," 90.

21. Howard Cohen, "Overstepping Police Authority," *Criminal Justice Ethics* 6, no. 2 (Summer/Fall 1987): 52–60.

22. Ibid.

23. Ibid., 52, 53.

24. Ibid., 53.

25. Ibid., 54.

26. Ibid., 59.

27. Roger Wertheimer, "Regulating Police Use of Deadly Force," in *Ethics, Public Policy, and Criminal Justice*, Frederick Elliston and Norman Bowie, eds. (Cambridge, Mass.: Oelgeschlager, Gunn, and Hain, 1982), 97.

28. The National Commission on Law Observance and Enforcement, *Report on Lawlessness in Law Enforcement* (Washington, D.C.: Government Printing Office, 1931), 5.

29. Wertheimer, "Regulating Police Use of Deadly Force," 95.

30. Ibid., 98.

31. Ibid., 96.

32. Ibid., 99.

33. Ibid., 107.

34. Ibid.

35. *Standards for Law Enforcement Agencies*, sec. 1.3.3, 1-2.

36. Wertheimer, "Regulating Police Use of Deadly Force," 109.

37. "NW Sex Assaults Raise Question: Should Police Warn Area Residents?" *Washington Post*, January 18, 1988.

38. Ibid.

39. Ibid.

Chapter 6: Public Corruption for Profit

1. Robert Bolt, *A Man for All Seasons* (New York: Vintage Books, 1962), 4.

2. J. A. K. Thomson, trans., *The Ethics of Aristotle: The Nicomachean Ethics Translated* 4.7 (Hammondsworth, Middlesex, Eng.: Penguin Books, 1958), 132.

3. *Virtue's Friend: Essays on Subjects Connected with the Duty and Happiness of Mankind*, 3d ed., vol. 1 (Ormskirk, Lancashire, Eng.: R. Cocker, 1816), 114.

4. Frederick A. Elliston and Michael Feldberg, eds., *Moral Issues in Police Work* (Totowa, N.J.: Rowman and Allenheld, 1985), 251.

5. Iris Murdoch, *The Sovereignty of Good* (New York: Schocken Books, 1971), 59.

6. CBS News, *60 Minutes*, November 22, 1987, vol. 20, no. 10, 10.

7. CBS News, *60 Minutes*, February 14, 1988, vol. 20, no. 22, 3, 4, 5.

8. Ralph Lee Smith, *The Tarnished Badge* (New York: Arno Press, 1974), 191, 192.

9. Ibid., 193, 194.

10. Ibid., 194.

11. Ibid., 212.

12. Jerry Knight, "Give Us That Old-Fashioned 'Honest Graft,'" *Washington Post*, June 21, 1988.

13. Arthur Niederhoffer, *Behind the Shield: The Police in Urban Society* (Garden City, N.Y.: Doubleday, 1969), 70.

14. Ibid. (quoting from Mort Stern, "What Makes a Policeman Go Wrong," *Journal of Criminal Law, Criminology, and Police Science* 53 [1962]: 98–99).

15. Ibid., 97 (quoting from William A. Westley, "The Police: A Sociological Study of Law, Custom, and Morality," ii; later published as *Violence and the Police: A Sociological Study of Law, Custom, and Morality* [Cambridge: MIT Press, 1970]).

16. Niederhoffer, *Behind the Shield*, 98, 99.

17. Julian B. Roebuck and Thomas Barker, "A Typology of Police Corruption," in *Social Problems* 21 (1974): 425. See also Thomas Barker and Julian B. Roebuck, *An Empirical Typology of Police Corruption: A Study of Organizational Deviance* (Springfield, Ill.: Charles C. Thomas, 1974).

18. Mark Pogrebin and Burton Atkins, "Probable Causes for Police Corruption: Some Theories," in *Police and Law Enforcement* 3, Robert J. Homant and Daniel B. Kennedy, eds. (New York: AMS Press, 1985), 215. Pogrebin and Atkins summarized the view of Wallace Sayre and Herbert Kaufman, in *Governing New York City: Politics in the Metropolis* (New York: Russell Sage Foundation, 1960), and the concern of the 1967 President's Commission on Law Enforcement and Administration of Justice.

19. Ibid.

20. Ibid., 212.

21. Ibid.

22. Morris S. Thompson, "Miami Vice: Police Trafficking in Drugs," *Washington Post*, February 7, 1988.

23. "Miami Jury Convicts Two in Drug Ripoffs," *Washington Post*, February 10, 1988.

24. Thompson, "Miami Vice."

25. Robert Daley, *Prince of the City: The True Story of a Cop Who Knew Too Much* (Boston: Houghton Mifflin, 1978).

26. *Virtue's Friend*, 15, 17, 18.

27. Michael Feldberg, "Gratuities, Corruption, and the Democratic Ethos of Policing: The Case of the Free Cup of Coffee," in *Moral Issues in Police Work*, 267.

28. Patrick V. Murphy and Thomas Plate, *Commissioner: A View from the Top of American Law Enforcement* (New York: Simon and Schuster, 1977), 213.

29. Feldberg, "Gratuities, Corruption, and the Democratic Ethos of Policing," p. 276; referring to William K. Muir Jr., *Police: Streetcorner Politicians*, chap. 3 (Chicago: University of Chicago Press, 1977).

30. Lawrence W. Sherman, "Becoming Bent," in *Moral Issues in Police Work*, 259, 260; referring to Ellwyn R. Stoddard, "'The Informal Code' of Police Deviancy: A Group Approach to 'Blue-Coat Crime,'" *Journal of Criminal Law, Criminology, and Police Science* 59, no. 2 (1968).

31. New York City Commission to Investigate Allegations of Police Corruption and the City's Anti-Corruption Procedures, *The Knapp Commission Report on Police Corruption* (New York: George Braziller, 1972), 4.

32. Herman Goldstein, *Policing in a Free Society* (Cambridge, Mass.: Ballinger Publishing Company, 1977), 193, 194 (quoting the *Knapp Commission Report*, 65).

33. CBS News, *60 Minutes*, February 14, 1988, 4, 5.

34. Leonard Schecter with William Phillips, *On the Pad: The Underworld and Its Corrupt Police, Confessions of a Cop on the Take* (New York: G. P. Putnam's Sons, 1973), 278.

35. Albert A. Seedman and Peter Hellman, *Chief!* (New York: Avon Books, 1974), 175.

36. Patrick V. Murphy, "Spotlight," *National Centurion* 1 (1983), 57.

Chapter 7: Authority and Reform

1. John E. Acton, *Essays in Religion, Politics, and Morality*, vol. 3 of *Selected Writings of Lord Acton*, J. Rufus Fears, ed. (Indianapolis, Ind.: Liberty Classics, 1985), 570.

2. James F. Richardson, "Berlin Police in the Weimar Republic: A Comparison with Police Forces in the Cities of the United States," in *Police Forces in History*, George L. Mosse, ed. (London: Sage Publications, 1975), 86.

3. Jack Goldsmith and Sharon S. Goldsmith, eds., *The Police Community* (Pacific Palisades, Calif.: Palisades Publishers, 1974), 7.

4. Richard H. Ward and Robert McCormack, *An Anti-Corruption Manual for Administrators in Law Enforcement* (New York: John Jay Press, 1979), 4, 5.

5. *The Autobiography of Lincoln Steffens* (New York: Harcourt Brace, 1968), 280, 281.

6. Ward and McCormack, *An Anti-Corruption Manual*, 5.

7. Ibid., 79, 80.

8. Quoted in Herman Goldstein, *Police Corruption: A Perspective on Its Nature and Control* (Washington, D.C.: Police Foundation, 1975), i.

9. Ibid., 52.

10. "You Need to Know," *Baltimore Police Department Newsletter*, February 7, 1973.

11. Donald C. Pomerleau, "Whistle Blown on Police Payoffs," *Baltimore Police Department Newsletter*, October 31, 1973; reprinted with permission of the *Baltimore Sun.*

12. Herman Goldstein, *Police Corruption*, 30.

13. Ward and McCormack, *An Anti-Corruption Manual*, 9.

14. Ibid., 51.

15. Ibid., 67.

16. William K. Stevens, "Gains by Philadelphia Police Are Seen," *New York Times*, January 2, 1988.

17. "Ex-Narcotics Unit Officers Indicted in Philadelphia," *Washington Post*, July 20, 1988.

18. Quoted in Stevens, "Gains by Philadelphia Police Are Seen," 9.

19. Ibid.

20. Christopher Hepp, "Residents and Cops: Partners against Crime," *Philadelphia Inquirer*, February 3, 1988.

21. Ibid.

22. Quoted in Stevens, "Gains by Philadelphia Police Are Seen," 9.

23. Robert C. Wadman and Robert K. Olson, *Community Wellness: A New Theory of Policing* (Washington, D.C.: Police Executive Research Forum, 1991), chap. 1, 12.

24. Ibid., chap. 4, 6.

25. Ibid., chap. 8, 13, 14.

Chapter 8: Leadership and Character

1. Booker T. Washington, *Up from Slavery* (New York: Viking Penguin, 1986), 99, 100.

2. Hillary Robinette, *Burnout in Blue: Managing the Police Marginal Performer* (New York: Praeger Publishers, 1987), 4 (quoting Lance Morrow, "The Burnout of Almost Everyone," *Time* [September 21, 1981]).

3. Ibid., 5.

4. David Maraniss, "Death in the County Jail," *Washington Post*, January 10, 1988.

5. Tom L. Beauchamp, "The Justification of Reverse Discrimination," in *Moral Issues in Business*, 3d ed., Vincent Barry, ed. (Belmont, Calif.: Wadsworth Publishing, 1986), 391.

6. Ibid., 394.

7. Ibid., 391.

8. William T. Blackstone, "Reverse Discrimination and Compensatory Justice," in *Moral Issues in Business*, 399.

9. *Civil Rights Act, U.S. Code*, vol. 42, sec. 2000e-2(a).

10. American Enterprise Institute, "A Conversation with the Reverend Jesse Jackson: The Quest for Economic and Educational Parity," *AEI Studies* 209 (1978): 4.

11. Terry Eastland and William J. Bennett, *Counting by Race: Equality from the Founding Fathers to Bakke and Weber* (New York: Basic Books, 1979), 136.

12. Carl Cohen, "Why Racial Preference Is Illegal and Immoral," *Commentary* 67, no. 6 (1979): 42.

13. Quoted in *Atlanta Journal-Constitution*, September 22, 1974.

14. See Thomas Nagel, "Equal Treatment and Compensatory Discrimination," *Philosophy and Public Affairs* 2 (1973): 348–63.

15. *Congressional Record* 110, 1518.

16. Ibid., 1540.

17. Ibid., 7213.

18. *United Steelworkers of America v. Weber*, 443 U.S. 193, 208 (1979).

19. Harvey C. Mansfield Jr., "The Underhandedness of Affirmative Action," *National Review* (May 4, 1984): 28.

20. Ibid., 26.

21. Ibid., 30.

22. *DeFunis v. Odegaard*, 416 U.S. 312, 334, 336–37 (1974), William O. Douglas dissenting.

23. Thomas Sowell, "Are Quotas Good for Blacks?" *Commentary* 65, no. 6 (June 1978): 50.

24. For a discussion of how such factors affect the occupational representation of women, see Diana Furchtgott-Roth and Christine Stolba, *The Feminist Dilemma: When Success Is Not Enough* (Washington, D.C.: AEI Press, 2001).

25. Thomas Short, "A 'New Racism' on Campus?" *Commentary* 86, no. 2 (August 1988): 50.

26. *Shelley v. Kraemer*, 334 U.S. 1, 21–23 (1948).

27. Cohen, "Why Racial Preference Is Illegal and Immoral," 44.

28. "U.S. Remains Racist, Survey Respondents Say," *Greenville (S.C.) News*, August 8, 1988.

29. Joseph Califano, "Tough Talk for Democrats," *New York Times Magazine* (January 8, 1989): 29.

30. Charles Murray, "Affirmative Racism: How Preferential Treatment Works against Blacks," *New Republic* (December 31, 1984): 22.

31. *Janoviak v. Corporate City of South Bend*, 750 E.2d 557, 561 (7th Cir. 1984).

32. *Williams v. City of New Orleans*, 729 F.2d 1554, 1565 (5th Cir. 1984), Judge Thomas G. Gee concurring.

33. *United States v. Paradise*, 480 U.S. 149, 153 (1987).

34. *Johnson v. Transportation Agency*, 480 U.S. 616, 630 (1987).

35. *Wygant v. Jackson Board of Education*, 476 U.S. 267, 274 (1986).

36. *Davis v. City of Dallas*, 777 F.2d 205, 216, 225 (5th Cir. 1985). The court cited *Spurlock*, 475 F.2d 219, and *Kinsey*, 557 F.2d 837.

37. "A Disgrace to the FBI," *Washington Post*, January 26, 1988.

38. Ibid.

39. Ibid.

40. Ibid.

41. Eloize Salholz with Ned Zeman, "Going after Detroit's Rogue Cops," *Newsweek* (September 5, 1988): 37.

42. David C. Couper, *How to Rate Your Local Police* (Washington, D.C.: Police Executive Research Forum, 1983), 15.

43. Ibid. See also Peter B. Block and Deborah Anderson, *Policewomen on Patrol, Final Report* (Washington, D.C.: Police Foundation, 1974).

44. *Standards for Law Enforcement Agencies: The Standards Manual of the Law Enforcement Agency Accreditation Program* (Fairfax, Va.: Commission on Accreditation for Law Enforcement Agencies, 1984), 31-1 to 32-9.

45. U.S. Department of Labor, Employment Standards Administration, WH Publication 1462, September 1988.

46. Los Angeles Police Department, *Police Officer Recruitment Plan*, prepared by the Personnel Department of the Police and Fire Selection Division, June 1987.

47. Quoted by Ordway P. Burden, "Recruiting Police from College," *FBI Law Enforcement Bulletin* (March 1988): 1, 2.

48. Ibid., 2.

49. Ibid.

50. Ibid.

Chapter 9: Illegal Narcotics Issues

1. Robert A. Rutland et al., eds., *The Papers of James Madison*, vol. 10 (Chicago: University of Chicago Press, 1975), 10.

2. See, for example, Eric W. Single, "The Impact of Marijuana Decriminalization," in *Research Advances in Alcohol and Drug Problems* 6 (New York: Plenum, 1981): 406.

3. Lee P. Brown, "Strategies for Dealing with Crack Houses," *FBI Law Enforcement Bulletin* 57, no. 6 (1988): 6.

4. Timothy Egan, "U.S. Agents and Drug Fight in Seattle," *New York Times*, July 15, 1988.

5. "The Legalization of Drugs," policy paper for the Police Executive Research Forum, Washington, D.C., June 6, 1988, 3.

6. Peter Kerr, "The Unspeakable Is Debated: Should Drugs Be Legalized?" *New York Times*, May 15, 1988.

7. National Drug Policy Board, *Progress Report* (Washington, D.C.: National Drug Policy Board, July 1988), 2; citing the *National High School Senior Survey: Monitoring the Future*, conducted for the National Institute on Drug Abuse by the Institute for Social Research, University of Michigan, January 1988, tables 15 and 9.

8. Peter Kerr, "More People Found Opposing Drugs," *New York Times*, July 14, 1988.

9. George F. Will, "The Good Prohibition," *Newsweek* (June 20, 1988): 74.

10. Ovid Demaris, *The Boardwalk Jungle* (New York: Bantam Books, 1986), x–xii.

Chapter 10: Fundamentals of Character

1. J. O. Urmson, *Aristotle's Ethics* (Oxford: Basil Blackwell, 1988), 22.

2. Robert C. Wadman, Monroe J. Paxman, and Marion T. Bentley, *Law Enforcement Supervision: A Case Study Approach* (St. Paul, Minn.: West Publishing, 1975), 34, 35.

3. Ibid., 36.

4. William James, *Psychology: The Briefer Course,* Gordon Allport, ed. (New York: Harper and Brothers, 1961), 11. James's essay "Habit" is also reprinted in *The Writings of William James*, John J. McDermott, ed. (Chicago: University of Chicago Press, 1978), 9–21.

5. Ibid.

6. Ibid.

7. Lawrence W. Sherman, *Ethics in Criminal Justice Education* (Hastings-on-Hudson, N.Y.: Hastings Center, 1982), 17.

8. Ibid., 3.

9. Lawrence W. Sherman and the National Advisory Commission on Higher Education for Police Officers, *The Quality of Police Education* (San Francisco, Calif.: Jossey-Bass Publishers, 1978), 89.

10. Sherman, *Ethics in Criminal Justice Education*, 17, 18.

11. Ibid., 20, 21.

12. Immanuel Kant, *The Metaphysical Elements of Justice* (Indianapolis: Bobbs-Merrill, 1965), 36.

13. Matthew Lipman, *Philosophy Goes to School* (Philadelphia: Temple University Press, 1988), 69.

14. Sherman, *Ethics in Criminal Justice Education*, 3, 26, 32.

15. Carol Schlagheck, "Ida Man Helps Ohio Patrolman," *Ida (Ohio) Evening News*, February 24, 1988.

16. Urmson, *Aristotle's Ethics*, 77.
17. Ibid., 77, 78.
18. Harper Lee, *To Kill a Mockingbird* (New York: Fawcett Popular Library, 1962), 34.
19. Dorothy Uhnak, *Policewoman* (South Yarmouth, Mass.: John Curley and Associates, 1963), 20–22, 30.

Chapter 11: Moral Problems in Training

1. William James, *Psychology, The Briefer Course*, Gordon Allport, ed. (New York: Harper and Brothers, 1961), 12–15.
2. Brand Blanshard, *Reason and Goodness* (London: George Allen and Unwin, 1966), 417, 418.
3. James Boswell, from the conversation of June 13, 1784, in *Boswell's Life of Johnson*, Anne H. Ehrenpreis and Irwin Ehrenpreis, eds. (New York: Washington Square Press, 1965), 469.
4. "Police Blame ABC for Abrupt Raid," *New York Times*, April 11, 1988.
5. Malachi L. Harney and John C. Cross, *The Narcotic Officer's Notebook* (Springfield, Ill.: Charles C. Thomas, 1961), 135.
6. Ibid., 150.
7. Gerald M. Kaplan, ed., *ABSCAM Ethics: Moral Issues and Deception in Law Enforcement* (Cambridge, Mass.: Ballinger Publishing Company, 1983), v.
8. Malachi L. Harney and John C. Cross, *The Informer in Law Enforcement* (Springfield, Ill.: Charles C. Thomas, 1968), vii, viii, 5, 12.
9. Quoted in ibid., 20.
10. Irwin B. Nathan, "ABSCAM: A Fair and Effective Method for Fighting Public Corruption," in *ABSCAM Ethics*, 5.
11. Sissela Bok, *Lying* (New York: Pantheon, 1978), 18.
12. Sanford Levinson, "Under Cover: The Hidden Costs of Infiltration," in *ABSCAM Ethics*, 45, 58, 55.
13. Mark H. Moore, "Invisible Offenses: A Challenge to Minimally Intrusive Law Enforcement," in *ABSCAM Ethics*, 17.
14. Harney and Cross, *The Narcotic Officer's Notebook*, 152.
15. Ibid., 242.
16. William Shakespeare, *Othello, The Moor of Venice* 1.3, Marc Eccles, ed. (New York: Appleton-Century-Crofts, 1946).
17. Larry Lewis, "An Officer's Nightmare: Drug Role Became Reality," *Philadelphia Inquirer*, March 21, 1988.
18. Jonathan Rubinstein, *City Police* (New York: Farrar, Straus, and Giroux, 1973), 207.
19. Gary T. Marx, *Undercover: Police Surveillance in America* (Berkeley: University of California Press, 1988), 107.

20. Lon L. Fuller, *The Morality of Law* (New Haven, Conn.: Yale University Press, 1975), 159.

21. J. A. K. Thomson, trans., *The Ethics of Aristotle: The Nicomachean Ethics Translated* 10.3 (Hammondsworth, Middlesex, Eng.: Penguin Books, 1958).

22. William Ker Muir Jr., *Police: Streetcorner Politicians* (Chicago: University of Chicago Press, 1977), 191.

23. *The Ethics of Aristotle: The Nicomachean Ethics Translated* 3.7.

Chapter 12: Tragedy and Corruption

1. Immanuel Kant, *Foundations of the Metaphysics of Morals* (New York: Bobbs-Merrill, 1959), 46, 47.

2. Albert Camus, *Resistance, Rebellion, and Death*, Justin O'Brien, trans. (New York: Vintage Books, 1974), 5.

3. Bertolt Brecht, *Galileo*, Charles Laughton, trans. (New York: Grove Press, 1966), 110.

4. Walter Lippmann, *The Public Philosophy* (New York: Mentor Books, 1955), 27.

5. *Crimes Code of Pennsylvania*, secs. 502, 503 (Longwood, Fla.: Gould Publications, 1985), 19, 20.

6. David Maraniss, "Death of a Reputed Vigilante," *Washington Post*, September 21, 1986.

7. Joan Fleischman, "Ex-Cop: 'I enjoyed shooting dealers,'" *Miami Herald*, April 14, 1988.

8. William Safire, "Stalker's Last Case," *New York Times*, June 30, 1986. Safire was writing in the context of his analysis of the "Stalker Affair," so named by Deputy Chief Constable of the Greater Manchester Police John Stalker in describing his investigation of alleged abuses of authority and power by the Royal Ulster Constabulary. The case was much more complex and murky than popular published accounts made it out to be, but Safire's statement of principle was nonetheless correct.

9. Robert Bolt, *A Man for All Seasons* (New York: Vintage Books, 1962), 43.

10. Carl B. Klockars, "The Dirty Harry Problem," in *Moral Issues in Police Work*, Frederick A. Elliston and Michael Feldberg, eds. (Totowa, N.J.: Rowman and Allenheld, 1985), 55–62.

11. See Edmund Burke, *Reflections on the French Revolution and Other Essays* (New York: E. P. Dutton, 1951), 60.

12. Reinhold Niebuhr, *The Irony of American History* (New York: Charles Scribner's Sons, 1952), vii, viii, 5.

Chapter 13: Death and Bereavement, Deadly Force and Guilt

1. C. S. Lewis, *A Grief Observed* (New York: Bantam Books, 1976), 16.

Chapter 14: Taking Our Lives Seriously

1. Paul H. Appleby, *Morality and Administration in Democratic Government* (Baton Rouge: Louisiana State University Press, 1952), 67, 68.

2. Walter Lippmann, "A Theory about Corruption," in *Political Corruption: Readings in Comparative Analysis*, Arnold J. Heidenheimer, ed. (New York: Holt, Rinehart, and Winston, 1970), 296, 297.

3. Lon M. Fuller, *The Morality of Law* (New Haven, Conn.: Yale University Press, 1975), 5.

4. Ibid., 8.

Chapter 15: Fatalism, Microcosms, and Therapeutic Reductions

1. Immanuel Kant, *Lectures on Ethics*, Louis Infield, trans. (New York: Harper Torchbooks, 1963), 126.

2. *Trop v. Dulles*, 356 U.S. 86 (1958).

3. Howard S. Cohen and Michael Feldberg, *Power and Restraint: The Moral Dimension of Police Work* (New York: Praeger, 1991), 43.

4. Edwin J. Delattre and Scott R. Stripling, "Police Integrity and Public Expectations," *The Public Interest Law Review* (Durham, N.C.: Carolina Academic Press for the National Legal Center for the Public Interest, 1992), 47–62.

5. Selwyn Raab, "Report Says Police Tolerate Corruption," *New York Times*, January 2, 1994.

6. Francis E. Rourke, "Urbanism and American Democracy," *Ethics* 74, no. 4 (1964): 264.

7. Ibid., 265 (citing Josiah Strong, *The Twentieth Century City* [New York: 1898], 101, 102).

8. "Texts of Letters between Clinton and Baird," *New York Times*, January 23,1993.

9. "Baird's Withdrawal: What Some Americans Had to Say," *Atlanta Journal-Constitution*, January 23, 1993.

10. Victor LaCerva, *Let Peace Begin with Us: The Problem of Violence in New Mexico* (Santa Fe, N.M.: New Mexico Health and Environment Department, 1990); cited in Steve Terrell, "Country's Violent Crimes Rate Ranks High," *Santa Fe New Mexican*, September 16, 1990.

11. "A Scandal in the Cloister," *Newsweek* (July 23, 1990): 34.

12. Quoted in Carol Innerst, "'Sensitivity' Is Buzzword at Colleges," *Washington Times*, August 29, 1990.

13. "Feminist Woes," *Crisis* (September 1990): 4.

14. Quoted in David Streitfeld, "The Addiction Habit," *Washington Post*, August 28, 1990.

15. Ibid., citing the *Los Angeles Times*.

16. "Excerpts from Durenberger's Senate Testimony," *New York Times*, June 14, 1990.

17. Quoted in M. A. J. McKenna, "Experts to Debate Measures for Getting Moms off Drugs," *Boston Herald*, September 30, 1990.

18. Don Feder, "Sex Addicts: Newest Victims," *Boston Herald*, June 18, 1990.

19. David Gelman et al., "The Mind of the Rapist," *Newsweek* (July 23, 1990): 46.

20. Trish Hall, "Spas to Massage Both Body and Mind," *New York Times*, July 11, 1990.

21. Edward Silver, "This Alter Ego Helps Scripts Be Psychologically Sound," *New York Times*, July 1, 1990.

22. Juan Williams, "Hard Time for Rayful Edmond," *Washington Post Magazine* (June 24, 1990): 20.

23. California Task Force to Promote Self-Esteem and Personal and Social Responsibility, *Toward a State of Esteem* (Sacramento: California State Department of Education, 1990), vii, 2, emphasis added.

24. Ibid., 7, 10.

25. Ibid., 22, 23.

26. Ibid., 27.

27. From the National Assessment of Educational Progress, cited by Chester E. Finn Jr., "Narcissus Goes to School," *Commentary* 89, no. 6 (1990): 43.

28. From the University of Michigan's Institute for Social Research, ibid.

29. Gerald J. Pine and Asa G. Hilliard III, "Rx for Racism: Imperatives for America's Schools," *Phi Delta Kappan* (April 1990): 595.

30. Ibid.

31. Quoted in Eleanor Clift, "Peccadillo Politics and the New Rules of Conduct," *Newsweek* (April 9, 1990): 21.

32. Quoted in Ze'ev Chafets, "The Tragedy of Detroit," *New York Times Magazine* (July 29, 1990): 50.

33. Quoted in Jane De Hart-Mathews, "The New Feminism and the Dynamics of Social Change," *Women's America*, Linda K. Kerber and Jane De Hart-Mathews, eds. (New York: Oxford University Press, 1987), 451.

34. Douglas Martin, "They Are Gay, and Asking God to Save Them," *New York Times*, July 21, 1990.

35. Quoted in Linda Hayes Tischler, "Self-Help's Hottest Guru," *Boston Herald*, August 13, 1990.

36. Charles Krauthammer, "Defining Deviancy Up," Bradley Lecture, American Enterprise Institute for Public Policy Research, Washington, D.C., September 13, 1993.

37. Wilhelm Reich, *The Mass Psychology of Fascism*, 3d ed., Theodore P. Wolfe, trans. (New York: Orgone Institute Press, 1946), 51.

38. Daniel Patrick Moynihan, "Defining Deviancy Down," *American Scholar* 62, no. 1 (Winter 1993): 17–30.

39. Krauthammer, "Defining Deviancy Up."

40. Herbert D. Kleber, "On Current Approaches to Drug Abuse—Progress, Problems, Proposals," *New England Journal of Medicine* (1994): 362.

41. *Americans with Disabilities Act: Policy Guide* (Washington D.C.: Bureau of National Affairs, 1991), 19.

42. See Shelby Steele, *The Content of Our Character* (New York: St. Martin's Press, 1990), 74 (quoting from Ellison's novel, *Invisible Man*).

43. Derald Wing Sue and David Sue, *Counseling the Culturally Different*, 2d ed. (New York: John Wiley and Sons, 1991), 113.

44. Ibid., 117.

45. *U.S. Code*, vol. 20, sec. 951 (6). Section 953 of the legislation called for the establishment of a National Endowment for the Arts and a National Endowment for the Humanities within the National Foundation on the Arts and the Humanities. *U.S. Code*, vol. 20, sec. 953 (a).

Chapter 16: Ethical Ideals, Youth Violence, and Gang Enforcement

1. John Silber, *Straight Shooting: What's Wrong with America and How to Fix It* (New York: Harper & Row, 1989), 75.

2. Josh Barbanel, "More Students Are Violent at Young Age," *New York Times*, December 4, 1993.

3. Larry Rohter, "Florida Governments Move to Get Teen-Ager Curfews," *New York Times*, December 23, 1993.

4. William J. Bennett, "Getting Used to Decadence: The Spirit of Democracy in Modern America," keynote address, Heritage Foundation's twentieth anniversary, Washington, D.C., December 7, 1993.

5. James Q. Wilson and George L. Kelling, "Broken Windows: The Police and Neighborhood Safety," *Atlantic Monthly* (March 1982).

6. Connie Fletcher, *What Cops Know* (New York: Villard Books, 1991), 21.

7. "Should Crime Be Color Blind? Mayors Urge Removal of Race Data from Crime Stats," *Law Enforcement News* (December 15, 1993): 1, 10.

8. As William J. Bennett wrote: "During last year's Los Angeles riots, Damian Williams and Henry Watson were filmed pulling an innocent man out of a truck, crushing his skull with a brick and doing a victory dance over his fallen body. Their lawyers then built a successful legal defense on the proposition that people cannot be held accountable for getting caught up in mob violence. When the trial was over and these men were found not guilty on most counts, the sound you heard throughout the land was relief. . . . We are losing a once-reliable sense of civic and moral outrage." "Commuter Massacre, Our Warning," *Wall Street Journal*, December 10, 1993.

9. Sidney J. Harris, "Gangs Make Martyrs of Issues," in Robert K. Jackson and Wesley D. McBride, *Understanding Street Gangs* (Placerville, Calif.: Custom Publishing, 1990), 1.

10. Ibid., p. 11.

11. C. S. Lewis, *The Abolition of Man* (New York: Macmillan, 1947), p. 24.

12. U.S. Department of the Treasury, Bureau of Alcohol, Tobacco, and Firearms, *ATF Facts* (Washington, D.C.: Government Printing Office, monthly).

13. See, for example, American University's packet on conflict resolution. American University, "Anatomy of Confrontation," *Conflict Resolution* (Washington, D.C.: American University, n.d.), 4.

14. Evan Simpson, "Social Norms and Aberrations: Violence and Some Related Facts," *Ethics* 81, no. 1 (1970): 29.

15. Kathryn Girard, Janet Rifkin, and Annette Townley, *Peaceful Persuasion: A Guide to Creating Mediation Resolution Programs on College Campuses* (Amherst: Mediation Project at the University of Massachusetts–Amherst of the National Institute for Dispute Resolution, 1985), 7.

16. Ibid.

17. Ibid., 6.

18. Program on Negotiation at Harvard Law School, "Increasing HR Effectiveness: New HR Leadership Strategies for Managing Organizational Issues and Disputes," An Interuniversity Consortium, Harvard University, Massachusetts Institute of Technology, and Tufts University, October 15–17, 1990; April 29–May 1, 1991, p. 6.

19. Jacques Barzun, *Begin Here: The Forgotten Conditions of Teaching and Learning* (Chicago: University of Chicago Press, 1992), 14.

20. I was hopeful that the Police Executive Research Forum's projects on gangs and organized crime conspiracies, funded for two years late in 1993 by the National Institute of Justice and the Bureau of Justice Assistance, would prove valuable to police and sheriffs, legislators, and law enforcement agencies. PERF described the projects as follows:

> With funding from the National Institute of Justice, PERF is conducting a 24-month project to identify the relationships between traditional and newly emerging organized crime groups and youth gangs. The study will include an extensive review of the literature; a national mail survey to identify police perceptions of the nature of criminal group relationships; structured interviews regarding the nature of links between various crime groups with law enforcement and others in two cities impacted by chronic gang problems; and field studies consisting of interviews with gang members about the nature of criminal gangs, their structure and changes over time, such as their possible transition into groups that more closely resemble traditional organized crime.
>
> PERF has joined with COSMOS Corporation, a private sector think-tank, to develop a comprehensive problem-oriented approach to addressing the chronic gang problems that plague urban areas. The comprehensive strategy will be flexible enough to allow each locality to

tailor the approach to its needs and conditions. Funded by the Bureau of Justice Assistance, the project will be divided into four separate stages: STAGE I will consist of a national assessment of gang problems and local responses throughout the United States. STAGE II will focus on developing a problem-solving model that combines enforcement, prevention, and education. The model will provide analysis guidelines for each site to use to determine the program mix that best fits local conditions and gang problems. STAGE III will consist of training and technical assistance. The PERF/COSMOS team will develop training for police and other practitioners to assess their communities' needs and the nature of their own gang problems and to implement this approach in their communities. In STAGE IV, PERF and COSMOS will develop a technical assistance implementation plan and provide initial assistance to BJA–selected demonstration sites.

Police Executive Research Forum, "Active Projects," December 1993, Washington, D.C.

Such projects may advance knowledge and draw police into closer association regionally and nationally. If they succeed in doing so, they will help to improve policing generally and not only in controlling gangs.

Chapter 17: Police, the O. J. Simpson Trial, and Race

1. Ralph Ellison, *Shadow and Act* (New York: Vintage Books, 1972), 22.

2. Frank Bruni, "Alisa's [sic] Story: A Girl Trapped, Neglected, Tormented, Dead," *New York Times*, November 25, 1995.

3. Quoted in Marc Peyser, with Carla Power, "The Death of Little Elisa," *Newsweek* (December 11, 1995): 42.

4. Bruni, "Alisa's Story."

5. Gertrude Himmelfarb, "The Gender Card Loses," *Weekly Standard* (October 16, 1995): 15.

6. Reported in Gordon Witkin, with Timothy M. Ito, Monica Guttman, Scott Minerbrook, and Jill Jordan Sieder, "When the Bad Guys Are Cops," *U.S. News & World Report* (September 11, 1995): 20.

7. *California v. Orenthal James Simpson*, 1995 WL 109035, official transcript, March 15, 1995, p. 96, 97.

8. *California v. Orenthal James Simpson*, 1995 WL 550493, official transcript, September 6, 1995, p. 31.

9. Ibid., 15.

10. *California v. Orenthal James Simpson*, 1995 WL 106323, official transcript, March 14, 1995, p. 160.

11. Quoted in Fred Barnes, "The Shame of Lance Ito," *Weekly Standard* (October 16, 1995): 12.

12. Abigail Thernstrom and Henry D. Fetter, "From Scottsdale to Simpson," *Public Interest* 122 (1996): 23.

13. John J. DiIulio Jr., "100,000 O. J. Simpsons," *Weekly Standard* (October 16, 1995): 7.

14. Craig Hemmens and Rolando V. del Carmen, "The Vagueness of Reasonable Doubt," *Law Enforcement News* 21, no. 434 (November 30, 1995): 12.

15. Thernstrom and Fetter, "From Scottsdale to Simpson."

16. George F. Will, "A Political Caucus, Not a Trial," *Boston Globe*, October 6, 1995.

17. Oliver Wendell Holmes, quoted in Hiller B. Zobel, "The Jury on Trial," *American Heritage* 46, no. 4 (1995): 44.

18. Quoted in A. M. Rosenthal, "Contempt in Court," *New York Times FAX* (January 30, 1996): 8.

19. Ibid., 46.

20. Ibid., 47, 48.

21. Edward A. Flynn, "Police Officers Fall under Dark Shadow of Notoriety," *Quincy (Mass.) Patriot Ledger*, Saturday/Sunday, September 9/10, 1995.

22. Ibid.

23. Ibid.

24. "Why O. J. Simpson Was Found Not Guilty," *Jet* (October 23, 1995): 9.

25. Ibid., 56.

26. Ibid., 56, 57.

27. James T. McBride, "Looking for Clues: Law Enforcement News Surveys a 'Jury' of Experts to Assess the Impact of the O. J. Simpson Case on Law Enforcement and Criminal Justice," *Law Enforcement News* 21, no. 434 (1995): 8.

28. "Simpson Verdict Sets Back Los Angeles Police," *New York Times FAX* (October 5, 1995): 3.

29. Diane Weathers, "The Other Side of Johnnie Cochran," *Essence* (November 1995): 88, 146.

30. Larry C. Plummer, "The Problem of Bigotry and Hate Requires a Collective, Intentional Response," *Subject to Debate: A Newsletter of the Police Executive Research Forum* 9, nos. 10/11 (1995): 1, 6.

31. For further details, see Edwin J. Delattre and Daniel L. Schofield, "Combating Bigotry in Law Enforcement," *FBI Law Enforcement Bulletin* (June 1996): 27–32.

32. John Warner, "Examining, Not Exploiting, Recent Serious Lapses in Police Integrity," *Law Enforcement News* (September 30, 1995): 8.

33. Ibid., 8, 10.

34. "Officers Reported to Have Gang Ties," *Boston Globe*, October 8, 1995.

35. "A Crackdown on Police Criminality," *New York Times*, October 29, 1995.

36. "Corruption Scandal Surfaces in Atlanta—with Inside Help," *Law Enforcement News* (October 31, 1995): 7.

37. Ronald Smothers, "Atlanta Holds Six Policemen in Crackdown," *New York Times*, September 7, 1995.

38. Edmund Burke, *Reflections on the Revolution in France*, quoted from Russell Kirk, ed., *The Portable Conservative Reader* (New York: Penguin Books, 1982), 39.

39. *Federal Register* 60, no. 166 (1995): 44673–93.

40. Ibid., part 6, Office of Management and Budget, 44677.

41. Maria Puente, "Multiracial Families Want Identity Respected," *USA Today*, January 2, 1996.

42. Luigi Cavalli-Sforza, quoted in Adam Goodheart, "Mapping the Past," *Civilization: The Magazine of the Library of Congress* (March/April 1996): 47.

43. Lewis Hanke, *Aristotle and the American Indians: A Study in Race Prejudice in the Modern World* (Bloomington: Indiana University Press, 1970), ix.

44. John Leo, "The Color of the Law," *U.S. News & World Report* (October 16, 1995): 24.

45. Ibid.

46. Thernstrom and Fetter, "From Scottsdale to Simpson," 25, 26.

47. Kurt Mack, "O. J. Is Not a Black Hero," *Newsweek* (October 30, 1995): 20.

48. Allen J. Beck and Darrell K. Gilliard, "Prisoners in 1994," *Bureau of Justice Statistics Bulletin* (August 1995): 9, 10, 11.

49. Orlando Patterson, "Going Separate Ways: The History of an Old Idea— Why Farrakhan's Obsession with Race Is Bad for Blacks," *Newsweek* (October 30, 1995): 43.

50. Quoted in Michael Saunders and Ann Scales, "Blacks on Simpson: Community Speaks with Many Voices: Many Blacks in Boston See Vindication in Verdict," *Boston Globe*, October 6, 1995.

51. John Ellis, "A Shift to the Right," *Boston Globe*, October 7, 1995.

52. Ralph Ellison, *Invisible Man* (New York: Vintage Books, 1972), and Ellison, *Shadow and Act*.

53. Ellison, *Shadow and Act*, xix.

54. Ibid., 3–5.

55. Ibid., 8–9.

56. Ibid., 12.

57. Kwame Anthony Appiah, "Beware of Race-Pride," *Network News and Views* 14, no. 11 (1995): 22.

58. Ibid., 22.

59. Abraham Lincoln, "Second Inaugural Address," in *The American Intellectual Tradition*, 2d ed., vol. 1, 1630–1835, David A. Hollinger and Charles Capper, eds., (New York: Oxford University Press, 1993), 431.

Chapter 18: Public Service and Individual Conscience

1. Brand Blanshard, *Reason and Goodness* (London: George Allen and Unwin, 1966), 33.

2. Leigh Rivenbark, "Border Agents Sue over Sewage Exposure," *Federal Times* (April 8, 1996): 8.

3. Daniel L. Schofield, "Freedom of Religion and Law Enforcement Employment," *FBI Law Enforcement Bulletin* (June 1995): 28.

4. Ibid., 30.

5. Ibid.

6. Ibid., 31.

Chapter 19: Ethics in the Future of Policing

1. Roger Scruton, "Bring Back Stigma," *City Journal* (Autumn 2000): 68.

2. Paul Johnson, "Creative Destruction?" *Commentary* 109, no. 1 (2000): 68.

3. Charles Murray, "Prole Models," *Wall Street Journal*, February 6, 2001.

4. Scruton, "Bring Back Stigma," 68.

5. Ibid.

6. Ibid., 69.

7. Ibid., 71.

8. Ibid., 75.

9. *Ethics Roll Call* 7, no. 4 (2000): 1.

10. James Q. Wilson and George L. Kelling, "Broken Windows: The Police and Neighborhood Safety," *Atlantic Monthly* (March 1982).

11. Ibid.

12. Ibid.

13. Ibid.

14. Ibid.

15. Recheal Stewart-Brown, "'Mind Your Own Business' Is Bad Advice," in *Community Policing Exchange* (Washington, D.C.: Community Policing Consortium, November/December 2000): 1.

16. Wilson and Kelling, "Broken Windows."

17. David Barstow, "Officer, Hoping to Avoid Life Sentence, Admits He Tortured Haitian Immigrant," *New York Times*, May 26, 1999.

18. Tom Hayes, "Volpe: I'm the Real Victim," Associated Press, 1999, accessed at www.abcnews.go.com/sections/us/dailynews/volpe991101.html.

19. U.S. Commission on Civil Rights, *Police Practices and Civil Rights in New York City: A Report of the U.S. Commission on Civil Rights*, letter of transmittal by Mary Frances Berry (Washington, D.C.: U.S. Commisssion on Civil Rights, August 2000), x.

20. Quoted in Lou Cannon, "One Bad Cop," *New York Times Magazine* (October 1, 2000), accessed at www.nytimes.com/library/magazine/home/20001001mag-lapd .html.

21. David Dotson, "Culture of War," *Los Angeles Times*, February 27, 2000.

22. Erwin Chemerinsky, in collaboration with Paul Hoffman, Laurie Levenson, R. Samuel Paz, Connie Rice, and Carol Soble, *An Independent Analysis of the Los Angeles Police Department's Board of Inquiry Report on the Rampart Scandal: Prepared at the Request of the Police Protective League*, September 11, 2000, p. 7.

23. Beth Shuster and Vincent J. Schodolski, "Poor Morale Rife in LAPD, Survey Finds," *Los Angeles Times*, September 8, 2000.

24. We may be tempted to say that the Rampart Division outrage is not so heinous as police scandals in which larger numbers of police have been implicated. In July 2000, for example, the governor of Rio de Janeiro fired 353 police, many of whom had been convicted of crimes including car theft, drug trafficking, and murder and had been allowed to continue in the police department for years while their legal appeals languished in the court system. (See "Cleaning House," in *Ethics Roll Call* 7, no. 4 [2000]: 5.) It is true that where larger numbers of police are involved, the moral ethos of the department as a whole will be worse, but not the outrageousness of the actions. The moral quality of an act is distinct from questions of quantity. A single murder is a moral outrage, just as framing one person is a moral outrage. The immorality of acts is not determined by quantification.

25. Edward Albert Shils, *The Calling of Education: The Academic Ethic and Other Essays on Higher Education*, Steven Grosby, ed. (Chicago: University of Chicago Press, 1997), 70, 71.

26. U.S. Commission on Civil Rights, *Police Practices and Civil Rights in New York City*, iv.

27. Ibid., 19.

28. Ibid.

29. Ibid., 14.

30. Patrick M. Kelly, "College Education as an Entry Level Requirement for Law Enforcement" (position paper, Florida Criminal Justice Standards and Training Commission), 3.

31. Ibid., 4.

32. U.S. Commission on Civil Rights, "Dissenting Statement of Commissioners Carl A. Anderson and Russell G. Redenbaugh," *Police Practices and Civil Rights in New York City* (Washington D.C.: U.S. Commission on Civil Rights), 111, 112, 114.

33. Stephen Kurkjian, "Education Costs Soar for Police," *Boston Globe*, February 13, 2001.

34. John Passmore, *The Philosophy of Teaching* (London: Gerald Duckworth, 1980), 37. This is one of the best books ever written on teaching and learning, the nature of open and closed capacities, the development of capacities, and the cultivation of habits. Educators and police trainers will find here a more comprehensive treatment

of those topics than space allows in *Character and Cops*. Passmore's writings are demanding but exceptionally instructive.

35. See Jacques Barzun, *Begin Here: The Forgotten Conditions of Teaching and Learning*, Morris Philipson, ed. (Chicago: University of Chicago Press, 1992). *Begin Here* contains a collection of very readable and extremely insightful lectures and essays by Barzun that police educators and trainers should come to know.

36. Gilbert Highet, *The Art of Teaching* (New York: Vintage Books, 1950), 214, 215.

37. Edward J. Tully, "The Slippery Slope," *National Executive Institute Associates Leadership Bulletin* (May 2000), accessed at www.neiassociates.org. The essay includes the instructive analogy of "scruffy shoes" worn by police to "broken windows" in a neighborhood. Tully served as a special agent with the FBI from 1962 until 1993 and is executive director of the National Executive Institute Associates and the Major City Chiefs' Association.

38. "Sample Professional Traffic Stop Policy and Procedure," International Association of Chiefs of Police, 2, accessed at www.theiacp.org/pubinfo/pubs/stopsletter.htm.

39. Ibid.

40. Ibid., 3, 4.

41. Ibid.

42. Ibid., 3.

43. Bill Toohey, "Media Relations during a Hostage Standoff," in *Subject to Debate*, a newsletter of the Police Executive Research Forum (August 2000): 3.

44. Associated Press, "Tactics Questioned in Hostage Standoff," *Portland* (Maine) *Press Herald*, June 3, 2000.

Chapter 20: Terrorism and Policing

1. Jacques Barzun, *The Culture We Deserve* (Hanover, N.H.: Wesleyan University Press, 1989), 168.

2. Robert Schlesinger, "Hate Groups Applaud Terror Attacks, Watch Reaction Warily," *Boston Globe*, October 28, 2001.

3. Laura Parker, Kevin Johnson, and Steve Sternberg, "Evidence Supports Both Foreign, Domestic Theories," *USA Today*, October 30, 2001.

4. Antonio Regalado, "The Scientists Probing Terror Anthrax Trace Microbe's Family Tree," *Wall Street Journal*, November 8, 2001.

5. David Espo, "FBI Offers Profile of Anthrax Terrorist," *Portland Press Herald*, November 10, 2001.

6. Brian Fitzgerald, "Bioterrorism: Be Alert, but Not Anxious, Says City Expert," *B.U. Bridge* 5, no. 11 (2001): 1, 9.

7. Madeline Drexler, "Sowing the Seeds of Disaster," *Boston Globe*, October 28, 2001.

8. Joseph Lieberman, "After bin Laden, We Must Target Saddam," *Wall Street Journal*, October 29, 2001.

9. Ibid.

10. Parker, Johnson, and Sternberg, "Evidence Supports Both Foreign, Domestic Theories."

11. U.S. Department of Justice, Federal Bureau of Investigation, Counterterrorism Threat Assessment and Warning Unit, Counterterrorism Division, "Terrorism in the United States 1999: 30 Years of Terrorism, A Special Retrospective Edition," 23, 24.

12. George Will, "Now, Weapons of Mass Disruption?" *Newsweek* (October 29, 2001): 76.

13. Susan Sachs, "An Investigation in Egypt Illustrates Al Qaeda's Web," *New York Times*, November 21, 2001.

14. Middle East Media and Research Institute, *Terror in America* 24, Special Dispatch No. 297, November 7, 2001, accessed at www.memri.org.

15. Undated September 2001 letter to alumni and friends over signatures of Professors Judith D. Singer and John B. Willett, acting deans, Harvard University Graduate School of Education.

16. William Safire, "Infamy: Words of the War on Terror," *New York Times Magazine*, (September 23, 2001): 32.

17. Benjamin Netanyahu, *Fighting Terrorism: How Democracies Can Defeat the International Terrorist Network, 2001 Edition* (New York: Farrar, Straus, and Giroux, 2001), xxi.

18. John O'Sullivan, "Mincing Words and Reality," *Chicago Sun-Times*, September 25, 2001, accessed at www.suntimes.com/output/osullivan/cst-edt-osul25.html.

19. Daniel Pipes, "The Danger Within: Militant Islam in America," *Commentary* 112, no. 4 (2001).

20. Quoted from an attachment to a letter from John Silber to Edwin J. Delattre, November 14, 2001.

21. *U.S. Code*, vol. 18, sec. 2332b.

22. Ibid., sec. 2331.

23. "Captured Terrorist Manual Suggests Hijackers Did a Lot by the Book," *New York Times*, October 27, 2001.

24. Quoted in Benjamin Netanyahu, "Defining Terrorism," in *Terrorism: How the West Can Win*, Benjamin Netanyahu, ed. (New York: Farrar, Straus, and Giroux, 1986), 16, 17, 23.

25. U.S. Department of Justice, "Terrorism in the United States 1999," 13, 24.

26. Bernard Lewis, "Jihad vs. Crusade," *Wall Street Journal*, September 27, 2001.

27. President George W. Bush, "Address to a Joint Session of Congress and the American People," United States Capitol, Washington, D.C., September 20, 2001, accessed at www.fas.org/irp/news/2001/09/gwb092001.html.

28. Farouk El-Baz, "Terrorism's Goal Is Political Power," *Boston Herald*, October 7, 2001.

29. Rick Bragg, "Shaping Young Islamic Hearts and Hatreds," *New York Times*, October 14, 2001.

30. Thomas L. Friedman, "In Pakistan, It's Jihad 101," *New York Times*, November 13, 2001.

31. Katherine Ross, "New York Rejects $10 Million Donation from Saudi Prince," Associated Press, October 11, 2001.

32. *Al-Riyadh* (Saudi Arabia), October 15, 2001; translated and quoted in Middle East Media and Research Institute, "Saudi, Syrian, and Palestinian Authority Press Attack Giuliani and U.S."

33. *Al-Hayat Al-Jadida* (Palestinian Authority), October 17, 2001; translated and quoted in Middle East Media and Research Institute, "Saudi, Syrian, and Palestinian Authority Press Attack Giuliani and U.S.," *Terror in America* 19, Special Dispatch 291. (October 25, 2001), accessed at www.memri.org/sd/SP29101.html.

34. Lewis, "Jihad vs. Crusade."

35. "Notes Found after Hijackings," *New York Times*, September 29, 2001.

36. See J. Glenn Gray, *The Warriors: Reflections on Men in Battle* (Lincoln: University of Nebraska Press, 1990), 146, 147. Gray was a philosopher and a brilliant teacher at Colorado College. *The Warriors* was first published in 1959 as a reflection on Gray's experience as an infantryman and intelligence officer in four years of service during World War II. Chapter 5, "Images of the Enemy," describes "the crusader" for whom the enemy is "totally evil" and "for whom any mercy or sympathy is incongruous, if not traitorous. . . . [T]he crusader denies his humanity by making him into a devil."

37. *Nicomachean Ethics* 3.8, in *The Complete Works of Aristotle*, vol. 2, Jonathan Barnes, ed. (Princeton: Princeton University Press, 1984), 1763.

38. *National Strategy Review*, accessed at www.nationalstrategy.com/speakers/oneill.html.

39. Alexander Hamilton, James Madison, and John Jay, *The Federalist*, No. 41, Jacob E. Cooke, ed. (Middletown, Conn.: Wesleyan University Press, 1961), 275.

40. C. S. Lewis, "Learning in Wartime," in *The Weight of Glory* (San Francisco: Harper Collins, 2001), 49, 50.

41. International Association of Chiefs of Police, "Leading from the Front: Law Enforcement's Role in Combating and Preparing for Domestic Terrorism," accessed at www.theiacp.org.

42. Ibid.

43. "Since September 11: The Ongoing Betrayal of Liberty on America's Campuses," Foundation for Individual Rights in Education, Inc., accessed at www.thefire.org.

44. Stanley Kurtz, "Free Speech and an Orthodoxy of Dissent," *Chronicle of Higher Education* (October 26, 2001).

45. "War Profiteers II," *Wall Street Journal*, November 8, 2001.

46. Schlesinger, "Hate Groups Applaud Terror Attacks."

47. "Falwell Apologizes for Placing Blame," September 20, 2001, accessed at www.abcnews.com.

48. "Idiocy Watch," *New Republic* (October 29, 2001): 10.

49. Andrew Sullivan, "The Agony of the Left," *Wall Street Journal*, October 4, 2001.

50. Ibid.

51. Valerie Strauss, "Sept. 11 Prompts Lesson Review," *Washington Post*, October 1, 2001.

52. "Veep's Wife Champions Curriculum," Associated Press, October 5, 2001.

53. George Steiner, *In Bluebeard's Castle: Some Notes towards the Redefinition of Culture* (New Haven: Yale University Press, 1971), 108, 110.

54. Hamilton, Madison, and Jay, *The Federalist*, No. 8, 45.

55. Ibid., No. 23, 147.

56. See chapter 12 above, "Tragedy and 'Noble Cause' Corruption," where I have treated this point in detail.

57. U.S. Department of Justice, "Terrorism in the United States 1999," 50, 51.

58. Uri Ra'anan, "Vulnerabilities of the International Support Apparatus," in *Hydra of Carnage: International Linkages of Terrorism*, Uri Ra'anan, Robert L. Paltzgraff Jr., Richard H. Shultz, Ernst Halperin, and Igor Lukes, eds. (Lexington, Mass.: D.C. Heath, 1986), 229.

59. Netanyahu, *Fighting Terrorism*, 96.

60. U.S. Department of Justice, "Terrorism in the United States 1999," 24, 25, 27, 37.

61. George W. Bush, "Remarks by the President to the Warsaw Conference on Combatting Terrorism," White House, Office of the Press Secretary, November 6, 2001.

62. H.R. 3162.

63. "Terrorism Blamed for Rise in Robberies," *Charlottesville Daily Progress*, November 18, 2001.

64. "Discussion Draft: Local Law Enforcement's Role in Preventing and Responding to Terrorism," Police Executive Research Forum, October 2, 2001, p. 2, accessed at www.PoliceForum.org.

65. International Association of Chiefs of Police, "Leading from the Front," 3.

66. "Attorney General Ashcroft and Deputy Attorney General Thompson Announce Reorganization and Mobilization of the Nation's Justice and Law Enforcement Resources," November 8, 2001, accessed at www.usdoj.gov/ag/speeches/2001/agcrisisremarks11_08.htm.

67. Public Law 105-277, *U.S. Code*, vol. 28, sec. 530B.

68. Quoted in Tim Weiner, "The Building of a Network That Is Global and Reliable," *New York Times*, September 23, 2001.

69. Duncan Deville, "Foreign Terrorists Don't Belong in Court of Law," *Boston Globe*, October 26, 2001.

70. Ibid.

71. Griffin Bell, "The Constitution Doesn't Protect Foreign Terrorists," *Wall Street Journal*, September 26, 2001.

72. "President Issues Military Order: Detention, Treatment, and Trial of Certain Noncitizens in the War against Terrorism," November 13, 2001, accessed at www.whitehouse.gov/news/releases/2001/11/20011113-27.html.

73. Ibid.

74. Ibid.

75. Ibid.

76. Harold Hongju Koh, "We Have the Right Courts for bin Laden," *New York Times*, November 23, 2001.

77. William Safire, "Seizing Dictatorial Power," *New York Times*, November 15, 2001; Elisabeth Bumiller, "Raid Account, Hastily Told, Proves Fluid," New york Times, May 5, 2011

78. William Safire, "Kangaroo Courts," *New York Times*, November 26, 2001.

79. "Justice for War Criminals of Invisible Armies: A New Legal and Military Approach to Terrorism," *Oklahoma City University Law Review* 21, no. 1 (1996): 405.

80. *Uniform Code of Military Justice*, subchap. 2, sec. 812, art. 12; subchap. 10, sec. 906, art. 106; subchap. 10, sec. 906a, art. 106a, accessed at JAGLINK.jag.af.mil/ucmj.htm.

81. Ibid., subchap. 7, sec. 836, art. 36.

82. Ibid., subchap. 6, sec. 832, art. 32; subchap. 7, sec. 851, art. 51.

83. Ibid., subchap. 9, sec. 867a, art. 67a.

84. "President Issues Military Order."

85. Ibid.

86. "Law and Liberty," Online Newshour, October 26, 2001, Ray Suarez interview with law professors Clifford Fishman, David Cole, and former FBI special agent Harry Brandon, accessed at www.pbs.org/newshour/bb/congress/july-dec01/patriot_10-26.html.

87. Sam Howe Verhovek, "Americans Give in to Race Profiling: Once Appalled by the Practice, Many Say They Now Do It," *New York Times*, September 23, 2001.

88. Jason L. Riley, "'Racial Profiling' and Terrorism," *Wall Street Journal*, October 24, 2001.

89. Ibid.

90. See also International Association of Chiefs of Police, "Leading from the Front."

91. David Bright, "PERF Research Director Testifies on Racial Profiling Legislation," *Subject to Debate: A Newsletter of the Police Executive Research Forum* 15, no. 8 (2001): 3.

92. Kevin Johnson, "Justice Seeks to Question 5,000 Possible Witnesses," *USA Today*, November 14, 2001.

93. Jodi Wilgoren, "Prosecutors Begin Effort to Interview 5,000, but Basic Questions Remain," *New York Times*, November 15, 2001.

94. Fox Butterfield, "Police Are Split on Questioning of Mideast Men," *New York Times*, November 22, 2001.

95. I am indebted to Dr. John Howes, distinguished Australian philosopher, grammarian, and teacher, for locating and translating this quotation from Xenophon's Anabasis 2.6.30.

96. *Abraham Lincoln: Speeches and Writings, 1859–1865*, with notes by Don E. Fehrenbacher (New York: Library of America, 1989), 420.

97. *The Letters of William James Edited by His Son Henry James*, vol. 1 (Boston: Atlantic Monthly Press, 1920), 65.

Chapter 21: Ethics in Action

1. Fyodor Dostoyevsky, *Notes from Underground*, trans. Jessie Coulson (Harmondsworth, England: Penguin Classics, 1972), 29.

2. Dave Cullen, "The Depressive and the Psychopath: At Last We Know Why the Columbine Killers Did It," *Slate Magazine*, April 20, 2004, http://slate.msn.com./id/2099203 (accessed November 14, 2005). See also David Brooks, "The Columbine Killers," *New York Times*, April 24, 2004.

3. See, for example, Alice Miller, *For Your Own Good: Hidden Cruelty in Child-Rearing and the Roots of Violence*, trans. by Hildegarde and Hunter Hannum (New York: Farrar, Strauss, and Giroux, 1990).

4. Blaise Pascal, *Thoughts, Letters, and Minor Works*, trans. W. F. Trotter, vol. 48 of *The Harvard Classics Five Foot Shelf of Books*, ed. Charles W. Eliot (New York: P. F. Collier and Son, 1910), 133.

5. Dwayne Fusilier, correspondence with author.

6. Ibid.

7. Scott Glover and Matt Lait, "LAPD Settling Abuse Scandal," latimes.com, March 31, 2005.

8. See, for instance, D. Weisburd, and J. Eck, "What Can Police Do to Reduce Crime, Disorder and Fear," *Annals of the American Academy of Political and Social Science* 593 (2004): 42–65.; Committee to Review Research, "Effectiveness of Police Activity in Reducing Crime, Disorder and Fear," in W. Skogan and K. Frydl eds., *Fairness and Effectiveness in Policing: The Evidence* (National Research Council, 2004), 217–51; L. Sherman and D. Weisburd, "General Deterrent Effects of Police Patrol in Crime "Hot-Spots": A Randomized Control Trial," *Justice Quarterly* 12 (1995): 626–648.

9. Steve Sellers, "A Model of Federal, State, and Local Information Sharing," in *Protecting Your Community from Terrorism: Strategies for Local Law Enforcement*, volume 4 (Washington, D.C.: Police Executive Research Forum, 2005), 8–10.

10. The spread of these types of task forces would greatly improve the level of professionalism of police in the United States. Fortunately, there have been efforts to

facilitate the adoption of such task force–oriented strategies. The best example is Project Safe Neighborhoods, a federally funded initiative that has provided money to every state in recent years to fund antifirearm-crime task forces that combine the efforts of federal, state, and local law enforcement agencies. See http://www.psn.gov (accessed November 16, 2005).

11. "Protecting Justice," *Boston Globe*, February 7, 2005.

12. Fox Butterfield, "Guns and Jeers Used by Gangs to Buy Silence," *New York Times*, January 16, 2005.

13. Ibid.

14. Jerry Markon and Jamie Stockwell, "Two Convicted, Two Acquitted in Gang Slaying," *Washington Post*, May 18, 2005, A1.

15. Sellers, "A Model of Federal, State, and Local Information Sharing," 8–10.

16. "Troubles Deepen for a Troubled Police Force," MPNnow.com, April 29, 2009, www.mpnnow.com/greece/x1092989883/Troubles-deepen-for-a-troubled-police-force (accessed May 25, 2011).

17. See Report 9 of the Independent Commission on Policing for Northern Ireland, published at the conclusion of Constantine's three years as Oversight Commissioner: "The proposed revisions for the policing services in Northern Ireland are the most complex and dramatic changes ever attempted in modern history." Office of the Oversight Commissioner, December 2003.

18. Jim McMahon, e-mail message to author, September 30, 2005.

Chapter 22: From War Veterans to Peace Officers

1. J. Glenn Gray, *The Warriors: Reflections on Men in Battle* (Lincoln: University of Nebraska Press, 1959, 1970), 169.

2. Uniformed Services Employment and Reemployment Rights Act of 1994 (USERRA), 38 U.S.C. §§ 4301–4335.

3. Ibid.

4. International Association of Chiefs of Police (IACP), *Law Enforcement Leader's Guide on Combat Veterans: A Transition Guide for Veterans Beginning or Continuing Careers in Law Enforcement* (Alexandria, VA: IACP, 2010), 4.

5. Samuel F. Wright, "Another New Appellate Case Shows USERRA Has Teeth," *ROA Law Review* 0864 (December 2008), available at www.roa.org/site/PageServer?pagename=law_review_0864.

6. Ibid.

7. *Petty v. Metro Government of Nashville–Davidson County*, 2008 U.S. App. LEXIS 17549 (6th Cir. August 18, 2008), available at http://caselaw.findlaw.com/us-6th-circuit/1291168.html.

8. Ibid.

9. Kansas City Police Department, "Administration of Leave, 732—Military Leave," *Personnel Policy Series* 700.

10. Topeka Police Department, "The Deployment Challenge: Preparing for the Military Deployment and the Return of Officers to the Topeka Police Department."

11. Colorado Springs Police Department, "General Order 1968, Section 19: Military Support Officer, Employee Well-Being."

12. Ibid.

13. "Servicemembers Civil Relief Act Overview," Military.com, www.military.com /benefits/legal-matters/scra/overview.

14. Ibid.

15. Quoted in Gregg Zoroya, "Despite Efforts, No Letup in Marine Attempted Suicides," *USA Today*, June 7, 2010.

16. Ibid.

17. Ibid.

18. Ibid.

19. Julian E. Barnes, "Soldiers' Suicides Tied to Problems at Home," *Wall Street Journal*, July 30, 2010.

20. Ibid.

21. Judy Keen, "States Try to Link Up Vets with Federal Government Benefits," *USA Today*, April 9, 2010.

22. Private correspondence with author.

23. Andrea Elkon, "Military Readjustment and PTSD," presentation, August 3, 2010.

24. Jonathan Shay, *Achilles in Vietnam: Combat Trauma and the Undoing of Character* (New York: Simon & Schuster, 1995).

25. Ibid., 3.

26. Ibid., 3, 4.

27. Ibid., 16–20.

28. Ibid.

29. Ibid., 67.

30. Ibid., 66.

31. Ibid., 198.

32. IACP, *Combat Veterans and Law Enforcement: A Transition Guide for Veterans Beginning or Continuing Careers in Law Enforcement.*

33. Gray, *The Warriors*, 43, 9, 1.

34. Ibid., 26–29.

35. Ibid., 27.

36. Ibid., 42, 46, 51.

37. Ibid., 81.

38. Ibid., 191–93.

39. Ibid.

40. Ibid.

41. Ibid.

42. Matt Gallagher, *Kaboom: Embracing the Suck in a Savage Little War* (Philadelphia: Da Capo Press, 2011), 84.

43. Bing West, *The Wrong War: Grit, Strategy, and the Way Out of Afghanistan* (New York: Random House, 2011).

44. West, "Meanwhile, in the War in Afghanistan . . . ," *Wall Street Journal*, April 9–10, 2011.

45. Ibid.

46. Ibid.

47. Sebastian Junger, *War* (New York: Hatchette Book Group, 2010), 47, 48, 79, 120.

48. Ibid., 160–61.

49. Shay, *Achilles in Vietnam*, 23.

50. Gray, *The Warriors*, 169.

51. Jon Ostendorff and Nanci Bompey, "VA Scopes Out Medical Needs of Female Veterans," *USA Today*, March 1, 2011.

52. Kirsten Helmstedt, *The Girls Come Marching Home: Stories of Women Warriors Returning from the War in Iraq* (Mechanicsburg, PA: Stackpole Books, 2009), 72.

53. Ibid., 75.

54. Guy Sajer, *The Forgotten Soldier* (Dulles, VA: Potomac Books, 2000), 431, 448, 465. Guy Sajer is a pseudonym of Guy Mouminoux; he chose "Sajer" because it was his mother's name before she married. Some academic historians dispute the accuracy of *The Forgotten Soldier*, but U.S. Army and Marine Corps training programs include it in reading lists.

55. J. Glenn Gray, "A Review of The Forgotten Soldier," *New York Times Book Review*, February 7, 1971. See also Douglas E. Nash, "The Forgotten Soldier: Unmasked," *Army History* (Summer 1967).

56. "State Transition Assistance Advisors," TurboTAP.com, available at www.turbotap .org/portal/transition/resources/press/Frequently_Asked_Questions.

57. "Which of the following do you think is the most important thing for Congress to concentrate on right now: job creation, the wars in Iraq and Afghanistan, the federal budget deficit, illegal immigration, health care, or something else?" CBS News/*New York Times* Poll, January 15–19, 2011, available at www.pollingreport.com /prioriti.htm (accessed May 6, 2011).

58. "Which of the following do you see as the most important issue facing the country right now? Immigration. Health care. The federal deficit and government spending. The war in Afghanistan. Unemployment and jobs," Bloomberg National Poll, March 4–7, 2011, available at www.pollingreport.com/prioriti.htm (accessed May 6, 2011).

59. "What do you think is the most important problem facing this country today?" CBS News/*New York Times* Poll, April 15–20, 2011, available at www.pollingreport.com /prioriti.htm (accessed May 6, 2011).

60. Charles L. Griswold, *Forgiveness: A Philosophical Exploration* (New York: Cambridge University Press, 2007), 204–207.

61. John Schwartz, "Defendants Fresh from War Find Service Counts in Court," *New York Times*, March 15, 2010.

62. Kimberly Hefting, "Iraq, Afghanistan Veterans Struggle to Find Jobs," WashingtonPost.com, March 1, 2011.

63. Schwartz, "Defendants Fresh from War Find Service Counts in Court."

64. Jacques Barzun, "Columbia University's ROTC Shame," *Wall Street Journal*, March 10, 2011.

65. Ibid.

66. "ROTC Homecoming," *Wall Street Journal*, April 26, 2011.

67. Fahmida Y. Rashid, "The Return of ROTC to Columbia," Villagevoice.com, April 6, 2011, www.villagevoice.com/2011-04-06/news/the-return-of-rotc-to-columbia.

68. Sean Gregory, "The Price of Free Speech," *Time*, October 9, 2010, 31–34.

69. Ibid.

70. *Snyder v. Phelps* et al., 562 U.S. ___ (2011) (Roberts, J., concurring).

71. Ibid., (Alito, J., dissenting).

72. Adam Liptak, "Justices Uphold Hateful Protests as Free Speech," *New York Times*, March 3, 2011.

73. Peter Schworm, "Justices Uphold Funeral Protests," *Boston Globe*, March 3, 2011.

74. *Snyder v. Phelps* et al. (Alito, J., dissenting).

75. Richard L. Eubank, "Court Sends Chilling Message," *USA Today*, March 3, 2011.

Appendix B: Internal Affairs and Integrity

This essay, published in the July 20, 1995, issue of the John Jay College of Criminal Justice's *Law Enforcement News*, was originally given as a keynote speech at the June 14–15, 1995, Internal Affairs Conference of the New York City Police Department.

1. John Fletcher Moulton served as minister of munitions for Great Britain during World War I. The passages included here are drawn from "an impromptu speech" he gave at the Authors' Club in London "some years before his death" in 1921. The speech was published under the title "Law and Manners" in the *Atlantic Monthly* (July 1924): 1–5. I am indebted to John R. Silber for his treatment of the work of Lord Moulton in his 1995 Boston University Commencement Address, "Obedience to the Unenforceable."

2. Alexander Hamilton, James Madison, and John Jay, *The Federalist*, No. 6, Jacob E. Cooke, ed. (Middletown, Conn.: Wesleyan University Press, 1961), 31.

3. *Commission Report*, Milton Mollen, chairman (New York: Commission to Investigate Allegations of Police Corruption and the Anti-Corruption Procedures of the Police Department, July 7, 1994), 51.

4. John E. Acton, *Essays in Religion, Politics, and Morality*, vol. 3 of *Selected Writings of Lord Acton*, J. Rufus Fears, ed. (Indianapolis, Ind.: Liberty Classics, 1985), 570. Lord Acton is better known to the general public for his 1887 observation, "Power tends to corrupt, and absolute power corrupts absolutely."

5. Hamilton, Madison, and Jay, *The Federalist*, No. 57, 384.

6. U.S. National Commission on Law Observance and Enforcement, *Report on Police* 14 (Washington, D.C.: Government Printing Office, 1931): 17. This study is also known as the Wickersham Report, after the commission's chairman.

7. *Commission Report*, 65.

8. Edwin J. Delattre, "Public Corruption for Profit," in chapter 6 in this book (Washington, D.C.: AEI Press, 2002), p. 83

9. Rudolph W. Giuliani and William J. Bratton, *Police Strategy No. 7: Rooting Out Corruption; Building Organizational Integrity in the New York Police Department*, June 14, 1995, 6 ff.

10. Hamilton, Madison, and Jay, *The Federalist*, No. 57, 386, 387.

11. Walter Lippmann, "A Theory about Corruption," in *Political Corruption: Readings in Comparative Analysis*, Arnold J. Heidenheimer, ed. (New York: Holt, Rinehart, and Winston, 1970), 296, 297.

12. Edwin J. Delattre, *Character and Cops: Ethics in Policing*, 2d ed. (Washington, D.C.: AEI Press, 1994), 271.

Index

About the Author

Edwin J. Delattre is president emeritus of St. John's College in Annapolis, Maryland, and Santa Fe, New Mexico; dean emeritus of the Boston University School of Education; and professor of philosophy emeritus at the Boston University College of Arts and Sciences. He was president of St. John's College from 1980 to 1986; director of the National Humanities Faculty from 1976 to 1980; and professor of philosophy at the University of Toledo from 1968 to 1976. Dr. Delattre received a BA in philosophy from the University of Virginia and a PhD in philosophy from the University of Texas.

Dr. Delattre has served on the boards of many academic institutions, professional organizations, and government agencies. He is former chairman of the National Advisory Board of the Fund for the Improvement of Postsecondary Education and former vice chairman of the National Council of the National Endowment for the Humanities, and he has recently completed a five-year term of service as a member of the Massachusetts Board of Education. He has been a frequent lecturer at the FBI Academy in Quantico, Virginia, and at police academies and law enforcement seminars and conferences worldwide. Dr. Delattre served for five years as chairman of the Boston University/Chelsea Public Schools Partnership. He has served on the Quaker Chemical Corporation Board of Directors since 1984. In 1973, he received the University of Toledo Outstanding Teacher Award.

Dr. Delattre is the author of two books, *Education and the Public Trust* (1988; 2d edition, 1992) and *Character and Cops: Ethics in Policing*, now in its sixth edition, and of numerous newspaper and magazine articles on ethics in daily private and public life—including parenthood and moral education of the young and ethics in higher education, law enforcement, government, and business. He has also published articles on excellence in the humanities and liberal arts education; on the governance of educational institutions; and on illegal narcotics, organized crime, urban gangs, and related domestic and international policy issues. Since 1975, Dr. Delattre has spent thousands of hours with police and law enforcement personnel on duty.